MW00614602

GLOBAL INFORMATION TECHNOLOGY AND SYSTEMS MANAGEMENT

KEY ISSUES AND TRENDS

Editors

Prashant C. Palvia
Shailendra C. Palvia
Edward M. Roche

 Ivy League Publishing

IVY LEAGUE PUBLISHING
P.O. Box 7225
Nashua, NH 03060-7225
Phone: (603) 891-0669

Copyright © 1996 by Ivy League Publishing, Limited
Library of Congress Card Catalog Number: 95-77455

ISBN: 0-9648382-0-6

Printed at: Courier Companies Inc., Westford, MA.

Global Information Technology and Systems Management:
Key Issues and Trends

Table of Contents

SECTION II . NATIONAL INFRASTRUCTURE CULTURE AND DEVELOPMENT

SECTION III. GLOBAL INFORMATION TECHNOLOGY ARCHITECTURES

SECTION IV. GLOBAL SYSTEM DEVELOPMENT AND OUTSOURCING

SECTION V. GLOBAL SUPPORT SYSTEMS AND TECHNOLOGIES

SECTION VI. GLOBAL INFORMATION TECHNOLOGY STRATEGY AND MANAGEMENT

SECTION VII. GLOBAL INFORMATION TECHNOLOGY APPLICATIONS AND CASES

DEDICATION

Prashant and Shailendra would like to dedicate this book to the loving memory of their father Dr. Chandmal Nanalal Palvia -- teacher, researcher, consultant, and UN Adviser -- who left for his heavenly abode on July 14, 1993.

ABOUT THE EDITORS

Dr. Prashant Palvia is Professor of Management Information Systems at the university of Memphis. He is the Editor-in-chief of the journal of Global information Management. His research interests include international information systems, strategic information systems, database design, and software engineering. He has published over forty articles in journals such as MIS Quarterly, Decision Sciences, communications of the ACM, Information & Management, Decision Support Systems, and ACM Transactions on Database Systems.

Dr. Shailendra Palvia is an Associate Professor at the Long Island University. His research interests include management of the systems development process, mode of use in problem solving, implementation issues for MIS/DSS, and global information systems. Shailendra has published in refereed journals such as Communications of the ACM, MIS Quarterly, Information & Management Journal of Global Information Management, International Information Systems. Dr. Palvia has been invited for talks in USA, Europe, and Singapore.

Dr. Roche worked in management consulting for 9 years with the Diebold Group and Booz-Allen & Hamilton, Inc. He was an associate editor for the journal of International Information Systems. He is a contributing editor to Transnational Data Report, and a book review editor for the Journal of Global Information Management. He is the author of two books: "Managing Information Technology in Multinational Corporations" and "Telecommunications and Business Strategy". He founded the IFIP Working Group 8.7 Informatics in International Business Enterprises.

PREFACE

The nineties have witnessed an almost explosive expansion of businesses into global markets. As we move towards the next millennium, multinational corporations continue their quest for global business expansion and entry into new world markets. We will continue to witness zealous strategizing by national econmies to integrate into global economy. Products such as automobiles, electronic appliances, textiles, and computer hardware & software have become truly global products in that that the raw materials may be procured anywhere , the product manufactured anywhere, and the final product sold everywhere in the world. The global phenomenon has had tremendous impact on organizational growth and survivability, and is destined to be irreversible. Large and growing organizations simply have no choice, but to "go global".

Information technology has played a key role in the drive of businesses into "going global". Early books and publications (albeit, only in the last five years or so) provided early directions to practitioners and researchers in the application of information technology (IT) for globalization. Nonetheless, the global phenomenon is accelerating at a brisk pace, and the technological advances are racing at exponential rates. Without a doubt, the rapid advances in information technology, e.g., Asynchronous Transfer Mode (ATM), mainframes on a chip, Enterprise Servers, the Information Superhighway (Internet and the World Wide Web), RISC (Reduced Instruction Set computing) technologies, RAID (Redundant Arrays of Information Devices) and optical storage media, Virtual Space Collaborative Technologies, software factories in developing countries, and many others, have proven to be critical enabling resources in this globalization phenomenon of unprecedented proportions. To borrow from Richard Nolan's stage theory of IS evolution, we are in a stage of rapid contagion of IT into global business, having moved on from the initiation period. The contagion period calls for a careful reevaluation of the issues, and attempts to bring control and maturity to the field.

This book's goal is just that. While, the previous studies provided early directions for scholars and practitioners, the collection of chapters in this book written by authorities recognized in the emerging global IT field provides an updated, comprehensive, and rigorous treatment of the subject. It summarizes current experiences, offers managerial insights, and incorporates foundational perspectives. Different chapters, to different degrees, examine significant issues from several perspectives, i.e., the views of the practitioner, the educator, and the researcher. This multi-perspective goal was achieved by inviting proposals from distinguished authors, consultants, and practitioner in the field. Invitations to write the chapters were made after carefully screening the proposals in terms of their quality and relevance to the book. Each submitted chapter is original and was written specifically for the book. Each chapter submission went through a thorough review process, and several revisions. While every chapter is worthwhile reading in and of itself, some readers may focus on specific chapters based on their own interests.

The book contains 27 chapters organized into seven sections to introduce the subject matter in a logical order to maximize pedagogical effectiveness. The approach may be characterized as an "outside-in", or "top-down" or "goal directed" approach. The reader is first familiarized the various issues and factors impacting global IT application, before management and strategies are described. A brief overview of each section is provided below; detailed overview is provided in the introduction preceding each section.

In the first section, consisting of six chapters, the IT environment is described in different parts of this world. An understanding of the environment is absolutely essential before explication of issues and strategies. The first chapter provides key IS issues in different parts of the world, and is followed by chapters focusing on specific countries.

The second section, consisting of five chapters, elaborates more on the theme of the first chapter and looks at issues of national infrastructure, economic development, culture, and law and regulations related to IT application. Issues of technology, telecommunications, culture, and transborder data flows are presented.

Starting with the third section, the book starts to introduce solutions, methods, and strategies for global IT application. The third section contains three chapters, and discusses the various IT architectural forms that may be used in implementing global IT. More importantly, various issues, that may impact the selection of a particular architecture, are thoroughly discussed.

The fourth section has three chapters and examines various global system development strategies. The first chapters provides various tactics and strategies for global IT development. The remaining two chapters are on international outsourcing, an option being exercised by an increasing number of firms.

The fifth section, containing four chapters, begins to examine the role of management support systems and emerging technologies in global applications. Among support technologies, groupware and DSS/ES/EIS are examined. Two leading technologies are evaluated in terms of their support and impact on the global organization: EDI and Internet. Internet provides tremendous futuristic possibilities for electronic commerce.

The sixth section has three chapters and discusses global IT management and strategy. Strategies include: providing global customer service and assessing the role and impact of IT. An instrument is provided to assess the strategic applications of IT in a global firm.

Finally, the seventh section includes IT applications and case studies. These applications drawn from Seagate Technology, citibank, and General Motors demonstrate how organizations have implemented the ideas of previous chapters in building successful and vibrant global organizations. The emphasis in these chapters is on the global application and impact of information technology.

The book will have **significant value** for four constituencies: students in universities and colleges, educators, researchers, and managers in corporations. It would be **ideal** for a graduate level (master's or Ph.D.) course or a junior/senior course dealing with international aspects of information technology management. Many schools now have a program in international business or specific courses in international IT; the book is ideally suited to serve their needs. The book can also be used as a companion text for courses in management of information technology resources, advanced IS courses, or executive MBA courses. The book will also be of significant value to senior executives and IS managers, as many of the chapters provide practical ideas and case studies for the global utilization of information technology. Finally, the book will be useful to educators in incorporating the global dimension of IT in their lectures, and to researchers in pursuing research in the international IT arena. The global dimension of IT is not a passing fad; it is here to stay well into the future. Educators and researchers will be prudent to learn about new challenges and opportunities in this exciting field.

The editors will like to express the sincerest form of gratitude to the chapter authors. While, we provided coordination and direction for the overall work, it is the individual authors' original work which is reflected in the book. They worked diligently in targeting the chapters to the needs of our readers, presenting contemporary material, and responding to our extensive comments in a timely fashion. We also thank the staff of Ivy League Publishing who kept pushing us with swift deadlines, and kept us on track. They are primarily responsible for being able to complete this project in just a year since its inception. We would also like to thank Mr. Choton Basu and Mr. Ajay Chawdhry, graduate students at The University of Memphis for their valuable assistance in copy editing.

Finally, we take responsibility for any errors that might have crept in inspite of our best efforts. We will like to ask our readers to point these errors so that they can be corrected in subsequent prints and editions. We also welcome any feedback that will improve the quality of the book. With the fast pace of globalization and IT developments, we expect to prepare and publish the next edition in three to four years, and so any comments will be helpful and will be greatly appreciated.

Prashant C. Palvia, Memphis
Shailendra C. Palvia, Long Island
Edward M. Roche, New York

SECTION-1

THE GLOBAL INFORMATION TECHNOLOGY ENVIRONMENT

In the spirit of the top-down or outside-in approach used for this book, the first section focuses on IT issues at world, region, and country levels. IN order to fully exploit the potential of IT applications in far flung regions of the world, multinational companies (MNCs) must understand the disparate cultural, economic, political, and infrastructural conditions that exist in different parts of the world. Such an understanding can help them in devising appropriate business and IT strategy for the headquarters as well as foreign subsidiary organizations.

First chapter by Palvia and Palvia synthesizes the various IS issues studies conducted for different regions and countries of the world over the last decade. The regions include North America, Europe, and Africa. The countries covered by these studies include Australia, Hong Kong, India, Singapore, Taiwan, UK, and USA. The authors' concrete contribution is in describing the existence of significant differences in issues between developed, newly industrialized, developing, and under-developed nations of the world.

The remaining five chapters articulate trends and issues in specific regions and countries of the world. Ewan Sutherland analyzes the dramatic changes in the European telecommunications industry with particular attention to the cases of UK, Germany, Hungary, and Bulgaria. He concludes that the old order of bureaucratic government controlled PTTSs (Post Telegraph and Telephone companies) is being replaced by entrepreneurial and efficiently run private telecommunications companies. In chapter three, Lee Gilbert traces the evolution of robust and state-of-the-art telecommunications infrastructure in Singapore within a span of fifteen years and attributes the phenomenal success to sound government policies and actions. He goes on to make recommendations for other nations in the region by asserting that national TC infrastructure and computer policies are inseparable and ought to be pursued together. In chapter four, Dr. Alkier explores the potential of using internet as the underlying structure for a global electronic marketplace. This exploration is done in the context of Austrian international businesses. She outlines the importance of accompanying government activities and industry initiatives for the success of internet as the global electronic marketplace. In chapter five, Elia Chepaitis makes a case for lack of data quality as being the most serious impediment to IS applications development in many emerging markets, including Russia. Finally, in chapter six, Rover, Tigre, and Fagundes analyze the diffusion of information networks among Brazilian firms. They identify global and local factors that contribute to the successful implementation of these networks. They also offer implications for industrial policy.

1 Understanding The Global Information Technology Environment: Representative World Issues

Prashant C. Palvia
The University of Memphis, USA

Shailendra C. Palvia
Long Island University, USA

As an increasing number of businesses expand their operations into international markets, in order to succeed they need to understand the considerable cultural, economic, and political diversity that exists in different parts of the world. For these reasons, while information technology is a critical enabler and many times driver of global business expansion, it cannot be applied uniformly across the world. This chapter is aimed at analyzing the key information systems/technology (IS/IT) issues identified during the last decade in different regions of the world. Spurred by periodic key IS issues studies in USA, several researchers have attempted to do the same for many other countries. We summarize many of their findings, and provide insights into the various differences and similarities among countries. A precursory model is developed to help understand the underlying causes into the nature of the issues. Elements of a more detailed model, worthy of further exploration, are also presented.

INTRODUCTION

During the past few years, the world has witnessed an unprecedented expansion of business into global markets. The idea of a "global village," envisioned by McLuhan (1964), has finally come true. At the same time there is realization that information technology (IT) has played a crucial role in the race towards globalization. IT has been a critical enabler of globalization in most cases and a driver in some cases. Today, multinational corporations and governments increasingly rely on information technology (IT) for conducting international business. Therefore, in order to fully exploit the vast potential of IT, it is extremely important for corporate executives and chief information officers to understand the nature of global information technology environment.

In this chapter, we aim to provide not only this understanding, but also provide insights into the nature of world IT issues.

Reports of key management information systems (MIS or IS) and IT[1] management issues have continually appeared in the United States. For example, a stream of articles of MIS issues in USA has appeared in the *MIS* Quarterly (Ball & Harris 1992; Brancheau et al. 1987; Dickson et al. 1984; Niederman et al. 1991). A study by Deans et al. (1991) identified and prioritized international IS issues in US based multinational corporations. As technology is assimilated into other countries, researchers have begun to identify IS/IT issues in these countries. Several such studies have appeared recently: representative examples include: North American and European issues (CSC Index 1995), Canada issues (Carey, 1992), Australia issues (Watson 1989), Hong Kong issues (Burn et al., 1993), India issues (Palvia & Palvia 1992), and Singapore issues (Rao et al. 1987). Such studies are perceived to be of value as they not only identify issues critical to determining strategies for organizations, but also provide direction for future MIS education, practice, and research.

A comparison of the cited studies reveals that the key IS issues in different countries vary to a considerable degree. In order to fully exploit IT for global business, it is imperative that the key IS issues of different countries are identified and dealt with appropriately in the conduct of international business. While an examination of IS issues of the entire word is impractical and infeasible, and even the data are not readily available, we summarize issues from a few countries selected on the basis of their level of economic development. Four categories of economic development are defined: advanced, newly industrialized, developing (operational), and under-developed . This classification is somewhat parallel to that used by many international agencies (e.g., the United Nations). Countries discussed in this chapter loosely fit this classification.

While some level of generalization is possible based on the countries discussed herein and is intended, we need to clearly point out the limitations. The chapter does not cover the entire world. Only a few countries are surveyed and while they may represent many other countries, they do not represent all. Second, the classification of a country into one of the above four classes may be disputable, and furthermore, there is certainly a range within each class. Lastly, some countries may simply defy our classification scheme (e.g., Russia and the former socialist nations).

KEY MIS ISSUES IN ADVANCED NATIONS

Advanced and industrialized nations include the United States, Western European countries, Japan, and Australia among others. Key IS issues have been systematically and periodically researched in the United states over the past fifteen years (Ball & Harris 1992; Brancheau et al. 1987; Dickson et al. 1984; Hartog & Herbert 1986; Niederman et al. 1991). As of this writing, an effort is underway at the MIS Research Center at the University of Minnesota to compile a contemporary list of key IS issues in USA based on a Delphi study to obtain opinions from IS

Rank	Description of Issue
#1	Building a Responsive IT Infrastructure
#2	Facilitating and Managing Business Process Redesign
#3	Developing and Managing Distributed Systems
#4	Developing and Implementing an Information Architecture
#5	Planning and Managing Communication Networks
#6	Improving and Effectiveness of Software Development
#7	Making Effective Use of the Data Resource
#8	Aligning the IS Organization within the Enterprise
#9	Recruiting and Developing IS Human Resources
#10	Improving IS Strategic Planning
#11	Managing the Existing Portfolio of Legacy Applications
#12	Measuring IS Effectiveness and Productivity

Source: *Janz, B.D; Brancheau, J.C. and Wetherbe, J.C. Key Information Systems Management Issues. MISRC Working Paper, University of Minnesota. 1994.*

Table 1: Key Issues In Information Systems Management - USA (1994)

Rank	Description of the Issue
#1	Aligning I/S and corporate goals
#2	Instituting cross-functional information systems
#3	Organizing and utilizing data
#4	Re-engineering business processes through I/T
#5	Improving the I/S human resource
#6	Enabling change and nimbleness
#7	Connecting to customers/suppliers
#8	Creating an information architecture
#9	Updating obsolete systems
#10	Improving the systems-development process
#11	Educating management on I/T
#12	Changing technology platforms
#13	Using I/S for competitive advantage
#14	Developing an I/S strategic plan
#15	Capitalizing on advances in I/T
#16	Integrating systems
#17	Cutting I/S costs
#18	Providing help-desk services
#19	Moving to open systems
#20	Improving leadership skills of I/S management

Source: *The Eighth Annual Survey of I/S Management Issues, 1995. CSC Index Group.*

Table 2: Key Issues In Information Systems Management - North America (1995)

executives (Janz et al. 1994). Preliminary rankings from an intermediate step of this study are shown in Table 1. While a few new issues have appeared in the new list (e.g., business process re-engineering), there is not a substantial departure from the 1991 list of issues reported by Niederman et al. (1991). Also, as reported by CSC Index (1995), the IS issues in Western Europe are very similar to the North

Rank	Description of the Issue
#1	Instituting cross-functional information systems
#2	Improving the I/S human resource
#3	Re-engineering business processes through I/T
Tie	Cutting I/S costs (tie)
#5	Creating an information architecture
#6	Aligning I/S and corporate goals
#7	Improving the systems-development process
#8	Educating management on I/T
#9	Organizing and utilizing data
Tie	Changing technology platforms (tie)
#11	Integrating systems
#12	Using I/S for competitive advantage
Tie	Enabling change and nimbleness (tie)
#14	Developing an I/S strategic plan
#15	Connecting to customers/suppliers
Tie	Providing help-desk services (tie)
#17	Moving to open systems
#18	Updating obsolete systems
#19	Determining the value of information systems
#20	Capitalizing on advances in I/T

Source: The Eighth Annual Survey of I/S Management Issues, 1995. CSC Index Group.
Table 3: Key Issues In Information Systems Management - Europe (1995)

Rank	Description of Issue
#1	Improving IS Strategic Planning
#2	Building a responsive IT infrastructure
#3	Aligning the IS organization with that of the enterprise
#4	Promoting effectiveness of the data resource
#5	Using IS for competitive advantage
#6	Developing an information architecture
#7	Improving data integrity and quality assurance
#8	Improving the quality of software development
#9	Increasing the understanding of the role and contribution of IS
#10	Planning for disaster recovery

Source: Pervan, G.P. Results from a study of Key Issues in Australian IS Management. 4th Australian Conference on Information Systems. September 28, 1993. University of Queensland, St. Lucia. Brisbane, Queensland.
Table 4: Key Issues In Information Systems Management - Australia (1993)

American issues (Tables 2 and 3). This similarity is also seen in Australian issues (Table 4) and West Europe issues that were reported by Watson and Brancheau (1991). As the 1991 issues study by Niederman et al. is well-known, meets methodological rigor, and is widely distributed, it will be discussed below as representative of IS issues of advanced nations.

Key Issue Ranks

A ranked list of IS management issues as reported by Niederman et al. (1991) is shown in Table 5. These issues were captured by a three-round Delphi survey of senior IS executives in the US. It should be noted these ranks represent the opinions of the members of the Society for Information Management (SIM) . Typically, the SIM membership is comprised of large private organizations. The top ten issues are reviewed below. The review draws heavily from the Niederman et al. article.

Rank	Description of Issue
#1	Developing an Information Architecture
#2	Making Effective Use of the Data Resource
#3	Improving IS Strategic Planning
#4	Specifying, Recruiting, and Developing IS Human Resources
#5	Facilitating Organizational Learning and Use of IS Technologies
#6	Building a Responsive IT Infrastructure
#7	Aligning the IS Organization With That of the Enterprise
#8	Using Information Systems for Competitive Advantage
#9	Improving the Quality of Software Development
#10	Planning and Implementing a Telecommunications System
#11	Increasing Understanding of Role and Contribution of IS
#12	Enabling Multi-Vendor Data Interchange and Integration
#13	Developing and Managing Distributed Systems
#14	Planning and Using CASE Technology
#15	Planning and Managing the Applications Portfolio
#16	Measuring IS Effectiveness and Productivity
#17	Facilitating and Managing Decision and Executive Support Systems
#18	Facilitating and Managing End-User Computing
#19	Improving Information Security and Control
#20	Establishing Effective Disaster Recovery Capabilities

Source: Niederman, F., Brancheau, J. C., and Wetherbe, J. C. Information Systems Management Issues for the 1990's. MIS Quarterly. December 1991.

Table 5: Key Issues In Information Systems Management (1991)

Rank 1. Information Architecture: An information architecture is a high level map of the information requirements of an organization. Also called the enterprise model, it provides the overall framework to guide application development and database development. It includes the major classes of information (i.e., entities), and their relationships to the various functions and processes in the organization. The steps included in enterprise modeling include functional decomposition, entity-relationship diagrams, and planning matrices (McFadden & Hoffer 1994).

Rank 2. Data Resource: Data should be regarded as a vital resource for an organization, especially for the information systems function and application development. Data and information are corporate resources, and not in the domain of an individual or a subgroup, but for the benefit of the entire organization. Firms collect massive amounts of not only data internal data but also vast amounts of data from external sources, such as customers, suppliers, government and other firms. These data should be properly harnessed and leveraged for optimizing the benefit to the organization. The establishment of large corporate data bases, as well as the emergence of firms specializing in specific types of databases (e.g., Dow Jones, Compuserve, Compustat, Data Resources, etc.) underscores the value of the data resource.

Rank 3. Strategic Planning: Strategic IT planning refers to IT planning that supports business goals, missions, and strategy With the role of IT elevated to a strategic tool for obtaining competitive advantage and achieving superior performance, the need for strategic IT planning is of paramount importance. Yet, strategic planning remains a thorny issue for both senior IS and non-executives. The rate of technological change requires the ability to develop quick courses of action at economical costs, before they become obsolete. Further exacerbating the situation is rapid organizational change as well as environmental change outside the organization. In spite of the difficulties, this issue has remained one of the top issues in all previous key issue studies.

Rank 4. IS Human Resources: Human resources for IS include technical as well as managerial personnel. This issue reappeared in the top ten list, after an absence in the previous study of 1986. This factor includes such concerns as planning for human resources, hiring, retaining, and developing human resources. While there is no acute shortage of IS talent, the rapid technological change creates shortage of specialized skills. For example, object oriented programmers are in short supply and in great demand at the present time. Another phenomenon of the last decade which has serious implications for human resources is IS downsizing and outsourcing. Organizations need to decide which IS functions can be outsourced to external vendors and which need to be retained in-house. These decisions have strategic implications for the company.

Rank 5. Organizational Learning: This issue calls for continued organizational learning about the applications of information technology, and productive use of information systems. Historically, information systems have been initiated by IS managers, and they have been the purveyors of information technology. However, the organizations that prosper will have to make proper use of information technologies and will have to use IT in the whole organization. As recent examples will indicate, line managers are taking initiatives for the development of IT applications, and end user computing is becoming pervasive. These trends bode well for organizational IT learning; however, such applications need to expand to a broader range of companies.

Rank 6. Technology Infrastructure: Infrastructure includes such components as organization's diverse computers, telecommunication networks (both LANs and WANs), databases, operating systems, system software, and business applications. A new issue that emerged in the 1991 study, it refers to the development of a sound technology infrastructure that will support business strategy and organizational goals. The appearance of this issue may have again been driven by strategic concerns. A lack of a coordinated strategy for technology infrastructure may have prevented companies from taking timely advantage of business opportunities as they emerged.

Rank 7. IS Organization Alignment: The organizational positioning of the IS department within the company has a direct impact on its effectiveness. In early days of computing, IS was relegated to Accounting or Personnel departments, and had the image of a service/overhead function. While that image has been mostly erased, there are still issues relating to its proper alignment. For those, who view IS as a strategic function, IS department has moved up in the organizational hierarchy. Large companies today have positions such as Chief Information Officer (CIO) and vice-president of information technology. Another issue relating to alignment is the question of centralized, decentralized, or distributed IS organization. Technology can effectively support any option; the key issue is that the IS organization should be consistent with the company organization and philosophy.

Rank 8. Competitive Advantage: Information technology and information systems in a firm can be used in ways that provide a decided advantage over its competitors. Early examples of firms using IT in such manner include American Airlines, United Airlines, American Hospital Supply Co., and Merrill Lynch. The eighties provided a major thrust for using information technology as a source of competitive advantage. This issue still ranks among senior IS executives as one of the top issues. Information systems dubbed as "strategic information systems" are targeted towards customers, suppliers, or competitors, and are an essential part of a company's competitive strategy. While targeting information systems at external entities is one source of competitive advantage, other sources include using IT for organizational redesign, improving organizational effectiveness, streamlining of business processes, and integration of business activities.

Rank 9. Software Development: The development of software represents a major expenditure for the IS organization, yet it remains fraught with problems of poor quality, unmet needs, constant delays, and exceeded budgets. At the same time, the organization is presented with more options: in-house development, software packages, and outsourcing. Newer developments, e.g., software engineering methodologies, prototyping and CASE tools, promise to provide some much-needed help. However, the organization is further challenged as they have to constantly evaluate new technologies and development paradigms, such as distributed processing, visual languages and object oriented programming. For example, much of the new development is being done using the C++ or similar programming languages.

Rank 10. Telecommunication Systems: Telecommunication systems provide the backbone for an organization to do business anywhere anytime, without being constrained by time or distance. While the earlier focus in telecommunication systems was on connecting users to a centralized mainframe computer, the renewed emphasis is on providing connectivity between different computing centers and users, who are widely dispersed geographically, and many times globally. Telecommunication networks also need to substantially multiply their bandwidth in order to carry all types of signals: data, graphics voice, and video. Challenges that face the implementation of telecommunication systems include huge financial investments and lack of common industry standards. Yet, for those who have implemented backbone networks, the rewards have been tremendous.

Other Issues: Issues ranked just below the top ten include understanding the role of IS, multi-vendor data interchange and integration, managing distributed systems, and planning and using CASE technology. It is apparent that these issues have a strategic orientation, and relate to planning and successful use of emerging technologies in the organization.

KEY MIS ISSUES IN NEWLY INDUSTRIALIZED NATIONS

Several countries have made rapid economic growth in just over a decade. These countries have emerged as the "newly industrialized countries (NICs) " and are now beginning to prosper. While the precise categorization of any country into any class is somewhat contentious, and is also subject to movement over time, countries like Taiwan, Hong Kong, Ireland, South Korea, and Singapore fall into this group. The latest key issue results that are available from some of these countries are included in the chapter. Singapore issues were reported by Rao et al. (1987), Hong Kong issues by Burn et al. (1993), and Taiwan issues by Wang (1994) and Palvia and Wang (1995). The Singapore results are shown in Table 6, and Hong Kong results in Table 7. Once again, there is a certain degree of similarity between these country issues. We discuss only the Taiwan issues as representative of issues of newly industrialized countries, as it is the most recent study of all and one of the authors was directly involved with it.

Rank	Description of Issue
#1	Measuring and improving IS effectiveness
#2	Facilitating and managing end-user computing
#3	Keeping current with new technology and systems
#4	Integrating OA, DP, and telecommunications
#5	Training and educating DP personnel
#6	Security and control
#7	Disaster Recovery Program
#8	Translating IT into competitive advantage
#9	Having top management understand the needs and perspectives of MIS department (IS role and contribution)
#10	Impact of new technology on people and their role in the company

Source: Rao, K.V., Huff, F.P. and Davis, G.B. Critical Issues in the management of information systems: A Comparison of Singapore and the USA. Information Technology, 1:3, 1987. pp.11-19.

Table 6: Key Issues in Information Systems Management - Singapore (1987)

Rank	Description of the Issue
#1	Retaining, recruiting and training MIS/IT/DP personnel
#2	Information Systems/technology planning
#3	Aligning MIS/DP organization
#4	Systems Reliability and availability
#5	Utilization of data resources
#6	Managing end-user/personal computing
#7	Application software development
#8	Information systems for competitive advantage
#9	Telecommunications technology
#10	Integrating of data processing, office automation, and telecommunications
Tie	Software quality assurance standards

Source: Burn, J; Saxena, K.B.C.; Ma, Louis.;and Cheung, Hin Keung. Critical Issues of IS Management in Hong Kong: A Cultural Comparison. Journal of Global Information Management. Vol. 1 No. 4, Fall 1993.p. 28-37.

Table 7: Key Issues In Information Systems Management - Hong Kong (1989)

Key Issue Ranks

The key IS issues in Taiwan were obtained by conducting a survey of senior managers in Taiwan, who were well-versed in technology (Wang 1994; Palvia & Wang 1995). Responses were obtained from 297 managers on a 7-point likert scale on 30 issues. The majority of the respondents were IS executives. A wide range of organizations, both in terms of size and type of business, were represented in the study. The ranked list is provided in Table 8. Once again, we focus on the top ten issues.

Rank	Description of Issue
#1	Communication between the IS department and end users
#2	Top management support
#3	IS Strategic planning
#4	Competitive advantage
#5	Goal alignment
#6	Computerization of routine work
#7	IT Infrastructure
#8	System Integration
#9	Software development productivity
#10	System friendliness
#11	Security and control
#12	Software development quality
Tie	IS Standards (tie)
#14	Data resource
#15	IS funding level
#16	IS role and contribution
#17	User Participation
#18	Recruit, train, and promote IS Staff
#19	Information architecture
#20	Placement of IS department

Source: Palvia, P., and Wang, Pien. An Expanded Global Information Technology Issue Model: An Addition of Newly Industrialized Countries. The Journal of Information Technology Management. Volume VI, No.2, 1995. p.29-39.

Table 8: Key Issues In Information Systems Management - Taiwan (1994)

Rank 1. Communication between IS Department and End Users: Communication between these two groups of people is necessary as one group is the user and the other builder. End users in Taiwan seem to be not able to specify their information needs accurately to the IS group. They also have an unrealistic expectation of the computer's capabilities and expect the IS staff to quickly automate all of their operations. At the same time, IS employees may lack a good understanding of the organization's business processes, and use terminology that end users do not understand. The communication problem between the users and the IS community is further aggravated due to the low level of communication skills among IS graduates.

Rank 2. Top Management Support: Top management support is required as IS projects require major financial and human resources. They also may take long periods of time to complete. As such, the call for top management support is pervasive in the MIS literature. Taiwan is no exception. Top management support was found to be especially important in encouraging the use of microcomputers in Taiwan (Igbaria, 1992). Senior management is expected to demonstrate its support by both allocating suitable budget for the IS department, and by showing leadership and involvement. At the same time, top management support will strengthen the IS department by helping acquire the support of other functional departments. Without strong top management endorsement and support, the IS department would have little chance to achieve its mission.

Rank 3. IS Strategic Planning: IS strategic planning in Taiwan is difficult due to rapid changes in technology, lack of familiarity with IS planning methodologies, inadequate understanding of business processes, short term orientation of firms, absence of successful domestic planning models, top management's unwillingness to provide adequate funding to implement strategy, and lack of top management support for the planning process. Lack of appropriate strategic planning in other countries have had the effect of producing system failures and creating uncoordinated "islands of automation".

Rank 4. Competitive Advantage: In the private sector, several retail, wholesale, transportation, and media firms have begun to build information systems that can be utilized to make new inroads, create business opportunities, and enable an organization to differentiate itself in the market place. Even public organizations have made progress. Stories of how public organizations (e.g., a government-run hospital and the administrative office of a village) use IT to improve their administrative effectiveness and reduce the waiting time of clients, have been reported. The aggressive promotion of IT by the government has helped to further raise the IS practitioner's consciousness of the competitive impacts of information technology.

Rank 5. Goal Alignment: The needs and goals of the IS department can often be at odds with the organizational goals. A major incongruence results in potential conflicts and sub-optimization of IS resources. The IS staff is often interested in developing large scale and technically advanced systems which may not meet the needs of the business and the end users. In order to assure goal alignment, senior management needs to clearly communicate the organizational goals, policies, and strategies to the IS staff. In fact, a carefully crafted IS strategic planning process (issue #3) would facilitate goal alignment.

Rank 6. Computerization of Routine Work: In USA, computerization of routine work (such as accounting functions and transaction processing) was the first priority and was done in the sixties and seventies. Even though, Taiwan is classified as a newly industrialized country, the extent of computer usage in business is far behind that in USA. As a paradox, the production of IT products has had a striking growth in Taiwan, while the businesses themselves have been slow in adopting the technology. In a sense, the IS evolution in many organizations is still in the Nolan's initial stages (Nolan, 1979). For these organizations, automation of routine work (i.e., transaction processing systems) is evolving, yet critical.

Rank 7. IT Infrastructure: In vibrant economies, a responsive IT infrastructure is vital to the flexibility and changing needs of a business organization. The technology infrastructure issue is exacerbated by a combination of evolving technology platforms, integration of custom-engineered and packaged application software, and the rigidity of existing applications. Many Taiwanese organizations are gradually realizing that building an infrastructure, which will support existing business applications while remaining responsive to changes, is a key to long-term enterprise productivity.

Rank 8. Systems Integration: Integration of various system components into a unified whole provide benefits of synergy, effectiveness, and added value to the user. Many IS managers in Taiwan are recognizing the need to integrate the "islands of automation" (e.g., data processing, office automation, factory automation) into an integrated single entity. In the past, the execution of systems integration had encountered great difficulty due to lack of IS standards, insufficient technical ability, and inadequate coordination among functional departments. However, open systems, networks, client/server architecture, and standardization of IT products (promoted by the government) are expected to make systems integration easier in the future. .

Rank 9. Software Development Productivity: Productivity is measured simply by the ratio of outputs to inputs. On both outputs, e.g., the quality and magnitude of software produced, and inputs, e.g., total time to complete a project and the total man-hours, IS has had a dismal record. In interviews conducted during the research process, both IS professionals and end users complained that it takes excessively long to build and modify applications. The speed of development is not able to keep pace with changing business needs. Possible explanations and reasons that were stated include: insufficient technical skills, high IS staff turnover, lack of use of software productivity tools, and inadequate user participation. However, new software technology seems to offer hope, e.g., CASE tools, object oriented languages and visual programming languages.

Rank 10. System Friendliness: Ease of use and user-oriented features are essential to the success and continued use of a software product, as the popularity of graphical user interface (GUI) will testify. Unfriendly and difficult-to-use systems encounter strong resistance from end users at all managerial levels in Taiwan The development of a friendlier interface is critical not only for the success of the software and hardware vendors, but also for the ultimate acceptance by the end user.

Two reasons can be subscribed for the significance of this issue in a non-advanced country. First, the users may be comparatively unfamiliar and untrained in the use of information technology. Second, a lot of software is imported from the advanced nations of the West and may not necessarily meet the human factor requirements of the host nation.

Other Issues: Issues rated just below top ten included: information security and control, and software development quality. As organizations in Taiwan increase the use of IT for business operations, there is a greater risk of disclosure, destruction, and contamination of data. The high turnover of IS professionals causes great concern for managers that proprietary information may be disclosed to competitors. Probable reasons associated with software quality problems include: lack of business process understanding and technical skills of the IS staff, high turnover among IS staff, and inadequate user participation. Issues rated at the bottom include: open systems, distributed systems, telecommunications, CASE, and experts systems. While these technologies have been introduced in Taiwan, their implementation is in a primitive stage. Also, end-user computing was rated low, as it is not prevalent in the country. However, as employees and the general population acquire greater computer literacy due partly to government efforts, this issue is expected to become more prominent.

KEY MIS ISSUES IN DEVELOPING NATIONS

Countries which can be loosely qualified as developing countries include: Argentina, Brazil, India, and Mexico. These countries have been using information technology for a number of years, yet their level of IT sophistication and types of applications may be wanting in several respects. For example, La Rovere et al. (1996) report that Brazil faces several difficulties in network diffusion. Many of these are caused by lack of integrated policy towards informatics and telecommunication industries, and paucity of quality training programs. Similar obstacles are faced by many of the other Latin American countries. In Pakistan, Hassan (1994) describes environmental and cultural constraints in utilizing information technologies. With the emergence of many eastern block countries out of closed and guarded environments, and the general trends towards globalization, information is now available about the IT readiness of these countries. Much of this information is derived from individual experiences, general observations, and case studies (e.g., Chepaitis, 1994; Goodman, 1991). Yet, many of them seem to face similar problems.

Russia and other former Soviet Union countries defy a natural classification into any of our four classes. In fact, the World Bank places the former socialist countries in a separate category in and of itself. In their commentary, Goodman and McHenry (1991) described two sectors of Soviet computing: the state sector which included development and deployment of a full range of highly sophisticated computers, and the mixed sector of private, state, foreign and black-marketing activities which were struggling in the sustained use of information technology. Roche (1992) made similar observations. While giant centrally planned enterprises were created that emulated technological developments of the West, little computer equipment was either designed for or used by management and consumers. Thus, while Russia and former Soviet Union countries have made great strides in selected technological areas (e.g., space program, and aerospace industry), the general consumer sector and management have lagged behind significantly in IT utilization. As many reports would indicate, Russian IT issues are therefore characteristic of issues in developing countries. According to Chepaitis (1994), lack of adequate supply of quality information and poor information culture are IS issues reflective of Russia.

A prioritized list of ranked issues based on a systematic study is available for India. We present these results as an example of issues from a developed country.

Key Issue Ranks

The key IS issues in India were obtained by Palvia and Palvia (1992) and were based on data collection from top-level and middle-level Indian managers. These managers either worked directly with computers and information systems, or had been exposed to them by other means. The issues were first generated using the nominal grouping technique and brainstorming, and were then ranked by participant managers in two seminars in India. A fully ranked list is provided in Table 9; the top issues are discussed below. The discussion draws primarily from (Palvia & Palvia 1992) and (Palvia et al. 1992).

Rank 1. Understanding and Awareness of MIS Contribution: An appreciation of the benefits and potential applications of MIS is absolutely necessary for successful IT deployment. There is a general lack of knowledge among Indian managers as to what management information systems can do for their business. The need for computer-based systems is neither a high priority nor widely recognized. Unless the potential contribution of MIS is clearly understood, advances in technological resources are not likely to be of much help. The lack of understanding is partly due to the traditional reliance on manual systems. The ready availability of a large number of semi-skilled and skilled personnel makes the operation of manual systems satisfactory, and prevents management from looking at superior alternatives.

Rank 2. Human Resources and Personnel for MIS: Higher national priorities and lower priorities assigned to IS development have caused the neglect of IS human resource development. India is somewhat of an enigma in this regard. In the last several years, India has become a primary location for international outsourcing contracts; yet there is a great demand and shortage within the country for those trained in developing business

Rank	Description of the Issue
#1	Understanding/Awareness of MIS contribution
#2	Human Resources/Personnel for MIS
#3	Quality of Input Data
#4	Educating Senior Managers about MIS
#5	User Friendliness of Systems
#6	Continuing Training & Education of MIS Staff
#7	Maintenance of Software
Tie	Standards in Hardware and Software (tie)
#9	Data Security
#10	Packaged Applications Software Availability
Tie	Cultural and Style Barriers (tie)
#12	Maintenance of Hardware
#13	Aligning of MIS with Organization
#14	Need for External/Environmental Data
#15	MIS Productivity/Effectiveness
#16	Applications Portfolio
#17	Computer Hardware
#18	MIS Strategic Planning
#19	Effect of Country Political Climate
#20	Telecommunications

Source: Palvia, P. and Palvia, S. MIS Issues in India and a Comparison with the United States: Technical Note. International Information Systems. Vol. 1 No.2 April 1992.pp 100-110
Table 9: Key Issues In Information Systems Management - India (1992)

information systems. While many universities and educational institutes are attempting to meet the burgeoning demand, some of these efforts may be misdirected from an IS point of view. The current emphasis on education seems to be on technological aspects rather than on the application of IS concepts to business needs.

Rank 3. Quality of Input Data: Information systems rely on accurate and reliable data. The age-old adage of GIGO (Garbage In Garbage Out) is well known in MIS, and directly impacts the quality of IS. This issue has also been seen in Russia (Chepaitis, 1994) and other developing countries. While not reported as a key issue in US studies, it appears that developing countries have inferior input data due to several reasons: lack of information literacy and information culture among workers as well as a less-than-adequate infrastructure for collecting data. Some managers reported experiences of excessive errors in data transcription as well as deliberate corruption of data.

The underlying causes may be mistrust of and intimidation caused by computer processing, resulting in carelessness, apathy and sabotage.

Rank 4. Educating Senior Managers about MIS: This issue suggests a possible response to the top-ranked issue dealing with the lack of understanding and awareness of the role of MIS in organizations. It appears that senior managers do not truly understand the full potential of information technology. They need to be educated not so much about the technology per se, but more so about its many applications in business. For example, besides transaction processing, IT can be used for building executive information systems and strategic systems. Exposure to such possibilities by way of education and training can provide new and innovative ideas to managers to utilize IT fruitfully. In the authors' opinion, any education must be supplemented with business cases and some hands-on training.

Rank 5. User Friendliness of Systems: The appearance of this issue in a developing nation may be attributed to several factors. First, the users in a developing nation are generally novices and untrained in the use of information technology; thus they may not be at ease with computer interfaces. Second, much of the software and systems are imported from western and advanced nations. This software is geared to the needs of their people and may not be user-friendly as per the needs and cultural backgrounds of users in the importing nation. A hypothesis can be made that the ergonomic characteristics of an information system are at least partially dependent on the cultural and educational background of the people using them.

Rank 6. Continuing Training and Education of the MIS Staff: The education issue comes up once again, this time in the context of MIS personnel. Rapid advances in technology and a lower level of IT preparedness in developing countries put further pressure on MIS personnel to keep pace with the technology. Another challenge here is to not only provide training on the technology but to be able to do that from a business perspective. Specifically, two of the problems reported were: many current training plans attempt to train a large number of people simultaneously at the expense of quality, and there is a lack of proper training available for MIS professionals in business functions.

Rank 7 (tie). Maintenance of Software, and Standards in Hardware and Software: These two related issues were tied in rank. Maintenance refers to fixing and updating production software when there are bugs or new requirements. Maintenance is a problem because of inadequate resources and competition for resources from new applications. Compared to developed nations, developing nations suffer from an inadequate supply of trained programmers. The problem is compounded if the majority of the software is purchased as packaged software. The maintenance effort is likely to be high if the quality and applicability of the purchased system is low. The quality of a system depends, in part, on the existence and enforcement of hardware and software standards, which brings us to the next issue.

The issue of standards in hardware and software is an important one in developing countries, as much software and hardware (especially hardware) is imported from other countries. The problems of hardware/software standards are compounded manifold when one is buying hardware and software produced by different vendors in different nations, each with its own proprietary systems. While some international standards exist (e.g. in programming languages and telecommunications); the ultimate challenge will be to develop an exhaustive set of standards, and then to be able to enforce them.

Rank 9. Data Security: An organization's data is a valuable corporate resource, and needs to be protected else it may be abused to the organization's detriment. Data contained in manual systems was not very vulnerable to breach of security due to either unavailability of ready access or inordinately long access times. As a result, many information workers have developed poor practices and habits in data handling. With computerized systems, this attitude can cause severe data security and integrity problems. Newer controls and security provisions, which were unheard of in manual systems, may need to be built which may themselves cause resistance in adoption.

Rank 10 (tie). Packaged Applications Software Availability, and Cultural Barriers: These two issues were tied in rank. Off-the-shelf packaged application software provides an inexpensive alternative to in-house development. All around the world, a lot of software is purchased off-the-shelf. An inadequate supply of MIS personnel (an issue discussed earlier) further necessitates an increased reliance on packaged software. While much packaged software is now being made available, there is need to develop more that meets the specific business requirements unique to developing nations.

Culture plays a role in the application of information technology (Ein-Dor et al. 1993), although sometimes in subtle ways. For example, in one governmental office, secretaries and clerical people were mandated to use word-processing equipment. But as soon as the mandate was removed, they went back to typewriters and manual procedures. Apparently, they trusted their age-old equipment more, and it gave them a greater sense of control. Chepaitis (1994) provides the example of Russia, where people have never gathered, shared, and managed bountiful information. As a result, information is often hoarded for personal gains rather than freely shared or invested.

Other Issues: Issues ranked just after the ones discussed above included maintenance of hardware and alignment of MIS with the organization. Many organizations are getting personal computers, and their maintenance sometimes becomes a problem due to limited vendor presence and delays in procuring parts. Aligning of MIS with organization is an issue of moderate importance. According to an Indian manager, beyond alignment, the organizational culture and philosophy itself has to change to accept the role of MIS. Applications portfolio is not a major issue as most businesses are in the initial stages of information systems growth and are in the process of computerizing basic operations. For the same reasons, MIS strategic planning was not rated high, and telecommunications was considered not of immediate interest but more a concern of the future.

KEY MIS ISSUES IN UNDERDEVELOPED NATIONS

Underdeveloped or basic countries are characterized by low or stagnant economic growth, low GNP, high levels of poverty, low literacy rates, high unemployment, agriculture as the dominant sector, and poor national infrastructure. While precise categorization is difficult, subjective and arguable, countries like Bangladesh, Cuba, Haiti, Jordan, Kenya, Nigeria, Iran, Iraq, and Zimbabwe may be included in this group. Note that countries may move in and out of a particular class over time. In this chapter, we use two African countries: Kenya and Zimbabwe as examples of under-developed nations.

Key Issue Ranks

The key MIS issues of Kenya and Zimbabwe were reported by Palvia, Palvia, and Zigli (1992), and were based on a study completed by Zigli in 1990. The methodology used in Zigli's study was based on the India study by Palvia and Palvia (1992). The same questionnaire, with minor modifications was used to collect the data. A number of in-depth personal interviews with senior information systems executives were conducted utilizing the questionnaire for data collection and as the basis for discussions. Information was also gathered from local trade publications and other secondary sources.

The computing industry in both countries at the time appeared to be competing in an environment that was strongly influenced by government and lack of "hard foreign currency". The hard currency situation was exacerbated by the virtual absence of indigenous hardware and software production, resulting in an inventory of outdated hardware and software. In addition, IT was accorded a very low priority by the government. As a result, purchases of equipment were being made from wherever possible, leading to mixed vendor shops and associated problems. Given the basic nature of IT adoption in these countries, only seven issues emerged with any degree of consensus. These are shown in Table 10 and are discussed as per the 1990 study reported in (Palvia et al. 1992).

Rank 1. Obsolescence of Computing Equipment: Of greatest concern was the state of obsolescence of most computer equipment. The need for state of the art equipment is urgent and was a critical concern for the IS executives. The current inventory is aging fast and simply does not meet the requirements of most businesses. A major contributing factor is the balance of trade and more specifically, the shortage of "hard foreign currency". These computers were state of the art twenty years ago but no longer. Not much progress has been made in 20 years. In fact, some regression may have occurred. These computers have now gone through two or three iterations of emulation's, and both efficiency and effectiveness have suffered. The short-fall of computer equipment not only affects the private sector but the public sector as well. Overall, national infrastructures of both countries appear ill-prepared to advance information technology to bring it to par with the rest of the world.

Rank	Description of Issue
#1	Obsolescence of Computing Equipment (hardware)
#2	Obsolescence of Operating and Applications Computer Programs (software)
#3	Proliferation of Mixed Vendor Shops (hardware and software)
#4	Availability of Skilled MIS Personnel and opportunities for Professional Development for MIS Managers and Non-Managers
#5	Possible Government Intervention/Influence in Computer Market
#6	Establishment of Professional Standards
#7	Improvement of IS Productivity

Source: Palvia, P., Palvia, S., and Zigli, R.M. Global Information Technology Environment: Key MIS Issues in Advanced and Less Developed Nations. In The Global Issues of Information Technology Management, edited by S. Palvia, P. Palvia, and R.M. Zigli, Idea Group Publishing, 1992.

Table 10: Key Issues In Information Systems Management Underdeveloped Nations Of Africa (1992)

Rank 1 (tie). Obsolescence of Software: The inventory of software (including operating systems and application programs) is also quite dated. Most of the packages are of the word processor and spreadsheet variety, or their emulations. Only recently have relational databases been introduced into both countries. The acute shortage of "hard foreign currency" precludes firms from purchasing software from overseas vendors, and further leads to exceptionally high rates of software piracy (especially for microcomputers). Major systems development is a rare occurrence. There seems to be simply no concept of integrated business systems, e.g., in manufacturing or accounting. However, some contemporary software is being introduced on a limited scale. For example, the relational database package Oracle is now being distributed in both countries by local software firms.

Rank 3. Proliferation of Mixed Vendor Shops: There are many vendors to choose from within one country, let alone the number of vendors in the entire world. While competition among vendors should raise the quality and reduce the cost of technology acquisition, it may also cause severe problems if vendor selection is not done carefully. Due to lack of coherent policies on part of the government and the firms, many purchases of hardware and software are made on an opportunistic and ad-hoc basis from whatever source and vendor that happens to be available at the time. This has led to the proliferation of mixed vendor shops. Of course, mixed vendor shop has added to the problems of IS management, operation, and maintenance. Mixed vendor shop was seen as a major detriment to efficiency and productivity by a number of firms in the interview sample.

Rank 4. Availability of Skilled MIS Personnel and Professional Development: There is a shortage of people with computing and systems skills. Finding trained personnel and keeping existing information systems people current with the latest advances in IT are vital concerns of information systems managers in these less developed nations. They are too few qualified people, and they are being spread too thin. This issue has implications for the educational system of under-developed nations: they must incorporate education and training in high technology areas, do it fast, and keep their programs constantly updated lest they become obsolete again.

Rank 5. Possible Government Intervention in the Computer Industry: In economies dominated by government control, there is always the risk of government intervention in the computer industry thereby threatening to reduce competition and increasing the probability of a monopoly. While a selected few may benefit from government actions, the larger business community tends to suffer. Such intervention may occur in the form of issuance of import licenses to new, local businesses in an effort to encourage their growth. Unfortunately, these new firms sell their licenses to existing, larger vendors. Both the sellers and the buyers realize substantial profits. Another example of government action is the mandated markups on imported parts and equipment. As a result of these markups (equaling or exceeding 100%), virtual cartels have emerged, and the cost of computers, computer peripherals and computer software have become one of the highest in the world.

Rank 6. Establishment of Professional Standards: The lack of professional standards threatens the entry of non-professionals and untrained people into the MIS field, thereby further aggravating the IS quality issue. Therefore, the professional data processing societies in these two countries are very anxious to gain "official" approval authorizing them to establish or participate in the establishment of standards of behavior and expertise for MIS professionals. The establishment of such standards will go a long way towards the development of better quality IS products. It should also improve productivity, the subject of the next issue.

Rank 7. Improvement of IS Productivity: Productivity is a concern in these two nations as a result of lack of professionalism, lack of access to state of the art productivity tools, and deteriorating hardware and software. In general, the productivity concern seems to extend to all aspects and areas of information systems. Over the last decade, there has been considerable emphasis on productivity in the advanced nations, and serious efforts have been made to enhance productivity (e.g., in the use of fourth generation languages, and CASE tools). However, in the less-developed countries, while being recognized as a problem, productivity appears to take a back seat to often more pressing problems.

Other Issues: The existence of archaic hardware and software and the inability to acquire modern resources have caused an ever-widening technological gap and thereby a loss of competitiveness of the domestic businesses that depend upon such equipment. Erosion of the competitive position of firms was an issue expressed by several local executives. Another issue cited by some executives is the question of the local manufacture of hardware and software. This appears to be a polarizing issue. The foreign based vendors, as one would expect, oppose the local manufacture, while users and the government favor it. However, software development may be a prime determinant in the evolution of information technology in less-developed nations, as in the case of India and Philippines.

What was equally surprising were the issues not mentioned by the participants. For example, understanding of MIS by senior executives did not emerge as an issue of significant concern. Using IS for competitive advantage is another issue that did not surface in the interview process. In general, the strategic dimensions of information technology do not seem to be as important as the operational issues.

A MODEL OF GLOBAL INFORMATION TECHNOLOGY ENVIRONMENT

In summary, we have presented key IS management issues for representative countries in each of the four classes, and made comments about several other countries. Space considerations prevent us from discussing results from other countries that might be available. For example, key issues not discussed in this chapter, but investigated and available in the literature, include the following countries: United Kingdom (Galliers et al., 1994), Gulf countries (Badrii, 1992), Estonia (Dexter et al., 1993), and Slovenia (Dekeleva & Zupancic, 1993).

In any case, our discussion shows that there are major differences between issues of different countries, and few commonalties. There were more common issues between USA and Taiwan, and fewer between other countries. As an overall impression, it seems that advanced countries are driven by strategic needs, developing countries by operational needs, and under-developed countries by infrastructural needs. Based on this observation, Palvia et al. (1992) posited an initial model of country specific MIS issues based on economic development of the country. This model classified countries into three categories based on the level of economic growth. These categories are: advanced countries (e.g., United States, Canada, Japan), developing/operational countries (e.g., India, Russia, Argentina, Brazil), and under-developed/basic countries (e.g., Kenya, Chile, Iran, Nigeria). They acknowledged that the placement of a country into a particular category is subject to some debate, and that countries may change categories over time. Nevertheless, they were able to make some broad generalizations on the nature of IS issues based on economic growth of a nation. According to the model, the level of information technology adoption increases from one stage to next, i.e., from underdeveloped to developing to advanced nations. Quite striking are the types of MIS issues at each stage of economic development. In the underdeveloped countries, the infrastructural issues dominate (e.g., the very availability of computer hardware, operating and applications software, and human resources for MIS). In the developing countries, operational issues are paramount (e.g., management's awareness of MIS capabilities, human resource development for MIS, quality of data, standards). Advanced country issues are characterized by strategic needs (e.g., information architecture, data resource management, strategic planning for MIS, organizational learning).

While the Palvia et al. (1992) model appears to be generally sound, the Taiwan study included in this chapter and experience from other countries has led us to refine the model (see figure 1). Another class of countries has been added to the original three-way classification. Several countries have emerged as the newly industrialized countries (NICs) in the last decade and are now prospering.

Examples of such countries include Taiwan, South Korea, Hong Kong and Singapore. If we extrapolate the Taiwan issues to NICs in general, then the majority of NIC issues are somewhat unique and different from other classes. To reiterate, representative NIC issues include: communication between IS department and end users, top management support, software development productivity, goal alignment, and security and control. Clearly, most of these issues are above the routine operational and infrastructural issues faced by organizations in under-developed and developing nations. Yet, they are lower in their strategic orientation as compared to the advanced nations. These issues then can most appropriately labeled as "management and control" issues reflective of growing technology adoption. In a sense, the refined "global information technology environment" model is correlated with the Nolan stage model (1979), which posited the need for a control stage to contain and manage the proliferation of IS activities in an organization. The main difference is that our model explains the nature of IT conditions and practices based on economic conditions in different countries.

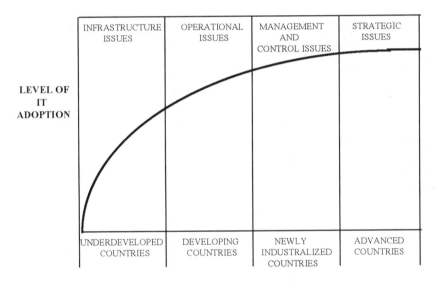

LEVEL OF ECONOMIC GROWTH

Figure 1: A Model Of Global Information Technology Environment

The addition of NICs into the model is also supported by the "management and control" oriented policies being exercised in these countries. For example, Taiwan, Singapore, and South Korea have one or two government agencies which coordinate and implement explicit national IT plans since the 1980s. These three country governments explicitly promote and manage the production and use of IT products. Computerization is a national goal and essential to maintaining the competitiveness of the national economy in the global environment.

The model depicted in Figure-1 provides a first attempt in understanding the complex global IT environment. We recognize that there are limitations and other elements may be necessary for a finer understanding of the global IT environment, or the environment of any particular country. For example, the inclusion of Russia and socialist countries under the "developing/operational" country class may be an object of concern for some. Singapore might also be a special case, as it is not really a country, but a city-state, and has a benevolent ruler form of government. Nevertheless, the above model may be a starting point for an organization considering expansion into other world markets, and attempting to evaluate the role and use of information technology in its pursuit.

Basic elements of a more complete model for global IT environment are offered in figure 2. Some summary comments are made about this model here; more elaboration and expansion are subjects of further investigation. Besides, level of economic growth, other factors critical to information technology adoption by firms in a country include its culture and political system. National culture comprises of the values, beliefs, and behavior patterns dominant in a country, and has a strong influence on institutional and organizational patterns of behavior. Ein-Dor et al. (1993) presented a framework for the role of culture on IS, and presented some culturally sensitive findings. Shore and Venkatachalam (1995) explored the impact of culture on systems analysis and design issues. Based on the emerging literature on international and cross-cultural IS, it is a reasonable argument to make that national culture would have an impact on IS priorities.

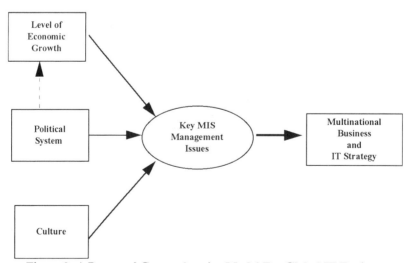

Figure 2: A Proposed Comprehensive Model For Global IT Environment

The politically system and government policies also have an impact on the IT readiness of a nation, as can be seen in the startling differences found among western countries, Russia, eastern Europe countries, and pacific rim countries. The government, inspired by its political beliefs, may take a hands-off (yet supportive) approach towards IT developments (as in USA and other free economies). On the other extreme, in spite of all good intentions, the government may impose a wide array of overly restrictive policies (as in some communist countries). As another alternative, the government may pursue an aggressive policy of rapid technology growth, and provide necessary incentives and infrastructure to firms (as in Taiwan, Singapore, and South Korea). The dotted line shown in figure 2 indicates that the political system of a nation also has an influence on its economic growth. Finally, as shown in the model, a good understanding of the global IT environment will be a key factor in the development of a suitable business and IT strategy of the multinational firm.

CONCLUSIONS

Reports of information systems management issues in different parts of the world are useful to organizations as they begin to plan and implement IT applications across the world. In this chapter, we have presented IS issues for many countries, and have examined the issues in USA, Taiwan, India, and Kenya & Zimbabwe in greater depth. The word is a large place, and attempting to understand the critical issues in every single country, or even selected countries, would be an arduous, perhaps an imprudent task. Instead, we have divided countries into four classes, and have provided an example in each class. An elementary model for the global IT environment has been postulated based on this categorization. While generalizations are fraught with risks, the provision of such a model will allow practitioners and researchers alike in a preliminary assessment of the criticality of the various IT issues in different regions of the world. In closing, we would like to exhort others to pursue the following lines of investigation:

1. Develop and validate sound models that seek to explain the country issues. A simple model was presented in figure 1. Elements of a more comprehensive model may include economic growth, national culture, and political system as causal factors, among others (as in figure 2).

2. Evaluate the predictive ability of such models as well as report on the use of the models for prediction. While descriptive studies are helpful in identifying the key issues of individual countries at a point in time, this can be an enormous and time-consuming proposition given the number of countries on the globe and the temporal nature of the issues. However, if

the determinants of the key issues are known, then a preliminary
estimation of the issues will be easier to make.

3.   Use the model for focused research. For example, if culture is identified as
one of the factors influencing IT needs, then it can be explored in more
detail both in terms of culture components and IT components that are
influenced by it.

4.   Develop a comprehensive universal instrument and methodology that can
be applied globally to identify the key IS issues. This instrument should
then be administered simultaneously (or approximately in the same time
frame) by a group of researchers in different countries. One of the
limitations of previous "key issue" studies is that they have used different
questionnaires, different time frames, and different methods to assess the
issues. While difficult, this undertaking will be very helpful in obtaining
reliable results.

5.   Develop specific practical implications and uses of the "key issues" results?
How can they be incorporated into the formulation of national policy,
corporate policy or IS policies within an organization?

Endnotes

1.   The terms: management information systems (MIS), information systems (IS), and
to some degree information technology (IT) are used interchangeably.

References

Badri, M. A. Critical Issues in Information Systems Management: An International Perspective.
International Journal of Information Management. Vol 12, 1992, pp. 179-191.

Ball, L., and Harris, R. SMIS Members: A Membership Analysis. *MIS Quarterly*, Vol 6, No 1, March 1982,
pp. 19-38.

Brancheau, James C., and James C. Wetherbe, 1987. Key Issues in Information Systems Management. *MIS
Quarterly*, March, pp. 23-46.

Burn, J., Saxena, K.B.C., Ma, L., and Cheung, H.K. Critical Issues of IS Management in Hong Kong: A
Cultural Comparison. *Journal of Global Information Management*, Vol 1, No 4, Fall 1993, pp. 28-37.

Carey, D. Rating the Top MIS Issues in Canada. *Canadian Datasystems*, June 1992, pp. 23-26.

Chepaitis, E.V. After the Command Economy: Russia's Information Culture and Its Impact on Information
Resource Management. *Journal of Global Information Management*, vol 2, no 1, Winter 1994, pp. 5-11.

CSC Index. *Critical Issues of Information Systems Management for 1995*, Cambridge, Massachusetts, 1995.

Deans, P.C., Karawan, K.R, Goslar, M.D., Ricks, D.A., and Toyne, B. Identification of Key International
Information Systems Issues U.S.-Based Multinational Corporations. *Journal of Management Information
Systems*, Vol. 27, No. 4, Spring 1991, pp. 27-50.

Dekeleva, S., and Zupancic, J. Key Issues in Information Systems Management: A Delphi Study in Slovenia. In: DeGross J. I.; Bostrom, R. P.; Robey, D., Eds. *Proceedings of the Fourteenth International Conference on Information Systems,* Orlando, FL, 1993.

Dexter, A. S., Janson, M. A., Kiudorf, E., and Laast-Laas, J. Key Information Technology Issues in Estonia. *The Journal of Strategic Information Systems.* June, 1993, vol 2, No 2, pp. 139-152.

Dickson, G.W., Leitheiser, R.L., Nechis, M., and Wetherbe, J.C. Key Information Systems Issues for the 1980's. *MIS Quarterly,* Vol 8, No 3, September 1984, pp. 135-148.

Ein-Dor, Philip, Segev, E., M. Orgad, 1993. The Effect of National Culture on IS: Implication for International Information Systems. *Journal of Global Information Management,* Winter: 33-44.

Galliers, R. D., Merali, Y., and Spearing, L. Coping with Information Technology? How British Executives Perceive the Key Information Systems Management Issues in the mid-1990s. *Journal of Information Technology.* Vol 9, No 3, 1994.

Goodman, S.E. Computing and the Resuscitation of Romania. *Communications of the ACM.* Vol 34, No 9, September 1991, pp. 19-22.

Goodman, S.E. and McHenry, W.K. The Soviet Computer Industry: A Tale of Two Sectors. *Communications of the ACM.* Vol 34, No 6, June 1991, pp. 25-29.

Hartog, Curt, and Martin Herbert, 1986. 1985 Opinion Survey of MIS Managers: Key Issues. *MIS Quarterly,* Dec., pp. 351-361.

Hassan, S.Z. Environmental Constraints in Utilizing Information Technologies in Pakistan. *Journal of Global Information Management,* vol 2, no 4, Fall 1994, pp. 30-39.

Igbaria, M., 1992. An Examination of Microcomputer Usage in Taiwan. *Information & Management,* 22: 19-28.

Janz, B., Brancheau, J., and Wetherbe, J. Key Issues in IS Management. Working Paper, *MIS Research Center,* University of Minnesota, 1994.

La Rovere, R.L., Tigre, P.B., and Fagundes, J. Information Networks Diffusion in Brazil: Global and Local Factors. in *Global Information Technology and Systems Management: Key Issues and Trends,* edited by P. Palvia, S. Palvia, and E. Roche, Ivy League Publishing, New Hampshire, 1996.

McFadden, F.R., and Hoffer, J.A. *Modern Database Management,* 4th Edition, Benjamin Cummings Publishing Company, California, 1994.

McLuhan, M. *Understanding Media: The Extensions of Man,* McGraw-Hill, New York, 1964.

Niederman, Fred, Brancheau, James C., and James C. Wetherbe, 1991. Information Systems Management Issues for the 1990s. *MIS Quarterly,* Dec., pp. 475-495.

Nolan, Richard L. 1979. Managing the Crisis in Data Processing. *Harvard Business Review,* vol. 57, no. 2 (March-April). pp. 115-126.

Palvia, P., and Palvia, S. MIS Issues in India, and A Comparison With the United States. *International Information Systems*, April 1992, pp. 100-110.

Palvia, P., Palvia, S., and Zigli, R.M. Global Information Technology Environment: Key MIS Issues in Advanced and Less Developed Nations. In *The Global Issues of Information Technology Management*, edited by S. Palvia, P. Palvia, and R.M. Zigli, Idea Group Publishing, 1992.

Palvia, P., and Wang, P. An Expanded Global Information Technology Issues Model: An Addition of Newly Industrialized Countries. *Journal of Information Technology Management*. Vol VI, No. 2, 1995, pp. 29-39.

Rao, K. V., Huff, F. P., and G. B. Davis, 1987. Critical Issues in the Management of Information Systems: a Comparison of Singapore and the USA. *Information Technology*, 1 (3): 11-19.
Roche, E.M. *Managing Information Technology in Multinational Corporations*. MacMillan Publishing Company, New York, 1992.

Shore, B., and Venkatachalam, A.R. The Role of National Culture in Systems Analysis and Design. *Journal of Global Information Management*, vol 3, no 3, summer 1995, pp. 5-14.

Wang, P. Information Management Systems Issues in the Republic of China for the 1990s. *Information & Management*, vol 26, 1994, pp. 341-352.

Watson, R. T., 1989. Key Issues In Information Systems Management: an Australian Perspective - 1988. *Australian Computer Journal*, 21 (3): 118-129.

Watson, R.T., and Brancheau, J.C. Key Issues in Information Systems Management: An International Perspective. *Information & Management*, vol 20, 1991, pp. 213-223.

2 The European Telecommunications Industry: Trends Analysis and Future Forecast

Ewan Sutherland
University of Wales, UK

Telecommunications are undergoing a major change in Europe. In the past, telecommunications policies and structures were controlled by rigid and inefficient entities such as the Post, Telephone and Telegraph (PTT) authorities and government run monopolies. Driven by increasing competition, globalisation, and adoption of new technologies in today's world, the European Telecommunications industry is responding to make its operations more efficient and effective to meet new customer needs and expectations. This chapter provides a careful analysis of the industry, first in the European Union and its single internal market. Then, it looks specifically at the happenings in the United Kingdom, Germany, Central and Eastern Europe, Hungary, and Bulgaria. Most countries have introduced major reforms in this dynamic industry, especially UK and Sweden. There are a few countries that lag behind, and they have a reluctance to admit competitors. Overall (with the exception of a few countries), the future of telecommunications appears to be bright in Europe.

INTRODUCTION

The 1990s are seeing continuing dramatic changes in the European telecommunications industry, transforming its appearance, structure and practices, eroding what were once unquestioned certainties. Globalisation, as a result of new customer needs and the adoption of new technologies, combined with radical changes in the attitude of governments are sweeping away the old order. This chapter examines the European telecommunications industry, with particular attention to the cases of the United Kingdom, Germany, Hungary and Bulgaria as examples of the many different issues and problems.

The rigidities of the old market and industry structures were legendary. Clearly defined national markets were controlled by Post, Telephone and Telegraph authorities (PTTs) and supplied by national manufacturers or by the local subsidiaries of multi-national corporations. Integration with manufacturing—found in the USA with AT&T and in Canada with Bell Canada Enterprises (BCE)—was unknown in Europe. That function had been preempted by governments, though seldom performed very efficiently. Attention to the needs of customers was a concept of little relevance; products and services were devised and supplied as PTTs saw fit.

Integrated Services Digital Network (ISDN) was the last example of a large scale development driven by the PTTs. It dates back some fifteen years and was originally an attempt to achieve a technically advanced service over the existing copper cables in the local loop. Today efforts are being made to provide television-quality video in those same copper cables known as Asymmetric Digital Subscriber Loop (ADSL). The extremely long gestation period for the development of the ISDN standard meant that it had ceased to be state-of-the-art when hardware and services were finally introduced. The growth of personal computers meant a difficult fight to persuade computer manufacturers to produce ISDN adapter cards, an indication of how the market was changing. Transmission capacity has increased and the telecommunications market has become scarcely recognisable, leaving ISDN barely relevant. Perhaps the most telling criticism of the PTTs was their ineffective marketing of ISDN. The jokes about ISDN tell the story: Interfaces Subscribers Don't Need and I Still Don't Need it.

No longer can a PTT roll out a service with the certain knowledge that customers will gratefully accept it or that they can be manipulated into accepting it by adjustments to the tariffs. PTTs now face true competition from global telecommunications and computer companies, based on servicing genuine customer needs.

Change

Dramatic changes are occurring in service provision, brought about by new customer demands, in technological capability and through entrepreneurial pressure. Customers are increasingly looking for global or at least pan-European services. Some businesses want highly sophisticated services such as global virtual private networks, while others prefer to buy large capacity digital 'pipes' (e.g., 'dark fibre' at 2-5 Gbps) with which they can build their own networks. However it is provided, telecommunications plays a vital rôle in the provision of services and, combined with computers, is essential in strategic information systems and business process redesign [Sutherland, 1994].

The technology comes with ever shorter product life cycles and consequently greater risks of commercial failure. In the past PTTs could rely on their control of standard setting processes and their powers of enforcement. Today it is increasingly obvious that the traditional standardisation process is too bureaucratic and too slow to keep up with changes in technology and markets. The recent re-organisation of the International Telecommunications Union (ITU) seems unlikely to keep pace with changes in the marketplace where *de facto* standards have growing dominance. It is not yet clear whether telecommunications companies can successfully compete against computer corporations, now that their respective markets have collided.

Country	Company	Date(s)	Amount (Bn)	Method	Residual state holding
United Kingdom	Cable & Wireless	1981-1983		Floatation	0%
United Kingdom	British Telecom	1983-1993		Floatation	0%
Hungary	Matav	1993-1996	US$ 2	Sale+ Floatation	21%
Denmark	Tele Denmark	1995	DKr 19	Floatation	52%
Netherlands	KPN	1994-1996	US$ 4	Floatation	0%
Czech Republic	SPT Telecom	1995	US$ 1.5	Sale	75%
Portugal	Telecom Portugal	1995	US$ 0.9	Sale	72%
Spain	Telefonica	1995	US$ 1.5	Sale	20%
Greece	OTE	1995	US$ 0.5	Floatation	75%
Italy	STET	1995	US$ 7	Floatation	25%
Belgium	Belgacom	1995	US$ 2	Sale	75%
Germany	Deutsche Telekom	1996	DM 15	Floatation	51%
France	France Télécom	1998?		Floatation	51%
Ireland	Telecom Éireann	1999?		Sale	50%
Switzerland	PTT Telecom	1999?		Floatation	49%

Source: Financial Times and Public Networks Europe.
Table 1: Privatisations in Europe

Privatisation has moved from the political avant-garde to become accepted practice. This has been accentuated by a new generation of technologies and the globalisation of service provision to match customer needs. Few countries are welcome in the state-owned monopoly of another country, equally few can afford to fund the global expansion of their own PTT. The capital necessary for that expansion is much more easily raised through flotation than extracted from governments or customers. European countries are at differing stages in privatising their PTTs, with even Albania considering selling its PTT (see table 1). The only remaining resistance is from trades unions, most notably in Greece and France.

In an era of global super-carriers, PTTs can be divided into two categories, a few very large potential survivors and the remainder which must search for international partners. Only a few organisations can hope to survive as a significant or even dominant partner in a group, for example, BT. For the majority of PTTs in Central, Eastern and Western Europe, the best hope is a continuing local rôle in the delivery of services for an international group, in which they are a minor partner or a service unit.

The old pattern is consigned to history. Today there is a free market already established in customer premises equipment and competition can be seen in a growing number of market segments. Although only Sweden and the UK have genuinely free competition, other countries are gradually joining them.

The structure of this chapter is to look first at the European Union and its single internal market. The United Kingdom is the most open market in Europe and often used as an exemplar. Germany is the largest market and one where competition has proved more difficult to introduce. Thereafter, the transition economies of Central and Eastern Europe are examined. Hungary is an instance of substantial growth and progress, whereas Bulgaria has allowed an initially strong position to weaken. The conclusion examines the patterns of regulation, technology and globalisation across Europe.

THE SINGLE EUROPEAN MARKET FOR TELECOMMUNICATIONS

Within the fifteen nations of the European Union (EU) there is a wide range of service provision. For most countries in north-west Europe there is limited growth in voice telephony, though some southern European countries are growing more rapidly as they try to catch up (see figure 1). Much faster growth in the telecommunications industry is found in mobile telephony and in the Asian and Latin American markets. Telefónica de España, for example, has bought into telephone companies in Latin America for their growth potential, rather than their installed base.

The market for digital mobile telephony is thriving, in both Groupe Speciale Mobile (GSM) and Personal Communication Network (PCN). What is noticeable in figure 2 is the variation, which is accounted for by the national regulatory practices, rather than by factors such as disposable income or economic development. Mobile telephony licences are attracting a variety of new entrants, from manufacturers such as Motorola, to utilities such as Veba and computer companies such as Olivetti.

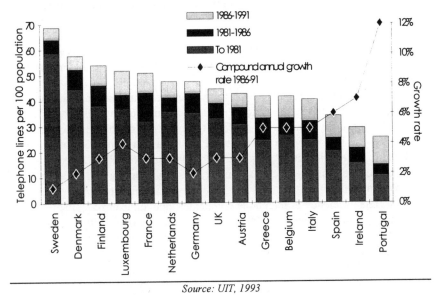

Source: UIT, 1993
Figure 1: The Growth Of Telephony In the European Union

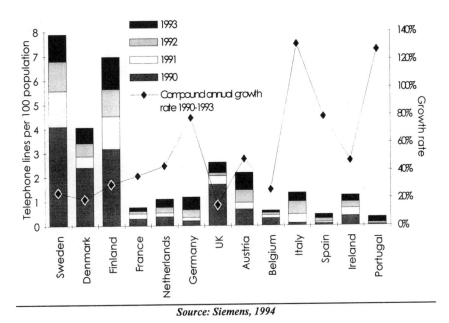

Source: Siemens, 1994
Figure 2: Growth Of Digital Mobile Telephony In the European Union

The growth of GSM mobile telephony service was aided by a Memorandum of Understanding sponsored by the European Union, co-ordinating the introduction and interworking of GSM. Directives have obliged member states to licence a second, competing GSM operator and have forced the early granting of a PCN licence. All of which attack the historical dominance of the PTT. [EC, 1994]

An important trend has been the formation of international alliances, for example, BT linking with Tele Danmark, Telenor and Telecom Finland. Uniworld has been created by AT&T linking its WorldSource service with Unisource, the latter being a joint venture of Telia (Sweden), Koninklijke PTT Nederland, Telefónica de España and the Swiss Telecom PTT. One new rival, Hermes Europe Railtel BV, is a joint venture formed by European national railway companies.

The efficiency of telephone companies can be measured, albeit crudely, in terms of telephone lines per 100 employees (see figure 3). Whilst most share a gradual improvement, there are dramatic differences in the efficiency of the individual telephone companies, with poorer figures for the Mediterranean countries and the former Marxist-Leninist states of Central and Eastern Europe. Some of the differences can be accounted for by differing levels of digitalisation of central office switches, since automation produces enormous

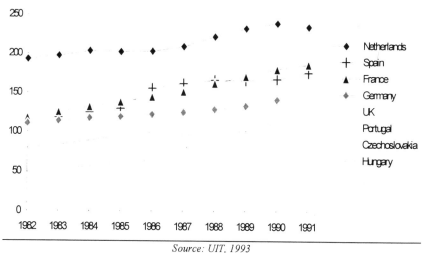

Source: UIT, 1993
Figure 3: Telephone Lines Per 100 Employees

savings in staff costs. An organisational focus on the customer can also lead to reduced staffing. More complex changes are being introduced under the banner of business process redesign. While employment in traditional PTTs is declining and this trend is set to continue, there is some compensating growth in their newer rivals and in the distribution chains, for example, in telephone shops and mobile telephone dealerships.

Apart from the adoption of new technology, the major force changing the environment for telephone companies has been politics. The European Union has adopted pro-active policies for the creation of a single market in telecommunications with significant lowering of entry barriers. The European Commission (EC) has even used threats against member states under Article 90 of the Treaty of Rome in order to force the introduction of competition, for example, in customer premises equipment. Its aim is the creation of a market for services and products which spans the European Union. Overall it seeks to promote the transition from distinct national markets to a single and highly competitive market. Telecommunications policy is handled within the framework of Open Network Provision which has evolved considerably as the politics has unfolded and more member states have accepted that competition and not monopoly is the best, perhaps, only policy. It was even included in the Maastricht Treaty. [EC, 1987; EC, 1993]

National monopolies for voice telephony end on 31 December 1997. There are optional derogations for Greece, Ireland, Portugal and Spain until 2002 in order that they may 'catch up' by further expansion of their national networks. Data communications companies and value-added service providers are now allowed to lease lines from any supplier and the European Union is considering ending the restrictions on the monopoly provision of telecommunications infrastructure by the national PTTs. Telephone companies are losing lucrative international revenues to International Simple Resale (ISR) and the growth of services such as 'calling cards' and 'call-back'. The other losers in this are hotels, which take substantial profits on calls.

Access by foreign companies is usually on a reciprocal basis only, which limits the activities of telecommunications companies from the USA. One justification for this was that until recently European PTTs have had great difficulty in obtaining licences in the USA, since they were automatically designated dominant carriers. Many European countries have been very defensive on behalf of their PTTs, being justifiably afraid of the more innovative and customer-focused North American telecommunications companies. Equally, the USA has been vociferous in demanding access to European Union markets, especially for its equipment suppliers which complain about tendering procedures. US-based telephone companies can obtain licences in some sectors in some European Union member states, but outside Sweden and the UK it is somewhat patchy. Recent changes indicate a growing openness to foreign competitors.

Regulation in member states of the European Union is slowly passing from ministers and government officials to quasi-independent agencies, though some are still closely linked to PTTs and to politicians. The convergence with broadcasting is of growing significance, notably in problems of dealing with Video on Demand (VoD), where the collision of market sectors is particularly evident (see figure 4). This is especially complex because there are state owned television channels. The European Commission is playing an increasingly important rôle in co-ordinating the adoption of new technologies and moves to the *Infobahn*, *Infostrada* or Information Superhighway. Importantly this is not to be by subsidy, but by the creation of an appropriate environment for commercial developments. [HLCIS, 1994]

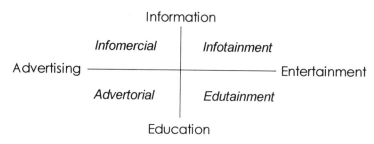

Figure 4: Services On The Infobahn

Across the European Union the single market in telecommunications is being completed. National governments, the Council of Ministers and the European Commission are working to ensure the delivery of advanced services to the poorer regions. They are also encouraging European collaboration in the development of the technology and its applications. The telecommunications companies are obliged to cope in environments which are very different from the recent past. The new conditions of competition necessitate the development of international collaborative ventures, while acquiring a customer focus, as the following examples show.

The United Kingdom

The United Kingdom has been at the forefront of privatisation, because of the position taken by the Thatcher Administration (1979-1992). British Telecom, the former telecommunications arm of the Post Office, was a key and early target of privatisation, yielding very large sums of money over a number of years. Since 1992 the market has been opened to almost free competition, 57 licences were issued in the period to the end of 1994, together with a further 90 voice telephony licences for cable television franchisees. The 1990s have seen increasing public anxiety and doubts about the success of privatisation policies, though generally focused on sectors other than telecommunications. One criticism has been over the salary of the chief executive of BT.

Cable and Wireless (C&W), the old 'Imperial Carrier', was nationalised by the Attlee Administration in 1947. In 1981 it was privatised, ahead of BT. C&W has grown solidly over the last decade (see figure 5). Today it seems increasingly likely to be absorbed into an international grouping, not least because there seems to be a lack of strategic alignment within the C&W group. Cable & Wireless had abortive discussions with AT&T in 1993 and,

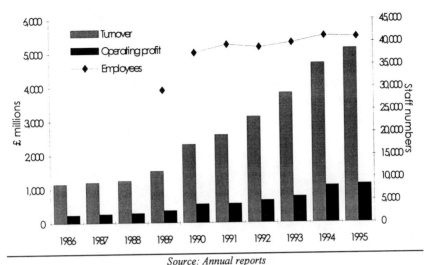

Source: Annual reports
Figure 5: Growth of Cable & Wireless plc

allegedly, with BT. In late 1994, it sold a 10.5% stake to Veba, a large German industrial grouping. The stock market value of Cable & Wireless has often been said to be that of its 57.5% share of Hong Kong Telecommunications, making a break-up or take-over attractive and, perhaps, inevitable. In 1995 Cable and Wireless announced a move into marketing telecommunications for specific industry sectors; its first venture, for the oil industry, was launched with Schlumberger.

In order to create competition in the UK domestic market, Mercury was conjured up to be the second player in a genteel duopoly which ran from 1982 to 1992. Initially Mercury was owned jointly by Cable & Wireless (40%), British Petroleum (40%) and Barclays Bank (20%). In 1986 it became a wholly owned subsidiary of Cable & Wireless, effectively its operating arm in the UK. Then in 1992 Cable & Wireless sold a 20% stake in Mercury for £480 millions to BCE, the Canadian manufacturer and operator. A 50% stake in its subsidiary, Mercury Personal Communications Ltd, was sold to US West—this company offers a PCN service under the brand-name 'one2one'.

Mercury grew slowly but solidly in the UK market, attaining some ten percent market share (see figure 6). By 1994, Mercury was seen to be under considerable commercial pressure from rivals, for example, BT and newcomers such as City of London Telecommunications (COLT) in the City of London and WorldCom and MFS Communications on Trans-Atlantic business. Mercury was not helped by its unimpressive record of quality of service, having for too long focused on competing on cost. Customers had learned from dealing with Mercury what a free market in telecommunications was like and were better able to manage multiple suppliers. In late 1994 Mercury replaced its chief executive and began the painful process of reducing its workforce of 11,400 to some 8,000. Perhaps symbolically, it sold its public payphone business and gave up direct sales of telephone equipment.

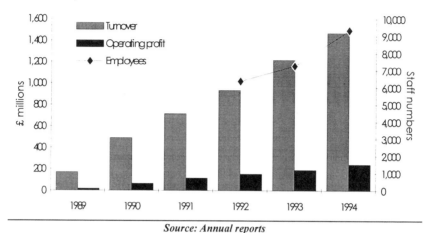

Source: Annual reports
Figure 6: Growth Of Mercury Plc

Advances in technology created the potential for new services which in turn allowed additional competition. The most conspicuous example being in mobile telephony which was initially offered by Vodafone and Cellnet (a joint venture between BT and Securicor) using analog technology. In 1993 the first of the new digital GSM services was launched by Vodafone, with Cellnet following in 1994. Both offer extensive coverage of continental Europe through exchange agreements. Vodafone has expanded overseas, by joining consortia bidding for mobile telephone licences in continental Europe.

In the early 1990s four licences were issued for Telepoint, a mobile telephone service with no incoming calls. All failed due to lack of consumer interest and the service was allowed to die quietly and quickly. The most recent licences for mobile telephony have been for PCN services, marketed as one2one and Orange, aimed at a mass market.

Another newcomer is Energis Communications Ltd which launched its service on 15 September 1994. It is a subsidiary of National Grid plc, which operates the electricity grid in England and Wales, which is currently jointly owned by the privatised Regional Electricity Companies (RECs). National Grid plc is due to be floated on the stock market in the near future. Energis used the electricity grid to build a telecommunications network of some 3,500 kilometres, by wrapping fibre optic cable round the earth (or ground) wire slung between electricity pylons. In addition to offering services to larger customers such as the BBC and at smaller and medium-sized enterprises,

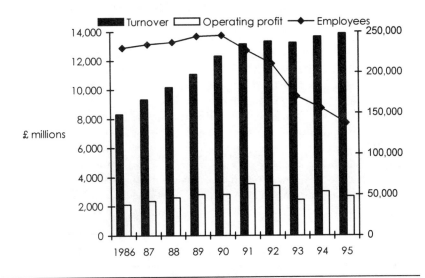

Source: Annual reports
Figure 7: BT Plc Turnover And Profits

Energis aims to resell capacity to other telephone companies which do not presently have infrastructure in the UK, such as AT&T and Telia. In November 1994, Scottish Telecom, a subsidiary of Scottish Power, one of the Regional Electric Companies (RECs) and a partner of Energis, launched its own telecommunications service aimed at the Scottish market. Many of the RECs have interests in cable television franchises.

Despite a growing number of rivals, BT continues to make immense profits, the subject of considerable domestic criticism and demands for even lower residential tariffs despite considerable reductions forced by the regulator (see figure 7). The other side of this success has been the massive reduction in staff at all levels in BT, aided business process redesign with Gemini Consulting to improve its business operations.

Part of the profit has been channelled into international expansion, notably in its US$ 4,300 millions deal to buy 20% of MCI in order to form a global venture. Together they offer Concert, a one-stop shop for global telecommunications services and, to date, the only such alliance to have been approved by the regulators. BT has the potential to be a successful international competitor, though its failed attempt in the 1980s to absorb the Canadian PBX manufacturer Mitel is a warning of the problems involved.

The licence for BT does not permit it to broadcast entertainment services until 2001 or later. This has been the subject of complaint by BT and a matter of political debate. BT has been experimenting with Video on Demand, including field trials currently underway with a wide range of partners. It clearly intends to develop commercial services as soon as practicable. [House of Commons, 1994]

Foreign direct investment in UK telecommunications is limited but growing. Primarily this is through the presence of US carriers participating in cable television franchises. Many of these now offer telephone services, a market expected to continue growing rapidly (see Table 2). Additionally, US West is a partner with Mercury in one2one and purchased Thomson Directories, publishers of Yellow Pages, for £70 millions in 1994. Reversing the pattern of Cable & Wireless, Hutchison Whampoa of Hong Kong operates Orange, the second PCN mobile telephone service, and formerly operated Rabbit, one of the abortive Telepoint services. In late 1994, AT&T was granted a full telecommunications licence for the United Kingdom, though to date its operations are very limited. Some years ago AT&T acquired ISTEL, a supplier of value-added services in the UK.

	1991	1992	1993	1994
Households passed	1,343,557	1,954,829	2,786,202	4,116,212
Households connected	268,812	440,162	611,423	915,592
Telephone exchange lines installed	21,225	106,989	314,381	741,146

Sources: Cable Communications Association.
Table 2: Cable Television And Telephony In The United Kingdom

International Simple Resale (ISR) has now been licensed in the UK, with reciprocal licensing in the USA. This had the immediate effect of cutting trans-Atlantic tariffs and will maintain the pressure to lower prices still further. The domestic consequence of this has been to put pressure on companies to lower long-distance tariffs within the UK, while internationally it both draws traffic to the UK to take advantage of the low tariffs and puts pressure on other European telephone companies to lower their own tariffs.

After more than ten years of the UK Telecommunications Act (1984) and a major review in 1992 there seem to be signs of success. Services are cheaper, more readily and more quickly available, including advanced services. The barriers to entry are falling and there are plenty of aspiring market entrants, though the success of domestic start-ups remains an open question. BT is competing in the global market and is seen to be a very significant player. The one serious criticism is the continuing dominance of BT. The UK is ahead of other European countries in terms of opening up its market. While it is difficult to judge on technical issues, it seems to be on a par with the USA. [Sutherland, 1995]

Germany

Germany has faced some quite different issues from the UK and in important respects is unique. Until recently, the government of Chancellor Kohl had made little progress towards the privatisation of Deutsche Bundespost (DBP) Telekom and had been slow in the creation of a truly competitive market—finally it seems to be doing that.

The DBP was an arm of the bureaucracy, under the *Bundesminister für Post und Telekommunikation* (BMPT) and embedded in Article 87 of the Constitution, requiring cross-party agreement for changes which proved difficult to obtain. It was not sufficiently appreciated by the politicians that telecommunications carriers would have to be international in scope and that the very survival of Deutsche Telekom, necessitated its privatisation.

The 1987 Report of the commission chaired by Professor Dr Eberhard Witte was split along party political lines. One important point was agreed, that the telecommunications monopoly was not included in the *Grundgesetz*, unlike the Deutsche Bundespost itself. In 1989 the Bundestag approved the *Poststrukturgesetz*, with the separation of Postdienst, Postbank and Telekom, within a new structure for the DBP. The monopoly was then limited to voice telephony and infrastructure, with the opening of markets in value added services and mobile telephony. This was in line with European Union policies which Germany had initially seemed to resist. Further reforms in 1994 legally separated Deutsche Telekom from Postbank and Postdienst, with the shares transferred to a Bundesamt and the BMPT being transformed into a regulator. The appointment of a number of politicians to the supervisory board of Deutsche Telekom has raised fears that at a time when the organisation needs to be given more freedom it will continue to be subjected to political control and interference. [Pfeiffer and Wieland, 1990]

Deutsche Telekom AG is due to be privatised in two tranches in mid-1996 and 2000 because at an estimated value of around DM 80 billions, it is much more than the market could digest at one time. Its floatation is being co-ordinated with that of Lufthansa, the state airline, to ensure that the market is not subjected to unnecessary stress. An alternative strategy would have been to link Deutsche Telekom with Siemens; vertical integration with its main supplier of switching and transmission equipment. Siemens is the owner of a substantial cash mountain and one of few firms which could afford to take a large stake. If this approach had been followed, it would have been sensible to separate the cable television activities and to privatise these separately, in order to increase competition in the market, breaking them up into *Länder* or municipalities and allowing them to offer telephony in competition with Deutsche Telekom. As it is, the combination of telecommunications and cable television is causing regulatory problems, since Deutsche Telekom so easily dominates the German telecommunications market in both telephony and in cable television. (See figure 8)

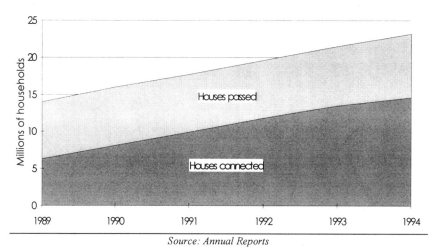

Source: Annual Reports
Figure 8: Deutsche Telekom Cable Television

A serious problem for the German government has been to ensure that the introduction of competition would not reduce the value of Deutsche Telekom when it is floated—money needed by the government. Yet, for the company, privatisation may have come too late to allow it to compete as an international telecommunications operator. Evidence from AT&T and from BT suggests that it takes a very long time to reshape the organisational culture and to devise a workable business strategy in the new global environment, involving a few necessary mistakes. Both have undergone considerable changes in organisational culture and have invested heavily in business process redesign.

The links between Deutsche Telekom and France Télécom to form Atlas and with Sprint to form Phoenix may represent a strategic route forward. If these alliances are ever approved by regulators in the European Union and the USA, it would create a telecommunications company of formidable size. Changes in the legal status of France Télécom makes a cross-holding of shares possible. The joint venture also presents real, even daunting challenges in organisational reforms, accentuated by national differences and sensitivities. France Télécom remains very close to the French government and *étatisme*, the leading rôle of the state, is deep in its culture. If this fails—a not improbable outcome, because of the cultural differences—Deutsche Telekom will be in very deep trouble, since the other consortia will be in place. It faces tough competition abroad and in the domestic markets, accentuated by the conditions for this approval of the deals, which require further and substantial opening of their domestic markets.

The deals are intended to provide Deutsche Telekom and France Télécom access to the US market and to make available in Europe the marketing skills of Sprint. The aims include the provision of one-stop shopping and pan-European services such as 800 freephone, calling cards, virtual private networks, data and voice networks. Deutsche Telekom has made other moves abroad, acquiring a share of Matav, the Hungarian PTT (see below), and in operations in the Ukraine. In May 1994 it bought a 16.6% stake in the *Société Européene des Satellites* for £180 millions, which as Astra broadcasts fifty television channels to Europe.

In anticipation of the opening of the German market in 1998, a number of players are moving into position. BT has formed an alliance with Viag, the owner of the electricity company in Bavaria. Thyssen has gone into partnership with Bell South, while RWE has established links with AT&T, Mannesmann and the Deutsche Bank. Veba, an industrial grouping which owns a large regional electricity company, has formed a range of alliances, including an arrangement to lay cable along the tracks of the state railway company, Deutsche Bahn, and with Cable & Wireless (see figure 9). In addition, Veba has the following telecommunications holdings:

- E-Plus (PCN, Germany) 28.5%
- Teleport Europe (VSAT, Europe) 49.7%
- Infomobile (paging, France) 10%
- MiniRuf (paging, Germany) 40%
- Concepta (cable television, Switzerland) 100%
- Helvesat (cable television, Switzerland) 100%
- Iridium (LEO, global) 10%
- Bouygues Telecom (PCN, France) 15%

A source of yet further competition lies in the municipalities which are entitled to build networks, for example, the city of Frankfurt with MFS Communications of the USA.

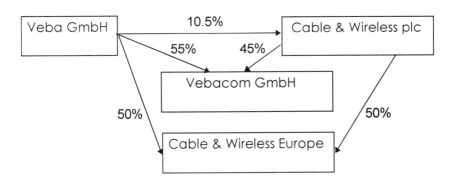

Figure 9: The Alliance Between Veba Gmbh And Cable & Wireless Plc

The totally unexpected re-unification of Germany in 1989, *die Wende*, with the effective annexation of the former Deutsche Demokratische Republik (DDR), presented massive difficulties in telecommunications. The poor quality of telecommunications in the former DDR was a major obstacle to the investment necessary to restart the economy. In particular the lack of lines linking the two Germanys was a severe bottleneck—only 1,450 lines in 1989, but increased to 34,000 by the end of 1991. The newly merged Deutsche Bundespost Telekom and Deutsche Post Telekom, handled problems commendably at a technical level through Program Telekom 2000. The targets were to install 7.2 million main lines, 5 million cable television connections,

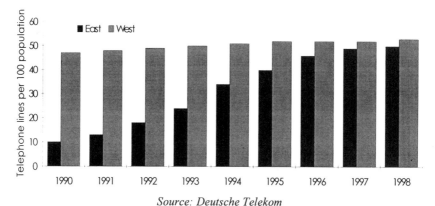

Source: Deutsche Telekom
Figure 10: Telephony In Germany

300,000 mobile telephone connections (with 90% coverage of the *neue Bundesländer*), 68,000 public coin and card phones and 50,000 Datex-P connections (see figure 10). Much of the early work was contracted out on turn-key projects. [Sacher, 1992; Schnöring and Szafran, 1994]

Germany is transferring some DM 60 billions to pay for the wiring and switches in the *neue Bundesländer*, in the period 1991 to 1997. At present there is no evidence of when, if ever, there will be a payback from the development of the *neue Bundesländer*. Increased competition, seems certain to make it even more difficult for Deutsche Telekom to recover its investment. Moreover, the economies of the *neue Bundesländer* remain weak with high levels of unemployment.

At the political level the decision making was unimaginative, the opportunity to introduce competition was largely ignored or fudged. A second GSM cellular service, D2-Privat, was licensed to a consortium led by Mannesmann (51.3%), including Pacific Telesis (26%) and Cable & Wireless (5%). This competes with Deutsche Telekom's DeTeMobil. A new mobile PCN service which began operation in the *neue Bundesländer* was licensed to E-plus, operated by Bell South, Vodafone, Veba and Thyssen. It would have been possible to have created a new telephone company for the *neue Bundesländer* and to allow it to compete with Deutsche Telekom in the western *Länder*, but this was too radical for government of Chancellor Kohl. The chosen solution was fast, extremely so, and substantially protected the interests of Deutsche Telekom and its traditional manufacturers. It was driven by national need, with more than a little consideration of party politics.

The Bundeskartelamt ruled in May 1994 that Deutsche Telekom had illegally cross-subsidised Datex-P (its packet switched data network) with DM 1.9 billion in the period 1989 to 1993. This ruling opened the way to rebalancing telecommunications tariffs more generally and increasing the competition in the German market. The dominant suppliers in the market for value-added services are Deutsche Telekom, Veba and Mannesmann, after some recent consolidation. Leased lines in Germany have been notoriously expensive, though they have begun to fall in price, for example, for a 2 Megabit per second leased line from DM 760 per month in 1991 to DM 240 in 1992 and to DM 170 in 1994. The tariffs have been based on volume of traffic, providing poor quality of service and value for money.

One of the real lessons of the 1990s has been that the Deutsche Bundespost has not been efficient for years, even decades. West Germany has been a surprisingly heavy investor in telecommunications with spending rising to DM 15 billion per annum in the late 1980s (see table 3). There is little evidence of more sophisticated or superior service which should be the reward of such high levels of spending. Vast sums have been channelled into cable television. The evidence from PA [1994] and elsewhere is that Germany is paying prices as much as four times the international average for its central office switches. The only rational explanation is that the expenditure was some sort of indirect subsidy to German telecommunications manufacturers.

	Units	1980	1981	1982	1983	1984	1985	1986	1987	1988
Revenues	billions	26.0	27.7	28.8	30.1	31.9	33.7	35.3	37.0	37.4
Investment	billions	9.4	10.7	11.2	11.3	12.9	14.8	14.9	15.5	15.7
Investment /Revenue	%	35.9%	38.5%	39.0%	37.5%	40.4%	43.8%	42.3%	41.8%	41.9%
Investment per line	DM	455.3	490.4	497.1	481.6	527.8	580.9	590.4	573.5	564.0
Investment per capita	DM	151.91	173.01	182.15	182.98	210.99	241.66	244.79	250.00	256.46

Source: ITU, 1990, page 39

Table 3: German Investment In Telecommunications

As a result of the prolonged monopoly the German consumer, residential as well as business, has been poorly served. This is changing as competition is beginning to be seen and by 1998 could be fierce. Foreign competitors are being allowed to compete from 1998 and seem ready and enthusiastic. Deutsche Telekom AG, finally freed from the PTT structure and soon from governmental control, is trying to make a rapid change, to a focus on customers. Yet it will take years to shed its image as a Kafkaesque bureaucracy. It is becoming a truly international operator, where it must prove itself able to adapt to operations in foreign countries and in joint ventures. Its Atlas and

Phoenix joint ventures with France Télécom and Sprint are high risk projects with, perhaps, a hint of panic in the search for partners.

Central And Eastern Europe

The state of the telephone networks in Central and Eastern Europe before they came under Soviet domination in the late 1940s was one of very limited development. Under Marxism-Leninism, telephone networks were part of the bureaucracy, fully controlled by the state. The mechanisms used were very similar to those of the UK and West Germany, though the purposes were different. Largely in ignorance of its economic significance, the telephone network was seen as a vehicle for passing down commands from the state planning apparatus. Successive five-year plans had very modest targets for the growth of telephone production and installation (see figure 11). In each country the industry was controlled by a sponsoring ministry, which regulated both the manufacturing industry and the provision of 'services', though without necessarily co-ordinating the two. While some Asian and African countries suffered from the inability to invest in telecommunications; Eastern Europe decided not to do so, as a matter of policy. [Sutherland, 1992]

For most people public call-boxes were the main means of access to the telephone network, but these were usually antiquated, unreliable and poorly maintained. The principal alternative was the less than surreptitious use of an office telephone for personal calls. For many, these are still the only means of access to the telephone network. The other popular use of telecommunications, was the telegram, something all but eliminated in Western Europe by the pervasive penetration of telephones and facsimile machines. British Telecom ceased to offer the service in October 1982. Danes and Germans send only 0.08 and 0.02 telegrams per capita per annum, compared with 0.8 in Hungary and 1.2 in Bulgaria, while the figures for the former USSR were even higher.

In the mid-1980s the Council for Mutual Economic Assistance (CMEA or Comecon) began a multi-national effort to build its own digital telephone exchange, aided by espionage efforts in the West. This failed because of the lack of technological capability, especially in the design of the chips and software, but also because of problems of co-ordination. PTTs were left relying on obsolete and labour intensive electro-mechanical equipment. They could not readily import equipment from the West, where they faced CoCom export restrictions, which limited purchases of equipment and doubled the price.

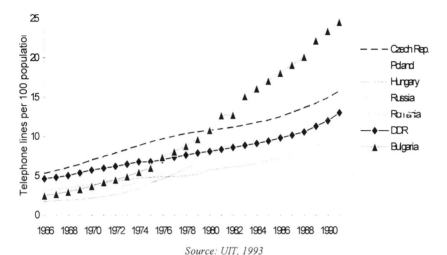

Source: UIT, 1993
Figure 11: Telephony In Central And Eastern Europe

Since 1989, developments in Central and Eastern Europe have relied on the goodwill of the international funding bodies (European Bank for Reconstruction and Development, European Investment Bank and the World Bank) and on the creation of opportunities which fit the strategic interests of international telephone companies and manufacturers. Thus the options are severely constrained. Until economic growth has been achieved for several consecutive years, the ability to extract full-price costs for services remains limited to a few customers in obviously identifiable niche markets. Consequently, service providers are sensibly concentrating on those most able to pay, for example, in supplying multinational corporations with services such as the satellite-based Very Small Aperture Terminal (VSAT) and new entrepreneurs with mobile telephones. All countries have now built digital overlay networks with new international gateways, substantially improving the quality of the telephone service. However, they are taking longer to replace central office switches and local cabling.

Mobile telephony was initially focused on the adoption of the Scandinavian standard, Nordic Mobile Telephone (NMT). The equipment was available relatively cheaply and the frequencies were not allocated to other users. Increasingly, service providers are looking to GSM for pan-European services and PCN is expected to follow in due course. The cheaper alternative of paging systems is also proving attractive, including the pan-European Ermes system.

Political and economic uncertainty limits the moves of the international telecommunications companies, which are unaccustomed to such an environment, notably in the former USSR. There has been considerable divergence of approaches, breaking up the old grey uniformity of Eastern Europe which are illustrated in the cases of Hungary and Bulgaria.

Hungary

Of the former Marxist-Leninist states, Hungary had one of the worst telecommunications infrastructures, with the remarkably low density of eight telephone lines per 100 population. It was particularly poor in urban centres, since the PTT had concentrated on servicing rural communities, though many of these had manual exchanges with operators available only during the working day. The reforms introduced since 1989 have allowed Hungary to move into the forefront of telecommunications in Central and Eastern Europe and it has now aligned its policies with those of the European Union.

Magyar Tavkozlesi (Matav), the Hungarian national telecommunications company, was separated from posts and broadcasting in 1990 but retains its monopoly on international traffic until 2000. Matav was never going to be a major international player like BT or AT&T, moreover it was burdened with massive domestic problems. It had little choice but to look for international partners both for capital and expertise. The sale of a minority holding in Matav attracted considerable international attention, especially in the USA, and delivered a remarkable sum of money. Ameritech and Deutsche Telekom acquired one-third of Matav in December 1993 for some US$ 875 millions and a commitment to spend US$ 4,300 millions up to 2002, beating STET (Italy) and a joint venture between France Télécom and US West. The new shareholders quickly gained control of the management and contrived to block an early attempt to float a tranche of Matav shares on the Budapest Bourse in order to allow reorganisation prior to the floatation, in the hope of raising the eventual value of the share issue.

While Matav has 85% of the market, the remaining 15% was separately licensed to a number of international telephone companies in fifteen different municipalities. Together these companies paid US$ 80 millions and are committed to invest a further US$ 200 millions.

A joint venture between US West and Matav, known as Westel, has operated a mobile telephone service since 1990 using the NMT standard. By the end of 1993 this had won some 40,000 subscribers. In March 1994, Westel launched 'Eurofon' a GSM service, fully compatible with other European GSM services and with reciprocal agreements signed with many other European countries. A second GSM licence was issued to Pannon, a consortium led by Unisource.

The opening up of mobile services, the construction by Matav of a digital overlay network, foreign investment and managerial expertise allowing an organisational transformation together put Hungary in a very strong position. The sale of a strategic stake in the national PTT has since been copied in the Czech Republic and in Belgium. Regulation has been devised in the light of experience in the UK and in consideration of the aspiration of Hungary to become a member of the European Union. The economy is relatively strong and has been successful in redirecting itself from facing east to looking westward, supported by a modernised market in which international telephone companies are important players.

Bulgaria

In contrast to Hungary, Bulgaria was in a much stronger position up to 1989 and to the collapse of Marxism-Leninism. Admittedly the equipment was electro-mechanical and the quality of service was poor, but a level of 24 telephones per 100 population was unmatched in the Soviet sphere of influence. Bulgaria was the only CMEA country with its own packet switched data network (X.25) in place prior to the political changes; using switches bought from Siemens. Todor Zhivkov, the Party Secretary, had successfully pushed the development of information technology manufacturing industries.

However, the slow and often faltering pace of political change since 1989 has meant that Bulgaria has been seen as a relatively unattractive market for international telephone companies. This is accentuated by the poor general state of the Bulgarian economy, which is primarily agricultural. The election in December 1994 of a quasi-reformed communist party to government did not help. Despite delays, the restructuring and reform of the PTT, the construction of the digital overlay network and improved international links are now well advanced. These have been supported by the World Bank, European Bank for Reconstruction and Development and the European Investment Bank. However, the sale of the Bulgarian Telephone Company (BTC) or even a substantial part of it remains a distant prospect, tied to a political reluctance to face up to privatisation in general—at least to official privatisation.

Only one NMT mobile telephone licence was issued, in order to minimise the loss of revenue to the BTC. The licensee is Mobikom, a joint venture between the Bulgarian Telephone Company (39%), Cable and Wireless (49%) and the Radio Electronics Systems Factory of Sofia (10%), with a further 2% held by private Bulgarian investors. Its 'Mobifon' service went live in December 1993, initially limited to Sofia. A licence for GSM was issued in mid-1994, the recipient was a domestic military-industrial combine, Tron, which seems unlikely to achieve an operational service, given its lack of expertise.

One significant problem in Bulgaria was the political desire to try to save Incoms, a local manufacturer of telecommunications equipment. Under the *ancien régime*, Incoms had manufactured large numbers of electromechanical telephone exchanges, based on a very old AT&T design. This type of manufacture employed tens of thousands of people, primarily because of a substantial export trade to CMEA countries and especially to the USSR. With the end of the CMEA, Incoms lost this export trade completely and there was little local demand. Recent purchases of exchanges have been by open international tender with limited local manufacturing in joint ventures with leading international suppliers. Attempts were made to find a western partner for Incoms, eventually settling on Siemens. However, it was slowly and painfully realised, that never again would telecommunications manufacturing be a major employer in Sofia.

The position in Bulgaria in 1995 is slightly disappointing, its edge over the other CMEA countries is gone. Reform though slow, has been effective. Yet, there is little competition and foreign direct investment is very limited.

CONCLUSIONS

There has been a remarkably rapid shift towards a truly global industry, for manufacturers, for service providers and for customers, and many are still adjusting to the changes. The single European market for telecommunications is taking shape, led by the United Kingdom and Sweden. Where some countries lag behind, it reflects a reluctance to admit competitors. The old world of direct provision by the state in national markets and of integration with manufacturers through procurement is gone forever. While there are local variations, the main evidence of national markets is as political and regulatory entities and a residual of dominance of former PTTs.

One indicator of the changes is the Swatch 'Beep' available in several European countries. It is sold for around £100 by the leading Swiss fashion watch manufacturer. The Beep is a combined watch and radiopager, with no rental charge—the costs being met from the initial purchase and the call to activate the pager.

For subscribers in countries such as Belgium and Austria, the future in telecommunications is very good. The population is relatively densely packed and prosperous, so that it can easily be reached and is worth serving with mobile services, tele-shopping, video-on-demand and everything else. By comparison, for PTTs the future is bleak. Automation and globalisation are depleting their workforces. They face competition from big international players such as AT&T and joint ventures such as Atlas, BT-MCI and Unisource, plus the many specialist players in mobile telephony and value-added services. They face the economies of scale and scope of those corporations and the development of global brand names in telecommunications, most notably AT&T. Consequently, it is difficult to see a future for the smaller and medium-sized PTTs, other than as integrated units within a global telecommunications operator. Such is the size of these global operators that most companies are quickly lost within them. BT and AT&T have a head start as a result of their much earlier privatisation and divestiture. The US presence in Europe is limited, in places experimental. AT&T has taken a long time to develop its strategy. The RBOCs have acquired some interests on what appears to be an opportunistic basis, mainly in Central and Eastern Europe. NTT remains absent, while its future is debated in Japan.

There is little evidence of integration between manufacturing and service operations. This may indicate a reluctance on the part of manufacturers to enter mainstream telecommunications or it may be delayed by the fierce competition in the market for central office switches and the massive changes these firms have had to face in their distribution channels. Nonetheless BCE has taken a stake in Mercury and Alcatel seems interested in taking stakes in Belgacom and France Télécom. Moreover the most common method of privatisation, through a public and often highly political sale of shares, discourages such holdings by foreign manufacturers.

Developments in the UK and in Germany show the growing involvement of electricity companies, while in France water companies have moved into telecommunications. More complex relationships occur in cable television. There is certainly no reluctance to enter the market..

These changes are occurring in a setting which is fundamentally political, slowing them down. It is not easy to achieve the consensus necessary to change the rules of the game, whether in the coalition government of Germany or in the European Council of Ministers. Many politicians neither accept the dogma of the free market nor immediately grasp the necessities of globalisation in the way that they see the importance of providing phones to the sick or the elderly. It is too easily seen as "selling the family silver" or simply giving it away, especially where it involves foreigners. For all that, they do recognise the issue of industrial competitiveness and consequently, and the need to drive down the costs of telecommunications.

Acknowledgements

John R. Beaumont (Energis Communications Ltd, London), George McKendrick (INTUG, London), Bill Martin (RMIT, Melbourne) and Svetoslav Tintchev (World Bank, Washington, DC).

References

European Commission. *Green Paper on Telecommunications*. EC, Brussels, 1987. [COM (87) 290.]

European Commission. *Review of Telecommunications Services*. EC, Brussels, 1993. [COM (93) 543 Final (15.11.1993).]

European Commission. *Green Paper on Mobile Telephony*. EC, Brussels, 1994. [COM (94) 154 Final (27.4.1994).]

DTI. *Competition and Choice; telecommunications policy for the 1990s*. HMSO, London, 1991. [Cm 1461]

HLCIS. "European and the Global Information Society; recommendation to the European Council" CEC, Brussels, 1994. [Known as the Bangemann Report.]

House of Commons. *Trade and Industry Committee, Third Report, Optical Fibre Networks*. HMSO, London, 1994. [HC (1993-94) 285-I, II, i, ii, iii, iv, v]

OFTEL. *A Framework for Effective Competition?* Office of Telecommunications, London, 1994.

PA. *Study of the International Competitiveness of the UK Telecommunications Infrastructure.* Department of Trade and Industry, London, 1994.

Pfeiffer, Günther and Wieland, Bernhard. *Telecommunications in Germany; an economic perspective.* Springer-Verlag, Berlin, 1990.

Schnöring, Thomas and Szafran, Uwe. "Telecommunications in Eastern Germany; a success story of East-West integration". *Telecommunications Policy* 1994 (18:6) 453-469.

Siemens. *Internationale Fernmeldestatistik.* Siemens AG, München, 1994.

Socher, Johann. "Networks and Services in Germany's New Eastern States" *Proceedings of Conference on Telecommunications in Central and Eastern Europe, 2-3 July 1992, London.* IBC Technical Services Ltd, London, 1992.

Sutherland, Ewan. "The Demands for Networks and Services in Central and Eastern Europe" *Proceedings of Conference on Telecommunications Central and Eastern Europe, 2-3 July 1992, London.* IBC Technical Services Ltd, London, 1992.

Sutherland, Ewan. "Computers and Competitive Advantage: the strategic management of information systems" pp 215-240 in Stubbart, Chuck *et al.* (editors) *Advances in Managerial Cognition and Organizatinal Information Processing Volume 5.* JAI Press, Greenwich, Connecticut, 1994.

Sutherland, Ewan. "Globalisation and Competition; lessons from the United Kingdom" *Proceedings of Telecom '95.*, Union Internationale des Télécommunications, Geneva, 1995.

UIT. *Annuaire Statistique.* Union Internationale des Télécommunications, Geneva, 1993.

3 A Framework for Building National Information Infrastructure: The Evolution of Increased Reach and Range in Singapore

A. Lee Gilbert
Nanyang Technological University, Singapore

This chapter portrays the rapid evolution of telecommunications and computing infrastructure in Singapore, from an inadequate POTS network in 1977 to an advanced nationwide "electronic highway" by 1992. This network will simultaneously and interactively deliver data, voice, and graphics or video images. The author traces the impacts of the convergence between information and communications technologies, and shows why emerging trends in the structure of the international telecommunications services industry lead to increasing needs for coordination and integration among national telecommunications and IT policies. Finally, the chapter compares the evolution of policy for the Singapore national information infrastructure to current trends in other Asia-Pacific nations.

INTRODUCTION

National information technology infrastructure serves the broad public interest and is also a basic economic factor serving commercial and industrial interests. Basic national infrastructure systems include roads, sea and air ports, water, sewer, electrical power, and telecommunications utilities, plus activities for designing, constructing, and regulating the use of such facilities. Advanced infrastructure systems include those which add value to the basic infrastructure: research and development, establishing and monitoring industrial standards, and information-based support activities such as trade facilitation. Because the economic behavior underlying investment in and operation of infrastructure allows non-users to enjoy many of the benefits without participating in the costs, markets providing capital for infrastructure investments tend to be inefficient (Gotlieb, 1984). Thus, governments must often initiate, fund, and operate nearly all basic infrastructure, and may also contribute to advanced infrastructure through subsidies, market protection, or other interventions (King, J. et al., 1994).

This pattern is dynamic: as an economy develops, demands on its infrastructure tend to become more differentiated and capital-intensive, trends which motivate many governments to intervene, for example by deregulating or privatizing certain activities.

The main elements of a national telecommunications infrastructure include lines linking local subscribers to switching systems, overseas lines providing two-way access to subscribers in foreign countries, and customer premise equipment such as telephones, PBX switches, and facsimile machines providing an interface between the user and the system. Advanced elements include high capacity (ISDN, broadcast television, or CATV) channels distributing information as data, pictures, or video, and mobile voice and data services (Wellenius, 1977), machine-readable data resources, and intelligent terminal equipment such as workstations and personal computers. Strong public interests and inherently high fixed costs for wire-based systems lead to public provision of basic services in most countries, and to extensive regulation virtually everywhere. This chapter studies interactions among contextual factors and policy interventions, proposes a model mapping the features of alternate policy regimes to the balance between supply and demand over time, and applies this model to a longitudinal analysis of the Singapore case, and to policy trends in other Asian nations.

Singapore as a Petri Dish for Policy Analysis

Singapore portrays a rapid series of policy transitions in a small, well-controlled environment. Independence in 1965 focused the young nation's infrastructure policy on building basic facilities to attract multinational corporations, which would bring needed capital, technology, and jobs. The national telecommunications system, along with schools, roads, and air and sea ports, was a major policy element. Soon, rapid economic growth accelerated demand for switching and transmission capacity. By the mid-1970s services were inadequate to support a transition to an economic strategy based on export-led industrialization, tourism, and financial services. The state-run Telecommunication Authority of Singapore (later Singapore Telecom) developed international satellite and undersea links, while upgrading its local network. By 1989 Singapore could offer modern telecommunications services, rated by the World Competitiveness Report well above all other non-OECD nations (Schwab & Lorange, 1989). This remarkable transition from laggard to leader required not only heavy investment, but a series of rapid transitions in the policy approach.

The economic role played by telecommunications shifted following arrival of the first computer in Singapore in 1963. While computer use expanded in the mid-1970's, few were interconnected. The Committee on National Computerisation (CNC) formed in 1980 established the first formal information technology policy (Tan, 1984). The CNC derived its goals from the economic strategy developed in the late 1970s. This economic plan did not explicitly link the two elements, and telecommunications was not a major CNC theme (Ng, 1979).

A visible link emerged in 1986, when a high-level Economic Committee identified improved information communication infrastructure as a key element of the new national IT strategy. The Committee stressed domestic needs for advanced services such as telemetry and integrated services digital networks (ISDN) to provide access to data and information, and for international telephone and facsimile services, and noted that while Telecom should continue to provide basic infrastructure and manage service delivery, "we should, whenever possible, privatize the provision of telecommunications services" (report of the Economic Committee, 1986, p.151). The resulting 1986 National I.T. Plan (Tan et al., 1986) identified a need for improved connectivity in the national telecommunications network infrastructure and shifted the future role of information technology from productivity tool to competitive weapon. This era led to implementation of an island-wide ISDN network, and accelerated development of strategic value-added applications such as the TradeNet documentation system.

By 1990, the focus of economic policy expanded beyond attracting OECD-based multinationals to embrace the rapidly developing Asia-Pacific region (Economic Development Board, 1991). The IT2000 Plan announced by the National Computer Board in 1992 extended the role of IT beyond the nation's borders, initiating an era of convergence in telecommunications, broadcast, and computer policies (National Computer Board, 1992). This "Intelligent Island" policy vision is built on a National Information Infrastructure (NII) supported by broadband ISDN (B-ISDN) services providing "bandwidth-on-demand" to link users, computing resources, and content (Sung, 1987).

Thus, the Singapore case portrays three shifts in the focus of IT policies: from an initial concentration on basic telecoms services to standalone computing, followed by efforts to create convergence between these two, and more recently recognition of the interdependence and interaction among computing, carriage, and content. The case also portrays shifts in the approach used to form and deploy the financial, technological and organizational assets necessary to build the national information infrastructure. Each policy regime is distinguished by its institutional approach to defining the role in capital formation played by equity, earned revenue, borrowing, and capital markets; the roles played by the public and private sector; and by foreign versus local enterprises. Each regime develops new institutions to regulate or influence the supply of and demand for IT resources. The following section explores these themes in greater detail.

THE DYNAMICS OF NATIONAL INFORMATION TECHNOLOGY POLICY

As the new nation grappled with independence, Singapore policy toward national information infrastructure focused first on meeting needs for basic telecommunications services, then on building modern infrastructure to attract multinational corporations, and more recently on advanced network facilities to extend the island nation's economic reach and range. These policies evolved in line with changes in technology, progress in national development, steady growth in the economic and social importance of the information service sector, and fundamental shifts in global economic structure. In the post-Vietnam war era, *technology* simultaneously advanced and became more standardised through the rapid maturation of all-digital, microprocessor-based radio and electronic network, fiber-optic, and multimedia technologies (Janczewski & Targowski, 1994). Many Asian countries, especially the East Asian "tigers," made significant progress toward *development* of an industrial base, accompanied by rising personal incomes. The resulting transformation from diverse traditional societies subsisting in separate agriculturally-based economies to rapidly modernizing societies functioning in integrated industrial and consumer economies generated demand for new services, and for the information imbedded in or constituting these services. Finally, the evolution of a *global economy* fundamentally altered the economic, organizational, and production structures of multinational firms (Dunning, 1993), restructured the basis of the competitive advantage of nations (Porter, 1990), and increased the global demand for timely business information. These trends altered both the ends of policy, and the means by which it was implemented.

Policy Interventions: Governance of the Telecommunications Industry

As the diffusion of information technology is directly related to the availability of telecommunications infrastructure, governance in this sector is a logical starting point (Gurbaxani et al., 1991). There are at least four possible telecommunications service delivery patterns: (Sutherland, 1992).

A typical *state monopoly* acquires capital resources through the national budget, patterns the skills-based bureaucracy needed to operate its system after the public service, develops simpler technologies in-house, and acquires more complex technology from foreign suppliers either as an outright purchase, or via cooperative arrangements (e.g., some form of licensing). This pattern describes most Asia-Pacific operators prior to 1980.

Prior to deregulation, the AT&T Bell System in the USA was the largest *regulated private monopoly*. AT&T could use its revenues to fund capital projects. Its market power also provided sufficient income to fund technology development and production of even the most advanced equipment. Although its local service delivery organisation was geographically decentralized, its long distance services provided much of its income, and funded its R&D efforts at Bell Labs. While many Asian governments have "privatized" their telecoms agencies in recent years, they retain significant equity (and thus control).

By far the most common pattern is some form of *regulated competition*, in which segments of the market are served by competing firms.

This pattern may be mixed: in the USA, basic local services are provided by monopolies, while firms compete to provide value-added services such as mobile communications, long distance services, etc. Such firms may obtain capital from financial markets or by issuing equity to shareholders.

The neoclassical economic paradigm promotes ***unregulated competition*** to enable many buyers and sellers with free access to information to optimize the efficient exchange of goods. The assumptions underlying this theoretical school are a poor fit with the economic realities of delivering goods (especially highly specialized services such as data) via a network-based infrastructure. Nevertheless, such a market may be taken as a goal state, which even if not fully attainable, should be pursued to the extent possible.

Given this typology, and bearing in mind the sharp differences between the ways we use telephones and computers, two difficult policy questions are [1] which path to select in proceeding from a state monopoly toward the goal of a free market, and [2] how to deal with the convergence between telecommunications and computing technologies?

Non-Regulatory Interventions

Some interventions, such as tax credits, measures to attract overseas technology suppliers, or new university courses, affect the technology supply. Others influenced demand, such as subsidies for consulting services and mandates that the Civil Service automate transaction processing systems. The patterns reflect economic policies, which have evolved since independence. In the late 1960s, a new government hoped to generate and maintain stable employment for all workers. To meet this need, the state intervened to woo multinational corporations, for their capital, technology, management systems, and access to overseas markets (Quah et al., 1985). In the 1970s, the policy intervention repertoire expanded to embrace subsidies to encourage training and automation to increase productivity and improve quality, and to fund technology transfer. By 1992, the strategic focus shifted from manufacturing to services, from being a low-cost source of unskilled labour to providing advanced industrial and professional skills, and from acting as passive receptor of foreign technology, capital, and management to a new role as a regional hub to package and redistribute capital, manpower, technology, and other resources. The range expanded beyond Singapore's traditional markets in North America and Europe to include geographically nearer but less accessible regional economies (Sung, 1987). Government intervention expanded to include privatizing the state-owned telecommunications operator, major new institutions to guide research and development, various forms of assistance to local firms venturing abroad, and greatly expanded postgraduate technical and business education.

DEVELOPING A NATIONAL INFORMATION INFRASTRUCTURE

The 1991 National Technology Plan signaled a new technology policy with specific targets for infrastructure, rather than the more general goals of the 1986 IT Plan or 1992 IT2000 plan. Targets included increasing the numbers of research scientists and engineers, doubling R&D expenditure, and balancing public and private participation in R&D efforts. The new National Science and Technology Board (NSTB), armed with more than a billion dollars, is responsible for guiding the nation toward these goals. The "Intelligent Island" policy vision will rebuilt on a National Information Infrastructure (NII) through B-ISDN-based "bandwidth-on-demand services," as modeled below (Lim, 1994).

Exhibit 1: Singapore's National Information Infrastructure (NII)

The base of the NII model represents a large, heterogeneous network infrastructure supporting the common network services layer, which provides standard functions such as access control, transaction engines, groupware, and various general- and special-purpose intelligent agents. This base is bounded by two critical "soft" elements, a policy and legal context within which technical infrastructure and applications operate, and a standards regime which mediates between the current and future technological contexts. National applications, of which the best-known is TradeNet, run in this transparent environment.

Small size and limited R&D experience limits a nation's capacity to develop the new technologies required to build this infrastructure. To acquire such tools, Singapore leveraged its long-term relationships with the multinational corporations investing in production and distribution activity within its borders. These global firms not only employ its workforce and patronise its financial, business service, and logistics industries, but act as a major channel for acquiring new technology. For example, in 1981 IBM helped set up the Institute for Systems Science (ISS), a postgraduate training and research facility to diffuse knowledge about systems design and management techniques (Motiwalla & Gilbert, 1989).

Later, AT&T helped ST become one of the first operators outside North America to install advanced 5ESS switching technology. AT&T then became NCB's partner in the Information Communications Institute of Singapore, supporting its mission to "develop the human, information and technological resources necessary to help realise Singapore's IT vision and masterplan to become an advanced information and networked society" (Information Communication Institute of Singapore, 1994).

By exploiting such external linkages, Singapore was able to lead in implementing country-wide ISDN service and offer a standardised, relatively high-bandwith, integrated digital access capability (Lian, 1991) to provide service-on-demand access to its customers. The country now plans to lead the way to B-ISDN, using frame-based ATM technology (Ramkumar & Kazmi, 1993) to support the far higher transmission rates required for videoconferencing and interactive multimedia services, then to distribute pay-per-view TV and other services on demand (Gengo Tazaki & Yong, 1992).

These ambitious plans are based in reality. Singapore progressed rapidly through the initial stages of ISDN development, fully digitising transmission, introducing common channel message based signaling with its digital switching, then digitising all portions of its local loop serving major business and industrial districts. ST then introduced ISDN termination services which could be interworked with its existing services, and in parallel, continued digitizing its entire switching network, meanwhile gaining ISDN experience. ST also successfully implemented mobile communications service initiatives, for which the economic and market features are very different. Fixed costs to provide and use ISDN are at least an order of magnitude greater than cellular. An organization investing in ISDN capability receives benefit only on links to other ISDN users, while individuals who buy or rent pagers and handphones can link to any user of a wire-based telephone system. These features tend to emphasize demand-pull for wireless, and supply-push for ISDN services.

Demand-Pull and the NII: Wireless Services

Mobile services such as radio telephones and pagers first appeared in the early 1970s, although use began to expand only following installation of cellular systems during the 1980s. Today, GSM digital cellular services (implemented in 1993) facilitate call roaming services for Singapore-based subscribers in Malaysia, the US, and Europe. With 24,000 subscribers to its Callphone services, ST is one of the more successful operators of CT2 services. Singaporeans are now one of the world's highest per capita users of cellular mobile telephones, and the highest users of radio pagers. These factors increase demand for terrestrial and wireless call capacity, bandwidth, and reach to provide a strategic platform for the continuing evolution of wireless digital services. A confluence between several factors suggests a potential for Singapore to become a world leader in mobile applications: [1] development of miniaturized data capture, display, and packet-switched radio modem technologies, accompanied by light but powerful batteries and power management systems, critical to widespread diffusion and use of handheld wireless terminals (Personal Data Assistants); [2] spectacular improvement in data compression technologies, enabling rapid transmission of images over wireless channels, [3] the emergence of personal-communications services (PCS) technologies which promise to increase the power available to mobile users, and decrease the cost per minute of talk time; [4] the rising penetration of mobile telephones and radio pagers, providing a pool of users for more advanced services; [5] the composition of the Singapore workforce, with its many workers who collect and transfer data; [6] the widespread use of multiple languages based on Roman or other character sets and on Chinese ideograms, forming a base for many of the languages used in East Asia (Lau et al., 1990); and [7] a long history of cooperation between its government and the multinational corporations owning and diffusing new technologies. Taken together, the first three promise to "sweep through global telecommunications in the same way as the personal computer roared through the computer industry in the 1980s," (Economist, 1993) while the latter factors position Singapore as a lead market for new PCS-based services, a breeding ground for advanced management techniques, and (given precisely targeted local R&D efforts (National Science & Technology Board, 1991)), a potential source of advanced technologies for use in the region, roles consistent with current government economic and technology development strategy (EDB, 1991).

Supply-Push and the NII: ISDN Services

The future prospects for ISDN depend on two key factors: [1] whether the ISDN architecture is sufficiently robust to incorporate new technologies (e.g., ATM); and [2], developing and diffusing global standards to enable decentralized design, development, and implementation of new applications which offer sufficient benefits to attract a critical mass of users. Assuming sufficiently robust architecture, demand for ISDN-based services will originate from four main drivers: [1] *globalization* of markets and production drives transaction volume growth and creates new needs to visualize information to close cultural gaps; [2] economic development alters *demographic* patterns, with growing prosperity, greater life expectancy, and a shift to leisure activities leading to demands for greater information exchange and higher video and audio quality; [3] a generally higher business *velocity* in industries such as retailing, making information exchange more time-critical; and [4] the rapid emergence of information *technologies* and enabling *applications* of ISDN to address new needs emerging from these driving forces, which vary by industry. Figure B portrays these relationships for eight key sectors of the Singapore economy.

INDUSTRY Domain	CONTEXTUAL DRIVERS			TECHNOLOGY Domain Enabling Applications
	Globalization	Demographics	Velocity	
Advertising	Rising economies of scope	Rising personal income, salary	Client interaction	Teleconferencing Imaging
Financial Services	Increasing scope *and* scale economies	Rising Asian managerial class	Response to customer	ATM, Imaging, VAN, VPN
Logistics	Increasing economies of scope	Globalization of production and consumption	Service level, Capital utilization	VAN, Global Positioning Systems, Cellular
Media Services	Increasing choice of media	Declining share of print media	Interaction w/ customer	Videotex, Video-on-Demand
Printing	Rising demand for service quality	Broader diffusion of knowledge	Turnaround time	EDI, Imaging Teleconferencing
Manufacturing	Increasing scope *and* scale economies	Outsourcing tasks (programming) to low-wage nations	Inventory costs, Time-to-Market	CAD-CAM Virtual Private Networks, EDI
Retailing	Increasing competition	Rising consumer incomes	Inventory Turnovers	Teleconferencing Imaging

Exhibit 2: ISDN Service Demand as a Function Of Context

Contextual forces in the industry domain drive demand for new applications, such as teleconferencing, virtual private networks, and interactive multimedia, while improved performance and lower cost drive demand for ISDN to replace existing services. For example, even though low labor costs are a primary basis for competition in the global printing industry, printers based in a country with strong IT infrastructure can seek niches where data acquisition skills, response time, and quality are more critical than cost, then develop ISDN network-based EDI, imaging, and teleconferencing applications to improve customers service. In the global logistics industry, costs for physical activities (transport and warehousing) are essentially variable, while many of the costs to acquire, disseminate, and use knowledge (about transport modes and tariffs, customs regulations, and packing requirements) are fixed. This economic structure gives rise to economies to wider service scope (Chandler, 1990), thus enabling a small Singapore firm such as YCH (NCB, 1992) to develop network-based applications which support an expanded range of services to meet the logistics needs of its multinational customers at a price lower than their internal costs.

The lesson of this simple framework is that as the driving forces rise in each key industry, new technologies appear to meet these emerging needs, and generate demands for services, such as broadband ISDN. The Association of Southeast Asian Nations (ASEAN) countries represent a market of 300 million people. Singapore, as the trading hub for this rapidly evolving economic region, will experience these emerging forces before other ASEAN members. Singapore offers a relatively advanced supply of ISDN services, and is a lead market for ISDN-based services, albeit on a small geographic scale. Singapore's experience may provide useful lessons for providers based in other markets.

Cellular and ISDN services are complementary: broadband packet-switched (ATM) ISDN services provide both speed and high capacity at low cost, while digital cellular can serve the "local loop" for mobile terminal users. The combined effect of all-digital and advanced cellular services on quality will "make the phones we use seem like two cans joined by a string," while enabling telephone service operators to "jump into new businesses and roll out new services with unprecedented ease and speed (Kupfer, October 3, 1994)." For example, in 1995 CATV provider Singapore CableVision launched a video-on-demand distribution trial to homes via its digital-cum-analog glass fiber and coaxial cable network, initiating a head-to-head conflict with the planned ST launch of ISDN-based VOD services (*The Strait Times*, October 10, 1994, p. 10). The regulatory challenge is to create a policy environment which simultaneously encourages innovation while protecting investors in existing services. The demands for governance generated by shifting supply and demand forces are likely to vary among nations with different economic structures, technological capabilities, and institutional structure (Sinha, 1995).

THE EVOLUTION OF INSTITUTIONS TO GOVERN THE INFRASTRUCTURE

As the earlier sections show, Singapore's policy goals have been addressed by its evolving regulatory and control structures, capable of:

- an initial emphasis on government funding and control of its investment,
- followed by a gradual transition to a limited form of regulated competition, accompanied by the differentiation of service delivery and regulatory roles *and*
- the emergence of a legal structure competent to handle complex information production issues related to access, accuracy, privacy, and ownership.

The institutional framework in which telecommunications services operate evolved with changes in goals. In overcoming a lack of natural resources to compete with other newly industrialized countries, Singapore first exploited its inherited strategic location and developed its population and basic infrastructure. However, the basic infrastructure of the other Asian "tigers" soon reached comparable levels. Direct labor and raw materials were now smaller portions of production costs, new technologies diffused rapidly throughout the region, and the comparative advantage enjoyed earlier in the economic development cycle began to decline (heng & Low, 1992). The response to this challenge was institutional reform.

From independence to 1974, the Singapore Telephone Board (STB) provided internal telephone services, while the Telecommunication Authority of Singapore (TAS) provided international services. Both were incorporated as statutory bodies. As the economy expanded, STB became unable to meet growing demand for services, and by the middle 1970s, over 33,000 applicants were waiting for telephones (Sung, 1990). This was one of the many symptoms prompting the 1974 absorption of STB, in which TAS acquired not only exclusive rights to serve both domestic and international markets for telecommunications services, but power to exercise licensing and regulatory functions, levy rates, rentals, charges, and fees, plus broad powers to enter private and state land and to conduct international negotiations in the course of its business (Sung, 1990). However, its powers were not unbounded, and the Ministry of Trade and Industry lobbied for aggressive rate reduction and service expansion policies, while criticizing TAS service performance targets (Ng, 1979). Preparing for the future provision of cheap and reliable electronic mail services, TAS absorbed the Postal Service department in 1982, when the expanded Singapore Telecom organisation became responsible for all postal and telecommunication services. The next stage in the institutional evolution of Singapore's telecommunications infrastructure is its passage into privatisation, a decade of transition to Era III beginning in 1994.

Economic planning emerged in Singapore during the late 1970s to support efforts to raise the value-added to its economy by its workforce. However, explicit technology planning is a more recent phenomenon. The 1986 National IT Plan identified general goals, such as upgrading the national telecommunications infrastructure and developing human resources to support IT and information communication. Although the government channeled financial and managerial resources toward these objectives, subsequent development of the IT and telecommunications sectors were largely parallel, with relatively little integration between the efforts of the National Computer Board (NCB) and those of organisations (such as Singapore Telecom) under the Telecommunications Authority of Singapore. Among the major outcomes of the 1986 IT Plan was the 1990 implementation of TradeNet, a value-added network which accelerates trade documentation and facilitates access to trade-related data. The NCB took a lead role in planning and implementing TradeNet (Neo, 1994).

NCB's 1992 announcement of IT2000 aligns the IT sector to the NT Plan, and proposes far higher level of integration among computing, telecommunications, and economic and social activities than in the previous plan. The major telecommunications-related policy target is developing a national information infrastructure (NII) to allow the use of advanced technologies such as digital cellular mobile, smart cards, and broadband networks to support national applications projects such as "intelligent homes," "smart schools," centres for distance learning, and "intelligent highways" (NCB, 1992). Other institutions responded to the NCB plan with focused studies such as the 1994 Library 2000 report, envisioning the national library as a distributed network of libraries and information resource centres which support the advancement of Singapore. The NII, as outlined in the IT2000 report, will be developed and implemented through an organizational framework to coordinate the efforts of NCB, Singapore Telecom, and Singapore Broadcasting. As these three powerful organisations have little history in working together, the government formed a high level steering committee to guide them.

The 1991 National Technology Plan moved Singapore into a new era. The NT Plan set specific targets, rather than the general goals of the IT Plan. These included increasing the numbers of research scientists and engineers, doubling R&D expenditure, and balancing public and private participation in R&D efforts. The new National Science and Technology Board (NSTB), armed with more than a billion dollars, is the agency responsible for guiding the nation toward these goals.

NSTB allocates its resources to achieve leadership in specific areas, develop scientific manpower, assist private sector R&D efforts, and build soft infrastructure capacity (e.g., technology information and legal services) needed to commercialize the fruits of its investments. NSTB divided target technologies into three groups based on their potential economic contribution and maturity, including telecommunications-related technologies. Group I technologies include EDI networks, videotex, value-added networks, and local and wide-area networks. R&D efforts are to focus on fully exploiting the value derived from use these relatively mature technologies. Group II technologies, expected to bring benefits in two or more years, include wireless technologies and ISDN. The R&D goal for Group II is to acquire or develop capabilities in these areas quickly. For Group III, the aim is to track development of specific emerging technologies, and prepare to move quickly as they become relevant to economic growth (NSTB, 1991). Certain NSTB activities have immediate effects: NSTB-funded Technet provided a gateway to global Internet resources, software, and specialized local research databases.

Through a strategic alliance between Singapore Telecom and Fujitsu, the island nation moved one step nearer its policy vision of "Bandwidth-on-Demand". Operating at 600 Mbps, the two year trial was aimed at refining the delivery model for broadband ISDN. Target applications include LAN/WAN interconnection services, real-time transfer of graphic images (including full-motion video-on-demand), high-speed data transfer, HDTV, and multimedia services. Large international organisations such as multinational corporations, and local organisations with special needs such as universities, hospitals, and research facilities are expected to be early entrants into this new B-ISDN marketplace (Dhilawala, 1994).

POLICY IMPACTS

These policy measures affected local use, access to international networks, and the availability of value-added services. From less than 60,000 telephones at independence, the network grew to connect over 270,000 telephones by 1974, and more than one million today. Singapore now has the second highest level of telephone installations per capita in Asia, after only Japan. Its network now accesses more than 200 countries, via satellite-based access to INTELSAT, and a variety of submarine cable-based access sources (International Telecommunications Union, 1995).

Any small nation is vulnerable to impacts from its larger neighbors, and Singapore has vigorously defended its citizens and their culture from those foreign influences which its government felt were undesirable. The government forbids private use of satellite receiver dishes, screens foreign video cassettes, and censors television programmes. However, the future application of these paternalistic policies to the new media age of Internet and 100 television channels is far from obvious (Ang, 1995).

While ST expected multinationals to take the lead in signing up for ISDN services, a few local private sector leaders saw access to the ISDN network as an opportunity to gain competitive advantage. Xpress Print, a family-run printing business employing 150 staff, is one such case. This low-profile Singapore-based firm is a market leader in printing financial and stock market reports. Such documents are both highly confidential and time-sensitive, and the firm's reputation for speed and accuracy enabled it to corner more than half the world market for this highly specialized service. When CEO Fong Kah Kuen introduced IT to firm operations in 1986, the average turnaround time was seven days. With desktop publishing technology in the prepress stage, and by integrating high-speed modems to communicate with clients, Xpress is able to print reports in full color within 24 hours of receiving the contents. Xpress also uses videoconferencing and screen-sharing applications, supported by the high ISDN data rates, to enable clients to view proof reports and make pre-production changes and corrections (wong, 1994).

However, the national investment in ISDN, fast approaching US$ 5 billion, can be justified only through widespread, high-volume use (Koh, 1993). The initial take-up of ISDN was slow, attributed by ST to a lack of suitable terminal equipment (McClelland, 1990). In sharp contrast, subscriptions to cellular radio-based services have accelerated, making Singapore a world leader in per-capita use. Despite minor setbacks, the impact of telecommunications policy has been strongly beneficial, particularly in economic terms. Generally, growth in IT investment is highly correlated with growth in national GDP and productivity, supporting the notion of IT-led development (Kraemer & Dedrick, 1994). The telecommunications-led information service sector represents a significant share of national income, and an even larger share of its service exports, while telecommunications equipment export is an increasingly large share of machinery and equipment exports (Kuo, Low & Toh, 1989). The external effects are even more impressive: by 1993, the Geneva-based World Competitiveness Report rated Singapore's employees highest (among non-OECD nations) in terms of computer literacy, its firms second only to Hong Kong in the use of IT to support strategy, and its national telecommunications infrastructure highest in terms of the extent to which it meets business needs (Schwab & Lorange, 1993). These IT-related factors contributed heavily to its 1994 evaluation of the Singapore economy as the world's second most competitive, lagging only the much larger USA (Schwab & Lorange, 1994).

A Contingency Model for Integrated IT Policy

Exhibit 3 depicts a dynamic contingency model of policy regimes governing access to telecommunications markets. The model reflects a need to match service supply with demand. At best, monopolies efficiently allocate resources only when demand is low, and the supply of resources is weak. Open markets efficiently allocate resources only when the national supply is strong enough to compete with foreign suppliers, and market growth is high enough to absorb slack resources within a reasonable time. Other conditions call for different approaches to governance: if demand is strong, but the local supply is weak, joint ventures with foreign suppliers fill service gaps while transferring technology and operational knowhow. When supply is stronger than demand growth, market protection will ensure the financial health of local operators, while joint R&D ensures a continuing supply of new technology and the knowledge needed to transfer, adapt, and apply it.

Each shift in Singapore's economic strategy demanded reconfigured infrastructure, particularly telecommunications services. The multinational corporations seeking an environment conducive to business required Singapore to provide factors of production, appropriate laws, governmental support, and a generalized basic infrastructure. Rising prosperity generated demand for additional services, and telecommunications service supply contributed to economic growth, a causal two-way link suggesting that inadequate service capacity could have been a severe constraint to rapid economic growth (chen & Kuo, 1984).

To understand links between policy and new services, it is useful to consider the impact of Singapore policies on wireless and ISDN-based communications services. Singaporeans are now among the world's highest per capita users of cellular mobile telephones and radio pagers. Similarly, the country installed the world's first nation-wide ISDN network in 1989, 110 years after becoming the first city in the region to set up a local telephone network to support its role as an entrepot trading centre. While all are telecoms-related information technologies, they are used in different contexts and require different technical and organizational infrastructure. Telecommunications is a technology-based service industry, in which new service offerings often involve acquiring new technologies, then mutually adapting organizational capabilities and technologies to meet emerging market needs. Value-added services use computers to "package" telecommunications and information-related services. For example, Singnet now provides owners of palmtop computers a wireless access path to stock prices and their E-mail accounts. With more than 30,000 subscribers to Internet services, the island nation leads Asia in per-capita E-mail addresses. The business value of such services depends on the parties (or processes) on the network, the scarcity value of the information provided, the extent to which its packaging meets user needs, and network speed and reliability. John Sviokla of Harvard characterizes these elements as context, content, and infrastructure, and points out that because IT alters the way these work together, IT infrastructure makes it possible to create new "marketspace" opportunities independent of geographic location (Sviokla, 1994).

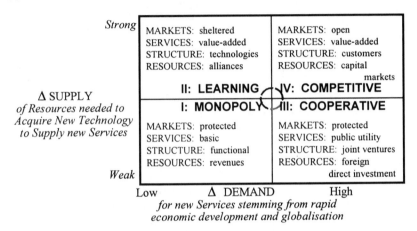

Exhibit 3: Four Telecommunication Policy Eras

The Singapore IT infrastructure evolved through three distinct eras, each focused on different goals, to maintain alignment with the national economic strategy. In the near term, Singapore will adopt <u>Competitive</u> policies to govern those specific services, such as CATV and wireless, where its policymakers view competition as a means to serve public interests, for example by lowering costs or improving service quality. For the long term, the government is building up new institutions to govern a fully competitive market.

Comparing Policy Trends in Singapore to Other Asian Nations

With independence, government policy for national infrastructure in Singapore focused on building facilities which would attract multinational employers, balancing a need for jobs with equally important needs for public safety, in a *Monopoly* regime. During this era, the sector was organised to meet an urgent shortage of line capacity through massive investments in infrastructure. In the late 1970s, as its success began to erode traditional comparative factor advantages derived from low labour costs, Singapore shifted to a strategy based on increased levels of efficiency and skill needed to increase local value-added to manufacturing and services, and shifted to a ***Learning*** regime to attract the needed new technology. In this era, the national telephone monopoly was reorganised to support a shift in economic strategy toward value-added services, electronic mail and facsimile services were added, and the national postal service was absorbed. Around 1990, the target evolved once more, as policymakers laid plans for a "global city in the first league of developed countries within 30 to 40 years" (Economic Planning Committee, 1990), and shifted to a ***Cooperative*** regime to facilitate the strategic alliances required to extend the reach of the economy beyond its borders. The service focus shifted outward toward improved linkages with external markets, while the management focus shifted toward greater internal efficiency and competitiveness, with institutional moves to liberalise service markets and gradually privatize its national telecommunications services provider (Kuo et al., 1989). Exhibit-4 traces Singapore's information infrastructure policy through three of the four eras:

Not every nation in the region adopted the policy regime which best fits its context. For example, India's earlier self-sufficiency policy not only barred foreign competitors from its markets, but barred its equipment suppliers and service providers from learning to meet world standards. However, the policy regimes of many Asian nations, such as Indonesia and Thailand, are aligned with this framework, as indicated in Figure D.

In sharp contrast, India relied for many decades after independence on its massive internal economy and heritage of elite educational institutions to support its policy of self-reliance, following precepts laid down by Mahatma Gandhi and later extended by Nehru to the industrial sector. While this policy approach enabled India to fulfill the basic needs of many of its stakeholders, it sharply limited the ability of Indian industry to benefit from trends toward globalization of markets and international standards, and thus hindered its emerging information technology industry (Dedrick & Kraemer). For example, despite the ability to design and produce simple and rugged telecommunications equipment suitable for use in its rural villages, the state-dominated equipment sector made no effort during the 1980s to design, develop, or produce products suitable for export. As a result, the Indian economy was slow to benefit from the rapid expansion of the telecommunications service sector in Asia.

This pattern now appears to be changing. In India as in Singapore, new links between industrial development and telecoms policy are emerging. The government has recently shown willingness to abandon its traditional policy of technological self-reliance, and has taken active steps to encourage technology transfer from foreign sources (Krishna, 1992). Also, the government now provides soft loans to developing economies to encourage export of rural exchanges (Pyramid Research, 1995). The introduction of limited competition has improved service levels, in terms of access and service quality. Such reforms, motivated by an overall trend toward economic liberalisation and technological advances in the sector, require sharply increased public investment (Jain, 1993), which India's economy is sufficiently large to provide.

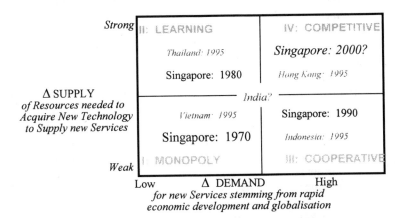

Exhibit 4: The Dynamics of IT Policy Regimes

Recent developments make the Vietnam case interesting. Policymakers must address four main challenges to building a national information infrastructure comparable to that of other ASEAN members: [1] raising sufficient capital, [2] integrating the diverse technology types currently in use, [3] reforming excessively complex and inefficient administrative processes, and [4] developing its technical and management skills (Chotrani, 1995). With spending plans approaching US$ 3 billion over the next five years, Vietnam now faces stiff competition from other expanding Asian economies, which must find about ten times this amount over the next ten years for telecommunications, and even more to fill growing needs for energy, transport, sanitation, and water treatment facilities (Asiaweek, 29 September, 1995). Ten years ago, the national network was fashioned from obsolete Soviet and French gear. Largely obtained through aid mechanisms, the current inventory of digital switching equipment is new but incompatible (gilbert, 1996). Although officials claim the deregulation process is underway, overseas investors see the lack of basic governance mechanisms (such as a telecoms law) as a critical gap. Manpower development, on the scale necessary to maintain the national network, is perhaps the most critical task. With 3,000 IT professionals today, Vietnam hopes to add 20,000 by the end of this decade. This may be difficult within the institutional tradition of Vietnamese academy, which typically provides advanced training to a small number of students through close supervision by a senior faculty member (Interviews, Hanoi Technological University, January, 1995).

Following years of enjoying protected markets, the state-owned equipment suppliers in *Indonesia* now face major foreign competitors, while its service markets are open to foreign entrants. After years of neglect, telecommunications service in *Thailand* was boosted by massive upgrades in switching and transmission capacity, via a series of Build-Operate-Turnover projects operated by international joint ventures (Ruchadaporn & Gilbert, 1995).

Hong Kong is an extreme case. Its colonial government tended toward a hands-off, free market approach, and did not invest in Civil Service IT reform or other institution-building measures. The result has been a healthy telecommunications industry offering quality services at low prices, but slow progress toward building information systems, such as Trade-Link, to complement Hong Kong's physical infrastructure. East Asian experiences are generally consistent with the model: in **Japan**, privatisation reduced cross-subsidies, leading to dramatic changes such as higher local tariffs and lower tariffs for long distance services. **Korea** moved early to privatize telecoms, removing many major financial constraints to development of the sector, and helping to raise capital for expansion (Kim et al, 1992).

Although these highly divergent cases portray sharp contrasts in approach, some broad patterns emerge: While more industrialized nations are in the process of deregulation to encourage increased competition, they retain strong regulatory positions on carrier services, yet relax these for value-added operators. Developing nations demonstrate high correlation between personal income and telecoms service access. It is unclear whether per capita GDP is cause or effect: most likely, these factors interact.

CONCLUSIONS

The Singapore case reveals two lessons: first, national telecommunications and computer policies are inseparable, even when their formulation is not well-integrated; second, IT policies are dynamic, and shift as the internal and external context changes. Infrastructure is obviously an important source of economic and social value, even though it is difficult to quantify precisely the economic value of information services. The strong, two-way, link between economic growth and investment in telecommunications infrastructure (Karlsson, 1993) resonates with the theoretical views of Robert Reich (Reich, 1991) who sees human capital and infrastructure as key determinants of development, and of Michael Porter, who identifies a strong link between economic success and the development of national infrastructure and support services (Porter, 1990).

Information infrastructure policy is at an important intersection in the development of technology, policy, and industry structure. As telecommunications and information services are increasingly critical to user organizations, users must make strategic choices about when to invest in new capabilities. Because the technology is developing faster than it can be implemented, providers must make strategic choices regarding their investment in new technology-enabled service offerings. By intervening in such choices, information infrastructure policy shapes supply and demand. Singapore, recognizing a need to coordinate all policies guiding technological support to its information-dependent economy, moved to integrate its computerisation, IT industry, and telecommunications policies in support of its economic strategy

(Motiwalla & Yap, 1992). Implementation required the government to exploit close relationships with multinational corporations to acquire the necessary technologies, then build institutional capacity to adapt and diffuse these technologies. This led to the rise of a new organisation, the National Computer Board, which competed for influence first with a more-powerful telecommunications agency, then with the state-owned TV broadcaster. As the mushrooming use of computers became widespread, and gradually converged with telecommunications, NCB took a lead planning role.

To generate a credible IT2000 plan, NCB involved private sector leaders, an innovation unlikely to emerge from the more traditionally oriented skills bureaucracies of the national telecommunications or broadcast monopolies. Here the institutional implication lies in the multiple sources of control and influence held by policymakers over the public and private sector organisations who will adopt the planned services supported by the national network. Universal access to advanced telecommunication services and a new generation of network-based institutions are critical to the success of the IT2000 strategy. Separation of physical from electronic trade networks will require new institutional solutions to create an advanced electronic trading environment in ASEAN, then linking the region to the wider global economy. Technology management and the effective use of information technology are central managerial concerns of the 1990s. Singapore's economic success results partly from building its capabilities in these factors, and partly from being able to influence organisations to use these capabilities.

References

Ang P.H. (1995). Control and censorship in the information age: A Singapore perspective. Presented at the *Workshop on Chances and Risks of the Information Society*. Singapore, 18-20 September 1995.

Chandler, A.D. (1990). *Scale and scope: The dynamics of industrial capitalism*. Cambridge: Belknap Press.

Chen, H.T. & Kuo, C.Y. (1984). Telecommunications and economic development in Singapore. Institute of Culture and Communications working paper, East-west Center, Honolulu.

Chotrani, R. (1995). Vietnam's IT Revolution. *Vietnam Business News*. Pilot issue, 1995, p.16.

Chotrani, R. (1995). Vietnam's Telecoms Challenge. *Vietnam Business News*. Pilot issue, p.8.

Dedrick, J. & Kraemer, K. (1992). *India's quest for self-reliance in information technology: costs and benefits of government intervention*. CRITO working paper. University of California, Irvine.

Dhilawala, S. (1994). Internal research documents. Singapore: Datapro Corporation.

Dunning, J. (1993). *Multinational enterprises and the global economy*. Wokingham: Addison Wesley.

Economic Development Board (1991). *Singapore: The Next Lap*. Singapore: Times Editions.

Economic Planning Committee (1990). *The Strategic Economic Plan: Towards a Developed*

Nation. Singapore: Ministry of Trade and Industry.

Economist (1993). The end of the line. *Telecommunications Survey.* October 23rd, 1993.

Gengo Tazaki & Yong Y.C. (1992). Distance learning system using ISDN. *Proceedings of PTC '92.* Honolulu, January 1992.

Gilbert, L. (1995, January). [Interviews]. Vietnam: Hanoi Technological University.

Gilbert, L. (1996). Wireless infrastructure in Vietnam. *Proceedings of PTC '96,* in press.

Gotlieb, C. (1984). *The economics of computers.* Englewood Cliffs, NJ: Prentice Hall.

Gurbaxani, V. et al. (1991). Government as the driving force toward the information society. *The Information Society, 7,* 155-185.

Heng, T.M. & Low, L. (1992). Information technology and telecommunications to achieve national goals in Singapore. presented at the *Conference on Dynamic Asian Development,* Seoul, March-April 1992.

Information Communication Institute of Singapore. (1994). Singapore: ICIS.

International Telecommunications Union (1995), *Yearbook,* Geneva: ITU.

Infrastructure: how to find $1.5 Trillion. *Asiaweek,* September 29, 1995, p.28.

Jain, R. (1993). Review of policy changes in the Indian Telecom Sector--Implications for decision makers. *JGIM, 1 (*3), 33-43.

Janczewski, L. & Targowski (1994). Toward a global telecommunications policy. *JGIM, 2,* 2, 30-41.

Karlsson, Jan (1993). Dynamics of economic telecom growth. *Transnational Data and Communications Report,* July/August 1993.

Kim, C. et al. (1992). Korean telecommunications development. *World Development Review, 26* (12), 1829-1841.

King, J. et al. (1994). Institutional factors in information technology innovation. *Information Systems Research, 5* (2), 139-169.

Koh, B.W. (1993). Singapore Telecom Organisation for the 1990s. *Transnational Data and Communications Report.* July/August 1993, pp.20-23.

Kraemer, K. & Dedrick. (1994). Payoffs from investment in computer technology--lessons from the Asia Pacific region. *Proceedings of ICIT '94.* Kuala Lumpur, August 1994, pp.3-23.

Krishna, S.D. (1992). The challenge of introducing advanced telecommunications systems in India. In Palvia and Palvia (Eds.) *The global issues of information technology management.* Harrisburg PA: GITM Idea Publishing.

Kuo, E., Low, L. & Toh, M.H. (1989). The Singapore telecommunications sector and issues affecting its competitive position in the Pacific region. *Columbia Journal of World Business, 24,* 1, 59-71.

Kupfer, A. (October 3, 1994). The future of the phone companies. *Fortune,* 59-64.

Lau K.T. et al. (1990). Asian language processing. *Journal of the Singapore Computer Society, 3* (2), 65-78.

Lian, B.L. (1991). The development of telecommunications in Singapore to support the information age. *Proceedings of Challenges for the Telecommunications Sector in the Asia Pacific Region.* Bangkok, March 1991.

Lim, E. (1994). Major national infrastructure initiatives. *Journal of the Singapore Computer Society, 6* (1), 21-30.

McClelland, S. (1990) Singapore: The Asian Teleport. *Telecommunications [International Edition], September,* 108-113.

Motiwalla, J. & Gilbert, L. (1989). Managing the information revolution. In Sandhu and Wheatley (Eds.) *Management of success--The moulding of modern.* Singapore: ISEAS.

Motiwalla, J. & Yap, M. (1992). Systems integration at the national level--a research agenda. *IEEE Proceedings 1992,* Singapore: IEEE. 366-371.

National Computer Board [NCB] (1992). *A Vision of an Intelligent Island: IT2000 Report.* Singapore: Singapore National Printers.

National Science & Technology Board [NSTB] (1991). *Windows of opportunities--National Technology Plan 1991.* Singapore: Singapore National Printers.

Neo. B.S. et al. (1994). *Singapore TradeNet.* working paper. Singapore: IMARC

Ng, M. (1979). *Highlights of Singapore's economic development plan for the eighties.* working paper. Curriculum Development Institute of Singapore.

Palvia, S. & Neo B.S. (1996). Using a flexible IT architecture for total logistics management. In Neo B.S. (Ed.) *Exploiting information technology for business competitiveness.* Singapore: Longman.

Pyramid research (1995). *Telecom Markets in Vietnam, Laos and Cambodia.* Cambridge: Pyramid.

Porter, M. (1990). *The Competitive Advantage Of Nations.* New York: Free Press.

Quah. J. et al. (1985). *Government and politics of Singapore.* Oxford: Oxford University Press.

Ramkumar, V. & Kazmi (1993). How intelligent networks will change the way Singaporeans do business by year 2000. *Proceedings of ITWorks '93.* Singapore, October 1993.

Reich, R. (1991). *The work of nations: Preparing ourselves for 21st century capitalism.* New York: Knopf.

Report of the Economic Committee (1986). *The Singapore Economy: New directions.* Singapore: MTI, p.151.

Ruchadaporn & Gilbert, L. (1995). Information technology-led development--can the lessons be learned? *Informatics in the Public Sector.*

Schwab, K & P. Lorange (1989). *World competitiveness report.* Geneva: World Economic Forum.

Schwab, K & P. Lorange (1993). *World Competitiveness Report.* Geneva: World Economic Forum.

Schwab, K. & P. Lorange (1994). *World Competitiveness Report.* Geneva: World Economic Forum.

Sinha, N. (1995). Regulating telecommunications in developing countries: an institutional analysis. *Proceedings of PTC '95*, 370-377. Honolulu.

Sung, S.M. (1987). *Telecommunications development and evolution of manufacturing and service industries.* Geneva: Forum 87.

Sung, S.M. (1990). Leveraging telecommunications for strategic applications. *Proceedings of the National IT Applications Conference.* Singapore 1990.

Sutherland, E. (1992). Telecommunications in Eastern Europe. In Palvia and Palvia (Eds.) *The global issues of information technology management.* Harrisburg PA: GITM Idea Publishing. 73-97.

Sviokla, J.(1994). Managing in the marketplace. *Harvard Business Review,* November-December.

Tan C.N. (1984). A strategic perspective of the CSCP. *Proceedings of the CSCP Seminar.* Singapore: NCB.

Tan C.N. et al. (1986). National IT Plan--A Strategic Framework. *Proceedings of the 20th Institution of Engineers.* Singapore.

The Straits Times. October 10 1994, p. 10.

Wellenius, B. (1977). Telecommunications in developing countries. *Telecommunicaions Policy, 1(*4), 289-297.

Wong. E. (1994, October 5). Speedy Does It. *The Straits Times. p.23.*

4 International Business Opportunities on the Information Superhighway: An Austrian Perspective

Lore Alkier
New York University, USA

Global networks and the Internet in particular are major enabling factors for the globalization of markets and new types of organizations. User-friendly services transform the Internet into a viable business place and cause impressive growth rates in new business and private users. This chapter shows how governments in the US and Europe react to these changes and how the Internet as a business place developed over the last years. It then outlines several possibilites to take advantage of the Internet for international business purposes. These business opportunities are presented within a case study of Austria. In addition to showing how firms can address the challenges of the Internet as a global marketplace the case study also proposes accompanying government activities and industry initiatives to prepare Austria for the "Information Society".

INTRODUCTION

Global business is usually considered a domain of multinational enterprises, large in terms of revenues, the number of worldwide subsidiaries, or employees. However, in many industries this notion of a global corporation might not be useful any more. Converging consumer tastes in industrialized countries and the resulting similarities in buying behavior seem to favor small and flexible players that can adapt quickly to changing trends. Technological developments - especially in the computing and telecommunications industry - are also changing traditional organizations drastically and offer business opportunities in global markets for small competitors.

While global proprietary networks had an important impact on the international operations of multinational corporations, the Internet is often re-garded as the enabling technology for smaller competitors in the global market-place. Over the last years the Internet has evolved into a valuable - but still largely neglected - information source, connecting users to government agencies, libraries, databases, and much more and thus making the initial steps of market research affordable for smaller competitors. As the chairman of Assurance

Medical Inc. in Dallas, a $2 million enterprise, put it when he searched for information on alcohol-related problems in Argentina on the Internet (Business Week, 1995): "Some of the best information we just stumbled on as we were surfing around." But the Internet is surely not a "one-way street". It is increasingly being used to support distributed workgroups (IEEE Spectrum, 1992) and serves as a virtual marketplace linking businesses and customers. As a result of these developments new types of organizations emerge that are frequently referred to as virtual organizations (Davidow et al, 1995; Poon et al, 1995), networked organizations (Jarvenpaa et al,1994; Inc., 1993), temporary organizations (Innovation, 1995), negotiated organizations or vertically integrated conglomerates (Lucas et al, 1993).

So far only few corporations are actively redesigning their operations around global electronic markets as a strategic goal. Electronic commerce on the Internet is still in an experimental stage and readily usable application programs as well as widespread Internet know-how are scarce. Furthermore there is only little knowledge about user demographics and consumer behavior on the Internet, and security concerns as well as legal uncertainties are keeping firms from venturing into on-line business at a faster pace.

In the following sections we will discuss how the "Information Superhighway" affects the traditional business environment. We will introduce government initiatives designed to enhance the competitiveness of the national economy by building a national telecommunications infrastructure and will then give an overview of the current state of the Internet as a global marketplace. By means of a case study we will also look at possible actions on different economic levels to enhance the competitiveness of a nation in a global marketplace.

INFRASTRUCTURE INITIATIVES

Competitiveness in the global business environment is closely associated with linking business partners and consumers electronically.[1] In order to meet the rising demands in telecommunications bandwidth and services governments all over the world are developing strategies to improve the existing telecommunications infrastructure. Two of the most influential infrastructure initiatives, in the US and the European Union, that directly affect 16 of the world's 20 largest telecommunications operators, are outlined below and show the growing concern of industrialized nations regarding their technological competitiveness. Other infrastructure initiatives were started in Japan (Dialog, 1994), Australia, and Canada. A description of their impact especially on SMEs in those countries can be found in (Poon et al, 1995).

USA

By today's international standards the telecommunications infrastructure already in place in the US is very advanced. Extensive fiber-optic and cable networks connect a much higher percentage of businesses, households, and educational institutions than in any other country. But the services envisioned by the proponents of the "Information Superhighway" or the "National Information Infrastructure" (NII) still demand much higher bandwidths to every household than are available today.

One of the first politicians to recognize and promote the future telecommunications infrastructure requirements, Al Gore, created the term of the "Information Superhighway" which stands for his vision of:

"... a seamless web of communications networks, computers, databases, and consumer electronics that will put vast amounts of information at users' fingertips. Development of the NII can help unleash an information revolution that will change forever the way people live, work, and interact with each other." (NII Advisory Committee).

According to a study by the US Computer Science and Telecommunications Board [11] the main characteristic of this infrastructure has to be *openness* in several respects: universal connectivity for users, open access for information and network providers, and the possibility of technological change as well as contents changes.[2]
The evolution of the NII in the US is closely linked to the development of the Internet, which will be discussed later. Kettinger [34] describes this evolution as a multi-step development with four phases that can be observed over the years:

- Rather experimental *special-purpose networks*, often in a technical research environment, are managed at an ad hoc basis. They are typically funded by research grants.

- *Wider diffusion* is achieved through substantial government or industry funding and by broadening the reach of the networks. Networks may be operated by consortia and achieve higher capacities.

- High capacity networks enable *broad participation,* eventually by businesses. Substantial changes occur in the scope of applications used, the pricing mechanisms used, and the private sector as the typical source of funding. Management of the networks is shifted to the private sector.

- Eventually a multi-gigabit network infrastructure will be *available to the public* and developments will be market-driven, especially by telephone, cable, and computer companies, and the entertainment industry.

While the initial situations of countries may vary this US example of achieving the NII can serve as a model for other countries planning similar infrastructure developments.

European Union

The European Union has recently shown much concern about Europe's position in the global marketplace. An area regarded as a particular weakness is the overpriced and heavily regulated telecommunications sector. Compared to the US Europe faces serious challenges on its way to a common telecommunications infrastructure: it has yet to overcome the fragmentation of the telecommunications market and the existing monopolistic structures, and to agree on common standards. In most European countries the full liberalization of telecommunications services cannot be expected before 1998.

Compared to the US (34 PCs per 100 citizens) the penetration of European households with computers is relatively low (10 PCs per hundred citizens), as is the number of households with cable TV that could carry additional telecommunications services (25% in Europe vs. 60% in the US) as reported in European Commission (1994). Within Europe these numbers differ enormously from country to country. The heterogeneous market with many languages spoken and very different infrastructure levels does not encourage trans-European services like home shopping or home banking, video on demand, and other entertainment offers for consumers. European businesses are also believed to be less aware of the trends and opportunities with regards to telecommunications than their US counterparts. This is especially true for Europe's 12 million small and medium sized enterprises that need to manage their business resources more effectively to remain competitive.

In May and June 1994 first recommendations (European Commission) and a follow-up action plan (Commission of the European communities, 1994) regarding Europe's way into the "Information Society" were presented to the European Council and the European Parliament. These reports cover regulatory and legal aspects, networks, basic services, applications, social, societal and cultural aspects, and promotional activities to increase public awareness.

To demonstrate the potential of a common European networking infrastructure and to stimulate further initiatives from the private sector the recommendations emphasize ten application areas that could strengthen the industrial competitiveness, create new jobs, promote new forms of work organization, improve the quality of life and quality of the environment, respond to social needs, and raise the efficiency and cost-effectiveness of public services (European Commission, 1994).

Among the main EU business concerns in the envisioned Information Society are SMEs. The proposed actions are expected to increase the competitiveness of SMEs compared to larger corporations, and to ease the relationship with administrative organizations. These goals should be achieved by the following means:

"Promote the widest possible use of telematic services (E-mail, file transfer, EDI, video conferencing, distance learning, etc.) by European SMEs, with links to public authorities, trade associations, customers and suppliers. Raise the awareness of added value services, and communications in general, among SMEs. Increase access to trans-European data networks." (European Commission, 1994).

It is expected that the private sector will provide the necessary trans-European value-added services tailored for SMEs over existing ISDN networks. According to EU plans 40% of all SMEs with more than 50 employees should use telematic services by 1996.

The recommendations to the European Council emphasize the necessity to act quickly and on a common European basis. They also raise concern whether the Information Society "...will be a strategic creation for the whole Union, or a more fragmented and much less effective amalgam of individual initiatives by Member States...." (European Commission, 1994). The report repeatedly demands that actions have to be taken at a European level with entrepreneurial mentality and that public funding, subsidies, or protectionism are not intended or encouraged.

THE INTERNET

As discussed above the construction of the Information Superhighway or the Information Society, whatever it may be called in different countries, is well under way. Today the concept closest to the intentions of the Information Superhighway, in terms of its global reach, its heterogeneous user groups and its enormous business potential is the *Internet*. Although many other on-line business initiatives are also in place (such as on-line services in the US, or public videotex systems in many European countries) most of them are aimed at national audiences and do not extend their services across borders. Furthermore all major on-line services either provide Internet access already or are in the process to do so. We assume that the distinction between on-line services and Internet services will further diminish. Within this chapter we will therefore focus our discussion solely on the Internet.

Internet Demographics

With the number of Internet participants growing exponentially, accurate and up-to-date information about the Internet is almost impossible to get. The number of hosts connected to the Internet in January 1995 is estimated at 4.8 million (according to the ISOC[3] host count as). This number more than doubled since December 1993 (2.2 million hosts) and is believed to reach more than 100 million in 1999. Accordingly the number of networks connected to the Internet rose from 21,430 (December 1993) to 46,318 (January 1995). While the number of Internet hosts and networks can be somewhat accurately determined, experts disagree on the number of Internet users, which is often estimated as ten users per host.[4] This estimate would set the number of Internet participants at almost 50 million.

While the Internet is still "the" communications tool for universities, it is estimated that businesses already run more than 60% of all networks connected to the Internet. This rapidly growing user group has very different networking needs and expectations than the research community, and eventually the business involvement is going to change the Internet profoundly.

Internet Services

The basic network services on the Internet are:

- remote login to computers via the *telnet* protocol,
- file transfer across networks using *ftp,*
- and the exchange of messages between Internet users via *electronic mail.*[5]

Newsgroups and mailing lists are other important means of exchanging ideas and discussing problems. They initiated the involvement of many companies in customer-related Internet activities, e.g. in the computer industry, because they provide an excellent mechanism to get immediate customer feedback or to participate in high-level technical discussions.

Despite all these services and many others that have not even been mentioned the Internet has largely remained a convenient tool for the scientific community and has only been marginally used for commercial activities. The most important reasons have been the lack of graphical user interfaces to improve user-friendliness on one hand and the lack of indexing and searching tools to locate information on the other.

The one service that changed user demographics on the Internet profoundly, is the *World Wide Web* (also called *Web* or *WWW*). Together with graphical user interfaces like NCSA Mosaic or Netscape, the Web allows users to access distributed information just by following predefined links. The concept allows not only to present static information of various types (text, graphics, pictures, audio, video) but also allows to attach forms, transfer files, query databases, use remote application programs and other Internet services from within the Web. Businesses and non-commercial organizations soon recognized the Web's ease-of-use. Within less than two years after the introduction of the WWW the number of servers that can be accessed from around the world is already approaching 30,000, while it was just 100 in mid 1993 (Business Week, Feb., 1995).

The suddenly discovered business potential of the Internet and particularly the Web led to a noticable shift in user demographics. As comprehensive surveys (Gupta, 1994-95; Investor's Business Daily, 1995; Pitkow et al, 1994) done in 1994 and 1995 show, the early Web users were predominantly male (90%), and from the university sector (51%), or working in a technical profession (27%). 30% of the respondents were commercial users. These numbers shifted significantly towards private users and businesses in the 1995 survey, partly because browsers like Netscape have been introduced for personal computers and major on-line services started offering Web access in 1995.

With large numbers of novice users and many new Web servers announced every day, search tools have become indispensable. The latest developments in information retrieval on the World Wide Web are so-called *agents* like Web spiders, robots, and wanderers that use different methods to fill information requests. Some well-known search engines are: W4 (World Wide Web Worm, http://www.cs.colorado.edu/home/mcbryan/WWWW.html), Web Crawler (http://www.webcrawler.com), Lycos (http://www.lycos.com), and Harvest (http://harvest.cs.colorado.edu). Several Web servers even provide collections of different search engines, e.g. CUSI, the Configurable Unified Search Engine, at http://web.nexor.co.uk/public/cusi/cusi.html). Other most helpful tools are *meta-lists* of Web sites. The best known such meta-list is Yahoo (http://www.yahoo.com), a collection of links to World Wide Web sites, that allows easy access to distributed resources by arranging them in a hierarchical menu structure.

AUSTRIA - A CASE STUDY

After looking at general business trends, government policies, and the rising impact of the Internet we will now use Austria as an example to address potential activities by

* individual businesses,
* industries,
* and the government

in order to participate successfully in the global marketplace. We will first give a brief overview of Austria's economic position and telecommunications infrastructure, discuss Austria's NII plans, and look at the current state of Internet usage by Austrian businesses. From that perspective we will then give an overview of the many possibilities to use the Internet for gaining access to international markets.

Economic Position

The CIA World Factbook 1994, accessible via the Internet [9], describes the Austrian economy as occupying market niches in European industry and services. The Austrian government has recently undertaken efforts to liberalize the economy especially by means of a tax reform, by major privatizations, and by liberalizing cross-border capital movements. Although the opening of eastern European markets increases competition, Austria should benefit from its long-term relations to many eastern European countries, its geographic proximity to these markets, and its risk-reducing hard-currency policy. After a strong economic growth period, fueled by the German unification, GDP growth slowed down considerably until 1994. Austria's economy is currently undergoing major changes after joining the European Union in 1995. EU regulations about the free movement of people, capital, and goods and services between member states have to be implemented. On the other hand Austria struggles to keep welfare benefits within budgetary limits while supporting an aging population.

A comparison with other members of the European Union shows that Austria's average business has slightly more employees than EU firms. Very small firms (up to 9 employees) account for 85% of all Austrian businesses, while the average within the European Union is even higher (92%). 13.6% of all corporations in Austria have 10 to 99 employees (7.4% in the EU). Only 1.3% (Austria) vs. 0.6% (EU) have more than 100 employees. Of the 3 million Austrians in the workforce 57% are employed in the services industry, industry and crafts employ 35%, agriculture and forestry 8%. As of 1993 Austria ranked number 21 in worldwide exports. Austria's main trade partners are European countries: In 1994 63% of all Austrian exports (Austrian Schilling (AS) 512 billion) went to the European Union (mostly to Germany), 13% to Eastern Europe, 9% to EFTA countries, 7% to Asia, 4% to North America, and 4% to other regions of the world. With the exception of an export decline in 1993 Austria's exports have been rising steadily. However, Austria regularly reports a foreign trade deficit - AS 116 billion in 1994 - the largest part of it with the European Union.[6]

Telecommunications Infrastructure

The telecommunications sector in Austria is strongly regulated by the federal government and will remain largely under government control until 1998. By then - according to EU-wide deadlines - the full liberalization of telecommunications services in all member countries will be in effect.

Today telecommunications is the only profitable business division of the Austrian PTT, while mail service and the public bus transportation system are both highly unprofitable. By the end of 1994 about two thirds of all telephone lines were switched to digital service, in cities the availability is almost 100%. Although ISDN is theoretically available to many PTT customers, the actual percentage of ISDN users is discouraging. While the monthly ISDN surcharge of approximately $40 for a private ISDN line is rather low, the high tariffs even for local calls prohibit intensive Internet "surfing". For somebody using the Internet or another on-line service for only one hour per day at day-time calling rates, the monthly local calling charges alone would be $120. The additional cost of the necessary PTT-approved ISDN modems contribute to the little success so far.

The following table compares Austrian calling rates internationally [41]:[7]

Country	Local calls Cost per hour	Long-distance calls (nationwide, > 100 km) Cost per minute	International calls to U.S.A. Cost per minute
Austria	40.0	5.3	12.6
Germany	16.5	4.7	14.1
Switzerland	31.0	12.6	8.5
Great-Britain	36.3	1.6	9.5
U.S.A.	1.0 (per call)	2.1	7.5

This table shows that on average European telephone rates are by far higher than in the US. Austria is in the top ranks of the countries surveyed: it has not only the highest rates for local calls, but also ranks second in the other two categories. These high rates are among the most important reasons why the use of telecommunications services in Austria, and in Europe in general, are notably lower than US usage rates.

Leased lines are priced according to capacity and distance: a 64 Kbps line costs about $80 per kilometer and month within a local calling area, but regional rates might be as high as $1600 per month, thereby giving businesses in urban areas considerable cost advantages.[8] As an Internet access provider, Telecom, a partnership between the Austrian PTT and an industry partner, charges $2,700 per month for a 128 Kbps leased line ($5,400 for 256 Kbps), if the line is within 5 km of an access point, which is usually the case in urban areas. In contrast the US consortium CommerceNet charges $150 per month for a 128 Kbps line [3]. For high capacity networking needs the Austrian PTT offers a 34 Mbps country-wide Metropolitan Area Network connecting all nine state capitals in Austria.

So far the PTT had few incentives to offer telecommunications services at competitive rates or to strengthen their customer-orientation. Only the rates for international calls had to be adjusted due to foreign competition.

The Development of a National Information Infrastructure in Austria

First efforts to offer additional telecommunications services in Austria were made by US-based long-distance telephone companies that offer call-back systems for international calls at US telephone rates. Meanwhile Austrian corporations, that already have an extensive terrestrial infrastructure in place, are making considerable infrastructure investments. State-owned utility companies and the federally regulated Austrian Railroad have intensified their exploration of new business opportunities, especially by providing telecommunications services through their already existing networks.

Domestic and international joint ventures are working on projects to provide terrestrial telecommunications services, mobile telecommunications services in the upcoming European GSM network, cable TV, interactive TV, and other services (Der Standards -- 1994). One of two GSM network licenses in Austria will be open to foreign bids and several European and US-based telecommunications providers already showed their interest.

In 1994 several state governments together with the PTT and future telecommunications providers started projects to build regional fiber-optic "data highways" that will connect businesses to world-wide networks at low cost. One recent project in Salzburg aims at attracting businesses to rural areas by providing network access at local calling costs for about 80% of all private and commercial customers in the state of Salzburg.

The Presence of Austrian Businesses on the Internet

Austria's Internet activities started in the late 1980's with universities and other research institutions forming a nation-wide research network (ACOnet) that connects all Austrian universities to the Internet. After a long period of mainly research interest the number of private and commercial Internet users is rising rapidly. Businesses were partly attracted by the example of the scientific community, the computer industry, and the R&D divisions of large firms. But it was not until 1994 that the strong international media attention for the Internet made Austrian entrepreneurs and managers increasingly aware of new business opportunities.

Subsidiaries of multinational corporations were the first commercial users in Austria. The second notable user segment are Austrian multinational corporations like OeMV, Zumtobel, AVL List, or VOEST who use the Internet mainly for internal communications purposes (Trend, 1994). But lately the user-friendly graphical browsers for the World Wide Web attract new business and private users to explore the Internet.

In April 1995 the European Internet registration service organization, RIPE, reported more than 35,000 registered hosts in Austria, which accounts for roughly 350,000 users. For 1997 some industry experts expect more than 500,000 private and 200,000 business Internet users in Austria. The following table compares the Austrian numbers with other European countries and the US:

Country	Internet Hosts[9]	Households (in million)	Population (in million)	Hosts/ Households (in thousands)	Hosts/ Population (in thousands)
Austria	35,077	3.0	7.9	11.7	4.4
Switzerland	58,459	26	7.0	22.5	8.3
Germany	313,344	35.7	81.0	8.8	3.9
U.K.	271,236	23.0	58.1	11.8	4.7
US[10]	3,300,000	97.6	260.7	33.8	12.7

The table shows that Austria's start into broad Internet usage is certainly comparable to other countries within the European Union. While Switzerland comes closest to US standards within our comparison, Austria has almost the same penetration rate as the UK and a higher Internet density than Germany. Still the overwhelming percentage of users (experts estimate about two thirds) are associated with research institutions, but business and private users are now the fastest growing segments.

Together with booming user numbers the number of Internet access providers grew from one pioneer corporation that is on the market for about three years to nine Internet access providers in April 1995. Their service range starts with limited access by e-mail only, targeted at the private customer market, and includes full Internet access mostly for corporate clients. Prices for limited Internet access by e-mail start at $10 per month without time limits, and run higher for full Internet access (starting at $60 per month plus volume charges above a certain limit). While the number of Internet access providers grew rapidly the number of content providers, and especially on-line service providers is still very small. Currently CompuServe is the only US-based on-line service provider that is active in Austria and other European countries. Another on-line service provider, America Online, recently announced plans to enter the German speaking market in a joint venture with the German media corporation Bertelsmann AG.

Commercial Internet participants in Austria are still rather passive users of the services available, or they just started to experiment with network-based applications like the World Wide Web to get the attention of a larger audience. There are only few commercial Web servers already in use that are beyond the experimental stage, and seem to be professionally designed and maintained.

Between February and May 1995 about 20 new Austrian Web servers were announced on the Internet per month[9] with the total number of Web servers estimated by the author below 200 as of May 1995.   '

Month	New Web Servers (Total)	Research Servers	Business Servers
2/95	22	9	13
3/95	20	8	12
4/95	18	6	12
5/95	18	11	7

The firms that are currently maintaining Web servers on the Internet offer a broad range of services:

• **Internet access providers and service providers:** As already mentioned Internet-related services, spanning from technical solutions to seminars, Web server design and consulting for Internet marketing activities, are being offered extensively, mostly by small start-up companies.

• **Computing and telecommunications:** These companies partly overlap with the above mentioned Internet providers, since corporations such as IBM started to offer Internet access and related services through their existing global networks. Others are maintaining Web servers for public relations purposes, product information, customer service etc.

• **Publishing:** The Austrian publishing industry is very active in its Internet exploration and their Web servers reflect much of the international spectrum: "Der Standard", a nationwide daily newspaper, produces daily on-line versions (http://www.DerStandard.co.at/DerStandard) that are accessed frequently. The weekly business magazine "Wirtschaftswoche" also maintains (http://www.wirtschaftswoche.co.at/wirtschaftswoche) a Web server with several articles from every issue. Other publishers on the Internet are the Austrian Press Agency, magazines specialized in classified ads, publishing houses, and the Austrian Broadcasting Corporation. Although ambitioned the efforts by Austrian publishers are mostly experimental. Many expect no immediate return on their investments but try to get an early start and gain experience.

- **Electronic banking:** All major Austrian banks have been offering some sort of electronic banking software to their customers, mostly to their corporate clients, for several years. While first experiments with electronic banking for private customers over the Austrian videotex system, PAN, were unsuccessful, banks are now offering their first electronic banking applications via the Internet. Bank Austria, the largest Austrian bank, specifically targets the Austrian student market, currently the best connected and presumably largest user group on the Internet. Until December 1996 Bank Austria expects to attract 50,000 new on-line customers with this service.

- **Shopping:**
Distance shopping, whether by catalog, TV, or on-line is of little importance in Austria. On-line shopping on the Internet, as rudimentary as the possibilities are, experiences the same problems that companies encounter everywhere: although many Internet "surfers" browse the available Internet storefronts actual buyers are scarce. Within a few months several businesses started to present themselves and their products to potential customers either individually or mostly as part of an Internet shopping mall. The Web pages available as of May 1995 show that the necessary expertise from a marketing and design perspective is predominantly missing. So far the Web sites of the few companies present are of little interest and do not make users curious to check back. Customer feedback, requests for additional information, or orders are in most cases possible by sending e-mail, some firms provide on-line ordering forms.

- **Tourism:** Although the travel industry, an important industry sector in Austria, is present on the Internet, the interest in travel related information, as expressed in surveys, would call for a more intensive use of the Web in this specific industry. As of May 1995 Lauda Air and Austrian Airlines present their timetables and general information about travel destinations. Arrival and departure information, on-line booking or fare information were not available. Train schedules of the Austrian Railroad can be accessed via the public videotex system, PAN, but are expected to be available on the Web soon. Several hotels, travel agencies, museums, theaters, and city tourist offices present general information, quote rates, or offer a limited selection of travel packages. Additional information about Austrian cities and sights was made available by students. But most existing servers seem to be directed towards domestic users and do not present Austria to a foreign audience.

- **Information services, government agencies:** Many Austrian information sources such as library catalogs, economic data, and research data were made available by universities as an effort to share information with colleagues, or to present Austria and the own research institution to the scientific community. Professional organizations and government agencies are not yet widely represented on the Internet. One information provider with a very useful server is the Austrian Chamber of Commerce (http://www.wk.or.at/aw/wk_home/wkoehome.htm). Information about foreign countries, trade agreements, EU specific information, requests for bids etc. are especially designed to help Austrian

corporations find business opportunities abroad. Some federal and local government agencies are also setting up Web servers, e.g. the Ministry of Science and Research (http://www.bmwf.gv.at), the Viennese municipal board, or the Austrian Patent Office. Several international organizations with offices in Vienna are also present on the Internet.

Internationalization via the Information Superhighway

So far most Austrian business initiatives on the Internet started out of curiosity and technical interest rather than to pursue a well defined business strategy. Despite enthusiastic reports about the Information Superhighway firms have little knowledge about the possible benefits of joining the Internet and how to use this network for global competitive advantage.

Therefore firms currently concentrate on the domestic market. Starting with a limited range of activities helps them understand the basics of the Internet, learn about their competitors, and build the necessary expertise for future activities.

Once the Internet presence is established and the necessary expertise is available the Internet offers a broad range of business opportunities in an international context as well. Its design as an open globally accessible network makes it an excellent and low-cost *tool for communications and coordination as well as for marketing and sales.* The rapid worldwide deployment of the World Wide Web has made this aspect a viable and cost-effective possibility for businesses to present themselves in a global marketplace. Austrian businesses should take advantage of these opportunities to build new or strengthen existing ties with customers, especially in countries where Internet usage is already high.

The Internet as a Global Information Source and Communications Tool

Austrian firms planning to start international business activities or expanding their reach can use the Internet's enormous information and communications potential. Businesses can adopt a rather passive approach in their Internet usage by gathering freely available information, or they can actively participate in on-line discussions, conduct market research, or use the communications capabilities of the Internet to facilitate internal and external communications.

In general, countries with a well-established Internet presence already provide a great variety of publicly available information from many different sources that may be important to businesses entering new markets:

- industry information,
- foreign competitors and products,
- business partners,
- general information about foreign countries,
- Internet characteristics,
- consumer demographics,
- import regulations,
- and other regulatory issues.

Given its history the Internet provides a rich knowledge base for certain industries. Especially for *IT related questions* the Internet has become an essential source of advice and discussion. A broad range of mailing lists deals with almost every computing aspect and involves researchers, practitioners as well as IT or business consultants from all over the world. Over the years the research information available on the Internet broadened considerably. Disciplines like medicine or biotechnology have databases and discussion groups in place that serve as valuable sources of information for businesses in such industries.

Internet-specific information is of course particularly well represented. It covers the most recent developments and is indispensable for businesses considering to apply new Internet-based technologies, e.g. to implement on-line monetary transactions.

Industry-specific information on foreign markets is an other area of particular importance. Although the Internet will not replace personal contacts, or industry fairs and seminars, it is an additional source of information that can be accessed at any time and at low cost. A growing number of trade associations, international organizations, and government agencies in foreign countries provide lots of data and pointers to further information sources on Web servers, ftp servers, or gopher servers. But also the direct observation of competitors by visiting their Web sites, or by following discussions in newsgroups can give valuable input.

The Internet can also provide a firm with ***general information*** about potential foreign markets: mailing lists discuss foreign countries or regions, government agencies, international organizations like the OECD or the UN, or news services on the Web provide country-specific information from which further investigations can be made.

Companies interested in *on-line selling* to foreign countries can directly observe how the Internet is used in the target countries and investigate on-line the usage characteristics, cultural differences, attitudes towards security issues, data privacy, transborder data flow, and much more. Valuable information of this type is often made available by research projects, some of which we already mentioned earlier. They help to identify shifts in usage patterns and provide Internet demographics on a regular basis. They also give insight into attitude changes towards critical issues of electronic commerce as the usage of the Internet progresses. So far, much of this research is done in the US with strong participation of US Internet users. It may therefore not be broadly applicable but can at least help firms interested in the US as an export market.

The legal and administrative side of exporting seems to be the most difficult task for inexperienced exporters. Export permissions, import quotas, customs declaration procedures, legal responsibilities abroad such as minimum warranty requirements all demand considerable know-how. These issues have to be thoroughly researched before making strategic decisions about a lasting engagement in a foreign market. While some information of this kind is already available on Web servers (e.g. on the server of the Austrian Chamber of Commerce) many details need to be addressed individually. Using e-mail whereever possible for inquiries to government authorities, trade associations, Chambers of Commerce, or to contact foreign distributors, freight agents, and related businesses can speed up this process considerably and be a cost-effective way to prepare foreign operations.

Access to most of the information mentioned so far is provided mainly through newsgroups, Web servers, freely accessible databases, on-line publications and archives, library information systems, gopher servers, and WAIS servers worldwide. *Locating relevant information* easily and within reasonable time is becoming increasingly important. "Right now it is like an enormous library with no card catalog. People look around and leave." [21] is a common observation that has to be addressed in order to make the Internet useful for a larger audience.

The Internet as an International Marketing and Sales Instrument

MCI chairman Bert Roberts predicts that on the Information Superhighway "...you can have access to millions of customers. Products and services can be sold 24 hours a day. And since transactions are handled electronically, sales and distribution can be done much more cost-effectively" (Edupage, 2/3/95). His expectations are shared by many business leaders and the investments especially into on-line business transactions on the Internet are considerable. Despite these investments actual on-line sales lag far behind expectations (Blanning et al, 1995; Hansen, 1994).

Currently most of the money made on the Internet goes to access and service providers, the hardware and software industry, and Internet consultants, but industry analysts have no doubts about the future of electronic commerce.

Blanning and King (1995) report that catalog shopping currently is by far the most important form of distance shopping in the US with $53 billion in 1994, whereas TV shopping accounted for $2.5 billion. On-line shopping accounted for only $200 million in 1994, but forecasts by Goldman, Sachs & Co. (estimate the Internet market - including software, hardware, and services - to rise to $4.2 billion until 1997.

Besides a certain "everything for free" attitude (Forbes, 1995), that will change gradually as the number of business participants and consumers grows, firms have to take into account different consumer attitudes towards distance shopping in foreign countries. A recent study of European consumer behavior indicates that Europeans show very different shopping interests than US customers, especially in "...what are considered "precursor behaviors" to interactive television use, such as video rental, mail-order purchasing and home delivery of take-out food. While 75% of US homes with VCRs rent a movie at least once a month, only 40% of Western Europeans do. Only 21% of Europeans have take-out food delivered, and an even smaller percentage - 19% - of consumers in France and Britain express a strong interest in video-on-demand services" (Wall Street Journal, 1995). Another reason for consumers to use Web servers for browsing but not for shopping are the security and privacy concerns associated with transferring sensitive data over the Internet.

According to a study by the Yankee Group (Business Week, June, 1995) firms currently use the Internet for internal (30%) and external (49%) communications. The biggest growth rates are expected in advertising and selling products on the Internet. While only 8% of the firms surveyed currently advertise on the Internet, 33% have plans for the future. Direct selling to consumers is expected to rise from 5% today to 35% of all firms in the future.

Because of the media interest in on-line shopping the Internet is often perceived as "the" tool for *on-line sales*. But the possibilities of the Internet also encompass *pre- and post-sales activities* and corporations will have to examine carefully at what stage of their customer contacts the Internet can be useful.

Public Relations And Advertising: The most subtle way to approach potential customers on the Internet is to *participate in on-line discussions* that relate to a firm's products, services, or other areas of expertise. Businesses actively participating in discussions, offering solutions for customer problems, answering questions, reporting about new developments, or providing some other sort of information are usually leaving a positive impression on the newsgroup's subscriber base. Participation in on-line discussions also offers good chances for international recognition since many newsgroups are distributed worldwide. Most newsgroups use English as the common language, but in many cases firms will also find discussion groups about similar issues in the language of their target country.

For many products where this type of interaction may not be viable the *World Wide Web* provides an alternative. One possibility to attract broad attention immediately is the *design* of the Web server. Since many of today's

Internet users are very technology-minded word about new interesting sites is spreading rapidly on the Internet as well as in traditional news media. *Unique information* - even if it is not directly business-related - can also be a reason for visiting a Web site frequently. For a bookstore that might be links to foreign language magazines and newspapers available on-line or to on-line dictionaries, while a hotel chain might provide links to weather forecasts, foreign currency exchange rates, airline or car rental information, museums etc.

On-line Sales: Using the Internet for on-line business is an interesting opportunity in the *domestic* market as well as *internationally*. In the home market the additional distribution channel enables firms to address new customers and to offer extended shopping hours while at the same time speeding up the ordering and shipping process. In an international setting the Internet can expand a firm's reach to theoretically more than sixty countries without having to be physically present - which makes it especially appealing to smaller firms. Besides the expansion of the geographic reach the Internet enables:

•   24 hour on-line transactions without time-zone restrictions,

•   reduced cost of international transactions through electronic messages (e-mail, EDI, etc.),

•   fast order-processing through streamlined business processes,

•   fast international payment with secure digital cash or credit card transactions,

•   easy and inexpensive communications with customers and follow-up support.

So far not many products have been successfully sold over the Internet - or at least not yet - as many businesses are experiencing. While the US company 1-800 Flowers is pleased with the 30,000 daily hits of its Web site, these visits result in only 25 on-line orders per day. But there are also encouraging examples from the retail as well as the service industry: selling CDs, books, magazines, consumer electronics, hardware and software on-line has been quite successful as have been first tests of services by car rental companies, international express delivery services, and banks.

In general self-explaining, standardized and relatively low-priced merchandise is considered well suited for on-line selling. Mail-order merchandise typically meets these criteria and in the US we already see several examples of mail-order businesses opening up Internet branches. So far, most firms operate only domestically and either explicitly exclude international sales or refer browsers to customer service representatives for further inquiries about international shipping.

Besides opening their own domestic Web sites Austrian firms should consider joining well-established electronic shopping malls abroad. They could also join forces with businesses that offer products and services for similar consumer segments and build specialized "international shopping malls" to achieve *an immediate presence* in a foreign market.

To stay technologically ahead of the competition firms could participate in international research projects about the Internet as a marketplace. The most renowned research initiative with such an objective is *CommerceNet*, a consortium sponsored in part by US government research grants but also by its industry members. The overall CommerceNet objective is "to stimulate the growth of a communications infrastructure and marketplace that will be open, easy-to-use, oriented for commercial use and ready to expand rapidly" (http://www. commerce.net).

While on-line selling techniques are enthusiastically explored the *support of traditional business processes* does not get broad attention. Businesses can use the Internet's communications capabilities to establish and to maintain long- or short-term alliances and business networks, to work with local distributors and/or communicate with subsidiaries in foreign countries. Quick solutions for a single purpose might rely on basic services like e-mail and file transfer for non-standardized communications, while in a long-term business relationship access to the partner's order processing and logistics systems, groupware applications or EDI links can be added as needed.

Post-sales Customer Support: A 1994 IDC survey of the computer industry reports significant changes in customer service. Respondents named customer contact, especially technical support for their customers (87%), and software updates and patches (59%) as the most important reasons for on-line access by their companies [35]. While the computer industry has been pioneering these efforts [32], the penetration of private homes with computers slowly makes on-line customer support an interesting alternative for a growing number of industries.

For companies with worldwide customers electronic mail can be an excellent communications tool, both in terms of cost and timeliness. Services and products that need scheduled maintenance, need to be upgraded regularly, or manuals and technical documentation - in general technical products and services - are good candidates for on-line support. As mentioned earlier participation in discussion groups with prospective buyers and actual customers is an effective way of combining customer support with advertising.

Firms can make all kinds of existing applications available to their customers via the Internet. Always an excellent example of innovative IT use is Federal Express who in 1995 launched a Web-based application where customers can track the status of deliveries (http://www.fedex.com). Similar applications for querying replacement parts inventories, (re)scheduling deliveries, for maintenance appointments, and many other tasks can be offered to customers over the Internet as a cost-effective alternative to common practice.

Accompanying Activities at the Industry Level to Promote the Internet

The Austrian Chamber of Commerce, trade associations, industry consortia, and other organizations support the export activities of Austrian corporations with all kinds of services beyond basic information. They often organize symposia, visits of foreign corporations, or participate in trade fairs on behalf of their members. These organizations can use the Internet for several objectives: to fulfill their own communications and information needs, to electronically support the activities mentioned above, and to start initatives that promote international on-line business activities by Austrian corporations.

- Web servers with *general and industry-specific information* should be set up to make world-wide information sources easily available to firms at any time.[10] The Internet access should also enable firms to contact experts by e-mail, to form discussion groups for information exchange, or to search for specific information that is not available locally.

- Web servers should be designed that serve as *public relations and advertising* tools to get access to foreign customers and business partners. These Web sites can serve as electronic meeting points for domestic and foreign trade partners, a purpose that usually involves traveling to trade fairs or conferences. Businesses using these services often share common technological interests, which helps to establish regular operations on an electronic basis.

- Following the example of virtual conferences already held on the Internet trade associations could experiment with similar industry-specific *on-line conferences or trade fairs.*

- To acquaint especially smaller firms with the Information Superhighway *accompanying activities* should be considered. Samples of the information available on the Internet such as census data, statistics about domestic and international trade, government data, market research reports, etc. could be sent to firms on CD-ROMs or diskettes to promote electronic access to this type of information.[11]

- To promote the concept of international networks for forming business alliances and to *link international business partners* electronically trade associations should team up with business partners like telecommunications operators and content providers to offer specialized services for international business operations. A few such services like the Trade Point Network and World Trade Center Network - all based in the US - are already in use. A new service, the International Business Exchange (IBEX), has been announced by the US Chamber of Commerce. IBEX will eventually offer intelligent agents to match buyers and sellers automatically throughout the world [28].

Suggestions at the National Level

In order to participate successfully in a global marketplace government actions have to be taken to enable and support IT- and telecommunications-based business or industry initiatives. In addition to political, technical, and legal issues the government also has to prepare citizens for the challenges and opportunities of living in a global society. In some detail the issues that have to be faced on a national level are:

Competitiveness of Telecommunications Services: The liberalization of the telecommunications sector is well under way in the EU. The biggest European telecommunications carriers, e.g. the German PTT, are already being transformed into stock corporations and are moving aggressively into foreign markets. Small carriers like the Austrian PTT have to adopt a strong market and service orientation and will have to offer value added services as well as competitive rates to maintain their marketshare, especially with business customers.

Adherence to International Telecommunications Standards: The commitment to international standards ensures the interoperability and interconnectivity of services and provides a state-of-the-art infrastructure. The adherence to standards will be crucial for the success of telecommunications carriers, especially in small markets. Austria should be an early adopter of such standards so that it can offer new telecommunications services without delay.

Consideration of Global Communications in the Regulatory Framework: Global networks open up a multitude of questions concerning the protection of privacy, of intellectual property rights, transborder data flow, free speech and many other issues that are not included in existing legislation for electronic media. While the responsibilities of traditional publishers towards the accuracy of their sources are regulated, these issues are often unresolved for messages sent to Internet mailing lists or an on-line service provider. Clear and not overly restrictive regulations that allow the international use of basic information about customers while protecting sensitive data have to be introduced quickly.

Promote Austria as an International Business Center: With A state-of-the-art infrastructure under construction Austria has to improve its image in the world as a technologically advanced country that offers foreign investors a desirable position within Europe - with well established ties to the fast growing economies of the former Eastern Block, but also as a part of the European Union. Such an image campaign has to encompass a mix of activities and needs the commitment of the Austrian government. But especially with the information technology sector as the target, the image campaign should be accompanied by professionally designed information on the Web. In-depth information, discussion groups, pointers to other relevant Austria-specific data, and especially prompt reaction to personal inquiries can help to establish a positive image of Austria's commitment to global business and advanced telecommunications services.

Easy Access to Government Authorities: The Internet has a great potential to make the government more accessible for citizens as well as businesses. New ways of conducting business should not stop at the private level but should include easy access to government agencies, e.g. by using electronic mail for inquiries. This could significantly enhance the service level of government agencies as well as ease the burden of restrictive business hours.

Provide Information of General Interest: One way to promote the use of the Internet is to provide convenient and fast access to information that is needed frequently but is currently burdensome to get. Likely candidates are all sorts of directories like phone books, train schedules, business registers, stock market information, and other data of private and business interest. Although some of these data can already be accessed via a gateway to the Austrian videotex system, PAN, this service suffers from several technical restrictions.

Establish Research Projects in Internet - and Telecommunications-Related Areas: In the US the plans for the Information Superhighway created a new industry with small start-up companies that develop specialized tools, applications and services and often form alliances with businesses that use their services. In Europe such an industry has yet to develop. To satisfy the future needs for qualified researchers and software developers Austria should sponsor programs for developing applications and services for the Internet. Austria should also compete for European research grants and establish alliances with European research institutions for joint research projects.

Modernize Computer Literacy Courses: In order to promote the notion of a global community linked closer than ever before by telecommunications technology, and to establish an awareness of the impact that the Information Society will have on our lives "Internet skills" have to be included into the education of the future workforce. Know-how about the Internet as a tool for learning, business, and for everyday life, as well as a critical discussion of the dangers that accompany these developments have to be incorporated into curricula on different educational levels.

CONCLUSIONS

Business opportunities on a global scale have developed rapidly as improved services on the Internet become available and the numbers of commercial and private Internet participants explode. No other emerging industry ever had comparable flows of venture capital driving its research and the commercialization of new ideas.

As discussed above the Internet offers a broad range of possible uses for international business activities. A worldwide knowledge base and the "think tank" of millions of users can be addressed with questions and problems of all kinds. Especially for international operations the Internet's communications capabilities combine cost-effectiveness and productivity gains with open accessibility by business partners worldwide.

Using the Internet for international marketing and sales offers the greatest opportunities but also the biggest challenges. Current research can offer only hints which products and services correspond well with the fast changing user base and has few predictions which services will have lasting success on the Information Superhighway. The prospects for a wide variety of on-line business ventures are excellent, but firms will have to conduct their own market research before investing in Internet activities.

IS managers will increasingly be on the forefront of business decisions, as telecommunications and global networks change the design of organizations and business processes. MIS personnel therefore has to develop networking and especially Internet skills early to implement these changes as soon as they seem feasible. IS managers also have to spread the word about new ways of doing business within their organization and sometimes to their business partners as well.

Despite all uncertainties of a new medium there are exciting challenges ahead. Now firms have to set clear objectives about the role of the Internet within their business operations - ranging from the use as a strategic weapon in international competition to the use as a productivity tool. These objectives have to be part of the company's strategic IT and business plans and need the full commitment of top management **in order to make them happen.**

Endnotes

[1]Porter [40] emphasizes the importance of a modern telecommunications infrastructure for competing in foreign markets.

[2]Building this National Information Infrastructure is anticipated to cost more than $200 billion until 2004, while the current yearly infrastructure investments are estimated to be $60 million [23].

[3]The Internet Society (ISOC) defines itself on its Web homepage (http://www.isoc.org) as "... the non-governmental International Organization for global cooperation and coordination for the Internet and its internetworking technologies and applications. The Society's individual and organizational members are bound by a common stake in maintaining the viability and global scaling of the Internet. They comprise the companies, government agencies, and foundations that have created the Internet and its technologies as well as innovative new entrepreneurial organizations contributing to maintain that dynamic. The Society is governed by its Board of Trustees elected by its membership around the world."

[4]Some experts argue that the estimate of ten users per host is too high due to the many personal computers connected to the Internet. Others insist that the relationship of ten users per host underrepresents large corporations, that often use firewalls to protect their LANs and therefore have only few visible hosts on the Internet for hundreds or thousands of users.

[5]Electronic mail, which is largely responsible for the initial interest in global networking, is still the most important Internet service. According to ISOC data more than 1 billion Internet messages are exchanged every month. In terms of bytes exchanged over high-capacity backbone links file transfers account for the highest percentage of traffic on the Internet's NSFnet backbone [12].

[6]All economic data mentioned here are from [1], [2], and [44].

[7]All data are shown in Austrian Schilling. The current exchange rate for 1 US-$ is app. AS 10. All data except the calling rates for the US are from [41]. The US data were taken from the author's Nynex and AT&T telephone bills for January, 1995. The rates reflect the average cost of local calls within New York City, long-distance calls to Boston and international calls to Austria.

[8]Austria's and Germany's telecommunications tariffs for leased lines share the same problem of being highly overpriced. Bayer [3] cites the cost of a 2 Mbps leased line at a German university with DM 360,000, ten times as much as a comparable line in the US. In the US MCI recently reported testing the internal 2 Mbps broadband network of an electric plant as a model for delivering Internet access at speeds slightly higher than T1 (1.544 Mbps). The anticipated cost of $20 per month is far below the typical T1 access charges of $1,000 a month [27].

[9]The data are gathered by the Vienna University's Computing Center and can be accessed at http://www.ifs.univie.ac.at/austria/new.html. While it can be assumed that organizations are interested to announce their Web-servers on this page, this listing is not necessarily complete.

[10]It has to be noted that the Austrian Chamber of Commerce already provides very useful and up-to-date information on a broad range of topics on its Web server David (http://www.wk.or. at/aw/aw_info/aw_home.htm).

[11]According to a report in the Toronto Globe & Mail [19] Industry Canada sent 10,000 CD-ROMs with various trade information to small businesses in order to promote on-line business.

References

Austrian Chamber of Commerce. *Wirtschaftsgrafik 1994*. Wien, 1995.

Austrian Museum for Economic and Social Affairs. *Survey of the Austrian Economy 94/95*. Wien, 1995.

Bayer, R. Plädoyer für eine Nationale Informations-Infrastruktur. *Informatik-Spektrum* (1994) 17, pp. 302-208.

Blanning, R., King, D. *Internet and the Information Superhighway*. Tutorial, 28th Hawaii International Conference on Systems Sciences 1995.

Business Week. Cyberspace. February 27, 1995, pp. 78-86.

Business Week. Planet Internet. April 3, 1995, pp. 118-124.

Business Week. It's a small (business) world. April 17, 1995, pp. 51-56.

Business Week. Business on the Net? Not yet. June 26, 1995, pp. 100-101.

Central Intelligence Agency. *The World Factbook 1994*. Available from http://www.odci.gov/94fact/country/17.html

Commission of the European Communities. *Europe's way to the information society: an action plan. Communication from the Commission to the Council and the European Parliament and to the Economic and Social Committee and the Committee of Regions*. Brussels 19-07-1994.

Computer Science and Telecommunications Board. *Realizing the Information Future, A report submitted to the National Science Foundation by the Computer Science and Telecommunications Board of the National Research Council*. May 1994. Available from ftp://ftp.nas.edu/pub/reports /realizing_the_information_future

Data Communications. International SMDS to debut. March 1995, Vol. 24, issue 3, p. 18.

Davidow, W.H., Malone, M.S. *The Virtual Corporation*. New York, 1992.

Der Standard. Start für Datenhighway in Oberösterreich. 28.9.1994, p. 16.

Der Standard. EVN steigt in Telekommunikation ein. 15.11.1994, p. 21.

Der Standard. Telekommunikation: Ein Dreier-Wettlauf. 16.12.1994, p. 33.

Dialog. Bahn frei. No. 4, 1994, pp. 8-11.
        Edupage. MCI calls Internet the "Next Commercial Frontier" (from Atlanta Journal-Constitution 2/3/95, p. E3). Available from http://educom.edu/edupage.old/edupage. 95/edupage-02.05.95

Edupage. New CD promotes Info-Highway (from Toronto Globe & Mail, 4/26/95, p. B6). Available from http://educom.edu/edupage.old/edupage. 95/edupage-04.27.95

European Commission. *Europe and the global information society - Recommendations to the European Council.* Brussels, 26 May 1994. Available from http://www.earn.net/EC/bangemann.html

Forbes. Where's the money? January 30, 1995, pp. 100-108.

Gupta, S. *Consumer Survey of WWW Users.* Michigan Business School, 1994 and 1995. Available from http://www.umich.edu/~sgupta/ hermes.htm

Hansen, H.R. Implementing mass information systems: A Conceptual framework and guidelines. *CITM Working Paper* 94-WP-1004, University of California, Berkeley, 1994.

IEEE spectrum, E-mail at work. October 1992, pp. 24-28.

Inc. Twenty-eight steps to a strategic alliance. April 1993, pp. 96-104.*Inc.* Why every business will be like show business. March 1995, pp. 64-77.

Information Week. Testing Internet access - MCI teams with utility for 2-Mbps service. March 6, 1995, p. 64.
Information Week. Agent-based service joins electronic trading lineup. April 10, 1995, p. 32.

Innovation. Forming "temporary" companies to meet changing needs. (from [26]) Available from innovation-request@NewsScan.com, issue February 27, 1995.

Investor's Business Daily. Who's on the Net. April 3, 1995, p. A4.

ISOC. Internet Hostcount. Available from http://www.isoc.org/isoc/ charts/90s-hosts.txt,90s-nets.txt.

Jarvenpaa, S.L., Ives, B. *Digital Equipment Corporation: The Internet Company (A).* Available from CIS-FSERV@ube.ubalt.edu, filename: CASES.DIGITALWWW, 1994.

Jarvenpaa, S.L., Ives, B. The Global Network Organization of the Future: Information Management, Opportunities and Challenges. *MIS Quarterly.* Vol. 10, No. 4, 1994, pp. 25-57.

Kettinger, W.J. National infrastructure diffusion and the U.S. information super highway. *Information & Management,* Vol. 27, No. 4, 1994, pp. 357-368.

Levitt, L. Commercial Use of the Internet. *Proceedings of INET '95,* Honolulu, Hawaii, June 27-30, 1995. Available from http://inet.nttam.com /HMP/PAPER/128/txt/paper.txt

Lucas, H.C., Baroudi, J. The Role of Information Technology in Organization Design. *Working Paper STERN IS-93-48,* New York University, 1993.

NII Advisory Committee. *The National Information Infrastructure. Agenda for Action.* Available from http://sunsite.unc.edu/nii/NII-Executive-Summary.html

Pitkow, J.E., Recker, M.M. *Using the Web as a Survey Tool: Results from the Second WWW User Survey.* Available from http://www.cc.gatech. edu/gvu/user_surveys/survey-09-1994-html-paper

Poon, S., Swatman, P. The Internet for Small Businesses: an enabling infrastructure for competitiveness. *Proceedings of INET '95,* Honolulu, Hawaii, June 27-30, 1995. Available from http://inet.nttam.com/HMP/ PAPER/126/html/paper.html

Porter, M. *The Competitive Advantage of Nations.* New York, 1990.

Profil. Der Störfaktor Kunde. No. 5, January 30, 1995, p. 40.

Trend. Rein ins Netz. No. 11, November 1994, pp. 66-72.

Wall Street Journal Interactive offerings have less appeal in Europe than in U.S., survey says. June 20, 1995, p. A7A.

Wirtschaftskammer Österreich. *Österreichs Aussenhandel - Jahresergebnisse 1994.* Wien, 1995. Available from http://www.wk.or.at

5 The Problem of Data Quality in a Developing Economy: Russia in the 1990s

Elia V. Chepaitis
Fairfield University, USA

Data quality is the most serious obstacle to application development in many emerging markets, including Russia. This chapter examines cultural and economic factors in Russia which influence the development of information resources.

System design requires creative information strategies to compensate for and, if possible, alleviate data shortages. An ongoing evaluation of data deficits not only enhances the integrity of the systems analysis and design process, but also sustains a focus on competitive advantage.

As events unfold and information resources expand in the next decade, richer data models can be developed for enterprises. Russia is shedding the habits and institutions of a command economy, and individual organizations are accelerating the conversion from a command to a market economy, especially through global partnerships.

INTRODUCTION

Russia, the former center of the massive Soviet empire, is struggling in the 1990s to achieve stability and prosperity through a market-driven economy. Russia differs profoundly from most developing economies in geopolitical status, culture, infrastructure, and natural endowments. For example, Russia has three times the per capita GNP, twice the literacy rate, and thirty times the land mass as Morocco, which is a Muslim nation, an absolute monarchy, and a former French colony.

However, Russia shares a problem with many developing countries: effective information systems (IS) are scarce. In Russia and many developing areas, the salient obstacle to effectiveness is not a shortage of hardware, software, computer literacy, or adequate infrastructure. In fact, these resources are improving markedly, aided by development policy, private investment, education reform, and significant foreign assistance and alliances. Indeed, global transfers of communication and information technology (IT) have accelerated: cellular phones, faxes, desktop computers, VCRs, and copy machines are becoming commonplace in urban centers, even in Russian cities where the abacus is still in use.

In Russia and many emerging economies, the obstacle to effective application development is not insufficient IT, but a deep-rooted and neglected problem--poor data quality. Inadequate data quality curtails the effectiveness of electronic, oral and manual systems. In developing countries, concepts of legacy systems can be expanded to include not only inherited hardware, software, and people, but also data stores. Data quality is affected negatively by inefficiencies and cultural proscriptions left by vanishing and non-viable economic systems, and by distinctive traditional organizational structures, cost constraints, widespread information hoarding or deception, and chronic financial or monetary instability.

This chapter will discuss the centrality of data quality to economic development, the literature and the author's research methods, official and private information resources in Russia, and strategies to improve data quality in developing economies.

DATA AND INFORMATION POVERTY

Effective IS in Russia depend on a critical mass of robust data to support business information needs and manage crucial resources for economic development, yet Russia's environment is characterized by deep-rooted information poverty (Chepaitis, 1994). Information poverty can be defined first, as a paucity of useful information, and second, as an endemic condition, the lack of means to acquire the timely, accurate, and complete data needed to create useful information. In economic systems characterized by information poverty it is difficult to enhance data quality because existing data stores and collection processes are meager. Information poverty and data quality are intrinsically linked: the problem is circular and a conundrum.

Since improved information resources precede effective economic development, IS researchers, business enterprises, and public agencies have begun to accept as an absolute priority the amelioration of acute data deficiencies, even if this campaign predates the adoption of IT (Avgerou, 1991). Within both developed and developing economies, a reassessment of data quality provides an occasion to refocus profitably on the definition of data quality within specific organizations. Business re-engineering, quality movements, and global linkages have motivated IS researchers in the 1990s to challenge traditional definitions of quality which emphasize only accuracy. Total Data Quality Management (TDQM) research advocates equal concern for other characteristics which matter to the "data consumer" (Strong, Madnick, Redman, Segev, and Wang, 1994). Quality, or robust, data, must possess the contextual, representation, and accessibility value sought by the user; it should be relevant to the task at hand, readily interpreted, and both accessible to users and secured against damage and intrusion (Strong, Madnick, Redman, Segev, and Wang, 1994) (Figure 1).

The author's thesis is that improvements in data quality are vital to economic well-being and to enterprise development in Russia, but that information environment is so poor that the emergence of robust information resources will be slow and incremental. Russian entrepreneurs, foreign partners, and state authorities have low expectations for data improvement, based on their experiences of ubiquitous information poverty. These expectations are significant in Russia because data quality, as presented by Strong and Wang (Figure 1), is in the eye of the "data consumer", and the data consumer in Russia still defines data quality as accuracy.

However, for Russian and foreign enterprises engaged in business in Russia, an examination of data quality can initiate improvements in data enrichment which can accelerate substantially within the decade. To improve data quality,

| **Intrinsic Data Quality** |
| data have quality in their own right |
| e.g., accuracy, defect free |
| **Contextual Data Quality** |
| relevance and value of the data for the |
| task at hand |
| **Representation Data Quality** |
| format and interpretability of data |
| **Accessibility Data Quality** |
| accessibility and security of data |

Strong, Madnick, Redman, Segev, and Wang, 1994

Figure 1: Data Quality: The View of Data Consumers

existing data supplies and the business environment must be investigated to find: what types of data are unavailable; why is certain desired data uncollected, hoarded, or undervalued; is desired data delivered to the right users in an appropriate format; how relevant are fields for transactions, summaries, and decision making; how reliable and meaningful are temporal field values such as costs and prices; and how critical are data deficits for resource management, productivity, and competitive advantage? Is security neglected or problematic?

In Russia, a germane question is: how can managers and policy makers afford to develop value-adding IS and strategic information resources during turbulent times? How can IS improvement be supported in a period of macro-economic uncertainty? The author believes that Russia cannot afford to delay data improvements in the 1990s. The business climate is poor but improving (Aslund, 1995), and improved data quality can enable managers to evaluate swiftly emerging options for enterprise development and to establish performance measurements for both the short- and long-term.

Information systems constitute capital investments, spinning off cost-effective solutions in other functional areas. Also, systems development is educative for numerous stakeholders whose experience with quality systems and cross-functional goal-setting may be limited. As a bonus, sharing robust data and successful applications creates an atmosphere of communication and trust. Poor data quality and lack of access can perpetuate culture-based prejudices against open, available information. This prejudice hampers database design and administration, integrated application development, the distribution of telecommunication and information services, and information resource management. The definition of data quality can be enhanced in Russia by not only building on the past, but also capitalizing on discontinuities, revolutionary changes which present striking opportunities for early industry leaders and global partners (Kantrow, 1986). A powerful motivation to secure quality data for Russian enterprises is the need to create open, extended, and integrated IS and business systems for survival in a global economy: not only in export industries but also in domestic organizations who cannot compete with foreign imports (Tapscott and Caston, 1993).

LITERATURE AND RESEARCH METHODS

Data quality is identified by Palvia, Palvia, and Zigli (1992) as a pressing MIS issue in less-developed nations, and Avgerou (1991) emphasizes the need to assign top priority to improvements in data quality in economic development, to provide a foundations for information systems infrastructures. However, no field studies of data deficits or of projects to improve information resources have yet appeared on Russia.

Numerous authors examined the problem of information scarcities in Russia, for almost thirty years. Hardt et al. (1967), and Filatev, Buck, and Wright (1993), provide two complementary analyses of the impact of Leninist ideology on econometrics and data management, but the material is largely of historic interest. Brand (1994) discusses the deleterious impact of centralized planning on data in the Gorbachev era, from 1986 to 1991. Although data quality and information shortages are not the target of his research, Aslund (1995) provides a masterly account of Russian statistics in the 1990s which the author utilized in the following section on the relationship between the state and information poverty. Aslund searches through the transition from communism to capitalism for the emergence of reliable data in Russia, such as commodity prices published by the Moscow Interbank Foreign Currency Exchange (MICEX), and warns readers to be dubious about data published in new commercial journals such as <u>Komersant</u>.

Little Russian scholarship is available; the author had research privileges at the Lenin Library in 1994 and found empty shelves, missing collections and indexes, and no relevant publications in the available academic journals. The Lenin Library, the central repository for books and periodicals published in Russia, is comparable to the Library of Congress in the United States.

A steady stream of industry studies (Yergin and Gustafson, 1993) and descriptive journalism provides excellent background on business and information conditions in Russia. Also, Aslund (1995) finds that public studies sponsored by international groups or relief agencies such as the International Monetary Fund, the World Bank, the Organization for Economic Cooperation and Development, or the European Bank for Reconstruction are much more reliable than studies conducted by the Russian government or research institutions. In the next few years, international data will become available widely in Russia through E-Mail, and will vastly facilitate global research, partnerships, and commercial studies. Foreign business reporting is improving markedly, as seen in Russia 1994 by Chamber World Network, published in English, with the assistance of the German Chambers of Industry and Commerce; this publication contains a superior business directory and a series of statistics and Russian industry reports, intended for encourage foreign investors.

A large and valuable body of literature has emerged in the first half of the 1990s on data quality and on competitive advantage through strategic IS. Although these studies have not been applied to developing economies, several were useful in both research and consulting in Russia.

Work from the Massachusetts Institute of Technology's Total Data Quality Management (TDMQ) project provides not only rubrics for assessing data quality, but also strategies for continuous improvement which can be applied to enterprises doing business in Russia (Strong, Madnick Redman, Segev, A., and Wang, R.Y., 1994). Also, the author found the expanding literature on the relationship between quality IS and business re-engineering extremely helpful. Tapscott's and Caston's thesis holds that information technology (IT) cannot be exploited unless more open, extended, integrated, and flexible organizations are constructed. Paquin's and Turgeon's promotion of a customer-centered approach links quality IS and quality business practice in service industries, which are maturing rapidly and gaining in importance in Russia. Two recent books discuss data quality expertly and elegantly: Intelligent Database Tools and Applications (Parsaye and Chignell, 1993) and Quality Information Systems (Zahedi, 1995). Parsaye's and Chignall's three stages of information discovery (understanding, improvement, and prediction) might be applied fruitfully to applications within Russian enterprises to measure and monitor data quality. An examination of Zahedi's concept of continuous IS improvement is also valuable in weighing appropriate strategies for emerging economies.

Significant work has been done on culture and information systems, although most studies on developing countries focus on newly industrialized or pre-industrial developing countries, not the former Soviet Bloc. In Russia, the author has found cultural constraints in the adoption of IT diminishing, and cultural postures toward data quality and ownership of more significance.

Numerous scholars examine hardware and telecommunications improvements in emerging markets, including Russia and Eastern Europe (Clague and Rausser, 1992; Klebnikov, 1994). Roche (1992) has studied telecommunications for cost-savings and significant competitive advantage for multinational enterprises, but the impacts within developing nations have not been investigated in depth. Janczewski (1991) suggested that the construction of technical oases in Eastern Europe was necessary to permit a critical mass of enterprises to operate properly, rather than a campaign to improve the entire system. Chepaitis (1990) stated that whether local or systemic reform is attempted, technological solutions must be honed by local culture and material constraints in developing countries. A recent paper on culture and the information requirement determination process contains a superb bibliographical essay on multicultural IS (Leitheiser and Fouad, 1993).

Recent research on management strategies and global competitiveness often includes insightful treatments of information shortages and anomalies in Russia (Leitzel, 1993; Lawrence and Vlachoustsicos, 1993). Because Russia is of such major geopolitical importance, scholars can be expected to develop new lines of research as access to information opens. However, field studies in Russia are as risky as trade and investment in the 1990s, and nearly impossible for researchers who cannot speak Russian and are not working in supportive industries or institutions.

One comparative assessment assists researchers to rank and contrast countries' progress in IS development. In the 1970s, a three-tiered country classification of computer industry development potential by the United Nations divided nations into advanced, operational, and basic levels, and placed the Soviet Union in the second tier, with Hong Kong, Venezuela, Greece, India, Mexico, and others (Palvia, Palvia, and Zigli, 1992). It is clear in the 1990s that Russia has fallen behind those nations.

RESEARCH METHODS

The author conducted interviews with fifty-four Russian and foreign entrepreneurs, researchers, and policy-makers and visited scores of newly-formed businesses in Moscow, Irkutsk, Novosibirsk, Tomsk, and Kemerovo in 1991, 1992, and 1994 (Tables 1 and 2). The author theorizes that in Russia, even where IT is absent or primitive, seminal data quality improvements will occur at the organizational level, rather than in the public sector, and that well-communicated management commitments to data quality are central to effective IS and to economic development, even if data collection and processing techniques used in developed economies are not feasible.

From 1991-1994, the author peripatetically worked in Siberia, an area larger than the United States with a climate similar to Montreal in most cities, and established numerous contacts, especially in Kemerovo, a major industrial city with a population in excess of half a million people. Kemerovo is the source of significant attention from the central government because of export industries which yield hard currency and because of labor unrest under both Gorbachev and Yeltsin. The standard of living lags behind Moscow and St. Petersburg; Siberians often refer to the imperialism of European Russia and complain that they are treated like colonies, but they, in turn, are biased and occasionally violent toward numerous non-Russians. The author was evicted from an apartment for interviewing a Georgian greengrocer; Russians associate

Georgians with organized crime, and another occupant of the apartment, the owner, claimed that she was in physical danger.

Firm/Occupation	Type	Location
GEMMA, telecommunications, director	G	Irkutsk
Irkutsk State U., Rector Foreign Relat.	E	Irkutsk
AG garden tool manufacturing, intern	P/S	Kemerovo
ASM air cargo, management intern	P/S	Kemerovo
Chemmash, marketing services, manager	P/S	Kemerovo
Deputy Chief, City Administration	A	Kemerovo
Development, Junior Achievement, Dir.	A	Kemerovo
EC consultant, lumber	C	Kemerovo
Fedorev Regional library, operations	A	Kemerovo
Fedorev Regional library, acquisitions	A	Kemerovo
Garant insurance	P/S	Kemerovo
Georgian greengrocer	P/S	Kemerovo
Fata joint venture, industrial tools, sales	G	Kemerovo
Hospital intern/physician	P/S	Kemerovo
Informatica, Software development, intern	P/S	Kemerovo
Intourist Travel agent, manager	P/S	Kemerovo
Kemerovo airport, management intern	A	Kemerovo
Kemerovo Municipal ambulance dispatcher	A	Kemerovo
Kemerovo State University, vice rector	E	Kemerovo
Kuzbass Polytechnic U. Dean Econ.	E	Kemerovo
Knigi bookstore manager, buyer	P/S	Kemerovo
Krombank, deputy manager	P/S	Kemerovo
Kuzbass External Associates. director	G	Kemerovo
Kuzbass External Associates, dep. director	G	Kemerovo
Kuzbass Primapolis: shareholding firm	P/S	Kemerovo
Kuzbassocbank, board of directors	P/S	Kemerovo
The Professional, advertising	P/S	Kemerovo
PROMEST (import/export) director	P/S	Kemerovo
Raspadskaya coal, environmental engineer	C	Kemerovo
Restaurant manager	P/S	Kemerovo
Rhythm, tapes, audio supplies, manager	P/S	Kemerovo
Siemens sales manager	P/S	Kemerovo
Ziminka coal, mining tools development	G	Kemerovo
Sigma, Russo-Japanese consulting, Manager	G	Krasnoyarsk
Moscow Central Stock Exchange, Vice-Pres.	P/S	Moscow
Moskva bookstore	P/S	Moscow
Produce Farm, privatized sovkhoz, director	P/S	Moscow area
Distance education project, deputy director	E	Tomsk
Dom, small hotel owner	P/S	Tomsk
Tomsk Radiosystems, IS developer	E	Tomsk
Tomsk State U. Russian-Am. Exchange dir.	E	Tomsk
Siberian Adult Education Academy, dir.	E	Tomsk
YUGANSKNEFTEGAS, oil and gas, mgmt. intern	G	Tyumen
Kouchat fried chicken restaurant, Mgr.	P/S	Vladimir
KEY: A = Public Administrative P/S= Products or Services E = Education		
C = Consulting G = Global		

Table 1: Interviews with Russian Citizens 1991-1995 (44)

Questionnaires would have been the preferred method of data collection for this project, but these instruments are unwelcome and suspect in Russia, and inhibit open and ongoing communication, since they attract official attention. In fact, many Russians distrust and fear research which identifies individuals or enterprises by name.

Interviews in Russia had to be conducted with great informality, without tape recordings or even on-site note taking, both of which would hamper dialog and erect barriers to future contacts. Notes were reconstructed from memory off-site, occasionally after several hours had elapsed, and the author's records and laptop were kept in a secure apartment with a double iron door, due to widespread theft. Also, in 1994, carrying or using a laptop in public made subjects uncomfortable by drawing public attention to the research and interview process. These interviews took place on the street, in computer labs, on airplanes, predominantly in Russian, frequently with the assistance of student interns in Kemerovo.

Significant variations in attitude on account of differences in occupations, generations, and classes were obvious in three non-IS areas: the respectability of business occupations, the value of business education, and, most significantly, the probability that change in the next decade will probably be positive, rather than negative.

Titles, business logos, addresses, and even products and services changed rapidly from 1991 to 1995, and the author lost contact with numerous participants who are not included in Tables 1 and 2. Nonetheless, it has become dramatically easier to contact Russians via Fax, mail, and phone within the past three years, and Russians also became more voluble and less fearful of interviews.

The participants are classified according to their type of function or responsibilities: public administration (A), global business G, non-exported products or services (P/S), education (E), and consulting (C), although many firms and individuals engage in more than one type of function. Half of the respondents sell products or services, seven engage in global business, six in local administrative services, seven in education, and two in consulting.

Interesting strategies for dealing with information poverty emerged. YUGANSKNEFTEGAS, a mammoth oil and gas conglomerate, sent over 1,000 Russians abroad for business education, into environments in which business practice is mature and information resources are not scarce; most will owe years of service to YUGANSKNEFTEGAS and associated enterprises. Kuzbass External Associates also manages foreign business education for scores of interns from organizations which pay all educational costs, plus a commission, in hard currency. A more common strategy, for small enterprises, is to learn to do business with minimal, accurate data until conditions improve.

The participants were asked about four areas: business conditions in Russia, the goals of the organization, their information needs, and their information resources. By and large, except for the largest and most internationalized firms, the respondents expressed caution and modest optimism in all areas. Business objectives highlighted these seven priorities: stability, personal security, cost-control, solvency, and the acquisition of well-endowed partners, know-how, and business acumen. Six factors, which were in general more strategic than tactical, were apparently of secondary importance: growth, quality products or services, customer loyalty, price competitiveness, the acquisition of subsidiaries, and in-house innovation. The author was pleased with the simplicity and logic of the four questions. In general, attitudes and beliefs about contemporary business conditions affected the definition of organization goals, which in turn prompted well-focused examination of information needs and resources.

Firm/Occupation	Type	Location
Baptist missionary	P/S	Irkutsk
Boston Consulting Group, real estate	C	Irkutsk
Takanabe, Japanese, lumber, President	G	Irkutsk
INL International	G	Krasnodar
Dutch agronomist	C	Kemerovo
Fulbright, Library Science consultant	C	Moscow
Mercedes Benz, German manager	G	Moscow
Sister cities coordinator, US Embassy	A	Moscow
USAID housing rehabilitation, supervisor	P/S	Moscow
Central Asian consultant	C	New York
T.T.E., civil engineering, president Novokuznetsk	G	
Ohio State joint ventures Ph.D. research	E	Tomsk
Key: **A** = Public Administrative **P/S**= Products or Services		
E = Education **C** = Consulting **G** = Global		

Table 2. Interviews with Foreign Citizens Working in Russia (12)

A small group of foreigners working in Russia was also interviewed (Table 2), using the same four questions, and these interviews yielded significant insights into not only change, but the lack of change in cultural attitudes toward information sharing in Russia. These participants were struck by the lingering effect of the Soviet system, the popular distrust of profits, and widespread attitude that change will probably be for the worse. None had sufficient information resources in Russia, and all revised goals and responsibilities accordingly; most used advanced IT and external data resources, and all but one, the president of T.E.E., thought that the transition to a healthy market economy would require at least twenty years.

THE STATE AND INFORMATION POVERTY

Poor data quality in Russia's developing organizations is a deep-rooted liability exacerbated by three conditions: the lack of an established business culture, inadequate public data collection, and the continued impact of the previous Soviet system, especially the marked economic decline in the late

Brezhnev era, 1976 to 1985 (Filatev, Buck, and Wright, 1993; Clague and Rausser, 1992; Leitzel, 1993).

Economic historians, intelligence agencies, and Russian policy-makers do not know whether economic growth was slowing down, or whether the economy was contracting in the early 1980s (Brand, 1994). By the 1980s, the GNP had become a rough approximation, a ballpark figure, after two generations of fiction, double counting, and unexplained anomalies such as endemic shortages in the midst of excess capacity. Authoritarian and non-participatory planning disguised poor data quality and illogical decision-making, unlike any other Western socialist system (Brand, 1994). The Soviet system left unusable data stores, unmeasured social and environmental damage, and imbalances due to repressed consumption, forced savings, systemic underemployment and a widespread reluctance to share information. Incoherence and uncertainty cemented political control in the Soviet era, and were not only tolerated but nurtured: the planning elite did not want economic strategy to be understood and scrutinized, lest individual enterprises use data to achieve autonomy and competitive advantage (Brand, 1994).

Production was overreported in middle and late 1980s by as much as 5%, unofficial production and distribution was concealed, and Russia's announced GDP is still unreliable (Aslund, 1995). Since the collapse of the Soviet economy, there is less secrecy in public data gathering, and biases are more evident (Aslund, 1995). However, under Goskomstat, the State Committee of the Russian Federation on Statistics, data collection has deteriorated. Entire industries, from automobiles to housing, cannot rely on official statistics. After state enterprises are auctioned, privatization data becomes inaccurate when businesses split up. Employment statistics are mishandled, relying heavily on samples and on International Labor Organization (ILO) guidelines which are inappropriate for Russia in the mid-1990s (Aslund, 1995).

In addition, foreign trade statistics are unreliable because of widespread smuggling, bribery, and irregular registration procedures. Interstate trade statistics between members of the Commonwealth of Independent States are especially poor. similarly, intra-organizational commerce, especially intra-company loans and shared ownership are not tracked (Aslund, 1995).

Managers, academics, and foreign partners frequently complained about irrational government planning in the 1990s, and the inability to secure quality data because of ongoing political shifts. Data is inherently poor and cannot support decision making in an environment in which future costs cannot be calculated because of inflation, unexplained price increases, and interruptions in supply and distribution. Decision makers often refer to the value of business genius and instinct, and use heuristics, trial and error using what little data is available, to achieve *ad* hoc solutions to problems caused by corruption, shifting regulations and unexplained price increases. For example, the cost of shipping coal by rail suddenly increased 26% 1993 in the Muzbass region. In 1994, bus fares doubled, the free public telephone system was converted to a charge system, and international telephone rates increased 300%, all within periods of twenty-dour hours in Kemerovo. Fluctuating transport and communication costs deeply worry planners and investors in the provinces; the infrastructure is poor, private transport is uncommon, and substitutes for these services are unavailable.

Goskomstat's efforts to commercialize information have been underfunded; its work has been compromised by parliamentary and government interference, and Goskomstat makes little adjustment for estimated collection errors (Aslund, 1995). Yet authorities know that private production continues to be underreported for tax-avoidance and that many enterprises fail to register with national and local authorities to avoid taxes; as many as 50% of private enterprises may be unregistered (Aslund, 1995).

A recently-appointed taxman who began work last March, Sergei B., told the author that businesses resisted official discovery with force and that a number of his colleagues had been shot at; during the interview, he displayed his new uniform--an impressive greatcoat with highly visible gold braid. one new millionaire, who vacations regularly in Hawaii and Switzerland, a successful banker, exporter, and "consultant" drove the author to his dacha in a Land Rover with bullets rolling on the floor of the vehicle, and was greeted by a bodyguard carrying a shotgun--for protection from bandits, assassins, and confiscatory authorities, he said.

Goskomstat fails to collect data on private farming, private housing construction or remodeling, nor on most service industries, or consumer purchases (Aslund, 1995). Financial and monetary data is especially sparse, a legacy of the perennial neglect of monetary and financial data in the Soviet era, when the budget, monetary supply, and foreign debt were unpublished. The state has failed to collect data in the 1990s on the impact of inflation, bank failures, massive and unrecorded interenterprise borrowing, soaring bankruptcies, and privatized assets (Asland, 1995).

In Russia, the lack of primary data and secondary data, including public information stores, presents a serious problem for business planners. The author found entrepreneurs in lucrative new industries such as insurance, large appliances, household repairs, or commercial remodeling hard-pressed to define problems and opportunities because of widespread information poverty. For example, the Yellow Pages were first introduced in Russia, in Moscow only, in May, 1994. Moderately detailed city maps and monthly train schedules are frequently unavailable in Siberia due to "security reasons".

Conditions in a museum in Tomsk, a city closed to foreigners until 1991, are symptomatic of official Russia as a whole. The municipal museum houses a large collection of outstanding Western European paintings. The artists' signatures have been obliterated on each masterpiece in the collection; labels placed beneath the priceless paintings read simply: "By a Dutch Master", "By a French Master", "By an Italian Master", and so on. Data which could enhance the value and interest of these holdings exponentially has been mysteriously and crudely painted over; these defacements are symptomatic of a singular and idiosyncratic information environment.

BUSINESS CULTURE AND THE PRIVATE INFORMATION ENVIRONMENT

The Soviet experience bequeathed a deep distrust of statistics, a mania for secrecy, and a fear of private data ownership by individuals, lest the data owner seem to be self aggrandizing or subversive. Businesses often prefer to release minimal data, even to allies, not only to avoid tax authorities, but to maintain a low profile, exhibiting significant timidity. Numerous small businesses operate without signs on them or any identifying names, even on sales slips, although this has changed significantly from 1991 to 1995, especially in European Russia. The use of arcane identities such as YUGANSKNEFTEGAS, by a southern Urals oil and gas group or KEMNAG, for a Kemerovov shareholding group, is common and reminiscent of the Soviet era, but company names often offer even less intrinsic meaning to outsiders.

Pressure by authorities and local mobsters also inhibits easy data sharing between entrepreneurs, consumers, and potential business partners. In 1994, Siemens opened a dazzling electronic and appliance store in Kemerovo, but complied with an "unofficial request" to remove the sign on their storefront. No reason was given to the manager, and an Adidas outlet two blocks away continued to display their logo.

Russian entrepreneurs also maintain minimal accounting data not only because of exorbitant and shifting taxes and fees, but also because of enduring popular resentment of profits. Also, numerous commercial and financial advantages are transitory and optimized by secrecy. In Russia, numerous liquid or scarce assets, such as capital, extra apartments, automobile parts, or luxury items, often are kept off the books, because of fears of confiscation or theft.

The private motivation to improve data quality in Russia is sapped also by the short-term imperative to exploit pent-up consumer demand swiftly. Russians concentrate on opening new channels, filling product position gaps, blocking third-party access, protecting internal secrets, and hedging against risk as fast as possible, not on investing in quality resources and products. Since customers often purchase whatever becomes available, fearing shortages and inflation, entrepreneurs have scant interest in thorough data analyses of price, product, promotion, or place. The marked disinterest in market research, personalized advertising, and information ethics is not only a passing phenomenon in the transient *perestroika* era, but also a remaining Soviet bias that advertising is waste, quality is frivolous, and individual codes of behavior are superfluous.

A widespread lack of veracity among middlemen and facilitators, and also the temporality of Russian market solutions, reduce the value of private data. Business tactics are often experimental and survivalist, and remarkable discontinuity and metamorphoses in business structure and alliances characterize this revolutionary decade. Business planners and IS designers must deal with poor long-term linear vision and information fragmentation, and lack a critical mass of data which could support durable decision making.

Ironically, entrepreneurs concur vigorously if asked whether enhanced data would reduce the impact of endemic uncertainty and idiosyncratic behavior in Russian markets. For example, an egregious housing shortage often determines where consumers work, travel, and study, and also deeply affects family structure, disposable income, and eating preferences. In many cities, workers, including professionals, cannot be hired unless they can prove that they have secured an apartment. Productivity, labor supplies, and expansion into local markets would be enhanced by data from efficient underground housing markets (Katz and Rittenberg, 1992).

Another cultural prejudice against data sharing stems from the concept that power and position will be eroded if data is shared, a fear found in developed as well as developing countries (Constant, Kiesler, and Sproull, 1994). Data sharing in Russia is related inversely to political and economic dominance: the less information released, the more the dominance of upper echelon managers. Data ownership signifies status and authority in a nation with ubiquitous information poverty.

The impact of gangs and extortionists who dictate the terms of trade also impedes the collection of data on pricing and consumer demand. Organized crime and cartels bully retailers into set pricing, and discounting is also considered suspect and anti-social. In 1993 and 1994, fresh flowers, fruits, and vegetables began to enter Siberian markets twelve months of the year. If bruised, produce is discarded rather than discounted, and garbage bins are filled with wasted food. Produce never is sold at a discount nor distributed to the needy, in areas which had rarely seen fresh food imports prior to 1993, because criminals who control distribution demand uniform prices.

The vast cultural gap between data handling in the Organization of Economic Cooperation and Development (OECD countries and those in Russia affects data quality particularly at the strategic level. Strategic planning and decision making is difficult not only because of economic uncertainty and a lack of business experience, but also because of vestiges of Soviet culture in both the state and private sectors.

TWELVE FACTORS WHICH AFFECT DATA QUALITY

An examination of Russian conditions provides a list of cultural and contemporary conditions in emerging economies which may affect data quality.

Twelve factors related to market maturity and culture reduce data availability, accessibility, integrity, timeliness, and completeness in Russia. These factors, which contribute to both local and systemic information poverty include:

1. Unsuccessful and intrusive government planning and regulation;
2. Barriers to entry and dictated pricing in distribution, supply, or production;
3. Clandestine entrepreneurship, black markets, and barter;

4. Singular methods of managerial accounting, (for example omission of various overhead, depreciation, and maintenance costs, a common practice in Russia);
5. Unanticipated shortages and other tactics that inhibit consumption and disguise demand;
6. Political fear and widespread avoidance of information disclosure and sharing;
7. Inconvertible and unstable currency, nascent financial regulations, and a dearth of financial services;
8. A reluctance to divulge information without compensation or reciprocity;
9. Proprietary attitudes toward data ownership, IT, and IS training, by socioeconomic and political elites, including multinational and foreign controllers;
10. Rigid, hierarchical management styles featuring a marked reluctance to share information or to empower partners or employees through data sharing;
11. Communication behaviors such as a reliance on oral traditions in retailing, or the use of more than one language for business relations and record-keeping;
12. An emphasis on price and availability to the exclusion of quality, which discourages proximity to the customer and attention to preferences and trends.

Data quality is affected also by wealth, foreign partnerships, and other material and intellectual resources. Surprisingly, many multinational firms "wing it" in foreign markets and do not tackle the problem of data quality (van Mesdag, 1987). In Russia, foreign businesses often accept information poverty as part of the high risk of entering the huge untapped market and maintain highly speculative portfolio investments (Browning, 1995). These businesses operate at risk in an environment characterized by weekly currency, regulatory, and competitive shifts.

STRATEGIES AND SOLUTIONS

In Russia, an economy which has never experienced information plenitude, survivalist business practice and fortuitous personal connections are paramount. Data quality which users want is relatively modest, and applications seldom extend beyond operations, transaction processing, and summaries. However, accessibility is increasingly desired as organizations restructure, democratize, and create alliances, and as exposure to foreign business practices increases. However, as noted at the beginning of the chapter, most Russians identify data quality with accuracy at present, and this lack of appreciation for added data value reduces interest in both data quality and strategic IS.

However, in developing markets, the negative impacts of culture and historical experience on data quality can be diluted by self-conscious organization-wide culture shifts, quality processes, and technical elegance. Numerous occasions for change arise frequently in these dynamic economies. Shifts in management, financial restructuring, foreign aid contingencies, the initiation of strategic partnerships--all often offer ideal occasions for conversion and reform, although no event intrinsically guarantees quality improvements (Niamat and Nasierowski, 1995). Appropriate strategies to improve data quality require a sustained and enlightened effort to capitalize intelligently on moments of change.

IS development may provide an opportunity to discuss data quality theory and to experiment with novel business processes, especially if broad participation can be achieved. IS professionals, business partners, returning Russian management interns, and other allies who work closely with Russian enterprises can formulate convincing rationales for investments in data quality. Professional output, cost-cutting, and customer loyalty are central to enterprise prosperity. As electronic data interchange (EDI) creates more intricate coordination between global units, EDI partners can be motivated by positive incentives or threats to improve data quality standards and collection techniques.

Radical market and technology shifts appear to accelerate long-term potential to develop data resources, as long as local priorities are observed. Market information, case histories, or prototypes must be tested locally for profitability and low maintenance costs. In Russia, IS design and conversion through joint application development (JAD) holds promise since many economic units value tactical group decision making. JAD enhances legitimacy, responsibility, and design skills among participants who are expected to suggest refinements and expansions. The intellectual capital for software development in Russia is vast, since past training in mathematics, engineering, and science was superb. At present, however, domestic programmers cannot compete with the ubiquitous flood of illegal advanced software, and the future for software industry in Russia is in jeopardy (Specter, 1995). Also, formal business education or corporate training is needed to synchronize business planning and JAD.

Creative information strategies can compensate for and, if possible, alleviate poor data quality. An ongoing evaluation of data quality also sustains a focus on those business factors which enhance competitive advantage. Richer data models can be developed as Russia sheds the habits and institutions of a command economy. Domestically, highly competitive and expanding domestic service industries, ranging from automotive repair to waste disposal, are especially receptive to investments in data quality as the means to improve their customer focus (Paquin and Turgeon, 1994). Unfortunately, the prognosis for quality improvement is low in certain industries, even where vast consumer demand exists. In the 1990s, insurance, financial, and health care services struggle to achieve stability in Russia.

In some novel but critical activities, such as auditing air and water quality, radioactivity, or other critical environmental concerns, existing data quality is dangerously poor (Bater, 1989). Kuzbass External Associates (KEA) request not only tours of waste management facilities when they visit the United States, but also excursions to order or purchase literature on Russia's environmental problems.   Many large enterprises, including KEA, sponsor extensive foreign language training and education abroad for Russian students so that English E-Mail and imported periodicals can be understood, to compensate for domestic data shortages in some areas.   However, IS cannot succeed in environmental auditing using imported models, techniques and technologies developed in Western firms whose primary objective is compliance with existing regulations (Greeno, Hedstrom, and DiBerto, 1986).   Given Russia's massive environmental problems, Russia needs data and decision support which is not intended to keep a firm out of trouble, but to provide the tools for massive damage assessment, policy formulation, and clean-up processes.

CONCLUSIONS: QUALITY DATA, INFORMATION SYSTEMS, AND ECONOMIC DEVELOPMENT

The development of data resources, including data acquisition strategies, is a prerequisite for effective IS in every information environment. However, scholars and practitioners, who only recently began to consider IT transfer as IS turf, have often failed to identify information poverty as an IS problem Unfortunately, IS professionals generally lack experience with systems design and management in environments where robust data is non-existent or unshared.

However, this challenge is central to IS developers for two reasons. First, global information systems in varied information cultures must be developed, since these emergent markets present massive opportunity and valued partnerships in a world of shrinking markets and increasing competition. Second, IS alone provides the pragmatic and integrative functions which make IT and application transfers work.

In the past, information systems has ceded the study of entropy and inadequate data to economics, semiotics, communications, and referent business disciplines.   This research is, therefore, intrinsically multidisciplinary. Interdisciplinary aspects also surface since the roots of information poverty are frequently historical, political, and cultural, rather than technological, and since the ripple effect of inadequate information is far-reaching.   When computer systems are ineffective in developing business environments, the inability to utilize information systems exacerbates multiple economic, cultural, and technological deficiencies external to IS.

As the economies of the former Soviet bloc and of former European colonies mature and fold into global markets, robust and accessible data is pivotal to economic development and to effective foreign investment and aid. A critical mass of well located quality data for information resource management is central to long-term alliances and competitiveness in goods and services, both in home economies and also in world markets.   Because of a common triple legacy--a cultural bias against private data, poor public data stores, and a lack of competitive market experience, stable information resources cannot enhance other assets: capital, labor, plant, know-how, or inventory. Indeed, these resources are often depleted and ill managed to compensate for information deficits, turning information resource management (IRM) on its head.

Only in the past decade has IRM attracted practitioners and researchers in IS. Hardware and software have evolved to the point where data sharing on an unprecedented scale and in unlimited customized formats is possible. Data can be utilized, not only for traditional operations and reports, but also as an organizational asset which can optimize the management of multiple resources such as capital, know-how, labor, plant, and inventory. Skilled IRM can produce both virtual and actual increases in non-information resources, as well as marked improvements in the quality of those resources.

The potential for competitive advantage through data quality in Russia is massive in numerous industries. In an information-poor society, the organization with superior information resources is ideally positioned to build a value chain, reducing costs and increasing quality for customers through superior organization and streamlined activities (Porter, 1990). In an emergent market economy, consumers must soon be courted, and will be won through improved information-rich services and value-added features: enhanced supply and distribution, superior quality, cost-effective innovation, easy product or service maintenance, clear directions, attractive and durable packaging or casing, or associated services in areas such as communications, insurance, or finance.

Few domestic entrepreneurs expect to possess data with superior contextual relevance or elegant formatting for easy interpretation in the near future. Russians are leery of IS costs, unaware of external information resources, and unsure of the need for more than minimal security in 1995. Data consumers probably will become more acquisitive and ambitious with more experience, education, and economic stability.

Russians in 1995 routinely compare their country to the United States, composed of numerous peoples and languages linked by a common political system and one dominant language. However, ideology and ethnocentricity insulated and isolated Russia, and the economic environment is unique. Although rich in natural and human resources, Russia is ill-prepared to exploit either global markets or the information age. Improved communications, new opportunities, and global partnerships can accelerate quality systems development, but most Russian entrepreneurs are not yet optimistic or well-equipped to compete in global markets.

References

Aslund, A. (1995) How Russia Became a Market Economy. Washington, D.C. : The Brooklings institution.

Avgerou, C. (1991) Creating an information systems infrastructure for development planning. Proceedinqs of the Twelfth International Conference on Information Systems. New York 251-259.

Bater, J. (1989). The Soviet Scene: A Geographic Perspective. London: Edward Arno .

Behling, R. and Records, H. (1994-1995). Technology and international competition in the information age, Journal of Computer Information Systems.- (25:2), 50-55.

Brand, H. (1994) Why the Soviet economy failed: Consequences of dictatorship and dogma. ed. Moldman, M. 5th ed. Global Studies: Russia, the Europeasian Republics, and Central/ Eastern Europe.
Guilford, Ct: Guilford Press, 212-222.

Browning, E.S. (1995). Bold investors gamble on Russian stocks, New York Times (March 24, 1995), C1, C3.

Chepaitis, E. (1994). After the command economy: Russia's information culture and its impact on information resource management. Journal of Global Information Management (2:1), 5-11.

Chepaitis, E. (1990). Cultural constraints in the transfer of computer technologies. Mtewa, M. ed. International Science and Technology New York: St. Martins Press, 61-74.

Chepaitis, E. (1995), Information resources in Russia: A call to investigate a critical problem in international systems design. Northeast Decision Sciences Institute. Proceedings. Providence, RI. 180-183.

Clague, E. and Rausser, G.C. eds. (1992) The Emergence of Market Economies in Eastern Europe. Cambridge, MA, Blackwell.

Constant, D., Kiesler, S. and Sproull, L. (1994) What's mine is ours, or is it? A study of attitudes about information sharing. Information Systems Research (5:4), 400-421.

Greeno, J.L., Hedstrom, G.S., and DiBerto, M. (1985) Environmental Auditing: Fundamentals and Techniques. New York: John Wiley.

Filatev, I., Buck, T.M and Wright, M. (1993). The military industrial complex of the former USSR: Asset or liability? Communist Economies and Economic Transformation. (5:2), 187-2-04.

Hardt, J.P., Hoffenberg, M., Kaplan, N., Levine, H.S. (1967). Mathematics and Computers in Soviet Planning. New Haven: Yale University.

Janczewski, L. J. (1991) Factors influencing feasibility studies in under-developed countries. Managing Information Technology in a Global Society, Harrisburg, PA: Idea Group Nub-Ii-sFiEng, 35-43.

Kantrow, Alan M., ed. (1986) Why history matters to managers. Harvard Business Review (64)(1) January-February, 81-88.

Katz, B. S. and Rittenberg, L. eds.(1992). The Economic Transformation of Eastern Europe: Views from Within. Westport CT: Praeger.

Klebnikov, Paul. (1994) Russia--the ultimate emerging market. Forbes (153:4) February 14, 88-94.

Lawrence, P. and Vlachoustsicos, C. (1993). Joint ventures in Russia: Put the locals in charge. Harvard Business Review (81:1) January-February, 44-54.

Leithauser, R.L. and Fouad, N.A. (1993). An exploration of the role of diverse cultures on the information requirements determination process. Proceedings of the Fourteenth International Conference on Information Systems. Orlando, 35-45

Leitzel, J. "Russian economic reform: Is economics helpful?" (1993).Eastern Economic Journal (19:3), 365-378.

Niamat, E.M. and Nasierowski, W. (1995) Corporate turnaround: Dilemma for developing countries. Northeast Decision Sciences Institute. Proceedings. Providence, RI, 163-166.

Roche, E. (1992) Managing Information Technology in Multinational Corporations. N.Y.: Macmillan.

Palvia, P.C., Palvia, S. and Zigli, R.M. (1992). Global information technology environment: Key MIS Issues in Advanced and Less Developed Nations, The Global Issues of Information Technology Management. eds. Palvia, P.C., Palvia, S. and Zigli, R.M. Harrisburg, PA: Idea Group Publishing, 2-34.

Paquin, B. and Turgeon, N. (1994). Enterprises de Services: Gestion de la Qualite. Montreal: Agence d'ARC.

Parsaye, K. and Chignall, M. (1993) Intelligent Database Tools and Applications. New York: Wiley.

Porter, M. E. (1990). The Competitive Advantage of Nations. New York: Free Press.

Specter, I. (1995) Latest films for $2: Video piracy booms in Russia. New York Times, April 11, A3.

Strong, D. M., Madnick, S.E., Redman, T., Segev, A., and Wang, R.Y. (1994) Data quality: A critical research issue for the 1990s and beyond. Proceedings of the Fifteenth International Conference on Information Systems. New York. 500-501.

Tapscott, D. and Caston, C. (1993). Paradigm Shift: The New Promise of Information Technology, New York: McGraw Hill.

van Mesdag, M. Winging it in foreign markets. (1987) Harvard Business Review. (65:1), January-February, 71-74.

Yergin, D. and Gustafson, T.(1993). Russia 2010. Cambridge Energy Research Associates Report (CERA) N.Y.: Random House.

Zahedi, F. (1995) Quality Information Systems. New York: Boyd and Fraser.

6 Information Networks Diffusion in Brazil: Global and Local Factors

Renata Lèbre La Rovere and Paulo Bastos Tigre
Federal Univerisity of Rio de Jenairo, Brazil

Jorge Fagundes
Faculdades Candido Mendes-Ipanema, Brazil

The purpose of the chapter is to discuss information network's diffusion among Brazilian firms considering the impacts of globalisation, and the obstacles to their implementation. Benefits from network diffusion include cost-savings, productivity improvement, better market monitoring and customer service. Obstacles result from deficiencies in the infrastructure and regulation of the telecommunications sector. Global factors also affect network diffusion, since globalisation stimulates adoption of new organizational techniques to increase productivity and new competitive strategies with the formation of alliances at the global level.

This chapter describes how network diffusion takes place in Brazil's case and discusses the importance of global and local factors. The chapter is divided in five sections. In the first and second sections, Brazil's economy background and its IT industry conditions are described. In the third, IT network diffusion in Brazil in the services sector and in the industrial sector is analyzed. In the fourth, problems and issues in network diffusion are discussed. Finally, in the fifth section conclusions and implications for industrial policy are summarized.

INTRODUCTION

Information technologies are essential tools for competitiveness of firms that are following the new technological paradigm, which emphasizes the need for flexibility and velocity. Velocity of a firm is defined as the ability to answer promptly to modifications in quantities demanded by customers. Information networks produce a broad range of benefits for firms, from cost savings and productivity improvement to better market monitoring and customer service (Bar et.al. 1989, Porter and Millar 1990). What is meant by information networks is not only long-distance data communication networks but also local area networks.

Diffusion of information networks today is also influenced by globalisation. Globalisation is defined as "the emerging reality in the form of a transformation in the international environment and of the behavior of economic agents" (Michalet 1991). Globalisation comprises changes in firm behavior, such as adoption of new organizational techniques to increase productivity, and new competitive strategies with the formation of alliances at the global level. The convergence between informatics and telecommunications services has taken specific features in the context of globalisation (Dartois and Pouillot 1991). Therefore, the globalisation process must be considered to analyze network diffusion.

Nevertheless there are obstacles that may hamper diffusion of information networks among firms. In developing countries, low quality of the telecommunications infrastructure and regulation are common problems (Bharali 1994).

Brazil is an interesting case to analyze for several reasons. First, it is a large developing country with a strong presence of transnational companies in the economy. Second, Brazil has been reducing its trade barriers, thus forcing local companies to search for greater flexibility and productivity. Finally, the Brazilian government is committed to the formation of a trade agreement (Mercosul) that will attract more foreign investments to the country. The purpose of this chapter is to discuss network diffusion among Brazilian firms considering the impacts of globalisation, and the obstacles to its implementation.

BACKGROUND OF BRAZIL AND ITS ECONOMY

Brazil's national development strategy was based on an import substitution policy that generated a long period of economical prosperity beginning in the late 60's, when the yearly average growth rates were 7%. In this period GDP per capita grew at an annual average rate of 5.7% - 2.5 times as the average rates of the developed countries. There was also an increase of Brazilian international competitiveness. In the early 80s, Brazil had 1.36% of the total world trading, much more than the 0.87% observed in 1979. Besides, the export composition went through an upgrading process, that is, there was an increase of manufactured products from 38% to 44% of the total exports.

Nevertheless, in the early 80s there was a reversal in the economic growth cycle. The second petroleum crisis, the external indebtedness and the dinginess of the import substitution model caused a drastic reduction in the growth rates as well as a price inflation of 80% a month. As a result, during the 80s economical stagnation was followed by unsuccessful stabilization programs and unbalance of the public sector. Yearly investment rates decreased to a level as low as equipment depreciation, about 15% of GDP, while the GDP per capita did not change.

In the 90's, after a recessive period (1990-1992), the country presented a yearly average growth rate of 3%, mostly explained by the success of inflation control. Nowadays, the inflation rates are about 2% a month and the estimated growth rate in 1995 is about 4% a year. The national income per capita is US$ 3000. We can still observe some consequences of last decade's problems in the economy. In 1991, Brazil was not included in the list of the 25 biggest world exporters and in 1992 it was not even in the list of the 30 biggest world importers.

Despite this "lost decade," Brazil is the tenth largest economy in the world, with an estimated GDP of US$ 350 billion. It now has an open economy like developed countries. Average import tariffs are 20%. In 1990, exports represented 7.9% of GDP, and imports 5.2%. In 1993, Brazil exported US$ 38.7 billion and imported US$ 25.7 billion. Several enterprises of other nationalities are present in the Brazilian economy, particularly in the industrial sector as well as in technological dynamic sectors. Brazilian legislation is such that external direct investment conditions have been acceptable. In fact, transnational enterprises are responsible for 11% of the total economy capital, they participate in 32% of the production, offering 4% of the total formal employment of the country. These enterprises account for 83% of sales in the electrical devices sector and 78% of sales in the transportation sector.

IT BACKGROUND FOR BRAZIL

In 1990, the expenses in the acquisition of information technologies in Brazil were about US$ 2.6 billion, with an annual growth rate in relation to the previous year of 21.2% (OECD 1992). This amount represented 0.5% of GDP in 1990. The Brazilian market for IT is considered to be the largest among the developing countries, larger than the markets in countries like China (US$ 0.5 billion), South Korea (US$ 2 billion) and Mexico (US$ 1.2 billion). The national market represents less than 1% of the world market, estimated in 1990 in US$ 305 billion.

The composition of IT expenses of Brazil reveals a predominance of hardware equipment (56%), followed by software (32%), services (17%), and data communication (5%). This standard is not different from the one observed in the developed countries, where in average , hardware represents almost 50% of the total expenses in the IT market. However, Brazil never integrated its informatics and telecommunication policies. The absence of an integrated policy hampered IT diffusion since the telecommunications infrastructure is essential for developing data networks.

Informatics Sector

In the late 1970's, the development and manufacturing of computers were considered a key area for industrial development in Brazil. The informatics policy that lasted 15 years (until 1992) reserved the market of personal computers for locally owned firms. The aim was to both promote import substitution and to reduce technological dependence(Evans et.al.1992). Under protection, industry growth was impressive: local production of information technology equipment and software reached U$ 7 billion in 1989, with a high degree of endogenous industrial and technological production.

Overall figures for production and sales showed that in the late 1980s Brazil still had a larger computer industry than Korea. In addition, Brazil went further in the local production of computers such as mainframes, instruments and special terminals. However, as Evans and Tigre (1989) noted, there were substantial differences between the way in which the two countries related to the external market. While Brazil relied on its large protected market, Korean manufacturers focused on exports, thus inducing local firms to reach international competitiveness. In consequence, the Brazilian industry almost collapsed with the opening of the local computer market to imports.

The end of both tariff and non-tariff barriers to computer imports adversely affected the industry. The microelectronics segment has virtually disappeared while the manufacturing of microcomputers and peripheral equipment has seen a 50% fall in the early 1990's. Many Brazilian companies were taken over by multinational corporations interested in gaining access to existing market structures. Typically, the newcomers closed down production and development activities and shifted to imports to source the local market. The remaining local firms are oriented to more successful segments such as banking automation systems, software and telecommunications.

The impacts of the market reserve policies on the diffusion of information technologies are controversial. Although most critics argue that Brazilian users were forced to pay high prices for goods whose performance was often not up to international standards, the technological capabilities acquired by designing and manufacturing computers locally were a driving force in computer diffusion in sectors such as banking and industrial automation. Local production helped IT diffusion in a period when severe foreign currency restrictions prevailed.

Telecommunications Sector

Since the early 70's, Brazil's telecommunications sector is controlled by the Telebrás system. This state-controlled system includes a holding company, 26 state carriers and Embratel, a company in charge of interstate and international calls. Telebrás employs about 100.000 people and has a yearly turnover of U$ 7.8 billion, and it has grown since its creation at yearly rates of

11% (Wajnberg 1992). Private companies in Brazil can provide only a limited range of telecommunication products and services, such as switchboards for buildings, maintenance of public lines, paging systems, engineering services, satellite channels, operation of data networks and satellite systems, and value-added services. However, private participation in telecommunications is likely to increase, either through privatization of state carriers or deregulation.

Embratel provides long-distance data communication services, trough dedicated channels (Transdata) or packet transmission (Renpac). Renpac, the packet-transmission network, uses regular telephone lines, telex lines or dedicated channels for data transmission inside cities. Embratel also offers access to international databases, digital lines lease, e-mail, EDI, paging and trucking systems, as well as several satellite transmission services. The latter is mostly used by large firms, since its costs are relatively high compared to Transdata. Tariffs are fixed according to the service: while satellite use is charged according to time, Transdata users pay a flat rate per month. Renpac charges depend on the specific service provided: some are charged according to use, others are charged by month.

Embratel is implementing at present a five-thousand kilometer optical-fiber network that will provide connection to all state capitals within Brazil as well as connection to foreign countries in 1996. It is also planning to develop a broad-band ISDN and test it in the city of Brasilia this year.

Brazil has been experiencing a rapid growth in demand for telecommunication services. Demand is concentrated, as in other countries, in the services sector and in large firms. Two-thirds of Embratel's largest users are from the financial sector. Among the services provided by Embratel, data communications services are the ones growing faster: they jumped from 5% of Embratel's total receipts in 1983 to 31.8% in 1992, overcoming receipts obtained with local telephony. This rapid growth has been attracting new firms to the

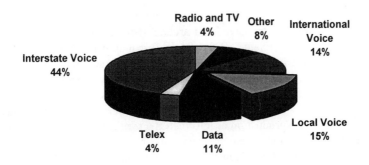

Figure 1: Composition of Telebrás' Revenues

Brazilian market. Telebrás is experiencing direct competition from global companies in value-added services. The latter are estimated to be a market of 60 million dollars in 1996. Interchange, an EDI firm, has seen its market grow from 500 thousand to 19 million processed documents in 1993 (Jornal do Brasil 3/10/94). Today, data transmission accounts for 11% of Telebrás' revenues (see Figure 1).

As for the composition of demand, Brazilian users have been reducing their demand for telex in favor of data communications, like in other countries. Reduction in equipment prices is also contributing to a shift towards more sophisticated services. For instance, between 1992 and 1994 the price of fax machines in Brazil fell 56%.

Overall, the reduction in import tariffs for informatics equipment and the growth in telecommunications investment is stimulating the diffusion of networks.

NEEDS AND BENEFITS OF NETWORK DIFFUSION

The Services Sector

The services sector has a great potential to use networks, since its activity has a high informational context. Miles (1987) observes that this high informational content is related to the sector's own features: immaterial products, production and consumption realized at the same time and production organization regulated by mechanisms beyond the market's logic.

Services may be classified according to the market to which they cater. Producer services are those linked to the physical infrastructure, like transportation and wholesalers. Mixed services cater not only to the physical infrastructure but also to the final user. Examples of these services are banks and insurance companies. User services are related to final users, like retailers and tourism companies. Finally, public services are those provided by the State.

Mixed Services. IT As A Competitive Tool: In the last 20 years, banks' yearly average returns have been around 16%, almost 50% superior to those of industrial firms (Exame 1993). Thus, Brazilian banks have had plenty of resources to invest in automation. Accordingly, banks started to automate their operations during the seventies. However, the pattern of network diffusion differs according to size. Large banks have built private networks, emphasizing on-line services based on satellite transmission and Transdata networks. Those banks also entered into production of informatics equipment during the Brazilian Informatics Reserve Period. Medium-sized banks have shared satellite channels and built networks based on Transdata. Small banks can not afford to use satellites, and thus use only Transdata. The latter began their automation later, during the eighties. The fall in equipment prices since the end of the Market Reserve has been stimulating small banks to build networks, especially LANs. The fact that each large bank has its own network hampers integration with other firms, especially retailers. The diffusion of electronic points of sale is therefore not so well developed as bank automation is.

Research by La Rovere (1995) in 15 banks that account for more than 50% of Brazil's agencies found that most banks consider IT as a competitive tool. Accordingly, 80% of banks have formal investment 033 plans for IT, where the main guidelines are extension of automation to all agencies, diversification and increase of services offered, increase in data transmission and processing capabilities and cost reduction. Expenses with data communications represent 2.5% of total expenses. The banks were required to list the main benefits and obstacles of long-distance networks (WANs and MANs) and local networks (LANs).

Benefits	% of answers
More availability of data	100.0
Quality increase	86.6
Velocity increase	86.6
Cost reduction	60.0
Workforce reduction	46.6
Obstacles	**% of answers**
Poor telecommunications infrastructure	93.3
High equipment cost	66.6
Lack of specialized workforce	26.6
Lack of scale	26.6
Lack of information about the system	20.0
Lack of customer interest	20.0
High cost of transmission channels	13.3

Source: La Rovere (1995), Based On A Sample Of 15 Banks
Table 1: Benefits And Obstacles Of Long-Distance Networks-Banking Sector

Emphasis on information quality and availability instead of cost reduction shows that for banks, IT are strategic tools for obtaining competitive advantages. Since banks' competition is based on diversification of services, availability of information becomes essential for competitiveness. However, diffusion of networks has several obstacles, especially inadequate telecommunications infrastructure and high equipment costs (see table I).

As for local area networks, their diffusion is more recent, stemming mainly from reduction in costs of equipment (personal computers and workstations) and software development. Most banks have LANs since the 80s, but the obstacles for their adoption differ from those for long-distance networks. Since the LANs cater to firms' organizational needs, the main obstacles to their implementation, besides high cost of equipment, are lack of specialized workforce and lack of organizational culture (see table II).

Albeit the price reduction in equipment, acknowledged by most interviewees, prices are still considered high. The results suggest that human resource development is a serious bottleneck to network diffusion in the banking sector, since both "inadequate technical assistance" and "lack of specialized workforce" are perceived as problems.

In conclusion, although banks are well advanced in use of IT, diffusion is limited by the size of the banks and inadequate telecommunications infrastructure. Most interviewees favor an increase in competition in the supply of telecommunication services, as a way to accelerate network diffusion in Brazil. As large users of telecommunications, the banks demand a wide range of services at competitive prices.

Benefits	% of answers
More availability of data	73.3
Velocity increase	66.6
Quality increase	66.6
Cost reduction	53.3
Workforce reduction	33.3
Obstacles	**% of answers**
High equipment cost	60.0
Inadequate technical assistance	46.6
Lack of organizational culture	46.6
High cost of software	40.0
High cost of transmission channels	33.3

Source: La Rovere (1995), Based on a sample of 15 banks
Table 2: Benefits And Obstacles Of Local Area Networks -- Banking Sector

Producer Services. The Case Of Transportation Companies: Diffusion of IT in the Brazilian transportation sector is characterized by the adoption of specific solutions for each sub-sector. Airlines were the first to automate their operations, following the international trend, and they still lead IT diffusion in transports. The most recent trend is alliances and code-sharing with international companies, sharing their reservation systems. Varig, for instance, will migrate gradually from its own transportation system (Iris 2) to Amadeus, used by Lufhtansa and other international airlines. Transportation companies typically start adopting IT in operational activities; they organize their networks following the structure of information distribution already in place.

In other subsectors IT diffusion is slow, due to structural difficulties. As observed by Barat (1993), there was a gradual deterioration of the transportation physical infrastructure between 1970 and 1990, due to cuts in public investment. Public investment fell from 1.6% of GDP in 1970 to 0.5% of GDP in 1990. Those cuts, by hampering the development of a planned transportation system, led to a fragmentation of networks and slowed IT diffusion.

Thus, in the transportation sector most firms are still on the early stages of IT diffusion, where IT is more considered as a tool to reduce costs and improve efficiency. Accordingly, only half of the companies analyzed in a survey (La Rovere 1995) had a formal informatics investment plan. Existing plans are very modest when compared to the banking sector and include: upgrade equipment, training of workforce, install LANs and automate management procedures. Most firms use long-distance networks to support operations, but the operational network is not connected to management departments. For instance, the federal railroad company has a network to control trains that is not able to transmit operation reports to the management's network, which is more recent. Managers have to read printed reports from the operational network before making decisions, which results in a considerable loss of time.

When asked about benefits of long-distance networks, most firms mentioned the same benefits. Divergence concerning the obstacles, on the other hand, reflects the diversity of situations in the sector (see table III).

Benefits	% of answers
More availability of data	80.0
Velocity increase	70.0
Quality increase	70.0
Cost reduction	20.0
Workforce reduction	10.0
Obstacles	**% of answers**
Poor telecommunications infrastructure	40.0
High cost of transmission channels	30.0
Inadequate technical assistance	20.0
Lack of resources to invest	20.0
Lack of specialized workforce	10.0
Other reasons*	40.0

*Source: La Rovere (1995), based on a sample of 10 companies. * Other obstacles mentioned: no transmission channels, incompatibility of equipment and transmission lines, procurement practices, problems with suppliers and lack of software.*

Table 3: Benefits And Obstacles Of Long-Distance Networks - Transportation Sector

As for LANs, only half of firms surveyed had them at 1993. Table IV shows major benefits and obstacles to implementation.

The results confirm the findings for the banking sector: the main obstacles to network diffusion stem from an inadequate telecommunications infrastructure and from deficiencies in training. The latter leads employees to view introduction of IT with distrust, which contributes to an organizational culture that does not favor network diffusion.

Consumer Services: The Case Of Media Companies In developed countries, IT diffusion in the media sector has two main characteristics: the first is a fast IT adoption in tradi tional activities of the firms (Miles 1988). The second is an increase in cross-sector competition, blurring the boundaries between the sectors' activity.

In Brazil, media and publishing companies have been investing heavily in informatics during the last three years, to cope with an increased need for velocity. Investment varied with the type of service: publishing companies, more prone to market fluctuations, increased their investments at a smaller rate. IT diffusion, on the other hand, is lessening boundaries between the different branches of this sector. Thus firms are adopting IT not only to enhance their competitiveness inside their activity but also be able to compete in other areas. The most characteristic example is newspapers creating on-line news agencies. Therefore, firms in the media and publishing sector in Brazil are at the stage of IT adoption where IT is used to redefine the scope of their business.

Benefits	% of answers
More availability of data	50.0
Velocity increase	40.0
Quality increase	40.0
Cost reduction	20.0
Obstacles	**% of answers**
Lack of organizational culture	50.0
Lack of specialized workforce	40.0
Inadequate technical assistance	30.0
High cost of equipment	10.0
High cost of software	10.0

Source: La Rovere (1995), based on a sample of 10 companies
Table 4: Benefits And Obstacles Of Local Area Networks -- Transportation Sector

The trend observed by Miles (1988) regarding IT adoption in traditional activities of firms is also happening in Brazil. In newspaper companies, network diffusion started in the mid-eighties. Large newspapers started to use Renpac during this period, and the increasing importance of Brasilia after democracy was reinstalled stimulated network diffusion.

In some cases companies develop their own software and applications, to connect different equipment to the network. The network was set up following the distribution of information already in place. The newspaper's main office is connected by a long-distance network to Brasilia and other large cities, and uses a LAN to compose the paper. Both networks brought significant reductions in editing time and paper costs. Smaller newspapers use LANs to speed production and offer faster services (like ads) to clients. Newspapers are also creating on-line news agencies, which are growing very fast. The main benefit brought by networks to this activity is increased velocity of information and diversification of services.

In publishing companies, IT adoption is linked to the need for improved production organization and product innovation. Publishing companies use IT to increase production velocity, control stocks and have links with retailers.

Television companies use long-distance networks to coordinate programs and ads broadcasted. As in other media companies, networks were first used in operations, then to support management decisions. In Brazil, the use of networks in management departments of TV companies started in 1990.

Finally, IT diffusion is stimulating the growth of on-line data dissemination services. Those companies sometimes are linked to companies that already had another activity in the media sector, like newspapers.

Use of IT in the media sector is essential due to high informational content of the activity. Most media companies surveyed (La Rovere 1995) have formal informatics plans, whose main guidelines are: integration of images and text; integration of operations; creation of on-line databases or alliances with on-line news agencies. Thus, media companies are already in the latest stages of IT diffusion, redefining the scope of their activity to increase their market share with the help of networks. The main benefits and obstacles of long-distance networks for media companies are described on table V.

Benefits	% of answers
More availability of data	72.7
Velocity increase	72.7
Quality increase	45.4
Cost reduction	63.6
Workforce reduction	9.0
Obstacles	**% of answers**
High cost of transmission channels	63.6
Poor telecommunications infrastructure	45.4
Inadequate technical assistance	18.1
Lack of specialized workforce	18.1
Lack of customer interest	9.0
Lack of scale	9.0

Source: La Rovere (1995), based on a sample of eleven companies.
Table 5: Benefits And Obstacles Of Long-Distance Networks -- Media Sector

Media companies spend more on communications than other companies of the services sector surveyed. Media companies started to use LANs by the end of the eighties, but they still have problems concerning organizational culture (see table VI).

The results confirm Aksoy's (1991) suggestion that IT diffusion trajectories depend mainly on the agents' capacity to articulate their informational needs as standardized procedures. Thus, organizational culture is essential for network diffusion.

Diffusion of Networks in the Industrial Sector

The Brazilian industrial sector is relatively low intensive in IT use when compared to the services sector. Among the twenty largest users of Embratel, only Autolatina (a joint venture between Ford and Volkswagen) is from the industrial sector. Two main reasons account for this. The first is related to the nature of industrialized products, which have less informational content than services. The second is related to the sluggish growth during the nineties. Instability of the economy, lack of good prospects and a protected market delayed decisions concerning modernization of production.

Benefits	% of answers
More availability of data	81.8
Velocity increase	45.4
Quality increase	27.2
Cost reduction	27.2
Obstacles	**% of answers**
Lack of organizational culture	45.4
Inadequate technical assistance	27.2
High cost of software	27.2
Lack of information about the system	18.1
Lack of specialized workforce	18.1
High cost of transmission	9.0
High cost of equipment	9.0

Source: La Rovere (19950, based ona sample of eleven companies
Table 6: Benefits and Obstacles of Local Area Networks--Media Sector

Network use in the industrial sector depends on the firm's size and operational logic. We made a survey concerning IT diffusion in leading firms in automobile, footwear, and electronics manufacturers. Among these sectors, automobile manufacturers use more IT because they are subsidiaries of global companies that increasingly compete at the global level. Automobile manufacturers are using networks to support just-in-time production and respond quickly to changes in the market. These firms are thus in the intermediary stages of IT diffusion, using IT to redesign their relations with clients and providers. The leading firms in the sector have their own IT companies, have a strong vertical integration and use networks to link their plants in Brazil and connect them with subsidiaries and the main company overseas. Those firms use intensively Transdata, Renpac and satellite, especially to support EDI, database use, e-mail, and data transmission. Use of LANs is more recent, mainly to exchange messages, graphics, and documents inside a plant.

In 1994, only 50% of providers of products and services to the automobile manufacturers were connected in a network. This hampered benefits associated with networks in the whole sector. The automobile manufacturers are putting pressure on their providers so that they start at least to use EDI, to speed operations. Mercedes-Benz has done so successfully and obtained substantial savings on stocks. We observed that providers are a stage behind automobile manufacturers in IT use, because they view networks mainly as a tool for organizational changes, while manufacturers want to redefine relations with clients and providers. Therefore the industrial sector still lags behind the services sector in network use.

As for obstacles, firms consider that high transmission costs, high equipment costs and the precarious telecommunications infrastructure are the main problems. Firms also complain about lack of specialized workforce. Finally, lack of organizational culture is also a problem.

The new projects concerning IT applications in the automobile industry all relate to its global character. GM, for instance, is setting up a satellite link with Argentina, to coordinate production inside Mercosul, the trade block formed by Brazil, Argentina, Paraguay and Uruguay.

The footwear sector is another interesting case to observe IT diffusion, since in Brazil this sector has grown mainly because of exports. The leading firms in the sector have a complex structure of distribution and sales, with points of sale overseas, and rely on strong relationships with few providers. This structure is reflected in their network: sellers send daily reports to the company's main office, reducing drastically the time required to prepare an order. In contrast, setting up a network with providers did not produce significant results, because supplies for footwear do not require detailed specifications nor intensive dealings. Firms prefer to use fax rather than e-mail in their relation with providers.

The main benefits of network use perceived by firms are cost reduction, increased velocity and integration in product development. Main obstacles to network diffusion in the footwear industry were inadequate telecommunications infrastructure and lack of transmission channels.

As in the automobile sector, the leading firms in the electronics sector are global firms. Only 43% of the firms in the sector use long-distance networks, due to the high number of small and micro enterprises in this sector. The leading firms (Ericsson and Xerox do Brasil) have been using networks for the last 10 years, to connect with other subsidiaries in Brazil and overseas. Main benefits from network use are increased efficiency in production, increased velocity, support to management decisions and integrated development of products and services. Xerox developed a network with providers centered in its plant at the city of Manaus, for just-in-time production, total quality management and shared development of parts. Ericsson has an international network involving its main operations, and plans to establish an integrated voice-data system, to extend EDI and teleconference, currently limited to Brazil, to the rest of the world.

In conclusion, globalisation is an important factor for network diffusion in the manufacturing sector. Leading firms in the use of IT are either firms that are subsidiaries of global companies or firms that have a high export share in production.

The Public Sector

The main difference between the public sector and other branches of the services sector relates to the former's organizational culture. Public service is not drawn only by a search of efficiency, since it is strongly affected by other factors. Bureaucrats fail to see clearly the results of their production since they have to provide diversified services on a broad time span. Bureaucrats also tend to be risk-averse (Stiglitz 1988), and have management decisions influenced by political factors (Vickers 1965).

The wide range of public services introduces differences in decision processes. State companies that are subject to potential competition from private firms tend to emulate those firms' behaviors, while public organizations, i.e., institutions involved in "classical" State activities like research foundations, urban planning agencies, libraries, etc., have centralized decision processes.

Our survey (La Rovere 1995), based on a sample of nine public institutions, showed that network diffusion depends not only on resources to invest -- which have been scarce in the Brazilian public sector in the last 20 years -- but also on organizational culture, which shapes IT use. The lack of such a culture is the more important obstacle to network diffusion in public organizations.

State companies have fewer problems with organizational culture than public organizations since they face competition from private firms and thus try to update their management philosophy. Today most state companies are adopting quality programs and are trying to disseminate an organizational culture aiming to increase efficiency. This is not the case with public organizations, where the bureaucratic rationale still prevails. Thus, Brazilian public organizations are still far from using IT to support changes in work and decision processes. However, understanding among public managers of the benefits brought by IT is increasing.

Thus, an increase in IT diffusion in the Brazilian public sector will depend not only on more resources to invest but also on a reform of management within the public sector.

PROBLEMS AND ISSUES IN NETWORK DIFFUSION

The development of new technologies and services combining informatics and telecommunications is giving ample "windows of opportunity" for work reorganization and improvement in competitiveness. However, most surveys aiming to assess the impact of IT on productivity do not establish a clear economic benefit. Impacts are more easily identified in specific firms or sectors where there is either a large increase in productivity or a diversification of products and services.

A possible explanation for this paradox is the existence of a break-even point, after which IT produces macroeconomic benefits. In other words, IT benefits for the economy are perceived only when a significant number of economic agents is linked to networks and adopt organizational procedures that permit full exploitation of IT opportunities.

This hypothesis is coherent with Schumpeter's (1939) ideas about diffusion of new technologies. In Business Cycles, Schumpeter argues that innovation can produce monopolistic profits for innovating firms, but it will have few impacts on the economy's productivity. The latter will increase only when innovations diffuse in the productive sector.

If we look at recent surveys about economic impacts of IT, the high speed of diffusion contrast sharply with the slowness of productivity increase. Robert Solow stated once that "IT was everywh033 ere, except in productivity indicators," based on his observation of the US, which has a higher rate of computers and telephones per capita compared to other developed countries but lagged behind in productivity in the 80"s. This paradox was challenged by Brynjolfsson and Hitt (1993), who demonstrated that IT investment has a significantly higher return than investment in other capital equipment. The authors suggest that investment returns can be assessed only after structural changes in use and supply of IT are in place, which where not complete during the 80s (hence the apparent "productivity paradox").

Therefore, economic benefits of IT are more easily identified when we consider a firm's strategy rather than production. Bar (1990) sustains that telecommunications and informatics promote a revolution in the strategic conception of economic activity. Cane (1992) corroborates this statement suggesting that IT use not only increases product quality and velocity and flexibility of operations but gives innovators' advantages linked to schumpeterian profits. Cost reduction is a secondary benefit in this case.

We discuss in this section factors that impact network diffusion. Our recent survey about IT diffusion in Brazil (Tigre et alli 1994) observed that potential benefits of networks depend on three basic conditions. The first relates to organizational changes in firms that use networks. The second is linked to the diffusion of networks among a wide range of economic agents. The third is linked to the development of the telecommunications infrastructure, including investments and changes in regulation. While the first condition is essentially local, the second and the third depend also on global factors.

Network Diffusion and Organizational Change

Organizational changes are essential to introduce new technologies. These changes include not only a reorganization of the firm structure but also modifications in culture and skill of personnel. Networks provide opportunities to save time that can only be fully exploited by the redesign of processes and the integration of stages of production.

Introduction of networks benefits firm divisions that depend largely on communications inside and outside the firm. Organizational changes that complement network diffusion include reduction of hierarchical levels, reorientation of decision processes and reorganization of work processes. These changes are not easy to implement since they challenge already established production and management routines, as well as division of power. Nevertheless, if firms do not adopt changes they risk to crystallize inefficiencies previously present. Usually firms tend to view networks as tools to provide solutions to their present problems, failing to perceive the potential to major changes in the firms' organization. In such a case, adoption of networks does not differ from automation of procedures that was characteristic of the early stage of IT diffusion.

Introduction of organizational changes depend on the development of technical capabilities in management of information systems and system engineering. While the former effectively combines technologies and organization procedures, the latter develops abilities to widespread use of networks. What is observed in practice is that firms do not consider organizational changes when introducing networks. This leads to high introduction costs and long learning periods.

Outward Network Diffusion

An important issue for network diffusion is the definition of technical standards, which at present is not complete since IT are still evolving very fast. Albeit standardization efforts lead by institutions like the International Standard Organization, what frequently happens is the imposition of standards by leading firms, especially those who are important at the global level.

The uncertainties associated with the use of new technologies leaves telecommunication operators and network users with no clues about the best solution. Technologies that are adequate for rich countriesain where development is centered in cities may not be the best solution for poor countries with large agricultural activities. Even when standards are defined, network applications may be developed considering local necessities. Therefore, it is important to develop a local technological capability to maximize benefits provided by networks.

On the other hand, the globalisation process implies that network developers and providers have to look at technological trends at the global level to ensure integration with the rest of the world. At present, three trends are important. The first is the digitalization of the telecommunications network, with the introduction of new switching stations, optical-fiber networks and satellite transmission. This trend enables the set-up of intelligent telecommunication networks that can be more easily managed by providers, thus increasing options and reducing costs to users. Digitalization of telecommunication networks also creates opportunities for firms to create new services, such as selling databases from their own networks to other firms. Therefore this trend further stimulates network diffusion among firms.

A second important trend is the growth of wireless communications, such as mobile telephony and low-orbit satellite networks. This trend is challenging the concept of natural monopoly that used to justify public ownership or regulation of telecommunication services. As privatization of telecommunications is spreading among developed countries, users have more options to choose telecommunication services and thus setting a network more adequate to their needs. Other advantage associated with wireless telephony is cost reduction. For instance, Telebrás estimates that mobile telephony can reduce a voice terminal cost in Brazil from the present U$ 2.000 to about U$ 600 (Telecom, March 1994).

The third trend is related to innovations in terminals and computers that at the same time make networks more user-friendly, thus stimulating their diffusion, and increase flexibility of the network.

These innovations are essential to widespread use of IT, since productivity gains from IT depend on a break-even point. Benefits stemming from IT are not linear, since it is only when a significant number of economic agents become users and form a cluster of firms that the competitive advantages provided by IT are fully exploited. For instance, in the industrial sector, when a firm is linked by EDI with providers and clients, it becomes possible to implement an electronic "just-in-time" system. In the financial sector, the greater the number of firms electronically connected to stock markets, the nearer the sector is to the neoclassical utopia of instant information.

Development of Telecommunications Infrastructure

The upgrading of the telecommunications infrastructure is also an essential condition for diffusion of networks. This upgrading involves digitalization, cost reduction and increase in the number of services supplied.

The inadequacy of the telecommunications infrastructure is a major problem for most Brazilian firms. In health and education, lack of telephone lines is the main obstacle to develop networks (Dantas 1994). Present experiences in these areas show that service automation and network development is improving quality of services provided as well as management procedures. The networks can also provide reduction in costs by guaranteeing information more easily. These experiences are nevertheless limited by the precarious telecommunications infrastructure and telecommunications tariffs.

Improving the telecommunications infrastructure not only requires more investment but also needs changes in regulation. Present rules concerning public telecommunications operators do not favor a competitive behavior. Areas open to private firms are limited and rules concerning private firm's operation are unclear.

Maculan and Legey (1994) note that the telecommunications infrastructure, at the global level, is being de stabilized by new technologies, by the demand of new services and by changes in the competitive environment for operators. As a consequence, new regulation frameworks, alliances and strategies are being tested so that the necessary structural changes are promoted. This includes a redefinition of priorities, changes in areas open to private firms and the establishment of a regulatory entity in charge of regulation and control.

In Brazil, the changes observed at the global level as well as the problems concerning the present telecommunications infrastructure define a need for a reform of the telecommunications sector, which is being considered by the new Government. However, little attention is being given to regulatory issues. Brazil may eventually follow the example of other Latin American countries by merely substituting private for public monopolies in telecommunications. Such a reform would not necessarily favor widespread network diffusion.

CONCLUSIONS: IMPLICATIONS FOR INDUSTRIAL POLICY

Our research found that network diffusion in Brazil is centered in the services sector and in large firms, be they private or public. Network diffusion varies in each sector according to its informational requirements. Most firms use networks not only to improve operational procedures but also to support management decisions. Most applications are used in long-distance networks inside Brazil. The firms are also using LANs, which are essential to organizational changes.

Our findings suggest that companies in Brazil increasingly perceive the benefits associated to network diffusion, but face several difficulties. The difficulties mentioned above result from several factors. First, Brazil has failed so far to have an integrated policy regarding informatics and telecommunications industries. Although Brazil for a long time had protective policies regarding informatics equipment production, its policies concerning telecommunications were subject to public budget constraints. In addition, there are distortions in Brazil's educational infrastructure that take their toll on workforce training.

Technical schools are few and quality of basic education is low. Few companies can afford systematic training programs in an environment of uncertainty about inflation, high interest rates and high costs due to fiscal complexity. Finally, the Brazilian telecommunications sector is organized in a complex way that provokes inefficiencies. As a result, setting up a data network, that involves a coordination between the local and the national carrier that leads to conflicts.

As for global factors, while globalisation is important for network diffusion in the industrial sector, it is not for most firms in the services sector. This is because in Brazil the services sector is dominated by local firms. Global factors may become important as Brazil reduces protective rules for local firms, as is happening in the banking sector.

Several problems must be addressed if Brazil wants to obtain benefits from network diffusion. It is necessary to expand the telecommunications infrastructure, as well as the range of value-added services. Solutions may include increased participation of the private sector and of global firms. Inefficiencies are not necessarily the result of public ownership of telecommunications, since several local carriers have positive results. They are rather a consequence of the gap between increasing demand and restriction in investment, coupled with regulation of the public sector that put limits to the carriers' competitive capacity. Therefore, a more flexible regulation for the public sector and the formation of alliances with the private sector should be the main goals of the policy concerning telecommunications. Government should also stimulate diffusion of IT in general. Our hypothesis about the break-even point suggests that collective benefits depend on the number of network users. It is necessary to diffuse an IT culture in firms with high informational content but slow adoption of networks, like small firms in the services and manufacturing sectors. On the other hand, firms that are subsidiaries of global companies and thus have already an intense use of IT can be agents of diffusion of networks.

References

Aksoy, A. (1991) 'Computers are not Dynamos - Frontiers in the diffusion of information technology', Futures, May.

Bar, F. (1990) 'Configuring the Telecommunications Infrastructure for the Computer Age: the Economics of Network Control' Berkeley Roundtable on the International Economy (BRIE) Working Paper 43.

Bar, F.,Borrus, M., and Coriat, B. (1989) 'Information Networks and Competitive Advantages: The Issues for Government Policy and Corporate Strategy' Final Report of the OECD-BRIE Telecommunications User Group Project, Seminar Information Networks and Business Strategies, Paris, 19 and 20 October.

Barat, J.(1993) 'Serviços de Infra-Estrutura em Transportes e Competitividade', in Coutinho, L., and Ferraz, J.C. (eds) Estudo da Competitividade da Indústria Brasileira, MCT/FINEP/PADCT/UNICAMP/IEI-UFRJ.

Bharali, U. (1994) 'Meeting Communication Technology Needs for DC's: a case for partnership in technology development' Information Processing '94, IFIP Transactions A-53 vol. II, North Holland.

Brynnjolfsson, E. and Hitt, L. (1993) 'New Evidence on the Returns to Information Systems' MIT Sloan School, Cambridge, Massachusetts, October.

Cane, A.(1992) 'Information Technology and Competitive Advantage: Lesson from the Developed Coutries'. World Development Volume 20 Number 12, December.

Dantas, M. (1994) 'Telecomunicações, Cidadania e Serviços Públicos: Aspectos Conceituais e Experiência Brasileiras', in Tigre, P. et alli. Telecomunica7ões: Mudança Tecnológica e suas Implicações Econômicas, Sociais e Institucionais. Research Report IEI/Embratel.

Dartois, O and Pouillot, D. (1991) 'La Globalization dans les Télécommunications'. Commission Of The European Communities, Fast Programme, Dossier prospective n°a 2, vol. 10.

Evans, P., Frischtak, C., and Tigre, P., (eds) (1992) High Technology and Third World Industrialization: Brazilian Computer Policy in Comparative Perspective, Research Series/Number 85, University of California at Berkeley.

Evans, P., and Tigre, P., 'Going Beyond the Clones in Brazil and Korea: A Comparative Analysis of NIC Strategies in the Computer Industry' World Development Vol.17 Number 11, November.

La Rovere, R.L., 'Tecnologias da Informação no Brasil: o Caso do Setor de Serviços', Research Report to CNPq, Rio de Janeiro, March.

Maculan, A. and Legey, L. 'Um novo Sistema de Regulação das Telecomunicações no Brasil: As experiências internacionais e os elementos para reestruturação dos serviços de telecomunicações' in Tigre, P. et alli Telecomunicações: Mudança Tecnológica e suas Implicações Econômicas, Sociais e Institucionais. op.cit.

Michalet, C.A. (1991) 'Global Competition and its Implications for Firms' presented at Technology and Productivity: the Challenge for Economic Policy, OECD.

Miles, I.(1988) Home Informatics:Information Technology and the Transformation of Everyday Life, Pinter Publishers, London.

Miles, I. (1987) 'Information Technology and the Services Economy', Oxford Surveys in Information Technology vol.4, Oxford University Press.
Organization for Economic Cooperation and Development - OECD (1992) Regulatory Reform, Privatization and Competition Policy". Paris.

Porter, M.E., and Millar, V.E. (1990) 'How Information Gives You Competitive Advantage', in Mac Gowan, W., (ed.), Revolution in Real Time: Mannaging Information Technology in the 1990's, Harvard Business Review, Boston.

Schumpeter, J.A. (1939) Business Cycles: a Theoretical, Historical and Statistical Analysis of the Capitalist Process, New York, McGraw-Hill.
Stiglitz, J.E. (1988) Economics of the Public Sector , Norton &Co. New York .

Tigre, P. et alli.(1994) Telecomunicações: Mudança Tecnológica e suas Implicações Econômicas, Sociais e Institucionais. Research Report IEI/Embratel

Vickers, G.(1965) The Art of Judgement: a Study of Policy Making, Chapman&Hall, London.

Wajnberg, S. (1992) 'Acesso ao Mercado, Barreiras e Expectativas: o caso do Brasil' Ministério das Comunicações.ain

SECTION-2

NATIONAL IT INFRASTRUCTURE, CULTURE, AND DEVELOPMENT

What are the challenges in developing information systems in host (subsidiary) countries or developing global information systems that span several countries?. Chief among these are the national IT infrastructure (or lack thereof), economic development level, costs of factors of production, cultural aspects, and legal issues. Some of these were discussed in the previous section with reference to specific countries. This section makes an introspective examination of these factors, and offers possible solutions and strategies to overcome the bottlenecks.

The section consists of five chapters. The first chapter by Chrisanthi Avergou discusses the problems, opportunities and challenges faced by developing nations in integrating with the global economy. She focuses on the IT and telecommunications weaknesses of these nations and proposes a number of policy issues necessary to improve the situation. The next chapter by Amitava Dutta reviews the state of telecommunications infrastructure in developing countries of Latin America and Asia. He also examines the reforms implemented in this sector in terms of privatization attempts and implementation of regulatory structures. While privatization trends have generally improved the pace of growth, problems exist in terms of lagging development of regulation, and disparity between urban and rural telecommunication services. Amitava goes on to extrapolate important lessons for telecommunications reform in developing countries.

Barry Shore, in his chapter, sensitizes the reader on the role of culture in the development and operation of global information systems (GIS). He emphasizes that an information-culture gap may exist between the headquarters and the host organization, and must be bridged for GIS success. He examines the various factors (including national culture, as defined by Hofstede) that may influence the information culture, categorizes information culture into four classes, and suggest some practical solutions to address the gap. In the next chapter, Effy Oz reviews data privacy and transborder data transfer laws in different countries, especially Europe. While protecting privacy, such laws hinder the free flow of information across borders, and have an impact on the organizational IS strategy. Oz also examines international attempts to harmonize legislation. Finally, in the last chapter of the section, Paul Alpar examines different technological   alternatives for business-to-business   electronic   commerce   and   business-to-consumer electronic commerce. He evaluates the business viability of each alternative in the European Union using factors from a framework that he developed, called "communication cost economies (CCE)" framework. Similar analyses may be conducted for other parts of the world.

7 How Can Information Technology Enable Developing Countries to Integrate into the Global Economy?

Chrisanthi Avgerou
London School of Economics, UK

The developing countries are faced with new opportunities but also enormous difficulties in their effort to utilize IT and telecommunications in order to become integrated in the emerging global economy. In this chapter we discuss the current situation regarding the IT and telecommunications capacity of developing countries, and highlight the main problems that they need to overcome, namely, increasing disparities with industrialized countries, difficulty in achieving value from the utilization of IT, and exacerbation of social problems of underdevelopment. We argue that these problems are unlikely to be resolved by the globalization processes alone, and discuss policy actions that a variety of institutions need to undertake.

INTRODUCTION

Undoubtedly, the most prevalent socio-economic phenomenon in the 1990s is globalization. There is a great deal of research and debate on the exact nature of the trends constituting globalization, focusing on a variety of its manifested aspects, such as emerging new organizational forms, cultural change, political and institutional development, or geographic re-distribution of industrial activities. Almost without exception all such studies recognize the enabling role of IT and telecommunications, although they do not necessarily clarify in what way do these technologies contribute to the observed or foreseen changes.

However, most studies of globalization examine the phenomenon from the perspective of a few economically advanced parts of the world, excluding from careful consideration the changes happening in developing countries. There is still little understanding of the way multinational corporations deploy information technology in their subsidiary companies around the world, and the role information systems play in their business strategy (Ives and Jarvenpaa, 1991). There is even less understanding about information systems which support business partners located in different countries. Research from the perspective of developing countries - rather than multinationals - about the information systems capacity of the subsidiary companies in developing countries, and the resulting technology transfer, is almost non-existing. Roche's study of 25 American corporations [1992] confirms widely held concerns about very unequal distribution of computer equipment and control over information resources.

Many analysts of the globalization trends predict pessimistically that the position of developing countries within the global economy is going to get worse [Castells and Henderson, 1987]. There are fears that globalization may result in disruption of the social fabric and further marginalization of whole regions within the world economy [Swamy, 1994]. In contrast, the literature of information systems tends to assume that the current trends are beneficial to the developing world, offering opportunities for economic growth to all countries. Perhaps such an attitude is appropriate for professionals and academics who aspire to guide action rather than only observe, explain and predict. If unfounded, however, it runs the risk of misdirecting government policy and company strategy.

This chapter examines the efforts of developing countries to take up IT in order to participate in the emerging global economy. The following questions are addressed: What do the current globalization trends mean for developing countries? What is the capacity of developing countries to exploit the potential of IT and telecommunications to their advantage within the global economy? What can be done to improve the capacity of developing countries to take up and utilize successfully IT and telecommunications?
Analysis of these questions is followed by discussion of required policy. Considering the diversity of socio-economic conditions of the developing countries, it would be unrealistic to attempt to make general recommendations of what should be done. The aim of this chapter is to highlight the issues involved and the options available, rather than to suggest particular courses of action to be followed.

GLOBALIZATION FROM THE PERSPECTIVE OF DEVELOPING COUNTRIES

Globalization in its most general meaning has been defined as a process which cuts across national boundaries, integrating and connecting communities in new space-time combinations (Hall *et al*, 1992). The term takes a variety of more specific meanings in the different disciplines studying it. The most relevant of them for the purpose of this chapter are the following:
One widely accepted conception of globalization highlights the trend towards freer trade, and the flow of finance, labor, and commodities among countries. It also refers to the flow of data which seem to be critical for the operations of organizations today, allowing the connection of the activities taking place in distant localities. Flowing capital, technologies, people, ideas and images constitute the restructuring processes of the contemporary economy (Castells, 1989; Lash and Urry, 1994).

Another meaning of globalization refers to the increasingly more significant role attributed to multinational corporations in the current economic regime. Numerous studies deal with the activities of multinationals, analyze their performance, and speculate on their impact on the socio-economic system of individual countries and regions. Different types of corporations have been studied by many authors in various disciplines, and although no consistent terminology is established, Bartlett and Ghoshal's (1989) analysis is frequently cited. Bartlett and Ghoshal distinguish among three types of firms operating across national borders: multinational firms, operating their foreign subsidiaries as a loose federation or nearly autonomously in order to be able to respond to local needs and national opportunities; global firms, applying strict control in order to co-ordinate world-wide activities and gain from standardized products manufacturing processes and operations; international firms, pursuing rapid diffusion of innovations from parent company to subsidiaries world-wide while allowing for local adaptation. A fourth type, transnational firms, are identified as those organized as integrated networks and seeking to retain local flexibility as well as global integration and diffusion of innovations (Bartlett and Ghoshal, 1989).

In business studies, a third meaning of globalization is discernible, referring to increasing partnership among companies around the world, irrespective of distance. The most frequently quoted example is the sub-contracting of software production by American and European companies to Indian software firms in Bangalore. Another example illustrating this phenomenon is the production of televisions by the Japanese Hitachi, described by Browne [1994]. Hitachi estimates the numbers and models of products their distributors in the United States will need in six weeks. According to this information, an order is issued to a Singaporean subcontractor who manufactures the specified transistors. The transistors are shipped to a subcontractor in Malaysia who assembles circuit boards. The circuit boards are then shipped to another subcontractor in Taiwan who, according to Hitachi's mix instructions, assemble controller chassis. The chassis from Taiwan, a number of components ordered from Hitachi affiliates in Japan, and other components made by a Dutch company in the United States are all shipped to Mexico to be assembled in television sets, tested, and packaged and finally shipped to the distributors in the United States. Examples like Hitachi's network of partners demonstrate a new pattern of production activities around the world, which opens new opportunities for relations between multinational corporations and companies in developing countries.

Finally, in the domain of communications, politics and culture, globalization refers to trends manifested in mass media and institutional patterns of behavior. Often this notion of globalization has negative connotations, implying the spreading of a mass culture dominated by American influences, and a disintegrating effect on personal identity. It is usually considered a manifestation of the homogenization brought about by the modernization process. Most studies, though, present a complex process of tension between the particular and the communal, on the one hand, and the universal and the impersonal, on the other (Robertson, 1992; Larrain, 1994; Friedman 1994; Appadurai, 1990). Universalizing tendencies lead ethnic groups to reaffirm their differences and become attached to their locality, rather than resolving national or other local or regional identities (Hall, 1991).

All these forms of globalization, heavily relying on information technology, have direct impact on developing countries. Increasing flows of trade and capital, new and more sophisticated strategies of multinational corporations for the expansion of their business, often seeking to subcontract parts of the production process to partners in distant locations, and increasing exposure among diverse cultures create a new economic and social structure in the world, within which the economies and societies of the developing countries have to find a place.

But what opportunities for economic growth do these trends provide to developing countries, and how can they be empowered to achieve socio-economic development within the new dynamic world regime? The literature does not provide a clear answer to this question. Geographical circumstances, such as local availability of material resources of special quality or at lower costs, appear to matter a great deal. Also, differences in entrepreneurial ability, scientific and technical know-how, and social attitudes appear to play a more significant role as factors determining the structures of production than in the past. However, there is still uncertainty about how globalization favours certain places over others, and only limited policy guidance can be derived from the analytical studies of the current globalization phenomenon.

A number of cases of local policy for the development of technical infrastructure and institutional forms are discussed in the literature, such as the cases of 'flexible specialisation' in the European regions of Baden Wurttemberg, and Emilia-Romagna in Europe [Cooke and Morgan, 1992], or the cases of the newly industrialized countries of the Far East. Such studies indicate the significance of social and institutional factors in addition to economic and technological measures, without however leading to a uniform theory of effective institutional intervention, organizational forms, and business management practices.

A different combination of socio-economic and cultural factors seems to be responsible for each of the successful cases. For example, while some cases indicate the significance of small and medium enterprises (SMEs) as possessing the necessary flexibility to provide the variety and quality of products and services demanded in today's market, others suggest the supremacy of large corporations, which can utilize new technology to achieve the required flexibility in production, as well as exploiting the power of their human and financial resources to determine favourable relations with suppliers, clients, and regulatory institutions. Indeed, it has proved almost impossible to imitate the successful cases. Rather, a contingency approach seems to be required, to assess the options available under the specific circumstances of a country or region, and to work out an appropriate program of measures.

Perhaps the only aspect for which there is certainty in all studies of the globalization trends is that an IT infrastructure is necessary for participating in the global economy. Nevertheless, it is equally well known that developing countries lack IT resources as well as information resources. They can only gradually and with great opportunity costs acquire such resources. Even then, the results are uncertain. Investing in IT does not guarantee either economic growth or social improvement. The experience of the industrialized countries demonstrates that governments need to make sustained efforts for socio-economic restructuring (OECD,1988), and companies need to have capacity for competent management in order to search for and work out organizational changes (Strassman, 1985; Applegate, 1994) in order to exploit the technological potential. Moreover, there is inadequate understanding of what governments should do to promote IT innovation and derive benefits from it (King *et al*, 1994). Thus, crucial and difficult as it may be, it is not enough for developing countries to acquire IT resources. It is necessary also to address the question of how such technical resources can be effectively utilized within their socio-economic context, and *vis a vis* the global socio-economic trends.

Required institutional interventions and appropriate organizational changes are aspects of the 'technology transfer' process which have been largely neglected in the IS literature for developing countries. It is on these issues that the remainder of this chapter is going to focus. The following section examines the current ability of developing countries to link the acquisition of technical capacity with appropriate institutional and organizational measures for its effective exploitation.

INFORMATION TECHNOLOGY AND TELECOMMUNICATIONS CAPACITY OF DEVELOPING COUNTRIES

A Few Impressive Successful Cases

There are countries which are successfully exploiting the opportunities offered by IT to overcome economic underdevelopment and to achieve significant competitive advantage in key sectors of their economy. The most frequently quoted example is Singapore. With limited natural resources but a strategic geographic location, since the early 1980's the government of this city state has masterminded and implemented a policy for the development of a highly advanced telecommunications and IT infrastructure to improve its position in transport services, and to attract foreign investment. South Korea is another example of a country which developed an IT policy as part of its successful sustained efforts to gain a favorable place in the global economy.

Efforts to Address the Challenge

Encouraged by such cases of spectacular economic growth, and recognizing the significance of IT and telecommunication, an increasing number of developing countries are adopting relevant programs of actions. Such measures vary from deregulation and encouragement of foreign investment in telecommunication services (for example: Mexico and Uruguay in Latin America, and Philippines), government initiatives in promoting innovative IT applications and information services (for example Egypt), or state investment in IT and telecommunications (Brazil, India, Malaysia). Up to now, the developmental results of most such efforts are debatable, but in few cases actually monitored and analyzed. Case studies of the implementation and impact of IT development programs are rare, in contrast to the large number of publications reporting ambitious initiatives and innovative applications of computers and networks (see for example chapters in Bhatnagar and Odedra, 1992; Harasim, 1994).

Extensively discussed are those few among the developing countries which have been making efforts to establish indigenous IT production and to compete in the global IT market, particularly hardware and software. As far as hardware in concerned, notable are the cases of Taiwan and South Korea whose successful industrialization included the re-engineering and low cost production of personal computers. Much more discussed in the literature are the cases of India and Brazil, countries with substantial industrial capacity and sizeable domestic markets, which for more than a decade since the late 1970's have tried to foster an indigenous hardware manufacturing industry through protectionist policy, but they did not withstand international competition [Evans *et al*, 1992].

Many more countries have been trying to develop a competitive software industry, which unlike the hardware and telecommunications industries appears to have low barriers to entry. Many developing countries have a substantial labor force suitably skilled for computer programming and design tasks while their salaries are a fraction of those required in industrialized countries. This provides scope for entering the international software market with a considerable advantage of lower production cost.

However, the software business is complex and its success depends on many more factors than cost-effective programming. It is almost inseparable from services, such as business consultancy and maintenance support, it requires considerable marketing capacity, and benefits from partnerships with powerful computer companies. Thus, the most successful software companies continue to be based in California, which in terms of labor is one of the most expensive regions of the world. Most developing countries can exploit their low labor cost advantage by gaining contracts from multinational software companies [Heeks, 1992; Meadows, 1995]. Within the new logic of the global economy such activities are certainly heralded for the employment opportunities they offer and their potential developmental impact.

The Technological Desert

Still, there are many countries and large regions of the world which have not been able to address the challenge of the new information and telecommunication technologies in any effective way. The diffusion of IT in many regions of the world, such as Africa and parts of Africa and Latin America is still very low (Rigg and Goodman, 1992; Odedra *et al*, 1993). Moreover, there is concern about the low success rate of IT projects in developing countries (Odedra, 1990).

A number of countries, facing widespread poverty and fundamental human development problems have no adequate resources available to address themselves to questions of advanced technology. Others have paid lip service with pompous ministerial documents on the significance of IT for modernization, but failed to take relevant decisions and effective actions. Computers have often been considered as luxuries and their imports have been subject to high tariffs in many African and Latin American countries.

Overall, the weak IT and telecommunications infrastructure of developing countries within the global economy is too obvious. Estimates that the developing countries have only 5% of all computers, and that they use less than 10 percent of stationary orbit, or that the African continent has as many telephone lines as the Netherlands, indicate the order of magnitude of the disparity, even if their accuracy and methodological rigour is unclear (Frederick, 1994).

Such severe lack of IT resources is undoubtedly a fundamental problem which is rightly acknowledged by everybody concerned with development. International development agencies include IT support for their development programs, and indeed, in many poor countries most IT equipment and software, other than that of the multinational corporations operating there, has been provided by international donors and is used predominantly in the public sector.

However, it is important to recognize that the problem of scarcity of resources is compounded by further difficulties, which need to be addressed both in research and action: first, the current disparities within the global economy are getting worse; second, developing countries face serious problems in achieving developmental benefits from the implementation of IT and telecommunications; and third, the development of IT capacity under the pressures and opportunities of globalization trends exacerbate existing internal inequalities between the urban and the rural, and between the elite and the unprivileged.

The Problem of Increasing Global Disparities

It is often argued that gross disparities in the world's IT resources can be overcome by the advent of new generations of IT and telecommunication technology. First optimistic predictions were made in the early 1980's, when the availability of microcomputers and user friendly software increased the accessibility of computers dramatically. Similar optimistic views are repeated in the 1990s concerning the emerging possibilities of global networking. However, there is concern that disparities are getting worse.

Despite gradually improving technical possibilities, developing countries continue to decline into more marginal positions in the world economy. Industrialized countries develop their IT and telecommunications infrastructure much faster than developing countries, and the gap of resources continues to widen. Business companies and government administrations in industrialized countries have been in à much more advantageous position to recognize the value of IT as a competitive weapon than companies in developing countries. Indeed, this technology has been developing in the research laboratories of industrialized countries and multinational corporations, in response to their own requirements. In a much more disadvantaged position, business firms in developing countries are struggling to exploit a technology that is transferred from another context.

There is also concern that within the *fora* of the global economy and politics, developing countries face marginalization and decreasing influence. Tracing the history of decisions regarding the creation of the global IT and telecommunications infrastructure, Hamelink (1994) finds that the developing world today have much more limited capacity to protect their interests. He examines the regulatory instruments - such as conventions, resolutions, codes and recommendations - produced by international governmental and non-governmental organizations - such as United nations agencies, GATT, OECD, business interest organizations, technical organizations and professional interests organizations - with regards to mass communication, telecommunication, data communication, intellectual property protection and technology transfer. Such instruments determine the practices through which the spread of IT and telecommunications is governed or is expected to be governed.

Hamelink's study concludes that in the domain of world communication politics, actions are increasingly shaped by trade and market standards and less by political considerations. The locus of policy making is shifting from governments to associations of private business actors. This trend implies increasing marginalization of developing countries, which lack strong representation in such institutions. As a result, developing countries are less active participants in decisions regarding the diffusion and exploitation of IT and telecommunications than they used to be. Indeed Hamelink gives the examples of issues such as regulation on transborder data flows and national sovereignty, international information order, and technology transfer rights, which featured prominently in the agenda of negotiations in the 1970's, and were significantly influenced by the concerns of developing countries. Developing countries tend to be raw data exporters (with possible risk of sovereignty) and importers of expensive information processed in industrialized countries [Sauvant, 1986]. This led a number of countries in the 1970's and early 1980's to adopt protectionist policies regarding the transfer of data across their borders [UNCTC, 1983]. Although no significant improvements regarding the flows of raw and processed data is discernible in the 1990's, the issue of transborder data flow ceased to concern national sovereignty, and is discussed is discussed predominantly information by advanced economies and their corporate actors in terms of rights of free trade.

Hamelink tries to explain this shift and suggests that the concessions developing countries made over the years were not only a result of coercion from the powerful, but also expectations that a free trade regime may ultimately be more beneficial regarding development than a regulatory regime. This may be true, particularly considering the dysfunctionalities of third world politics. However, for the time being developing countries are in the weakest position they have ever been to influence world decisions regarding the IT and telecommunication technologies. Historically, there is little evidence that a free market regime resolves on its own development problems such as poverty, illiteracy and poor health conditions.

The Difficulty of Achieving Value from the New Technologies

IT has the potential of enormous developmental benefits. In almost all sectors it can increase productivity, add to the quality of manufactured products, improve management decision making, and open new business opportunities in the same way as it has done in industrialized countries. In certain service industries, such as airlines, IT applications are standards which are necessary in order to operate in business. More generally, the services sector, which at present has the highest value added potential, can only be developed with an elaborate IT infrastructure. In addition to such business and wealth creation potential, IT in developing countries is expected to improve the effectiveness of the public sector. This is particularly significant not only because of the size of the government administration in developing countries but also because government institutions have a key role to play in planning and implementing development programs. Creating and maintaining databases for planning purposes, implementing modelling applications, and establishing information channels and information processing systems for the monitoring of development programs such as re-forestation, rural poverty relief, or repatriation of refugee population could do miracles in countries such as Mozambique, or Zambia. Moreover, innovative applications of even modest hardware and telecommunications could empower health experts, teachers, and social workers to provide services to the unprivileged.

But against the realities facing most developing countries, the above benefits prove to range from the non-feasible to the utopian. It is well established in the IS literature that harnessing the potential of technology is a socio-technical process which cannot be abstracted from its organizational context. And the context of developing countries has not proved suitable to foster effective applications of IT.

Studies have shown that after delivery, systems are often under-utilized and do not contribute significant improvements to the performance of organizations (Odedra, 1990; Odedra *et al*, 1993; Madon, 1991; Foster and

Cornford, 1992). Government efforts to improve the performance of the public sector have been particularly disappointing, at best demonstrating efficiency improvements in bureaucratic tasks (Kaul *et al*, 1987). While many publications present the launching of projects with ambitious modernizing effects, such as informed decision making and development planning (Han and Render, 1989; Mansaray, 1992), there are few after-implementation studies and they tend to suggest that the expected impact on the effectiveness of the government institutions in developmental activities is not realized (Madon, 1991). Although there is no stream of research regarding post-implementation failures and the causes of ineffectiveness of various IS projects, there is substantial evidence that in addition to inadequacies of technical expertise, there are organizational and cultural problems.

The development of information systems, according to literature developed in industrialized countries, requires a methodical process to identify organizational needs that can be fruitfully served by an IT application, to manage projects for the application of IT in the tasks of the organization, and to work out the necessary organizational adjustments. Successful IT applications are developed in relation to sustained efforts for the transformation of organizational structures, ways of working, and decision making. It is well documented that such a 'rational' process is complicated by political behavior of the actors involved - managers, technical experts, and end users - and that many successful IT applications involve *ad hoc* and idiosyncratic decisions and actions. Overall, however, empirical studies and analytical debate have contributed to the development of a body of know-how which is useful in most western organizations.

The rationality of such a process, however, is often incompatible to the prevailing norms of organizations in developing countries. Against the 'ideal process' model originated in research in the west, the conditions met in many IS projects in developing countries are dysfunctional. For example, most organizations in developing countries, such as government bureaucratic institutions and entrepreneurial family-owned businesses, have no tradition of formal planning, and little capacity of organizational reform on the basis of requirements analysis. Strategic decisions are either political, therefore not amenable to the analytical logic of organizational requirements, or intuitive based of the talent of entrepreneurs and mistrusting formal management practices.

Recognizing that the problems faced in developing information systems are organizational and cultural, often leads analysts to suggest the need for organizational reform and change of traditional social norms. Many organizations in developing countries are so clearly dysfunctional in relation to their declared mission, that calls for reform seem totally convincing. Moreover, cultural aspects such as unquestioning obedience within hierarchical structures of status, irrespective of the merit and validity of a decision or a command, impede the development of fundamental qualities of development, such as initiative and problem solving capacity. Nevertheless, such an attitude is flawed both in ideological and practical terms.

Ideologically, the tendency to advise for reforms aiming to create conditions similar to those experienced in industrialized countries is a manifestation of the modernist approach of imitation. Such an approach, has been repeatedly criticised in the literature of development studies, although it continues to be the dominant development paradigm followed by development agencies and, at least in rhetoric, by many governments. Practically, modernizing organizational reforms and interventions to change behavior driven by cultural norms tends to create a snowball of resistance, either overt or covert, and fails to serve the purposes of effective IS development.

Thus, the transfer of methods, models and organizational practices, may impede rather than facilitate the utilization of the potential of IT in developing countries. More significantly, by making efforts to learn the ways IT is used in industrialized countries, organizations in developing countries fail to discover ways that can serve their own requirements (Avgerou, 1995).

The Problem of Increasing Internal Disparities

The dispersal of economic activities by globalization trends does not follow any uniform pattern. To the contrary, it contributes to agglomerations of industries and services in particular geographic locations. Instead of a decentralized economic structure that the notion of the 'electronic cottage' evoked in the early 1980s, economic geographers find evidence that telecommunications and IT facilities give rise to global cities, that is a small number of sites of immense concentration of economic power (Sassen, 1994). Rural areas and many cities that were once major manufacturing centers tend to suffer declines.

A trend that contributes to a geography of centrality and marginality is particularly undesirable for developing countries where there is already a large gap between the rich and the poor. The new service industries relying heavily on IT and telecommunications require highly educated people and pay them unusually high salaries. In contrast, the earnings of manual workers and unskilled labor sink even further. In countries with high illiteracy rates, such trends can only sharpen existing extremes.

The city of Bangalore in India already demonstrates the problem. It is estimated that there are more scientists and computer engineers per square mile in Bangalore than any place on earth except California, Oxford and Cambridge; many of them employed by multinational companies. The city has almost a 'western' feel about it. However, the city's affluence has attracted a vast influx of immigrant workers from other neighbouring states, particularly from rural areas. The situation has led to the creation of slum conditions which are getting worse by the day, with frequent riots among laborers of different culture. The city has achieved a leading edge in the high technology telecommunications market but social problems have been aggravated and the divide between the have and the have nots has been exacerbated.

POLICY ISSUES OF INFORMATION TECHNOLOGY IN DEVELOPING COUNTRIES

The problems suggested by the discussion above cannot be resolved by the global market forces alone. Indeed, no country relies only on the laws of demand and supply for telecommunications and IT innovation, and the governments of some of the most successful countries, such as Japan, Singapore, and South Korea have been particularly interventionist either for the development of a competitive IT industry, or for the promotion of a network of effective applications, or both. In USA, the most profound proponent of the free market regime, the influence of the government has been crucial in such areas as: computer purchasing in state administration during the early days of computers; research through its military programs; active involvement in international negotiations, as indicated above; and more recently with the initiative to promote the development of the 'information highway'. However, in other cases, such as in the UK and France until the early 1980s, India and Brazil in the 1980s, government leadership in IT innovation was largely unsuccessful, and indeed these countries abandoned or relaxed their policies to allow more scope for market competition (Land, 1990). In the meantime, the policies of a variety of institutions other than national governments complement the market forces. In Europe, the most influential visions and actions at present come from the institutions of the European Union.

It would be inappropriate to attempt generalizations about effective IT and telecommunications policy. As argued above, the effects of technology are not deterministically derived from the inherent capabilities of the technology itself. Rather, they depend on the socio-economic processes within which they are elicited. And, as was suggested in the discussion of globalization above, no universal theory exists to determine how a country can achieve its developmental goals by participating in the currently emerging global economy. The search for IT policies and actions which are feasible and can benefit a country has to be linked to the assessment of a country's options under the global socio-economic trends. IT policy making should not ignore the developmental dilemmas already facing the country and it should assess undesirable effects that may be caused by the contemplated actions.

Having such a contingency perspective in mind, general policy recommendations are dangerously oversimplistic and unjustifiable. Also, seeking templates of successful programs, such as the cases of the newly industrialized countries, runs the risk of leading to misguided reliance, rather than developing the capacity of making effective decisions. Thus, this chapter discusses the nature of IT policy, not specific policies that can guarantee success. Two aspects of IT policy are considered: the policy making body (who makes the policy), and the policy content (what objectives to pursue).

The Policy Making Body

The literature of IS in developing countries tends to discuss only the role of national government policy. It ignores the context of multiple and diverse initiatives and actions that affect the extent and the way IT and telecommunication is diffused in an area, and the effects that can be achieved by their diffusion. However, the infrastructure of information and IT in developing countries is created under the influence and/or the direct initiatives of various agents involved in development. The most influential agents are national governments, regional associations of countries (such as the European Union, NAFTA, the MERCOSUR, or the Commonwealth) international aid organizations (such as the World Bank, United Nations agencies, the IDRC), aid agencies of individual industrialized countries (such as the USA AID), or non-governmental organizations, multinational corporations, and large national companies.

The limited view of IT policy as the responsibility of national government alone reflects the dominance of the nation state as the main legitimate and effective decision making forum regarding development. It is widely accepted that, as part of the globalization trends, the dominance of the nation state is eroded by both supra-national and sub-national social entities and organizations. In many countries there is a long history of conflict between 'central' government and 'local' government, or between the interests of different geographic regions of the country. Often, the policy making capacity and administrative competence of central government does not match its formal power. In such cases, policy by authorities at either a smaller or at a larger geographic scale may be much more effective. Thus, for example, more relevant lessons may be derived by a local or city government authority from analyzing the case of Singapore, than by a central national government.

Surely, the national state continues to be the most visible and perhaps in general terms the most powerful mechanism in making and implementing decisions affecting the socio-economic conditions of communities all around the world. Nevertheless, a much more complex arena of decisions and actions is emerging from the processes perceived as globalization, and any analysis which does not attempt to comprehend and address this complexity runs the risk of being grossly mistaken.

An IT policy affecting an area, a community, or a region's industry and social conditions is rarely to be found in a comprehensive strategy expressed in a single document. It usually comprises relevant decisions, initiatives and programs of a number of policy making institutions. Despite attention to well publicised national government IT policies that have been presented in a comprehensive form - such as that of Singapore or Japan - the documents produced in most countries stating their IT policy bear little relation to the real struggle of the organizations of the region to acquire and effectively utilize IT capacity. A broad notion of IT policy needs to be adopted, which encompasses the interests, visions or directions followed by the variety of institutions whose measures, initiatives, interventions and regulations affect the development of an information, IT and telecommunications infrastructure in a geographic area and the way such an infrastructure is utilized.

The Policy Content

Another question to be addressed is what actions can contribute to the creation of an information, IT and telecommunications infrastructure capable of serving development in the contemporary international context. In other words, what areas should IT policy cover? The following list includes the areas of policy suggested in the literature as relevant to developing countries:

The Creation of Data Repositories with Surveys, Organization of National Archives, or Links to International Databases: However, just creating data resources is not enough; promotion of their use and facilitation of access and communication to categories of potential users is particularly crucial. In places which are not data rich there is usually no established tradition of making use of data in professional and decision making activities. Decisions are not necessarily based on consideration of formal data. They are often the outcome of political negotiations, tradition, and informal communication. In most developing countries, the cry for data comes from expatriate development planners rather than local decision makers. Under such conditions, data repositories artificially created may have no impact on practices of decision making and planning. Critical issues here are what data need to be collected, in what form; how can western decision making rationality be effectively blended with traditional or political leadership and administration; what training in retrieving and using data is required, and what networking facilities are desirable and feasible.

Measures to Encourage and Promote Availability and Effective Use of IT in Strategic Economic Sectors: To the extent that a region is working to integrate with the global economy, IT resources are necessary, and must be utilized effectively. Thus, for example, reducing tariff obstacles on import of computers, promoting the development of local market of hardware, software and services are some of the necessary steps.

More difficult is the task of promoting effective utilization of these technologies. To some extent this issue too is technical. Efficient and cost-effective electricity and telecommunication infrastructure must be available in order to be able to utilize IT. More significantly, initiatives which provide incentives and show innovative ways for local business and administration to take up the technologies can be very useful.

For example, a study of the United Nations agencies UNDP and UNIDO in Cyprus suggested that the creation of consortia of small firms to develop a form of flexible specialization is an appropriate strategy for the structure of the economy of the island and its socio-economic conditions. Following these recommendations, local development institutions, such as a bank specializing in financing business activities with developmental potential, started to play a key role in the formation of consortia. Promoting the principles of flexible specialization provides a platform for using IT and telecommunications. It makes easier for local entrepreneurs to realize that computers can do more than making their routine administrative work faster; it becomes the means for re-organizing and doing business with suppliers and customers.

The Creation of Telecommunications Infrastructure: In most parts of the world telecommunications are well recognized as an industry of its own, as fundamental for the development of many other service industries, and as an important public service. It is this triple significance that causes policy dilemmas to governments and international authorities alike. Again the main issue is how can developing countries acquire the telecommunication facilities necessary to be part of the global economy, and pursue their developmental aspirations.

For places with inadequate telecommunications infrastructure in the hands of inefficient state monopolies, the suggested solution is usually deregulation. Indeed, strict regulations and restrictions for the provision of services which technologically are extremely dynamic can only be an obstacle. Many non-governmental organizations have taken innovative initiatives and developed cost effective networking means that can serve as examples of enriching the communications field for economic and social benefits.

However, deregulation is often understood to mean privatization, and complete surrender of the telecommunications services to market forces. There is no certainty that such an approach can serve either the globalization or the developmental objectives of a country or a region. The laws of demand and supply may not secure the services required in the particular socio-economic conditions of a region, or for a particular plan to promote the integration of a region in the global economy by fostering some industrial activities. A genuine concern of policy makers should be to secure telecommunication services which can be cost-effective and widely available, rather than prohibitively expensive for the capacity of the local industry and exclusively targeted to particular user groups.

Moreover, deregulation, does not mean no regulation. To the contrary, abolishing the monopolistic regime on telecommunications requires much more sophisticated legislation, both at international and national levels, in order to secure effective provision of services. The significance of this area of policy is highlighted in Hamelink's study mentioned earlier, which shows the diverse interests involved and the existence of a gap regarding policy actors capable of promoting the interests of developing countries' communities.

Development of Skills Required to Exploit the Potential IT can Provide in the Emerging Global Economy: The most obvious skills needed are technical, that is expertise to develop, maintain, use, and manage IT and telecommunications systems. However, such skills can prove useful only if there is a demand for them.

Demand often comes from multinational corporations which have the management skills to incorporate them in their production processes. But a major challenge for developing countries is to be able to utilize IT in local business firms and administration. To that end, the development of awareness about the potential value of new technologies and training on using it has to be part of broader education programs as well as specialized degree curricula. This is another difficult area for many developing countries. There is a tendency to imitate syllabuses developed in industrialized countries, which often have little relevance to the conditions of the local economic activities, and sometimes are seen as being in conflict with the values of their overall education system.

As in most countries all levels of education are controlled by the government, the issue of appropriate IT education is primarily a matter of government policy. They can take initiatives for the development of relevant curricula. They can also encourage educators to explore how IT fits within the local culture. International institutions can also play a significant role. So far they are mainly providers of technical courses. They can, however, make a much more valuable contribution. There is need for sensitization to cross-cultural aspects regarding the use of technologies which handle information and communication. It is important to avoid the situation where the spread of IT is identified with the provocation of the domination of 'western' culture. Initiatives for the creation of the means (such as courseware, multimedia applications, and culture sensitive syllabuses for IT use) so that IT education becomes a conveyer of respect of otherness rather than unquestioning imitation in the one extreme, or parochialism in the other, can be particularly valuable.

Research and Development: Efforts to enlarge the potential of new technologies in order to gain competitive advantage require substantial financial, knowledge, and organizational resources. Developing countries have found it too difficult to match the research establishments of the industrialized countries, and most have abandoned research and development efforts of any significant scale. In a knowledge intensive era, and in an economy which has made innovation the core value adding activity, absence of research and development is detrimental.

Although it is unlikely that developing countries can build the research capacity of the American institutions and achieve any breakthrough in computer and telecommunications technology, there are various ways of creating or participating in centers of excellence and of achieving innovations needed by their industries and communities. Globalization can play a facilitating role, as it provides the communication means and creates an unprecedented climate of collaboration among scientists.

Moreover, it is necessary that developing countries foster research and development to address the exploitation of IT to meet their own needs. Such research usually concerns the application of existing technologies rather than the discovery of new ones. At present IT is enormously flexible. Yet, it has been applied predominantly in ways that serve the circumstances of industrialized countries. Almost all systems development methods, information systems management practices, and computer applications originate in research that concerned the requirements of professionals and users in the context of industrialized countries. There is ample evidence that transfer of such methods and applications in the context of developing countries is ineffective. Lack of appropriate methods and tools may be the main reason for the disappointing results of technology transfer discussed above.

It is not surprising that research on implementation and effective utilization of information systems is almost non-existent in developing countries. There needs to exist a critical mass of technology - and technology related frustration - in order to appreciate that technology alone does not lead to the promised benefits, and that the utilization of technical capacity is a socio-technical process which needs to be organized as such, and supported by appropriate methods and practices. However, as most countries develop substantial technology assets, research on methodical practices, organizational processes, and management actions that should be followed in order to exploit the potential of new technologies in the local context is of paramount importance.

Promotion of Information Technology Related Industries: These comprise microelectronics, hardware, telecommunications equipment, network operation, value added services, software production, related consultancy services, and information services.

Although only a small number of developing countries have sought to claim a position in the international hardware manufacturing industry, as mentioned above, many countries participate in some of the other IT related industries, trying to compete either in the global or their regional market. Since the 1970's developing countries have been the site of production for multinationals of microelectronics and telecommunications equipment, because of their cheaper labor. Much more scope seems to exist in the service industries.

A major issue regarding the development of local IT industries is whether bending the free trade principles is necessary or beneficial. It is generally believed that fostering a local industry requires initial support by measures such as protection from competition of imported products or preferential purchasing by major customers. Both these measures are strongly opposed by international organizations representing business interests, although they have been practised by most countries' governments in relation to some of their industries.

Apart from the politics among institutions involved in setting the rules of doing business in the global economy, a major issue is the effectiveness of such policies. Protective policies may stifle the domestic market by offering a limited range of products and services, often of inferior quality and overpriced. Local customers of protected IT industries find themselves in disadvantage against their competitors. Subsequently, they cannot maintain the level of demand of IT products and services that can enable local IT industries to reach the manufacturing economies of scale needed to compete in the global market. Avoiding such a vicious circle requires careful assessment of the dynamics of demand and supply that few regulators can do.

Another debatable issue of policy which causes similar dilemmas is the regulation of intellectual property rights. The industries of software and services require a legal framework that recognizes and protects ownership of intellectual property. It is often argued, however, that countries with low diffusion of IT have more to benefit from a regime which allows unauthorized copying of software and intellectual products, that from safeguarding the interests of the producers. Spreading of IT can only lead to further demand and thus, in the longer term, benefit the IT industry. As diffusion of IT increases, lack of legislation protecting the ownership rights of software discourages software producers and stifles the supply of quality software. Initiatives regarding regulation of software property rights should be a matter of careful judgement and timely interventions, rather than a universal law.

Social and Legal Measures to Avoid Undesirable Effects and Pursue Developmental Goals: The diffusion of IT and telecommunications, and the globalization processes they support bring about risks of worsening the quality of life of various groups of people. In industrialized countries, concern about undesirable effects of IT, such as unemployment, disparities in terms of capacity to participate in an IT intensive society, challenge of the right of privacy, and new forms of fraud and crime has led to a variety of measures, partly legal and protective and partly empowering and proactive.

In developing countries, the risks are higher because of the weak social and economic position of large proportions of population. The issues here are moral, political, and economic. Morally, the gross inequalities between those capable of participating in the knowledge-intensive global economy and those who cannot, and therefore are marginalized and sunk in poverty, are unacceptable. Politically, such a polarization leads to resentment and conflict. Economically, in a knowledge-intensive society, human resources are the most valuable asset and must be empowered.

Thus, the social problems of developing countries remain a major issue which is unlikely to be resolved automatically by the globalization processes. Nor can they be treated as an issue concerning the governments of developing countries alone. The forces of globalization, which involve immigration, erosion of national government, and emergence of new centers of power, make the social problem of underdevelopment a global problem. So far the world institutions have been rather unimaginative and unable to find effective policy initiatives to confront such issues. This is an area which might require radically new visions.

SUMMARY

Globalization concerns developing countries as much as the industrialized countries. The information and telecommunication technologies which enable the processes of the global economy have spread to every corner of the world, either through the activities of multinational corporations or by local institutions and entrepreneurs. Yet, in this chapter, we argued that the position of developing countries is particularly weak in the globalization process. As far as IT and telecommunications infrastructure is concerned, there are severe disparities in availability of technology, control of technology, and in capacity for effective utilization. Moreover, social problems of underdevelopment tend to be exacerbated by the concentration of economic activities in the few geographic locations rich in IT and telecommunications facilities.

There is no evidence that either the disparities regarding IT and telecommunications or the accentuated social problems of underdevelopment can be resolved by the course of globalization itself. To the contrary, economic geographers tend to produce evidence of further marginalisation of most of the developing world, and new internal inequalities both in the industrialized and the developing countries.

As isolation from the global economy seems to be no option for any region, policy measures are required to remedy the current undesirable situation. We need to consider not only national governments as policy makers in this field, but a variety of institutions which, in the process of globalization, emerge as legitimate actors influencing the diffusion and utilization of IT and telecommunications.

Finally, we discussed a number of policy areas. Of these, there is one which concerns primarily professionals managing and developing information systems: sponsoring the search for practices and technology uses that are appropriate in the local organizational and socio-cultural context. To a large extent, this is a matter of approach that can be followed by individual professionals. However, it is not sufficient to rely on *ad hoc* approaches on the basis of the experience of individual practitioners. The search for appropriate practices needs to be adopted and institutionalised by professional bodies, influential research centers, and international organizations. Concerted efforts are needed for a shift of paradigm from transferring practices that are considered successful in industrialized countries to searching for practices that are effective in the local context. Such efforts may empower organizations in developing countries to utilize effectively the powerful information and telecommunications technologies and integrate in the global economy.

References

Applegate, L.M., 1994, Managing in an Information Age: Transforming the Organization for the 1990's, in Baskerville, R., Smithson, S., Ngwenyama O., Degross, J.I., (eds) *Transforming Organizations with Information Technology*, North-Holland, Amsterdam, pp 15-94.

Appadurai, A., 1990. Disjuncture and Difference in the Global Cultural Economy, in Featherstone M. (ed) *Global Culture. Nationalism, Globalization and Modernity. A Theory, Culture & Society Special Issue*, SAGE Publications, London.

Avgerou, C., 1995, Transferability of information systems and organisational practices, in the proceedings of the 4rth IFIP WG 9.4 conference, *Information Technology and Socio-Economic Development: Challenges & Opportunities*, Cairo.

Bartlett, C.A., and Ghoshal, S., 1989, *Managing Across Borders: The Transnational Solution*, Harvard Business School Press, Boston.

Bhatnagar, S.C., and Odedra, M., 1992,*Social Implications of Computers in Developing Countries*, Tata McGraw-Hili

Browne, H., 1994, For Richer, For Poorer: Shaping US-Mexican Integration, Latin American Bureau, London.

Castells, M., 1989. *The Informational City, Information Technology, Economic Restructuring and the Urban-Regional Process.*. Blackwell, Oxford.

Castells, M., and Henderson, J., 1987, Techno-economic Restructuring, Socio-political Processes and Spatial Transformation: a Global Perspective, in Henderson, J and Castells, M., (eds) Global Restructuring and Territorial Development, Sage Publications, London, pp 1-17.

Cooke, P. and Morgan K., 1992, *Regional Innovation Centres in Europe* (Report to the Department of Trade and Industry, University of Wales, Cardiff)

Evans, P.B., Frischtak, C.R., & Tigre, P.B., 1992, *High Technology and Third World Industrialization: Brazilian Computer Policy in Comparative Perspective*, University of California, Berkeley.

Forster, D., and Cornford, T., 1992, Evaluation of Health Information Systems: Issues, Models and Case Studies, in Bhatnagar, S.C., and Odedra, M.,*Social Implications of Computers in Developing Countries*, Tata McGraw-Hill, pp 304-318.

Frederick, H., 1994, Computer Networks and the Emergence of Global Civil Society, in Harasim L.M., *Global Networks, Computers and International Communication*, MIT Press.

Friedman, J., 1994, *Cultural Identity & Global Process*, Sage, London.

Hall S., 1991, The local and the Global: Globalisation and Ethnicity, in King A., (ed), *Culture, Globalization and the World-System*, Macmillan, London, pp 41-68

Hall, S., Held, D., and McGrew, T., 1992, *Modernity and its Futures*, The Open University and Polity Press, Cambridge.

Hamelink, C.J., 1994, *The Politics of World Communication*, Sage, London.

Han, C.K., and Render, B., 1989, Information Systems for Development Management in Developing Countries, *Information and Management*, vol 17, no 2, pp95-106

Harasim L.M., 1994, *Global Networks, Computers and International Communication*, MIT Press.

Heeks, R., 1992, Strategies for Indigenising IT Production in DCs, in Bhatnagar, S.C., and Odedra, M., *Social Implications of Computers in Developing Countries*, Tata McGraw-Hill, New Delhi, pp 110-123.

Ives, B., and Jarvenpaa, S., 1991, Applications of Global Information Technology, Key Issues for Management, in *MIS Quarterly*, March, pp 33-50.

Kaul, M., Patel, N.R., and Shams, K., (eds) 1987, *Searching for a Paddle: Trends in IT Applications in Asian Government Systems*, Asian and Pacific Development Centre, Kuala Lumpur.

King, J.L, Gurbaxani, V., Kraemer, K.L., McFarlan, F.W., Raman, K.S., Yap, C.S., 1994, Institutional Factors in Information Technology Innovation, *Information Systems Research*, vol 5 number 2, pp 139-169.

Knippers Black, J., 1991, *Development in Theory and Practice, Bridging the gap*, Westview Press, Boulder.

Land, F.F., 1990, Viewpoint: The Government Role in Relation to Information Technology, *International Journal of Information Management*, vol 10, pp 5-13.

Larrain, J., 1994, *Ideology & Cultural Identity: Modernity and the Third World Presence*, Polity Press, Cambridge.

Lash, S. & Urry, J., 1994. *Economies of Signs & Space*. SAGE publications, London.

Madon, S., 1991, The Impact of Computer Based Information Systems on Rural Development: A case study in India, PhD Thesis, London University.

Mansarray, M.L., 1992, ASYCUNDA: A Framework for an Integrated Socio-Economic Development of ECOWAS, in Bhatnagar, S.C., and Odedra, M., *Social Implications of Computers in Developing Countries*, Tata McGraw-Hill, New Delhi, pp 244-260.

Meadows, C.J., 1995, Software Development capabilities - A comparative Analysis: India vs. the Philippines, in the proceedings of the 4rth IFIP WG 9.4 conference, *Information Technology and Socio-Economic Development: Challenges & Opportunities*, Cairo.

Odedra, M. 1990, The Transfer of Information Technology to Developing Countries, PhD Thesis, London School of Economics

Odedra, M., Lawrie, M., Bennett, M., and Goodman, S., 1993, Sub-Saharan Africa: a Technological Desert, in *Communications of the ACM*, vol 35, no 2, pp 25-29.

OECD, 1988. *New Technologies in the 1990s. A socio-economic Strategy*. Paris.

Rigg, M., and Goodman, S., 1992, MercoSur: Reconciling Four Disparate Information Technology Policies, *International Information Systems*, vol 11, no 3, pp 73-86.

Robertson, R., 1992. *Globalisation - Social Theory and Global Culture*, SAGE Publications, London.

Roche, E.M., 1992, The International Crisis in Transnational Computing, in Bhatnagar, S.C., and Odedra, M., *Social Implications of Computers in Developing Countries*, Tata McGraw-Hill, New Delhi, pp 81-98.

Sassen, S., 1994, *Cities in a World Economy*, Pine Forge Press, California.

Sauvant, K., 1986, *International Transactions in Services: The politics of Transborder Data Flows*, Westview Press, Bouldes, Colorado.

Strassman, P., 1985, *Information Payoff, The Transformation of Work in the Electronic Age*, Free Press.

Swamy, D.P., 1994, *The political Economy of Industrialisation - from self-reliance to globalisation*, Sage Publications, New Delhi.

UNCTC, 1983, *Transborder Data Flows and Brazil*, United Nations Centre on Transnational Corporations, New York.

8 Telecommunications Infrastructure in Developing Countries: Privatization Trends

Amitava Dutta
George Mason University, USA

A good *telecommunications infrastructure is of strategic importance to nations in today's global economy. Developing nations, where telecommunications service has usually been provided by a government run monopoly, have experienced significant and chronic deficiencies in their infrastructure. To raise capital, increase efficiency, modernize and expand infrastructure, many developing nations are reforming this sector. In this chapter we survey the mechanics of reform in selected Latin American and Asian countries in an attempt to compare and contrast their general approaches. The former group has embraced reform more extensively and rapidly, with even basic service being privatized in several cases. Asian countries have been more cautious and slow in their privatization attempts, but the trend is clear. Customer premise equipment, mobile services and value added services tend to be opened to competition at an early stage of reform. Privatization of basic service requires careful crafting of performance contracts and restructuring of the government monopoly prior to sale. Exclusive rights for 5-10 years are also needed to attract qualified private operators for basic service. A major impediment in reform has been the slow pace of regulatory developments, which has often lagged behind the introduction of privatization or competition. Still, by various measures, privatization has resulted in major improvements. Judging from the experience of Latin American countries however, where privatization has been in place for several years, expansion of rural service continues to be difficult despite regulatory and contractual efforts towards that end.*

INTRODUCTION

Today, information is regarded as a basic factor of production along with land, labor and capital. The increasing information intensity of economic activity, coupled with the globalization of capital flows, manufacturing and other activities, has caused a strong demand for more reliable, cheaper and advanced telecommunications services (Nulty 1989). Telecommunications facilitates the networking of people and ideas, reduces costs and increases productivity (Saunders, Warford And Wellenius 1993). It is now considered strategic at the firm, national and regional level. In fact, in industrialized nations, corporate strategy includes a careful enunciation of telecommunications strategy. Countries with poor telephone service and inadequate advanced services cannot participate effectively in the global marketplace.

This is particularly true for developing countries[1] (DCs). Governmental administration, delivery of social services and various economic activities all use telecommunications. In recent years, achieving a good telecommunications infrastructure has been identified by many DCs as a high priority objective. There was a realization that without telecommunications infrastructure, broader economic reforms would be more difficult to implement. Over the last four or five decades, other infrastructure sectors such as energy and transportation had been viewed as basic and received considerable attention and share of funds in government planning. Telecommunications had never quite been accorded that high priority. As a result, the sector suffers from some chronic problems. The level of investment has been lower than that needed to meet pent up demand for a long time. This is a result of capital and foreign currency shortages and competing demands for development funds. The rare operational surplus may be appropriated for other purposes, preventing reinvestment in the telecommunications sector. These state owned enterprises often use inadequate accounting methods and controls, have insufficient financial and administrative autonomy from the government, and have very little incentive to control costs or improve customer service. Remuneration is often not performance based, tariffs do not reflect cost structures, and the ratio of employees to number of telephone lines (15 per 1000 lines) is high compared to that in industrialized nations (6 per 1000 lines).

To address these problems, many DCs are attempting to remove the government from the operation of this sector and leave it more and more in private hands. The sector reforms involve change along the following dimensions (i) increasing the participation of the private sector in the operation and financing of telecommunications services (ii) shifting government's role to one of setting policy and regulation (Wellenius, Stern, Nulty & Stern 1989). This change will introduce market forces which will, it is so thought, improve efficiency and customer service. However, how does one ensure that private enterprise also undertakes the developmental goals of the former state owned enterprise, such as putting telephones in rural areas, goals which are potentially unprofitable? Given the economies of scale in telecommunications and the interconnection requirements for universal service, how does one ensure that competition truly flourishes? Reform has to achieve balance among these conflicting aspects of privatization. In this chapter, we will summarize the mechanics of sector reform in several Latin American and Asian Countries to compare and contrast them, as well as to identify success factors.

Special Characteristics of Developing Countries

Telecommunications sector reforms have not been limited to DCs by any means. The breakup of AT&T in the U.S. in 1984, and the introduction of competition in Japan, New Zealand, and the United Kingdom are examples of this trend in industrialized nations. These reforms have introduced new complexities for residential and business customers in terms of service and price structure, but have also accelerated investment, broadened user choices and reduced prices. However, DCs have some distinctive characteristics that make reform even more complex. First, their core telephone infrastructure has very low average densities (about 2 telephones per 100 persons), and even lower densities in rural areas (less than 0.1 per 100). Reform needs to ensure that expansion of *basic voice facilities* will occur in addition to nonbasic (data, cellular etc.) services, even though the latter are more profitable for operators. This is in contrast to many industrialized countries, where reform is being carried out with an adequate core infrastructure already in place. For example, when the government began allowing competition in nonbasic services in the former West Germany, there already was a reasonably well established core infrastructure.

Second, DCs have very large rural populations with limited ability to pay for services. To have significant developmental impact, it will be necessary to provide basic service to such rural areas as much of the DC economies are rurally based. Third, DCs do not have well developed capital markets. As a result, even if domestic savings rates are high, there does not exist efficient mechanisms to channel these funds for telecommunications infrastructure investments. The variety of debt instruments are limited and the public's equity holdings are often concentrated in a few wealthy parties. Thus, creative mechanisms will need to be developed to finance the enormous outlays required for infrastructure development. From the viewpoint of foreign investors or operators specifically, concerns include government instability, foreign exchange controls, and limitations on repatriation of profits or capital. Fourth, DCs do not have much experience in developing or enforcing regulation that will be crucial to sector reform. Since government was both the monopoly operator and the regulator, there really was not much scope for this expertise to develop. Regulations need to be such that they achieve developmental goals (such as universal access) while still providing sufficient incentives to private organizations to participate in the building of this sector (Wellenius 1989).

Industrialized Nations' Interest in DC Sector Reforms

Equipment vendors, telecommunications operators and market investors in industrialized countries have all shown considerable interest in the telecommunications reforms of developing countries. Market investors see the potential for healthy returns from meeting the large pent up demand. Telecommunications operators in industrialized countries have been experiencing pressures on their profit margins and market shares as a result of liberalization in their own markets. AT&T, Bell South, MCI, British Telecomm, Nippon Telephone & Telegraph, Siemens, Fujitsu and others have all been pursuing opportunities in DCs. They are eager to explore new markets and establish a presence in specific regions of the world. DCs represent a large market for telecommunications equipment and services. This mutual interest has also manifested itself in multilateral arrangements among individual countries such as the North American Free Trade Agreement (NAFTA) and the General Agreement on Trade and Tariffs) GATT. The Uruguay round of GATT contains a framework specifying basic rules for trade in services, and contains a special annex for telecommunications. NAFTA contains similar provisions for telecommunications (Field 1994). The importance placed on telecommunications in both NAFTA and GATT reflects not just the interest of telecommunications vendors, but also of other major global industries like electronics and banking.

Telecommunications is essential to "business without borders" where one can take advantage of differential land, labor or capital costs. Business functions like marketing, manufacturing and distribution may now be dispersed globally. Thus, large multinational organizations need to be able to configure and maintain their networks to coordinate these different functions under rapidly changing business circumstances. The huge variation in regulatory regimes across different countries and the vast difference in service availability across them cause delays in building global networks and additional complexities and costs in managing them. In short, there are many parties interested in the telecommunications sector reforms of DCs.

DIFFERENT APPROACHES TO SECTOR REFORM

The pace and scope of telecommunications sector reforms has varied substantially among different regions of the developing world. It got an early start in Latin America, with privatization of the state owned enterprise being completed in Chile as early as 1987. Mexico completed a large part of its reform in 1990. Reforms are also in various stages of planning or implementation in a host of other Latin American countries including Bolivia, Peru, Brazil and Panama. The Asian market is much larger in terms of potential number of lines, but reforms have come somewhat more slowly over there. With the exception of Hong Kong, there seems to be more reluctance to relinquish governmental control of basic service over to private domestic or foreign operators as compared to Latin American countries. India has decentralized control over its once monolithic Post & Telegraphs Department, is setting up joint ventures for cellular services, and is considering opening up basic service to competition. The Philippines is introducing competition to international services, and China is introducing reforms that may allow private investment. So the trend towards private sector participation is clear, although actual progress is slow.

One major area of the developing world that has not been examined in this chapter is sub-Saharan Africa. There does not appear to be substantial sector reform efforts underway in that region. In most cases government is still the monopoly provider of all services, although in a few instances the customer premise equipment (CPE) market (telephones, FAX machines, answering machines, PBXs etc) has been opened up to competition. We are also omitting some of the newly independent countries in Central and Eastern Europe which could clearly be considered to be DCs. That region has also attracted a lot of attention from foreign telecommunications operators and vendors as well as businesses in general. The one difference here is that there may be export restrictions in place to some countries of the former Soviet Union. However, the two regions we have selected to examine in this chapter will suffice to point out the general issues and trends associated with sector reform. This is based on detailed accounts of these individual countries in (Wellenius & Stern, 1994).

Reform in Latin America

Telecommunications in Latin America has undergone perhaps the most sweeping and speedy reforms among different developing regions. Chile, Argentina, Mexico and Venezuela privatized quickly by about 1991. Government has been transforming its role to one of regulation and policy setting, leaving operations to the private sector. As part of sector reform, many Latin American countries have actively courted foreign investment capital and foreign telecommunications operators. This is interesting in light of the traditional wariness of many developing countries towards foreign control of key domestic industries. We now summarize (see Figure-1).

Argentina: Argentina has undertaken a very rapid reform effort starting in early 1989. The state owned enterprise ENTel (Empresa Nacional de Telecommunicaciones)[2] was to be divided into two regional companies, each being guaranteed monopoly over basic services for seven years. Two separate companies would provide international services. The CPE market and data/value added services would be opened to competition right away. Franchises would be awarded for cellular service. In November 1990 a consortium led by STET (Italy) and France Telecom took ownership and operational control of the northern regional company. The southern regional company was taken over by a consortium led by Telefonica (Spain). Remaining shares were sold over the next two years to employees, subscribers, existing rural telephone cooperatives and the general public. A review of these different stages of Argentina's privatization effort may be found in (Lanuza 1992) and (Petrazzini 1995).

Labor productivity figures (10 employees per 1000 lines), internal management structures, collection, contracting and purchasing all improved after reforms. An *executive decree* established CNT (Comision Nacional de Telecommunicaciones) in June 1990, as a regulatory agency located within the Ministry of Economy. Partly due to the rather rapid pace of reform, CNT was not able to develop basic guidelines in a timely manner and introduction of new services and extension of basic services to new areas was delayed. Like its counterpart Chile, (see Figure 1), CNT faced the problem of being housed within a large ministry with other responsibilities.

33	2767	96	13	6050	Arg
7.5	1099	26	48	680	Bol
154	8512	63	23	2770	Bra
13.6	757	65	15	2730	Chi
33.4	1139	75	29	1330	Col
85	1958	66	26	3470	Mex
20.2	912	77	9	2910	Ven
A	B	C	D	E	

A= pop. (1992) millions   B=Area, SqKm (,000)
C=Tel. lines/1000 population (1990)
D=% pop. in rural areas (1992)
E=GNP/capita (1992) $

	CPE	Basic Voice	MOBL Cell	PRIV NET	VANs	INTL VOIC	REGL AGNC.
Argentina							
Bolivia		P		E	E	C	
Brazil				C	C		
Chile							
Colombia		P		C		C	
Mexico							
Venezuela							

	Competitive, many entrants		Autonomous entity
	Competitive, # limited by design		Semi-autonomous entity. Some ties to govt. monopoly provider
	Govt. monopoly provider		Govt. regulator-operator
	Private, unlimited term	P	Privatization under consideration
	Private, limited term exclusivity	C	Competition authorized or under consideration
		E	Policy still emerging

FIGURE 1. SUMMARY OF LATIN AMERICAN REFORMS

Brazil: Although reforms in Brazil have not been as radical as those in other Latin American countries included in this section, we summarize some of Brazil's efforts since it has the second largest (next to China) telephone network within the developing world in terms of absolute numbers. However, its telephone density, about 6 per 100 in 1990, is well above the developing country average and that of China. Although there has not been a deliberate planned effort to reform the entire sector like say Chile or Argentina, some action was taken around 1990 to introduce competition in this market. Users could build and operate their own networks, in parallel with TELEBRAS (Telecommunicacoes Brasileiras S.A.). Also, new mechanisms for private investment in the public network, such as by community cooperatives, were allowed. The dominant provider for basic services is TELEBRAS. It is a holding company of 29 operating companies, one for each state and EMBRATEL (Empresa Brasileira de Telecomunicacoes) the long distance/international communications company.

Overall, the approach in basic services appears to be to try and improve the efficiency of TELEBRAS while retaining government control. There has not been an effort to put a regulatory structure in place to foster more aggressive competition in the provision of different services. President Collor loosened market restrictions to allow competition in paging, cellular telephony, and private data networks (Silton 1994), (Dibble 1992). However, companies desiring to offer value added service needed to do so through a Brazilian firm. Equipment could be purchased from foreign firms only if comparable local units were not available. This cautious approach is closer to the reform approaches taken by some Asian countries, as will be seen later in the chapter.

Chile: Sector reforms started in the mid 1970's. Prior to 1975, telecommunications service was primarily provided by two state owned companies along with a few smaller ones. CTC[3] (Compania Telefonos de Chile) provided about 95% of the local lines, while ENTEL (Empresa Nacional de Telecommunicaciones S.A) operated international and long distance facilities. In the mid 70's, the CPE market was opened to competition and several small new companies were licensed to provide local service in competition with CTC in selected areas having substantial unfulfilled demand. SUBTEL (Subsecreteria de Telecommunicaciones) was established in 1977, as a part of the ministry of transportation, for technical regulation. Mechanisms for investment financing and a system for regulating monopoly tariffs were defined in 1987. Monopoly tariffs are revised on a five year cycle. The state began withdrawing from operational control over basic services by first selling some of its shares in CTC and ENTEL to company employees and the public in 1986. In 1987 international bids were made for a controlling interest in CTC. In 1989 the government sold its remaining CTC shares to the public and company employees. The controlling interest in CTC was sold to Telefonica de Espana in 1990.

Following reforms, telephone line annual growth rates increased to 20% in 1991 compared to about 5% in the 80's. Labor productivity went from 13 employees per 1000 telephone lines up to about 7 per 1000 lines in 1991. There is increased competition in nonbasic services (multiple cellular providers in cities, for example) and competition is even emerging in basic voice service. More recently, Chile has selected two cities, Talca and Curico, to test and then subsequently launch one of the world's first true multi-carrier services (Wittering 1994). Using the service, customers will be able to access one of six carriers (Bellsouth Chile, CTC Mundo, ENTEL, Telex Chile, TVI and VTR) licensed to provide long distance and international telephony, FAX and low speed data services.

Mexico: Reforms started here around 1989. Prior to 1989, the government had an operational (through a controlling interest in TELMEX) role in providing local, long distance and international communications services, as well as a regulatory role through the SCT (Secretaria de Communicaciones y Transporte). Modernization plans called for the privatization of TELMEX, restructuring tariff to promote financial self-sufficiency, competition in the CPE market, and competing regional cellular operators. Most of these policies were implemented during 1991-92. Tariffs were increased for basic service. A duopoly scheme was implemented for cellular service in each of nine regions, with one of the two licensees being a TELMEX subsidiary. As in Chile and Argentina, the CPE market and value added services were opened to competition right away. A controlling interest in TELMEX was sold to a consortium associated with France Telecom and Southwestern Bell. Privatized TELMEX was required to meet significant performance and network expansion obligations, but was granted monopoly over basic services till 1996 after which competition will be allowed. Several big-name competitors are preparing for entry once this monopoly ends on January 1 1997 (Moore 1994).

TELMEX financial and operational performance has improved since privatization. In 1991, number of telephone connections increased by 12.5 %, compared to about 5% annual growth in the 80's. However, according to regulatory authorities, TELMEX did not meet its performance obligations in 1994. Local calls became more expensive while long distance rates came down. New cellular operators were competing with TELMEX's cellular subsidiary.

Venezuela: Reforms were initiated in 1990, with plans to sell off CANTV (Compania Anonima Nacional de Telefonos de Venezuela), the government monopoly providing local and long distance service. To facilitate the sale of CANTV, an investment banking consortium was created. In march 1991, the government finalized the criteria for privatization, and established a base price of $900 million for 40% of CANTV shares. The government retained 49% of remaining shares to be sold over the near future, and 11% shares were set aside to be sold to employees. Two consortia participated in the public tender, including one led by GTE and the other led by Bell Atlantic, with the former winning with a bid of $1,885 million. It is useful to note that the government was actively interested in owner-operators, not just investors. Privatization was accompanied by establishment of CONATEL (Consejo Nacional de Telecommunicaciones) as the new regulatory agency. This agency was set up by executive decree, much like in Argentina, and faces some of the same problems in terms of lack of adequate resources to carry out its functions.

Like TELMEX in Mexico, the new operator of CANTV has a nine year monopoly on basic services, including long distance and international while having to meet aggressive development and service requirements.   For instance, the concession requires installation of 3 million new lines in addition to 640,000 replacement lines over the monopoly period. They also had to meet targets for improvement in operator response time, call completion rates and repair times. At the time of privatization, CANTV labor productivity was not particularly good, being around 12 employees per 1000 lines. In addition to monopoly privileges, the new operator was allowed to fully index tariffs to inflation on a quarterly basis. While monopoly privileges are in place for core service for several years, competition was introduced in the areas of cellular and value added services, and CPE.

The reforms in the Latin American countries are summarized in figure 1. While differences exist among the specific reform actions taken by these countries, they share some common characteristics. First, with the exception of Brazil, there did not appear to be an aversion to foreign control, financial and/or operational, of a critical national resource. In fact foreign participation was actively sought. There could be several reasons for this mind set in those Latin American countries that have undergone significant reform. One may be cultural. Strong cultural ties bind Italy, Spain and other Western nations with Latin American countries. The Spanish language is also a common bond. A second reason may lie in the ownership history of telecommunications organizations in many Latin American countries, which was characterized by extensive domestic as well as some foreign private ownership of telecommunications facilities. The state owned telecommunications enterprise only appeared much later, usually through nationalization or through consolidation of several small operators. CANTV in Venezuela, TELMEX, CTC in Chile, ENTel in Argentina are examples. Foreign operators such as ITT (in Argentina and Chile), LM Ericcsson (Argentina), had also been present. The ownership history is quite different for most Asian countries that will be examined subsequently.   The speed with which reforms were made in these Latin American countries is truly remarkable. While difficulties have arisen, and are to be expected, the improvements in service quality and efficiencies have been significant.

Sector Reform in Asia

The reform process in Asia has been much more varied and cautious compared to that in Latin America. In general, they have been more hesitant about allowing foreign control over basic services, and government has reduced its operational responsibility gradually.   Since our focus is on developing countries, we exclude Japan for purposes of this chapter. Hong Kong, Singapore[4], Republic of Korea, Taiwan and Malaysia have been pursuing economic development activities quite aggressively, and telecommunications is a central part of their overall plans. India, China, Vietnam have also been examining reform, but are not as far along in implementing them. Encouraged by reform efforts, and attracted by the market size, foreign operators and vendors have been wooing Asian countries over the last few years with offers of joint ventures and financing (Liden 1994), (Weiss 1994). A summary of sector reform (see Figure-2) in selected countries follows (Bruce & Cunard 1994).

China: The government of China has recognized telecommunications as being key to economic growth, and is cautiously reforming that sector. Foreign investment in the provision of services, however, is currently foreclosed. Nevertheless, as a result of decentralization efforts, the opportunity exists for arrangements between local operators and foreign suppliers of equipment. The (Ministry of Post and Telecommunications) MPT is organized in hierarchic fashion, with central and provincial administrative units (Lu 1994). Provincial and rural enterprises provide services and have a hierarchical reporting structure. The MPT began to decentralize in 1988, giving more power to the provincial units while making them more accountable for financial performance. However, revenue is collected centrally and then shared based on formulas rather than on tariffs. The main objective of reforms so far have been to introduce efficiencies in the MPT rather than competition into the sector. However, expansion plans are immense, forcing the government to examine more flexible arrangements for the provision of nonbasic services such as paging and domestic VSAT networks. Recently, there has been pressure to challenge the monopoly of the MPT (Tan 1994). The formal approval of two networks distinct from the Ministry of Posts and Telecommunications represents a major shift in this direction (Ure, 1994), (Clifford, Apr. 1994), (Chang 1994). The government is finding it necessary to allow some limited competition and the entry of profit making organizations in its effort to raise the telephone density to its target of 8 per 100 by year 2000 from its current level of about 2 per 100.

India: India's average telephone density is quite low (0.6 per 100 in 1990). The DOT (Department of Telecommunications) is both the operator and regulator. Most of the reform efforts to date have consisted of restructuring components of DOT. For example, some independent business units have been set up within DOT, such as VSNL (Videsh Sanchar Nigam Ltd.) for overseas service and MTNL (Mahanagar Telephone Nigam Ltd.) for some urban areas, but they do not have the autonomy they need over revenues or costs. There has also been a recommendation that DOT's operations be organized into five regional operating companies and one company providing interregional service. Manufacturing of domestic telecommunications equipment is encouraged. C-DOT (Center for Development of Telematics) has been set up to stimulate domestic manufacturing, specially of rural switches. This is at the expense of constricting the importation of switching and other equipment from abroad. In 1992, following the election of a new government, the government moved ahead with the awarding of several cellular licenses. Like in China, some government agencies, such as Indian Railways and ONGC (Oil and Natural Gas Commission) are setting up their own private networks as overlays. The problem of developing an adequate regulatory structure that will provide incentives for introducing rural service still remains.

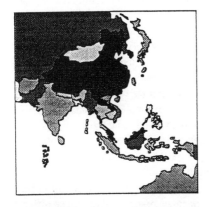

1162	9561	4	73	470	Chi
5.8	1	434	6	15360	HK
884	3288	6	74	310	Ind
184	1904	6	68	670	Indon
44	99	310	26	6790	Kor
18.6	330	89	55	2790	Mal
64	300	10	56	770	Phi
2.8	1	385	0	15730	Sing
58	513	24	77	1840	Tha
A	B	C	D	E	

A=pop. (1992) millions   B= Area. SqKm (,000)
C= Tel. lines/1000 population (1990)
D=% pop. in rural areas (1992)
E= GNP/capita (1992) $

	CPE	Basic Voice	MOBL Cell	PRIV NET	VANs	INTL VOIC	REGL AGNC.
China	○	☆	○c	☆c	☆c	☆	✊
Hong Kong	○	➤	○	○	○	➤	✊
India	○	☆p	○	☆c	☆c	☆p	✊
Indonesia	○	☆	☆c	☆E	☆E	☆c	✋
Korea	○	☆p	☆c	○c	○c	○c	✊
Malaysia	○	➤	○	☆c	☆c	○	✋
Philippines	○	➤	○	○	○	○	✊
Singapore	○	➤	➤	☆p	○	➤	✊
Taiwan	○	☆	☆c	☆c	☆c	☆	✊
Thailand	○	☆p	○	☆	○	☆E	✊

FIG 2. SUMMARY OF ASIAN REFORMS

Emerging worldwide mobile satellite services may offer one way of addressing this problem (Benton 1994), although the projected per/minute rates appear prohibitive for all except the business traveler. In all of these activities, one can see attempts to provide alternatives to DOT run operations. However, a comprehensive reform plan is yet to emerge, and the privatization of basic services appears to be a long way off. Nevertheless, in the eyes of domestic and foreign investors (and operators) India still remains an attractive prospect in terms of the size of the market.

Indonesia: Indonesia's telephone density is very low, about 0.6 per 100 in 1990, and its geography also presents some challenges for infrastructure development. In Indonesia, government is exploring ways to develop infrastructure through contracting with private entities, although it has been cautious about loosening control over state owned monopolies (Business Asia, Jun. 7 1993). Much like Thailand, the government is inclined to be the dominant, if not sole, provider of basic telecommunications services. But there is room for private investment in cellular and satellite services. In 1991, the government organization Perumtel was reorganized as a wholly government owned joint-stock company, PT Telkom. The latter is attempting to improve its organizational structure. It is being organized into several regional and one long distance company, with these different units having more independence to manage costs and revenues. Strategic investors are being sought to participate in these subsidiaries. PT Indosat , also a wholly government owned joint stock company, provides international services via INTELSAT. Cellular and paging services are provided through joint ventures between PT Telkom and two private investors. In Jan 1993, a new company PT Satelindo was established to provide international, cellular and satellite services using existing satellite capacity and developing additional capacity for the latter (McBeth 1994). Development of regulation is still evolving slowly as full competition is yet to develop. (Usually, the onset of competition forces a country to address the regulatory issues in a hurry).

Korea: Korea has a high telephone density at about 31 per 100 persons (1990). Nevertheless, the government has been engaged in sector reform for some time (Kim and Ro 1993). On January 1, 1991 the Korea Telecommunications Authority (KTA) was changed from a government authority to a state owned company, Korea Telecom, to facilitate ultimate privatization. The Government retains controlling interest, and is cautious about foreign equity ownership. To limit influence of large conglomerates, no single shareholder can own more than 10% shares of Korea Telecom. In August 1991, new telecommunications law established different classes of service providers to facilitate regulation. They are General Service Providers, Special Service Providers, and Value Added Service Providers. Competition is emerging in different areas. For example (Data Communications Corporation of Korea) DACOM's monopoly on data services was ended in 1992. As of December 1991, DACOM could provide international voice services, once the sole domain of Korea Telecom. Korea is moving to introduce competition in mobile services, the current provider being Korea Mobile Telecomm. DACOM and Korea Telecom are barred from the mobile sector.

Restrictions on ownership of providers of value added services were removed in 1994 after strong trade pressure, but foreign ownership restrictions in the general service provider category continue. In 1994 it was also announced that new domestic and foreign operators will be allowed to participate in the intercity telephone market provided they do not restrict geographic coverage to only profitable areas (Business Korea Jul. 1994).

Malaysia: Government began the reform process in 1984, by separating operational and regulatory roles of the Ministry of Energy, Posts and Telecommunications. Actual separation was effected in 1987. Telecom Malaysia became the operational arm, and was a wholly government owned company. Shares in Telecom Malaysia were offered to private hands in stages, first to private Malaysian institutions, then to the public at large. Some blocks of shares were retained for institutional investors, and a block was reserved for employees of Telekom Malaysia. Recently, the government has issued a number of facilities-based, cellular and paging licenses. Telekom Malaysia will face competition from other private Malaysian companies (e.g. Binariang) who have obtained licenses to provide local public network services. Technology Resources Industries is another company that plans to position itself as a rival to Telekom Malaysia in international services. A third competitor (Time Telecommunications) is currently laying fiber-optic cable to compete with Telekom in domestic long distance and international services. The new telecommunications policy announced in May 1994, introduces more competition to the sector and reduced the hold of the state monopoly (Astbury 1994) The regulatory institution in Malaysia is evolving along with competition in the sector.

Philippines: The telecommunications sector in the Philippines has a tradition of private ownership and regulation similar to the US. Telephone densities are low (1 per 100 in 1990). The private owners have close relationships and have considerable political clout. The dominant provider of domestic services is the privately owned (PLDT) Philippine Long Distance Telephone Company. However, the number of people waiting for lines is chronically high even in relatively affluent urban areas. But there are more than 70 telecommunications companies in the country. Multiple carriers are authorized to provide international services, domestic telex, FAX and leased-line services. Two international gateways have been authorized to Eastern Telecommunications Philippines Inc. (ETPI). However, ETPI needs access through PLDT to service most of its customers. Five companies have been granted permits to provide domestic satellite services. PLDT has resisted moves to reduce its dominance by resisting interconnection with new providers. However, its monopoly has ended and it will have to cope with increasing competition in the wake of recent efforts by the government of President Ramos (East Asian Executive Reports Apr. 1994), (Bromby 1994). Policy makers created an independent regulatory body (NTC) National Telecommunications Commission responsible for issuing new licenses and use of the radio spectrum. But the major problem continues to be operational and financial relationship between PLDT and new service providers.

Singapore and Hong Kong: International trade and financial services is critical to both Singapore and Hong Kong given their strategic locations, small size and lack of physical natural resources. Both countries place enormous importance on good telecommunications capabilities. However their approaches to sector advancement have been quite different, with Hong Kong emphasizing private enterprise in basic as well as non-basic services (Clifford Feb. 1994). Singapore is adopting a strategy similar to that in the Latin American countries, with liberalization being first introduced for non basic services.

In Hong Kong, Cable & Wireless (CW) has a monopoly on basic service through its holding company Hong Kong Telecom (HKT). These monopolies expire in 1995 and 2006 for domestic and international services respectively. In anticipation of the entry of new firms, HKT has been restructuring itself and becoming more customer oriented (Business Asia, Aug. 30 1993). There is strong competition in mobile (cellular and paging) services. The Hong Kong government awarded 3 licenses in late 1993 for domestic fixed network service, and set up the regulatory body OFTA (Office of The Telecommunications Authority). It will have the power to resolve disputes about interconnection among new entrants and HKT. One looming uncertainty for Hong Kong is the role China will play in this reform process after 1997 (Lee 1994). It is possible that the Chinese government will want to exert more control over the development of this sector in Hong Kong, although its propensity for control may be tempered by its desire to have access to the huge profits that could be generated by extensive liberalization.

The telecommunications sector in Singapore is dominated by ST (Singapore Telecomm), which has been enormously successful (Chwee-Huat 1992). On April 1, 1992, ST was transformed into a wholly government owned corporation. 11% of its shares were floated in Nov. 1993. ST has aggressively reinvested profits into operations. It has been able to do so by maintaining a tariff structure for local access that has supported investment in that sector. Contrast this with the artificially low and sometimes distorted tariff structures in many of the Latin American and Asian Countries where the sector suffered from chronic under investment. ST's cash reserves have not been expropriated by other branches of government. Singapore presents a rather unusual example where a dominant government controlled telecommunications provider has remained nimble enough to respond to emerging pressures from the marketplace. However, that dominance will be tested as ST looks to become a player on the world stage in providing network services, since other countries may want reciprocal freedom to provide network services in Singapore.

Taiwan: The sector is still predominantly monopolistic and Taiwan has been much more slow in introducing reforms(Chen 1994). Regulatory and operational responsibility both lie with the government through the DGT (Directorate General for Communications). Foreign firms have supplied equipment for other non-basic, cellular and paging services, but control remains with DGT. Some value added services are allowed to be provided on a competitive basis, but only domestically. Even partial foreign ownership is not allowed in telecommunications providers. Furthermore, the DGT has not yet been restructured as a government owned corporation in preparation for privatization. Taiwan is considering reform through the categorization of services into basic (type-1) and enhanced (type-2). Type-1 services would remain under the monopoly control of a restructured DGT, while type-2 services could be opened for competition.

   Thailand: Reform has taken the shape of seeking private investment with government retaining control of the sector. TOT (Telephone Organization of Thailand) is the primary provider of domestic communications services. CAT (Communications Authority of Thailand) provides international, telegraph, domestic satellite and packet switching services. The Thai economy is growing fast and the backlog of subscribers waiting for connections has exploded, despite a doubling of lines between 1986 and 1991. TOT and CAT are therefore making arrangements with private investors to develop cellular telephone and paging services.   Because of organizational and political constraints, the Ministry of Transport and telecommunications began exploring BTO (Build Transfer Operate) options. It did settle on a bidder who chose British Telecom (BT) as the foreign operator to construct the facilities. This was changed after a political coup in 1991. NYNEX replaced BT as the foreign operator, with the operational entity being known as TelecomAsia. TelecomAsia has been very successful in meeting its obligations, and its earnings prospects remain very favorable (Asia Money March 1994). CAT and TOT continue to have operational and regulatory responsibilities. Before CAT and TOT are finally privatized, these two responsibilities will have to be separated into distinct organizations just as they were in many Latin American countries.

   Compared to sector reforms in Latin America, reforms in most Asian countries have been more varied and slow. There appears to be a richer variety of financing alternatives that have been explored as governments, seek to maintain operational control while obtaining private investment.   The regulatory mechanisms also appear to be developing more slowly. This may be due to the fact the competition is entering the sector in a more controlled manner over a longer period.   The speed of many Latin American reforms often forced immediate attention to regulatory matter. The different reform activities in Asia discussed in this chapter are summarized in Figure 2.

RECOMMENDATIONS FOR SECTOR REFORM

   For convenience, let us separate two related aspects of sector reform - (i) which sector areas to open to competition, how and when, and (ii) how to address regulatory issues. Based on the country specific actions mentioned earlier in the chapter, we summarize those steps which were critical to the success of sector reforms for many developing nations.   In short, the steps seek to introduce competition into non-basic services fairly rapidly, while managing the transformation of basic services from a government monopoly to regulated private monopolies. The latter is particularly difficult since it involves dismantling long standing traditions and organizational structures. It is necessary to emphasize that several specific details for many of these steps will need to be tailored somewhat differently for each developing country. However, they do identify a broad range of possible actions that can be considered while making reforms.

- Open up the CPE market to competition during the earliest stages of reforms. It is a large market, and opening it to competition sends strong signals to investors and private operators about the government's commitment to sector reforms. Also, the CPE market is relatively fragmented, even for large and expensive units such as PBXs, reducing worries of monopoly abuses and other barriers to entry. Joint venturing with foreign partnership can be engineered through policy, in order to build up domestic capability in this area.

- Very early on in the reform process, set up a regulatory entity that is authorized through legislation. If the entity is created by executive edict rather than through legislation, then there is always the concern that it may be dissolved or otherwise altered with relative ease. Ensure adequate financial resources for this entity through government funds or through appropriate surcharges on revenue generated by private operators in the sector. The independence of this regulatory entity from the executive, or a dominant government monopoly provider, and its perceived power to monitor and enforce compliance with regulation is critical to the success and stability of reforms. It is just as important to have properly qualified and experienced personnel in this regulatory entity. Realistically however, the necessary regulatory experience is hard to find.

- Permit competition in facilities-based private network operations from an early stage. This, combined with a liberalization of the CPE market, will improve the ability of large domestic businesses to meet their information processing needs without having to wait for a full infrastructure to be built by a dominant basic services provider. Moreover, being facilities-based, these operators would be expanding overall infrastructure. (Facilities based operators own the facilities they operate, as opposed to resellers of capacity).

- Open up domestic mobile services (e.g. cellular, paging) to competition at an early stage. The initial beneficiaries will be large businesses, who could justify the higher prices for these services in terms of their higher reliability and coverage compared to existing local land line service. As a critical mass of business users develops, prices will come down, gradually bringing it within reach of individuals and small business. However, important regulatory issues have to be resolved - such as the number of cellular licenses per service area, and the process of awarding these licenses. In developing countries, where the wait time for a telephone line can be several years, cellular offers a good way to satisfy unmet demand from business and affluent individuals, once again expanding infrastructure.

- Restructure the state owned telecommunications monopoly to a corporate structure, with the government initially holding all shares. This structuring is an essential preparatory step for privatizing basic service. It allows potential private investors or operators to evaluate the financial health of the organization being privatized. and to put a value on its shares. This step also provides an opportunity to introduce operational efficiencies which can result in increased value during sale. Through this preparatory restructuring, it is also possible to divide the once monolithic government entity into multiple entities, which are then privatized separately.

- Target the sale of shares to an appropriate collection of stakeholders. These include individual domestic investors, institutional domestic investors and international investors. A portion of shares should be reserved for sale to employees of the former government entity as part of the process of gaining their support for privatization. The sale should be staggered over time to attract the appropriate population of stakeholders at each stage. It may be desirable to place an upper limit on individual share holdings, given that in many developing countries, wealth is concentrated in a few hands, although this would limit the amount of capital that could be raised.

- If controlling interest is to be transferred to a private operator as a result of the sale, it is necessary to specify well ahead of the sale, detailed performance requirements that have to met by the operator, and how the government will measure performance. In return, the controlling party should be assured monopoly privileges for a period of time (5-10 years), after which time, competition should be allowed. Infrastructure expansion to suburban areas (or even rural areas) can be mandated through these performance requirements, although rural expansion requirements have generally been minimal.

- Consider Build-Transfer-Operate (BTO) or Build-Operate-Transfer (BOT) as alternative ways of introducing private sector participation in the expansion of basic infrastructure. These mechanisms offer a compromise where private capital can be tapped while the government still retains some control over telecommunications operations. In BOT, private entities are responsible for building infrastructure, following which they have rights to operate facilities for a specified period (earning profits during this period). After this period, operational rights transfer back to the government.

The nature and success of telecommunications sector reform is closely tied to general economic and political reform activities. We have chosen to focus on the mechanics of telecommunications reform in this chapter. However, the influence of general economic and political conditions is evident when one contrasts telecommunications reform say in Singapore with that in Hong Kong or China with India. These conditions must be considered when evaluating different mechanisms for reform.

Implications of Reform

Figures 1 and 2 pictorially portray the reform activities described earlier in the chapter. We have attempted to make the symbols meaningful. The circle with multiple arrows signifies a competitive market with many players. A circle with three arrowheads also signifies competition, but with the number of players being limited by design. The star represents a government monopoly. Other symbols are identified in Figure 1.

In both Figures 1 and 2, the trend towards increased participation by the private sector, in the form of operators and/or investors, is quite clear. When this fact is combined with the numbers for population and telephone densities listed for most of the countries in those two figures, the immense size of these markets becomes apparent. The growth potential for private companies entering these markets is considerable. For market investors (i.e. those interested in telecommunications purely for investment purposes, not for operational control), they represent opportunity for attractive returns. In fact, judging from the performance of some of the Latin American companies (e.g. TELMEX, CTC), the confidence of market investors appears to have been amply justified. Opportunities for market investors exist in several Asian countries as well - (e.g. Malaysia, Thailand, Singapore). However, notice in Figure 2 that liberalization of the telecommunications sector in most Asian countries has concentrated on CPE and non-basic services. Moreover, development of regulatory structures is at an early stage. Issues such as interconnection among different providers (both rates and access rights) and restrictions on cross subsidies between monopoly and competitive components of the same organization have yet to be addressed. This is of concern to market investors when service in the sector is being provided by a mixture of competitive and monopoly entities, as it has significant impact on profitability.

For strategic investors (i.e. those interested in operations as well as ownership), the Latin American countries are a far more attractive prospect at present compared to Asian countries mentioned in this chapter. These investors are certainly interested in new markets and attractive returns on investment. However, they often have an additional interest - that of developing an infrastructure that provides one stop shopping for international telecommunications service to multinational business customers. The various international alliances that are developing among different telecommunications companies (e.g. British Telecom and MCI) are evidence of this trend. A comparison of Figures 1 and 2 shows that privatization and competition is prevalent in more sector areas (basic, cellular, private networks etc.) for the Latin American countries as compared to Asian ones. This makes it easier for a provider to offer an integrated array of services making the provider more attractive to business customers who are trying to set up global networks. Currently, the main opportunities for strategic investors in Asian developing countries are in the areas of mobile (e.g. paging, cellular) communications and, to a lesser extent, international voice/data services. Privatization of basic service in the most populous Asian countries (China, India, Indonesia) does not appear to be likely within the next five years.

Figures 1 and 2 also have some implications for international voice and data services. Note how in these two figures, whenever we have a government monopoly (star symbol) providing domestic basic service, we generally also have international voice service provided by a government monopoly. Further, the figures show competition in international voice is less prevalent than in other sector areas such as mobile services or private networks.   There should be less distinctions made between voice and data international services from a regulatory standpoint; i.e. both should be opened to competition at a more rapid pace.   Good international telecommunications service makes a developing country more attractive to multinationals and it also facilitates participation by the country in the global economy.   While there has been a trend towards competitive provision of international data services, international voice tends to get treated in the same way as domestic voice for purposes of regulation and introducing competition.   However, there is no need for this linkage - in fact one can argue for international and   domestic   basic   service   to   be   treated   quite   differently ,   with competition/privatization being introduced to international voice more rapidly.

We close this section by raising one question that is particularly relevant to telecommunications sector reform in developing countries. Will privatization further widen the disparity between urban and rural telecommunications service? Figures 1 and 2 show several developing countries (including the three most populated ones) with a high percentage of rural population. The experience of several Latin American countries shows that despite privatization, expansion of rural infrastructure continues to lag significantly behind urban expansion. Performance specifications in contracts with private monopoly providers often have nominal requirements for rural expansion. Expansion of rural service will continue to be a difficult challenge in sector reform efforts, and as yet there is not enough evidence to show which specific reform mechanisms might be effective in accomplishing this goal while at the same time introducing private enterprise into the provision of basic service. In terms of technological alternatives, VSAT (Very Small Aperture Terminals) systems are being considered (Mesch 1992) for rural service. The possibility of using INTELSAT based networks for providing rural service has not been explored as aggressively as it might be. With the increasing deployment of transoceanic fiber, the use of satellites for primary transoceanic links is on the decline.   The economics of satellite capacity for rural voice communications may therefore be becoming more favorable. When one considers the high opportunity costs of delay together with the actual system costs, satellite based techniques may turn to be more attractive than terrestrial based links since they offer the possibility of reducing the time needed to extend basic service to rural areas.

SUMMARY

In this chapter, we began with a description of the chronic deficiencies of the telecommunications sector in developing countries. Technological advances in computing and telecommunications have changed both the supply and demand structures of this sector. Individuals, businesses and governments are finding themselves increasingly dependent on timely information to participate in the global economy. However, government is unable to finance modernization and expansion of the infrastructure from its own coffers. Hence the need for reform. The broad objective of reform has been to increase private sector participation in ownership and operation of networks and redefine the role of government to one of policy setting and regulation. We have summarized reform activities from selected countries in Latin America and Asia to illustrate steps taken by them, and have then attempted to make some recommendations for sector reform.

In our opinion, the single biggest impediment to sector reform has been the slow evolution of regulatory structure. Part of the reason is a scarcity of personnel experienced in regulatory matters. DCs are usually liberalizing other sectors in addition to telecommunications, making this scarcity even more acute. In some cases, the regulatory agency has not had the necessary autonomy or resources. In any event, regulatory agencies in DCs need to prioritize their objectives - monitor monopolies for abuses, encourage competition, encourage widespread availability of communications, or manage the mix of monopoly and competitive services etc.. These objectives are related, but the regulatory instruments chosen would be different depending on which ones are deemed more important. For instance, simple rate based regulation is useful in achieving the monitoring objective, but it does not provide the proper incentives to achieve high levels of innovation and service. Structural separation and cost allocation mechanisms may be necessary to manage a mix of monopoly and competitive services when cross subsidies can distort the market These are just a few examples of the variety of regulatory mechanisms that can be employed.

Endnotes

[1] We will use the term "developing country" somewhat loosely in this chapter to include low and middle income countries as defined by different international agencies.

[2] Prior to 1948, when most of the telephone system was nationalized, private companies had been active in that sector with the main operator having been a subsidiary of ITT.

[3] CTC itself was formed by merging several small private operators. It became a joint venture of International Telephone & Telegraph (ITT) and the state, but was taken over by the government in 1974. So it did not have a long history of being a pure state owned enterprise.

[4] While it is probably not appropriate to consider Hong Kong and Singapore as developing nations, their telecommunications reforms offer interesting lessons and contrasts.

References

"TelecomAsia: A Major New Force in Telecommunications," *AsiaMoney*, Mar 1994, v5n2, p30-31.

Astbury S.(1994) , "Malaysia: The Victor in The Skies," *Asian Business*, Aug, v30n8, p9.

"Telecoms Deregulation in Hong Kong: No Time to Waste," *Business Asia*, Aug 30 1993, v25n18, p6-7.

"Indonesia: No Sign of Free-Market Mania," *Business Asia*, Jun 7 1993, v25n12, p5.

Benton D. (1994), "MSS Systems Advance Telecommunications in India," *Satellite Communications*, Nov, v18n11, p18.

"Free Competition Declared for Intercity Business Phones," *Business Korea*, Jul 1994, v12n1, p33.

Bromby R.(1994) , "The Philippines: A Challenge Awaits," *Telecommunications*, Jan 1994, v28n1, p37-38.

Bruce R.R. and Cunard J. (1994), "Restructuring the Telecommunications Sector in Asia," in *Implementing Reforms in the Telecommunications Sector*, ed. B. Wellenius and P. Stern, (World Bank, Washington DC).

Chang H.F. (1994), "Lian Tong: A Quantum Leap in the Reform of China's Telecommunications," *Telecommunications Policy*, Apr, v18n3, p206-210.

Chen B.S. (1994), "Taiwan: Reform at a Snail's Pace," *Telecommunications Policy*, Apr, v18n3, p229-235.

Chwee-Huat T. (1992), "Singapore Telecom: From Public to Private Sector," *International Journal of Public Sector Management*, v5n4, p4-14.

Clifford M. (1994), "Communications: Ringing in Change," *Far Eastern Economic Review*, Feb, v157n5, p40-42.

Clifford M. (1994), "China: A Questions of Money," *Far Eastern Economic Review*, Apr 7, v157n14, p47-48.

Dibble A. C. (1992), "Telecommunications Deregulation in Brazil Rings up Sales for U.S. Firms," *Telephony*, April 6 1992, v222n14, p25-32.

"Philippine Telecommunications: Deregulation Crowds The Field," *East Asian Executive Reports*, Apr 15 1994, v16n4, p6.

Field A. (1994), "Current Developments in the FCC: Telecommunications and the NAFTA," *Law & Policy in International Business*, v25n3, p1145-1151.

Kim J.C. and Ro T.S. (1993), "Current Policy Issues in The Korean Telecommunications Industry," *Telecommunications Policy*, Sept/Oct, v17n7, p481-492.

Lanuza, Luis M. Gonzales (1992), "The Argentine Telephone Privatization," *Telecommunications Policy*, Dec 1992, v16n9, p759-763.

Lee P.S.N. (1994), "China's Role in Hong Kong's Telecommunications Deregulation," *Telecommunications Policy*, Apr, v18n3, p254-264.

Liden J. (1994, "Telecommunications: Those Who Tread the High Wires," *AsiaMoney*, v4n10, p28-35.

Lu D. (1994), "The Management of China's Telecommunications Industry," *Telecommunications Policy*, Apr, v18n3, p195-205.

McBeth J. (1994), "Indonesia: Ready for Competition," *Far Eastern Economic Review*, Jan, v157n1, p48-49.

Mesch G. (1992), "Salinas' Rush for 'Bypass Technologies' ", *Satellite Communications*, Dec v16n12, p20.

Moore M.A. (1994), "Star Wars in Cyberspace Mexico," *Business Mexico*, v4n10, p20-23.

Nulty T.E. (1989), "Emerging Issues in World Telecommunications," in *Restructuring and Managing the Telecommunications Sector*, ed. B. Wellenius, P.A. Stern, T.E. Nulty, R.D. Stern, A World Bank symposium (Washington DC: World Bank , 1989).

Petrazzini B.A. (1995), *"Privatization of Telecommunications Services in Latin America: The Case of Argentina,"* forthcoming in The Privatization of Infrastructure in Developing Countries: Lessons from Latin America, Ravi Ramamurti ed., 1995

Silton, Michael M. (1994), "Brazil Revamps Telecom for Global Competition," *Business Communications*, v24n5, p53-56.

Saunders R.J., Warford J.J., Wellenius B. (1993), *Telecommunications and Economic Development*, The Johns Hopkins University Press, Baltimore & London, 1993.

Tan Z. (1994), "Challenges to the MPT's Monopoly," *Telecommunications Policy*, v18n3, p174-181.

Ure J. (1994), "Telecommunications, with Chinese Characteristics," *Telecommunications Policy*, v18n3, p182-194.

Weiss E. (1994), "Privatization and Growth in South East Asia," *Telecommunications*, v28n5, p95-101

Wellenius B. (1989), "Beginnings of Sector Reform in the Developing World," in *Restructuring and Managing the Telecommunications Sector*, ed. B. Wellenius, P.A. Stern, T.E. Nulty, R.D. Stern, A World Bank symposium (Washington DC: World Bank , 1989).

Wellenius B. (1994), "Telecommunications Restructuring in Latin America: An Ovrview," in *Implementing Reforms in the Telecommunications Sector*, ed. B. Wellenius and P. Stern, (World Bank, Washington DC).

Wellenius B., P.A. Stern, T.E. Nulty, R.D. Stern (1989) *Restructuring and Managing the Telecommunications Sector*, ed., A World Bank symposium (Washington DC: World Bank).

Wellenius B. and P.A. Stern (editors), *Implementing Reforms in the TC Sector*, (Wasington D.C. The world Bank, 1994).

Wittering S. (1994), "Chilean Domestic vie for Global Customers," *Communications International*, v21n10, p20-23.

9 A Conceptual Framework to Assess Gaps in Information Systems Cultures Between Headquarters and Foreign Subsidiaries

Barry Shore
University of New Hampshire, USA

Multinational corporations (MNC's) must rely on information systems to link headquarter organizations with subsidiary organizations in host countries throughout the world. Establishing this link may be complex for several reasons including the fact that national cultures may influence the IS cultures of both the headquarters and subsidiary organizations. Differences between these IS cultures may produce an IS culture gap which, if ignored, may interfere with headquarters' ability to use common IS applications. This chapter identifies the issues associated with this gap, develops a conceptual framework that focuses on the practices contributing to this gap, and concludes with implications for management. Addressing these issues will help to reduce conflicts, improve technology transfer, and achieve a more effective use of applications in the far flung organizations of MNC's.

INTRODUCTION

Information and telecommunications systems, and the ability to transfer and use these technologies in foreign subsidiaries, are central to the mission of multinational organizations (Kedia and Bhagat, 1988; Roche, 1992). Without these technologies, multinationals would find the consequences of time zones, currencies, languages, and legal systems extremely difficult to manage. But even more important, they would find it impossible to integrate their world-wide operations, a process essential to achieving the economies of scale and competitive advantage critical to today's world-wide markets.

Employing these technologies in subsidiary organizations can be very difficult. While the steps that need to be taken to assure effective use of IS technology are usually very clear to headquarters, the foreign subsidiary may find it very difficult to comply. Transfer of technology may get bogged down as management in the subsidiary organization and end-users resist efforts to change the practices with which they are familiar. As a result, transfer may take considerably longer than expected or may fail altogether. Even after an application has been successfully transferred, its routine day-to-day use may be disappointing. Maintenance may also be a problem, as the subsidiary resists intrusions on its operations. This is not to suggest that all organizations face these problems. Many efforts to transfer and use an application in foreign subsidiaries experience about the same degree of success or failure as do transfers to domestic subsidiaries. But problems, often beyond the scope of those experienced at home, frequently plague overseas projects.

In one Fortune 500 organization studied by the author, the full range of outcomes occurred, from total success to total failure. To integrate essential corporate functions, headquarters established a "common systems" group whose purpose it was to implement common sales, financial, and manufacturing applications throughout the world. But several years after this project was initiated only one-third of the world-wide sites were successfully using these applications. Another one-third were still having problems with implementation, while the last third found it impossible to begin.

Technical factors certainly contribute to these problems: a subsidiary may lack experience with information technology; technical support may be unavailable; and the telecommunications infrastructure may be inadequate. But technical factors alone cannot fully explain why problems occur when linkages are attempted between headquarters and subsidiary organizations. What needs to be considered is that these organizations may exist in very different national cultures and that different preferences for IS practices may exist within these cultures. Linkages which attempt to integrate these organizations may therefore be subject to cultural as well as technical failure.

This chapter explores the way in which national culture influences IS culture. It begins by placing the issue of IS culture within the context of the global IS literature, and then summarizes the work on national culture, organization culture, and IS culture. Next a conceptual framework is developed which integrates national culture with IS culture. Then the framework is used to explore the interaction between headquarters and subsidiary IS cultures, and explain why these linkages might fail. The chapter closes with implications for management.

LITERATURE REVIEW

Global IS research can be classified by geographic range (Ein-Dor, Segev, Orgad, 1993). Single country studies focus on IS issues within one country, often describing information systems indigenous to that area (Babbington, 1987; Odedra-Straub 1993; Hassan, 1994). Multiple country studies address the issues or specific practices in several countries, usually drawing comparisons and often implicating the role of national culture as well as other variables. For example, Azuma and Mole (1994) studied and compared software development practices between Japan and the European community. Other multiple country studies suggesting the role of culture include the work of:

Dagwell and Weber (1983), who found differences in designers working in the U.S. and the U.K.; Kumar and Bjorn-Andersen (1990), who found differences between Canadian and Danish designers; and Couger et al. (1990), who found differences between U.S. and Singaporean IS professionals.

Several studies have also focused on multinational organizations, often addressing issues of strategy and structure. Many of these studies involve the development of conceptual models with little empirical support (Ein-Dor, Segev and Orgad, 1993). Bartlett and Ghoshal (1989) identify four strategies which a business may pursue: multinational, global, international, and transnational. Cheung and Burn (1994) extend this model to IS and differentiate among three forms of Multinational Corporations (MNCs). They suggest that a multidomestic MNC views the world as a composition of a number of different domestic markets and delegates all decision making authority to its subsidiaries. A global MNC views the world as a single market and attempts to exercise control over its internal business processes, often ignoring the implication of differences associated with the subsidiary's culture and markets. Paramount to this strategy is the centralization of decision making authority at headquarters and the emphasis on economies of scale and cost efficiencies. Transnational MNCs are positioned between these extremes and must balance the tension between the forces for global integration and national responsiveness. Ives and Jarvenpaa (1991) study the challenges faced by senior mangers at multinational corporations. They found four common approaches for managing global information technology, in general confirming the framework developed by Bartlett and Ghoshal.

Because these studies have concluded that IS issues and practices differ among countries, a case can be made for the inclusion of national culture as one variable in any framework which attempts to address the linkages between headquarters and its subsidiaries, regardless of multinational structure. This is confirmed by Kedia and Bhagat (1988) who contend that it may be necessary to consider the impact of different national cultures on the ability of the headquarters organization to successfully transfer an application to its subsidiaries. It therefore seems appropriate at this stage in trans-national theory building to explore the influence of national culture on the IS cultures of headquarters and its subsidiaries.

Little work, however, has been done on IS culture. Cooper (1994) studied IS culture and concluded that there is significant support for the potential impact of culture on information technology implementation. Davenport et al. (1992) in their study of information culture in U.S. organizations, conclude that IS and the information made available from these systems is often used politically, sometimes contrary to the best interests of the organization. Both studies, however, ignore the role of national culture.

But the literature stops here. No studies have been conducted which explore the impact of national culture on IS organizations and how the differences between headquarters and subsidiary IS cultures may account for the difficulties in linking both organizations. Before developing a conceptual framework that attempts to bridge this gap, it is important to review the literature on national and organizational culture.

NATIONAL CULTURE

Hofstede (1980) defines culture as a set of mental programs that control an individual's responses in a given context. Parsons and Shils (1951) define it as a shared characteristic of a high-level social systems. It can also be defined as the shared values of a particular group of people (Erez and Earley, 1993). National culture reflects the core values and beliefs of individuals formed during childhood and reinforced throughout life (Lachman, 1983; Triandis, 1995). According to Hofstede (1980), it shapes the type of organizations and the nature of social structures in a society. Several other models of national culture have been suggested in the literature. These include: Kluckhohn and Strodtbeck (1961); Rokeach (1973); and McClelland (1961). Hofstede's model (1980) suggests that national culture can be defined through four dimensions. Utilizing data from 116,000 questionnaires, administered in 40 countries, he identified these four dimensions as: power distance, uncertainty avoidance, individualism-collectivism, and masculinity-femininity.

Power Distance is the degree of inequality among people, from relatively equal (small power distance) to extremely unequal (large power distance). *Uncertainty Avoidance* is the extent to which a society feels threatened by uncertain situations and avoids these situations by providing career stability, establishing formal rules, and not tolerating deviant ideas. *Individualism-Collectivism* contrasts a social fabric in which each individual takes care of himself or herself with a social fabric in which groups take care of the individual in exchange for his or her loyalty. *Masculinity-Femininity* reflects whether the dominant values are associated with the collection of money and things, which Hofstede classifies as masculine, as contrasted with values associated with the caring for others and the quality of life, which he classifies as feminine. Of these four dimensions, power distance and uncertainty avoidance are considered dominant in studying organizations within a particular culture (Hofstede, 1981).

Hofstede (1980) describes four classifications of culture measured by combinations of power distance and uncertainty avoidance. These classifications represent regions or quadrants into which organizations within a specific culture can be placed. The first quadrant, called the *family* by Hofstede, is characterized by cultures displaying a high degree of centralization (high power distance) combined with a lower level of formalization (low uncertainty avoidance). The second quadrant, called the *market*, includes cultures which are neither centralized (low power distance) nor formalized (low uncertainty avoidance). The third quadrant, called the *machine*, is characterized by a high degree of formalization (low uncertainty avoidance) and decentralized power (low power distance). The fourth quadrant, called the *pyramid*, is both centralized (high power distance) and formal (high uncertainty avoidance).

Erez and Earley (1993) explain why Hofstede's model has been widely used to study organizations: they contend that it is not only 'approachable', but is sufficiently clear and parsimonious to lend itself to empirical tests. Research which has used this model as a framework includes papers by Kedia and Bhagat (1988), who use it to develop a conceptual model of technology transfer, and Shore and Venkatachalam [1995], who use it to develop a conceptual model of systems analysis and design. However, Hofstede's model has been criticized in at least two areas: one, the model is based on and specific to a single organization (IBM) and hence raises the question of generalizability; and two, the four dimensions used in the study are insufficient by themselves to study all aspects of culture. Addressing the first criticism, Erez and Earley (1993) argue that national culture reflects an individual's core values and beliefs, and it is these values that dominate corporate or organizational culture. They maintain that organizations can, at best, exert influence over an individual's peripheral values and beliefs. Using this argument it is reasonable to suggest that the Hofstede model can be generalized to all organizations throughout the world, not just IBM. To address the second criticism, Hofstede introduced a fifth dimension, namely long-term vs. short-term orientation, in his later studies (Hofstede, 1991). Others have developed completely different sets of cultural variables while some have added variables to Hofstede's model (Kedia and Bhagat, 1988). Criticisms notwithstanding, the Hofstede model is very useful. Organizations located in a particular country can be placed in their appropriate quadrant, making his model a very practical tool for initiating cultural analysis. Several of the countries studied are listed in Table 1 together with the quadrant to which they belong.

MARKET	MACHINE	PYRAMID	FAMILY
Denmark	Finland	France	Hong Kong
Sweden	Switzerland	Japan	Singapore
Ireland	Germany	Mexico	India
New Zealand	Israel	Greece	Philippines
USA	Argentina	Arab Countries	West Africa
Great Britain	Costa Rica	Korea	Malaysia

Table 1: Examples of Countries which can be grouped into Hofstede's Quadrants

Hofstede's model has also been criticized because it can be interpreted to suggest that common cultural characteristics can be observed in all organizations within a specific national culture. But this is certainly not the case. Organizations characterized by high power distance exist in low power distance cultures, for example. Clearly the range in any culture can be wide. Accordingly, Hofstede's model, and its use in this chapter, is intended to suggest only the general tendencies observable in a culture; variations are expected. Without the ability to make these generalizations, the development of a simple conceptual framework would be limited.

ORGANIZATIONAL CULTURE

Organizational culture can be defined in many ways. Smircich (1983) defines it as the set of key values, guiding beliefs, and understandings that are shared by members of an organization. Schein (1985) defines it as a pattern of basic assumptions that has worked well enough to be valid, and therefore to be taught to new members as the correct way to perceive, think, and feel about organizational problems.

Organization culture can also be expressed in many ways. Deal and Kennedy (1982) suggest that the manifestation of organizational culture can be classified into four categories, each one peeled off, like the layers of an onion, until the core values are exposed. They include: (1) symbols, or the words or objects that carry a specific meaning within the organization; (2) heroes, or the persons highly prized as models of behavior; (3) rituals, or the collective activities that are socially essential in an organization; (4) and core values.

Hofstede, Neuijen, Ohayv and Sanders (1990) contend that there is no consensus about the definition of organizational culture. Most authors, they assert, will agree that it is: (1) holistic, (2) historically determined, (3) related to anthropological concepts, (4) socially constructed, (5) soft, and (6) difficult to change. To clarify its definition and introduce empirical evidence to a field dominated by what they criticize as "in-depth case studies," Hofstede et al studied ten organizations in Denmark and the Netherlands. They concluded that organizational values are partly determined by nationality, industry, and task. Furthermore, they concluded that while the popular literature insists that shared values represent the core of organizational culture, their factor analysis suggest that the way values affect ordinary members of an organization is expressed through practices. Practices represent what "is" in contrast to values which represent what "should be." An example of a value, in the context of an IS group, might be wide-spread participation in systems development. A practice might be the inclusion of functional mangers on all major IS development teams.

While Hofstede et al contend that organizational culture is partly determined by national culture and practices, others place even more emphasis on national culture alone. Erez and Early (1993) argue that organizations do not possess cultures of their own, but are formed as a result of societal cultures. Triandis (1995) suggests that organizations may have a weak effect on an individual's peripheral values, but have no long-lasting effect on core or deep-seated values. Corporate culture may therefore only affect an individuals peripheral values while leaving core values, those learned early in life, intact (Erez and Earley, 1993).

In summary, organizational culture can be defined as a set of shared values, basic assumptions, and practices in an organization. It is historically constructed and difficult to change. While it is generally agreed upon that national culture affects core values, the influence of organizational culture is primarily limited to peripheral values.

INFORMATION CULTURE

Extending the work of Hofstede et al on organizational culture, IS culture can be defined as the set of values and practices shared by those members of an organization involved in information activities including MIS professionals, managers and end-users. Examples of practices in a specific organization might include:

- Exclusive use of UNIX operating systems.
- Limitations in end-user involvement during a development effort. Commitement to protoyping methodologies in systems development.
- Minimum support for end-user computing.
- Requirement of IS approval for all PC purchases.
- Limited access by end-users for the purpose of updating databases.

Copper's study (1994) is the only work which directly addresses IS culture. He asserts that an IS culture may resist technologies which realign status, power, and working habits, especially when they may violate some of the group's shared values. IS culture, he contends, may be more or less compatible with certain information technologies and to the degree to which it is less compatible, consequences may occur which include, resistance to change, implementation failure , or disappointing results.

In building a model of IS culture, Cooper uses the competing values framework developed by Quinn and Rohrbaugh (1985). This framework emphasizes the competing tensions and conflicts inherent in groups. Two major conflicts include: (1) the need for *order* versus the ability to be *flexible*, and (2) the focus on either the demands of the *internal* social and technical systems of the organization versus a focus on the *external* world beyond the boundaries of the organization. When combinations of these conflicts are considered, four cultural archetypes can be defined: survival, productivity, stability, and human relations. The *survival* archetype is characterized by an organization that is flexible and external. Its leaders can adapt to a changing environment and are willing to take risks in the search for opportunities. The *productivity* archetype is characterized by an organization that is responsive to its external environment and prefers order. These organizations are very efficient, and nearly all decisions are driven by rational-economic considerations. The *stability* archetype is characterized by the need for order and internal focus. There is a high degree of formalization, and leaders tend to be cautious, emphasizing technical issues. The *human relations* archetype is characterized by flexibility and an internal focus. Emphasis is on informal roles rather than a formal structure, and maintenance of the organization is a primary goal.

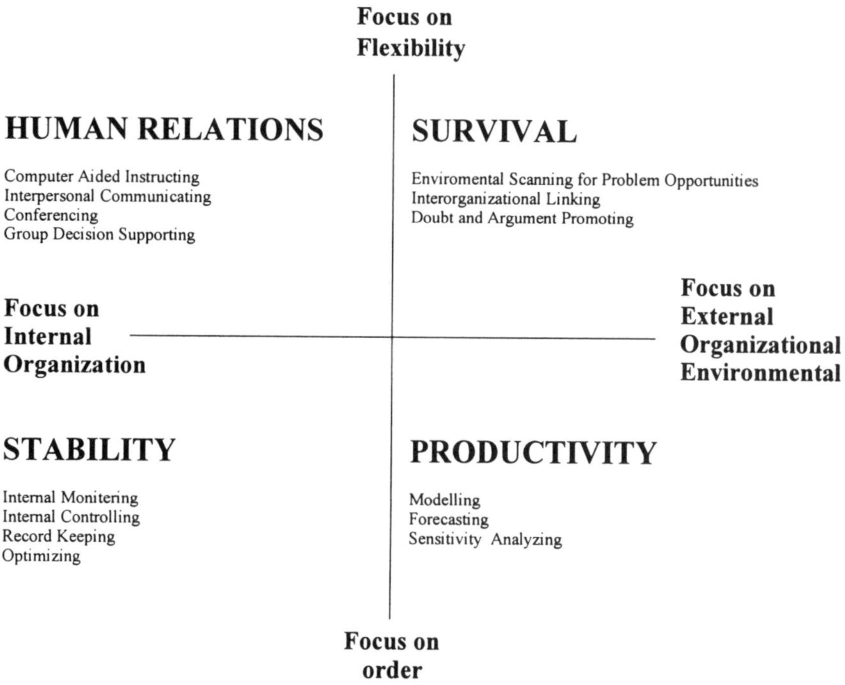

Focus on
Flexibility

HUMAN RELATIONS   SURVIVAL

Computer Aided Instructing   Enviromental Scanning for Problem Opportunities
Interpersonal Communicating   Interorganizational Linking
Conferencing   Doubt and Argument Promoting
Group Decision Supporting

Focus on   Focus on
Internal   ———————————————————————————————————— External
Organization   Organizational
                                                           Environmental

STABILITY   PRODUCTIVITY

Internal Monitering   Modelling
Internal Controlling   Forecasting
Record Keeping   Sensitivity Analyzing
Optimizing

Focus on
order
[Adapted from Cooper, 1994]
Figure 1: Organizational Practices Related to Cultural Archetypes.

Cooper's model is summarized in Figure 1. He associated several practices with each of the archetypes. The survival archetypes include such practices as scanning the external environment for project opportunities and inter-organizational linking. The productivity archetype is compatible with applications that facilitate organizational planning, directing and goal setting. Stability archetypes are more likely to emphasize applications which stress measurement and control such as accounting systems, cost-variance reporting, budgeting, and other record keeping applications. Human relations archetypes are compatible with systems which provide interpersonal communication and cooperation such as teleconferencing, electronic mail, and group decision support. Applications associated with this archetype must build or reinforce the social values of its members.

In summary, Cooper suggests that the culture of the IS organization is an important variable in the implementation process and that it is necessary to determine how the proposed new technologies, methods, and procedures conflict with the cultural values and practices of the IS organization. While his model provides useful insight into the role of culture in IS organizations, it fails to take into consideration the influence of national culture.

INFLUENCE OF NATIONAL CULTURE ON INFORMATION SYSTEMS CULTURE

Mapping National Culture on Information Systems Culture

To establish a link between national culture and IS culture, it would be useful to determine the extent to which Hofstede's model of national culture can be mapped onto the competing values model as it is applied to IS culture by Cooper. If successful, the competing values model could be used as the basis for an IS culture framework reflecting national culture. Such a mapping, however, is difficult because there is no direct relationship between Hofstede's dimensions of power distance and uncertainty avoidance and the archetypes of IS organizational culture including stability, productivity, survival, and human relations. To some extent, it could be argued that stability archetypes may be more compatible with organizations in the machine and pyramid quadrants since high uncertainty avoidance might suggest the need to maintain a stable organization. But even organizations in the family quadrant would need to maintain stable organizations in order to protect their "family" structures. Productivity archetypes may be more compatible with organizations in the machine quadrant, since they emphasize the improvement of efficiency and the reduction of uncertainty. Survival archetypes may be more compatible with organizations in the market quadrant, since the willingness to take risks is an important component of this archetype. Finally, human relations archetypes might be more compatible with organizations in the market and family quadrants since formal structures are not emphasized and teamwork is common.

There are at least three problems with this attempt to map culture onto archetypes. First, as suggested by the stability archetype, more than one archetype is likely to exist in each quadrant. Second, the characteristics of each archetype may vary from quadrant to quadrant. For example, in the market quadrant the human relations archetype may emphasize informal structures, widespread participation from end-users, team approaches, and the widespread use of group enhancing technology such as e-mail and decision support systems. But in the family quadrant, human relations may imply strong top-down management emphasizing the maintenance of the corporate family at all costs. The third criticism is that, unlike Hofstede's study, there is no empirical evidence to suggest the feasibility of such a link.

To summarize, national culture can be traced to IS culture, but when Hofstede's national culture model is mapped onto the competing values IS culture model, the results do not suggest a clear association between national culture and organizational archetypes. Rather than use the competing values model, it seems more appropriate to apply Hofstede's work on national and organizational culture directly to IS culture.

Identification of Information Systems Practices

Hofstede's model of national culture (1980), the model of organizational culture suggested by Hofstede et al. (1990), and Coopers model (1994) of IS culture will be used to develop a framework which relates national culture to IS culture. Hofstede's national culture model will be used to establish four quadrants into which IS practices will be placed. These practices, suggested by the work of Hofstede et al. (1990) and Cooper (1994), can then be used to define an 'expected' IS culture for organizations whose geographic location places them in one of these four quadrants. The method chosen here, to identify practices common to organizations in each quadrant, was to survey the global IS research literature for studies which identify specific IS practices, and then place these practices in the appropriate quadrant. The results are summarized in Figure 2.

The *market quadrant* includes cultures which are neither centralized nor formalized. Cooper (1994) obtained his data primarily in the U.S. and his work suggests that organizations in this culture scan the environment for project opportunities. Mouakket, Sillence, and Fretwell-Dowling (1994) found evidence of end-user participation during the development process in the United Kingdom. The use of groups or teams in North America was observed by Wetherbe, Vitalari and Milner (1994). Connectivity and widespread access in the U.S. was reported by Nelson, Weiss and Yamazaki (1992). Wetherbe, Vitalari and Milner (1994) found a reliance on distributed processing in North America, and innovation in the U.S. was suggested by Couger (1990).

The *machine quadrant*, which includes cultures that are not centralized but highly formalized, is compatible with practices more likely to improve existing IS operations rather than innovate or reengineer. This was the conclusion reached by Schwarzer (1995) in a study of German firms. Both Schwarzer (1995) and Ein-Dor and Segev (1992) also suggest the difficult process of balancing distributed and centralized architectures in organizations in Germany and Israel. This struggle can be related to the conflict between low power distance, suggesting the acceptance of distributed architectures, and high uncertainty avoidance, suggesting a preference for centralized data to minimize risks of unauthorized access and fraud.

The *family quadrant* is characterized by a high degree of centralization but low formalization. A study by Sicar and Rao, (1986) suggests IS organizations in Singapore are highly centralized. Limited end-user involvement was found in Hong Kong by Burn et al. (1993). Sicar and Rao (1986) also found limited use of networking and distributed processing in Singapore, with similar conclusions drawn by Goodman and Green (1992) for the Middle East. Lack of equality among team members was found in East Africa by Odedra-Straub (1993). Again these practices are compatible with these cultures which are characterized as highly centralized but not formalized.

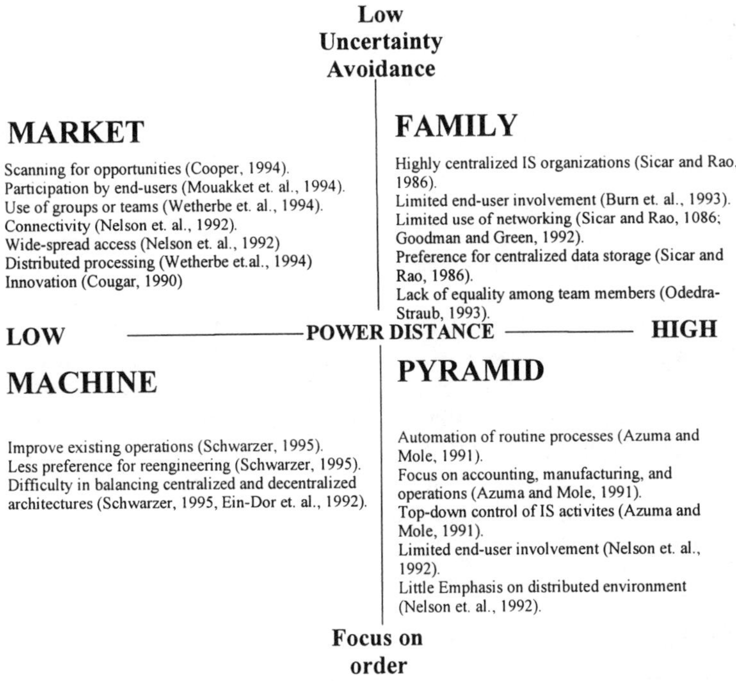

Low
Uncertainty
Avoidance

MARKET

Scanning for opportunities (Cooper, 1994).
Participation by end-users (Mouakket et. al., 1994).
Use of groups or teams (Wetherbe et. al., 1994).
Connectivity (Nelson et. al., 1992).
Wide-spread access (Nelson et. al., 1992)
Distributed processing (Wetherbe et.al., 1994)
Innovation (Cougar, 1990)

FAMILY

Highly centralized IS organizations (Sicar and Rao, 1986).
Limited end-user involvement (Burn et. al., 1993).
Limited use of networking (Sicar and Rao, 1086; Goodman and Green, 1992).
Preference for centralized data storage (Sicar and Rao, 1986).
Lack of equality among team members (Odedra-Straub, 1993).

LOW ————————————POWER DISTANCE———————— HIGH

MACHINE

Improve existing operations (Schwarzer, 1995).
Less preference for reengineering (Schwarzer, 1995).
Difficulty in balancing centralized and decentralized architectures (Schwarzer, 1995, Ein-Dor et. al., 1992).

PYRAMID

Automation of routine processes (Azuma and Mole, 1991).
Focus on accounting, manufacturing, and operations (Azuma and Mole, 1991).
Top-down control of IS activites (Azuma and Mole, 1991).
Limited end-user involvement (Nelson et. al., 1992).
Little Emphasis on distributed environment (Nelson et. al., 1992).

Focus on
order

Figure 2: Practices of IS Organizations Classified into Hofstede Quadrants

The *pyramid quadrant* is characterized by high centralization and high formalization. Azuma and Mole (1991) in the study of Japanese firms found an emphasis on the automation of routine processes in manufacturing, accounting, and operations. They also found an emphasis on top-down control of IS activities. Nelson, Weiss, and Yamazaki (1992), also studying firms in Japan, found limited end-user involvement and a preference for centralized architectures.

In summary, the work of Hofstede et al. and Cooper on national, corporate and IS culture was used to develop a framework expressing the influence of national culture on IS culture. Studies from the literature were used to identify specific practices associated with these cultures. Unfortunately, the number of studies which could be used were limited. Future research will hopefully overcome this shortcoming.

INTERACTION OF HEADQUARTERS AND SUBSIDIARY INFORMATION SYSTEM CULTURES

While national culture has been shown to influence IS culture, other factors, as suggested by Hofstede et al. (1990) also contribute. These other factors may include the competitive environment, business strategy and structure, and portfolio of IS tasks. The competitive environment, even when the same products are sold, may not be perceived in the same way by both organizations. Headquarters may perceive competition as much more intense than its subsidiary, or perhaps the reverse may be true. IS strategy and structure also play an important role in the interaction between the two organizations. Global MNCs, because they are highly centralized and treat the world as one market, may require more compliance from its subsidiaries and therefore have less flexible IS cultures. Multi-domestic MNCs, because they see the world as many markets, may have more flexible IS cultures and may demand less in the way of compliance from its subsidiaries. The portfolio of tasks is also a factor in establishing IS culture. For example, an organization that uses simple record keeping and reporting applications may have developed a very different IS culture than one which uses a broader range of applications from transaction processing to executive support systems. Figure 3 summarizes the way in which these factors influence the development of IS cultures in both the headquarters and host organizations. Meyer (1993) suggests that a cultural gap occurs when behavioral asymmetries exist between international work groups. Accordingly, the term IS culture gap, used in this chapter, will refer to the asymmetries between headquarters and subsidiary IS cultures.

When IS linkages between headquarters and its subsidiary encounter problems, the presence of this gap may be expressed by headquarters IS personnel in indirect ways. They may complain that the foreign subsidiary: is unwilling to take ownership of the application; doesn't understand the importance of the system; is staffed with people who are 'stuck in their ways'; and doesn't see the big picture. IS management at the subsidiary location, on the other hand, may complain that headquarters doesn't understand that their problems are different, and can't see things from their point-of-view.

It is undoubtedly difficult to operationalize the concept of a gap and measure its magnitude. Kedia and Bhagat (1988), addressing this issue, suggest that the greatest problems can be expected when applications are transferred between developed and developing countries. Perhaps it is reasonable to suggest that the IS culture gap may increase as the difference between power distance and uncertainty avoidance scores between headquarters and foreign subsidiaries increase.

Figure 2 can be used to establish an understanding of the IS practices which contribute to this gap. Consider, for example, a multinational company with headquarters in France about to introduce manufacturing control software to one of its subsidiaries in the United States. According to Table 1, France is located in the pyramid quadrant. It is therefore characterized by high power distance and high uncertainty avoidance. The U.S., located in the market quadrant, is associated with low power distance and low uncertainty avoidance. Practices in the pyramid quadrant, summarized in Figure 2, suggest limited acceptance of a distributed environment, top-down control, and limited end-user involvement. Practices in the market quadrant suggest a greater tolerance for

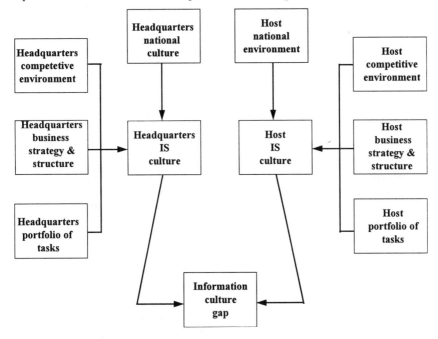

Figure 3: Factors Which Influence Organizational Culture Gap

distributed processing, wide-spread access, and end-user involvement. Consider that the new manufacturing application assumes a centralized subsidiary IS structure, little end-user involvement, and centralized architectures. If the IS culture of the subsidiary organization in the U.S. strongly reflects the values of the market quadrant, several conflicts are likely to arise. Subsidiary users in the U.S. may react negatively to strong top-down management, which may be expressed in the methods and procedures associated with the new application. For example, in high power distance cultures like France, there may be more restrictions on the freedom given end-users to initiate data entry and schedule changes.   Consider also that U.S. participants may expect to take more responsibility for the system, prefer wide access to data, and expect their views on the application to be taken into consideration.   For all of these reasons an IS culture gap can be expected to develop.

Attempts may be made to resolve the conflicts associated with this gap. Headquarters may try to influence and change the culture by transferring headquarters personnel to the subsidiary location or by training managers and end-users, or they may choose to ignore the gap and hope that the subsidiary organization will eventually adjust to the demands imposed by the application. Perhaps the subsidiary organization may even make changes in its own culture in an effort to close the gap.   Because, as Hofstede contends, culture changes slowly, the gap may close slowly, if at all.   Furthermore, the efforts to close this gap will succeed or fail to the extent that core values are respected and left intact. When core values of power distance, uncertainty avoidance, individualism-collectivism, and masculinity-femininity are threatened, conflict between headquarters and the subsidiary may be extremely difficult to resolve.

IMPLICATIONS FOR MANAGEMENT

Several implications can be drawn from this framework and are summarized in Table 2. National culture affects IS culture and IS practices in organizations. An IS group in a British organization, for example, can be expected to be influenced by British culture, while an IS group in France can be expected to be influenced by French culture. Culture can be measured by many dimensions.   Two of these dimensions, which appear related to organization culture, include power distance and uncertainty avoidance. Accordingly, IS practices in the British group may be influenced by the low power distance of the British culture while IS practices in the French group may be influenced by high power distance associated with French culture.

When national culture, IS culture and IS practices at the headquarters operation differ from the culture and practices at the subsidiary operation, an IS gap is likely to occur. The wider the gap, the more difficult it may be to establish effective linkages between these organizations. IS gaps, however, are easy to neglect. It is easier to blame problems on: technical issues, inadequacy of telecommunications systems, unsatisfactory end-user training, uncooperative subsidiary organizations, and the absence of persons at the foreign subsidiary who might 'champion' the IS application.

Management must avoid the temptation to place too much emphasis on technical problems or even 'unsophisticated' end-users. They must address cultural issues directly by raising culturally sensitive questions early in the planning process. "How might the subsidiary culture, which is high in power distance, react to the introduction of a manufacturing system that requires end-user involvement." If the headquarters operation is in a low power distance culture, then end-user involvement, demanded of the subsidiary may be a difficult request to make.

Answers to these and other culturally sensitive questions must be studied carefully, and the conclusions used to develop a cultural/technical strategy for improving the chances of a successful IS linkage. In most cases this plan must acknowledge that culture changes slowly. Incremental change rather than abrupt change may have a higher likelihood of success.

There can be many benefits associated with a carefully crafted cultural/technical plan. By focusing on these differences and developing strategies to resolve them, headquarters management has the opportunity to: limit conflict, decrease implementation time, reduce costs, improve transfer success, and minimize disappointing results.

1. National culture can exert a strong influence over IS culture and IS practices in organizations.

2. Power distance and the avoidance of risk-taking are dimensions of national culture which can be expected to influence these practices.

3. When national culture, IS culture, and IS practices at the headquarters operation differ from the culture and practices at the subsidiary organization, an IS gap occurs, and the establishment of effective IS linkages can become difficult.

4. IS gaps are easy to neglect. It is easier to blame problems on: technical issues, local infrastructure problems, uncooperative host organizations, and the absence of persons at the foreign subsidiary who might 'champion' the IS application.

5. Headquarters must raise culturally sensitive questions with the intent of exploring this potential source of conflict. They must ask how cultural dimensions such as power distance and uncertainty avoidance might affect practices such as end-user involvement, distributed data architectures, networks, users access to data, and teams.

6. Answers to these and other culturally targeted questions must be carefully studied and the temptation to focus solely on the technical issues avoided.

7. The insight gained from these answers must be used to develop a cultural/technical IS strategy for establishing or improving IS linkages.

8. IS culture changes slowly. The strategic plan must take this fact into consideration.

9. There can be many benefits to a cultural/technical IS plan: conflict can be reduced; Implementation will almost certainly be faster; IS costs may be lower; transfer success rates will increase; and the effective use of the system can be expected to improve.

Table 2: Implications for Management

CONCLUSIONS

The purpose of this chapter has been to link the role of national culture to the IS culture of headquarters and subsidiary IS organizations. While there has been work done on national culture and organization culture, the influence of national culture on headquarters and subsidiary IS cultures has been ignored. Given the explosive growth in global business, it seems appropriate to add this dimension to the evolving theory of global information systems.

To provide a more concrete framework in which to study the influence of national culture on headquarters and subsidiary IS cultures, this chapter has suggested that the identification of IS practices associated with organizations in a specific culture embodies the values and beliefs of that national culture. Furthermore by grouping these practices into one of four Hofstede quadrants it then becomes possible to predict the nature of the IS culture gap that may be expected, when national cultures are crossed.

While the quadrants into which these practices were grouped were limited to two cultural dimensions, including power distance and uncertainty avoidance, the goal was to keep the conceptual framework as simple as possible, but at the same time robust enough to provide insight. This is primarily a framework which suggests general directions. There will always be examples of headquarters/subsidiary interactions which extend across cultures but experience few problems, and there will be examples of failed alliances within the same national culture. However, the object of the conceptual framework developed here is not to accommodate the full range of possible outcomes but to: provide insight; promote consideration of culture early in the management process; anticipate conflict; and improve the likelihood of a successful headquarters/subsidiary alliance.

References

Azuma, M. & Mole, D. (July 1994). Software Management Practices and Metrics in the European Community and Japan: Some Results of a Survey. Journal of Systems Software, 26(1), 5-18.

Babington, E.A. (1987). Installing a Computerized Planning System in Ghana. Long Range Planning, 20(4), 110-117.

Bartlett, C.A. & Ghoshal, S. (1989). Managing Across Borders: The Transnational Solution. Boston, MA: Harvard Business School Press.

Burn, J., Saxena, K.B.C., Ma, L. & Cheung, H.K. (Fall 1993). Critical Issues of IS Management in Hong Kong: A Cultural Comparison. Journal of Global Information Management, 1(4), 28-37.

Cheung, H.K. & Burn, J.M. (Summer 1994). Distributing Global Information Systems Resources in Multinational Companies-A Contingency Model. Journal of Global Information Management, 2(3), 14-27.

Cooper, R.B. (1994). The Inertial Impact of Culture on IT Implementation. Information and Management, 27, 17-31.

Couger, D.J. (1990). Ensuring Creative Approaches in Information Systems Design. Managerial and Decision Economics, 11.

Couger, D.J., Adelsberger, H., Borovits, I., Zviran, M. & Motiwalla, J. (1990). Commonalties in Motivating Environments for Programmer/Analysts in Austria, Israel, Singapore, and the USA. Information and Management, 18, 41-46.

Dagwell, R. & Weber, R. (November 1983). System Designers' User Models: A Comparative Study and Methodological Critique. Communications of the ACM, 26 (11), 987-997.

Davenport, T.H., Eccles, R.G. & Prusak, L. (Fall, 1992). Information Politics. Sloan Management Review, 53-65.

Deal, T.E. & Kennedy, A.A. (1982). Corporate Cultures. Reading, MA: Addison-Wesley.

Ein-Dor, P., Segev, E. & Orgad, M. (Winter 1993). The Effect of National Culture on IS: Implications for International Information Systems. Journal of Global Information Management, 1(1), 33-44.

Ein-Dor, P. & Segev, E. (January 1992). End User Computing: A Cross Cultural Study. International Information Systems, 1(1), 124-137.

Erez, M. & Earley, P.C. (1993). Culture, Self-identity, and Work. New York: Oxford University Press.

Goodman, S.E. & Green, J.D. (August 1992). Computing in the Middle East. Communications of the ACM, 35(8), 21-25.

Hassan, S. (Fall 1994). Environmental Constraints in Utilizing Information Technologies in Pakistan. Journal of Global Information Management, 2(4), 30-39.

Hofstede, G. (Summer 1980). Motivation, Leadership, and Organization: Do American Theories Apply Abroad? Organizational Dynamics.

Hofstede, G. (1981). Culture and Organizations. International Studies of Management and Organizations, X(4), 15-41.

Hofstede, G., Neuijen, B., Ohayv, D. & Sanders, G. (1990). Measuring Organizational Cultures: A Qualitative and Quantitative Study Across Twenty Cases. Administrative Science Quarterly, 35, 286-316.

Hofstede, G. (1991). Culture and Organizations: Software of the Mind. London: McGraw-Hill.

Ives, B. & Jarvenpaa, S.L. (March 1991). Applications of Global Information Technology: Key Issues for Management. IS Quarterly, 33-49.

Kedia, B.L. & Bhagat, R.S. (1988). Cultural Constraints on Transfer of Technology Across Nations: Implications for Research in International and Comparative Management. Academy of Management Review, 13(4), 559-571.

Kluckhohn, C. & Strodtbeck, F. (1961). Variations in Value Orientations. Westport, CT: Greenwood Press.

Kumar, K. & Bjorn-Anderson, N. (May 1990). A Cross-Cultural Comparison of IS Designer Values. Communications of the ACM, 33(5), 528-538.

Lachman, R. (1983). Modernity Change of Core and Peripheral Values of Factory Workers. Human Relations, 36, 563-80.

McClelland, D.C. (1961). The Achieving Society. Princeton, NJ: Van Nostrand.

Meyer, Heinz-Dieter. (1993). The Cultural Gap in Long-term International Work Groups: A German-American Case Study. European Management Journal. 11,1, 93-101.

Mouakket, S., Sillence, J.A.A. & Fretwell-Dowling, F.A. (April 1994). Information Requirements Determination in the Software Industry: A Case Study. European Journal of Information Systems, 3(2), 101-111.

Nelson, R.R., Weiss, I.R. & Yamazaki, K. (October 1992). Information Resource Management within Multinational Corporations. International Information Systems, 1(4), 56-83.

Odedra-Straub, M. (Summer 1993). Critical Factors Affecting Success of CBIS: Cases from Africa. Journal of Global Information Management, 1(3), 16-31.

Parsons, T. & Shils, E.A. (1951). Toward a General Theory of Action. Cambridge, MA: Harvard University Press.

Quinn, R.E & Rohrbaugh, J. (1983). A Spatial Model of Effectiveness Criteria: Towards a Competing Values Approach to Organizational Analysis. Management Science, 29(3), 363-377.

Roche, E.M. (1992). Managing Information Technology in Multinational Corporations. New York: Macmillan.

Rokeach, M. (1973). The Nature of Human Values. New York: Free Press.

Schein, E.H. (1985). Organizational Culture and Leadership. Jossey-Bass, San Francisco.

Schwarzer, B. (Winter 1995). Organizing Global IS Management to Meet Competitive Challenges Experiences from the Pharmaceutical Industry. Journal of Global Information Management, 3(1), 5-16.

Shore, B. & Venkatachalam, V. (1995). The Role of National Culture in Systems Analysis and Design. Journal of Global Information Management. 3,3.

Sicar, S. & Rao, K.V. (1986). Information Resource Management in Singapore: The State of the Art. Information and Management, 11, 181-187.

Smircich, L. (1982). Concepts of Culture and Organizational Analysis. Administrative Science Quarterly, (28), 339-358.

Triandis, H.C. (1995). Culture: Theoretical and Methodological Issues. in M.D. Dunnette and L. Hough, Eds., Handbook of Industrial and Organizational Psychology, 2nd ed., Vol. 4, Consulting Psychologists Press, Palo Alto, CA.

Wetherbe, J.C., Vitalari, N.P. & Milner, A. (Spring 1994). Key Trends in Systems Development in Europe and North America. Journal of Global Information Management, 2(2), 5-20.

10 Challenges in International Data Transfer

Effy Oz
Wayne State University, USA

Free flow of information is one of the corner stones of free trade and economic growth. Communication networks now connect millions of commercial organizations throughout the world. Ostensibly, the networks could contribute immensely to the welfare of businesses, but there still exist technical, language, legal and other barriers that prevent genuinely free flow of data and information across borders. The chapter reviews the different types of hurdles. In particular, we elaborate on the one gap that is seemingly hardest to bridge: different views on protection of privacy. Strict laws in European countries forbid U.S. businesses to tap private data. This prevents free flow of information within multinational corporations and hinders marketing efforts of organizations that wish to target their products and services to selective consumers in foreign countries. The chapter reviews cross-border data transfer laws of different countries and the international effort to harmonize legislation.

INTRODUCTION

The availability of telecommunication networks is vital to the world's economy. Networks cover almost every country on planet earth. CSNET consists of some 200 host computers providing service to government and private research institutions in the U.S., Canada, Australia, France, Germany, Israel, Japan, Korea, Sweden and England. SWIFT (Society for Worldwide Interbank Financial Telecommunications) and CHIPS (Clearing House for Interbank Payments System) are operated by banks and credit institutions. Airline reservation systems service airlines worldwide. EURONET, in the European Economic Community, serves European countries and is connected through gateways to US and Canadian networks. TRANSAC (France), ACSNET (Australia), IPSS/PSS (England), NORDIC (Scandinavia), Junet (Japan), and VNIIPAS (the formerly Soviet Union) are connected through gateways to form one huge meganetwork (Madsen, 1989). Bitnet, the academic network, connects thousands of universities around the world. Soon, the meganetwork will expand to millions of users in the People's Republic of China. INTERNET has grown from an American network to a global network whose size no one knows, but it is considered the largest network. It is estimated over 20 million computers access the network parts of which are quickly being transformed to commercial use in addition to its original scientific and other non-commercial utilization.

Technically, the world's business community can collect, maintain, and transfer data as if there were no national borders. Technically, but not legally. In an age when information is so important for the development of new markets, many countries restrict the free flow of information between their territory and other countries.

Some countries forbid the transfer of classified data to other countries. They rationalize that information is wealth as is cash and tangible assets. Information has the power to give one country a political and technological advantage over another and, as a result, transfer of data threaten a nation's security. It is legitimate for a government to prohibit foreign access to research and development data, financial information, and other information that may jeopardise economic, political, or cultural interests, or even compromise the nation's sovereignty.

Economists, however, agree that one of the most important conditions for the world's economic growth is the free flow of information. Also, the restrictions on data transfer interfere with the smooth running of multinational companies. The number of these companies is growing. For these companies, restrictions on international data flow amount to not less than a restriction of data transfer from one department to another.

What are the issues left to be resolved? Fortunately, the standardization issues have been largely resolved. For example, ISO's model protocol OSI has been accepted by North-American and West-european nations as the model of choice, and the Asynchronous Transfer Mode (ATM) is now agreed upon as the standard for Integrated Services Data Networks (ISDN). Seemingly, there are still several hurdles on the route to inclusive and free transborder data flow (TDF).

THE HURDLES

As shown in Table 1, there are several types of problems that must be resolved. Some are technical in nature, e.g., connectivity and security. The rest have to do with cultural, political, and economic interests. It is those areas where the greater difficulties lie.

Connectivity

Connectivity to Internet, let alone to other networks, is still not available in several countries in Africa (e.g., Zaire and Sudan). Only four countries have full Internet connectivity. The rest either have e-mail access only, or no access at all. On the Asian continent, Syria, Iraq, Iran, Mongolia, Mianmar (formerly, Burma), Vietnam and North-Korea have no access at all. To the dismay of many MNCs, many of the technical difficulties are the result of arbitrary legislation, as explained later.

Connectivity	Several countries in Africa and Asia
Security	MNCs and trade partners
Language	Blocks: North-America, Europe, Australia and South Africa; Russia, Bulgaria, an Greece; Arab World; Asian Countries
Political and Economi Constraints	Various countries
Legal Issues • Technical • Privacy	Constraints on use of hardware and software North-America vs. Western Europe

Table 1: Transborder Data Flow Issues

Security

Security of the data transferred and access control is still weak. Standard techniques for network security such as the data encryption standards have been found inadequate for international networks, and many companies are using proprietary techniques for network security (Saraswat and Gorgone, 1993).

Language

Language is predominantly a problem of writing, i.e., the letters used. While in the Americas and most of the European continent the Latin alphabet is used, the situation is different in other parts of the world: Cyrillic, Chinese, Japanese, Arabic and other writing systems pose a difficulty in communicating data from the source. It is relatively easy to exchange data between parties that use Latin letters and Arabic numerals. However, data from sources in non-Latin-based scripts must be translated into Latin letters. Quantities transmitted from Arab countries must be translated into Arabic numerals (as ironic as this may sound).

Political and Economic Constraints

Political and economic constraints of some kind still exist in various countries. A survey of seventy-three U.S. companies with global computer networks revealed that almost 70% encountered some kind of politically imposed constraint that affected their ability to manage the network and to transfer data across international borders. The most common constraint involved requirements to use foreign telephone networks (Steinbart and Ravinder, 1992). Many of the legal constraints are actually the legislative means to protect the political independence and economic interests of some nations.

Legal

Legal problems include all the laws and regulations that nation states have passed which prohibit effective use of hardware, software, and data in telecommunications in general, and in international communications in particular. Quite a few countries have passed laws that force businesses to use only domestically manufactured hardware. Predominant among the countries is Brazil. This country also forbids businesses to use software developed by foreign companies, unless the prospective user establishes that no equivalent local software exists (Ewer, 1992). Consequently, hardware and software incompatibilities hamper transborder data flows between different organizational units of MNCs.

Both in south America and Europe, telecommunications is strictly regulated. In many countries, there is a single service provider, and, usually, that provider is a government agency (e.g., the postal service), or a commercial organizations enjoying a monopolistic status on behalf of the government. The provider charges exorbitant fees (reaching four times the American fee) and dictates the technical opportunities.

In addition to the economic and security issues, barriers to transborder data transfer are predominantly the result of the nations' different approaches to the issue of privacy. The purpose of this chapter is to review the current status of cross-border data transfer laws, the impact of the laws on international business, and the effort of international organizations to harmonize the laws and reach an international agreement.

LITERATURE REVIEW

Crossborder data transfer has been predominantly the concern of the legal and business communities. As the technical issues have been resolved, recent literature addresses other, non-technical issues. Authors expressed several concerns of governments: economic changes and shifts in balance of payment, preservation of sovereignty, undesirable political influence, cultural imperialism, compromise of national security, and privacy. To some extent, there exist also the problem of language. All, or some of these concerns are discussed in virtually every book and article on transborder data transfer (Basche, 1983; Butler, 1983; Chandran, Phatak, and Sambharaya, 1987; Coombe, 1983; Deans and Kane, 1992; Greguras, 1980; Oz, 1994; Sauvant, 1984; Tsanacas, 1985).

In one survey (Ewer, 1992), fifty-nine U.S.-based MNCs reported their difficulties in TDF with the local governments. They listed difficulties in the following areas.

Restrictions on Data Transferred

These restrictions include:
• Regulations that protect personal privacy

- Restrictions on the flow of non-personal data
- Monitoring of data transmission content
- Regulations that allow unusual access (by the government) to sensitive corporate information

Restrictions on Hardware, Software, and Telecommunications

Some of theses restrictions are:
- Requirements for use of locally produced hardware and software
- Import controls on hardware and software
- Excessive tariffs on data communication hardware
- Discriminatory rates on and access to public telecommunication networks
- Inconsistent technical standards
- Requirements to process data within the country
- Restrictions on leased line interconnections

Restrictions on Installation and Maintenance

Main restrictions under this category are:
- Unusual administrative delays in obtaining required government approvals in data communications endeavors
- Restrictions on business visas for vendors of choice to service data communications hardware

The respondents were asked to mention which type of "difficulty" they have encountered, where "difficulty" meant inability to receive service, unexpected delays, or restrictions imposed on resources that would otherwise be available to the company. Ranking the countries by frequency of citing the various difficulties, Table 2 provides a list of countries in descending order of difficulties faced with respect of TDF.

While many of the problems have been resolved through negotiation and mutual agreement sponsored by the United Nations and other international organization, one still remains unresolved: privacy (Oz, 1994). If the U.S. and Europe agree on the issue of privacy, they will form such a large economic and political block (in terms of TDF) that the rest of the world will have to comply with their principles. Thus, it is so important to understand the privacy problem and find ways to resolve it. (Interestingly, despite the importance we attach to privacy, the value is not even mentioned in the constitutions of the US and many other countries. Yet, a majority of the democratic nations try to protect privacy.)

National governments have different approaches to the issue, as is reflected in their laws. Some are willing to forego some privacy for the sake of freer flow of information and better marketing. Others restrict any collection of private data without the consent of the individual. Recent literature on transborder data transfer is intertwined with discussion of privacy (Deans and

Kane, 1992; Oz, 1994; Tsanacas, 1990; Weinrich, 1990). The following discussion focuses on the main barrier to international flow of information: the disharmony of privacy protection laws.

Rank	Country/Region	Rank	Country/Region	Rank	Country/Region
1	Brazil	6	Taiwan	11	Japan
2	Germany	7	Central Americal	12	Switzerland
3	Mexico	8	Argentina	13	Spain
4	France	9	India	14	Canada
5	United Kingdom	10	Italy	15	Australia

Source: Adpated from Ewer, 1992
Table 2: Ranking of Contries by TDF Difficulty

Although much of the literature deals with TDF as an issue for Multinational Companies (MNCs) (e.g., Sambharya and Phata, 1990; StŸck and Schroeder, 1994), from a stand-point of the world economy, this is an issue for the entire business community. Indeed, for a MNC, TDF is tantamount to transferring data from one department to another, and therefore they face a more immediate challenge than uni-national corporations, but the difficulties prevent more effective international cooperation among businesses in general.

LAWS GOVERNING DATA PRIVACY AND TRANSBORDER DATA TRANSFER

To a large extent, laws governing cross-border data transfer stem from a nation's approach to the privacy of its citizens and organizations. Over thirty nations have data privacy laws, and many more are considering either regulations or national legislation. Austria, Denmark, France, Germany, Norway, and Sweden enacted their laws in the 1970s. Luxemburg, England, and Holland joined in the 1980s. On other continents, Canada and New Zealand enacted privacy statutes. Almost all of the West European countries have laws that protect private data. Data protection laws may be classified according to three criteria:

(1)   the sector whose data bases are protected: only the private sector, or both the private and public sectors;

(2)   the manner of storage of data protected: only automated (read: computerized), or both automated and manual storage;

(3)   the legal entity that is protected: only natural persons, or both natural and legal persons, i.e. organizations.

Except for the American and Canadian acts, the laws apply to both the public and private sectors, i.e. both government and private organizations are subject to the same regulations of collection, maintenance, and disclosure of personal data. Over half the laws (including the US federal statute) encompass manual as well as computerized record-keeping systems. A minority of the laws apply to legal persons.

Countries that favor protection of data on legal persons argue that it is difficult to separate data on individuals from data regarding the business activities that are performed by the individuals. This is especially so with respect to small businesses. For example, the financial information of a small business also reflects information about the person, or a small group of people, who run the business. Also, a large corporation may unfairly compete against a smaller firm if it has access to the smaller firm's data (Deans and Kane, 1992). Denmark, Austria, and Luxemburg are among the countries that protect the privacy of legal persons' data.

Comparison of Privacy Laws in U.S.A and Europe

Privacy legislation in the US has taken place predominantly at the federal level. The US Congress passed a series of laws in the 1970s and 1980s to tighten the rules of collection, maintenance, and dissemination of personal data: Fair Credit Reporting Act of 1970, Privacy Act of 1974, Right to Financial Privacy Act of 1978, Privacy Protection Act of 1980, Electronic Funds Transfer Act of 1980, Debt Collection Act of 1982. The laws require federal agencies to inform individuals the purpose of soliciting their data, how they will be used, and to whom they may be transferred. Individuals have the right to peruse their records which are held by federal agencies.

Further more, under the Freedom of Information Act of 1966, citizens have access to many types of information maintained by the federal government even if the information does not relate to them, personally. In this respect, the law is more progressive than those of other countries. The US Congress truly tries to follow the motto "let the government know as little as possible about the people's affairs; let the people know as much as possible about the government's affairs."

The picture is completely different with respect to the private sector. In the name of free enterprise and competition, private organizations are restricted only in their handling of health and financial data. And even in this area, the protection of individual records is quite limited. For example, credit bureaus tap private accounts in banks and other credit agencies daily (Oz, 1994).

In Europe, sensitivity to privacy issues seems to be greater than in the US. European privacy laws restrict collection and maintenance of data on individuals more than their American counterparts. There is also a different approach to enforcing these laws. American governments settle for signing bills into laws. The citizen is then expected to take his or her case to court and prosecute it according to the appropriate federal or state law. For example, the federal Privacy Act of 1974 leaves it to the offended individual to privately bring his or her civil case to court. In contrast, European governments established supervisory boards to ensure adherence. For example, the British government established an agency called the Data Protection Registrar. Individuals who feel their privacy has been violated can file a complaint with the Registrar who then can take action against the violator, based on the Data Protection Act of 1984. The Dutch, too, have a Data Protection Registrar. The Registrar heads the Data Registration Chamber, a government body supervising the observance of Holland's Data Protection Act of 1989.

Another salient difference between the US and Europe concerns entities that privacy laws regulate. In the US, privacy laws regulate mainly governments, and, to a lesser extent, financial institutions. In many European countries, the same law restricts both governments and private enterprises without distinction. The European approach has been to pass sweeping laws rather than to target specific sectors. In the private sector, the statutes are not limited to credit and medical data.

There is also a different approach to the scope of protection with respect to foreign nationals. Among the countries that have established data privacy laws, only the US and Canada exclude foreign data subjects from the scope of their protection (Greguras, 1980).

French and Swedish Privacy Laws

Unlike in the US, in Europe the collection and maintenance of personal data by the private sector is a highly sensitive issue. In European Community countries such activity is restricted. The French Data Processing, Data Files, and Individual Liberties Act demonstrates these principles (Coombe and Kirk, 1983). It provides:

1. Personal data, i.e. information about an identified or identifiable individual, deserve special protection and should not be stored in an automatic manner (e.g. in a computer) without the data subject's   consent.
2. Personal data may be collected only for lawful purposes. Data   subjects should be advised about the nature of data collected, the consequences of a failure to supply it, and the intended recipients of the data.
3. A data subject should be able to determine whether an automatic processing system contains information about that subject and, if it does, to gain access to the data and correct inaccuracies.
4. A private enterprise or a public authority processing personal data in an automatic manner must declare the details of the   information system to the National Data Processing and Freedom Commission, the regulatory authority created by the Act. The Commission will make the particulars of the system public.
5. Personal data should not be disclosed to unauthorized third parties.

6. The Commission is authorized to subject transborder data flow to prior authorization in order to ensure adherence to the Act's underlying principles.

The Act provides protection of personal data which reveal racial origin, political, philosophical, and religious opinions, union membership, and criminal convictions. The National Data Processing and Liberties Commission was established to ensure that automatic processing is carried out in accordance with the law. The French law also requires that any corporation or individual who intends to use a computer for storage and processing of personal data declare their intention to the Commission. The corporation, or individual, must pledge that the processing meets the legal standards. For example, inadequate security controls is a criminal offense on the operator's part. The operator's application for permission to use the automated system must specify:

1. the party making the application and the party empowered to make decisions regarding the processing or, if such party resides abroad, its representative in France;
2. the characteristics, purpose, and type of the processing;
3. the department(s) that will do the processing;
4. the department through which the individual's right of access is exercised and the steps taken to facilitate exercise of that right;
5. the categories of people who, on account of their duties or for the needs of the department, have direct access to the data recorded;
6. the types of data processed, the sources thereof, and the time during which it will be stored, as well as the recipient of the data, or the categories of recipients authorized to receive such data;
7. the linkages, interconnections, or other methods of correlating such data, as well as transfer of the data to third parties;
8. whether the processing is destined for dispatch of data between France and another country.

The Commission maintains information sufficient for any person to make inquiries about data kept in the system. The law affords similar, but not equal, protection to individuals and organizations on whom data are stored. Individuals may object to inclusion of personal data concerning them in a data bank, unless the law designates such recording in the public interest.

The Law severely restricts the use of computer programs for decision making when in connection with personal data: "No governmental or private decision may be based on automatic processing of data which describes the profile of personality of the person concerned." This, for example, would prohibit a bank from using a decision support system in deciding whether to extend a loan to an individual.

Sweden, too, established a supervisory body for data protection. The Data Act of 1973 established the Data Inspection Board. All private and public organizations must register their databases and are not allowed to send, or transmit, out of the country certain types of data regarding private citizens.

The French and Swedish laws are quite restrictive. In other countries, e.g. Germany, England, and Holland, the law leaves a measure of private self-regulation to the operators of automated data processing systems. For example, the German Federal Data Protection Act requires every private organization employing at least five people and using automated data processing to appoint a data controller. The data controller ensures compliance with the Act. This officer, who reports directly to the chief executive officer of the corporation, must take the following actions:

1) maintain (a) a description of stored personal data, (b) a record of the reasons for their use, (c) a list of regular recipients of the data, and (d) a description of the data   processing system;
2) ensure that data processing software is used properly;
3) inform the employees who are involved in data processing of the requirements of the Act and related regulations; and
4) assist and advise in the selection of employees assigned to processing of personal data.

Due to potential conflicts with management, data controllers are assured immunity against adverse actions that management may take against them because of the performance of their duties. Data controllers, therefore, enjoy a semi-autonomous status.

The German Federal Data Protection Act mandates the following principles:

1) Individuals have to be notified when identifiable data concerning them are stored in the organization's automated system. Personal data may be tored only upon the individual's consent in writing (or otherwise because of special circumstances).
2) Personal data may be stored only if such storage serves the purpose of a contractual relationship of trust with the subject. If this condition is not met, the corporation may store data on a person only if such act does not harm the person's data protection interests, and if it is done to safeguard the legitimate interests of the organization.
3) Disclosure of personal data to a third party must serve a contractual relationship of trust between the organization and the subject, and is necessary to safeguard the legitimate interests of the organization, the third party, or the public.
4) Individuals have the right to scrutinize data that a corporation maintains on them, challenge the relevance and accuracy of the data, and demand corrections of erroneous records.
5) Transborder transmission of personal data is permitted only upon the subject's consent.

Comparison of Different European Privacy Laws

Unlike the French law, which restricts collection of personal data, the German law starts the protection upon storage of the data. Seven of the 12 European Community (EC) countries have laws that restrict the flow of individual data. The harshest exist in some German federal states. Generally, the data protection laws forbid organizations to pass on data without the consent of the individual. Table 3 summarizes the main foreign personal data protection legislation.

As is evident, the nations have enacted laws that are not fully compatible. Each law reflects the nation's political and economic interest, and its legal system. TDF restrictions will depend on the laws of origin and destination countries as depicted in Figure 1. The laws differ with respect to data covered by the regulations, type of processing system, categories of confidentiality, enforcement mechanisms, and restrictions on crossborder transfers. Usually, an origin country allows transborder data transfers when the destination country has a compatible law. However, countries have different approaches to transborder data flows. For example, Germany allows transborder transmission of personal data if the subjects consent. French law leaves the decision to its National Data Processing and Freedom Commission. The commission may prohibit transborder flow, but the French law does not specifically grant the option of consent to the data subject. This allows the Commission to restrict transborder data flow on the basis of national, not personal, interests. Sweden does not allow census, payroll, or personnel data to be transmitted to the US because these types of data are not protected under US law as they are in Sweden.

Figure 1: Destination countries with less restrictive data protection laws than those of the origin country are barred from receiving personal data

ATTEMPTS TO HARMONIZE THE LAWS

These conditions hinder development of international trade, and especially hurt MNCs. Therefore, international organizations try to harmonize the laws. The EC has considered a uniform law that will prohibit the transfer of personal data without the individual's knowledge and agreement. There are two problematic points in the draft. One is how to treat countries that are not signatories to the Council of Europe agreement on data protection, especially with respect to international use of credit cards. The other stems from an article in the draft that states: "An individual shall not be subject to an administrative or

	Austria	Canada	Denmark Public	Denmark Private	France	Germany	Iceland	Israel	Luxembourg	Norway	Sweden	UK
cope of application												
Central Government	Y	Y	Y	N	Y	Y	Y	Y	Y	Y	Y	Y
Province/States	Y	N	Y	N'	Ya	Y	Y	Y	Y	Y	Y	Y
Private sector	Y	N	N	Y	Y	Y	Y	Y	Y	Y	Y	Y
Covers all info traceable to identifiable individuals	Y	Y	Y	Y	Y	Ya	Nb	N	Y	Y	Y	Y
Information collected and /or processed using computers	Y	Y	Y	Y	Y	Y	Y	Y	Y	Y	Y	Y
Limits placed on personal data collection	Y	Y	Yc	Y	Y	Yd	Y	Y	Y	Y	Y	Y
Personal information must be collected for specified legitimate purpose	Y	Y	Y	Y	Y	Y	Y	Y	Y	Y	Y	Y
Individuals have right of access to inspect personal information	Y	Y	Y	Y	Y	Ya	Y	Y	Y	Y	Y	Y
Sensitive personal details specified (collection only with data subject's knowledge and consent)	N	N	Y	Y	Y	N	Y	N	Y	Y	Y	Y

KEY: Y=Yes, N=No

a Covers information concerning private affairs, such as financial situation of individuals
b Covers information on an individuals personal status intimate affairs, economic position, and vocational qualifications
c Collection of personal data limited unless it is " natural part of the normal operations of an enterprise"
d Personal information collection is permissable if it serves the purpose of a contractual relationship or there is a legitamate interest in (a business) storing it
e State laws may be enacted that for personal data maintained by the public sector

Source: Pipe, R. Westin, A.F., "Employee Monitoring in Other Industrialized Democracies," report prepared for Office of Technology Assessment; Oz, E., Ethics for the Information Age. Wm.C. Brown, Dubuque, IA 1994.

Table: Main Provisions of Foreign Data Protection Laws

private decision involving an assessment of conduct which has, as its sole basis, the automatic processing of personal data defining his profile or personality." This provision, which is stipulated in the French law, renders the use of a computer as a decision aid illegal. No automated decisions as to credit, admittance to a college, and the like would be permitted.

The Organization for Economic Cooperation and Development (OECD), an international body, has drawn guidelines for handling personal information. The guidelines are:

1) an organization should have the consent of an individual to use information about the individual;
2) the organization should collect only relevant, accurate and timely data, related to the purpose for which they are to be used;
3) the organization should identify to the individual the purposes for data collection;
4) re-use of data for new purposes should be restricted if the data subject does not give consent, or if other legal authority is not given;
5) reasonable safeguards should be kept;
6) the organization should disclose practices with respect to the collection, storage and use of personal data;
7) individuals should have the right to access information about themselves
8) the organization should be held accountable for compliance with data protection measures.

The OECD guidelines have been adopted by EC countries and the federal government of Canada. The Canadian government called on private industries to voluntarily follow them (Campbell, 1987). Adoption of the principles by other countries may ease the legal transborder flow of data, which is so important for the world's economy.

Similarly, the United Nations outlined eleven guidelines as a minimum to be incorporated into national legislation (Deans and Kane, 1992):

1) *Lawfulness and fairness.* Data has to be collected and processed in a legal and fair manner, without violating the Charter of the United Nations.
2) *Accuracy.* Whoever collects data is obliged to ensure its accuracy, relevance, and timeliness.
3) *Purpose specification.* The purpose of holding the data should be made known to the data subject before it is created. The data should be approved by the subject, and not be held beyond the period of time in which it fulfills the purpose.
4) *Interested person access.* Data subjects have the right to inspect data about them. The cost is to be borne by the entity maintaining the data.
5) *Nondiscrimination.* Information about race, ethnic origin, sex life, political opinion, union or association membership, or religious or other beliefs should not be compiled except as provided in Principle 6.

6) *Power to make exceptions.* Exceptions are provided only in the case of national security, public order, or public health, as provided in the nation's internal law. However, the exceptions shall not violate the International Bill of Rights.

7) *Security.* The entity maintaining the data must protect it against natural dangers, accidental loss or destruction, and unauthorized access.

8) *Supervision and penalties.* Every national law must designate the authority responsible for supervising and enforcing these principles.

9) *Transborder data flows.* The free flow of data should not be restricted unless there are no reciprocal safeguards provided by each country's legislation.

10) Field of application. The principles apply to both private and public data, which is maintained both in manual or automated form, and which applies to both natural and legal persons.

11) *Application of the guidelines to personal data kept by governmental international organizations.* The principles apply to personal data kept by international governmental organizations with adjustment made for the differences between internal staff data and external third party data.

These principles may be classified under the three major actions: collection, maintenance, and use of data:

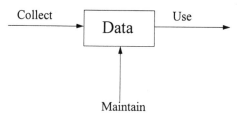

Figure 2: Stages in Data Collection and Use

Collect: From individuals and from other organizations;
                    For an identifiable purpose and only for that purpose;
                    For a set period of time;
                    With the subject's consent;

Use: For the declared purpose;
                    With the subject's consent;

Maintain: For the set period of time;
                    With permission to the subject to scrutinize and correct;
                    With ample security and with access only on a "need to know" basis.

Currently, there is no international agreement on these principles.

REMAINING OBSTACLES

In recent years, European Community countries made great strides toward agreement on these issues. Economic interests and the drive to create what some call "The United States of Europe" force these nations to reach an agreement. Also, to a certain extent, they all share an approach that favors protection of individual data. The difference relates to the extent of the protection, the inclusion of organizations in the protection, and means of enforcement.

In 1992, the Council of Europe considered a proposal that would harmonize the laws of the member nations. This would be good for Europe, but not necessarily for its trade partners, because the proposal states that individual member states should not permit data to flow to a country which does not provide adequate data protection for privacy (Boehmer and Palmer, 1993). While the Data Protection Directive is expected to resolve inter-European differences, the gap between the European approach and the American attitude toward personal data is unlikely to guarantee an agreement between the two blocks on data transfer. American businesses emphatically claim that it is their right to collect individual data and use it in their operations.

Consumer and civil rights advocates have voiced their objection to this view. Some even suggested the Federal Government adopt the concept of a data protection agency as practiced in Europe. This would require the registration of every computer database containing private data with the Government, an idea that corporate America would fiercely resist. Also, despite the occasional protest against junk-mail and telemarketing, there has not been significant popular pressure on legislators to restrict the private sector in its collection and dissemination of personal data. While the Europeans are closing the gaps among their own laws, they are determined to not allow the sharing of personal data with countries that do not comply with their own principles, whereby hurting American and Canadian corporations.

A similar situation exists in Canada and Mexico. With the implementation of the North American Free Trade Agreement (NAFTA), we will see two economic blocks that cannot share personal data. In fact, corporations in some European countries are not prohibited from using North American personal data, while they are not allowed to share theirs with organizations in North America. This gives them a significant advantage.

In most of Asia, Africa, and South America, there are no laws that restrict transborder transfer of data. (Some west-African countries passed laws restricting transborder flow of information, but their political and economic position renders the laws unenforceable.) However, computerization in these parts of the world lags behind, and does not allow efficient and effective collection of individual data by private organizations. Almost all of the recorded private data are in government data bases. The governments of these countries are unlikely to release personal data for use by foreign corporations.

The obstacles described here limit several types of activities that are vital for expansion of international trade. The most important of these activities are presented in Table 4.

Use of personal data for target marketing
Use of employee data to improve human resource management in MNCs and international hiring
On-line crossborder examination of credit-worthiness
Business EDI (Electronic Data Interchange)
Consolidation of financial and accounting information of MNCs

Table 4: Activities Facing Difficulties

Target marketing is fast becoming a favorite method in which organizations market their products and services. Sorted records allow companies to concentrate their effort only on those organizations and individuals that are likely to purchase what the companies have to offer. In the U.S., targeted marketing has been proven to be a very efficient and effective approach.

MNCs shuffle personnel, especially executives, among facilities in different countries. Computerized human resource systems are used to select the best candidates for a position in another country. The maintenance and manipulation of a consolidated human resource database is limited or impossible under the laws of many countries.

It is difficult for financial institutions to evaluate the credit-worthiness of organizations and individuals from countries that limit transborder data transfer because is is against the law to transfer the parameters used by the institutions to grant credit. This is particularly so when financial institutions wish to grant unsolicited credit, e.g., in the form of credit cards.

At least 50% of U.S. companies already use some kind of EDI. The practice is also spreading in Europe. However, crossborder EDI is quite limited due to restrictions imposed by data privacy laws.

MNCs must submit consolidated financial reports. The task would be significantly easier if data privacy and other restrictive laws where relaxed.

CONCLUSION

Although great strides have been made to open the lines for freer flow of data across national borders, there are still technical and legal issues that cause difficulties. While the resolution of the technical issues is mainly a matter of financial investment, the legal issues are anchored in cultural differences among the nations regarding the protection of their citizensÕ privacy. Protection of data privacy has a great impact on international trade. Unless an international agreement is reached, we may witness restrictions on international data flow which may have grave consequences for international trade. Currently, the main loser of this situation is corporate America, who cannot tap data banks in the huge European market.

It has been claimed that crossborder transfer of individual data constitute less than two percent of all international data transfer, and, therefore, the problem may not be so severe. However, we must look at the potential volume of such activity had the laws been relaxed. Of course, American companies do not tap databases containing personal and small organization data in Scandinavia, Germany, and France. They are not allowed to. If they only could, undoubtedly, they would use these resources.

It is difficult to speculate on future developments. We may expect two blocks in terms of international transfer of private data. On one hand, we will have the North American block, possibly joined by South American countries. This block will follow the U.S. approach to private data: free use and crossborder transfer. On the other hand we will se the European Union, possibly joined by East European countries, who subscribe to restrictive use and transfer of private records. It is impossible to say what approach Asian and African countries will take.

References

Basche, J., "Information protectionism," *Across the Board*, Vol 20, 1983, pp. 38-44.

Boehmer, R.G., and Palmer, T.S., ÒThe 1992 EC Data Protection Proposal: An Examination of its Implications for U.S. Business and U.S. Privacy Law,Ó *American Business Law Journal*,   Vol 31 Iss 2, September 1993, pp. 265-311.

Buss, M.D.J., "Legislative threat to transborder data flow," *Harvard Business Review*, Vol 62 No 3, 1984, pp. 111-118.

Butler, P.F., "Countries move to control foreign, domestic data flow," *Business Insurance*, November 14, 1983, pp. 49, 52.

Campbell, G., "New awareness of privacy issues coming: CIPS," *Computing Canada*, Vol 13, No 11, May 28, 1987, p. 1.

Chandran, R., Phatak, A., Sambharya, R., "Transborder data flows: Implications for multinational Corporations", *Business Horizons*, Vol 30 No 6, 1987, pp. 74-82.

Coombe, G..W., Jr., Kirk, S.L., "Privacy, data protection, and transborder data flow: a corporate response to international expectations," *The Business Lawyer*, Vol 39, November 1983, pp. 33-66.

Deans, P.C. and Kane, M.J., *International Dimensions of Information Systems and Technology*, PWS-Kent, 1992, pp. 86-87.

Ewer, S.R., ÒWhose Borders Are Barriers to financial Data Communications?" *Financial & Accounting Systems*, Vol 7 No 4, Winter 1992, pp. 5-10.

Sambharya, R.B. and Phata, A., "The Effect of Transborder Data Flow Restrictions on American Multinational Corporations," *Management International Review*, 30(3), 1990, pp. 267-290.

Greguras, F.M., "Computer networks and data protection law," *Computer Law Journal*, Vol. 2, Fall 1980, pp. 903-907.

Madsen,. C.W., "The World Meganetwork and Terrorism," *in Computer Security in the Age of Information*, W.J. Caelli (ed.), Elsevier Science Publishers B.V. (North-Holland), 1989, p. 345.

Oz, E., *Ethics for the Information Age*, Wm.C. Brown Publishers, Dubuque, Iowa, 1994.

Oz, E., "Barriers to International Data Transfer." *Journal of Global Information Management*, Vol 2 No 2, Spring 1994, pp. 22-29.

Saraswat, S.P., and Gorgone, J.T., "The Issues and Policy Implications of Transborder Data Flow on Multinational Corporations,"*Information Strategy: The Executive Journal*, Vol 9 Iss 2, Winter 1993, pp. 48-53.

Sauvant, K.P., "The growing dependence on transborder data flows," *Computerworld*, Vol 18, June 25, 1990, pp. ID19-ID24.

Steinbart, P.J., and Ravinder, N., "Problems and Issues in the management of International Data Communications Networks: The Experience of American Companies," *MIS Quarterly*, Vol 16 Iss 1, March 1992, pp. 55-76.

Stuck, J.M, and Schroeder, D.L., "Transborder Data Flows by U.S. Subsidiaries in Mexico and Hispanic South America: A Preliminary Regional Study," *Journal of International Business Studies*, 2nd Quarter, 1994, pp. 389-401.

Tsanacas, D., "The transborder data flow in the new world information order: Privacy or control," *Review of Social Economy*, Vol 43 No 3, pp. 357-370.

Weinrich, H., "Europe 1992: What the future may hold," *The Academy of Management Executive*, Vol 4 No 2, pp.7-18.

11 Communication Cost Economics: A Framework and its Application to Electronic Commerce in the European Union

Paul Alpar and Ulrich Hasenkamp[1]

Institute für Wirtschaftsinformatik

Philipps-Universität Marburg, Germany

In this chapter we develop a framework for the economic analysis of communication links that can support electronic commerce. First, we report some aspects of the state of telecommunication services and electronic commerce in the European Union. Then, we develop the theoretical framework. This framework is then applied to the analysis of two types of electronic commerce as they are conducted in Germany: electronic data interchange, as an example of business-to-business commerce, and electronic shopping, as a business-to-consumer commerce.

INTRODUCTION

Electronic commerce includes any action over electronic media that is related to an economic transaction. Thus, we consider an electronic inquiry about a product feature to be as much electronic commerce as a purchase order or an invoice delivery. However, not all forms of electronic commerce are discussed here but only commerce over networks where everyone (who pays) can participate. For example, commerce over a leased line between two subsidiaries of a firm or electronic funds transfer between banks over well-established specialized networks like SWIFT are not considered. In terms of technology, telefax and telex are not discussed although they are currently intensively used and certainly useful. Besides some of their technical limitations, the main reason for omitting them is that they use paper as an output medium and thus interrupt automated application to application data exchange or interactive use. Much of what is analyzed here is sometimes discussed under the term "electronic market place." We prefer the term electronic commerce as the broader term since there are many (potentially) electronic commercial transactions that do not take place under market conditions (e.g., electronic data interchange (EDI) between a firm and customs authorities).

Telecommunication is the infrastructure for electronic commerce. In the European Union (EU) it is still highly regulated and dominated by state-owned companies. These companies are slowly being privatized and forced to give up their monopolies but in most telecommunication segments there is still less competition than in the USA. Consequently, a smaller variety of services is offered and businesses and private households often pay higher prices for them. This situation has led to the continued existence of highly subsidized services, like Videotex[2].

This chapter concentrates on the situation in the Federal Republic of Germany (FRG), the most populous and economically powerful player in the EU. Developments in the FRG will strongly influence developments in other European countries since it is in almost all cases their largest trading partner. Of course, the developments in other large EU countries will be of similar importance, namely in France, the United Kingdom, and Italy. This does not mean that the smaller countries are slower to adopt new technologies. In the Netherlands, for example, there are more Videotex users per household than in the FRG (Hansen 1994). However, the telecommunication companies from larger countries, allied with each other and/or telecommunication firms from the USA, are predestined to become major players in the European telecommunications market.

CURRENT STATE OF TELECOMMUNICATIONS USE AND SERVICES

Two trading partners can electronically exchange:

a) information related to an economic transaction (e.g., price inquiry, product specification, delivery details, or a payment reminder),
b) the good (e.g., a software program) or service (e.g., remote computer diagnosis or information retrieval results) itself, or
c) the corresponding payment.

For a communication to be able to get from one partner to the other, several hardware and software components are necessary: a software application that can support electronic commerce, a communication protocol, and a physical network. A protocol is a set of rules for carrying out a communication process. Some of the protocols are standardized by official institutions, others are proprietary products developed by computer manufacturers, industry associations or other private organizations. Proprietary protocols are gradually superseded by standardized versions, namely those based on the ISO-OSI model or based on TCP/IP. We refer to a combination of the three components as a communication link. Factors not critical in making communication (link) decisions are omitted. For example, we leave out the particular computer operating system since relevant application and communication software is available for all common operating systems. There are still many options as to how to configure a communication link for electronic commerce. Thus, making the economically right decision is a difficult task. Figure 1 indicates some of the complexity of the task. It shows the currently available networks in Germany and the most common protocols and applications. Lines that connect the components indicate some of the combinations currently used.

Abbreviations:

CCITT	Comité Consultatif International Télégraphique et Téléphonique
Datex	Data Exchange (Public Digital Network)
EDI	Electronic Data Interchange
GEIS	General Electric Information Services
IBM	International Business Machines Network
ISDN	Integrated Services Digital Network
ISO	International Organization for Standardization
LAN	Local Area Network
MAN	Metropolitan Area Network
OSI	Open System Interconnection
TCP/IP	Transmission Control Protocol / Internetwork Protocol

Most of the physical networks shown on the top of Figure 1 are operated by German Telekom, a former branch of the post authority that has been privatized recently. Using their lines, other companies offer private networks, most of them with some added value. The IBM and GEIS nets are by far the most important such value added networks (VANs) for commercial applications. The near future will bring competition also in the field of physical networks as other carriers – mainly the utility and railroad companies – will extend their so far only internally used networks to become public physical networks. The last monopoly is scheduled to disappear in January 1998 when the barriers for competitive terrestrial voice communication will fall. The German part of the Internet is mainly run by the DFN-Verein, a science foundation. However, commercial and non-educational not-for-profit Internet service providers (ISP) are increasing their share of users and traffic volume.

The user of a specific service, e.g. e-mail, makes use of (1) software representing the service, (2) a protocol that is understood by his local software as well as by his partner's system, and (3) a network which is either a basic physical network or a VAN. The figure also shows that EDI, for example, as a service dedicated to electronic commerce is not tied to a specific set of protocol and network, but can be run on a variety of combinations that are not limited to the examples shown. The existence of gateways among the networks significantly increases available options for configuring communication links. For example, a Videotex user sending an e-mail message to a partner on Internet may partly unknowingly use the analog phone network, ISDN, the packet-switched network and a number of other physical networks on which Internet is

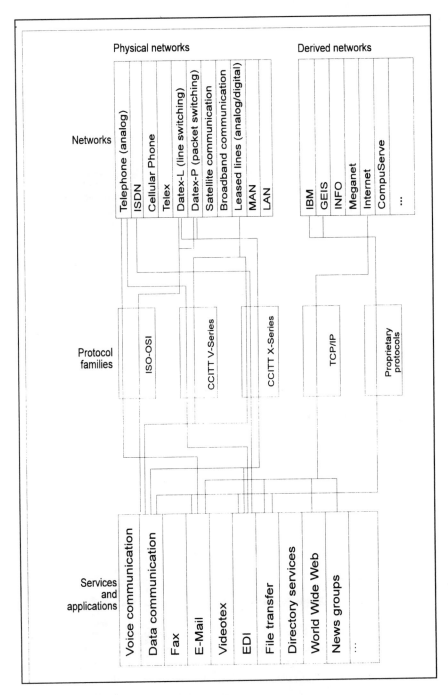

Figure 1: Networks, protocols, and application

run depending on the friend's location and access to Internet and the location of gateways. Communication options are also increased due to the possibility of embedding applications in other applications (e.g., file transfers can be embedded in e-mail).

The same communication links exist in other EU countries and the USA too; the main differences are in the volume of usage of different options. Exact figures for the usage of complete communication links do not exist but there are figures relating to specific network components and applications (see Table 1).

Country	Videotex subscribers (000)[3]	Internet hosts (000)[4]	Value of EDI-based business as a % of GNP[5]
Austria	19.6	20.1	
Belgium	11.0	12.1	1.4
Denmark	7.0	12.1	
Finland	100.0	49.6	
France	6,900.0	71,9	1.1
Germany	556.2	149.2	0.4
Greece	2.0	2.9	
Ireland	4.0	3.3	0.6
Italy	360.0	23.6	
Luxembourg		0.4	
Netherlands	340.0	59.7	2.3
Portugal	7.0	4.5	
Spain	500.0	21.1	0.4
Sweden	40.0	53.3	1.4
U.K.	67.0	155.7	2.3
Total EU	8,913.8	639.5	1.0
U.S.A.	5,555.0[6]	2,044.7	

Table 1: Electronic Commerce Indicators

Some of the figures in Table 1 are based on rough estimates (e.g., value of EDI-based business) but even the "objective" figures are questionable.[7] Once such figures are determined the next question is how to compare them for different countries. They can be related, for example, to the Gross National Product (Arnum 1994) or the number of households (Hansen 1994) to account for different sizes of countries in terms of economy or people.

Small businesses play an increasingly important role in the FRG. While big business is shrinking its labor force to become lean, the number of people employed in small businesses is increasing. Small businesses in the FRG are often export-oriented. Electronic commerce has great potential to support their operation and growth. In a survey of businesses under 500 employees, with 231 responding firms, fully 9.5% were already using EDI in late 1993[8]. It is likely that just the number of small businesses using EDI is greater than the total number of EDI users as estimated by some experts (the estimate for the FRG is 2,500 firms, Electronic Trader 1995).

Even if the real figures of EDI use may be higher than assumed by some observers, still only relatively few businesses already practice EDI (except in some specific industry branches). The adoption of EDI has been characterized as disappointing by its proponents (Sarson 1994, Steel 1994) given that UN/EDIFACT, as an example, has been adopted by ISO in 1987. That development was based on more than ten years of experience with other EDI standards like the British TRADACOM. In contrast to that, the adoption of Internet-based services has surely been explosive, even if the exact figures are hard to collect. However, so far little of its tremendously increased usage is towards commerce (Marion 1995). Many reasons for both developments have been offered. A theoretical framework may help to better structure and assess these reasons.

THEORETICAL FRAMEWORK

Companies wishing to conduct electronic commerce face the problem of choosing the right communication link. This is a challenge because of the many possible configurations (see Figure 1) and the often complicated price schemes for use of services provided by national telecommunication companies or private suppliers. Therefore, some theory to guide the decision-making process can be quite helpful.

One perspective useful for understanding the choice of telecommunication linkages is transaction cost economics (TCE). It was developed (Coase 1937, Williamson 1981) to explain why companies choose a certain governance mechanism, i.e., organize their activities in a certain way. Malone and coworkers have used TCE to explain the emergence of electronic markets (Malone et al. 1987 and Malone et al. 1989). They hypothesized that the growing use of information and telecommunication technology will lead to more electronic markets. Newer literature (Hess and Kemerer 1994, Webster 1995) indicates this hypothesis may need to be revised. One explanation for slow emergence of some types of electronic markets may be the lack of some non-technological preconditions (Reimers 1995). These could be membership rules that prevent free-riding and create trust (e.g., prevent market members from making unserious bids).

The **choice of a communication link** is different from the choice of a governance mechanism for the business function in need of the communication.

On one hand, these choices can be considered independent of each other. Let us assume that a firm wants to issue most of its purchase orders using EDI. The choices of a medium for EDI and the EDI format need to be made whether the purchasing function is retained in the firm or outsourced. On the other hand, communication costs of various governance options can vary significantly and thus influence the governance decision. TCE is of interest in our context because the characteristics that drive the governance decision also drive the decision for a communication link. These characteristics applied to communication are: the operating costs, expected communication frequency over the link, uncertainties related to the communication link, and the specificity of assets needed for the establishment and operation of the communication link.

Communication Frequency is relevant since the costs of setting up an electronic communication link for rare communications probably cannot be recuperated. For example, setting up an EDI relationship with a supplier from whom we buy once a year, probably will not pay off.

Uncertainty related to a communication link can result from a lack of reliability of the communication infrastructure, from potential intrusions by unauthorized parties, or from unfair behavior by authorized parties (e.g., a partner could claim not to have received a communication if an automatic receipt acknowledgment cannot be given). The higher the uncertainty the less likely the communication will be carried out electronically if costs of communication failure are high. If the costs of failure are low uncertainty has a low impact. For example, if a request for proposals for a commodity product is posted to an electronic news group on Internet, it is of little concern if some subscribers of the news group do not receive it in due time or not at all.

Specificity of Assets in a communication link depends on the level of standardization of the link's components. Standardization does not stand here necessarily for a formally accepted standard but for some technology or business practices that have been adopted by many organizations. The lower the specificity the more likely it is the assets can be used for various communications with various partners. This leads to lower average communication costs. Another advantage of lower communication link specificity is lower vulnerability to opportunistic behavior by communication partners or infrastructure providers. For example, if a supplier sets up an expensive communication link that is tuned to communication with his largest customer his dependency on that customer increases. The automotive industry delivers "real-life" examples for such a development (Webster 1995).

The relationship between a communication and a transaction, defined as an exchange of a good or service, is such that communications are a subset of a transaction. A transaction includes all exchange activities: search for a supplier, closing of a contract, delivery of a good or service, and corresponding payment. These are the main phases; in some cases a more refined structuring of the exchange is needed and loops may occur (e.g., product specifications may be changed and renegotiations conducted). When we shift our view from a single communication to a communication link the question arises which parts of a business transaction can be covered by that link. Thus, the characteristic of **transaction coverage** needs to be added to the characteristics derived from TCE. We refer to this framework as communication cost economics (CCE).

One could explicitly name other characteristics of communication links but most of them can be subsumed under the ones already mentioned. For example, integration capability of an application and the whole communication link with other applications is certainly important but this issue actually needs to be considered under the topic of asset specificity. Clearly, a solution that cannot be integrated (with acceptable efforts) with other applications represents an investment with high asset specificity. The possibilities of global electronic commerce are of special interest and we therefore extend the "core" CCE framework by the characteristic of a communication link to be **suitable for global commerce**, i.e., commerce across country borders and continents. Table 2 summarizes the extended CCE framework.

operating costs
communication frequency
uncertainty
specificity of assets
transaction coverage
suitability for global commerce

Table 2 : Variables That Determine Communication Cost Economics

The analysis of alternative communication links will be split into two parts based on the link's possible primary use: for business-to-business commerce or for business-to-consumer commerce. The main distinctions between these types of commerce are the frequency of communication (which is considered to be relatively low between two particular partners in the latter case) and the relative anonymity[9] of at least the consumer in the latter case. This does not mean that businesses never trade with occasional partners. In that case simply the business-to-consumer scenario applies.

BUSINESS-TO-BUSINESS COMMERCE

EDI is the most important form of business-to-business electronic commerce. Other examples of business-to-business commerce are exchange of unstructured information via e-mail or on-line applications. For example, BMW, the German car manufacturer, lets BMW dealers access parts databases via Videotex using the closed user group option (meaning that other Videotex users cannot access this information).

EDI is increasingly done on the basis of UN/EDIFACT, but the biggest share is still performed using other protocols. Besides historical reasons it is claimed that industry-specific standards for EDI are more economical.

While older industry-specific formats have no relation to the UN/EDIFACT standard, there is now a tendency to define industry-specific standards as "subsets" of UN/EDIFACT. This means the messages resemble the "official" ones, but cannot be processed by standard EDIFACT converters. The rationale behind the definition of subsets is to minimize the overhead, e.g. omit segments of the official message type that do no apply to the given industry. The drawback is the necessity for a firm to install multiple converters if it wants to communicate with partners outside its specific industry. The advocates of UN/EDIFACT point out that not one company communicates only within their own industry, but all have business relations with many different partners. This calls for a universal industry-independent protocol. Based on this state of affairs, we analyze one option with an EDI format based on negotiations between two partners (this option is referred to henceforth as "tailored" EDI), as one extreme, and all other options with a broad standard like UN/EDIFACT. Industry-specific standards lie between these two extremes.

We chose for further analysis communication links that are currently most prevalent ones plus one with great future potential (Internet). For communication links that use networks of the German Telekom (telephone, Datex-P, and ISDN) the use of the X.400 protocol is assumed. The proprietary VANs usually use their own protocols (e.g., SNA on IBM networks). On the Internet EDI messages can be embedded in e-mail which is transported with the Simple Mail Transfer Protocol (SMTP).

One may expect that determining operating costs is easy since these are tangible costs. However, both the private and state-owned providers of telecommunication services have complicated price schemes that make comparison shopping difficult. In addition, customized pricing is provided for large international customers. Therefore, we calculated monthly operating costs on the basis of two scenarios: one with a low monthly volume (LV) of EDI messages (a message to five partners per working day) and one with a high monthly volume (HV) of messages (100 partners per day). In both cases we assume that the average message length is 2,000 Bytes which approximately corresponds to an EDIFACT message. We assume that the message is sent further than 100km away (but within FRG) and a line speed of 9600 baud for telephone and Datex-P. ISDN speed is 64000 baud.

For communication links that use networks of the German Telekom (telephone, Datex-P, and ISDN) we also assume the use of the service called Telebox400. This service implements the X.400 protocol and, since recently, transmission set splitting. The latter means that messages for five partners, for example, can be sent in one message and that the Telebox400 will split and send them to the correct partner. For the Internet option the costs are based on access through an ISP. Service intialization costs are not considered in any case since they should be negligible in the long run. Communication frequency is omitted from explicit consideration since it is less a characteristic of a communication link than of the actual needs of a user (firm). However, it is included in the calculation of operating costs as discussed above. To be concrete and concise we show the prices in Germany in DM. In 1994 the average exchange rate was DM 1.62 for one US $.

Set-up costs are not considered since they strongly depend on the individual firm and are partly driven by the explicitly discussed communication characteristics of our framework. Costs of DM 18,900 for the implementation of an EDIFACT capability are given in the literature (Miebach and Schneider 1994). This figure contains software and labor costs but no hardware costs. The set-up costs for EDI tailored to the specific needs of two partners and a few transaction types are lower than for the EDIFACT capability. This cost relationship is reversed when new partners or new message types are added. The reversal is especially pronounced when adding new partners. For each new partner new negotiations about the exchange format and other work are necessary. In terms of our framework: the lower asset specificity of standardized EDI gives it relatively quickly advantage over tailored EDI.

We did not further analyze the use of the line-switching network (Datex-L) or leased lines as these options are too expensive in the general case. They are only of interest if other uses in addition to EDI exist. Videotex as a vehicle for EDI was excluded because of its current inflexibility. Table 3 shows our evaluation of the analyzed communication links. The reasoning for our evaluations follows: The asset specificity of standardized EDI is medium because there is not one generally accepted standard but many different "standards" are in use. Tailored EDI exhibits, of course, high asset specificity. Uncertainty of analog telephone lines is medium because of noise and they are relatively easy to tap. On Internet uncertainty is even higher because information travelling on it can be systematically attacked at many points on its way. To make it safe for commercial use one needs to use encryption which for some users seems to be too much of a burden as long as it does not happen automatically. Actually, encryption should be used for sensitive communication on any network since all networks are vulnerable to attacks.

Standardized EDI via telephone and X.400
Specificity   medium
Uncertaintymedium
Coverage   limited search, no shipping, mainly order and pay
Global   yes, at additional costs (e.g. FRG to USA DM 0.53 per 2KB)
Operating costs   LV   90   HV   368

Standardized EDI via packet-switching (Datex-P) and X.400
Specificity medium
Uncertaintylow
Coverage   limited search, no shipping, mainly order and pay
Global   yes, at additional costs (see above)
Operating costs   LV   533   HV   936

Standardized EDI via ISDN and X.400
Specificity medium
Uncertaintylow
Coverage   limited search, no shipping, mainly order and pay
Global   yes, at additional costs (see above)
Operating costs   LV   122   HV   349

Standardized EDI via proprietary VAN (and ISDN to VAN)
Specificity medium
Uncertaintylow
Coverage   limited search, no shipping, mainly order and pay
Global   yes, at additional costs
Operating costs   LV   564   HV   2190

Standardized EDI via Internet (e.g., e-mail and SMTP)
Specificity medium
Uncertaintycurrently high, unless extra efforts
Coverage   full coverage in combination with other Internet services
                     (e.g., search via World-Wide-Web, shipping via File Transfer
                     Protocol)
Global   yes, at no or additional costs (depends on the ISP)
Operating costs   LV   60   HV   360

Tailored EDI via any of the above network and protocol combinations
Specificity   high
Uncertaintyas above depending on the chosen network
Coverage   as above depending on the chosen network
Global   yes, costs depend on the chosen network
Operating costs: higher than the corresponding option above because no
                     transmission splitting possible

Table 3: Business-to-business Communication Links[10]

Based on the analysis, the best communication link for communication with several partners, even for low volumes, seems to be standardized EDI via ISDN and Telebox400. A survey says though that the majority of users in the FRG communicate via proprietary VANs (Electronic Trader 1995). There are several reasons for this seemingly uneconomic behavior. First, the improvement of the Telekom's Telebox400 service, making it basically a VAN, and agressive marketing of ISDN are so recent that they could not have had an impact on the decisions of the surveyed firms. Second, the same survey suggests that the network provider was often chosen because other partners or competitors were already using it. Third, the proprietary VAN providers still offer services not available from the Telekom (e.g., consulting in the set-up phase). Fourth, since the survey probably mainly includes larger firms the global support capability of proprietary VANs carries more weight. Unlike in the USA, we are not aware of any use of Internet for EDI in Germany so far. We have included the option because we believe that it will be a very interesting option, especially for global business, once the currently considered standards for EDI via e-mail are accepted and the security issues are resolved. Thus, we believe our framework will correctly predict the real behavior by firms once all the options are working and known to users.

In general, our framework can be used by a decision-maker to assess his specific needs in terms of the attributes of the framework and to try to match his needs with the most suitable communication link(s). The decision-makers need to determine the communication assets specificity and communication uncertainty they can tolerate, the transaction coverage and global support needed, and the available budget. This profile needs to be compared with the characteristics of available communication link options. For example, if a user considers certain data not sensitive, the uncertainty of Internet does not need to bother him. Or, if the user buys or sells products or services that cannot be distributed electronically, the capability of Internet to support distribution is of no help to her.

The exact measurement or evaluation of most of the variables of the framework is almost impossible which makes the matching process between the communication needs and the communication links difficult. Therefore, the Analytic Hierarchy Process (Saaty, 1980) or a similar procedure for multiobjective problems could be used. The decision makers could, for example, determine the most appropriate communication link through pairwise comparisons of the links along the criteria of the framework.

BUSINESS-TO-CONSUMER COMMERCE

In this section, we focus on the process of electronic shopping. Other electronic commerce could be, for example, customer support or product delivery. Four basic alternative approaches to electronic selling are of interest: Videotex, cable TV, on-line services like CompuServe, and Internet. Interactive cable TV is just entering its experimental stage with users in Germany. There is no reliable information to predict its acceptance, costs, and other important characteristics relating to this alternative. It is also not known whether cable TV operators will offer Internet access or other data services. Therefore, we do not consider this option further. On-line services do not yet play a significant role in Europe. While some of them do have a significant number of subscribers (CompuServe has 100,000 subscribers in Germany) most of their shopping offerings are tuned to the North American market. Thus, this option is also disregarded from detailed analysis. New on-line services are planned for Europe (Microsoft, Europe Online and a European version of America Online) and they certainly will change the market place. However, their planned services are not yet known well enough to make reliable predictions about their impact.

Shopping on Internet can take several forms. For example, someone can offer a product by posting a sales ad to the appropriate (business oriented) news group. Then, a consumer could buy the product or place a bid with an e-mail message. From the several options to conduct commerce on Internet we will analyze shopping via the World Wide Web (WWW). Thus, two alternatives are currently and in the near future important in the EU: Videotex and Internet. Table 1 shows that in many countries the number of Internet users (given the number of hosts) must be higher than the number of Videotex users. In some countries, like France, the number of Videotex users is still higher than the number of Internet users. In all countries, the volume of commerce via Videotex must be much higher than via Internet, given the currently few European sellers on Internet. On one hand, the number of suppliers on the Internet is growing. On the other hand, especially in the FRG, Videotex service is being enhanced. Thus, the race is open.

The monthly operating costs are split here into costs of a business (seller) and costs of a consumer (buyer). The consumer cost for Internet given in Table 4 is the currently lowest full access flat price. The consumer price scheme for Videotex use is a bit complicated. The cost in the table is calculated based on following assumptions: one hour usage during peak time (Mo-Fr, 8a.m-6p.m.), three hours off-peak, and about DM 18 for charged services (e.g., information look-up, search in out-of-region computers, receipt of e-mail from Internet). In both cases we assume that the consumer uses a PC with a modem and dials in via an analog telephone line using a local phone number at a certain baud rate. Therefore, the phone call costs are about the same (for comparable services) and omitted.

For sellers a number of options exist in both cases and price schemes vary a lot. This is especially true for Internet. Options exist from everything done in-house to everything outsourced. Prices may depend, for example, on volume transmitted, volume stored at an ISP, or distance the information travelled. The high and volume-sensitive prices may actually slow down the proliferation of WWW-technology, especially the use of non-textual information. The calculation of seller costs can be quite strange, e.g., if a consumer's ISP uses a different network than the seller's ISP. Depending on where the gateway between the networks is located, the seller could be charged an international distance fee even if the consumer, seller, and the points of presence of their ISPs are all in the same city. Further, some ISPs charge a percentage fee for sales consumated through them. Thus, we give here an exact price for Videotex and just compare the costs of Internet to this price. For Videotex, we assume that the seller uses the German Telekom's computer for the storage of pages and that the pages are callable nation-wide. Like in the former section, we give prices in Germany as a concrete example and, again, in DM.

Table 4 shows our characterization of communications links for electronic shopping. We leave frequency out since it is not a characteristic of a communication link itself. Determination of frequency of commercial communications by consumers is difficult in any case. When a person visits several electronic news groups on Internet some of which are recreational and some of which are commercial in nature how should this be counted? How should browsing the WWW be counted when a person enters several shops in an electronic mall at different detail levels (check home page only, check product offerings, check price of specific products)? If we only count actual purchases as commercial transactions we omit a significant portion of total transaction costs, the search costs. We assume the CEPT protocol for Videotex since the new multimedia-capable protocol, KIT, developed in the FRG, is currently used by only a very few sellers. However, it should be noted that in the long run CEPT has no chance of survival since its graphic capabilities do not match the quality achievable in WWW. CEPT is even less capable of effectively supporting sounds or virtual reality applications.

Shopping via Videotex, CEPT, and Datex-P and/or ISDN

Specificity	high
Uncertainty	medium
Coverage	everything
Global	no
Consumer costs:	40
Seller costs:	720

Shopping via WWW, Hyper Text Transfer Protocol, and Internet

Specificity	medium
Uncertainty	high as long as encryption is not built-in in browsers
Coverage	everything with a help of other Internet services
Global	yes, perhaps at additional costs for sellers
Consumer costs:	35
Seller costs:	two or more times as much as Videotex

Table 4: Business-to-consumer Communication Links

We consider the specificity of Videotex from the seller's point of view to be high because he has no alternative to Telekom if he is not happy with the service provided. A switch to a private on-line service would require considerable reprogramming. In the case of Internet, a seller could change the

ISP without need for any software modification (even the seller's Internet address could remain the same if it was a virtual one). It should be noted that the issue of support of global business would be judged somewhat differently if the analyzed Videotex service were the French one. That service is available in several countries and therefore capable of international commerce support (Cats-Baril and Jelassi, 1994). However, its international spread is in no comparison to Internet, both in terms of countries serviced and in terms of users per country (except for France as its home).

In addition to the attributes of our framework, currently the important question for consumers is what items or services are they mainly looking for. Some catalog merchandisers and many banks are found on Videotex; small retailers, high-tech suppliers, bookstores and especially out-of-country sellers are found on Internet. The situation will change when sellers create presence on the network where they are not present yet and when full Internet connectivity from Videotex is implemented (announced for Fall 1995). Then, the question for consumers will be whether the Videotex services not available on Internet are worth the price of using Videotex as the on-ramp for Internet (since using Internet via Videotex will automatically incur usage time and special service fees). For consumers who often shop electronically Internet seems to be cheaper than Videotex. It certainly offers access to more suppliers (world-wide) though some important services (like local banking) are missing in most locations. For global suppliers or suppliers who want to geographically increase their reach to consumers Internet is the only option. A current advantage of Videotex for national business is its control and billing for information provision by the Telekom. Credible "middle-men" of that rank are still to emerge on Internet.

CONCLUSIONS

In both segments, business-to-business and business-to-consumer, there is considerable activity going on in the EU. While much of this activity comes as catching up to developments in the USA, there are also important developments originating in Europe. WWW is such an example; although it was originally mainly designed for collaborative work, it is turning up to be a major driver for Internet and its commercial use. In Videotex use EU seems to have a lead over the USA but the future shape of this service is not clear. On one hand there will be more competition from private on-line services (and Internet). On the other hand, when the European telecommunication companies become more privately than state-owned Videotex will probably not be supported where it does not pay for itself. The usage of EDI seems to grow constantly in the EU and the USA, even if at slower speed than hoped for by many. New developments, e.g., EDI via Internet or interactive EDI (synchronous EDI-based communication between applications) and new areas of use (e.g., education and health-care) should further boost the growth of EDI use.

As we have shown, there are numerous choices for setting up electronic commerce links between trading partners. Our CCE framework can help to analyze these options in a particular context. The advantage of such a framework is that it is independent of particular technologies and current service providers. It will remain applicable when current methodologies are modified, new methodologies arrive, or new telecommunication service providers enter the market.

Endnotes

[1] The authors wish to thank Holger Rohde for effective research assistance and Ed Roche for helpful comments on an earlier draft of the chapter

[2] Videotex is an interactive service which, through appropriate access by standardized procedures, allows users of Videotex terminals to communicate with databases via telecommunication networks (ITU-CCITT 1984). Originally the terminals were TV sets supported by a decoder and a telephone which provided access to the analog telephone network as the transportation facility. Dedicated devices instead of the TV set and the decoder are also used. Today, in the FRG, a PC equipped with a modem is the terminal of choice. In France, dedicated devices, called Minitel, are still in wide use. The "standardized procedures" used in Europe are referred to as CEPT, named after the organization that established the standard (Conférence Européenne des Administrations des Postes et des Télécommunications). The content of the databases is perceived by the user to be organized as a hierarchy of pages. He navigates through this hierarchy mainly by specifiying page numbers. However, interaction through forms is also possible so the user can shop or bank using Videotex.

[3] (Hansen 1994);he calls them users but there are often more usersper one subscription(e.g., in the FRG there are 1.5 users per one private subscriber)

[4] M. Lotter's figures as reported in (Arnum 1994)

[5] forecasted for 1997 by Dean (1995)

[6] refers to subscribers of on-line services like Compuserve

[7] For example, the number of Internet hosts can be deduced from the network numbers assigned by InterNIC, it can be extrapolated from a survey, or it can be calculated based on the number of "reachable" hosts (M. Lottor, see above). Each of these approaches bears problems. For example, hosts that are not registered can also get information into the Internet and not all registered hosts are active (Claffy et al. 1994). Further, people try to calculate the number of Internet users by multiplying the number of hosts by a number between 3.5 and 10 which is also a rough estimate at best.

[8] The respondents were representative of the whole population of appr. 270,000 small businesses in the FRG in terms of the number of employees but the percentage of EDI users in the sample cannot be simply extrapolated to the total population.

[9] The degree of anonymity depends on the application. For example, when consumers call up product information via World Wide Web the business usually does not know

who did it. However, if a consumer shops through the same facility and identity and some additional information will be known to the business.

[10] Assumptions: "specifity" and "uncertainty" are low, medium, or high; "global" is yes or no. "Coverage" is given as an enumeration of things done with the condidered communication link.

References

Arnum, E. "Internet growth continues unabated," *EEMA Briefing*, October 1994, 16-17.

Cats-Baril, W.L. and Jelassi, T. "The French Videotex System Minitel: A Succesful Implementation of a National Information Technology Infrastructure," *MIS Quarterly*, March 1994, 1-20.

Claffy, K.C., Braun, H-W., and Polyzos, G.C. "Tracking Long-Term Growth of the NSFNET," *Communications of the ACM* (37:8), August 1994, 34-45.

Coase, R. H. "The Nature of the Firm," Economica, Vol. 4 (1937), 386-405.

Dean, R. "Der europäische Messaging Markt," Notes from the talk at the Conference "Enterprise Messaging" organized by Connector GmbH, April 10-12, 1995.

Electronic Trader, no author, "Germany: Careful approach pays off," February 1995, 26-27.

Hansen, H.R. "Implementing Mass Information Systems, Conceptual Framework and Guidelines," Arbeitsbericht No. 11, Wirtschaftsuniversität Wien, 1994.

Hess, C.M. and Kemerer, C.F. "Computerized Loan Origination Systems: An Industry Case Study of the Electronic Markets Hypothesis," *MIS Quarterly*, Sept. 1994, 251-275.

ITU-CCITT: Telematics Services: Operations and Qualities of Service. Recommendation F.160-F.350, Red Book, Genf, 1984.

Malone, T.W., Yates, J., and Benjamin, R.I. "Electronic Markets and Electronic Hierarchies," *Communications of the ACM* (30:6), June 1987, 484-497.

Malone, T.W., Yates, J., and Benjamin, R.I. "The Logic of Electronic Markets," *Harvard Business Review*, May-June 1989, 166-170.

Marion, L. "Who's guarding the till at the CyberMall?" *Datamation*, February 15, 1995, 38-41.

Miebach, J.T. and Schneider W. "Untersuchung zur Evaluierung des spezifischen Nutzens von EDIFACT auf Basis eines EDI-Implementationsmodells," *Wirtschaftsinformatik* (36:6), Dezember 1994, 557-569.

Reimers, K. "Markets for Electronic Markets? The Non-market Preconditions of Electronic Markets," *EM - Electronic Markets*, January 1995, 12-13.

Saaty, T.L. The analytic hierarchy process. New York: McGraw-Hill, 1980.

Sarson, R. "Richard Sarson looks back," *Electronic Trader*, November 1994, 30.

Steel, K. "Another Approach to Standardising EDI," *EM - Electronic Markets*, September 1994, 9-10.

Webster, J.L.Y. "EDI: A Pessimistic Viewpoint," *EM - Electronic Markets*, January 1995, 6-7.

Williamson, O.E. "The Economics of Organization: The Transaction Cost Approach," American J. of Sociology, Vol. 87 (1981) 548-577.

SECTION-3

Global Information Technology Architectures

At the core of any multinational enterprise lies the information technology arcitecture - layers of networks, geographically dispersed islands of data processing, and a complex distributed environment which is difficult to manage or even measure adequately. Just as in classical architecture for buildings and public spaces, the 'information architect' must work to shape form from function, and thereby help to create an environment for social efficiency and effectiveness in the virtual workplace. One of the most difficult and fundamental problems is that of headquarters to subsidiary coordination. As shown in the chapter by Steven Simon, the control of extended enterprises is dependent upon how well the information technology and communications system functions for users. Rick Gibson presents a view of a way corporations might go about planning their global IT architecture, a process which is difficult to do well because of the difficulties in determining user requirements and translating them into specifications for such large systems. It is interesting, in this respect, that multinational corporations based in different parts of the world tend to approach these problems in a unique way, as demonstrated in the chapter by Janice Burn and H.K. Cheung, who have made an extensive study of information technology architectures in the territory of Hong Kong.

12 An Informational Perspective on the Effectiveness of Headquarters-Subsidiary Relationships: Issues of Control and Coordination

Steven John Simon
Oklahoma City University, USA

This chapter provides a framework for examining the alignment of a multinational corporation's (MNC) structure and strategy with it's information architecture. Four levels of MNCs are examined in the context of effectiveness of headquarters-subsidiary relations. Traditional information architecture factors are enhanced with organizational and cultural variables that more completely explain an MNC's optimal information architecture alignment. The concepts of control and coordination are utilized to illustrate various strategies that firms undertake to accomplish their objectives. The integration of business and information factors is accomplished within the control/coordination matrix. Examples of MNC alignment are provided to demonstrate the potential outcomes of various strategic options.

INTRODUCTION

This chapter examines the effectiveness of the relationship between the headquarters and the subsidiary of a multinational corporation (MNC) and its information architecture. Specifically, the chapter investigates the relationship between such effectiveness and 1) two key processes of integration: coordination and control and 2) introduces a framework to provide the organization with direction for selecting the optimum information architecture. There are several forces that have pushed companies to embark on globalization of its business: the lowering of trade barriers, the existence of unexploited economies of scale beyond the size of national markets, the rise of competition (which raises the need for a global strategy), competition from low cost producers, decreased transportation costs, and ease of global communications. These forces have led to an evolution in MNC strategies which yield structures ranging from the highly centralized *global* enterprise to the dispersed *transnational* organization. While many factors have been examined with respect to the MNC, reliance on information technology is common across all organization structures.

The multinational has three broad categories to classify its goal for attaining competitive advantage. The firm must achieve efficiency in its current activities, it must manage the risks that it assumes in carrying out those activities, and it must develop internal learning capabilities to be able to innovate and adapt to future changes. The MNC has three sets of tools for developing competitive advantage. The firm can exploit the differences in input and output markets among the many countries in which it operates. It can benefit from scale economies in its different activities. It can exploit synergies or economies of scope that may be available because of the diversity of its activities and organization (Ghoshal 1987).

All of these tools compel the MNC to balance the degree of control and coordination between headquarters and subsidiaries while requiring the firm to extensively utilize its information technology infrastructure.

Galbraith (1977) contends that increasing organizational information processing capacity is the only way to cope with increasing complexity and uncertainty without reducing performance standards. As companies expand overseas and face greater complexity and uncertainty, to maintain performance they must increase their information processing capacity (Neo 1991). Yet unbridled and unguided IT investments can contribute to poor returns on investment and systems that are not properly aligned with the MNC's organizational and cultural structure. It is therefore critical that the MNC develop an information architecture that is aligned with the firm's strategy as well as its structure.

The headquarters-subsidiary relationship is one of increasing importance. Effective management of this relationship has emerged as one of the key challenges for managers of these enterprises. More industries in which MNCs compete have increasingly become globalized. As industries become more global, the management of the linkages among the units of the MNC becomes more critical for international competitiveness (Porter 1986). This suggests that communication and information technology should become of greater importance to these firms as their environment becomes increasingly competitive. Bartlett and Ghoshal (1986) note that MNCs are beginning to move away from having all subsidiaries act only as implementers and adapters of strategic directives from headquarters toward having some subsidiaries take on different roles of strategic responsibility. Having strategic responsibility dispersed throughout the MNC creates greater demands on the headquarters-subsidiary relationship and implies the need for enhanced fit between corporate strategy and information architecture.

The multinational corporation is, by definition, comprised of subsidiaries that are located in different nation-states. The existence of international operations suggests that a transactional advantage must exist for the central control of such operations, as compared with each operation being controlled by separate management. Williamson (1975) suggests that markets and firms are alternative instruments for conducting transactions and the choice of instrument will be determined by the relative efficiency of each. An important implication of this theory of the MNC is the recognition that fundamental to the existence of a foreign subsidiary is an interdependence between the subsidiary and its parent. The subsidiary exists as an alternative to the market, for which the purpose is the execution of transactions. The MNC increasingly faces multipoint competition which requires a response from a highly integrated unit. Therefore, competitive actions throughout multinational corporations have become interdependent. Competitive positioning, in these MNCs, is based on the collective organization respective of location or organizational composition (Prahalad and Doz 1987). Management of the firm's integrated subunits to achieve competitive actions suggests the need for an information architecture that is closely aligned with firm strategy and structure.

The concepts of control and coordination are introduced and explained from an international strategy perspective with their effects on information systems described at the end of each section. Next, the trade-off between control and coordination is explored. The text introduces the control/coordination matrix and its direct affect on the degree and intensity of information and knowledge flows within the organization. An exploration of information architecture follows this section. Factors from IS studies are augmented with variables which help to explain the special conditions from the international environment. Finally, information architecture variables are introduced into the control/coordination matrix. This process illustrates the *ideal* alignment of information architecture with MNC strategy and structure. Several examples for each category of MNC structure are provided to illustrate real-world models.

CONTROL

Control is seen as a process which brings about adherence to a goal or target through the exercise of power or authority. Control is also used to manage the integration of activities within the MNC. The importance of control as an integrating mechanism within organizations stems from the fact that it reduces uncertainty, increases predictability and ensures that behaviors originating in separate parts of the organization are compatible and support common organizational goals (Egelhoff 1984). A wide range of organizational devices exist to manage activities. These devices may be classified as either bureaucratic mechanisms or personal integrating mechanisms. Bureaucratic integrating mechanisms are constraints or parameters imposed on subsidiaries by headquarters for the purpose of managing or tracking subsidiary performance, usually in the form of standardized reporting procedures. Table 1 illustrates common control mechanisms. High instances of control are designed to give the organization a sense of direction, helping to coordinate interdependent subtasks at dispersed locations. Bureaucratic mechanisms may limit operational flexibility and have an impact on information architecture by restricting the flow of information between headquarters and subsidiaries and more especially between the subsidiaries themselves. The reduced communication results in increased *efficiency* of the headquarters-subsidiary relationship, which is important given the cultural and geographic distances inherent in operating internationally. These mechanisms are used presumably by all organizations and are considered a least costly means of managing interdependence, especially in cases where interdependence is relatively low (Roth and Nigh 1991). In cases where interdependence is considered high, bureaucratic integrating mechanisms must be supplemented with personal integrating mechanisms. Personal integrating mechanisms operate through socialization, which internalizes rules and desired behaviors by the individual rather than imposing them externally. These mechanisms overcome the limitations of formal structure through the development of shared norms and values. Organizations also utilize output and behavior control as a supplement to institutional norms and values. A requirement for this type of behavior modification in a widely dispersed multinational corporation is the creation of flexible, open channels of communication, in this case provided through the organization's information architecture.

Control mechanisms can be expected to vary with the structure of firms operating in the global environment. These mechanisms include centralization and formalization of departments and decision making. Firms will seek to align their control mechanisms with their strategies and structures in hopes of attaining competitive advantage. To achieve these advantages, the configuration of the firm's information architecture must reflect the firm's strategic objectives. For instance, a firm whose headquarters wishes to exert a high degree of control over its subsidiaries might structure its information architecture with one way information flows. These information flows allow data in the form of reports to flow from the subsidiary to the headquarters, but knowledge in the form of decisions flows from headquarters to the subsidiaries. In this type of information architecture one would expect to find little if any information flow between subsidiaries[1]. On the other hand, a firm's strategy based on low levels of control might seek an information architecture designed to provide dense two-way communication. A system of this nature could promote closeness of contact between headquarters and subsidiary and perhaps enhance information and knowledge flow between subsidiaries. Contact might be initiated by any party and this system could be one in which the parties are regarded more as equals.

The degree of control sought by an MNC can have its roots in the culture and origin of the home country. Eglehoff (1984) found that U.S. MNCs tend to measure more quantifiable and objective business measures whereas European MNCs tend to measure more qualifiable business measures while determining adherence to corporate standards. U.S. MNCs also seek more precise plans and budgets with greater centralized decision making authority. Given Eglehoff's finding one might assume that U.S. MNCs would likely be structured around larger central staffs with the highly centralized information processing capacity required to make comparisons and generate feedback.

COORDINATION

Coordination is a part of all organizations that have a certain degree of specialization or differentiation among their parts, mandating some sort of coordinated effort across them. A mechanism

Control	Coordination
-Centralization	-Decentralization
-Formalization	-Departmentalization
-Output and Behavior Control	-Planning Systems
-Performance Tracking Systems	-Lateral and Cross - Department relations
-Standardized Reporting Systems	-Informal Communication
	-Socialization

Table 1: Common Mechanisms of Control and Coordination

of coordination can be considered any administrative tool used for achieving integration among different units within an organization. Coordination as compared with control should be less direct and less costly (Cray 1984). Coordination is not a direct intervention into the activities of the subsidiary; rather, the subsidiary's activities are embedded into the larger organizational context. This type of integration allows activities of the subsidiary to be consolidated within the organization through establishing intraorganizational associations rather than through a direct exercise of power or authority (Roth & Nigh 1991). In the MNC, coordination involves sharing and use by different facilities of information about activities within the firm's value chain. The greater the level of interdependence within the organization, the greater the need for integration of the subsidiary units. This is true especially in cases of manufacturing MNCs whose subsidiaries perform sequential tasks in the manufacturing sequence. Kogut (1985) suggests that the coordination of value activities provides critical competitive advantage for the multinational corporation. The MNC's distinctive competency is based on its 1) differential capabilities to perform value activities and 2) ability to capture comparative advantages through coordinating activities between different country locations.

Table 1 illustrates common coordination mechanisms utilized by organizations. Structural or formal mechanisms include the grouping of organizational units and the decentralization of those units as well as decision making authority. More informal and subtle coordination mechanisms encompass the use of lateral or cross-department relations. The use of teams, task forces, and committees are the most prevalent examples of this form of coordination. Other common mechanisms consist of personal contacts among managers and socialization which helps build organizational culture and shared norms.

The essence of coordination is the communication and processing of information (Malone et al 1987). Therefore, a firm's ability to coordinate a worldwide business successfully is contingent upon the creation of appropriate organizational structures and relationships within which flows of information can take place efficiently and effectively (Galbraith 1977). The effectiveness and efficiency of these information flows should be directly related to the alignment of the firm's information architecture with corporation's strategy and structure. According to March and Simon (1958), there are two general ways of achieving coordination - by programming behavior and by communication and feedback so that adjustment can be made. This chapter is concerned with communication and feedback between members of different subunits. Communication can be utilized to reduce uncertainty with regard to work flow contingencies, promote joint decision making, facilitate corrective action, and provide a conduit to share knowledge throughout a globally dispersed organization.

In information technology, uses of coordination for strategic advantage are seen in interorganizational systems which electronically link activities of firms at different stages of the value chain. MNCs with high levels of coordination can be characterized by mutual dependence between headquarters and subsidiaries with higher degrees of cooperation and joint problem-solving. Innovations in information technology in the past two decades have greatly reduced coordination costs by reducing both the time and cost of communicating information and knowledge (Karmi and Konsynski 1991). The reduction in coordination costs have in turn accelerated changes in the global market place and encouraged MNCs to modify their organizational and information structures to take advantage of market opportunities.

An MNC whose strategy seeks to leverage a high degree of coordination between its subunits might elect to develop an information architecture that promotes a broad two-way communication flow between headquarters and subsidiaries as well as open communication between the subsidiaries themselves. This type of organization might have a product that is adapted for specific markets and requires information systems to promote information/knowledge sharing between subunits.

COORDINATION / CONTROL TRADEOFF

The preceding two sections assume that the roles of the integration processes - control and coordination - are distinct and separate. In reality the applications of control and coordination are performed in concert with one another. What is the relationship between them and how is it associated with the strategic aspects of information architecture? The concept of the trade-off between control and coordination form the basis through which the MNC's strategy can be explored.

To some extent control and coordination work as substitutes for one another in that each can integrate the subsidiary into the firm. The use of varying degrees of either control or coordination and more especially their use together will help determine the firm's strategic orientation. For instance, in cases when the subsidiary is likely to deviate from overall organizational policy, when predictability is high, or if the organization views the world as a single market one would expect control to be high. In this case, the information architecture of the MNC could be designed to help direct the downward flow (from headquarters to subsidiaries) of information and knowledge, centralize decision making authority and minimize costs. In other situations, the firm might provide a product adapted to each individual market or operate in an environment requiring substantial local involvement. Additionally, environmental influences in the form of market or governmental pressures for local responsiveness could affect firm strategy. As external or environmental conditions increase, in number or degree, the headquarters unit becomes more flexible with subsidiaries, as the cost of applying control increases. To counteract increasing costs, MNCs employ more coordination throughout their organization, which in turn affects the development of the information architecture.

Control and coordination respond to organizational variables in different ways and with differential strengths. A number of factors have contributed to the level of coordination and control required by an organization. Some of these factors include structure of the MNC's industry, technology, foreign commitment to the corporation, profitability, and location of the MNC's subsidiaries (Cray 1984). It is the variety of the associations of factors and the degree of application of control and coordination which will anchor the decision for information architecture selection. Control and coordination are related to factors of transnational integration in MNCs. One indicator of the degree of transnational integration is the relative volume of intrafirm resource flows; the two most important intrafirm flows are products and technology (Kobrin 1991) and the transfer of knowledge (Karimi and Konsynski 1991). Gupta and Govindarajan (1991) posit that this intrafirm knowledge flow can be arrayed along the following two-dimensional space: (1) the extent to which the subsidiary engages in knowledge inflows from the rest of the corporation and (2) the extent to which the subsidiary engages in knowledge outflows to the rest of the corporation.

At the subsidiary level, if a high level of control exists with little coordination, headquarters may be viewed as intervening directly in the management of subsidiary operations while conveying little concern for a bi-directional exchange of knowledge. Subsidiary interaction with headquarters may be dominated by formalized reporting structures, one way knowledge flows, and increased administrative demands placed on the subsidiary without recognizing the subsidiary's contributions. This arrangement could be supported by a corresponding information architecture that provides the one way information flows with decision making authority highly centralized. It is critical that the application of control and coordination (in this instance high control with low coordination) be matched to the appropriate information architecture. Failure to align a suitable information architecture with the strategy objectives of the MNC will result in an organization out of balance and unable to use their information systems effectively.

An examination of Figure 1 provides insight into the control/coordination trade-off experienced by the MNC. The control/coordination matrix is the basis of the framework which will be utilized to plot the MNC characteristics and help determine information architecture. For illustrative purposes, the matrix will be introduced depicting intrafirm knowledge flows discussed above. Starting with the top left cell - high control/low coordination - we see that the subsidiary has high knowledge inflows from the headquarters with low knowledge outflows to headquarters and other subsidiary units. As the matrix demonstrates, this is an example of a parent company exerting high levels of control over its subsidiaries with low levels of coordination. This structure places decision-making authority and mechanisms at the headquarters level with subsidiaries playing a subservient role. The top right cell - high control/high coordination - suggests a situation where the communication of knowledge exists throughout the organization at all levels. This arrangement requires an information architecture that promotes open, two-way knowledge flow, with all units freely exchanging knowledge to enhance competitive position. The lower left cell - low control/low coordination - illustrates an organization where knowledge flows are of minimal value. A *laissez-faire* approach characterizes the attitude of the headquarters to subsidiary decision making. The bottom right cell - low control/high coordination - denotes a firm which values communication of knowledge between subsidiary units with minimal direction from headquarters. In this case, the headquarters unit would exert minimal control over subsidiaries with those subsidiaries in constant communication exchanging knowledge.

High		
C	High inflows from headquarters	High inflows from headquarters and other subsidiaries
O	Low outflows to headquarters and other subsidiaries	High outflows to headquarters and other subsidiaries
N		
T	Low inflows from headquarters	Low inflows from headquarters
R		
O	Low outflows to headquarters and other subsidiaries	Moderate outflows to headquarters High outflows to other subsidiaries
L		
Low		**High**

Figure 1: Subsidiary Knowledge Flows

INFORMATION ARCHITECTURE

A number of definitions have been suggested for information architecture (IA). IS corporate planners regard information architecture as a means of bringing together internal and external data processing groups, of merging data processing, office automation and telecommunications (Wardle 1984). Information architecture is a high-level map of information requirements of an organization. It is a personnel, organization, and technology independent profile of the major information categories used within an enterprise (Brancheau et al 1989). Allen and Boynton (1991) view IA as a set of policies and rules that govern an organization's actual and planned arrangements of computers, data, human resources, communications, software, hardware, and management responsibilities. They suggest that there are two approaches for developing an IA. The technical driven strategy approaches IA from a bottom-up perspective. This approach is fast and innovative. The business strategy, on the other hand, takes a top-down perspective to IA, concentrating on a strategic methodology targeting synergy, feasibility, and fit.

In a 1991 study of international IS managers, Watson and Brancheau discovered that IA ranked fifth in overall importance. Architecture differs from design in that architecture provides a long-term goal and represents the overall design target and direction for a particular aspect of information processing (Devlin and Murphy 1988). Wardle (1984) also examines IA from both technology and business driven perspectives. Table 2 provides architecture definitions from both perspectives. It is this long term, overall design perspective that this chapter utilizes.

AN INFORMATION ARCHITECTURE MODEL

Studies have investigated the factors of IA in fairly common terminology. These common factors, explained below, form the basis from which most IA studies are constructed (Table 2).

These general factors, while sufficient for a domestic organization, leave a number of gaps in areas of critical interest to the multinational corporation. The gaps are a result of the differences in the environment, conditions, and strategies of the MNC. The IA factors for the MNC will be classified according to the technical-driven verses business-driven dichotomy and are derived from the list initially compiled by Gibson (1994).

The information architecture model (see Figure 2) depicts the relationship of business driven IT factors, control and coordination needs, and the organization's information architecture. The model indicates that business factors, found on the left side of Figure 2, are independent variables. These independent variables influence as well as are moderated by an organization's varying need for

Data:	Classification and organization of internal and external data resources employed by the company.
Application:	Structure and relationships of current and future applications both vertically and horizontally in the company.
Communication:	Flows of data within an organization, and between the organization and the outside world.
Technology:	Structure and relationship of the hardware devices and system software forming the technological infrastructure.

Table 2: Common Architecture Factors

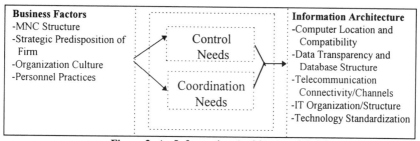

Figure 2: An Information Architecture Model

control and coordination. The information architecture components are dependent variables. These components are in part a result of the organization's choice and extent of business factors and its trade-off between its control and coordination needs. The following sections discuss the factors and components found in the information architecture model.

Technology Driven Information Architecture Factors

Computer Location and Compatibility: Survey data indicated that regardless of their strategy, MNCs concentrated their data processing resources in their home country (Roche 1992) - implying a high degree of centralization. Olson and Chervany (1980) suggest that the placement of computing resources is not affected by organizational factors and is primarily an economic decision. Vast changes have occurred in the information technology market place since the Olson and Chervany study. Prices of systems have dropped precipitously while processing power of computers has increased geometrically. The decision to purchase a specific brand of computer by the MNC can be driven, in some cases, by the conditions imposed by the host government or the dynamics of the local market. With the current compatibility of hardware and software, the key for the MNC should be the compatibility of data and information exchange, not the location or types of systems. Given this argument, this study will de-emphasize this factor.

Data Transparency/Database Structure: This factor measures the ability of the distributed database management system to support access and retrieval of data. The structure of the database management system has the power to link dispersed parts of the organization while providing information in varying degrees to corporate subunits. This structure should be highly correlated with overall MNC strategy. The options for the structure of the database management system are explained below:

Centralized: The data and database management system software is located in the headquarters unit. More importantly, the manpower and expertise to manage the system is positioned at headquarters which restricts the subsidiaries' direct access to and manipulation of data.

Decentralized: This arrangement disperses the data and the data base management systems throughout the organization's subsidiaries. This organization of data requires one subsidiary to contact the headquarters which in turn polls another subsidiary to obtain the required information. Placing the data closest to its point of use is wise but this configuration slows the dissemination of information and is recommended for organizations having minimal contact between subsidiaries.

Linked: The linked database configuration could be considered an intrafirm system similar to interorganizational systems (IOS). This organization connects the systems of the subsidiary units to the central data base of the parent organization. Subsidiaries are then free to access whatever information that the parent permits.

Integrated: This arrangement provides a system of shared data and data base processes. Data is disseminated and data base management systems are dispersed throughout the organization, similar to the decentralized configuration. The difference is that all the organizational units, both headquarters and subsidiaries, are interconnected. Integrated architectures allow each unit to access data at any place in the organization at any time providing a global pool of information to each unit. The MNC supported by this integrated structure clearly values the open exchange of information and knowledge above all other intrafirm flows and would rely on a very high degree of coordination.

TC Connectivity Channels: Communication channel width has been suggested as an organizational mechanism to combat uncertainty (Daft and Lengel 1986, Daft and Macintosh 1981). Global firms are characterized by an environment of higher uncertainty as the MNC operates in multiple markets and increasing interdependencies. Given these environmental factors, MNCs would be assumed to have communications channels that are capable of handling the increased information load required for highly interdependent operations and conditions of high uncertainty. Yet these global environmental factors can be expected to vary depending on the strategy of the firm. This study utilizes information/knowledge flows (Gupta and Govindarajan 1991, Korbin 1991), in both direction and intensity, as a means of suggesting a link between architecture and firm strategy. The key here is not the technology that delivers this product, as new technologies such as asynchronous transfer mode (ATM) create wider channels that are more accessible and inexpensive, but rather control and coordination as they impact connectivity. A topology of communication channels and expected delivery technologies are listed below.

Narrow Channel: MNCs with narrow communication channels are characterized by low flows of knowledge between headquarters and subsidiaries. Firms utilizing a narrow communication channel are expected to have low control and coordination requirements. These organizations rely on mixed T-1 lines or leased lines that are shared by multiple users, yielding reduced costs but diminished capabilities.

Medium Channel: A combination of low knowledge inflows/high knowledge outflows or high knowledge inflows/low knowledge outflows portray the communication channel of these MNCs. These firms have mixed control and coordination requirements, e.g. low control/ high coordination or high control/low coordination. Dedicated T-1 lines are utilized by firms at the lower end of the spectrum with T-3 lines employed by organizations at the upper end of the spectrum.

Wide Channel: MNCs exploiting wide communication channels require a system to support the most extensive and highly complex knowledge flows. These firms rely on cutting edge technology to support their requirements, utilizing frame relay and asynchronous transfer mode (ATM) which are very promising to provide high speed delivery of different types of traffic.

Information Technology Organization/Structure: Strategic alignment of a firm's IT organization and its strategy is of a critical concern for both domestic and multinational firms. This is of even greater importance to the MNC as the alignment of the firm's information processing requirements and organizational structure is a key element required to optimize the firm's value chain activities (Ghoshal and Noria 1989). This chapter draws upon a topology organized by Karimi and Konsynski (1991). Their topology categories IT structures into the four types listed below.

Centralized Federation: This IT organization is characterized by one-way knowledge flows from the headquarters to the subsidiary unit. Information flows from the subsidiary to the headquarters do exist but are restricted to procedural data flows such as sales reporting data.

Decentralized Federation: Both information and knowledge flows in this structure are quite informal. The organization supported by this structure is composed of highly autonomous national companies that have little interaction with either headquarters or other subsidiaries. Information flows can be characterized by procedural information similar to that found in the centralized federation with knowledge flows almost nonexistent.

Coordinated Federation: Subsidiaries in this organization operate in areas that require extensive modification of products for use in their markets.   These subsidiaries are forced to rely on their parent company for new processes and ideas.   This dependency requires an extensive knowledge flow from the headquarters to the subsidiary.   Since the subsidiaries operate in an independent manner, in widely differing markets, we expect to find little in the way of knowledge flows between the subsidiaries.

Integrated Network: This structure is the most complex of the four types in the topology and resembles that of a matrix organization.   It is characterized by conditions where subsidiaries and headquarters are considered as equal partners, information is dispersed throughout the organization, and widely used two-way communication channels are common.   Subsidiaries operating under this structure have been referred to as holographic, suggesting that as with a hologram, each piece contains a complete image of the whole (Hagström 1990).   Knowledge and information flows are extensive and occur throughout the organization at all levels.

Technology Standards: Technology standards can significantly effect the interconnectability of an organization's information system.   The degree of standardization within an MNC's information system will be driven by the desired to exchange data or knowledge as well as the firm's business strategy.   MNCs seeking high levels of either coordination or control and desire to transfer data/knowledge, regardless of direction, will endeavor to standardize systems and procedures.   The transnational or networked firm represents an organization with the most profound standardization requirements, utilizing continuous two-way flows to conduct daily operations.

MNCs search for standardization can be hampered by governmental regulatory requirements which vary from region to region, industry standards, and the varying market conditions, especially the availability of products. Firms should seek to standardize their information architecture structure, data, and procedures. Note that standards are not hardware specific and should be instituted throughout the organization without regard for varying regional factors.

Business Factors Impacting IA

Organizational theory suggests that as organizations mature they tend to become more mechanistic, that is less flexible and adaptive.   Yet, when organizations are driven by more competitive and turbulent environments, they need to become more adaptable and organic (Slevin and Covin 1990).   Lee and Liefer (1992) posit a reciprocal relationship between organizational characteristics and information systems.   Information systems (IS) influence organizational characteristics and, at the same time, organizational dimensions affect IS structures. The following business/organizational characteristics are considered in the model.

MNC Firm Structure: MNCs, to a varying degree, utilize their dispersed subunits to learn about the environment and the firm's own resources through the delegation of responsibilities. Kogut (1985) suggests that organization structure does not only channel information and delegate authority; it, in fact, provides a system by which information and organizational knowledge are created. The strategy an MNC adopts will in effect determine its application of control and coordination choices. A number of topologies have been proposed to classify overall organization structure of firms operating in the global environment. The most widely recognized of those topologies is based on the global/transnational continuum developed by Bartlett and Ghoshal (1989). Their framework of firm type was used by Jarvenpaa and Ives (1991) to classify decision-making structures in their investigation of global information technology "fit." This chapter also adopts the Bartlett and Ghoshal topology to explain strategic positions of MNCs with regard to applications of control and coordination and information architecture. A brief description of each classification is summarized below.

Global: This organization is driven by the need for global efficiency, while having structures that are more centralized in their strategic and operational decisions. Their unit of analysis is the world and their products and strategies are developed to exploit and integrated a unitary world market (Bartlett and Ghoshal 1989, p. 14). As a result of this centralized structure the majority of decisions are made at the headquarters level and propagated to the subsidiaries. A structure of this nature suggests a strategy based on high levels of control and low levels of coordination.

International: Transferring and adapting the parent company's knowledge or expertise to foreign subsidiaries is the hallmark of this MNC structure. The parent retains influence and control, but less than in a classic global structure; national units can adapt products and ideas (Bartlett and Ghoshal 1989, p. 14). This structure continues to exploit knowledge on a worldwide basis, using high levels of control coupled with high levels of coordination.

Multinational: A structure developed which allows the company to be sensitive and responsive to the different national environments is the characteristic of the multinational firm. This organization manages its subsidiaries as though they were components of a portfolio of multinational entities (Bartlett and Ghoshal 1989). Given the independence of the subsidiaries operating in this organization the headquarters exercises low control and low coordination.

Transnational: This organization seeks a balance between the pressures for global integration and the pressures for local responsiveness. Adaptation to all environmental situations is key to the philosophy of this firm, utilizing knowledge and two way information flows throughout the organization. Its strategies force the firm to have structures considered both centralized and decentralized simultaneously. Transnational firms have higher degrees of coordination with low control dispersed throughout the organization.

Strategic Predisposition of the Firm: The strategic disposition of a firm is shaped by a number of factors: the circumstances of its birth, the leadership style of top management, past administrative practices, the myths and folklore that have endured in the organization, etc. (Chakravarthy and Perlmutter 1985). This chapter draws upon four distinct predispositions of an MNC from Heenan and Perlmutter (1979):

Ethnocentrism: All strategic decisions are guided by the values and interest of the parent.

Polycentrism: Strategic decisions are tailored to suit cultures of the varied countries in which the MNC operates.

Regiocentrism: This predisposition tries to blend the interests of the parent with that of the subsidiaries at least on a regional basis.

Geocentrism: Integration of diverse subsidiaries through a global systems approach is the hallmark of this predisposition.

Organizational Culture/Personnel Practices: The orientation of the MNC's culture and personnel practices will have a significant impact on the information architecture. These factors affect the mind set of managers as well as perpetuation and evaluation standards of managers and employees and can be expected to vary widely across organizational types as the MNC adapts to environmental pressures. Alignment of this factor with organizational strategy must occur to achieve continuity of performance of systems and personnel. Four specific MNC cultures are outlined below.

Home country culture: This mind set would most likely develop home country nationals for positions everywhere in the world and apply home standards for evaluation of personnel throughout the organization. This limits the scope of organizational "thinking" and would be found in organizations offering identical products worldwide regardless of national market preference.

Host country culture: People of local nationality would be developed for key positions in their own country with local standards applied for evaluation at each subsidiary.

Regional culture: This culture performs the same as the host country but uses regional standards in the place of host country standards.

Global culture: This culture seeks to promote the best people everywhere in the world for positions throughout the world. Standards for promotion and evaluation are usually universal but weighted to suit local conditions.

INTEGRATION OF COMPONENTS: A MANAGER'S PERSPECTIVE

Organizations, especially MNCs, must begin to manage the evolution of a global information architecture that forms their infrastructure. So far, this chapter has established a framework from which to build an IA aligned with the existing structures of the MNC. The preceding sections created the control/coordination matrix and presented factors critical to assist managers in their selection process. The control/coordination matrix will now be enhanced to include IA factors, particularly the business-driven factors, in an effort to align the IA options with the organization's goals and requirements. Managers can safely assume that the structure of the firm will be in place before the creation of an IA. Therefore, the basis of this alignment discussion will be anchored in the MNC firm structure.

Figure 3 illustrates the placement of specific MNC business conditions in the appropriate cell of the control/coordination matrix. Cultural related factors are included with business conditions. Next, the information architecture configuration most closely aligned with the objectives of that MNC strategy is added to the cell. Descriptive features of the IT structure are placed in the cell to clarify role and alignment. These factors complete the picture of a firm's strategy and information architecture.

The following sections explain in detail Figure 3. Each section reviews the components of the MNC strategic type and the IA factors required to support that strategy. Real-world examples of MNCs representing different structural types are used to augment the discussion and fill in the matrix, thereby providing managers with examples of the desired alignment (see Figure 4).

Global Structure Information Architecture

The top left cell - high control/low coordination - is occupied by firms with a *Global* structure. Bartlett and Ghoshal (1989) suggest that these firms view the world as a single market and endeavor to sell a product with few modifications on a global basis. Operating under these assumptions, the headquarters does not require its subsidiaries to make decisions regarding product or procedures. Therefore, one would expect the communication channels to be dominated by one-way knowledge flows from the headquarters to the subsidiaries and information flows in the form of routine reports from the subsidiaries to headquarters. Given this arrangement, the system would be dominated by headquarters which would seek high levels of control, while requiring minimal levels of coordination between subsidiaries.

The *centralized federation* IT structure is very closely aligned with the global MNC structure. These information systems are highly centralized at the headquarters level with one-way top-down knowledge flows. Systems configured in this manner are considered to be *structure-enforcing*. These systems reinforce the traditional norms of the organization, often embedding organization policy in the system's logic (Fedorowitz and Konsynski 1992). Managers wishing to strengthen the position of the headquarters unit, maintain high levels of control over subsidiaries, or align their systems with a global MNC structure would be well advised to develop and implement systems of this design.

To complete this cell two additional cultural factors, *ethnocentrism* and *home country culture,* have been added. These factors clearly are aligned with the orientation of the global MNC structure. All strategic decisions are guided by the interests and values of the parent organization. Further, home

High	**Business Conditions** - Global - Ethnocentrism - Home country culture	**Business Conditions** - International - Regiocentrism - Regional culture
C **O** **N**	**IA Configuration** - Centralized data bases - Centralized Federation (Structure Enforcing)	**IA Configuration** - Linked data bases - Coordinated Federation (Structure Preserving)
T **R** **O**	**Business Conditions** - Multinational - Polycentrism - Host country culture	**Business Conditions** - Transnational - Geocentrism - Global culture
L **Low**	**IA Configuration** - Decentralized data bases - Decentralized Federation (Structure Independent)	**IA Configuration** - Integrated data bases - Integrated Network (Structure Transforming)

    Low   **High**

COORDINATION

Figure 3: Control/Coordination Matrix Aligned Information Architecture

country nationals are selected for all key positions with personnel evaluation criteria based on home country standards. Given that the global organization is aligned toward centralized processing systems with high levels of control at the headquarters level, these practices seem intuitive.

McDonalds Corporation is a textbook example of a global MNC, selling a product world wide with minimal modification across markets. Its actions with regard to its subsidiaries, both domestic and global, conform to the classic ethnocentric, home country culture orientation. The company's knowledge flows are top-down, with headquarters dictating decisions to subsidiaries. Information flows from the subsidiary units to the headquarters are in the form of routine sales and product mix data. The IT infrastructure - centralized data bases - and its information system expertise is located at the Oak Brook, IL headquarters. McDonalds is so ethnocentric that all standards - product, procedure, and personnel- throughout the world are based on the uniformity imposed by its headquarters' officials.   Host country managers are even brought to the headquarters training facility, Hamburger University, to becomes acclimated to the McDonalds' way of business.   Given McDonalds' global strategy, operating environment, and business practices, their information architecture seems to be aligned with their objectives.

Nippon Electronic Corporation (NEC) is another example of a global MNC. Their globally dispersed subsidiaries are strongly dependent on the parent company for strategic direction. Their information architecture is also aligned in a headquarters directed strategy similar to that of McDonalds. Yet, in the case of NEC, this proved to be a mechanism that blocked effective global innovation. In the 1970s, the Japanese managers of its US subsidiary detected "digital fever" in the US market. Unfortunately, Japanese managers at the headquarters failed to interpret the digital technology as anything more than a fad. Given that their systems were configured to support only routine information flows from their subsidiaries headquarters dismissed the opportunity to obtain "first-mover" advantages in the digital switch area. The failure on NEC's part was not the alignment of strategy and IA, but in their strategy and the rapidly changing environmental/market conditions. (Bartlett and Ghoshal 1990)

International Structure Information Architecture

The *International* firm structure occupies the upper right cell of the matrix in Figure 3 - high control/high coordination.   Parent companies of this MNC structural type rely on their subsidiaries to adapt their products to the preferences of the local markets in which they operate.   Analogous to the global firm, the international firm utilizes high density of knowledge flows from the headquarters to the subsidiaries.   Unlike the global firm, these MNCs demand high levels of knowledge flows from the subsidiaries back to the parent. These flows are required so that the parent company can maintain a data base on successful and unsuccessful product modifications given particular market conditions.   Specific information is then made available to the subsidiaries to assist them in future product adaptations. The high density of knowledge flow between the headquarters and subsidiaries requires the organization to maintain increased levels of both control and coordination to insure the vital flow of knowledge.

The *coordinated federation* IT structure also occupies the international firm structure cell. Information systems, including linked data bases, in this type of firm must be aligned to support subsidiaries relying on extensive knowledge flows from headquarters. Comparable to the centralized federation, we find that the majority of processing power and expertise is located at the headquarters level. The level of coordination is much higher in coordinated federation so that the headquarters unit has the ability to retrieve information from subsidiaries while supporting the knowledge requirements of the dispersed subsidiaries.   These systems can be characterized as *structure-preserving*, which result in changes to decision processes of managers but do not directly affect business processes which drive the organization. Headquarters' managers desiring to influence the decision making processes of their subsidiaries while still allowing the subunits the freedom to make their own decisions should consider this IT structure.

Regiocentric predisposition and *regional culture* characterize the international cell. Firms in this category align strategies to blend the interests of the headquarters with those of subsidiaries on a regional basis. These firms are distinctive in that they view the market environment as a series of "trade areas," placing less emphasis on geo-political boundaries, and greater emphasis on the similarities of market and consumer factors. Examples of "trade areas" include formally declared trade blocks such as the European Economic Union and the North American Free Trade Agreement, as well as any area a firm perceives with common characteristics towards their products. Personnel decisions are targeted towards the use of regional managers making decisions applicable to their specific area and being evaluated based on the area's criteria. The information systems desired to support these operations are highly controlled and coordinated to insure adequate knowledge flow for product adaptation. This coordinated federation of systems is designed to link all units with the powerful centralized processing of the headquarters unit.

SKF, the giant Swedish ball bearing manufacturer, has introduced information systems designed to improve vertical information flows (Hagström 1990). This is concurrent with its strategy of Regiocentrism and an information infrastructure built upon linked data bases. The headquarters unit in Sweden maintains a decentralized information systems development policy. However, this policy is subject to corporate guidelines and stringent regulations on standards for hardware, applications, and communications to facilitate information exchange between the subsidiary and headquarters. These decentralized systems have evolved into interorganizational information systems (IOS) between SKF and some of its suppliers and largest customers, e.g. Volvo (Hagström 1990).

IBM, a company that manufactures, markets, and services computers around the world is an MNC engaged in managing tremendous interdependencies. IBM has developed a system of headquarters directed concurrence mechanisms to manage the allocation of resources to projects and programs. This system of linked data bases and headquarters controlled lateral information flows have allowed the MNC to coordinate the management of dispersed operations and optimize the elements of its value chain to achieve competitive advantage. The company has been very successful in diffusing information, knowledge, and innovative ideas from one subsidiary to others throughout the organization by utilizing their information infrastructure.

Dow chemical utilizes its coordinated federation information structure to manage sourcing/allocation decisions. The headquarters conducts studies to determine optimal solutions for their sourcing/allocation situations based on the information provided by subsidiaries. The knowledge generated by the studies is then returned to the subsidiaries via the system of linked data bases. Dow executives describe the process as the global glue which holds the company together. The company interprets its structure as horizontal with flexible relations between subsidiaries created in part as a result of the linkage of the information architecture with corporate strategy (Whire and Poynter 1990).

Multinational Structure Information Architecture

Multinational firm structure occupies the lower left cell of the matrix - low control/low coordination. This firm's strategy is that of local responsiveness or allowing its subsidiaries to operate as relatively autonomous units. Given that the subsidiaries are operating independently, the organizational requirements for knowledge sharing is inordinately low which compels the organization to allocate resources to other areas. With a lower demand for intrafirm communication, systems will be less formal and extensive, dictating low requirements for control and coordination.

The *decentralized federation* IT structure is most closely aligned with the multinational's corporate strategy. The subsidiaries of this MNC structure operate as independent units which rarely have the need to share data. Therefore, the information systems in this cell are configured as decentralized or stand alone data bases. These systems can be characterized as *structure-independent.* They transcend organizational structure, neither requiring nor deliberately defying traditional norms (Fedorwitz and Konsynski 1992). These systems are ideal for managers preferring to have minimal interaction in their subsidiaries' decision making.

Polycentrism and *host country culture* have been added to this low control/low coordination cell. These factors are a near perfect fit for the multinational MNC's strategy of minimizing interaction with its subsidiaries. It is intuitive that an organization having a strategy tailored to meet the needs of the individual countries served by each subsidiary would modify personnel decisions to reflect each country's culture. One would also expect to find independently supported decentralized or stand alone data base operations sustaining widely dispersed subunits which require minimal interaction.

In a move to reverse Acer's tendency to act like other slow-moving corporations, the PC-clone corporation took a giant step and decentralized operations. Acer disintegrated the company into a collection of individual subsidiaries that could make their own decisions closer to the marketplace, with the slogan: "Global Brand, Local Touch" (Hamilton and Mark 1994). The change to polycentric or home country culture means that subsidiaries now run their own product and marketing programs while relying on their own internal stand alone data bases and locally developed information system's expertise. This change has realigned the organization's strategy and information architecture with the dynamic environment and allowed units like Acer US to become more competitive and profitable.

Unilever's decentralized strategy and approach to global business has given it the ability to sense and respond in innovative ways to local needs and opportunities (Bartlett and Ghoshal 1990). Its locally located subsidiaries have a history of creating products more suited to local markets than its internationally organized competitors. For instance, the company's laundry detergents did not sell well in markets like India, where laundry is done in water streams. The local subsidiary developed a technique to allow the detergents to be compressed into a solid tablet and sold in the market similar to a bar of soap. The independence of the subsidiary and the freedom to experiment without headquarters oversight provided breakthroughs which resulted in market innovation.

Transnational Structure Information Architecture

The final cell in the matrix, lower right - low control/high coordination - is characterized by the *transnational* organization. This evolving organizational form believes that each subsidiary unit is a reflection of the entire organization. Therefore, data, knowledge, and capabilities are dispersed throughout the organization, with each subunit having the ability to access and process information. To facilitate a system of this order - providing open two-way communications - demands a system that is very highly coordinated so that subsidiaries maintain communications links. Yet there must be little influence - low control - so that the units are free to determine their requirements and how to fulfill them.

The alignment of the *integrated network* IT structure and the transnational organization's strategy is illustrated by low control and high coordination. This holographic organization seeks to adapt to all global situations. This approach requires extensive communications and knowledge sharing between all units, which in turn creates additional knowledge as individual systems are connected to external data bases. Systems of this type are considered *structure-transforming* which facilitate a changing or matrix structure. These systems are more complex than any of the other system structures discussed so far and require much higher levels of coordination to guarantee free access to information which the firm considers its prime competitive weapon.

Transnational firms take a *geocentric* approach where subsidiaries are integrated into the whole global unit but each subsidiary is holographic, a reflection of the whole. A *global culture* promotes the best people throughout the world with standards highly adjusted to meet individual criteria. This structure disperses all assets throughout its organization, while its complex matrix structure requires extensive knowledge flows throughout the enterprise.

L.M. Ericsson has been able to develop an organizational climate that is cooperative and collaborative. This organizational climate has fostered subsidiary units that work together to develop and implement innovations. This MNC has made wide use of temporary assignments and joint teams which result in significant advantages, especially in research and development projects. Its use of integrated data bases and global communications has facilitated this concept which relies on a balanced two-way information flow (Bartlett and Ghoshal 1990).

Proctor and Gamble (P&G) is another MNC widely known for its use of work teams to promote globally-linked innovation. This globally-linked process captures the MNC's potential scope economies and harnesses the benefits of worldwide learning (Bartlett and Ghoshal 1989). The process requires an open flow of knowledge between team participants and is facilitated by highly integrated information systems and an organizational culture that promotes Geocentrism. The coordination of R&D teams from Europe, Japan, and the US permitted P&G to develop concentrated liquid detergents that met the specifications of several markets around the world. This effort led to the near simultaneous introduction of three uniquely formulated liquid detergents in Europe, Japan, and the US.

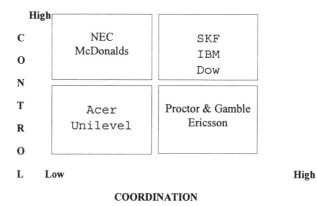

Figure 4: Control/Coordination Matrix MNC Examples

CONCLUSION

The alignment of strategy and information architecture is clearly a critical issue for managers of MNCs. As firms evolve from domestic to world-wide organizations operating in the dynamic global arena, the need to optimize their value chain activities in search of competitive advantage has placed increasing demands on corporate strategy and structure. This chapter has interpreted those demands as the trade-off between control and coordination. Differing corporate strategies and structures require distinct methodologies through which the headquarters interacts with its globally dispersed subsidiaries. The control/coordination matrix in Figure 3 illustrates that centralized, *global* organizations align their information architecture along high control, low coordination lines. This organizational configuration places systems and expertise in the headquarters unit, but as was seen in the NEC example, can produce undesirable effects in the form of missed opportunities. *Transnational* firms, located in the low control/high coordination cell are characterized by their intensive knowledge flows throughout the entire organization. This new organizational form disperses decision making to all levels and locations requiring an information architecture configuration that is decentralized yet highly integrated.

This chapter has introduced environmental and cultural factors to the information architecture equation. The alignment of information architecture with firm structure has proved critical to the success of both domestic and global firms. The dynamics of the environment and opportunities to expand into markets requiring extensive product modification of once local products is driving continued organizational structural evolution in MNCs. Information systems are in part responsible for that evolution. In domestic firms, information systems have been credited with influencing organizations to adopt broader and flatter structures. Many MNCs are moving toward adhocracy, or the networked organization. This organizational form is quite similar to the transnational organization. Such structural changes will require realignment of the information architecture. It is expected that this structural evolution will be driven by the use of task-teams. These teams are composed of globally dispersed experts organized to complete a specific project or achieve an explicit goal. Their physical proximity is not of concern as they will be linked via the organization's information systems. These task-teams, such as Proctor and Gamble's R&D detergent teams, will become the core of organizations that require quick action to the company's competitors and the dynamic operating environment while relying extensively on information architecture to maintain contact and exchange knowledge.

An understanding of business conditions, control/coordination needs, and information architecture factors can enlighten managers. This understanding provides managers with vital knowledge required to accurately plan their organization's information architecture so that their IA can best support the goals and overall strategy of the organization. The information architecture model (Figure 2) illustrates the relationships and presumed causal effects of the model's factors while the control/coordination matrix (Figure 3) provides managers with tools to plan and determine the organization's ideal information "fit." Managers can also use the matrix to design the structure of communication and data base systems to best suit the control/coordination needs of their organization. By comprehending the business factors reviewed in this chapter managers can interpret the composition of information support needs of their organization. The overall picture of the organization's information architecture provided by this study additionally provides the manager with a means to "sell" the use of information systems within their organization.

Research in the international MIS arena is in its infancy. Studies cited in this chapter draw mainly from the international business literature. The dynamics and complexities of the global competitive environment challenge many of the conclusions derived from domestic IS studies. Research must continue in the international IS area so that both researchers and practitioners understand the effects of the IS "glue" which holds MNCs together. The control/coordination matrix presented in this chapter explains only one aspect of the effect of IS on MNC strategy and structure. It is critical that knowledge flows between information system and international business researchers and practitioners multiply so that the small step taken in works like this are enhanced and provide true understanding of the phenomenon that is international IS.

Endnotes:

[1] In the context of this discussion, information flows might also be considered data flows, which take the form of standardized or routine reports. Knowledge flows, on the other hand, take the form of decisions and value-added information.

References

Alavi, M. and Young, G. "Information Technology in an International Enterprise: An Organizing Framework," In Palvia, S., Palvia, P., and Zigli, R.M. Eds. *The Global Issues of Information Technology Management*. Harrisburg: IDEA Group, 1992.

Allen, B.R. and Boynton, A.C. "Information Architecture," *Management Information Systems Quarterly*, December 1991, pp. 435-445.

Bartlett, C.A. and Ghoshal, S. "Tap Your Subsidiaries for Global Research" *Harvard Business Review*, November-December 1986, pp. 84-94.

Bartlett, C.A. and Ghoshal, S. *Managing Across Borders. The Transnational Solution.* Boston: Harvard Business School Press, 1989.

Bartlett, C.A. and Ghoshal, S. Managing Innovation in the Transnational Corporation. In Bartlett, C.A., Doz, Y., and Hedlund, G. Eds. *Managing the Global Firm.* London: Routledge, 1990.

Brancheau, J.C., Schuster, L., and March, S.T. "Building and Implementing an Information Architecture," *Data Base,* Summer 1989, pp. 9-17.

Chakravarthy, B.S. and Perlmutter, H.V. "Strategic Planning for a Global Business," *Columbia Journal of World Business*, Summer 1985, pp. 3-10.

Cray, D. "Control and Coordination in Mutlinational Corporations," *Journal of International Business Studies*, Fall 1984, pp. 85-98.

Daft, R.L. and Lengel, R.H. "Organizational Information Requirements, Media Richness and Structural Design," *Management Science*, 32(5), 1986, pp. 554-571.

Daft, R.L. and Macintosh, N.B. "A Tentative Exploration Into the Amount and Equivoclity of Information Processing in Organizational Work Units," *Administrative Science Quarterly*, 26, 1981, pp. 207-224.

Devlin, B.A. and Murphy, P.T. "An Architecture for a Business and Information System," *IBM Systems Journal*, 27(1), 1988, pp. 60-80.

Egelhoff, W.G. "Patterns of Control in U.S., UK, and European Multinational Corporations," *Journal of International Business Studies*, Fall 1984, pp. 73-83.

Fedorowicz, J. And Konsynski, B. "Organizational Support Systems: Bridging Business and Decision Processes," *Journal of Management Information Systems*, 8(4), 1992, pp. 5-25.

Galbraith, J.R.*Organizational Design.* Boston: Addison-Wesley Publishing Co., 1977.

Ghoshal, S. "Global Stratgey: An Organizing Framework," *Strategic Management Journal*, 8,1987, pp. 425-440.

Ghoshal, S. And Noria, N. "International Differentiation within Multinational Corporations," *Strategic Management Journal*, 10(4), 989, pp. 323-337.

Gibson, R. "Global Information Technology Architectures," *Journal of Global Information Management*, 2(1), 1994, pp. 28-38.

Gupta, A.K. and Govindarajan, V. "Knowledge Flows and the Structure of Control With Multinational Corporations," *Academy of Management Review*, 16(4), 1991, pp. 768-792.

Hagström, P. "New Information Systems and the Changing Structure of MNCs," In Bartlett, C.A., Doz, Y., and Hedlund, G. Eds. *Managing the Global Firm.* London: Routledge, 1990.

Hamilton, D.P. and Mark, J. "Acer Emerges as Global PC Power and Asian Pacesetter," *Wall Street Journal*, December 1, 1994.

Heenan, D.A. and Perlmutter, H.V. *Multinational Organizational Development: A Social Architecture Perspective.* Reading, MA: Addison-Wesley, 1979.

Jarvenpaa, S.L. and Ives, B. "Organizing for Global Competition: The Fit of Information Technology,"*Decision Sciences*, 24(3), 1991, pp. 547-574.

Karimi, J. And Konsynski, B.R. "Globalization and Information Management Strategies," *Journal of Management Information Systems*, 7(4), 1991, pp. 7-26.

King, W.R. and Sethi, V. "A Framework for Transnational Systems," In Palvia, S., Palvia, P., and Zigli, R.M. Eds. *The Global Issues of Information Technology Management.* Harrisburg: IDEA Group, 1992.

Kogut, B. "Designing Global Strategies: Profiting From Operational Flexibility," *Sloan Management Review*, Fall 1985, pp. 27-38.

Korbrin, S.J. "An Empirical Analysis of the Determinants of Global Integration," *Strategic Management Journal*, 12, 1991, pp. 17-31.

Lee, S. and Leifer, R.P. "A Framework for Linking the Structure of Information Systems with Organizational Requirements For Information Sharing," *Journal of Management Information Systems*, 8(4), Spring 1992, pp. 27-44.

Malone, T. W., Yates, J., and Benjamin, R. I. "Electronic Markets and Electronic Hierarchies," *Communications of the ACM*, June 1987, pp. 484-497.

March, J.G. and Simon, H.A. *Organziations.* New York: John Wiley, 1958.

Martinez, J.I. and Jarillo, J.C. "The Evolution of Research on Coordination Mechanisms in Multinational Corporations," *Journal of International Business Studies*, Fall 1989, pp. 489-514.

Neo, B.S. "Information Technology and Global Competition," *Information & Management*, 20, 1991, pp. 151-160.

Olson, M.H. and Chervany, N.L. "The Relationship Between Organizational Characteristics and the Structure of the Information Services Function," *Management Information System Quarterly*, June 1980, pp. 57-67.

Porter, M.E. *Competition in Global Industries.* Boston: Harvard Business School Press, 1986.

Prahalad, C.K. and Doz, Y.L. *The Mulitnational Mission: Balancing Local Demands and Global Vision.* New York: The Free Press, 1987.

Roche, E.M. *Managing Information Technology in Multinational Corporations.* New York: Macmillan, 1992.

Roth, K. And Nigh, D. "The Effectiveness of Headquarters-Subsidiary Relationships: The Role of Coordination, Control, and Conflict," *Journal of Business Research*, 23, 1991, pp. 1-25.

Slevin, D.P. and Covin, J.G. "Juggling Entrepreneurial Style and Organizational Structure - How to get your Act Together," *Sloan Management Review*, 31(2), Winter 1990, pp.43-53.

Wardle, C. "The Evolution of Information Systems Architecture," *Proceedings of the International Conference on Information Systems*, 1984, pp. 205-217.

Watson, R.T. and Brancheau, J.C. "Key Issues in Information Systems Management. An International Perspective," *Information & Management*, 20, 1991, pp. 213-223.

White, R.E. and Poynter, T.A. "Organizing for World-wide Advantage." In Bartlett, C.A., Doz, Y., and Hedlund, G. Eds. *Managing the Global Firm.* London: Routledge, 1990.

Williamson, O.E. *Markets and Hierarchies.* New York: The Free Press, 1975.

13 Information Technology Planning and Architectures for Networked Global Organizations

Rick Gibson
The American University, USA

Information technology has become indispensable for the effective and efficient conduct of business by networked global organizations. Paradoxically, spectacular advances in information technology capabilities have been accompanied by an inability to develop systems that satisfy the strategic information requirements of global firms. This disturbing paradox, encompassing interrelated phenomena such as the opportunities for the strategic use of information technology and the corresponding challenges of globalization, served as the staging area for this chapter.

This chapter provides a data-driven response to the overwhelming complexity of global information technology planning. The response is centered on a study that relates foreign subsidiary strategic roles and information technology architectures by empirically identifying patterns of information technology architectures that reflect the strategic planning considerations and contextual constraints of actual networked global organizations.

INTRODUCTION

The established disciplines of strategic management, international business and information systems have each contributed much to the practice of global management. Nevertheless, the search continues for a way to overcome the overwhelming complexity associated with global information technology planning.

Spectacular advances in information technology capabilities have been accompanied by an inability to develop systems that satisfy the strategic information requirements of global firms.

This chapter adopts a common technique for reducing complexity-- typology construction--which involves the grouping of observed systems into a finite number of types with some explanation of the factors that produce the different types. The typologies themselves serve no purpose, but do provide the opportunity to focus on one proposed solution--information technology architectures as constructs to facilitate the planning of systems that satisfy the strategic requirements of networked global firms.

For this study, international business firms were conceptually treated as interacting subsystems of domestic headquarters and foreign subsidiaries. This follows the approach taken by Gupta and Govindarajan (1991) whereby the international firm was modeled as a network of headquarters and subsidiary units involved in intra-corporate exchange in which the subsidiaries were distinguished by their distinct value chain configurations. Their suggested typology used value chain activities as distinguishing factors, yielding four distinct types: pure marketing, pure manufacturing, manufacturing-cum-marketing, and full value chain inclusive of research and development efforts.

In considering the value chain for a given subsidiary type, it is important to remember that it is a metaphorical *chain*, with implied linkages between the various required activities. Any subsidiary's activities depend on an information technology-enabled chain linkage to other primary and secondary activities conducted at headquarters or at other subsidiary units. The next section addresses the second typology needed for understanding global information technology capabilities, generic architecture types.

INFORMATION TECHNOLOGY ARCHITECTURE

Several researchers have espoused the benefits of an architectural approach for information technology planning during the next decade (e.g., Latham 1990, Targowski 1990, Allen & Boynton 1991, Watson & Brancheau 1991). Likewise, practitioners responding to the CSC Consulting Group surveys continue to place the creation of an information architecture among the top five management concerns. Representative of this architectural approach is Ives and Jarvenpaa's (1991) grouping of four patterns for managing global information technology. The first approach favored subsidiaries operating under their own information system initiatives, with architectures built using foreign standards and vendors. In direct contrast, a second approach is headquarters-driven, with corporate-wide information technology imposed on all subsidiaries. A third approach, labeled intellectual cooperation, has the salient characteristic of joint application development targeted at achieving innovation and flexibility. Finally, integrated global information technology requires a planned common information technology architecture to be concurrently efficient and responsive in global markets.

Adopting Targowski's (1990) concept of generic architecture types, Gibson (1994) used a comparison of six frameworks, shown in Table 1 to create composite descriptions of four information technology architecture types.

Sullivan (1982)	Processing-oriented	Data-oriented		Workstation-oriented	Integration-oriented
Earl (1989)	Delayed	Dependent		Drive	Delivery
Allen & Boynton (1991)	Low Road	Hybrid			High Road
Sankar, Apte & Palvia (1993)	1	2	3	4	5
Madnick (1991)	Minimal	Partial		Full Mainframe	Full Distributed

Table 1: Comparative Summary of Architectural Frameworks

Significant statistical results, which included cluster analysis, factor analysis, and multiple discriminant analysis, supported the premise of a seven-element definition of information technology architectures. As shown in Table 2, this

	Type I Decentralized	Type II Centralized	Type III Coordinated	Type IV Integrated
Computing Compatibility	Low	Low	Moderate	High
Data Transparency	Low	Low	Moderate	High
Communications Connectivity	Low	Low	Moderate	High
Applications Functionality	Low	Low	Moderate	High
Information Technology Planning (Strategic Role)	Low	Moderate	Moderate	High
Information Technology Organization	Low	Moderate	Moderate	High
Information Technology Control (Subsidiary autonomy)	Low	Moderate	Moderate	High

Table 2: Capabilities of Generic Architecture Types

multidimensional construct captures four distinct patterns as generic architectures. The names assigned to the four types are adopted from Bartlett and Ghoshal's (1989) patterns of global structures. Other researchers (e.g., Jarvenpaa & Ives

1993 and Konsynski & Karimi 1993) also adopted Bartlett and Ghoshal's strategy labels for information technology configurations and structures.

The next section describes how using this typology of four generic types to represent information technology capabilities makes it is possible to explore a proposed matching with the requirements that emerge from the four subsidiary strategic roles discussed earlier.

RESEARCH MODEL AND PROPOSITIONS

The general model in Figure 1 serves as a framework for answering the question: *Is it possible to utilize a typology of information technology architectures to facilitate the planning of information systems that satisfy the strategic requirements of global firms?*

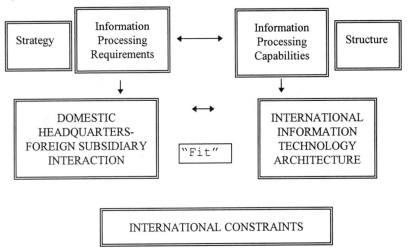

Figure 1: General Research Model

The basic structure of the model itself originates with a central tenet of the strategy literature, i.e., Chandler's (1962) classic strategy-structure paradigm, which suggests structural adjustments corresponding to variations in subsidiary strategic roles. Three decades later Egelhoff (1992) used information processing theory to express the relationship between an international firm's strategy and its organizational structure. He treated international strategy as a variable from which the information processing requirements for the organization might be determined. In like manner, the organizational structure became a second variable from which the derivation of information processing capabilities was possible. This approach simplified the examination of the corresponding fit ($\hat{U}$) between information technology requirements and capabilities as comparable phenomena.

This chapter takes Egelhoff's idea one step further. The information technology architecture becomes a variable derived from the information processing capabilities, which should fit the requirements that result from subsidiary strategic roles. International contextual constraints serve as antecedent factors that may explain the suboptimal information technology architectural choices commonly found in practice. By limiting the focus of analysis to the headquarters-foreign subsidiary dyad it was possible to alleviate confounding concerns related to organization size, and the complexity resulting from the occurrence of a variety of information systems and structures even within a single global firm. Thus, this study proposed an appropriate match between subsidiary strategic role and information technology architecture with full consideration of international regional constraints as critical success factors.

Several research efforts support the expectation of an "alignment" or "fit" between information technology and business strategy (e.g., Tavalolian 1989, Roche 1992, Karimi & Konsynski 1991, Sabherwal & Kirs 1994). The research propositions, detailed in Table 3, emerge from three sources: The model, the subsidiary information requirements suggested by Gupta and Govindarajan (1991), and more specific categorization of the information technology roles discussed by Roth and Morrison (1990).

As shown in the research model, these propositions must provide full consideration of international regional constraints that may affect the architectural choices of firms operating in the global arena. The specifics of the research methodology employed for empirically testing these propositions are presented in the next section.

RESEARCH METHOD

The research activities conducted in testing these four propositions had two distinct, yet interrelated phases. Considering the relative infancy of this area of study, the first phase adopted a case study framework that used interviewing as the specific qualitative data collection technique. Personal interviews were scheduled with the top-level information technology executive at four global firms. Ninety-minute interviews were conducted with questions leaving unspecified choices of answers open to the respondents. A detailed discussion of the results of this qualitative phase is beyond the scope of this chapter. However, it is pertinent to note that this initial field work provided the foundation for the second research phase, a mail survey of a larger sample of firms.

The sample was selected as representative of the population of successful international firms. The measure of success was based on the *InformationWeek* list of the five hundred American firms considered the largest and best users of information technology. The initial list of five hundred firms was reduced to two hundred and seventy-two firms that were currently operating in foreign countries. A 23% response rate was achieved by the survey and appropriate follow-up efforts.

DOMESTIC HEADQUARTERS-FOREIGN SUBSIDIARY INTERACTION	<==>	INTERNATIONAL INFORMATION TECHNOLOGY ARCHITECTURE
MARKETING SUBSIDIARY. The role assigned to this category of subsidiary is to market into a local trading area products that are developed and manufactured elsewhere. Activities range from simple importing to sophisticated marketing with extensive distribution, advertising, sales and customer support services.	<==>	TYPE I- Centralized. Large headquarters systems incompatible with subsidiaries. Low sharing of isolated data. Very low frequency and volume of routine data transmission. Local, cost reduction applications. Efficiency goals, non-strategic planning. Back room organization, no formal reporting. Tight control of subsidiary information technology.
MANUFACTURING SUBSIDIARY. This category of subsidiary produces a designated set of components or complete products for either a single country or an entire global market. Marketing and product development activities are undertaken by the headquarters unit.	<==>	TYPE II-Decentralized. Locally tailored, cooperative systems. Specialized databases. Low volume of routine and non-routine data transmission. Innovative applications, value maximization objectives. Middle management level organization, headquarters support but local control by subsidiary.
MARKETING-MANUFACTURING SUBSIDIARY. This subsidiary has a role as a product specialist that produces and markets a limited product line. Similarities in products, markets or basic technologies with headquarters result in frequent data communication exchanges between headquarters and the subsidiary. The subsidiary is self-sufficient in the value-added aspects of the product with strategic control over established products.	<==>	TYPE III-Coordinated. Self-reliant, compatible functional unit systems. Multiple local data systems, some data sharing. Moderate frequency and volume of routine data transmission. A few common functional area applications. Resource-based planning. Functional business unit organization. Headquarters-imposed budgetary control.
FULL VALUE CHAIN SUBSIDIARY. Capable of performing research and development activities in addition to marketing and manufacturing, this subsidiary acts as a miniature replica of the parent corporation and has the freedom and resources to develop entire lines of business.	<==>	TYPE IV-Integrated. Fully compatible, integrated systems. Continuously shared, highly transparent data. High frequency and volume of both routine and non-routine data transmission. Sharing of best practices applications. Integrated information technology and strategic planning. Complex, hybrid organization.

Table 3: Research Propositions

Questionnaire items defined to encompass each architectural element were combined by using unweighted averaging to produce an aggregate measure of the element for each company that responded to the survey. The seven architectural elements were treated as latent constructs and their operational labels were: computing compatibility, data transparency, communications connectivity, applications' functionality, planning, organization and control. Subsidiary strategic role was measured by a single categorical questionnaire item that provided a choice among four mutually exclusive value-chain configurations. For increased confidence, an alternate questionnaire item focusing on headquarters-subsidiary interaction was also included. A high degree of association between the two measures was found ($r = .97, p < .001$).

Research Results

The sixty-one firms represented by the completed surveys provided information from a variety of industries including: banking, manufacturing, chemical/petroleum, communications, computers/office equipment, conglomerates, non-bank financial, food, natural resources, services, and transportation. Most of the sixty-one firms responded with the requested data about two foreign subsidiaries. This provided a total data set consisting of one hundred and thirteen subsidiaries representing locations spread throughout the world including: United Kingdom, Brazil, Japan, Malaysia, Norway, Singapore, Hong Kong, Australia, Germany, Switzerland, Spain, Korea, Portugal, Pakistan, Netherlands, France, Scotland, Belgium, Italy, Ireland, Panama, and Mexico.

Table 4 displays the reported relationship between subsidiary strategic requirements and information technology architecture capability. Note that the subsidiaries are arranged down the table according to increasing completeness of the value chain activities and include the number of occurrences (n) of that subsidiary type.

A Chi-square test of independence ($c^2=32.109$, $p=.0002$) confirmed the statistical significance of the frequency of firms that reported an architecture-strategic role match. It was expected that the majority of the firms would fall along the diagonal in Table 4 because rational managers would strive for a fit between subsidiary strategic role and an appropriate information technology architecture type. Nevertheless, the mismatches (i.e., values not along the diagonal) came as no surprise given the existence of uncontrollable factors in the external international environment. An analysis of the findings about the four research propositions follows in the next subsection. The international constraints will be discussed further in a later subsection.

	Type I Decentralized	Type II Centralized	Type III Coordinated	Type IV Integratd
Marketing (*n*=31)	11	2	17	1
Manufacturing (*n*=25)	6	0	14	5
Marketing-Manufacturing (*n*=27)	2	3	19	3
Full Value Chain (*n*=30)	0	6	13	11
Number of occurrences of particular information technology architecture types (column totals)	19	11	63	20

Table 4: Architectures and Subsidiary Strategic Roles

Analysis of Propositions

The data concerning the distribution of information technology capabilities among subsidiaries is best analyzed by independently examining three views of Table 4: vertically, diagonally and horizontally.

Vertical Analysis: First, from a vertical viewpoint that focuses on the columns in Table 4, the distribution of information technology architecture types suggests a correspondence between foreign subsidiary requirements and architectural capabilities. Moving down the columns, as the subsidiary value chains become more complete, the coordination and control requirements of the multiple activities demand increases in information technology-enabled integration between headquarters and subsidiary units. For example, the information processing requirements of marketing subsidiaries are often limited to control of inventory and coordination of market intelligence. Conversely, the complete set of activities conducted at full value chain subsidiaries require architectures that enable high levels of integration. Overall, these empirical results support the expectation that information technology architecture choices would proceed rationally from comparatively low to moderate to high levels of overall capability.

The number of occurrences (*n*) of each category of subsidiary strategic role was uniformly distributed. Looking first at Type I-Centralized architectures, it is reassuring from a theoretical standpoint that, of the total of nineteen subsidiaries, eleven are linked with marketing subsidiaries. Similarly for Type IV-Integrated, the predominant linkage (eleven of twenty occurrences) was with full value chain subsidiaries, as expected.

The relatively low number of Type II-Centralized architecture occurrences suggests that this architecture type may serve as a transitional, rather than permanent information technology configuration for firms evolving globally. In direct contrast, the column totals shown for each architecture type highlight the prevalence of Type III-Coordinated architectures. The inclination of the subsidiaries, regardless of strategic role, to favor the Type III-Coordinated architecture type can be considered as evidence of the expansion of information requirements and capabilities imposed by operations in the international environment. By similar reasoning, the comparatively low number of Type IV-Integrated architectures may be partially accounted for by the long lead times, local infrastructure constraints, and higher levels of investment required for the development of architecture types with high levels of connectivity and integration.

Diagonal Analysis: Notable implications emerged from a cross-tabular analysis of Table 4. Nineteen of the twenty-seven marketing-manufacturing subsidiaries used Type III-Coordinated architectures as expected. The mismatched subsidiaries were evenly distributed among the three other architectural types. In contrast, most of the marketing subsidiaries were mismatched, most commonly as Type III-Coordinated architectures. This suggests that, in international environments, marketing subsidiaries can be expected to employ information technology architectures that exceed their information processing requirements. Moreover, this finding implies that the evolution of information technology in international firms would proceed from Type I-Decentralized to Type III-Coordinated, implying a proactive anticipation of the trend toward increasing information needs in the global environment.

For the proposed pairing of Full Value Chain subsidiaries with Type IV-Integrated architectures, the relatively large number of mismatched subsidiaries suggested two plausible inferences. First, the large number of subsidiaries with Type III-Coordinated architectures may indicate that the local manufacturing requirements predominate so, as yet, there are no additional perceived requirements for synergistic value-chain combinations of manufacturing, marketing and research & development activities.

Unexpectedly, the Type III-Coordinated architecture was prevalent along the entire range of value chain configurations. This occurrence is even more interesting in consideration of the fact that the survey was targeted at the leading users of information technology in the global environment. This finding further emphasized the apparent difficulty, even among leading firms, in achieving the optimal international information technology configuration.

Horizontal Analysis: An attempt to concentrate on the horizontal rows in Table 4 requires an additional refinement, accomplished by assigning weights to the architecture types that reflect their capability to enable headquarters and foreign subsidiary interaction. As shown in Table 5, Type I-Decentralized architectures, with low elemental values were assigned a weight of 1. In like manner, architecture

Types II, III, and IV were assigned weights of 2, 3, and 4 respectively. An index can then be calculated as a weighted average involving the number of observed occurrences of architecture types and their relative degree of integration as indicated by the assigned weights (*w*). For example, across the marketing subsidiary row the calculation of the information technology architecture index of integration would be:

$$\text{Index} = [(11 \times 1) + (2 \times 2) + (17 \times 3) + (1 \times 4)] / 4 = 2.26$$

	Type I- Decentra lized *w*=1	Type II- Centraliz ed *w*=1	Type III- Coordin ated *w*=3	Type IV- Integr ated *w*=4	I n d e x
Marketing	11	2	17	1	**2.26**
Mfg	6	0	14	5	**2.72**
Mkting-Mfg	2	3	19	3	**2.85**
Full Value Chain	0	6	13	11	**3.27**

Table 5: Architecture Types and Integration Index

It is noteworthy that increases in the index (i.e., 2.26 to 2.72 to 2.85 to 3.27) paralleled the increasing completeness of the firm's value chain activities at the subsidiary location. It is also interesting to note that the rate of increase in the level of integration of the information technology platform increased at differing rates. The index jumped by approximately 0.5 between Types I and II and between Types III and IV, but by only 0.1 between Types II and III.

Analysis of International Constraints

Prior research (e.g., Deans et al., 1991) suggests that important factors constraining the strategic choice of the information technology architecture in the international environment include at least the following five constraints: Hardware restrictions, vendor limitations, transborder data flow restrictions, substandard telecommunications, and applications' idiosyncrasies such as exchange rate volatility.

Five-point (1=rarely to 5=always) questionnaire responses were utilized to capture the extent to which these five constraints adversely affected the subsidiaries within the past three years. A linear probability model, referred to a logit analysis, served to analyze the responses. Hair et al. (1992) define a logit as the natural log of the ratio of two frequencies--in this case, the frequency with which the information technology structure was either a match or a mismatch with the subsidiary strategic role. The natural logarithm (ln) of the number (N) of occurrences of the *main effect* (i.e., structure-strategy match) that also report adverse *interaction effects* due to international constraints can be expressed as:

$$\ln(N) = \mu + \lambda_{main} + \lambda_{interaction}$$

Where Lambda (l) is the average logarithm of the frequencies in a particular category minus the grand mean and Mu (m) is the average of the logarithms of the frequencies in all the categories. Since the corresponding Lambda values are equal in value but opposite in sign, the main effect can be multiplied by two. Recalling that the logarithm of a ratio is equal to the difference of the individual logarithms, we can compute the logit model for the for match/mismatch frequencies as:

$$\ln(N_{match}/N_{mismatch}) = 2(\lambda_{main} + \lambda_{interaction})$$

By reversing this mathematical process using the definition of the natural logarithm it is possible to predict the probability of occurrence. Furthermore, since the probability of a mismatch is the same as one minus the probability of a match, the logit procedure makes it possible to compare the probability of the occurrence of a match expressed as an odds ratio calculated as:

$$\frac{\text{Probability (match)}}{1 - \text{Probability (match)}} = e^{2(\lambda main + \lambda interaction)}$$

Recall that the survey data results indicated forty-one of the one hundred thirteen subsidiaries had a match between information technology architecture and subsidiary strategic role--thus, the match/mismatch ratio is 41/72. Table 6 provides the Lambda coefficients, obtained by using a non-linear maximum-likelihood estimation procedure, for each of the international constraint parameters and the calculated logarithm ratio of match/mismatch.

Overall, these findings support the expectation that within the international environment, several factors act to constrain attempts to match of information technology architecture and subsidiary strategic role. It is noteworthy that the transborder data flow constraint was not quite significant at the 95% confidence level. Regarding the other four constraints, it can be reported with a high degree of confidence that the probability of such a match was significantly greater in the absence of the international constraints. Possible explanations for the observed patterns are addressed in the following subsections, which summarize the logit model predictions.

Constraint	Z-value	Main Effect (match)	Interaction Effects of International Constraints	
			Low effect	High effect
Restrictions on hardware acquisitions	2.556*	.33459	-.03084 1.83	-.30375 1.06
Lack of vendor support	3.049*	.33464	-.04642 1.78	-.28822 1.09
Transborder data flow restrictions	1.939	.22045	.18197 2.24	-.40242 0.69
Telecommunications infrastructure	2.981*	.29958	-.06269 2.06	-.36227 0.88
Currency conversion and exchange rate volatility	2.099*	.22849	.19515 2.33	-.42364 0.67
Significance * p < .05				

Table 6: Logit Analysis of International Constraints

Hardware Restrictions: Consider the possible effects of hardware restrictions such as import barriers on computers, or local product use requirements. The log ratio of a low effect equal to 1.83 suggests that under conditions of minimal constraints on hardware acquisitions for the foreign subsidiary there is a greater probability that a predicted match between the information technology structure and the subsidiary strategic role will occur. For instance, the predicted odds ratio of match/mismatch for the sample of 113 subsidiaries would be 73/40, with 73 matches and only 40 mismatches. In like manner, the log ratio value of 1.06 for high effect suggests that under conditions of high constraints on hardware acquisitions the predicted odds ratio of match/mismatch for the sample of 113 subsidiaries would be 58/55.

Local Vendor Support: In various places around the globe, certain hardware and software vendors are simply not represented. From a pricing and volume discount perspective, most major information technology vendors have not supported global sales efforts or maintenance contracts. They tend to approach marketing issues on a country by country basis due to lack of control over local conditions, demographics, and education levels. Apparently, for the international firms, additional effort and expenses are associated with attempts to acquire comparable global information systems capabilities. The log ratio of a low effect equaling 1.78 suggests that under conditions of low adverse effects due to the availability of vendor support the predicted odds ratio of match/mismatch for the sample of 113 subsidiaries would be 72/41. In like manner, the log ratio value of 1.09 for a high effect suggests that under adverse conditions due to the unavailability of vendor support the predicted odds ratio of match/mismatch for the sample of 113 subsidiaries would be 59/54.

Telecommunications Infrastructure: High levels of computer-mediated communication have been globally available for some time, with switched and private cables and satellite usage prevalent for data transmission. Although satellite technology successfully overcomes many problems, there still exist some constraints due to telecommunications infrastructure issues. Prohibitive pricing by foreign postal, telephone and telegraph agencies may push firms into information technology structures based on distributed processing and foreign vendor minicomputer acquisition. The log ratio of a low effect equal to 2.06 suggests that under conditions of low adverse effects associated with telecommunications infrastructure the predicted odds ratio of match/mismatch for the sample of 113 subsidiaries would be 76/37. In like manner, the log ratio value of 0.88 for high effect implies that under conditions of a high adverse effect due to a poor telecommunications infrastructure the predicted odds ratio of match/mismatch for the sample of 113 subsidiaries would be 53/60.

Currency/Exchange Rate Volatility: Unlike hardware acquisitions, standardization in applications areas is more difficult to achieve. Language and cultural differences may overwhelm may software packages and the economic aspects of the international domain, local competition, currency fluctuations, and inflation are important considerations. The log ratio for a low effect equal to 2.33 suggests that under conditions of low effect for this constraint the predicted odds ratio of match/mismatch for the sample of 113 subsidiaries would be 79/34. In like manner, the log ratio value of 0.67 for high effect suggests that under conditions of a high effect for this constraint the predicted odds ratio of match/mismatch for our sample of 113 subsidiaries would be 45/68.

IMPLICATIONS OF FINDINGS FOR MANAGERS

Having started with a paradox, this chapter now ends with prescriptions for information systems managers who are expected to deliver information technology solutions that consider foreign subsidiary strategic roles and international constraints. These managers must reconcile challenges and opportunities across three principal domains: strategic management, information technology, and international business. In response, these domains have been modelled in this chapter using a theoretical framework with three corresponding dimensions. First, the foreign subsidiary-headquarters relationship was used as a surrogate for global strategic planning. Second, a typology of information technology architectures served to limit the scope for capabilities discussions. Third, international constraints were examined as potential antecedent factors. The management implications associated with each of these dimensions are detailed in the following subsections.

Prescription #1: Build a Networked Global Organization

Global dynamics have refined the traditional framework for understanding the operations of international firms. For some time now, the organizational roles and corresponding activities assigned to the foreign subsidiaries of global firms have been severely limited--somewhat analogous to one-way, product delivery pipelines. Firms that previously found it acceptable to operate around the world with largely autonomous foreign subsidiary units are finding that they must now maintain coordination without losing responsiveness to local markets. Specific findings in support of this prescription include:

- The tendency of the subsidiaries (37%), regardless of strategic role, to adopt architecture types with capabilities in excess of the minimum required can be considered as evidence of the expansion of information requirements imposed by operations in the international environment.

The relatively low number (10%) of Type II-Centralized architecture occurrences suggests that this architecture type may be unsuitable for global operations, and serve only as a transitional configuration for firms evolving globally.

Prescription #2: Adopt an Architectural Approach

The empirical discovery of the need for information technology architectures to be aligned with business strategies can provide assistance with two problems commonly found in practice. One problem is that of obtaining the commitment and involvement of senior management in giving appropriate attention and resources to information technology initiatives. A second problem encountered by information technology managers is that of knowing when and what to change in their infrastructure. By using the technique of comparison of information technology architectures and subsidiary roles, managers can decide whether their information technology platform is lagging the business needs or whether the business roles were lagging the information technology opportunities provided. Specific findings in support of this prescription include:

- A Chi-square test of independence ($c^2=32.109$, $p=.0002$) provided statistical support for the reported architecture-strategic role match, which demonstrates that information technology must be an integral part of strategic business planning to enable coordination and cross-functional linkages.

- The index of integration jumped by approximately 0.5 between Types I and II and between Types III and IV, but by only 0.1 between Types II and III--thus suggesting the idea of a critical mass of information technology capability as a planning consideration.

- The high number of Type III-Coordinated (56%) and Type IV-Integrated (18%) architectures suggest that competitive advantage in international environments requires the principles of coordination and integration rather than the individualistic efforts of decentralized architectures. Information systems of multinational firms must function as dynamic architectural networks rather than engineered hierarchical structures.

Prescription #3: Anticipate International Constraints

Until very recently, information systems research has been conducted with inadequate consideration of the global environment. Some anecdotal and case study evidence exists concerning the role of information systems in global firms, which suggests an assumption that what works well in domestic systems can be transferred unchanged to foreign subsidiaries. This study has demonstrated that international contextual constraints serve as antecedent factors that may force suboptimal information technology architectural choices. Specific findings in support of this prescription include:

- The sub-optimal architecture mismatches (21%) came as no surprise given the existence of uncontrollable factors in the external international environment. Hardware restrictions, vendor limitations, substandard telecommunications, and applications' idiosyncrasies all proved significant at the 95% confidence level.

- The comparatively low proportion (37%) of Full Value Chain subsidiaries that have Type IV-Integrated architectures may be partially accounted for by international constraints, as shown by log ratio values ranging from 0.67 to 1.09 for high interaction effects.

CONCLUSIONS

Although it may be tempting to respond to global complexities by planning advanced information technology capabilities, two considerations are paramount. First, the current and future strategic requirements may not warrant the associated costs and risks. Second, contextual constraints embedded in the international environment may force suboptimal architectural decisions. The recognition that information technology architecture decisions are dependent on subsidiary business strategy choices and constrained by national differences encourages development of a strong relationship between corporate and foreign subsidiary managers.

References

Allen, B. & Boynton, A. (1991). Information architecture: In search of efficient flexibility. *MIS quarterly* 15 (December), 435-442.

Bartlett, C.A. & Ghoshal, S. (1989). *Managing across borders: The transnational solution.* Boston: Harvard Business School Press

Chandler, Alfred D. Jr. (1962). *Strategy and structure: Chapters in the history of the American industrial enterprise.* Cambridge: MIT Press.

CSC Survey. (1994). *Critical issues of information systems management for 1994.*

Deans, P.C., Karwan, K.R., Goslar, M.D., Ricks, D.A. & Toyne, B. (1991). Identification of key international information systems issues in U.S.-based multinational corporations. *Journal of management of information systems* 7 (Spring), 27-50.

Earl, M.J. (1989). *Management strategies for information technology.* New York: Prentice Hall.

Egelhoff, W.G. (1992). Information-processing theory and the multinational enterprise. *Journal of international business studies* (Third Quarter), 341-368.

Gibson, R. (1994). Global information technology architectures. *Journal of global information management.* (Winter), 28-37.

Gupta, A. & Govindarajan, V. (1991). Knowledge flow patterns, subsidiary strategic roles, and strategic control within MNCs. In *Proceedings: Academy of management annual meeting.*

Hair, J. F., Anderson, R.E., Tatham, R.L. & Black, W.C. (1992). *Multivariate data analysis with readings.* 3rd ed. New York: Macmillan.

Ives, B. & Jarvenpaa, S.L. (1991). Applications of global information technology: Key issues for management. *MIS quarterly* (March), 32-49.

Jarvenpaa, S.L. & Ives, B. (1993) Organizing for global competition: The fit of information technology. *Decision sciences* 24:3, 547-581.

Karimi, J. & Konsynski, B.R. (1991). Globalization and information management Strategies. *Journal of management information systems* 7 (Spring), 7-26.

Konsynski, B.R. & Karimi, J. (1993). On the design of global information systems. In S.P. Bradley, J.A. Hausman, & R.L. Nolan, R.L. (eds.) *Globalization, technology, and competition: The fusion of computers and telecommunications in the 1990s.* Boston: Harvard Business School, 81-108.

Latham, R.W. (1990). Systems architecture: Identifying strategic strikes, *Journal of systems management*, 41 (October), 28-30.

Madnick, S.E. (1991). The information technology platform, In M. Scott Morton (Ed.), *The corporation of the 1990s: Information technology and organizational transformation*, New York: Oxford University Press.

Porter, M.E. (1986). Competition in global industries: A conceptual framework. In M. E. Porter (Ed.), *Competition in global industries.* Boston, MA: Harvard Business School Press.

Roche, E.M. (1992). *Managing information technology in multinational corporations*, New York: Macmillan.

Roth, K. & Morrison, A. (1990). An empirical analysis of the integration-responsiveness framework in global industries. *Journal of international business studies* (Fourth Quarter), 541-564.

Sabherwal, R. & Kirs, P. (1994). The alignment between organizational critical success factors and information technology capability in academic institutions. *Decision sciences*, 25:2, 301-331.

Sankar, C., Apte, U. & Palvia, P. (1993). Global information architectures: Alternatives and tradeoffs. *International journal of information management* 13, 84-93.

Sullivan, C.H., Jr. (1982). Rethinking computer systems architecture. *Computerworld extra* XVI (November 17), 5-10.

Targowski, A. (1990). *The architecture and planning of enterprise-wide information management systems.* Harrisburg, PA: Idea Group Publishing.

Tavakolian, H. (1989). Linking the information technology structure with organizational competitive strategy: A survey. *MIS quarterly*, September, 309-317.

Watson, R.T. & Brancheau, J.C. (1991). Key issues in information systems management: An international perspective. *Information and management* 20 (March), 213-223.

14 Information Systems Resources Structure and Management in Multinational Organizations

Janice M. Burn and H.K. Cheung
The Hong Kong Polytechnic University, Hong Kong

This chapter examines the issue of how to manage information systems resources (ISR) in multinational organizations. It specifically reviews the arguments for alignment of organizational and ISR management structures (ISRMS), develops a model to test these theories and identifies the specific variables which have previously been thought to impact on these decisions.

The results of an exploratory study with a particular focus on the logistics industry suggests that many of the current concepts are out-dated and no longer relate to a global environment. It also suggests that management issues in general are not well understood in MNCs and more emphasis is given to resolving technical issues rather than social issues.

A number of additional issues are raised which may have greater influence in the search to develop effective and appropriate ISRMS and which also challenge the concept of alignment or 'fit' as a necessary pre-condition. A number of directions for future research are proposed.

INTRODUCTION

As the expanding global economy encourages the development of multinational companies (MNCs) so these organizations find themselves increasingly dependent on information systems (IS) for worldwide coordination and management. The emergence of such multinational IS (MNIS) intensifies the problems faced in IS management by introducing the issue of international management across a number of cultural and political barriers, coupled with the sheer immensity of MNIS services.

This chapter focuses on the structure and management of the IS resources in MNCs. Jarvenpaa and Ives (1993) conclude that different MNCs will use different strategies and structures in order to compete globally. They further conclude that these will force MNCs to deploy different MNIS structures in order to align these resources with the organizational management policies. They do not, however, suggest the organizational variables which will impact on the MNIS services structures and hence how IS resources should be managed.

This chapter considers these issues by first examining the different classifications of MNCs; the role and alignment of MNIS; and the organizational factors which will influence the structure and management of IS resources management. This is followed by a report of the findings from an empirical study to evaluate the influence of these variables in the context of MNIS structures, which suggests a number of issues that challenge current concepts and suggest new directions for future research.

MULTINATIONAL COMPANIES (MNCs)

An MNC is defined, in this chapter, as a company that has operations (or equity investment) in more than one domestic area, that is, a company that has one or more foreign affiliates or production facilities and is therefore involved in international management (Neo, 1991).

Compared with domestic management, international management has to face a much more complex environment, due to the fact that the MNC operates within and among different sovereignties; functions under widely different economic, legal, regulatory and cultural conditions; works with people of different value systems; acts across wide geographical distances; and competes in national markets varying in structure, population and area. These factors affect the coordination between headquarters and subsidiaries. Researchers suggest that the major differences in managing an MNC compared with the domestic one are the concerns related to distance, time, and additional variabilities in the multinational operating environment, such as the legal, cultural, economic and political dimensions (Deans & Kane, 1992; Roche, 1992).

They further contend that an MNC may face unique problems, challenges and opportunities not necessarily encountered by a domestic firm. Therefore, it is inappropriate to look at MNCs as extensions of domestic business. Generally, an MNC will experience two contradictory environmental forces: national responsiveness and global integration (Ghoshal & Nohria, 1993; Jarvenpaa & Ives, 1993). According to Porter (1986), it is the economic imperative which drives an MNC to integrate its global operations by reducing the differences in models of a product sold in different nations in order to accomplish economies on a global scale, global sourcing (Hass, 1992), and entertain multinational customers (Beckert, et al., 1990). However, there is a political imperative urging the MNC to respond to the local market sensitively by introducing variations, from one country to another, in product design, after-sales service and other technical parameters. By doing so, the MNC can satisfy different requirements from host governments, commit to the large number of non-global customers' demands and reduce costs in transportation, communication and storage.

As different MNCs face different environments (both internal and external), an MNC will experience different strengths of pressure exerted by the two imperatives and the balance of these imperatives will vary widely from business to business or even from company to company. The variations of the strength of the imperatives cause MNCs to have different degrees of international commitment, centralized control and decentralized autonomy. The different combination of these attitudes affects the adoption of different configurations by the MNCs.

MNC Classifications

One major problem faced by MNCs in operating their business internationally is how to overcome the regional differences in promoting their products or services in foreign markets. These regional differences can cause a serious conflict between the headquarters and the subsidiaries. Subsidiaries frequently demand more local autonomy for the modification of products or operations in order to fit into different of local markets. However, the headquarters require more central control to reduce the variations in the subsidiaries operations for easier co-ordination among subsidiaries and alignment with headquarters' policies. The extent to which decision making authority should be delegated to subsidiaries is generally the main source of conflict within the MNCs and is traditionally resolved by developing two forms of MNCs : global and multidomestic (Neo, 1991).

The *Global MNCs* view the world as a single market, therefore they attempt to control all the subsidiaries as a single entity and ignore the differences contingent to each subsidiaries' markets. Consequently, the decision making authority is concentrated in the headquarters, so that the entire business enterprise achieves economies of scale and cost efficiencies. This form of MNC is referred to as the centralized form of MNC.

Rosenzweig and Singh (1991) argue, however, that the global MNC presumes an unrealistic assumption of a homogenous and monolithic environment. An MNC does have to face the demands of specific local environments, so the MNC simultaneously confronts differing national environments. Accordingly, a diametrically opposite approach has been adopted by some MNCs : the *Multidomestic MNCs*, which view the world as a composition of a number of different domestic markets and delegate all the decision making authority to their subsidiaries. Each subsidiary acts as a single entity without recourse to maintain coordination with other groups within the MNC. This form of MNC allows variations in local environments faced by foreign subsidiaries and is referred to as the decentralized form of MNC.

Rosenzweig and Singh (1991) suggest that the multidomestic MNC does not consider the binding forces of subsidiaries, such as shared management, the strategic roles of each subsidiary in the overall organizational objectives and the ability to shift resources within the organization. Since, both central control and local autonomy are essential to MNCs, each MNC, to a certain extent, should have these characteristics incorporated in their companies' structures, strategies and policies. One response is to develop another form of MNC: the *Transnational MNCs*, which respect the tension between forces for global integration and national responsiveness. The transnational MNC can transfer products, capital, and knowledge between its central organization and foreign subsidiaries, and facilitate such transfers among the subsidiaries, to create competitive advantages in any of its markets from any combination of resources in the corporation. Under this arrangement, decision making authority should be partly centralized at the headquarters to look at the corporate strategic issues and be partly decentralized into the subsidiaries to take care of the local operational issues.

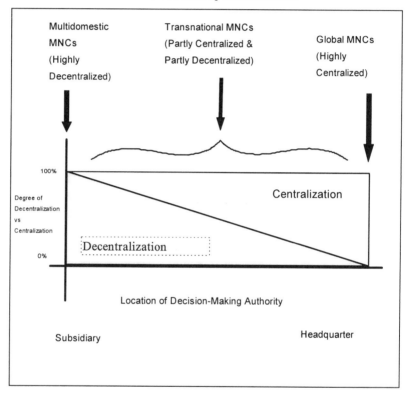

Cheung and Burn, 1994
Figure 1: MNC Continuum

According to the location of the decision making authority and the extent of centralization and decentralization, a simple continuum model shown as Figure 1 can be constructed. The multidomestic MNC and the global MNC are placed at the two extremes of this continuum to represent the fully decentralized and centralized structures of MNC respectively. The degree of centralization and decentralization will vary as the companies locate between the two extreme types of MNC structure. The transnational MNC should be placed between the two extremes.

This model can be directly related to that of Ghoshal and Nohria (1993) where they classify four environmental conditions faced by MNCs : (a) a *global environment* in which the forces for global integration are strong and for local responsiveness weak; (b) a *multinational environment* in which the forces for national responsiveness are strong and for global integration weak; (c) a *transnational environment* in which both contingencies are strong, and (d) a placid *international environment* in which both contingencies are weak. This classification is illustrated in Figure 2.

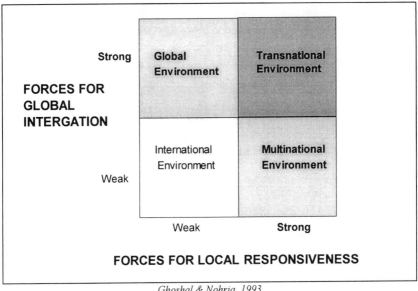

Ghoshal & Nohria, 1993
Figure 2: The Environment of MNCs : Classification of Business

In Ghoshal and Nohria's (1993) classification, "*multinational*" refers to the view of the world as different distinctive national markets where international companies have to deal with these local markets individually. This is equivalent to "*multidomestic*" as defined in this chapter.

In order to face the challenges in different MNC environments, different MNC structures should be adopted by companies. It is quite straight-forward for an MNC to adopt a global MNC structure in a global environment and a multidomestic MNC structure in a multinational environment. In an international environment, it is suggested that any MNC structure will be suitable, as the integration and diversification forces are both weak in this case. Whereas, in a transnational environment, the MNC should adopt a mix of centralized and decentralized structure in order to satisfy both forces. However, as the environment of any MNC is dynamic and moves from one quadrant to another, MNC executives should evaluate their external environment regularly to formulate suitable strategies for coping with environmental changes.

MULTINATIONAL INFORMATION SYSTEMS (MNIS)

An MNIS is defined as an IS which is operated or managed across two or more national borders, so that it has to deal with a heterogeneous national environment. Senn (1993) contests that an MNIS plays a pivotal role in the capability of firms to be successful in a global business community, as an MNIS has helped make it possible to execute strategy on a global basis, and an MNIS also offers the opportunity to increase competitive advantage. Roche (1992) further argues that the utilization of MNISs has been one of the key elements in making possible the development of entirely new international business strategies. MNISs therefore serve to address and resolve two strategic issues : coordination of worldwide activities and elimination of worldwide business barriers. Hence, a properly managed MNIS is a major critical success (or survival) factor for companies operating in the globalized environment.

Given that different types of MNCs should have different IS requirements, the design, implementation and management of MNIS resources presents complex problems of alignment. Below, we examine how an affiliation between the proposed MNC continuum and MNIS alignment could be achieved.

Alignment of MNIS

Previous debate on MNIS structural issues of MNCs has centred around two conflicting views : the centralization of MNIS in response to headquarters' needs to control their subsidiaries' activities; and the decentralization of MNIS to cope with the demand from subsidiaries to exercise freedom to react to local requirements.

Centralization of IS is referred to as *the policy and practice of allocating all IS resources (IS staff, hardware, software and data) in one of the company's business units to carry out various IS activities (e.g. systems development, systems maintenance, systems planning and systems management) and so provide the required IS services for the whole corporation.* Whereas, decentralization of IS is referred to as *the policy and practice enabling the individual business units in an organization to have delegated responsibility to acquire control over local IS resources and various IS related activities in order to satisfy their individual IS requirements without regard to other business units.*

In summary, the basic philosophy behind centralization is oriented towards top-down control, with an emphasis on efficiency and economies of scale (Dearden, 1987; Moad, 1989; Alter, 1990; Von Simson, 1990). On the other hand, decentralization is oriented towards bottom-up productivity, and stresses effectiveness and intangible benefits (Dearden, 1987; Kim, 1988; Bacon, 1990; Hodgkinson, 1990).

It is too simple to resolve the MNIS alignment issue by organizing MNIS either as centralized or decentralized, since in retrospect, neither the centralization nor decentralization approach has worked well. A more desirable option for MNCs lies in controlled decentralization giving subsidiaries more IS autonomy to carry out their business locally yet not to the extent of introducing incompatible systems. The IS structure which combines the features of centralization and decentralization is called distributed (or hybrid or dispersed) systems. The major goal of distributed systems is to allow parts of an organization to be more in control of their own operations and improve the use of computer resources by giving users more local control. So, theoretically, distributed systems render the benefits of both centralized and decentralized IS services.

The challenge to the IS resources manager is to achieve the 'best' combination of centralized and decentralized services for the particular organization (Olson & Chervany, 1980). Various MNIS structural alternatives have been proposed such as international, global, multinational / regional, collaborative and transnational (Roche, 1992), but very few guidelines have been developed to assist in selecting and implementing appropriate IS structures.

Although, Alavi and Young (1992) argue that centralized MNIS should be suitable for global MNCs, decentralized MNIS should be appropriate for multinational MNCs, and distributed MNIS should be chosen for transnational MNCs, there is no recipe for the perfect distributed structure. Each company must find its own balance between centralization and decentralization based on its overall corporate organization, industry competitiveness and market challenges (LaPlante, 1991). The MNIS structure should be aligned with MNC characteristics. The contingency view of IS and organizational alignment is supported both by arguments on organizational fit (Leifer, 1988) and information sharing (Lee & Leifer, 1992).

The 'organizational fit' concept uses the ecological view of organization and adopts the idea of 'survival of the fittest'. The organizational fit concept argues that IS alignment is extremely important for the organization to perform its business activities successfully. A mismatch of IS structure and the organization will decrease the effectiveness and efficiency of the company. In fact, Egelhoff (1991) has proposed an 'Information Processing Theory' to argue that the fit must be achieved between information processing capacity provided by MNIS structure and information processing requirement imposed by MNC characteristics.

The 'information sharing' concept uses the view that management should only be concerned with resources, such as data, which are shared by people, otherwise, individuals should take responsibility for their own resources. The information sharing concept argues that location of the information processing and storage should depend on the degree of sharing of information throughout the whole corporation. The higher level of data (information) sharing, the greater the need to place the processes and the data in the central headquarters; otherwise the processes and the data should be placed in local subsidiaries (Lee & Leifer, 1992).

Data should be situated near to the users but shared data should be the responsibility of a third party. In global MNCs, most data is shared throughout the whole corporation, therefore, all the data and MNIS functions should be established as a central function. However, in multidomestic MNCs, no data sharing is expected and only report summaries need be uploaded to the headquarters, so MNIS functions and data should be decentralized into local subsidiaries.

As previously argued, different positions in the MNC continuum represent different degrees of combined centralized and decentralized environments. Generally, IS functions should be organized as a mix of centralized and decentralized functions. The levels of this mix would be contingent on a number of organizational variables. The next section develops a framework through which organizational variables can be identified and related to the alignment and management of MNIS.

IS RESOURCES MANAGEMENT (ISRM)

ISRM can be interpreted as the *coordination and integration of IS related elements* in order for the IS to achieve its predefined goals. A research model for ISRM as shown in Figure 3 is proposed.

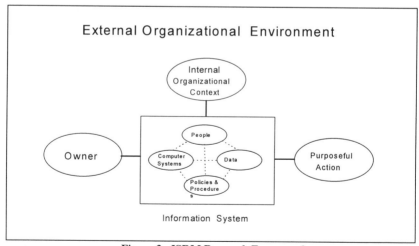

Figure 3: ISRM Research Framework

This model argues that IS is made up of a number of elements (people, data, computer systems, policies and procedures) and exists within an organization which is composed of the system owner, internal organizational context and purposeful action. The organization will also be subject to influence from the external environment. In order to manage IS resources effectively, it is important to handle the relationships between these elements harmoniously. The alignment of ISR structures and management is interpreted as the policies and procedures components of IS, and, therefore, it is important for IS researchers to study the relationships between other elements and the policies and procedures element.

Internal Organizational Context

The location of decision making, centralized or decentralized, should affect the information processing capacity required among various corporate units (Habib & Victor, 1991; Roche, 1992), hence, different degrees of IS centralization / decentralization are required. It is also the case that the greater the level of international involvement of the MNC, the greater the degree of heterogenous environment the MNC will face. IS decentralization can assist subsidiaries to cope with individual environments and also transform some of the variables into a standard format for headquarters.

Gates and Egelhoff (1986) argue that centralization is negatively correlated with the level of foreign product diversity in an MNC and the degree of product modification differences between subsidiaries. Since production processes for standard products should be the same throughout the world, it is more efficient to concentrate all vital activities, such as information processing, inventory control, decision making and product design, in one area to facilitate top management control. On the other hand, the production processes of diversified products should be different, so it is more effective to decentralize some activities, such as information processing, decision making and product design, into subsidiaries. Finally, Buss (1982) points out that different levels of IS maturity within the MNC will affect the subsidiaries in implementing their IS - where a high degree of differences exist, decentralization of IS services may be the only solution.

System Owner

A view of the world that is homogeneous will influence top management to adopt a global strategy, produce standard products and have a philosophy of full control over the subsidiaries and efficiently use resources. Whereas, a view of the world that is heterogeneous will lead top management to adopt a multidomestic strategy, produce diversified products and have a full autonomy philosophy for the subsidiaries. The resultant effect is that a centralized IS is more suitable for a company with a homogeneous view of world and a management philosophy of centralized control, but a decentralized IS is more appropriate for a company with a world view that is heterogeneous and a management philosophy of decentralized autonomy.

Purposeful Action (System Goal)

Centralized IS tends to facilitate efficiency in the use of company's resources, such as money, people and data, by sharing these resources among various units in order to maximize usage (Tavakolian, 1991). Centralization of IS can also help MNCs to supervise information access and achieve a large measure of control over subsidiaries. Centralized IS favors efficiency and control. Decentralized IS enforces the effectiveness of companies to react to external changes by providing essential information processing power to various units, so that subsidiaries can get sufficient information to make high quality decisions locally. Thus, decentralized IS focuses on effectiveness and autonomy.

Data

It is argued that the greater the degree of data sharing, the more centralized IS services should be in order to reduce data duplication and ensure data integrity. Researchers (Lee & Leifer, 1992) contest that all unshared data should be decentralized into subsidiary locations. This encourages the owners of the data to fully explore the potential of the IS in order to maximize the competitive ability of the MNC. Centralization also generates an environment where it is much easier to ensure data standards. In a decentralized environment, it is much easier to cope with different needs for data, file access and applications in the various subsidiaries.

People

Centralized IS services structure can assist in creating an attractive environment for specialized technical staff by providing richer technical IS career path opportunities. It is easier to reduce turnover and maintain a more professional, cheaper and high-quality operation. On the other hand, decentralization encourages the transfer of knowledge from IS staff to users and vice versa as expertise is located close to the users (Contractor & Narayanan, 1990). Moreover, the different level of technology development and education infrastructures of countries means that required IS skills may not be available in all countries or not to an equal standard. Hence, if suitably qualified IS staff are only available in a specific office, IS services should be centralized in that location. It can be decentralized if suitable IS staff can be found in subsidiary countries.

Computer Systems

The required hardware and software may not be available in all countries (Buss, 1982). The availability problem is further intensified by factors of national protectionism, transportation problems and so on. Therefore, centralization of resources will necessarily relate to the availability of such resources. If the required hardware or software is only available in the headquarters, IS services should be centralized otherwise it should be decentralized to facilitate technical support and development. Finally, centralized IS resources can reduce the cost of duplication; whereas, a decentralized IS can reduce the communications costs for the transfer of data between headquarters and subsidiaries.

External Organizational Environment

MNCs are often accused by host governments of using monopolistic power to crush competition, and of gaining favorable credit ratings for investment, thereby competing for scarce capital with domestic industry. Host governments have, therefore, sought to exercise control over multinational corporations operating under their jurisdiction (Negandhi & Palia, 1987). One of the ways by which they try to exercise control on MNCs is to require MNCs' technology and manufacturing processes to be adapted to local standards. This is more easily effected in a decentralized IS environment. Transborder data flow (TBDF) refers to the transportation of data from and to a country in any format electronically, magnetically or textually. Due to various reasons of security, protectionism and privacy, some countries prohibit the export of data in any format to other countries. As a result, MNCs are forced to decentralize IS. Furthermore, setting up IS services in subsidiaries will involve a huge amount of investment, therefore, the economic, political and social stability of the home and host countries should be taken into consideration in the centralization or decentralization of IS.

Where joint ventures exist, the foreign parties in an MNC may exert pressure to adopt their policies and standards, such that the MNC has to cope with two or more sets of policies and standards. Decentralization is one way to facilitate the MNC to implement different policies and standards at the same time. Subsidiaries can then carry out foreign policies and standards in order to adapt to local markets.

The greater the differences among countries, the greater are the difficulties for a single integrated MNIS to handle all regional differences, such as the differences in people's working styles and practices, legal systems, languages and so on. So, it is suggested that the greater level of differences among countries, the greater should be the level of decentralization.

Policies and Procedures

The policies and procedures component relates to how all of the above factors can be efficiently managed and the identification of the most effective structural model to support this management model.

The conclusions drawn from the above arguments are summarized as Table 1. In the next section, the results of a study to evaluate this research framework are discussed.

	Pressures to Centralize	Pressures to Decentralize
Internal Organizational Context		
Decision Making Style	Central	Decentral
Level of International Involvement	Low	High
Degree of Product Interchangeability Between the Local Affiliate and the Rest of the Multinational Groups	High	Low
Degree of Differences in the level of IS Maturity Among the Multinational Groups	Low	High
System Owner		
Management's Business Philosophy	Centralization (Full Control)	Decentralization (Full Autonomy)
World View	World is Homogeneous	World is Heterogeneous
Purposeful Action (System Goal)		
General Orientation	Efficiency	Effectiveness
Focus	Control	Autonomy
Data		
Degree of Data Sharing	Large	Small
Data Management Focus	Standardization	Local Variations
People		
Location of Expertise	Centralized Expertise to Maintain a more Professional, Cheaper and Higher-Quality Operation	Decentralized Expertise to Facilitate Knowledge Transfer between IS Staff and Users
Availability of IS Professionals	Suitable Qualified IS Staff cannot be found in Foreign Areas	Suitable Qualified IS Staff can only be found in Foreign Areas
Computer Systems		
Availability of Hardware and Software	Required Hardware and Software cannot be found in Foreign Areas	Required Hardware and Software can only be found in Foreign Areas
Cost	Reducing Duplication Cost	Reducing Communications Costs
External Organizational Environment		
Pressure from Host Government to Force Local Economic Involvement	Low	High
Transborder Data Flow Policies of the Host Government	Loose	Strict
Countries Stability	Host Countries are unstable	Home Countries are unstable
Outside Ownership	Low	High
Degree of Different Among Host Countries Environment (e.g. social value and language)	Low	High

**Table 1: Pressures of IS Centralization versus
Pressures of IS Decentralization**

THE STUDY

A questionanaire mail survey was carried out at the end of May, 1994. In this section, the operationalization and the results of the survey are examined. The questions in the questionnaire were based on the variables proposed in the previous section. At the end of August, 1994, seventy-five fully completed questionnaires were returned from MNCs. Of these, 28 were headquartered in USA, 16 in HK, 10 in Japan, 8 in UK, and Generally, the results of the survey show that most of the hypotheses, which were proposed earlier were not supported. Furthermore, some interesting phenomena were found. 13 in other locations.

The variables and hypotheses generated shown in Table 1 were analyzed separately over three dimensions : system development, system management and system operations. For each hypothesis and each of these three dependent variables, data was analyzed through three statistical tests. Table 2 shows the summary of the results.

Among the proposed nineteen variables, only three of them are shown to be related to MNIS resource management. The three variables are the degree of data sharing among the MNC groups, the degree of corporate-wide data standardization in the MNIS and the degree of differences in the IS stages in various MNC groups.

It can be argued that the current focus of MNIS resource management is purely based on technical rather than social issues. It may be that the complexity of organizational management of MNCs in the new global environment is not well understood. If the issues are not well understood, or, if they are in a state of transition, then the easier technical issues may be the first to be addressed.

Looking in more detail at the overall trends of centralization / decentralization, Table 3 shows that 56% of MNCs tend to have 61% - 100% of their applications developed decentrally. This phenomenum is quite understandable since different subsidiaries will have different local constraints, although conceptually they may be operated quite similarly. The differences in local constraints may relate to different national technological infrastructures, different national legislations and different national cultures. So, decentralized application development will be the preferred choice.

On the other hand, Table 4 shows that about half of MNCs are centralized in their IS strategy formulation in the range of 61% - 100%. Obviously, a centralized IS strategy is one of the most effective ways to synchronize the local strategies at different areas. Therefore, most of the earlier proposed variables are ignored with regard to IS strategy formulation. However, this policy may imply that strategy makers cannot understand the small, but essential, local requirements.

	Decentralized Systems development	Decentralized Systems Management	Decentralized Systems Operation
INTERNAL ORGANIZATIONAL CONTEXT			
Decentralized Management	Slightly support	not support	slightly support
High international involvement	slightly support	not support	slightly support
High product interchangeability	not support	not support	slightly support
Different IS stages	fairly support	slightly support	slightly support
SYSTEM OWNER			
Heterogeneous view	not support	not support	not support
Full autonomy preferences	slightly support	not support	slightly support
PURPOSEFUL ACTION (SYSTEM GOAL)			
IS oriented to effectiveness	not support	not support	slightly support
IS oriented to autonomy	not support	not support	not support
DATA			
Low data sharing	strongly support	fairly support	fairly support
Low data standardization	strongly support	fairly support	fairly support
PEOPLE			
Decentralized IS expertise	not support	not support	not support
IS skills in host only	not support	not support	not support
COMPUTER SYSTEMS			
H/W and S/W in host only	not support	not support	not support
Reduce communication cost	not support	not support	not support
EXTERNAL ORGANIZATIONAL ENVIRONMENT			
Great pressure from host	not support	not support	not support
Strict TBDF policy	not support	not support	not support
Unstable home	not support	slightly support	slightly support
Great foreign ownership	slightly support	not support	slightly support
Different hosts environments	slightly support	not support	slightly support

Key: The degree of support to the hypotheses in the following order
strongly>fairly>slightly>not

strongly support: the relationship of the two variables is supported by all 3 tests.
fairly support: the relationship of the two variables is supported by 2 tests only.
slightly support: the relationship of the two variables is supported by 1 test only.
not support: the relationship of the two variables is supported no tests.

Table 2: Statistical Summary of the Variables

Decentrally developed applications

	Frequency	Percent
100%	4	5.3
99% - 81%	26	34.7
80% - 61%	12	16.0
60% - 41%	4	5.3
40% - 21%	13	17.3
20% - 1%	12	16.0
0%	4	5.3
Total	75	100.0

Table 3: Frequency by Decentral Application Development

Decentrally formulated IS strategy

	Frequency	Percent
100%	5	6.7
99% - 81%	9	12.0
80% - 61%	10	13.3
60% - 41%	14	18.7
40% - 21%	16	21.3
20% - 1%	16	21.3
0%	5	6.7
Total	75	100.0

Table 4: Frequency by Decentral IS Strategy Formulation

Table 5 indicates that 72% of MNCs decentralize IS operations to their local subsidiaries to the extent 61% - 100%, thus minimizing the corporate impact which might arise from local aberrations. This policy allows for local technical expertise to respond more quickly to operational problems.

In order to investigate these results in more depth, four case studies were carried out in the express courier industry. Express courier companies were chosen because successful express couriers are truly multinational operators, and these companies rely heavily on IS technology to streamline their worldwide operations.

Decentralized other IS operations

	Frequency	Percent
100%	15	20.0
99% - 81%	29	38.7
80% - 61%	10	13.3
60% - 41%	8	10.7
40% - 21%	3	4.0
20% - 1%	8	10.7
0%	2	2.7
Total	75	100

Table 5: Frequency by Decentral IS Operations

CASE STUDIES

A decade ago the term 'express parcel' referred to an emergency parcel, today it refers to the high-speed guaranteed delivery of a parcel (Brown, 1990). In other words, the express business is very time sensitive requiring good coordination, communication and timeliness of key information between various parties involved in transporting the parcel.

The express courier companies basically differentiate themselves by the following factors (listed in decreasing order of importance) : reliability, service quality, speed and price (Bradley, 1990; Brown, 1990; Hastings, 1992).

In the express companies, service quality is usually referred to as the value-added services provided by the companies to their customers, such as parcel tracking, logistics management and direct access to the parcel delivery information by the customers (Tausz, 1992). The express companies now provide the value-added services through their advanced IS. Furthermore, IS also is a key for the express couriers to coordinate their worldwide activities.

Basically, express business can be sub-divided into three sub-markets : documents, package (small parcel) and cargo (heavy parcel). Each of these sub-markets are in different stages of the product life cycle as shown in Figure 4. The prediction is that there will be a decline in the document market due to the emergence of substituting technologies or concepts such as facsimile services, electronic mailing and electronic data interchange.

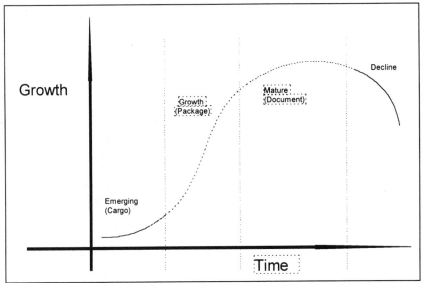

Figure 1: Product Life Cycle of Express Business

It is forecast that express services will be used as a method of distribution, not simply as a method of meeting urgent requirements. Therefore, express giants tend to provide integrated services in order to cater to the changing nature of the business from emergency services to logistical services. Raphael (1992) argues that there are several driving forces for the emergence of this integrated express service:

a. increase in demand for worldwide delivery of front office documents, where traditional cargo transportation is basically a 'back-door' business;
b. increase in demand of door-to-door service;
c. increase in desire of guaranteed service, as it is quite common for delay to occur in shipments in cargo industry;
d. increase in the value of shipments demands special attention up to individual mailing. So, more reliable and safe shipment services are requested, utilizing advanced technology for shipment tracking;
e. response to the need for worldwide delivery of time-sensitive emergency documents, such as medical, legal and financial documents.

Currently, the express industry is dominated by four global integrated express giants. Each of these has developed from a slightly different background, but as the organizations mature, they are tending to become similar in terms of services provided, particularly in the way that all of them are aiming to provide door-to-door movement of documents and parcels, worldwide, at all-inclusive rates. Therefore, they are going to differentiate themselves and compete by providing some value added services, such as logistic management, inventory management and parcel tracking. In the following sections, the details of these four companies are presented.

Companies Scenario

Company A: Company A is divided into three super-regions: America, Asia and Europe(Figure 5). A corporation is the U.S. headquarters. A International represents the other countries. Each of these super-regions is made up from a number of regions, and each region is composed of a number of countries. It is through this hierarchy that A manages its worldwide express industry. An IS subsidiary (namely A IS Company) in the US manages all IS usage throughout the whole organization.

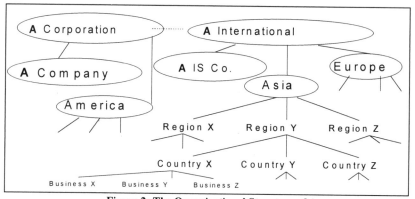

Figure 2: The Organizational Structure of A

Within each country, beside the worldwide express business, A may hold a number of business lines, such as intra-city express services, world mailing services and heavy cargo express services. Separate local companies may be established to handle each of these business lines.

The corporate headquarters of A in Europe is responsible for overseeing all business, while the local offices are responsible for running their operations autonomously. In other words, the task of strategic formulation is centralized in the European corporate headquarters, however, the approach to implement the centrally defined strategies locally is completely controlled by the subsidiaries management, so deviations can exist in local operations among the subsidiaries. Furthermore, subsidiaries can be claimed as quite independent, they can be viewed as partners in doing express business together. On the other hand, activities among the lower level offices will be coordinated by the upper level offices within the hierarchy of the organization. For example, regional offices act as a coordinator among subsidiaries to overlook their budgeting, business goals and business directions.

A views the worldwide express market as made up of a number of different markets, each of these markets will have variations, such as economic situation and business culture. However, A still aims to provide global services around the world, through its subsidiaries. All the financial data in the country offices is uploaded to the regional offices for consolidation, the results are subsequently uploaded to super-regional offices for further consolidation and finally data is uploaded to corporate headquarters.

Information Systems: In each office (country, regional and super-regional), there are IT departments organized to coordinate IT activities both within their own office and one level down offices. For example, the IT department in regional offices coordinate the activities in country offices. However, A IS Company, which reports directly to the corporate headquarters, was established to coordinate technology development worldwide and to act as the technological pioneer in exploring technologies for future use. The local offices (both regional and country) are responsible for the local technology deployment and implementation. Therefore, it can be claimed that IT strategies are formulated centrally, supported by the senior business management, and implemented decentrally by local IT departments.

In the application development aspect, the core applications, which are shared worldwide, such as customer services, services operations and accounting, are developed centrally and in some regional offices. Local IT departments are responsible for customizing the centrally developed core applications to satisfy local requirements and will also develop some applications to cater to some local user requests which cannot be handled by the core applications. The local applications developed from one subsidiary may be used by other subsidiaries if they find the applications are appropriate, but the transfer of applications must be subject to approval and certification of regional offices.

There is no direct data exchange among country offices except electronic mailing messages; data has to go upwards to regional offices and then downwards to the other country office. This arrangement of data exchange is due to two reasons : ease of control and communication cost.

Finally, the computer systems are decentralized in structure with a distributed database implemented throughout the corporate IS network, and each country office has its own machine. Currently, the local platforms are migrating from IBM S/36 machines to UNIX based machines to support open systems architecture, which is the ultimate IS design concept of the corporation. A only requires subsidiaries to use UNIX-based machines rather than forcing them to use a particular brand of hardware, as different locations have different hardware vendor advantages. They also have an IBM mainframe to serve as a database repository for the distributed database.

Company A prides itself on its decentralized operating style and UNIX provides the flexibility for them to expand and select hardware. This profoundly distributed system, a worldwide UNIX-based network, requires the software to be responsive, reliable, supportable and also easy to customize and extend at individual sites in countries where procedures are slightly different.

Company B: B is organized hierarchically as shown in Figure 6. At the base of the hierarchy is country level. A group of countries form a region and a group of regions form a division. At the top of the hierarchy is the corporate management which is located in the USA.

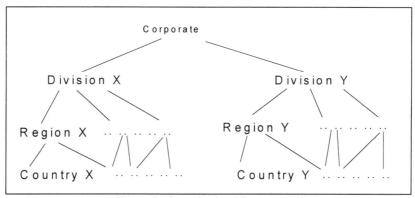

Figure 3: Organizational Structure of B

Direct contacts among subsidiaries are kept minimal, as, normally, strategic events involving two subsidiaries will be resolved through regional or divisional offices; however, for some business operations (for example, the transfer of parcels from one country to another country), the subsidiaries will communicate directly.

At each foreign subsidiary, a managing director is in charge of all decisions on local operational affairs. Decisions will be sought at the regional or divisional levels when problems cannot be resolved by the local managing director. Therefore, to a certain extent, the decision authority can be claimed to be decentralized into the foreign subsidiaries to cope with the site specific situations, however, strategic decisions are still centralized at the USA headquarters.

Most foreign operations are fully owned by B and only a few are in agent arrangements between B and local companies. Moreover, B provides global services, so that customers can purchase the same package of services across the globe from the various subsidiaries. They operate under the principle that all subsidiaries' operations are identical, therefore, no autonomy should be given to local operations. Limited autonomy is dictated by the degree of local pressures exerted by local governments, for examples some governments (such as USA) allow customs clearance electronically, but some governments (such as Hong Kong) do not yet allow electronic customs clearance.

B does not apply the same philosophy in its technology management; new technology can emerge anywhere within the organization and spread to other units.

Information Systems: Although, B has a centralized IS, it is in the process of decentralizing its IS into local subsidiaries using client / server technology. Currently, all data processing activities are centralized in USA, where nine IBM 3090 computers are located. All applications developed at the central site are supported by three production shops also based in the US.

Since the company uses identical operations worldwide to deal with package movements they also hold the view that data handling requirements should be identical and so support the need for centralized IT. The company runs their own satellites/leased lines global network and all data is sent through this for processing in the US.

In the local IS shops, there is little IT support, except for telecommunications. Therefore, the local shops have to either purchase software packages or develop customized software within their limited resources in order to cope with local variations. Things are, however, starting to change. The company has installed a system to connect its IS with some of their major customers and allow them to directly track the status of their packages from the centralized parcel tracking systems.

Because local and regional requirements cannot be handled by the US, IS is starting to become decentralized into the local offices. The intent is to gradually import the generic systems into regional specific software and let the local business requirements drive the IS development. After completion of decentralization, there will be an IT manager in each regional office responsible for IS development within the particular region.

Company C: The corporate structure of C is organized hierarchically as shown in Figure 7. At the base of the hierarchy is country level. A group of countries form a district, and a group of districts form a region. Regions are classified into North American regions or other regions. The North American regions are put under the management of domestic business and other regions are put under the management of international business. Finally, at the top of the hierarchy is the corporate level management. Direct contact among subsidiaries are kept minimal, as, normally, subsidiaries communicates through district or regional offices.

Top management believes that markets in different countries have different requirements and restraints. At each foreign subsidiary, a country manager is responsible for all decisions on internal affairs of that particular subsidiary provided that the decisions made are aligned with the direction or strategy set by the corporation. Therefore, the decision authority can be claimed to be decentralized into the foreign subsidiaries.

Information Systems: C is quickly catching up and passing many competitors in its effort to develop IS to help it manage its operations and provide new services to customers. They adopt a centralized approach in carrying out IS services. Most of the critical processes, such as parcel routing, are carried out by mainframes (IBM 3090 and compatible) located in the US. The major IS responsibility of subsidiaries is data input and verification. The remote sites upload input data to the mainframe through some means, for example, leased lines, satellite communications, and Public Data Networks (PDNs).

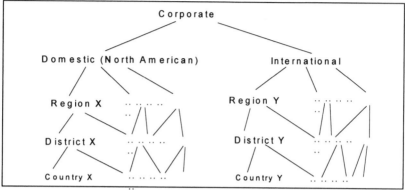

Figure 4: Organizational Structure of C

Not all foreign subsidiaries have the same level of IS maturity as the USA headquarters. The IS maturity is dependent on both the technological maturity in the countries and the size of the business in those countries. As a technology policy, the company will provide "technology and may be capital" for network facilities, such as very small aperture terminal links which the country would eventually take over. In return, the company gets the bandwidth it needs at wholesale rates.

Company D: Operationally, D is divided into four regions and each region is made up of subregions. Each subregion, actually, is a country office. Regions are managed by Regional Directors and subregions are administered by Country General Managers. The organizational structure of D is shown in Figure 5.

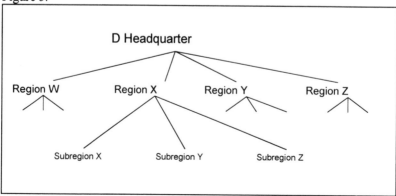

Figure 5: The Organizational Structure of D

Corporate headquarters seldom communicates directly with subregional offices, instead, corporate headquarters manages the subregional offices through regional offices. They believe that direct management between the headquarters and subregional offices may create two problems a) communications - as too many people will be involved in various operational processes; and b) a lot more labor resources required in the headquarters' office to coordinate activities among various regional offices. As a result, most of the authority has been devolved into regional offices. Headquarters is responsible for making mostly strategic decisions which affect the whole corporation, and regional offices are responsible for making mostly operational decisions which may only affect their own regions. Although the strategy formulation process is centralized in the corporate headquarters, local opinions from subregional offices are also gathered through formal meetings in various regional offices. Furthermore, a decentralized strategy implementation gives autonomy for various regions and subregions to localize the corporate strategies for adaptation to local environments.

The subregional offices can operate quite independently provided that they follow the corporate strategies. Moreover, there is no direct business communication between two subregional offices, all the communications between subregional offices have to go through regional offices. Subregional offices have to upload both financial summaries and financial details to the regional offices, and regional offices also have to do so to the corporate headquarters for financial consolidations.

Information Systems: There are no IS departments in the subregional offices. All IS issues in subregional offices are handled by two parties : a) a group of people, called Site Point Of Contact (SPOC), organized in each subregional office to handle local operational and house keeping issues, e.g. user ID requests, routing error and data backup; b) regional MIS departments which physically allocate a representative to each subregional office to oversee all local IS affairs. An MIS department is also established in the corporate headquarters to look after the corporate IS issues.

The responsibilities distribution between the corporate MIS department and regional MIS departments simulates the business responsibilities between corporation headquarters and regional offices. That is, the corporate MIS department is responsible for IS strategies formulation and MIS departments in regional offices are responsible for local implementation of IS strategies. The regional MIS departments are also responsible for several duties, such as local hardware deployment, communication lines set up between subregional offices and the corporate mainframe, application software training for local users, and reflection of local user requests to the corporate MIS department.

The corporate HP UNIX mainframe is located in UK with all application systems and database operated centrally in this machine. The applications development is also centralized in the UK office. The centralized approach is made feasible by a set company policy:

   a. before application development, a super set of systems requirements is formulated by gathering and including all local requirements.
   b. operation procedures of various local offices are forced to standardize to fit with the systems developed.
   c. regional MIS departments have to carry out systems acceptance procedures (testing and signoff) to ensure the developed systems satisfies their requirements.

Different governments impose different requirements in form of local laws on the subregional offices, such as the existence of value added tax laws in Taiwan but not in Hong Kong, which generates some special requests to the systems. The programming team in the regional MIS department will modify the centralized developed applications to meet these local special requests. The modified applications will be located and run on the mainframe.

For some local needs, which are not catered for by central development, local applications will be developed on local PCs or mini systems. However, there is a strong control on these local applications, as approval for development has to be obtained from the central MIS department. The transfer or exchange of local developed applications between local offices has to be performed through regional MIS and the subregional offices are not allowed to transfer the applications by themselves.

In short, D's IS resource management can be described as centralized IS development in UK office, centralized IS strategies formulation in corporate MIS department, and centralized IS operations in the UK office which controls the three mainframe computer centers in US, Australia and UK.

SCENARIO ANALYSIS

Due to the business nature of the express industry, each transaction involves at least, two subsidiaries in different countries, so to affect coordination the company is pushed to form a global structure. However, the local legal and cultural requirements oblige the company to localize, which pushes the company to form a multidomestic structure. Due to these contradictory forces, companies in the express industry should organize themselves neither as pure global MNCs nor multidomestic MNCs. Instead, transnational MNC should be the most optimal form as is the case of the four express giants. They still, however, have slightly different organizational structures as shown in Figure 6. In order to relate organizational differences with MNIS structures, the details of the company scenarios are studied and summarized in Table 6.

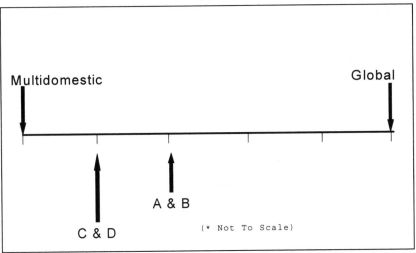

Figure 6: The Organizational Structure of the Four Express Companies

In the organizational dimension, all of the express companies have very similar attributes except in the methods of expansion. B, C and D expand their companies by acquiring local companies, which allow them to impose full authority on all local issues; whereas, A expands by joint ventures, which forces them to have lesser autonomy in dealing with local issues.

In the IS dimension, all four adopt centralized systems management (centralized strategy formulation with local implementation) in order to facilitate their systems coordination and synchronization in various subsidiaries. In the systems development aspect, only C purely centralizes all its applications (both universal and local) development, the others retain certain controlled local developments to cater for the small and specialized requests from the local users. Only A and D allow subsidiary developed applications to be used in other subsidiaries. Although minor differences can be observed in systems development practices, it can be concluded that all four utilize a centralized systems development approach. In the systems operations, only A uses a decentralized approach with decentralized computer systems, the other three use centralized IS operation with centralized computer systems. Figure 10 summarizes the IS comparisons.

	A	B	C	D
Organizational Dimension				
Date of Establishment	1969	1973	1907	1970s
Date of Internationalization	1972	1980s	1976	1975
Current Headquarters	Europe	USA	USA	Europe
Methods of Expansion	Joint venture, New establishment	Acquisition	Acquisition	Acquisition, PTTs' Consortium
Organizational Structure	4 layers' hierarchy (2 separate entities for USA domestic and International)	4 layers' hierarchy (1 entity to operate worldwide business)	5 layers' hierarchy (1 entity to operate worldwide business)	4 layer's hierarchy (1 entity to operate worldwide business)
Direct Contact between Subsidiaries	Minimal	Minimal	No	No
Geographical Strength	Far East, Australia	USA	USA	Australasia, Europe
Business Strategy Formulation	Centralized	Centralized	Centralized	Centralized
Business Strategy Implementation	Decentralized	Decentralized	Decentralized	Decentralized
IS Dimension				
IS Development	Centralized	Centralized	Centralized	Centralized
IS Strategy Formulation	Centralized	Centralized	Centralized	Centralized
IS Strategy Implementation	Decentralized	Decentralized	Decentralized	Decentralized
IS Operation	Decentralized	Centralized	Centralized	Centralized
Local Systems Development	Minimal	Minimal	No	With approval
Transfer of Local Development	With approval and certification	No	No	With approval from upper level offices
Direct Data Exchange	No	No	No	No
Computer Systems	Decentralized UNIX based machine with distributed database	Centralized IBM mainframes with local PCs	Centralized IBM mainframes with local PCs	Centralized HP UNIX mainframes with local minis or PCs

Table 6: Summary of the Four Case Scenarios

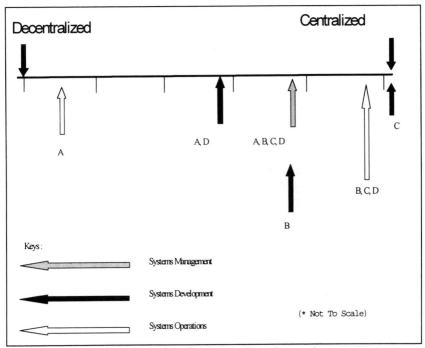

Figure 7: Comparisons of the Four Companies

These comparisons would suggest that an additional variable which directly impacts IS structures and resource management is the method of expansion employed by the organization. Expansion by acquisition gives B, C and D complete authority to discard the old systems from the purchased companies and extend the IS from the headquarters straightaway. This allows them to gain quick control and to become familiar with the new environment promptly. However, expansion by joint venture forces A to deal with some special requirements from the local partners, and different local partners may impose different requirements on different partnerships. Therefore, decentralized systems for A provide sufficient flexibility to cope.

CONCLUSIONS

MNIS are becoming increasingly important in today's globalized environment, but yet little is known about MNIS resource management. Although Jarvenpaa and Ives (1993) conclude from their research that different globally competing firms should exhibit different MNIS structures in order to improve their operational performance, they do not further inquire into which organizational variables in an MNC will affect the MNIS structure.

This study utilized both questionnaires and in-depth case analyses. According to results from the questionnaire survey, the most important factors in organizing MNIS are the degree of data sharing among the subsidiaries of the MNCs, the degree of corporate-wide data standardization in MNIS, and the degree of differences in the maturity in various MNC groups.

In addition, the case studies indicate that when companies show similar attributes in the three mentioned factors, there exists another less influential factor in determining the structure of MNIS : the degree of foreign ownership in foreign subsidiaries.

Perhaps more important than the supporting variables, however, were the findings that the majority of organizational variables proposed from prior research were found to have no support. They may not be relevant to the MNIS centralization / decentralization issue today because of the new dynamics of a global environment. One conclusion is that a number of these concepts are out-of-date.

Firstly, the improvement in education system and emphasis on rapid informatization in various countries causes the availability of IS expertise and IS skills in different countries to be irrelevant in considering the MNIS structure. Secondly, the reduction in inter-national protectionism to promote worldwide economic growth causes the pressure from host governments, strictness of TBDF policies and availability of required hardware and software to be irrelevant in designing the structure of MNIS. It also significantly lessens the effect of host differences. Finally, as the advancement of telecommunication technology decreases the cost per bit of transmissions, so the importance of the cost in telecommunication incurred in the MNIS will decrease and MNCs will not consider this variable in designing their MNIS resource management structures.

At the beginning of this chapter, two concepts, 'organizational fit' and 'information sharing' were discussed to support the idea that different organizational forms of MNCs should adopt different IS resource structures. The results of this study lends more empirical support to the concept of information sharing. The 'organizational fit' idea seems to be out-dated as the development of advanced technology has significantly reduced costs and improved processing power and information distribution.

This raises the question of what exactly are the factors which should influence MNIS resource management? The results reported in this chapter suggest that organizations are struggling to maintain internal consistency between IS functions and the organization. The external issues have been given scant consideration and may not even be understood. Certainly some of the existing ideas on MNIS resource management are based on a world view which is substantially outdated and more relevant issues need to be explored. These may include size or importance of foreign markets, patterns of geographical distribution of subsidiaries, and nature of clients. This study also has the usual limitation that it was conducted in only one area albeit covering a fairly wide spread of nationalities.

Replicative cross-cultural studies and longitudinal studies are needed to provide meaningful guidance to what may prove the major issue for MNCs in the very near future - the management of their Information Services Resources.

References

Alavi, M. & Young, G. "Information Technology in an International Enterprise : An Organizing Framework", in The Global *Issues of Information Technology Management* Palvia, S., Palvia, P. & Zigli, R.M. (eds). 1992. Idea Group Publishing.

Alter, A.E. "Intelligent Networking". *CIO* 3(5), 1990, pp. 51 - 60.

Beckert, B., Day, C.R., Jr., Knill, B. & Weimber, G. "Integrated Manufacturing : The EC'92 and Manufacturing Integration". *Automation* 37(11), 1990, pp. 2 - 30.

Bradley, P. "Package Express : A Study in How Free Markets Work". *Purchasing* 109(4), 1990, pp. 68 - 73.

Brown, M. "Pass the Pacel". *Management Today*, 1990, pp. 125 - 131.

Buss, M.D.J. "Managing International Information Systems". *Harvard Business Review* 60(5), 1982, pp. 153 - 162.

Cheung, H.K. & Burn, J.M. "Distributing Global Information Systems Resources in Multinational Companies - A Contingency Model". *Journal of Global Information Management* 2(3), 1994, pp. 14 - 28.

Contractor, F.J. & Narayanan, V.K. "Technology Development in the Multinational Firm : A Framework for Planning and Strategy". *R & D Management* 20(4), 1990, pp. 203 - 322.

Deans, P.C. & Kane, M.J. *International Dimensions of Information Systems and Technology*. 1992. Boston : PWS-Kent Publishing Company.

Dearden, J. "The Withering Away of the IS Organization". *Sloan Management Review* 28(4), 1987, pp. 87 - 91.

Egelhoff, W.G. "Information-Processing Theory and the Multinational Enterprise". *Journal of International Business Studies* 22(2), 1991, pp. 341 - 368.

Gates, S.R. & Egelhoff, W.G. "Centralization in Headquarters - Subsidiary Relationships". *Journal of International Business Studies* 17(2), 1986, pp. 71 - 92.

Ghoshal, S. & Nohria, N. "Horses for Courses : Organizational Forms for Multinational Corporations". *Sloan Management Review* 34(2), 1993, pp. 23 - 35.

Habib, M.M. & Victor, B. "Strategy, Structure, and Performance of U.S. Manufacturing and Service MNCs : A Comparative Analysis". *Strategic Management Journal* 12, 1991, pp. 589 - 606.

Hass, N. "A Global Report - The Indian Option". *Financial World* 161(2), 1992, pp. 50 - 51.

Hastings, P. "The Express Route to Contract Logistics". *Accountancy* 19(1182), 1992, pp. 68 - 69.

Hodgkinson, S.L. "Distribution of Responsibility for IT Activities in Large Companies : A Survey". *Research and Discussion Papers RDP 90/5, Oxford Institute of Information Management*, 1990.

Jarvenpaa, S.L. & Ives, B. "Organizing for Global Competition : The Fit of Information Technology". *Decision Sciences* 24(3), 1993, pp. 547 - 580.

Kim, K.K. "Task Characteristics, Decentralization, and the Success of Hospital Information Systems". *Information & Management* 19(2), 1988.

LaPlante, A. "Here Come the Hybrids : The Latest Shape for IS Organizations is a Mix of Centralization and Decentralization". *Computerworld* 25, 1991, pp. 24.

Lee, S. & Leifer, R.P. "A Framework for Linking the Structure of Information Systems with Organizational Requirements for Information Sharing". *Journal of Management Information Systems* 8(4), 1992, pp. 27 - 44.

Leifer, R. "Matching Computer-Based Information Systems with Organizational Structure". *MIS Quarterly*, 1988, pp. 63 - 73.

Moad, J. "Navigating Cross-Functional IS Waters". *Datamation* 35(5), 1989.

Negandhi, A.R. & Palia, A.P. "The Changing Multinational Corporation-nation State's Relationship : The Case of IBM in India". *PRIISM Working Paper, No. 87-002*. 1987.

Neo, B.S. "Information Technology and Global Competition : A Framework for Analysis". *Information & Management* (20), 1991, pp. 151 - 160.

Olson, M.H. & Chervany, N.L. "The Relationship Between Organizational Characteristics and the Structure of the Information Services Function". *MIS Quarterly* 4(2), 1980, pp. 57 - 68.

Porter, M.E. "Changing Patterns of International Competition". *California Management Review* 28(2), 1986, pp. 9 - 40.

Raphael, D.E. "Fly-by-night or Here to Stay ? - The Future for Air Express". *Long Range Planning* 25(2), 1992, pp. 52 - 62.

Roche, E.M. *Managing Information Technology in Multinational Corporation*. 1992. Macmillan Publishing Company.

Rosenzweig, P.M. & Singh, J.V. "Organizational Environments and the Multinational Enterprise". *Academy of Management Review* 16(2), 1991, pp. 340 - 361.

Senn, J.A. "Drivers of Globalization : The Intertwining of Business and Information Technology", in Khosrowpour, M. & Loch, K.D. (eds), *Global Information Technology Education : Issues & Trends*. 1993. Idea Group Publishing.

Tausz, A. "Integrators Go for Global Contracts". *Distribution* 91(10), 1992, pp. 38 - 46.

Tavakolian, H. "The Organization of IT Functions in the 1990s : A Managerial Perspective". *Journal of Management Development* 1(2), 1991, pp. 31 - 37.

Von Simson, E.M. "The 'Centrally Decentralized' IS Organization". *Harvard Business Review* 68(4), 1990.

SECTION-4

Global Systems Development and Outsourcing

The globalization of information systems has several implications: first, an information system can be developed jointly by developers located in various parts of the world, second, it may be operated and used anywhere in the world at anytime, and third the system may be both developed and used globally. The problems of development of large and complex software are legendry and well documented in the literature. The global dimension superimposes an extra layer of complexity on an already formidable task.

In the first chapter of this section, Nicholas Vitalari and James Wetherbe focus on practical strategies for global IS development based on years of international consulting experience. They suggest five tactics to implement the desired transnational model for a global firm to do business. They convincingly argue that IT has a key role to play in supporting these tactics. IS managers will be well-advised to examine the five recommended strategies for their global IS development. Section-7 provides practical flavor to these and many other strategies that MNCs like Seagate Technology, Citibank,and General Motors are employing to grapple with and succeed in dealing with GIS development and implementation.

Economic hardships and realities of the past decade have caused organizations to take a hard look at their IS budgets. As a result, many IS organizations have experienced downsizing and outsourcing. Firms increasingly rely on externally developed software. Drawing from his extensive consulting experience both inside and outside United States, Warren McFarlan discusses issues in international outsourcing. He divides these into two categories: software and operations. He discusses the impact of various factors one may consider in international outsourcing, and provides sound practical advice to managers based on their strategic motivation.

The last chapter in this section by Richard Heeks provides a thorough review of software outsourcing to India. India has become a major player in software outsourcing from developed to developing countries. He reviews outsourcing drivers, benefits, and costs to the client organization. A unique feature of this chapter is that it also examines the benefits and costs from the Indian sub-contractor's point of view. Benefits and cost reductions are not automatic, but require careful management and planning of the outsourcing process.

15 Emerging Best Practices in Global Systems Development

Nicholas P. Vitalari
CSC Index Research and Advisory Services, USA

James C.Wetherbe
The University of Memphis and
University of Minnesota, USA

With companies employing global structures to gain competitive advantages and ensure profitability, globalization of business is accelerating at a phenomenal rate. The primary objectives of this chapter are to explore the implications for companies going global and to identify the information technology (IT) infrastructure required to support global operations. This chapter draws upon previous work on the global management and the role of IT in global enterprise. Five operational tactics, accompanied by case examples, for implementing the predominant IT strategy are also presented. The chapter concludes with an extensive look at five strategies for successful global applications development, and the changing role of information systems (IS).

INTRODUCTION

Global business is accelerating at a phenomenal rate. Since 1950, world trade has proliferated over 700%, while world GDP has grown 400%. Rarely a week goes by where the balance of trade between the major countries of the world (frequently, the U.S.A. and Japan) is not a news item. Exports are key to that growth, with most countries today emphasizing exports and the balance of trade as a means and measure of economic growth and national vitality. In fact, one of the primary reasons for the imbalance of trade between the U.S.A. and Japan was Japan's concentration on exports (automobiles, electronics) for fueling internal growth, while the U.S.A. looked inward at its domestic markets. Whereas domestic markets may be saturated or limited, global markets often offer opportunities for profits and competitive advantage.

Companies are employing global structures to gain competitive advantages and ensure profitability. Some of the realized or expected economic benefits of globalization include:
- Economies of scale due to larger market for standardized products;
- Ability to locate value chain activities in locations offering strategic advantages low cost labor, skilled workers, financial markets, physical infrastructure, customer proximity; and

- Diversification of demand in multiple markets stabilizes overall firm performance in the face of economic fluctuations in individual markets

Chapter Overview

In this chapter, we explore the implications of companies going global and particularly the implications for information technology (IT), including the IT infrastructure required to support global operations. Using Bartlett and Ghoshal's model (1989) as the foundation, we examine four globalization structures employed by companies and Konsynski and Karimi's four approaches for aligning global structures with information management strategies. A discussion of the impact of companies' globalization on their industries and the ramifications for IT follows. The focus of the next section is the evolving IT strategy, examining five tactics for implementing the transnational strategy, supported by case examples. Five strategies for success in global applications development follow. The chapter concludes with a look at the changing role of IT and the future.

GOING GLOBAL: COMPETING IN THE INTERNATIONAL MARKETPLACE

What does the often used phrase *going global* really mean and why is it of interest from an information technology perspective? Looking at companies, going global means operating as a single, unified company worldwide, balancing resources across the entire company to implement a structure to compete with other firms and maximize total customer value. Operating as a global company entails different structures due to local, regional, national and worldwide economic, political, and social conditions. The structures determine a firm's management control systems, operations, and sales. Ultimately, they affect the development, deployment, and maintenance of information systems and the related infrastructure.

The role of IT in a globally operating company is a force for dissolving boundaries: time, distance, cultural, language, governmental, regulatory, organizational, customer, functional, competitor, to name a few. IT enables an organization to operate as if time and distance did not exist. The Internet, for example, blurs the boundaries of time and space and is an example of an emerging global infrastructure for the transport, storage, and retrieval of information and ultimately the conduct of electronic commerce. In reality, IT is an essential component for enabling firms to *go global* and critical to their success. Furthermore, IT is pivotal to the operation of the global marketplace itself. Using IT, for example, shipping ports, such as Singapore's TradeNet, can now provide in bound ships with clearances and other services based on digital manifestos accessible online. Similar devices and others will continue to evolve and further support new and more streamlined forms of global trading and transaction processing.

The rivalry between Firestone and Bridgestone, two tire manufacturers, demonstrates the competitive dynamics of going global. At one point in time, Firestone had 60% of the U.S. tire market along with a great reputation and strong brand identity. Bridgestone, on the other hand, was located in Japan with about 20% of the Japanese tire market. They sold tires in Europe (with market shares of 9% in Germany and 11% in England), Korea, Indonesia, and a variety of other places. While Bridgestone had a presence in many countries, they did not hold the predominant market share in any country.

Then Bridgestone became interested in entering the U. S. market. Advisors suggested they were *crazy*; that there was no way to do it successfully. But Bridgestone decided to enter the U.S. market and its first move was to undercut Firestone prices by 20%. To compete, Firestone had to drop its prices. What did Bridgestone do? Cut its prices another 5%. Firestone spent more money on advertising, to no avail. Firestone cut prices; Bridgestone cut prices another 5%. Firestone cut its prices again; Bridgestone cut prices another 5%. Firestone complained to the U.S. government; Bridgestone cut prices another 5%. Of course, the outcome was that Firestone's market presence was dramatically reduced.

Bridgestone accomplished this remarkable feat by raising their prices in other markets around the world using that as leverage to supplant Firestone in the U.S. As a result, Bridgestone/Japan became one of the *big three* tire manufacturers, competing with Goodyear/U.S. and Michelin/Europe.

Pressures Driving Localization

The global competitive landscape is also defined by many local factors. While many managers realize that local cultures and circumstances play a role in global competition, few realize the subtleties. For example, many managers realize the difference between doing business in Singapore as compared to France, but fail to recognize the importance from a global standpoint of conducting business in Midwest regions versus the Southwest region of the United States. Cultural and local subtleties exist within presumably homogeneous cultures. The astute global firm incorporates such features into their strategies. The following factors are some of the reasons for *acting local*, i.e., the pressures driving localization:

◊ Local languages   ◊ National, regional,protectionism
◊ Local cultures   ◊ Regulations, tariffs
◊ Local business practices   ◊ Communications weaknesses
◊ Local taste   ◊ Labor unions
◊ Local competitors   ◊ Transportation
◊ Proximity to local customer   ◊ Quality of local labor

Evaluating these pressures is most useful from the perspective of a particular industry by creating an industry overlay for the above list. For example, create an overlay using the consumer products industry, and more specifically the classic soap consumer industry. Which localization pressures from the list above would be pertinent? The first might be local competitors; with transportation second; then local taste. If a company is going to manufacture soap, local labor, proximity to the customer, labor unions, local business practices, cultures, and languages all become important.

The machine tools industry is another interesting example. Both Japan and Taiwan have been very successful bringing machine tools into North America. Regulations and tariffs on machine tools, for instance, are much less critical than they would be for the insurance or consumer products industries. The same is true for local taste, e.g., a mill is a mill; a bulldozer is a bulldozer, etc.

Thus, *acting local* is different depending on the industry; and there are important ramifications from an information technology standpoint. In a highly regulatory environment, for example, there is a high demand for information locally, which means unique information demands. Other examples of the need for local information include currency processing, tax laws, unique customer requirements, local deals with partners, or specific product formulas or services for local tastes.

Status of Globalization

The status of globalization in different parts of the world varies based on the indigenous situation in each of the areas, e.g., the general business climate, IT infrastructure, market characteristics, boundaries or obstacles. In North America, for example, micro-economies (i.e., the economic conditions and factors of a particular region such as the Midwest, the Research Triangle of North Carolina, southern California) are dominating the landscape of economic activity. In Europe, strong ethnic identities are a major factor requiring consideration during globalization. The evolving infrastructures in Latin America and Southeast Asia impact companies globalization efforts in those two regions. In Southeast Asia, *leapfrog computing* (rejecting the conservative, proven, evolutionary approach, and employing client/server technology, multi-media, i.e.,. whatever is state-of-the art) provides its own set of challenges to companies' with more traditional approaches. These factors are all pertinent to determining the best global structure to use when entering a new region or market, or when evaluating whether a current approach is working or not working effectively.

GLOBAL STRUCTURES MODEL

In 1989, Professors Bartlett and Ghoshal formulated a powerful framework to view global organizational structures based on observations in the marketplace. The model postulates that global firms move from a traditional, divisional organization, based on a domestic model of business, to a more elaborated and globally-compatible organizational structure as they gain experience and success in global markets. He argues that, in general, a global firm can be characterized into four strategic structures: 1) multinational, 2) global, 3) international, and 4) transnational (see Figure 1).

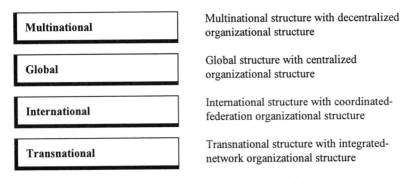

<table>
<tr><td>Multinational</td><td>Multinational structure with decentralized organizational structure</td></tr>
<tr><td>Global</td><td>Global structure with centralized organizational structure</td></tr>
<tr><td>International</td><td>International structure with coordinated-federation organizational structure</td></tr>
<tr><td>Transnational</td><td>Transnational structure with integrated-network organizational structure</td></tr>
</table>

Figure 1: Global Business Structures Model

Multinational Structure with Decentralized Organizational Structure

The multinational structure is likely the most prevalent approach used in the globalization process. Companies employing this structure have a headquarters base and operating units in various countries or markets. This structure might also be described as the *classic, domestically controlled model* which is really just an extension of a divisionalized organization.. There is little difference whether the company is headquartered in France, the U.K., the U.S., or Germany, the domestic company basically controls the rest of the global operations. Organizationally, there are fairly loose controls with strategic decisions made remotely. The lines of communication could be represented by inward flowing arrows from the remote business units to headquarters indicating that the remote sites funnel large quantities of information into headquarters. Strong financial reporting flow is a primary characteristic of the multinational structure; in fact, that is how control is exercised. Redundancy is a primary disadvantage because each site is performing its own activities. From an IT perspective, site autonomy creates difficulty for dissolving cross-functional boundaries. Cultural differences are also a factor.

Global structure with Centralized Organizational Structure

Used frequently by those firms which ventured early into *going global*, this structure involves a centralized organization with a global management perspective. The global structure involves a strong headquarters base and operating units in various countries or markets. The global structure presumes that headquarters knows best what is useful and valuable at distributed sites and that headquarters knows what is happening remotely, across many boundaries, e.g., different cultures, methods of operating, because all communication is outward from headquarters where all strategic decisions are made. This structure is difficult to maintain and keep stable. Information flowing one way allows little room for remote input, thus site differences and advantages are ignored operationally and, as a result, in information systems.

International Structure with Coordinated-Federation Organizational Structure

The international structure, a more contemporary approach, marries an international management perspective with an organization of coordinated federations, i.e., local units which have a federated relationship with each other. Assets and responsibilities are decentralized to the federations. Formal control systems exist, but the federations are more likely to work together for the good of their common customers with headquarters supporting and encouraging such an approach. However, with assets and responsibilities decentralized, coordination, sharing, and balancing of information or systems between units is difficult, although the possibility for some coordination between the two at least exists.

Transnational Structure with Coordinated-Federation Organizational Structure

The transnational structure is the most contemporary approach and has the most promise for the future. Management has a transnational perspective and the organization structure is weblike, an integrated network. Headquarters is highly involved in the complexities of both the coordination and the strategic decision processes. Capabilities, resources, and decision making are distributed to the remote sites. There are heavy flows of materials, people, information and technology. This structure is also characterized by internal labor and resource markets, high coordination costs; and absolute dependence on information systems and technology.

Bartlett and Ghoshal's framework is germane to our analysis for several reasons. First, the framework illustrates that as firms become more sophisticated, the organizational model moves to a more loosely-coupled, market-coordinated structure. The move to more differentiated, loosely-coupled organizational structures, that are more responsive to global markets, reflects the need for more diversity in global operations and more flexible responsiveness to local market demands. Fortunately, advances in information technology, particularly network and communications technology, provides the capacity to handle greater diversity in operations through integrated systems, E-mail, groupware, and Internet compliant web servers. Given these technology developments, a growing number of researchers on organization theory and the global structure of firms have argued that information technology affects the structure of the firm (see Miles and Snow, 1994; Venkatesh and Vitalari, 1992; and Ives and Jarvenpaa, 1991) and that ultimately firms will move to a more networked, loosely-coupled structure indicative of the transnational structure (see also Jarvenpaa and Ives, 1994; and Vitalari, 1990).

Second, as firms move to the international and transnational models, the control model changes by becoming more decentralized, permitting more local autonomy and local decision rights, but with the cost of more complex control and coordination systems. Third, although the ultimate transnational form is the most globally sophisticated, all forms are found at work today and have varying levels of success. Fourth, since the firm structure varies, particularly around control and coordination, it is likely that the underlying information systems strategies and infrastructure will vary according to each of the four structures.

Jarvenpaa and Ives (1993) examined empirically whether or not information technology structures varied according to Bartlett and Ghoshal's categories and found some support. Others, Alavi and Young (1992) have also postulated similar relationships between firm structure and information technology use. We would argue that, although the empirical data may be inconclusive, as networks and information technology become pervasive, the infrastructure to allow firms to operate in a more distributed but coordinated fashion will increase. It is further expected that global firms will be among the first to attempt to exploit these technological capabilities fully and thereby move them closer to the transnational model.

ALIGNING GLOBAL STRUCTURES AND INFORMATION STRATEGIES

In 1993, Konsynski and Karimi, took Bartlett and Ghoshal's framework and explored its implications for information systems. Konsynski and Karimi analyzed each of the four structures and proposed four different coordination strategies and the likely IS structure (see Table 1).

In the first example, the multinational strategy, Konsynski and Karimi contend that socialization is the key *Coordination/control strategy* to making this global structure work, i.e., people in the organization must believe this will work to overcome all the other issues working against it. And the correct IS structure is one of decentralization: stand-alone databases and processes, with information funneled back to the headquarters.

In the second example, *centralization* is the key Coordination/control strategy and IS structure, including centralized databases and processes. This translates to **strong** central control, and having the authority to mandate common systems. In fact, some research supports this approach as the best way to start in *going global*, and then move into the other dimensions gradually.

Business structure	Coordination/ control strategy	Coordination/ control mechanism	IS structure
Multinational/ decentralized federation	Socialization	Hierarchies: managerial decisions determine the flow of materials and services	Decentralization : stand - alone databases and processes
Global centralized federation	Centralization		Centralization: centralized databases and processes
International and interorganizatio-nal/ coordinated federation	Formalization	Markets: market forces determine the flow of materials and services	IOS: linked databases and processes
Transnational/ integrated network	Co-opting		Integrated architecture: shared databases and processes

Source: Konsynski and Karimi (1993)
Table 1: Alignment of Global and Information Management Strategies

Linking the databases and processes of interorganizational systems (IOS) is the third IS structure, facilitated through formalizing the interaction between organizational units, the federations. Coordination and control is done primarily through formal means, usually from headquarters. Since this is a very mixed model, linking together independent systems is probably the best approach from an IS development standpoint.

Finally, an integrated IS architecture with shared databases and processes is essential to aligning the global structures and informational strategies in the transnational model. The approach for accomplishing it is through co-opting   forming alliances.

From   an   information   systems   developer   perspective,   the coordination/control strategy is critical to success. For an IS developer in a multinational, decentralized federation, for example, the only way coordination can occur is through socialization of management   individual managers in the various countries or units have to have some sort of common, global vision. Otherwise, for example, if the developer goes to France to create a global system, the people there may be totally uncooperative because they see no need for what is being developed.

To facilitate globalization efforts, IS personnel must identify the coordination/control approaches in their organizations, and then determine how best to leverage them to accomplish having the various organization units share data and information, build common systems, etc. Often, there may be multiple approaches, e.g., some parts of the firm may be highly socialized and believe in the global process, others may be using the formal strategy, while still others are co-opting. The challenge is to find common concerns, common interests, or common values and form alliances accordingly.

GLOBALIZATION IMPACT ON INDUSTRIES AND INFORMATION TECHNOLOGY

While the global marketplace offers enormous potential for business growth, the key is understanding what the marketplace characteristics mean relative to implementing the four globalization strategies. Figure 2 presents the scale of opportunities on a global basis versus how extensive the demand is homogeneous (demand homogeneity).

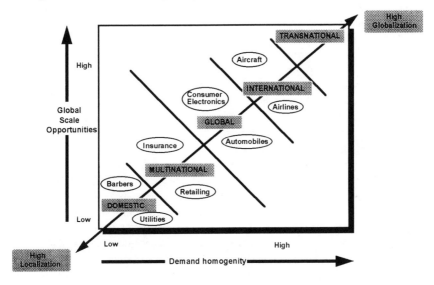

Figure 2: Globalization Impact on Industries

The objective of figure 2 is to show that as global scale opportunities vary, and as the demand for homogeneity varies, it is easier for companies to be successful with certain global structure models than with others. For example, a transnational model is better where global scale opportunities are high. And, correspondingly, if there is simultaneously a high homogeneous demand, the chances for success are even greater. The reason is that the more differentiation that exists within the global setting, the more difficult it is to coordinate. By contrast, it would be very difficult for a company to execute a transnational structure if all of its markets had different characteristics, different access requirements, different rates of growth, and different cultures. [Note: *Domestic* was added to this diagram as a global structure, with barbers and utilities as representative examples, just to show that having a completely domestic structure is almost impossible.]

This model also requires examination from an information systems perspective. For the Chief Information Officer (CIO) in an organization active in a few select, well-formed markets world-wide, e.g., French, Brazilian, New York, Los Angeles, Tokyo and Swedish markets (i.e., demand homogeneity is in the middle) with high scale opportunities in those markets (highly global), what is the best information systems strategy to use based on this model? Two examples of industries that fit this scenario well are the chemicals and petroleum industries. Regardless of whether they are selling petroleum, additives to consumer products, or adhesives, there are high global opportunities and mid-range demand homogeneity. So the best structure would be the Global structure.

Carrying that scenario further, consider what would happen in the chemicals industry if suddenly the business became highly localized due to an onslaught of *green ecology* legislation and severe enforcement of different regulatory requirements in each market. Would that make things more difficult for the CIO? The CEO? Often companies just pick a structure without considering these two dimensions and wonder why implementing it is so difficult, or worst case, unsuccessful. Or executives assume that information systems can overcome these fundamental structure problems. This model can be extremely useful in assessing a company's demand homogeneity and local opportunity, choosing the right structure, and determining the correct information systems model.

For the purpose of this chapter, Konsynski and Karimi's analysis suggests that we should observe different IS strategies and systems in the global marketplace across firms. Both Bartlett and Ghoshal's framework and Konsynski and Karimi's analyses suggest that in the long-run most firms will progress to the transnational model. The move to the transnational model is consistent with broader trends in organization structure and design discussed by Miles and Snow (1994), Drucker (1988), Vitalari (1992), and Lipnak and Stamps(1994), which emphasize the emerging network-orientation of organizational structures.

In the next section, we examine five tactics which characterize the move to the transnational organizational model among global corporations. The five tactics represent the linking of information technology capabilities with business process innovations that enable the more loosely-coupled organizational structure indicative of the transnational structure.

IMPLEMENTING THE TRANSNATIONAL MODEL

Figure 3 combines the pressures for localization, the pressures for globalization, and the four structure models, and illustrates the move to the transnational model. The transnational structure is effective when the pressures to globalize and localize are high because a company can maintain global economies and be locally responsive at the same time. Yet, it is also important to note that despite the movement toward the transnational model, some firms may find it useful to operate under other structures.

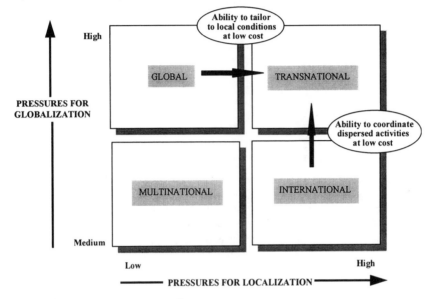

Figure 3: Global and Local Pressures vs. Structure Models

For example, if the pressures for globalization are medium (low was not used on the global scale because our research revealed there were no industries with a low need to go global) and pressures for localization are low, the multinational structure applies. The global structure works best where there is high pressure for globalization and low pressure for localization (homogeneous products). Where localization is high and the pressures for globalization are medium, the international model seems to fit best. Given the increasing pressures to globalize and localize simultaneously, the transnational model is evolving as the desired structure for companies and IT.

Five Tactics for Implementing the Transnational Model

Companies have used the five tactics presented in Table 2 to facilitate the implementation of the transnational model. Since these five tactics are most easily understood in the context of the experience of actual companies, the following applicable examples are pertinent.

1	Mass Customization
	(synergies through global research and development)
2	Global Sourcing and Logistics
3	Global Intelligence and Information Resources
4	Global Customer Service
5	Global Alliances

Table 2: Five Transnational Implementation Tactics

Mass Customization

In the book <u>Future Perfect</u> (1987), Stan Davis proposes the idea of product and service customization for an individual on a mass basis as being the ultimate end point of the information age. Currently, the most common examples of mass customization are found in the telecommunications, mass media, and consumer products industries, where some products and services are tailored for each consumer on the basis of unique needs (see Figure 4). When the concept of mass customization is applied in the global context, the firm looks at local requirements and attempts to customize products to those needs.

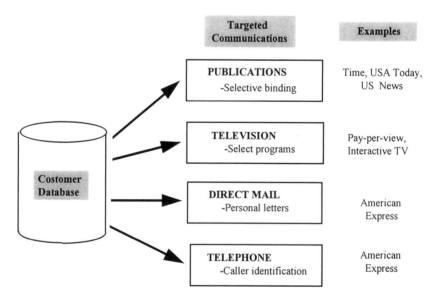

Figure 4: Mass Customization of Communications

For example, in the publications business, selective binding, wherein specialized advertising inserts or regional stories are inserted into the mass publication, is almost commonplace. Selective binding allows almost all national and international media firms to combine unique content of interest to local settings with common or *reusable* content that has mass appeal. Publications such as Time, USA Today, the Wall Street Journal, U.S. News and World Report, to mention a few, selectively bind inserts, advertisements, and stories to fit regional needs. USA Today, for instance, performs selective

on a centralized basis for the most part. Then, using satellite broadcasting technology, sends different versions of the newspaper all over the U.S.A., appealing to local readership, cultural tastes, micro-economies, and other regional factors. Selective binding technology is also seen in the creation of mail order catalogs based on the examination of regional and individual consumer profiles extracted from massively cross-referenced data warehouses.

Other examples include Frito-Lay which tailors product tastes to regional conditions. AT&T, MCI, and Sprint which provide different telecommunications services based on regional preferences. For example, AT&T's Pay-Per-View interactive TV division envisions using customer profiles, customer database, and regional information to develop customized programming down to the individual consumer level. With the advent of telephone caller-ID technologies, the capability to further refine the service that accompanies these products is expected to progress rapidly.

The common denominator in the mass communication strategy is the use of market information drawn from multiple sources on mass, regional and individual trends, preferences, and buying behavior. This information is collected in massive data warehouses, analyzed, and employed to form custom responses to individual and regional market needs. The use of information technology permits the global firm to collect, analyze, monitor, and respond in a targeted manner to unique conditions around the world.

TACTIC:	MASS CUSTOMIZATION / GLOBAL RESEARCH & DEVELOPMENT
CASE EXAMPLE:	Pharmaceutical
IT: ENVIRONMENT	Global database, global network (electronic conferencing, electronic mail)
OBJECTIVES:	• Scale economies in R&D, leveraging distinctive competencies • Local product externals with standard internals for scale economies in manufacturing
COMMENTS:	The IT environment and the first objective are particularly pertinent to the pharmaceutical industry, where R&D is going on all over the world and scientists need to keep in constant contact. Genetics research is another area where information is shared via global networks, e.g., over the Internet.

Table 3: Mass Customization. Global Research & Development Case Example

Table 3 provides an example of mass customization thinking employed in the pharmaceutical business where one firm has leveraged global research and development (R&D) activities occurring in regional locations.. The R&D activities are leveraged via interchange of information throughout the firm's wide-area network to optimize local product information with global manufacturing scale objectives.

Global Sourcing and Logistics

While mass communication seeks to meet customer requirements on a global basis, the global sourcing and logistics strategy seeks to optimize manufacturing cycle time and costs. Global sourcing and logistics attempts to obtain materials from vendors as close to the production site as possible and to establish global sourcing agreements with materials vendors who will guarantee material consistency and delivery schedules on a global basis. One growing addition to the global sourcing and logistics strategy is to create joint agreements to co-locate warehouse, manufacturing, and logistics facilities at optimized regional locations. Such ventures, which combine multiple companies, are feasible due to computer-based interorganizational systems.

TACTIC:	GLOBAL SOURCING & LOGISTICS
CASE EXAMPLE:	Benetton
IT ENVIRONMENT:	Global network, EPOS terminals in 4000 stores, CAD/CAM in central manufacturing, robots and laser scanner in their automated warehouse
RESULTS:	• Produce 2000 sweaters per hour using CAD/CAM • Quick response (in stores in ten days) • Reduced inventories (just-in-time)
COMMENTS:	Benetton captures information at its over 4000 electronic point of sale terminals, transmits it via the global network into their systems which control simple manufacturing, cuts the fabric robotically, dyes the fabric, assembles the finished goods and sends them to the automated warehouse, and ships the finished goods to the stores in response to the first step. Extremely quick response 10 days start to finish, with just-in-time inventory as a result. What is their secret? The United Colors of Benetton their advertising slogan provides the answer. By reducing styles and designs to a minimum, they can premanufacture most items, adding the <u>customer order color</u> later in the dyeing process. By simplifying 1) the product line and 2) their production, they are able to deliver to their customers on a global basis and cater to local taste.

Table 4: Global Sourcing & Logistics Case Example 1

Two firms exemplify the global sourcing and logistics strategy: The Gap and Benetton. Both firms have found success by: 1) simplifying the product; and 2) simplifying production to enable optimized global sourcing and logistics solutions. In both examples, the solutions depend heavily on the use of information technology. As seen in Table 4, Benetton has created a global telecommunications network which links point-of-sale information to manufacturing technologies through to the warehouse to create a global sourcing and logistics solution. Suppliers are expected to meet demand and delivery schedules and are provided information to meet logistics objectives. The Gap utilizes a similar strategy. In either case, local tastes, although strongly limited through product simplification, are supported.

Recently, the emergence of global logistics organizations such as Federal Express, Roadway, United Parcel Service, American President Companies, and others offer outsourced solutions which essentially take over the sourcing and logistics operation of major companies and assure that global operations can be optimized. Such shippers even implement a shipper terminated policy wherein suppliers' products are rejected if not received in time to meet agreed-to, just-in-time scheduling windows set by their customers.

Global sourcing is also seen in the global banking industry. Regional conditions abound and the condition affects the types of financial instruments and characteristics of financial services which are offered. Moreover, as the recent Barings Ltd. scandal indicates, the importance of financial information systems which are globally and regionally structured is paramount to a global financial institution's survival. Table 5 summarizes the global sourcing activity at Citibank, which uses its information systems to provide local conditions and global sources of funds information. Based on this information, Citibank can source local deals predicated on the best information from around the world.

TACTIC:	GLOBAL SOURCING & LOGISTICS
CASE EXAMPLE:	Citicorp
IT: ENVIRONMENT:	Global network
RESULTS:	Constructs a deal offering best rates and terms from offices around the world: • Several countries • Different currencies • Different tax jurisdictions
COMMENTS:	The product Citicorp is sourcing is money from any of their 90 branches, anywhere in the world. Their scenario involves having a customer come into a local branch to make a request for funds. The Citicorp customer service agent is able to create a portfolio (the above results) by having access to financial instruments available globally.

Table 5: Global Sourcing & Logistics Case Example 2

Global Intelligence and Information Resources

Maintaining the appropriate level of understanding of local and global conditions of the business prior to the advent of computer and communication technology was a daunting, almost impossible task. However, the ability to mount an effective campaign for global intelligence is now within the reach of most companies. The proliferation of Internet providers and other information network providers (e.g., CompuServe, America Online (AOL), Geisco) and the related growth in the off-the-shelf software (e.g., World Wide Web, HTML, TCP/IP, Netscape, Microsoft Windows, Lotus Notes) enables firms to establish, with relative ease, global intelligence networks with facilities for information collection, interchange, storage, and distribution inside and outside the companies.

Along with the proliferation of network capabilities has been the concomitant rise in information resources available on local conditions throughout the world. With the force of network externalities, the more sites created leads to more users and this in turn leads to more information resources at lower cost. Thus, as the worldwide digital infrastructure develops, the ability to effectively and efficiently conduct global intelligence increases rapidly. As evidence, consider a firm's radically greater access to local information resources in 1995 or later compared to operating globally in 1990. Various national governments have begun to monitor international digital transactions and the ingress and egress of data.

Hence, almost all global firms today maintain a collection of local databases assembled from internal and external sources. Many external providers offer customized data and will actually develop specialized filters and pipe the information into a firm's information systems. Tipsily, firms attempt to gather local intelligence on economic indicators, customers, business performance, competitors, and market conditions to make appropriate modifications to business strategies. From an information technology standpoint, the real differentiation among global firms is seen in the degree of seamless integration between the global intelligence activity and internal information sources and decision processes supporting company operations.

Global Customer Service

Major advances in global customer service depend on effective use of information technology. Many global industrial manufacturers depend heavily on suppliers which can provide a single global view of the customer. Global customer service is now a highly sought after competitive advantage. For example, a global manufacturer expects to know order status, delivery schedules, invoices, outstanding balances, and quantity of business on a global.
basis. The global manufacturer also expects consistent prices, consistent performance, and consistent quality. The service layer supporting global operations increasingly determines which suppliers are selected and which are

avoided. At the basis of global customer operations are global databases, common customer codes, sales force automation, interorganizational systems, and interconnected supplier systems with manufacturer's systems.

The same trends and conditions apply to other sectors. For example, investment banking and global retail banking success depend on global customer service operations. Customers of all types depend on access to financial resources anywhere, anytime. Similarly, the airline, hospitality, and telecommunications industries require global customer service operations. American Express Corporation, perhaps the preeminent global player in customer service, has offices with a full spectrum of financial and travel services all over the world. Table 6 illustrates some of the services offered by American Express. Although many travel companies and credit card consortia have copied American Express, it still stands out as best practice in global customer service.

Global Alliances

Global alliances have become commonplace, creating power for the companies involved. By allying and sharing key resources and assets, each company benefits in gaining quick access to new markets or by gaining new

TACTIC:	GLOBAL CUSTOMER SERVICE
CASE EXAMPLE:	American Express
IT: ENVIRONMENT:	Global network linked from local branches and local merchants to the customer database and medical or legal referrals database
RESULTS:	Offers companies faced with the common needs of traveling consumers (e.g., airlines, hotels, car rental, credit card usage, etc.), these customer service solutions: • World-wide access to funds • "Global Assist" Hotline • Emergency credit card replacement • 24-hour customer service
COMMENTS:	At the height of their operations, American Express was spending about one billion dollars a year on computing because their entire business is the information business. They had an early vision of what travelers would need, implemented it, and deliver it via a global network to airport kiosks and local branches. If someone loses a card, they send the information over the network and reproduce it locally. For cash advances, they comply with the local requirements on branch or non-branch banking. Regardless of the local requirements, they honor every request made of them. That's global customer service!

Table 6: Global Customer Service Case Example

skills and competencies. The airline industry offers several examples of global alliances and illustrates the necessity of information technology to deliver global business objectives. Almost all airlines have formed alliances to gain access to markets, provide new service levels to local customers, and encouragecustomer loyalty. As mentioned in the discussion on global sourcing, alliances provide an effective way to make use of resources without major investment and ownership. Table 7 illustrates the characteristics of the alliance formed by British Airways and U.S. Air. Other examples include KLM and Northwest, Delta and Virgin, and American Airlines and Quantas. Most importantly, such alliances are only feasible due to information technology that can track collections of data about customers including travel preferences and frequent travel awards.

Global Tactics Evolution

In the prior paragraphs, we reviewed five implementation tactics as separate approaches. In reality, each of the tactics is utilized in combination.

TACTIC:	GLOBAL ALLIANCES
CASE EXAMPLES:	British Airways / US Air KLM / Northwest Quantas / American
IT: ENVIRONMENT:	Global network (online reservation system)
RESULTS:	• Coordination of schedules • Code sharing • Coordination of flights • Co-ownership
COMMENTS:	Some of these alliances are a mixture of illusion and reality, e.g., British Air / US Air may be more of a merger than an alliance. But basically, these airlines are using their online reservation systems to form alliances through coordinating schedules and flights, and sharing codes and resources.

Table 7: Global Alliances Case Example

For example, a firm may use global information sources to gain customer understanding and then, in turn, use that information to establish and monitor a global customer services strategy. A global alliance may be used to take advantage of global sourcing abilities in the alliance. As firm sophistication rises with regard to global operations, one can expect the transnational firm to exhibit many of the tactics discussed, adding new ones as the global information technology infrastructure progresses.

Company	Result	System	Result Key Factors in Success or Failure
International computer and office products	Failure	Worldwide accounting system, deployed in 2-3 countries. Planned worldwide rollout stopped because of the level of customization being made for each country.	No strong global standards established. Culture did not support definition of standards. Regional autonomy.
Pharmaceutical	Failure	System to support mid-level pharmaceutical processes and clinical trials. System completed and implementation started. Rollout stopped and global deployment in review.	Could not overcome regional differences and barriers. Process-oriented applications are often difficult to deploy globally.
Auto-manufacturer	Failure	Manufacturing system for deployment in Far East, Europe and US regions. System highly customized for each region or region rejected.	Not invented here. Cultural differences and barriers.
Shipping	Success	Worldwide freight forwarding system 10+ sites	Uniform system deployed in multiple sites
Chemicals	Success	Manufacturing accounting success-package based	Single mainframe system with global standards used to support worldwide operations
Consumer products	Success	Financial applications built and then core functionality customized for 20-25 sites worldwide by central team	Reasonably standard core functionality with regional variations
Personal products	Success	Order entry and accounting system using primarily packages deployed in AS400 network worldwide	Reasonably standard product set with regional variations
International bank	Success	Trader decision support system built using object technology and rolled out simultaneously in New York, London, and Tokyo	High need and support for common system
Medical products	Success	Support system for self-directed teams. AS400 based systems linked to mainframe systems, built and supported centrally both installation and customization. Six sites.	Global standards
Consumer products	In process	Moving from a mix of some centralized systems with autonomous regions to global systems.	Uniform system deployed in multiple sites.
Air freight/courier	In process	Global distribution of a federation of systems (package and custom) using UNIX mainframe.	Expected to succeed because of global standards
Large financial services provider	In process	Central development using new technology and new organization structure. Objective is to replace distributed overlapping functionality with a single central system which will then be deployed worldwide with regional customization.	Very high risk. Uncertain. Clear senior business sponsorship but managed as an IT initiative with mixed business manager support.

Table 8: Composite of Global Case Studies

CRITICAL SUCCESS FACTORS FOR GLOBAL INFORMATION SYSTEMS

From our research, this collection of case studies represents a wide range of industries, successes and failures, the system(s) implemented, and the key factors attributing to success or failure of these globally operating companies (see Table 8). Some common denominators appear to be evident upon closer examination of the system implementation failures and of the successes. For example, a lack of standards and regional differences are two key reasons why implementation was unsuccessful. On the other hand, the companies tallied successes where standards were in place and adhered to, where regional differences were identified and incorporated, or where there was a high need for the system across business units.

In assessing these case studies as a whole, both successes and failures, the technology is rarely the driving factor tipping the scale either way. More likely, it is the *soft-side glitches* the management structure, the strategy of the organization, and then the cultural climate which dictate success or failure.

Other Global Issues

There are some issues which have not been dealt with effectively in any of the examples. Data was one of those issues; however, in all of the successful cases, data was dealt with either through a very elaborate enterprise data model or through specifying the database with aliases, etc. The application architecture issue is another area which has been omitted. However, the companies participating in the research identified the more critical issues presented in Table 9.

STRATEGIES FOR GLOBAL APPLICATIONS DEVELOPMENT

One of the key factors associated with success is following the right development strategy. Based on the cited case studies, research, consulting experience, and pertinent literature, the five strategies appearing in Table 10 offer success in developing global applications.

Issue	Facets	Discussion
Sorting It Out	Cultural vs. Organizational vs. Personal boundaries	Companies had difficulty distinguishing between cultural, organizational and personal issues. Oftentimes, organizational issues were more divisive than cultural issues. In fact, one company said they had greater difficulty building applications across domestic operations than in subsidiaries in other countries, i.e., the organizational boundary factor. Others indicated that personal barriers or personal problems created obstacles to building global systems.
Rates of Growth and Change in Markets and Regions	Status Market Position Capability	The different rates of growth and change in different markets and regions are another issue. The different statuses of the various globalization environments (e.g., North America, Europe, ...) affect globalization strategies. And a company may have different market positions in different regions with differing capabilities it can mobilize. Depending on what is happening in the markets, a company may be forced to operate in ways which it had not predicted.
Mandates and Leadership	Common communication, Common frameworks Common goals Common practices	This issue has to do with the extent to which solutions can be forced or mandated versus getting consensus. Contrary to the way we personally might like to believe this can be done, the research supports that the greatest successes occurred in organizations where strategies were mandated or implemented by a very strong leader and team. In the international trading system which was so successful, the need (information deficit) was so great that people just bought into it. So the issue is to what extent can a company establish common frameworks for communication, goals, and practices as a means to going global. Trying to get everyone to agree is not very expedient when a company is faced with extensive diversity, differences, and boundaries. Sometimes mandating a solution, while it does not ensure success, is the only feasible approach.

Table 9: Other Global Issues

1	Mandate use of best-in-firm application system
2	Use commercial off-the-shelf software packages
3	Cross-boundary development teams
4	Parallel development
5	Object class library strategy

Table 10: Five Strategies for Global Applications Development

Mandate Use of Best-in-Firm Application System

The basic philosophy behind this strategy is to search throughout the organization for the global application which best fits the business experience of every unit, i.e., the proven one, and then determine whether the common system can be modified into a single proposition which will be acceptable to all global units. The following questions must be asked:

Can it be globally deployed?

Does the architecture support it?

Is the right equipment available to support it?

To what extent is the application consistent with best practice?

What is available in the marketplace?

Is it feasible to mandate common use as the deployment option?

In addition to the above criteria, it is important to note that the best-in-firm strategy is based on several important assumptions: 1) The software provides the best match to the business process it supports; 2) It is better to modify the business organizations or processes to conform to the best-in-firm model; and 3) The firm can overcome local cultural and behavioral barriers to change and garner the appropriate level of acceptance.

A variation on mandating the best-in-firm is to transform the best-in-firm system with local modifications on an as needed basis. The same evaluation process identified above is used. Essentially, the common system is cloned, and limited, but agreed upon changes are made to the system according to local demands, and then a separate modified version is deployed locally. However, even if this strategy is managed correctly, the change and configuration management issues proliferate. In essence, the global firm ends up with a portfolio of many individual systems doing largely the same tasks, duplicating effort, and increasing the cost of maintenance in the long run. Thus, experience has shown that if the best-in-firm strategy is chosen, it is far better to alter the organization to fit the system rather than modifying the system for local conditions.

Use of Commercial off-the-Shelf Packages

Conceptually, this strategy is similar to the first strategy in that it starts with something rather than nothing   using a commercially available software package for global deployment and use. This approach has been very popular in Europe and is gaining in popularity in North America and elsewhere with packages offered by SAP. A.G., Oracle, PeopleSoft, Systems Software Association (SSA), and others. Many of the newer packages provide integrated enterprise solutions and can be configured extensively. However, best practice in package implementation recommends minimal modification to the package and that additionally required functionality not found in the package should be built independently and interfaced into the package. Often, the independent functionality is seen as *cocooning* the commercial package, and many packages now have application programming interfaces (APIs) to facilitate interaction with other packages and systems.

The commercial software package strategy includes the following steps:

- Use JAD (joint application development) methods to determine requirements and prototypes to validate requirements;
- Limit the number of vendors to be examined   do not attempt to achieve a perfect fit between software product and requirements;
- Test candidate packages and negotiate with vendor;
- Create a time box for the project (see Wetherbe and Vitalari, 1994, for a description of the time box approach to project management);
- Cocoon any changes in other systems to preserve package functionality, integrity, and future vendor-supported upgrades and modifications;
- Change the business process and organization to conform to package; and
- Adopt and enforce architectural assumptions and standards implied in the package.

The package approach has been successfully applied in a number of industries. A large global consumer products firm, a large global manufacturer, and a global petroleum products firm have used this strategy to completely revamp their operations and support global operations.
The consumer products company used IBM's AS/400 as their hardware, and rolled their application out in Southeast Asia, the U.S.A., Europe, and Latin America. The manufacturing company operates in Singapore, Japan, Korea, U.S.A., and three European areas. The petroleum firm was able to completely integrate European operations and establish standard operating procedures.

Cross-Boundary Development Teams

The philosophy behind this strategy is that obtaining support for global applications requires the appropriate leadership and the appropriate multicultural, multi-disciplinary team. The team leader is key, must be multi-cultural, and at least a benevolent dictator (dictator in the worst case). This strategy employs the following steps:

a) Identify and assemble multicultural and multidisciplinary team;
b) Assure team is composed of opinion leaders and has strong leadership;
c) Use JAD + Prototype + Time box to develop application;
d) Use progressive rollout strategy and clone rollout teams;
e) Incorporate local talent to build application anc use infrastructure.

Generally the core team is fairly small, eight to ten people. When the application building process commences, the team increases and incorporates local talent.

Research in this area included banks and a worldwide manufacturing company, headquartered in Sweden with divisions in the U.S.A. and the Far East. The manufacturing company, in particular, contended that once it moved to cross-boundary development teams, the application development process worked much more effectively. In fact, the company now uses cross-boundary development teams everywhere in the world. Recently, the manufacturer deployed a system in Louisiana/Alabama/Florida even using a cross-cultural team for building the system. Medtronic has used this strong leader, multi-cultural team approach very effectively.

Parallel Development Teams

This strategy differs from the previous three because the underlying philosophy emphasizes regional differences right from the beginning with hooks established later to create a global system. Strategy 4 approaches application development this way:

a) Local or regional teams are formed;
b) Local teams examine local requirements for application and infrastructure;
c) Separate systems are constructed;
d) Applications interconnections established via bridges or internal EDI;
e) Strong decoupling maintained.

This strategy relies on cooperation at the end to create the global system a multi-cultural, cross-boundary team comes together eventually. One variation had the local teams come together at a central site after developing their local requirements. At the central site they resolved differences, building the system with a certain percentage of regional differences, and then a common structure. Despite obtaining local input and having representation, the local representatives encountered problems upon return to their units, being accused of *selling out*, omitting strong regional preferences, and not bringing back the system the region wanted.

Object Class Library Strategy

The final strategy is the object class library strategy. This approach makes heavy use of object oriented technology, and approaches development following this methodology:

a)   Cross-boundary development teams work to develop local and global requirements;

b)   Version 1 object class architecture established;

c)   Search for relevant commercial class libraries;

d)   Fast-cycle development approach used to develop class libraries;

e)   Object class architecture refined   local and global class variations and standards established;

f)   Integration and rollout in concert with existing legacy architectures.

This strategy takes advantage of the fact that different object class libraries reflect the different local and global requirements and that there can be inheritance within the object structure. Once the common objects are identified, variations can be incorporated to reflect local requirements. The end result is a system that operates locally with global commonality.

Two very different examples of this strategy follow. The first example, a small, trading system using the NEXTStep development environment was very successful. The second example was a much more ambitious effort for a global order entry, order fulfillment system, with C++ being used in a client-server environment. The object class architecture was much more complex for the second project, but advantageous at the same time to balance the needs of both order entry and order fulfillment.

CREATING A TRANSNATIONAL IT DEPARTMENT

The extensive consolidation around *going global* requires that companies, and particularly IT personnel re-think their role in the organization. The global movement demands a shift from passive (order takers) to active (information sharers); from cost driven to value driven; from independent support to intimate partner. In the absence of a company-wide global business structure, research suggests that IT managers should create a prototype transnational IT department to effectively deliver and support IS in their organizations. The following four step approach provides one proven method for success:

- Conduct a skills inventory   identify centers of competence
- Define technology management principles, models, and standards (Get senior management endorsement when timing is right)
- Link up   expand the global network for information systems professionals and provide other mechanisms (e.g., meetings) for sharing and learning
- Look for opportunities for rationalizing systems and data center operations regionally and globally

CONCLUSIONS

In this chapter, we have examined a range of contemporary strategies employed by global corporations in the use of information technology. We have argued that the structure of the global firm differs substantially from strictly domestic firms and that this structure has an impact on the information technology strategies deployed. In addition, our observations of the global setting suggest that most firms with global objectives and operating models are moving over time to the transnational model. Interestingly, the transnational model more closely resembles some of the recent network-style organizational structures which are more team-based and flat in comparison to the classic, divisionalized structure.

We have noted that many of the firms observed in our work utilize at least five major tactics to leverage information technology for global purposes. In many cases, these tactics are also consistent with recent reengineering plays to take advantage of process simplification and the power of shared databases. Finally, we argued that the actual process of systems delivery and implementation plays a significant role in the use of technology in global operations. Change management, long an important issue in systems implementation, seems to play an even more important role in the successful implementation of global systems.

Finally, we have suggested that senior information executives in global firms begin to model their own IT organizations on the transnational model. By moving to the transnational model within the IT organization, IT managers and professionals will become familiar in a microcosm with the issues of network organizational design and operating in a highly distributed model. Perhaps more importantly, the transnational model closely resembles the IT models implied by various forms of IT outsourcing.

As firms approach the 21st century, it is becoming increasingly clear that technology is further blurring traditional boundaries and our sense of time and space. Perhaps in the long run, we will look back and consider the global firm an interesting anachronism for a point in time when human collaboration and organizational structures were limited by local traditions and low bandwidth communication.

References

Alavi, M. and G. Young, *Information Technology in an International Enterprise: An Organizing Framework*, Global Issues of Information Technology Management, P. Palvia, S. Palvia, and R. Zigli (Eds.), Idea Group Publishing, 1992, pp. 495-56.

Davis, S., Future Perfect, Addison-Wesley Publishing Company, 1987.

Drucker, P., *The Information-Based Organization*, The Harvard Business Review, January - February, 1988, pp. 45-53.

Ives, B and S. Jarvenpaa, *Applications of Global Information Technology: Issues for Management*, MIS Quarterly, March 1991, pp. 33-49.

Jarvenpaa, S. and B. Ives, *The Global Network Organization of the Future: Information Management Opportunities and Challenges*, Journal of Management Information Systems, Vol. 10, No. 4, Spring 1994, pp. 25-27.

Jarvenpaa, S. and B. Ives, *Organizing for Global Competition: The Fit of Information Technology*, Decision Sciences, Vol. 24, No. 3, 1993, pp. 547-580.

Lipnak, J. and J. Stamps, The Age of the Network: Organizing Principles for the 21st Century, Oliver Wright Publications, Inc., 1994.

Miles, R and C. Snow, Fit, Failure and the Hall of Fame, Simon and Schuster Inc., 1994.

Venkatesh, A. and N. Vitalari, *An Emerging Distributed Work Arrangement: An Investigation of Computer-based Supplemental Work at Home*, Management Science, Vol. 38, No. 12, December, 1992.

Vitalari, N., *Exploring the Type-D Organization: Distributed Work Arrangement, Information Technology and Organizational Design*, Research Issues in Information Systems: An Agenda for the 1990's, A. M. Jenkins et. al. (Eds.), Wm. C. Brown Publishers, 1990.

Wetherbe, J. and N. Vitalari, Systems Analysis and Design: Best Practices, West Publishing, 1994.

16 Issues In Global Outsourcing

F. Warren McFarlan
Harvard Business School, USA.

Companies are increasingly globally outsourcing Information Technology (IT) for a variety of reasons such as concern for cost and quality, lagging IT performance, supplier pressure and other financial factors. This chapter identifies those situations where outsourcing development work is likely to be successful and where it is likely to be problematical. It also identifies those environments where outsourcing IT operations makes sense and where it will produce little, if any, advantages. The author's final contention is that while much of the detailed work of IT can be outsourced, management responsibility cannot be outsourced and the job of the CIO is going to be more important in the next decade than it was in the last decade. This job, however, may involve more managing of relationships with staff.

INTRODUCTION

Since the 1992 publication of "Global IT Management" by Palvia, Palvia and Zigli, several dramatic changes have occurred which have profoundly impacted the global management of IT activities. Amongst the critical changes are the following:

1. A sustained 35-50 percent per year drop in the cost of chips, memory and other pieces of hardware which has profoundly impacted the economics of providing and linking IT services around the globe.

2. An explosion in the availability of cheap broad-band fiber which now reaches six continents, supplemented by satellite communications.

3. A surge in development of inter-organizational systems and global inter-connectivity. The recent prominence of the Internet ensures that this growth will accelerate rapidly.

4. The increasing reliance of firms on external software. The reality is that today less than one-tenth of one percent of the code used inside a company has been developed inside the company. The information systems organization for the most part has become an internal systems integrator.

5. Outsourcing has become a highly relevant alternative as companies like Xerox[1] and Kodak[2] have gone to international outsourcing of major pieces of their operations.[3]

As one looks to the future from this base, several points are clear. The first is that the evolution of the technology and cost performance will continue at the same or faster rates for a period in excess of 20 to 30 years. This will pose continual challenges for firms as they scan new alternatives and try to decide reliably when they should make specific investments. The need for accessing relevant outside expertise will intensify as firms try to manage software implementation risk on the one hand and exposure to being backwards in software features on the other hand.

Second, the spread and use of global networks will evolve much like the highway system of the 20th century or the railroad system of the 19th century. It is important to understand that each of these systems took 50 to 70 years to evolve and stabilize. In each case the end output of these technologies dramatically changed the structure of society in ways radically different from what the originators thought they were going to be. While railroad and highway predominantly impacted an individual country, airlines are an example of how different countries have been knit together by a technologically based system. The global information highway will have a similar deep and probably ill-understood impact at this time.

Third, outsourcing will be a massively growing business as firms find they have neither the expertise nor capital to develop solutions on their own to deal with the issues raised by the first two points. Much as the textile firms with their looms in the 14th century destroyed cottage weaving activities, a similar challenge lies before many IT departments today. Last year alone, over forty billion dollars of outsourcing contracts were written with a substantial increase expected this year. To use a more contemporary example, most companies in the 1880s generated their own electricity, but by 1910 were using the outputs of large utilities. The same phenomena is impacting the IT service's industry as we move towards the 21st century.

In looking at this phenomenon, I find it useful to sort it into two parts. The first are issues relating to the development of specific software-based applications. The second part concerns the centers of data processing operations and networks including the cost effective reliable maintenance of desktop devices. The following sections will discuss these two parts in detail.

SOFTWARE DEVELOPMENT

Realistically, the major part of a firm's software development has already been outsourced with little fanfare. Most firms today would not think of developing their own word processing software, operating system software, computer assisted design software, or local area networks (LAN) software. A very large industry of specialist firms has grown up to develop and provide these items. This industry thrives by being located close to highly skilled innovative pools of software talent. Realistically, the best technical software people in the world are attracted to these firms. They are where the action is.

At the same time, however, there remains a significant role for developing in-house software which takes these packages and links them directly to the specific needs of the firm. Additionally, firms also continue to execute very large customized development projects today because packages are not available for their needs. In the last several months, for example, the author has looked at a twenty-five million dollar order entry system and a thirty million dollar inventory and warehouse management systems project. In looking at these customized development projects, there are three important aspects which bear on their management and whether outsourcing is practical.[4]

Project Size

The larger the project in terms of dollar expense, staffing levels, elapsed time and number of departments affected by the project, the more appeal outsourcing has as the inevitable coordination costs in such an endeavor can be covered more easily by the larger base. Multimillion-dollar projects generally require less coordination costs per dollar of expenditure than $50,000 projects. A related concern is the size of the project relative to the normal size of the development group's projects. Very large projects in relation to the firm's experience base are highly risky. Outsourcing can help reduce the risk of projects which are much larger than the firm's normal experience, assuming that they can be appropriately structured.

Experience with Technology

The complexity of a project increases as the project team's and organization's familiarity with the hardware, operating systems, database management and project application language decreases. A technically skilled outsourcer familiar with these technologies can mitigate many of the risks of a project which otherwise might be too high risk for a firm to prudently execute.

Project Structure

For some projects, the nature of the task defines the processing, file structures and outputs completely from the moment of project conceptualization. Such projects can be classified as "highly structured." They are much easier to outsource and carry much less risk than projects whose outputs are more subject to the user-manager's changing judgment on desirable features. Business process reengineering projects are excellent examples of the kind of project where judgments are continually changing and thus, outsourcing them is very complex if success is to be achieved. Conversely, the outputs of highly structured projects are fixed and not subject to much change during the project's life. Consequently, these projects are much easier to outsource. A recently examined order management software project was an example of this work.

Domestic software outsourcing has been a part of the industrial scene for most of the past thirty years. International outsourcing of software development, however, is relatively new. Some of the major factors driving its growth today are the following.

In 1995, wide disparities exist in software developer labor costs around the world. This disparity of costs combined with cheap global communications has opened up the opportunity to move project development work around the globe cost effectively. For example, in India today, the cost of a client/server programmer is roughly $7,500 while a similar individual in the eastern US would run $75,000 or more. While it is clear that over time this gap will narrow, its existence today economically legitimatizes international software outsourcing. At the beginning of 1995, over a hundred thousand people in India were devoted solely to the development of software for companies in the USA and western Europe. *Exhibit 1* is a sample list of firms (from A to W) who have engaged in this practice. The combination of English as the prime language, a strong educational system, and good global communications has allowed this to happen. Similar things have occurred in the Philippines and minus the English capabilities, aggressive discussions are also taking place in China and the Russian Republic. Analysis of successful work to date suggests that international outsourcing software development is particularly good for large projects or for a sustained stream of maintenance activities on Legacy Systems. The coordination costs of setting up an arrangement are significant and thus, the larger the project is, or more the chance of several projects over a long term the more these costs can be spread.

Abbey National	Allied Vans	Anz Bank	Apple
Arthur Anderson	Ashton - Tate	AT&T	British Telecom
Britannia Building Society	Ciba-Geigy	Citibank	Consolidated Freightways
Data General	Digital	Dun and Bradstreet	Fireman's Fund Insurance
Hewlett Packard	IBM	John Deere	KPMG
Merrill Lynch	Microsoft	North West Water	Novell
Oracle Corp.	Price Waterhouse	Singapore Airlines	Swiss Air
Texas Instruments	Unisys	Verifone	Woolwich Building Society

Exhibit 1: Examples of Organizations Doing Major Development in India

Additionally, it should be noted that leading-edge software technology skills are readily available around the globe. The reality, for example, is that the senior cadre of many Indian software organizations were educated in the US or western Europe and either for family reasons or an inability to get a permanent visa, returned home to work with the competent graduates of local educational institutions. The hypothesis of an earlier period, therefore, that high technology projects could not be done globally has turned out to be fallacious. The real issues instead turn on the concept of structuredness. Where the end outputs are very clear or where only a few changes are likely to be required, global outsourcing of software development has been largely effective. Where the specifications are evolving or otherwise not clear and where there is substantial need for "give and take," e.g., in systems design, these arrangements have tended not to work out well. In one situation recently reviewed by the author, a business process reengineering effort for a chemical company generated a system containing 700,000 lines of code. The computer programs were completely debugged and operated flawlessly for an utterly "non-existent real world situation" (the specification needs had dramatically evolved during the time of project development). This suggests that large highly structured projects almost irrespective of the technology can be safely developed by a competent remote global partner with a high likelihood of positive results. Conversely, for projects which have elements of low structure and whose specifications are likely to evolve over time, the geographic distance turns out to be a real problem. These projects are best done either in-house or by a geographically close outsourcer. *Exhibit 2* summarizes these observations on outsourcing global system development.

		Low Structure	High Structure
Low Technology	**Large Project**	Poor Global Outsourcing Candidate	Good Global Outsourcing Candidate
	Small Project	Poor Global Outsourcing Candidate	Poor Global Outsourcing Candidate Unless Part of a Portfolio
High Technology	**Large Project**	Poor Global Outsourcing Candidate	Good Global Outsourcing Candidate if partner has technology skills
	Small Project	Poor Global Outsourcing Candidate	Poor Global Outsourcing Candidate Unless Part of a Portfolio and Partner has Technology Skills

Exhibit 2: Effect of Degree of Structure, Company-Relative Technology, and Project Size on Project Implementation Risk

MANAGEMENT IMPLICATIONS

For medium to large organizations, the opportunities posed by global software development are very significant and must be examined. In examining this domain, several important practices have emerged which significantly increase the likelihood of success.

1. Take the time to go visit the country if you have work that meets the above characteristics.   There are many very attractive firms who have strong

technical capabilities, but are still learning how to reach the USA/European market. If you deal only with firms who have a strong USA/European marketing presence, you will both miss key firms and potential development savings. The USA/European marketing costs of an Indian software firm for example are intense (the same as USA companies) and account for a significant element of their total project costs. Government agencies, such as for example, the electronics and computer export promotion council of the Ministry of Commerce in India can help you make the arrangements to see company premises and directly assess the people who will be working on the project. To get the most significant savings, the work needs to be done in the remote location as opposed to transplanting people to the purchasing firm's home country for a period of time.

2. Work on several modest projects with the global outsourcer before undertaking mega development efforts (to ensure quality). It takes a significant change in management process and mindset to shake down an appropriate work pattern that spans the globe.

3. Carefully check client references and financial stability. Similar to US software companies, while the barriers to entry for a new firm are low, the exit barriers are equally low. Track record and financial stability are important items in general and even more so given the geographic separation of the two organizations.

4. Understand that outsourcing of development is a practical alternative to full outsourcing (which includes data center operations, network operations, etc.). Given the cost savings, not surprisingly, most major systems integrators have developed systems and software development capabilities in remote low-cost, easily telecommunications accessible environments as a way to contain costs and get new business. This approach is used by some firms for new client/server applications, (so existing staff can maintain current operational code which they understand) and by other firms for their basic maintenance (so they can leverage their existing staff on the client/server applications of the future.)

5. Recognize that the global information highway means the export of knowledge workers job as it allows a balancing of global labor market inefficiencies. Realistically, you can expect the same internal hostility towards these moves as accompany any transfer of manufacturing facilities from one location to another. However, these are transition problems and if you don't do this where it makes sense, you will be at a severe competitive disadvantage.

OPERATIONAL OUTSOURCING

Driving Forces

A series of a factors drive the consideration of outsourcing one's global operational IT activities.[5] First and foremost is a genuine general management frustration over *IT costs and response time*. Trapped in a spending spiral to upgrade outdated legacy systems, they have no ability to manage new investments.

Second, are the difficulties a firm faces over installing *global standards on infrastructure* by its internal staff. Current estimates suggest that the average network costs of supporting a networked client ranges between $10,000 and $13,000 per year.[6] Today's new outsourcing arrangements are driving this cost down to the $4,000 to $5,000 per year level engendering major operating savings. Third, there is a rapidly growing industry of firms which have demonstrated the capability to do national outsourcing effectively and which are reaching towards the global market. These firms would include IBM, Andersen Consulting, Computer Sciences Corporation and EDS. Each of these firms, however, although deeply skilled in domestic market outsourcing has limited skills to date with which to run large global outsourcing arrangements. Selecting a viable experienced global vendor was the single biggest problem facing Xerox in 1994.

Fourth, is the need to simplify a firm's general management agenda. A number of firms under intense pressure in their markets and underlying technologies have gone back and reviewed their core competencies. In this review, they discovered that learning how to run data centers and stable global networks reliably and cost effectively is not something they needed to focus on as there are other firms who have genuine capabilities in this area. Realistically, management has only a finite attention span, and must husband it for the highly leveraged issues.

Fifth, significant financial issues are driving global outsourcing. The first is the opportunity to take assets off the firm's balance sheet. In many of these arrangements, the outsourcer acquires all the firm's computing equipment and networks for book value plus a goodwill premium. This allows the firm to make its investments only in highly firm specific assets. This is a major factor particularly for high target rate of return firms facing capital shortages. Also linked to it is the ability to take formerly fixed costs and turn them into variable costs. The outsourcer who handles many firms activities can deliver much greater variability in costs than an in-house operation, as the volumes of business rise and fall.

Sixth, often the only way to affect major internal cultural change is to transfer responsibility for the activity to an outsider. The dynamics of dealing with a third-party firm where hard cash passes hands is fundamentally different and more professional than dealing with an in-house IT activity. The author has personally observed several situations where multiple data centers needed to be collapsed and corporate standards enforced. The firm's internal IT unit simply did not have enough clout to make those things happen. When the firm went to an outsourcer, however, as part of the negotiating contract process, these problems disappeared. Finally, of particular importance to the medium-sized organization is its ability to get access to specialized technical skills in remote locations. The major outsourcers mentioned earlier all have much greater staffing and technical depth than you can expect in a medium-sized organization whose operations are relatively thinly spread around the globe. In aggregate, these points have driven global outsourcing of networks and data centers to the top of the multi-national firm's list of activities to consider. *Exhibit 3* summarizes these issues in showing the major drivers that led Xerox to outsource their overall networks and data centers.

---

1. Enabling the acceleration of data center consolidations by speeding up moves faster than it could accomplish with internal staff.

2. Gaining access to outside vendors' IT knowledge which was more specialized than Xerox possessed.

3. Enabling Xerox to take advantage of outside vendors' economies of scale in operations and purchase discount.

4. Allowing a much easier implementation and enforcement of standards than could be done by internal staff.

5. Allowing internal IT management to focus solely on new IT infrastructure and development by relieving them of custodial responsibility for maintaining the old system.

6. Permitting a much faster phasing down of Legacy systems.

7. Permitting sharper focus of Xerox's internal resources on its mission as "The Document Company."]

Exhibit 3: Reasons for Xerox Outsourcing Its Global IT Activities[7]

Associated Risks

There are, however, significant potential concerns and risks about global outsourcing of operations. The most deeply felt risk is usually articulately expressed by the firms' operations management that they are losing control over an important corporate resource. It is critical that this notion of control be dealt with pragmatically. The reality is that every organization depends deeply on the reliable operations of outsiders. Few firms could survive for more than a very few days when there are major collapses in their telephone service, electric power or water. The aforementioned utilities (none of which existed one hundred years ago) have responded to this need. IT operational outsourcing is simply another evolving potential example of this inter-dependence.

More important, the cost savings of outsourcing this activity needs to be carefully and pragmatically examined to ensure they are there. The larger an organization becomes, the more opportunities it has on its own to reach global scale efficiencies if they put their mind to it. This study needs to be done with a substantial element of pragmatic disinterested analysis. Realistically, since all of the outsourcers are profit-making organizations, if your firm is highly efficient, they will be the first to draw it to your attention by not wanting to bid on your work.

The stability of the outsourcing vendor is also very important. Disengaging from a relationship can be extremely difficult. Therefore, in recognition of this reality and the favorable economics of long-term contract operational outsourcing, contracts of eight to ten years are the norm. It is thus crucial that you satisfy yourself of your partner's long-term financial viability. This is particularly important in 1995 because at present there is no regulatory supervision of outsourcers. The earlier mentioned examples of electronic utilities, telephone companies and water utilities are now almost always regulated. It is the author's belief that similar regulatory moves will eventually come to this field. Perhaps the most important potential risk is for both sides to clearly understand the needs and issues at every level of management. Particularly in its early stages, outsourcing is very much a strategic partnership and a rich network of linkages needs to be set up ranging from very senior management in both organizations to quite junior levels. These linkages are important in the detection and management of the irritants in the relationship before they get out of control.

Strategic Relevance

In thinking through international outsourcing of development and operations, a critical issue is how strategically dependent the firm is on IT, both operationally and as a source of innovation/business transformation. *Exhibit 4* is a framework that demonstrates IT's strategic relevance to a company/business unit at a particular point in time.[7] The vertical dimension focuses on the company's current dependence on utterly reliable cost-efficient computers and/or networks. When networks collapse, to what extent is the firm able to keep its global operations and core services going with only minor disruptions, and to what extent is the firm severely impaired? When the Reuters news service goes down, an airline reservation system stops working or an ATM network collapses, the firm's core activities are immediately and brusquely stopped. Conversely, when a marketing information system or research center data analysis capability are interrupted for example for a week or more, the damage is not nearly so significant and in reality, negligible in most cases as people turn their attention to other activities.

The horizontal dimension on Exhibit 4 focuses on the strategic importance/impact of new systems and services currently under development. Are they absolutely core to the company's future viability, competitiveness, and survival or are they more in the category of useful but in a pinch postponable.

High		
	Factory	**Strategic**
	Outsourcing Presumption: Yes, unless company is huge and well managed	Outsourcing Presumption: No
	Reasons to consider outsourcing:	Reasons to consider outsourcing:
	· Possibilities of economies of scale for small and midsize firms. · Higher quality service and backup. · management focus facilitated. · Fiber-optic and extended channel technologies facilitate international IT solutions.	· Rescue and out-of-control internal IT unit. · Tap source of cash. · Facilitate cost flexibility. · Facilitate management of divestiture.
	Support	**Turnaround**
	Outsourcing Presumption: Yes	Outsourcing Presumption: No
	Reason to consider outsourcing:	Reasons to consider outsourcing:
	· Access to higher IT profession- alism. · Possibility of laying off is of low priority and problematic · Access to current IT technologies. · Risk of inappropriate IT architectures reduced.	· Internal IT unit not capable in required technologies. · Internal IT unit not capable in required project management skills.

CURRENT DEPENDENCE ON INFORMATION

Low   **Importance of Sustained, Innovative**   High
Information Resource Development

Exhibit 4: Strategic Grid for Information Resource Management

Outsourcing IT operational activities is generally attractive as it allows attention to be focused more crisply on core differentiating activities of the firm. It relieves the need for keeping on the payroll specialists who are both hard to find, and whose long-term career paths are difficult to plan. Important scale opportunities also exist for the small and mid-size organization (under $500 million sales). For example, in 1991 Air Products and Chemicals, using channel extendor technology, was able to close down a UK data center supporting 600 on-line European terminals and transfer the processing work to their Pennsylvania data center. This project saved them two million dollars a year. The process of conversion was so smooth that no one in Europe was able to tell when the conversion was made and over the next year, response time on the terminals either remained the same or improved.

As the size of the organization grows, however, the impact of these two ideas begins to diminish as companies can be economically self-sufficient in this domain (if they wish to be). For massive operations like American Airlines (who hasn't outsourced) and Xerox (who has), the challenge is for the outsourcer (whose core business is IT) to show they can bring more intellectual horsepower, discipline and cost control focus to the task.

When the applications' development portfolio is filled with maintenance work or projects which are valuable, but not vitally important to the firm, transferring these tasks to an outsourcer holds few strategic risks. When new systems development, however, is at the core of significant differentiation and/or massive cost reduction, the outsourcing decision comes under more scrutiny, particularly when the firm has a large, technically innovative, well-run IT organization.

Exhibit 4 shows that the presumption for outsourcing is *yes* for companies in the support quadrant. The cost savings for very large companies can be truly significant, as both focus and true professionalism can be brought to this often neglected area. Similarly, for firms in the factory quadrant, the presumption is *yes*, unless they are huge and perceived as exceptionally well managed. For firms in the turnaround quadrant, the issue is much more complex with the general presumption being *no*. Surrendering a source of major competitive leverage is a matter of real concern unless the firm lacks the size or will to properly maintain it. Since this competitive leverage often involves selecting radically different IT architectures like client-server, the operations function may be so transformed that it becomes very complex to negotiate a viable long-term operational outsourcing arrangement. The reality has been that these contracts have had substantial flexibility in their clauses. In these cases like General Dynamics[8] and Xerox, only partial outsourcing was done (of operations and Legacy maintenance), with a focus on keeping key development skills on the company's payroll. For companies in the strategic quadrant, the presumption is *no*; in the absence of a crisis of IT competence and assuming that the firm is able to attract a critical mass of skills this is a core differentiating/cost reduction competence which should be part of the firm's portfolio of skills.

For multinationals the problem is more complex than for domestic firms because of the legitimate differences in IT strategic impact among divisions and the very different resource capabilities in countries. For example, one international oil company outsourced its operationally troubled Brazilian subsidiary's IT activities while keeping their other country's IT activities in-house which were generally performing satisfactorily. Similarly, as technology and competitive circumstances evolve, firms may move from one position on the grid to another, and thus need to reconsider their outsourcing decisions. Firms, for example, under profit pressures after a period of sustained strategic innovation (in either the turnaround or strategic quadrants) are good candidates for outsourcing as a means to clean up their shops and procedures.

SUMMARY

What global outsourcing of operations and software development does not mean is elimination of the need for senior IT leadership in the firm. The CIO function is going to be more important in the next decade than it was in the past. Realistically, however, for many organizations the role is evolving from the manager of a large staff to managing a network of relationships. It is critical that the firm has someone who has an informed view of technology and how the various partners are supporting the firm.

Additionally, this function ensures that the long-term information architecture (networks, databases, etc.) of the firm is evolving appropriately to take advantage in a timely fashion of the new technologies. It is also responsible for identifying emerging technologies and ensuring that appropriate pilot projects are underway. While international outsourcing is growing, at the present moment it is impossible to definitively prove how successful it has been. It is known that a number of firms have done it and that their managers feel comfortable about the results. What, of course, is unknown is what would have happened had they really dug in and concentrated on transforming their international IT activities through internal resources and driven things forward in a positive way. Measuring success in short is very hard. The final observation as can be seen from this chapter is that outsourcing is a philosophy rather than a technique and it comes in many variations. It is a mix and match issue with various firms dealing with its different aspects over periods of time in quite distinctive ways. For firms who are laggard, however, and have not invested significantly in these IT technologies, this may be the only viable way to pragmatically get caught up.

Endnotes

[1] Xerox: Outsourcing Global Information Technology Resource, 9-195-158, 1995. Publishing Division, Harvard Business School, Boston, MA 02163.

[2] See "Kodak's Outsourcing Deal Brings Risks -- And Not Just for Kodak," **The Business Week Newsletter for Information Executives, August 1989;** and D. Norton, H. Pfendt, G. Biddle, and R. Connor, "A Panel Discussion on Outsourcing," **Stage by Stage,** 25 January 1990, pp. 13-16.

[3] For a critical discussion of the outsourcing phenomenon, see R.A. Bettis, S.P. Bradley, and G. Hamel, "Outsourcing and Industrial Decline,"**Academy of Management Executive**, February 1992, pp. 7-22.

[4] This taxonomy is described in Chapter 10, pp. 175-190 of *Corporate Information Systems Management:* J.I. Cash, Jr., F.W. McFarlan, and J.L. McKenney, Richard D. Irwin, Homewood, IL, 1992.

[5] See F. Warren McFarlan, Richard L. Nolan, **How to Manage An IT Outsourcing Alliance,** Sloan Management Review, winter 1995, Vol. 36, No.2.

[6] **A Guide for Estimating Client Server Costs,** R-810-105, april 18, 1994, Gartner Group RA's Services.

[7] for a discussion of the strategic grid, see F.W. McFarlan, J.I. Cash, and J.L. McKenney, **Corporate Information Systems Management** (Homewood, Illinois: Richard D. Irwin, 1992). McFarlan developed the framework in 1982. See F.W. McFarlan, J.L. McKenney, and P. Pyburn, "The Information Archipelago--Plotting a Course, "Harvard Business Review, January-February 1983, pp. 145-160.

[8] General Dynamics and Computer Science Corporation: Outsourcing the IS Function (A), (B), (C), (D); Boston: harvard Business School Publishing Division, 1993.

17 Global Software Outsourcing to India by Multinational Corporations

Richard Heeks
University of Manchester, UK

This chapter focuses on the outsourcing of software development by multinational corporations to Indian sub-contractors. This important and rapidly growing new trade is likely to exceed US$500 million in 1995/96. Key issues in this "global software outsourcing" (GSO) are reviewed and the principal quantitative and qualitative features are analysed. The varied forms of client/sub-contractor relationship are described and a trend identified for these relationships to move from loose to close collaboration, beyond that normally seen in other outsourcing relationships. Reasons for this trend are identified, as are the drivers/benefits behind global software outsourcing. Cost savings are not always present and the benefits picture looks less positive when viewed from the Indian sub-contractors' perspective. Future prospects for global software outsourcing are forecast and recommendations made to help clients and sub-contractors get the most from GSO.

INTRODUCTION

"Outsourcing refers to the concept of hiring outside professional services to meet the in-house needs of an organization or an agency." (Gupta and Gupta, 1992)

Virtually any aspect of the information systems function may be outsourced, but this chapter focuses on the outsourcing of software development to sub-contractors outside the client organisation's home country, in what will be termed "global software outsourcing" (GSO).

Two principal sets of ideas relate to GSO - that on outsourcing, and that on globalisation. Both are reviewed below within the context of key issues that emerge from the literature.

Determinants and Outcomes of Outsourcing

Outsourcing is growing rapidly. Estimates of market size vary considerably, but US-based organisations will outsource something like US$40 billion of information systems work in 1995, with a growth rate of 15-20% per year (Dué, 1992; Kindel, 1993; Patane and Jurison, 1994).

Globalisation - integrated production of goods and services in more than one country - is also increasing, mainly through the auspices of multinational corporations (MNCs). Over the past two decades, both the number of MNCs and the level of foreign direct investment have risen five-fold (UNCTC, 1988; Emmott, 1993).

How can the increase in both outsourcing and globalisation be explained?

A series of preconditions must be met if outsourcing is to take place. These include the presence of a modularised production process using standardised, stable technologies and skills. If outsourcing is to be globalised, there are further preconditions that include (Dunning, 1980; ILO, 1988; Dicken, 1992):

- technology to permit transport, communication and organisation of production at acceptable cost levels;
- acceptable quality of sub-contractor labour force;
- acceptable physical, linguistic and cultural "distance" between client and sub-contractor;
- an acceptable government policy framework and political stability in the sub-contractor's country.

One must also understand the "push" and "pull" factors that explain why outsourcing and globalisation are increasing. From theoretical constructs on trade, location, product cycles and technology, the "push" drivers can be divided into external and internal factors (Caves, 1982; Dicken, 1992; Parvatiyar and Gupta, 1993; Arnett and Jones, 1994).

External factors include declining demand for the client organisation's products or services, increased competition, ever-shortening product cycles, changes in production costs, labour problems, and pressures from governments at home and abroad.

Internal factors drive outsourcing and globalisation from within the client organisation. They may be negative, such as poor performance of individual units, lack of congruence between senior and IS managers, or identification of resources being diverted into non-strategic areas. The drivers may alternatively be more positive, such as new top management, changes in business direction, and new acquisitions.

Clients are also driven by the "pull" of various benefits that they hope to obtain from outsourcing and globalisation (Beamish, 1988; Apte, 1991; Takac, 1994):

- reductions in costs or development time;
- resources freed to be redirected into strategic initiatives;
- access to new skills, ideas and technology;
- access to new market opportunities;

• greater flexibility, especially in staffing.

One contentious aspect of this list is the centrality of costs to outsourcing and globalisation. Some (Fröbel, et al., 1980; Harding, 1993) argue that cost reduction is far and away the principal driver. Others (ILO, 1988; Gupta and Gupta, 1992) see it as an important issue, but not the only one. Others still (NCC, 1993; Dekleva, 1994) feel that cost reduction forms only a small part of the decision-making process.

Global outsourcing can bring significant benefits to the client, and these have been a main focus of discussion and writing on outsourcing.

> "Most notably, outsourcing is portrayed as a panacea for IS problems." (Lacity and Hirschheim, 1993)

However, this perspective is very limited. As pointed out by Dué (1992) and Lacity and Hirschheim (1993), outsourcing can bring considerable costs to the client, which may overshadow the benefits.

Costs and benefits can also be viewed from the perspective of the sub-contractor; a focus taken by some of the literature on MNCs and globalisation (Sauvant and Lavipour, 1976; Jenkins, 1987). As Dicken (1992) observes, viewpoints in this literature have tended to be quite strongly polarised either for or against multinationals.

In addition to describing drivers and benefits of global software outsourcing, this chapter therefore seeks to identify the costs and risks of GSO to client organisations. It will also examine costs and benefits from the viewpoint of the sub-contractors and their host nation.

The Outsourcing Relationship

Relationships between client and sub-contractor vary enormously. At one extreme, the outsourcing literature has dealt almost entirely with relations between independent actors. Sub-contracting in this context will be referred to as "external outsourcing".

At the other extreme, much of the literature on multinationals, at least until recently, has focused on very close relations in which the sub-contractor would typically be a wholly-owned subsidiary of the overseas client. Sub-contracting in this context will be referred to as "internal outsourcing".

Between these two extremes are many other points on the continuum, including strategic alliances and joint ventures with varying degrees of equity invested by the client.

The structures that set the framework for global software outsourcing need to be analysed. This chapter will therefore determine the nature of relationships found between GSO clients and sub-contractors.

Determinants of Outsourcing Relationships

Within the literature on software outsourcing, there has been a general assumption that the client/sub-contractor relationship will be a relatively loose one, with each party remaining independent of the other and interacting through the medium of contracts. However, there is growing realisation of the benefits that closer relationships can bring. Commentators are therefore advocating the building of tight alliances and even joint ventures between client and sub-contractor (Gupta and Gupta, 1992; Huber, 1993). Similarly, the literature on globalisation describes a general trend for multinationals to move from loose to tight co-ordination of their operations, partly through creation of sub-contractor subsidiaries (Blomström and Zejan, 1991; Emmott, 1993).

The main reasons cited for moving to a closer relationship are (Kirkpatrick and Yamin, 1981; Dicken, 1992):

- reduction in uncertainty about production availability, price, quality, post-sale maintenance, etc., and a desire for direct control over these factors;
- greater ease of transferring technology and skills, without losing knowledge and other intangible assets to potential competitors;
- access to sub-contractor intangible assets, such as knowledge of the local policy environment and production conditions;
- the ability to indulge in transfer pricing to avoid taxation;
- internal capture of benefits that would otherwise accrue to the sub-contractor;
- sharing of investments and risks;
- government regulations or incentives.

This chapter analyses whether a similar trend of change - from loose relationships to close collaboration - is found within global software outsourcing. It also identifies the factors which play a role in determining the type of outsourcing relationship chosen.

Source of Evidence

The evidence presented here derives from ongoing research work at the University of Manchester into the development of Asian software industries. This has included several periods of fieldwork in India and in Western nations and, unless otherwise indicated, figures and opinions presented here are drawn from fieldwork interviews and surveys. Indian data is supported by reviews of IT industry performance issued by the Indian computer journal, Dataquest (for example, Dataquest, 1994).

INDIA AND GLOBAL SOFTWARE OUTSOURCING

Global software outsourcing is growing rapidly, with perhaps US$1.5 billion-worth of contracts outsourced to developing countries in 1994. India has a significant proportion of this trade, and is the largest developing country base for GSO.

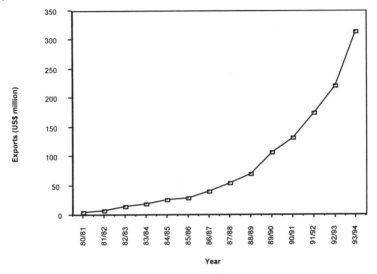

Figure 1: Software Exports From India

Software was first exported from India for an overseas client in 1974. Export growth was initially slow and the trade only became notable in the 1980s. Since then growth has been very strong, as indicated in figure 1. Exports have grown at an annual average rate of 40% from US$4.0 million in 1980/81 to US$314 million in 1993/94.

Perhaps 5% of exports are software packages or data entry services. The remainder consists of software services - software development, conversion or maintenance - for an overseas client.

These figures must be kept in perspective. India's exports form less than 0.15% of the total world computer services and software market, and the exports reported here represent the *gross* value of contracts undertaken. *Net* earnings for Indian firms are as little as 35% of gross because payments have to be made to cover overseas travel, subsistence, marketing, and import of hardware and software.

Divisions of Labour

Most software work outsourced to India has been characterised by two divisions of labour. Firstly, an international *locational* division of labour. Based on survey figures, one may estimate that just under 65% of software export development work takes place at the client's site overseas ("onsite"), and only 35% offshore in India.

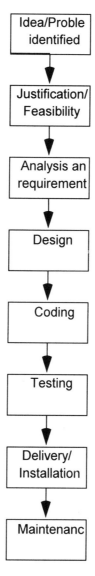

Figure 2: Software Production Stages

Secondly, there has been an international *skill* division of labour. Software development overall is highly skilled, but is often broken down into a series of relatively standardised production steps, as shown in figure 2.

This model highlights the skill division of labour within software production because the earlier stages of analysis and design require higher levels of skill and experience, whereas those of coding and testing are relatively less skill-intensive.

According to survey figures, at least 65% of contracts required only the provision of coding and testing services, while less than 35% involved all stages of software development from requirements analysis to development and installation. In other words, Indian workers are far more often used as programmers rather than as systems analysts or designers. They work to requirements and design specifications set by Western software developers.

Collectively, the two divisions of labour (i.e. the provision of onsite programming labour) are known in India as "body shopping".

Sub-contractors and Employees

By 1995, around 200 Indian software firms were active in global sub-contracting but the field was highly concentrated with the top two firms - Tata Consultancy Services (TCS) and Tata Unisys Ltd (TUL) - responsible for about 30% of all work, and the top eight players exporting roughly half of all software. Unlike small, new companies, these larger, longer-established firms have the ability to seek out overseas clients, and the reputation and marketing contacts to convince them to outsource.

In all, about 15,000 Indian software developers were involved in exports in 1994 but the skills profile of the industry was heavily skewed towards programming, as table 1 shows.

Worker Type	Indian Software Industry	Average US software
Project leaders	9%	14%
Analysts/designers	16%	47%
Programmers	75%	39%

Source: Interviews
Table 1: Breakdown of Indian Software Workers by Type

The Indian industry has thus been significantly "programmer heavy" compared to the needs of certain export contracts, which helps explain the international skill division of labour.

FORMS OF OUTSOURCING RELATIONSHIP

It was seen above that a wide variety of possible relationships can exist between clients and sub-contractors, set along a continuum. Analysing global software outsourcing to India, one can identify both the loose "external outsourcing" (contractual relationships between autonomous organisations) and the close "internal outsourcing" (contractual relationships between separate parts of the same organisation) described. To these must be added an intermediate form - known here as "alliance outsourcing" - a contractual relationship between organisations which, although nominally autonomous, are bound together in a close alliance.

All three forms are described in greater detail below. First, though, the type of firms involved in GSO will be analysed.

GSO Clients

"American information technology and financial services companies have moved much more quickly than their European counterparts to take advantage of offshore programming." (Tilley, 1990)

As a result, US multinational clients dominate software outsourcing to India, being responsible for around 70% of all outsourcing collaborations. A handful of European multinationals are involved, especially from the UK, with Japanese firms playing only a minor role so far.

According to client interviewees, the reasons for America's faster uptake are: greater awareness of GSO; fewer negative stereotypes about the capabilities of workers from developing countries; greater risk-taking; and more companies with a "global vision" or a tradition of global outsourcing.

The first multinationals to take the plunge into global software outsourcing in the early-mid 1980s had certain identifiable characteristics - higher than average willingness to take risks; one or two Indian staff among their senior managers (staff who often drove the initiation of outsourcing); heavy pressures to cut costs and/or a strategic vision of global competitiveness. Since then, general awareness of GSO has risen sharply and it has become less risky. As a result, a much wider variety of firms has become involved.

With the exception of Japanese firms, almost all major hardware multinationals are now outsourcing software development work to India. The software multinationals have been slower to get involved and, instead, have concentrated on setting up agreements with Indian firms which act as their local distributors. A few other types of multinational are involved, and the list of principal clients includes DEC, Hewlett-Packard, IBM, Fujitsu ICL, Siemens-Nixdorf, Texas Instruments, Unisys, British Telecom and Citibank.

Loose Relationships and External Outsourcing

In this form of outsourcing, the relationship between client and sub-contractor is merely that of trading. Neither client nor sub-contractor has any long-term commitment to the other, and they look ahead only as far as the end of the present contract. Because of the loose, transient nature of these relationships, it is not possible to estimate exactly how many of them take place, but one can gauge that they are relatively unimportant to, and relatively little used by, most of India's major software clients.

Close Collaborations

GSO contracts are not generally won by open tender in the market. Instead, taking the average of individual figures for all significant exporters, one finds 75% of output being sent to a single client with whom the Indian firm has some close outsourcing arrangement. Most of the remaining output is exported to other clients in close collaborations.

Year	Contracting Alliances	Joint Ventures	Wholly- Owned Subsidiaries
Pre-1984	3	2	-
1984	1	-	-
1985	-	-	1
1986	1	1	1
1987	2	4	-
1988	1	2	1
1989	3	2	2
1990	1	6	3
1991	6	2	2
1992	3	4	1
1993	6	3	-
1994	6	5	3
1995	1	1	-
Unknown	1	2	-

Source: Interviews and Dataquest surveys

Table-2: Number of Close Indian Software Export Collaborations Starting per Year

The degree to which Indian sub-contractors service only one client is even greater when they are just starting up, with many Indian firms being entirely reliant on their collaborator for contracts at first and only able to attempt diversification after several years of single client-dependent growth.

As Table 2 and Figure 3 indicate, the number of close outsourcing collaborations has grown strongly over the past decade. Cumulative figures exclude terminated collaborations. 1995 figures are partial and include collaborations with an "unknown" date. These collaborations have taken a number of different forms, as described below.

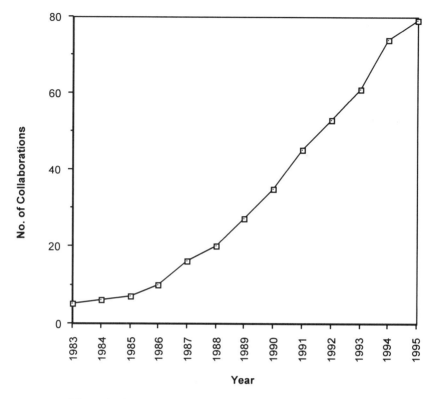

**Figure 3: Cumulative Total of Active, Close Indian Software Export
Collaborations**

Alliance Outsourcing

Informal Alliances: These exist between Indian software exporters and
contracting agencies overseas. Usually without offering any guarantees, the
agency will source most of its labour from the Indian company, while the Indian
company will obtain most of its contracts in that particular market through the
agency.

Many agencies are run by Indians living abroad, and they work by
accepting a contract from the end client and then sub-contracting it to the Indian
company, after extracting commission (typically 40%). Most Indian companies
use these agencies to some extent, especially when first getting started.

Contractual Alliances: These may not be completely formalised but
represent a close relationship in which the client is the main source for the Indian
firm's contracts. This type of arrangement exists between some hardware
multinationals and their Indian distributors, with a reciprocity such that the

Indian firm sells Western hardware and the multinational buys Indian software services, with both firms benefiting from both sides of the arrangement.

Internal Outsourcing

Joint Equity Ventures: The client typically owns 40% or 51% of the Indian sub-contractor's equity which are, respectively, the pre-1991 and post-1991 permissible maxima for most investors wishing to sell to the domestic, as well as export, market. A number of these companies were set up by hardware multinationals to sell computers to Indian customers and they have had only a secondary interest in software.

Roughly 10% of India's 1993/94 software exports came from joint ventures aimed specifically at software production; a further 30% came from joint ventures initially set up primarily for hardware production. Four of the top five software exporters of 1993/94 were joint ventures.

Wholly-owned Subsidiaries: These are comparatively rare, being only permitted for wholly export-oriented operations. By 1995, only fifteen had been set up, with a total investment of about US$30 million. They were responsible for 7.5% of 1993/94 software exports and included two of the top twenty exporters.

Movement Between Categories

Some Indian firms start in the GSO business as "headhunters" - finding suitable workers anywhere in India in response to a "shopping list" from an overseas contracting agency. As the Indian firm matures, it may hire its own staff but still take contracts from the agency for provision of onsite programming services.

Dissatisfaction with this type of relationship then leads both end client and sub-contractor to seek "disintermediation". Relations with the agency are broken off, and the Indian firm invests in its own US-based subsidiary or office, which deals directly with the client. The dynamic is therefore from loose to close collaboration.

Unisys provides a similar, but different example. As Burroughs in the 1970s, it tried out one simple external outsourcing contract with TCS. The success of this led rapidly to a contracting alliance lasting four years. Both parties were then sufficiently familiar with each other for a joint venture to be developed. As Tata Burroughs Ltd (now TUL), it began work in 1977 with 40% US equity, and Burroughs/Unisys became an "internal outsourcer".

Most multinationals have followed this format, starting with a trial contract in external outsourcing mode, moving rapidly to an alliance relationship followed, in a number of cases, by an internal outsourcing relationship involving equity investment.

This tightening of relationships is linked to changes in the divisions of labour described above. Once the Indian sub-contractor has carried out a few contracts for the same client and proved itself able to follow a set of instructions or specifications and to deliver on time and to the required quality, then it may be entrusted with a little more of the software development process and/or may be allowed to carry out more work offshore.

Indian software companies therefore move slowly up a "trust curve" with their clients, firstly taking on only the least skilled elements of software production, then also creating the design, and finally accepting responsibility for the entire software development process from feasibility onwards.

Similarly, with location, it becomes increasingly possible that work will be sent offshore. This trend has been encouraged by India's expanding access to international telecommunications links, by tougher US visa regulations, and by the recent anti-immigration court case brought against Hewlett-Packard and TCS in California (Heeks, 1995).

These changes are summarised in table 3.

	Initial Model	Maturation Model
Stage of Relationship	Initial	Mature
Type of Outsourcing	External	Internal
Type of Relationship	Contractual/Trade	Joint Venture/Wholly-owned
Skills	Programming only	Turnkey
Location	Onsite	Offshore

Table 3: Changes in Outsourcing Model Within Collaborations

The constant flow of new Indian entrants into GSO maintains the preponderance of the initial model and of contracting agency relationships. However, most *individual* client/sub-contractor collaborations have made the model change indicated in their first few years and moved some distance rightwards along the relationship continuum illustrated in figure 4, even though few have reached the extreme of the wholly-owned subsidiary.

Of the forms of collaboration shown, three predominate, listed below in decreasing order of importance to India-bound GSO:
• Semi-formal contracting and joint equity ventures with hardware multinationals.
• Informal sub-contracting arrangements with overseas contracting agencies.
• Wholly multinational-owned subsidiaries.

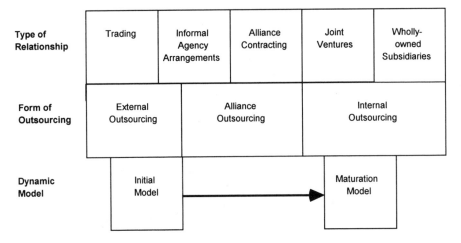

Figure 4: GSO Relationship Continuum

Relationships have therefore been closer than one would expect from the outsourcing literature, but less formalised, with less total ownership and more diversity, than represented in some past images of multinational globalisation.

FACTORS UNDERLYING GLOBAL SOFTWARE OUTSOURCING

Preconditions for Software Outsourcing

The first precondition for software outsourcing is the existence of software as a separate, "outsourcable" commodity with its own market. After a modest start, growth in that market became almost exponential from the late 1970s onwards, as shown in figure 5.

However, more than just the existence of a product market is required for production to be outsourced. As stated above, there must also be a modularised production process using standardised, stable technologies and skills. Without this, work specifications cannot meaningfully be transported outside the originating organisation, and intermediate deliverables cannot be defined and monitored.

As illustrated in figure 2, software development was fragmented into a series of relatively standardised production stages by the 1970s. At the same time, programming languages changed from being both manufacturer- and even computer-specific to being generic. Languages such as Fortran and COBOL

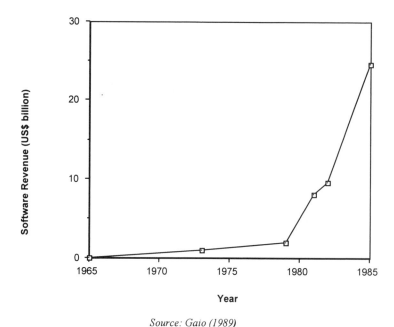

Source: Gaio (1989)
Figure 5: Birth of the Global Software Market

became quite stable standards that were widely taught and used, so extending the possibility for outsourcing of software skills.   This was assisted by the standardisation and relative stability of various computer operating systems.

Software therefore had the preconditions necessary for outsourcing from the late 1970s. Given the globalisation of the software market and of software standards, these are also preconditions for global outsourcing by multinationals. However, one must now explain why these firms considered sources in the Third World, like India.

Drivers Behind Outsourcing to India

Of the preconditions required for globalisation of software outsourcing, technology for transport between India and the West has been available for many years. India also has good quality programmers who speak English and are relatively well-attuned to Western culture and, despite its apparent turmoils, the country has been politically stable for many years.

However, India did lack two prerequisites of globalisation in the late 1970s.   Firstly, the international phone system was quantitatively and qualitatively so poor that there was effectively no technology to permit adequate communication and organisation of software production.   Until good telecommunications links (and plentiful hardware) became available from the late 1980s, onsite working had to be the norm.

Secondly, at least in the eyes of many potential clients, India lacked an acceptable government policy framework until the late 1980s. This explains why only the less risk-averse clients with insider knowledge of the country entered GSO before this date. Since 1986, the government has explicitly encouraged software outsourcing through its Department of Electronics by measures that include expanded infrastructural and human resource development.

Beyond these preconditions, there must also be drivers to explain software outsourcing to India. The general "push' and "pull" factors behind GSO were described earlier, and three of these are especially important.

The most obvious factor is the need for cost savings in production of software, spurred on by growing competition, rising costs and, in some cases, poor performance or the recognition of a competitive opportunity within the client organisation. Such savings are rooted in the salary differences between developed and developing countries. For example, software wages in the US throughout the 1980s and 1990s have been six to eight times higher than those in India.

Overall software development charges are not as competitive as these figures suggest because labour is by no means the only cost factor. Hardware and software prices, telecommunications and marketing costs are all higher in India than overseas, and office rentals, overseas travel costs and interest rates are high. For staff working onsite, an overseas allowance also has to be paid. This has typically been US$1900-2500 per month, a figure which will rise with growing implementation of two recent rulings on tax and wages by the US authorities[1].

Cost cannot be considered in isolation from productivity. Coding productivity figures for offshore software development in India vary widely but they have typically been 10-50% less than those of Western companies, with smaller Indian firms performing least well. The performance shortfall is caused mainly by lack of resources (computing equipment, support staff, uninterrupted power supplies) and of project management skills. Most large sub-contractors have started to use standardised scheduling, progress review and quality assurance techniques, so that they do not differ greatly from Western software firms. By contrast, many of the smaller firms admitted "we just plan as we go along".

On the other hand, when working overseas - as is the case for most contracts - Indian software developers achieve productivity levels at least as high as their Western counterparts and often higher by 20-50%. The same is true of quality and timeliness, with onsite work being "of an international standard" (Tilley, 1990). Offshore work within large Indian companies is of about the same standard but within smaller companies it has tended to suffer.

Adding all these elements together, Indian sub-contractors typically charge about 70% of Western contract rates for onsite work and 40% for work carried out offshore. There is, however, a considerable variation in charges, depending on the Indian company's size and reputation, on the level of adherence to US regulations, and on the presence or absence of an intermediary contracting agency.

The second main driving force behind multinational outsourcing to developing countries like India is that of "labour problems". In the context of software outsourcing, this has meant particularly a drive to cope with fluctuating staff needs, freezes on in-house recruitment and, above all, a shortage of skills in the client organisation and home market. For example, the gap between supply and demand for software development labour is estimated to be growing by 20,000 annually in the US (Widge, 1990). The consequence, apart from a large project backlog, has been a great desire of Western firms to exploit all possible sources of skills.

India has thousands of software developers who are well-educated, English-speaking, technically-proficient and available for export work. They are therefore an obvious source for those clients seeking to bridge their demand-supply gap. This has been especially so in the US, where some clients have "poached" contract workers from Indian sub-contractors by offering them full-time employment and a US resident's green card.

Finally, clients have outsourced to gain access to the local market. With India's IT markets growing rapidly and worth over US$1.1 billion in 1994, intense interest from overseas producers is only to be expected. Hardware multinationals, for example, have outsourced software work for the Indian market to local collaborators. The local firms develop software that is then integrated with the multinational's hardware and sold as a complete information system to Indian customers.

None of the factors cited - low production costs (with adequate productivity and quality), the skills shortage, and accessing Indian markets - imply a need for collaboration. Western clients can reap the benefits of GSO merely by recourse to basic trade, i.e. by external outsourcing. What, then, are the additional reasons which encourage clients and Indian companies to seek closer collaborations?

Factors Underlying Closer Outsourcing Relationships

Western clients could access local software workers and their skills through simple trade, but most have preferred collaboration because it offers greater control over the software production process. Multinational clients are able to transfer technology-related skills as well as standards of working - of communication, scheduling and delivery, documentation, quality control, and so on - by training their Indian counterparts. In return, the client receives a flow of commercial, technical, and government-related information from the sub-contractor. It will also receive equity if entering into a joint venture with the Indian firm.

Close collaboration means that the client retains sub-contractor staff as its corporate memory and that the Indian sub-contractor understands the foreign client's corporate strategy and culture well, which brings a greater assurance that the software developed for the client will match users' needs. Assurance and control are also essential if the client is to offer sub-contractor services to its own customers in the West.

Conversely, without a close relationship, globalisation is held back by the perception of risk, by uncertainty over available skills and standards, and by fears of a loss of control over the process. When first approaching global software outsourcing to India, clients are faced with such a high level of uncertainty that most feel they cannot afford the risks of alliances or internalisation. They therefore start with a simple trading contract. Only once risk and uncertainty have been sufficiently reduced does close collaboration then become advantageous to them.

In general, the closer the collaboration, the stronger the transfer of skills, information, standards and procedures has been. Multinational-controlled subsidiaries use the same manuals and methods as their parent companies, so that the latter are assured of product quality and timeliness. This helps explain why the subsidiaries have moved up the "trust curve" faster and taken on far more offshore, turnkey work than those not doing internal outsourcing.

Such work offers greater savings to the client than onsite, programming-only development, and internal outsourcing brings other financial gains. Software development in India can be highly profitable, and the client will share these profits if it invests equity. Similarly, "transfer pricing" is only possible with close collaboration, with evidence from interviews that a very few firms were employing this technique to avoid tax payments. They exploit the different tax years between India and their home country, over- or under-invoicing during the overlap period to create an appearance of low or non-existent profits.

However, it would be wrong to see the drive for close collaboration as deriving solely from the client. Indian companies are also keen for collaborations because they offer a way to circumvent the marketing and credibility barriers of open market competition by virtually, though not completely, guaranteeing export work. Indian firms are particularly motivated to seek the kind of long-term access to contracts that alliance and internal outsourcing provide, which removes the need to continually compete on establishing credibility and to have an expensive overseas marketing operation. Such collaborations also provide access to technology and associated skills.

The final factor pushing clients into closer collaboration has been Indian government policy, which has acted in two main spheres:
i. Procedures and attitudes. In the 1970s, India was known as the country that forced IBM to leave. As long as this image remained, multinationals preferred to trade at arm's length rather than get more closely involved. Over the 1980s and even more in the 1990s, bureaucrats' attitudes have changed from seeking to regulate foreign firms as much as possible, to encouraging them and cutting

away large swathes of red tape for those seeking collaborations. As a result, closer collaboration has become more attractive.

ii. Investment incentives. Although placed low on client interviewees' lists of decision-making factors, the special policy incentives available to those investing in wholly export-oriented software firms - 100% foreign ownership with hard currency accounts, full profit and dividend repatriation, duty-free and almost bureaucracy-free import and export - did encourage some multinationals to proceed with investment collaborations.

The Indian government has set limits on the proportion of foreign equity that can be invested in those joint ventures which sell to both export and domestic markets. However, this has had less impact than might be expected on the form of collaborations because control of subsidiaries is no longer determined by level of equity but by management and technology, as managers of various joint ventures made clear:

"Greater investment is not needed because we already have full control of both the company and its technology."

"To all extents and purposes, we treat our Indian unit managers as if they belonged to a 100 percent subsidiary."

"Modi Olivetti sees itself asa subsidiary of Olvetti, even though Olivetti does not hold a majority stake."

OUTCOMES OF GLOBAL SOFTWARE OUTSOURCING

Client Costs and Benefits

As described above, cost savings represent an important benefit of GSO for multinational clients. This benefit is under pressure, though, for a number of reasons that include:

- additional managerial, administrative and communications costs that outsourcing imposes;
- training and enculturation costs for some Indian staff;
- the tax and equal remuneration rulings in the US;
- occasional demotivation and consequent poorer performance of in-house staff who work alongside Indians.

Clients typically reported that they were shaving at least 10% off total costs by outsourcing to India when staff worked onsite. However, these reports often seemed to have ignored some of the more hidden costs of outsourcing and, as Jones (1994b) observes, very few clients have a clear picture of their pre-outsourcing costs to act as a comparator.

Outsourcers have definitely obtained greater cost saving benefits when work has gone offshore, back to India. However, as already noted, this can only be done once the client is sure that the sub-contractor can be relied upon in areas such as project management, productivity and quality.

The main benefit of onsite working is increasingly seen as access to a new skills pool. Even if not trained, Indian staff have shown themselves to be eminently trainable and some, at least, represent the cream of the Indian education system. Clients find themselves able to reduce their applications backlogs, or to target new business areas that they would otherwise have had to ignore because of the shortages of US software talent.

For example, Unisys computer sales representatives can go to a potential customer site in the US where, say, an IBM machine is currently installed. Thanks to the certainty of access to its Indian sub-contractor's labour pool, Unisys can promise to convert all existing IBM-based software to run on Unisys hardware and to develop any new applications the customer wants by the time the Unisys computer is installed. The assurance of being able to contract out such work also allows Unisys to retain corporate flexibility by keeping the number of its core staff low.

Clients have been far more ruthless with their sub-contractor than would be possible with American staff in meeting their own needs for staffing flexibility. The level of outsourcing can therefore rise or fall quite sharply as determined by the client's strategic business requirements.

The experience of benefits accruing to the client varies greatly depending on the nature of the sub-contractor. The weakest Indian firms bring only headaches by providing staff who do not match their résumés; staff whose "experience" consists of merely reading the manual; staff who cannot manage projects; staff who have technical but not interpersonal skills; and staff who quit part-way through.

In part, these problems arise from a lack of close contractual control by the client during outsourcing but sub-contractor evaluation prior to outsourcing is also critical in ensuring an adequate flow of benefits. Various sub-contractor criteria can be evaluated (Gupta and Gupta, 1992; Polilli, 1993; Jones, 1994a), including:

- cost;
- reputation;
- past work and past client satisfaction ratings;
- outstanding litigation and bad debts;
- service quality to be provided.

These criteria are hard to assess in the context of Indian sub-contractors. The hidden costs of outsourcing, for example, make true overall costs difficult to evaluate. Many of the established, reputable firms are unavailable because of their existing link with one client through alliance or internal outsourcing. Others are often too new to have any track record; their past clients may be hard to contact; and the sharp divide between export and domestic market work in India makes it unlikely that they can point to any relevant past work within India itself.

Other criteria - like the sub-contractor's human resource base or its knowledge of the client's business area - can also be difficult to gauge. Some Indian firms maintain large databases of "free agents" who can be pulled out of their existing firm to front a particular contract bid. These workers have no real allegiance to, and therefore do not reflect on the suitability of, any particular sub-contractor.

ISO 9000 "fever" has swept over India since 1993, with several of the top sub-contractors being certified. This is certainly a stamp of approval that clients can look to in trying to ensure that their outsourcing relationship will be beneficial, but some caveats need to be stated. Firstly, the vast majority of sub-contractors remain uncertified. Secondly, the intense competition between certifying organisations in India has led to certificates being issued solely on the basis of a company's *intention* to introduce quality assurance measures. It must be stressed that this only involves a very small minority of cases, but it has slightly devalued all Indian certification in the eyes of some clients. Lastly,:

> "ISO-certified organizations do not yet seem to have achieved quality results that differ significantly from similar organizations that are not certified." (Jones, 1994b)

This backdrop of evaluation uncertainty provides the reason why most client/sub-contractor relationships start with a single, simple, traded contract and only slowly migrate up the "trust curve". Hence, also, the clients who end up with all costs and no benefits because they outsourced a major contract to the first Indian firm that came along, spurred on by the media hype about India and unconscious of the need to tread warily.

Sub-Contractor Costs and Benefits

Outsourcing from multinationals has been a vital part of India's software export and employment growth. Without the multinationals, winning contracts would - for most Indian firms - have been very costly, difficult and time-consuming. The marketing and credibility gains that Western companies can bring may be complemented by investments in capital, technology and skills which provide new jobs and more highly-skilled offshore workers.

Unfortunately, however, some collaborations have only helped to perpetuate the persistent international divisions of labour and market concentration that characterise Indian software production. Losses of profits, staff and intellectual property rights overseas have also been seen.

All collaborations have involved some indirect investment of time or training, and a few clients have made substantial direct investments in sub-contractor joint ventures or subsidiaries. However, much of that investment has gone to pay for imported equipment rather than Indian goods or services. At the same time, the Indian government has itself had to invest large sums in the infrastructure of transport, telecommunications and other utilities to help attract foreign investors.

On the one hand, then, outsourcing collaborations are binding Indian sub-contractors more tightly into the global economy. On the other, there have been relatively few links to or from the Indian domestic economy in these collaborations. This use of Indian labour to boost the growth of Western firms and Western economies incurs a large opportunity cost when applications to meet many domestic needs are consequently ignored.

Collaborations have also been associated with a loss of self-determination. Individual firms (and, hence, the whole industry) fall victim to the weakness and vulnerability that come with dependence on foreign firms for markets, technology and skills. Sub-contractors have, for example, suffered considerably if their collaborator loses interest in outsourcing or suffers financial losses. Many are in a relatively weak bargaining position and they have been offered little choice over what contracts, what technology and what skills they are given access to.

There is a wider aspect to this in the growing foreign influence over Indian policy making. Because of outsourcing, multinationals have become a significant part of the Indian political economy in recent years and their presence is likely to constrain future government policy choices.

There can thus be no simple, polarised view either for or against collaborations from an Indian perspective. Both costs and benefits are seen, and these have varied between different firm types, collaboration types, market segments and historical timings.

RECOMMENDATIONS

Recommendations for Multinational Clients

GSO appears to be quite risky and cost-prone. A number of clients have experienced serious problems with their outsourcing. Where they do come, benefits do not arrive automatically, but only through careful management.

Outsourcing must therefore be well planned, with a clear strategic objective and with thought given to selecting only those projects which are appropriate for outsourcing, to true costs, to the in-house alternative, and to the impacts of outsourcing on in-house staff. There was some evidence from the client population, for example, that more successful clients were those who undertook GSO to India as a strategic business move rather than simply as an attempt to cut costs.

GSO should not proceed unless there is an adequate in-house outsourcing team, with sufficient project management skills to co-ordinate outsourcing and monitor it continuously during development, and with sufficient technical skills to make informed decisions. Ideally, an in-house understanding of India, its culture and its software firms is required. As a stop-gap on initial contracts, clients may rely on an agency with Indian experience.

Once a decision to outsource is made, it is obvious that trust and commitment to the outsourcing relationship are a key to greater benefits, but that these can only come if the sub-contractor is well chosen. As noted above, evaluation can be difficult. Nevertheless, there are some obvious guidelines:

- Look to the more well-established firms first. Newer, smaller sub-contractors may charge less but they bring much higher quality and contract completion risks.
- Look out for those sub-contractors who have invested in a US subsidiary or liaison office. This shows commitment that weaker firms will not provide.
- Look at formal ratings such as ISO 9000 or position within the US Software Engineering Institute's software process maturity model.
- Look at informal ratings such as "word-of-mouth" reputation within the industry or specific feedback from past sub-contractor clients.

Once a sub-contractor is chosen, part of building trust and reducing uncertainty for the client is good communications between all parties, plus good contract specification that should include:

- an unambiguous description of activities and skills required;
- details of timetable, deliverables and incentives or penalties;
- a clear set of performance measures, acceptance criteria and procedures covering, for example, what happens if staff leave half-way through the contract or if quality falls below acceptable criteria;
- a clear set of "Go/No Go" decision points;
- a clearly defined dispute resolution process;
- a statement of who will own intellectual property rights to the software developed;
- agreement on asset transfer, as when hardware is loaned to the sub-contractor;
- agreement on post-delivery maintenance;
- agreement on how to change the contract, given the need for flexibility.

Although a formal contract might not always be involved, all of these aspects are just as important when outsourcing internally.

Even with care taken over sub-contractor choice and contracts, uncertainty and risk will remain. Initially, then, outsourcing should focus on marginal, low-risk work such as a small maintenance or conversion contract. This should be used as a mechanism for judging which elements of the software development cycle the sub-contractor can deal with competently.

A set of formal mechanisms for transfer of skills and technology will subsequently be needed, such as planned training programmes that bring the

Indian team to the West or take the client's training team to India. With gradual deepening and tightening of the client/sub-contractor relationship, more strategic applications development can be outsourced.

Recommendations for Sub-Contractors

Outsourcing has been essential to the growth of Indian sub-contracting firms, yet it remains a process of inequality. The client holds most of the desired resources - market access, finance, skills, particular technologies - and can fairly easily get what it seeks - labour and/or local market knowledge - from a number of different Indian companies. Sub-contractors must therefore embrace outsourcing but must also seek to increase their negotiating strengths and the diversity of their activities.

Action can be taken on a number of fronts, including:

- Clients. If possible, sub-contractors can build relationships with more than one major client in order to spread their risks and reduce their dependency. Sub-contractors must pay just as much attention as the client to the contract and must try to get the most in terms of technology transfer from their client. Contracts will, though, achieve much less in this regard than a long-term commitment from the sub-contractor's management to building a high-quality, professional organisation that the client can rely upon.

- Form of relationship. Sub-contractors must adopt a strategic planning perspective to steer the organisation along the path from initial to maturation model. Whilst building up this close relationship with the client, some degree of financial and managerial autonomy must also be sought, if feasible. Sub-contractors need to retain autonomy by looking for alternative sources of finance, software skills training, and market information.

- Markets. Those sub-contractors who maintain a presence in both the export and domestic markets appear to fare better than those operating solely as exporters. The experience of one or two Indian firms indicates that it may be more beneficial to develop a broad base of contracts and experience within the domestic market and then move slowly into exports rather than focusing immediately on exports.

- Collaboration with other sub-contractors. This can take many forms, including merger (as yet still not easy within India) in order to create larger, stronger Indian players; "sub-sub-contracting" of export work from larger to smaller Indian firms; and the organisation of workshops to share negotiating experiences and skills.

- Collaboration with government. Sub-contracting firms must work together with government and encourage it to continue substituting for or complementing the inputs that Western multinational clients provide. Such state interventions include tax concessions, provision of venture and similar finance, funding of training courses, funding of Indian software R&D, provision of telecommunications infrastructure, and assistance with market research and marketing (Heeks, 1995). Government must also be persuaded to provide a secure legislative framework for contractual agreements and joint ventures.

CONCLUSIONS

During the 1970s, the first preconditions for global software outsourcing (software as a separate commodity; fast international transport; a modularised production process; standard and stable technology and skills) and for GSO to India specifically (high quality, Westernised labour; political stability) were put into place. With the final preconditions (communication and control technology; acceptable policy framework) ready by the late 1980s, GSO to India was ready for take-off.

Beyond these preconditions, GSO has actually increased so rapidly because highly competitive Western multinationals found they could access lo ver labour costs, a new skills pool and a new IT market. They could get access to these benefits through trade but have wished to move beyond trade to close collaborations.

In general, the closer the collaboration, the more it has provided: greater assurance about access to Indian workers, and access to sub-contractor information and equity; greater understanding of corporate needs; more successful transfer of skills, technology and culture; greater control over software production and quality; greater cost savings through offshore, turnkey work; and higher profits with lower tax payments.

It is clear, however, that the positive correlation between "closeness of relationship" and perceived benefits breaks down somewhat at the extreme. 100% ownership of the sub-contractor by the client is permitted but is not required in order to achieve internal outsourcing benefits. Many clients and sub-contractors therefore find a joint venture to be the optimal form of relationship.

For the client, collaboration without total ownership reduces investments, risks and responsibilities, as multinationals move to a regime of control through access to markets, skills and "techknowledge" rather than control through access to capital. This type of relationship also allows the client to create a leaner, more responsive organisational form in which only the basic core of skills necessary for control and strategic development are kept in-house, while all other activities are outsourced to provide greater flexibility and speed in coping with changing markets.

For the sub-contractors, joint ventures seem to provide the best balance of export and employment growth with satisfactory transfer of skills and some small degree of self-determination.

Returning to an issue raised earlier, one may also conclude that far more than just costs explain outsourcing and globalisation decisions. Cost savings are by no means always the principal benefit of outsourcing and, if labour and related costs were of overriding importance, one would expect both the locational and skill divisions of labour in software services exports to disappear because of the added cost advantages. The divisions are diminishing within individual collaborations but, with start-up firms often relying solely on US-based onsite programming, average change within the industry is much slower. Indian companies ought also to be global competitors in the software package market because they can produce at such low cost, yet they are not.

The fact that cost savings are not the sole outsourcing benefit, that labour divisions have persisted and that India exports very few packages shows that factors such as productivity, quality, timeliness, client-developer relationships, marketing, politics, and availability of skills and technology have often outweighed costs in shaping the nature of global software outsourcing.

Future Prospects for Global Software Outsourcing

The overall global software market is predicted to continue growing throughout the 1990s (Schware, 1992). There will be particular growth in two strong areas of GSO: software maintenance of "legacy systems", and software conversion as organisations move towards downsized and client/server environments.

There will be some limitations to global outsourcing: innovative, confidential, proprietary and strategic applications are unlikely to be outsourced except, perhaps, internally; recession may cause a slowdown in outsourcing growth; and too much global outsourcing may lead to protectionist reactions in developed countries (Gupta and Gupta, 1992; Milner, 1993). However, "All indicants suggest that the outsourcing trend will continue to gain momentum during this decade" (Lacity and Hirschheim, 1993).

The global software skills shortage will also continue. However, it is becoming a shortage more of analysts and analyst/programmers than of programmers, and countries like India may face difficulties if they rely mainly on supply of programming staff (Cole, 1994).

There has been growing automation of software development using software tools. This automation threatens programming jobs and outsourcing, particularly in the long term, and causes a greater need for analysts and designers in the medium term. In the short term, however, these impacts are more than compensated by the rising demand for software tool skills which India has usually been able to meet (Heeks, 1990). The increasing use of telecommunications technology is also increasing the opportunities for GSO.

GSO is likely to benefit in the near future from other technological trends such as rising program modularity (allowing individual parts of a larger development to be contracted out), more formalised methods for defining requirements (making it easier to transmit these from client to developer), and the spread of open systems (allowing software developed in one hardware environment to be easily transferred to a different platform).

Changes in product technology will also create new skills requirements and new markets. For the rest of the 1990s, networking, multimedia and client/server environments will be likely demand drivers.

For India itself, a principal threat may be competition from sub-contractors in other countries. India had the field largely to itself in the 1980s, but its main competitors are now China, Hungary, Ireland, Israel, Mexico, the Philippines, and Singapore. India is highly rated by clients and it can still rely on cost advantages compared to other locations. However, both government and sub-contractors will have to continue to work hard if it is to retain its pre-eminent position.

Endnotes

[1] According to the first, foreigners on the H1 visa (temporary work permit) must pay social security taxes of roughly 20% of income. According to the second, an equal remuneration ruling, H1 workers must be paid the same as the prevailing wage for Americans with a similar background. Many firms still try to work their way round these, assisted by confusion about counting allowances as income or not. However, a lot of contract workers have had to pay the tax and, if fully enforced, these rulings could significantly alter the economics and pattern of software outsourcing to India.

References

Apte, U. "Global Outsourcing of Information Systems and Processing Services," *Information Society* (7:4), pp. 287-303.

Arnett, K.P. and Jones, M.C. (1994) "Firms That Choose Outsourcing: A Profile," *Information & Management* (26:4), 1994, pp. 179-88.

Beamish, P.W. *Multinational Joint Ventures in Developing Countries*, Routledge, London, 1988.

Blomström, M. and Zejan, M. "Why do Multinational Firms Seek Out Joint Ventures?," *Journal of International Development* (3:1), 1991, pp. 53-63.

Caves, R.E. *Multinational Enterprise and Economic Analysis*, Cambridge University Press, Cambridge, UK, 1982.

Cole, L. "IT Skills Shortfall Hits Project Surge," *Computing* (30/6/94), 1994, p. 41.

Dataquest "The DQ Top 20," *Dataquest* (India) (1-15/8/94), 1994, pp. 40-206.

Dekleva, S.M. "CFOs, CIOs and Outsourcing," *Computerworld* (28:20), 1994, p. 96.

Dicken, P. *Global Shift: The Internationalization of Economic Activity*, Paul Chapman Publishing, London, 1992.

Dué, R.T. "The Real Costs of Outsourcing," *Information Systems Management*, Winter 1992, pp. 78-81.

Dunning, J.H. "Towards an Eclectic Theory of International Production," *Journal of International Business Studies* (11), 1980, pp. 9-31.

Emmott, B. "Survey of Multinationals: Creatures of Imperfection," *The Economist* (27/3/93), 1993, pp. 53-57.

Fröbel, F. et al. *The New International Division of Labour*, Cambridge University Press, Cambridge, UK, 1980.

Gaio, F.J. *The Development of Computer Software Technological Capabilities in Developing Countries: A Case Study of Brazil*, PhD thesis, University of Sussex, Brighton, UK, 1989.

Gupta, U.G. and Gupta, A. "Outsourcing the IS Function," *Information Systems Management*, Summer 1992, pp. 44-50.

Harding, E.U. "IS Explores Outsourcing," *Software Magazine* (13:9), pp. 28-29.

Heeks, R.B. "Fourth Generation Languages and the Indian Software Industry," in *Information Technology in Developing Countries*, S.C. Bhatnagar and N. Bjorn-Andersen (eds.), North-Holland, Amsterdam, 1990, pp. 251-63.

Heeks, R.B. *India's Software Industry: State Policy, Liberalisation and Industrial Development*, Sage, New Delhi, 1995.

Huber, R.L. "How Continental Bank Outsourced its "Crown Jewels"," *Harvard Business Review*, January-February 1993, pp. 121-29.

ILO *Economic and Social Effects of Multinational Enterprises in Export Processing Zones*, ILO, Geneva, 1988.

Jenkins, R. *Transnational Corporations and Uneven Development*. Methuen, London, 1987.

Jones, C. "Evaluating Software Outsourcing Options," *Information Systems Management*, Fall 1994, pp. 28-33.

Jones, C. "Globalization of Software Supply and Demand," *IEEE Software*, November 1994, pp. 17-24.

Kindel, S. "Blowing Through the Barrier," *Financial World* (162:14), 1993, pp. 24-26.

Kirkpatrick, C. and Yamin, M. "The Determinants of Export Subsidiary Formation by US Transnationals in Developing Countries," *World Development* (9:4), 1981, pp. 373-82.

Lacity, M.C. and Hirschheim, R.; *Information Systems Outsourcing: Myths, Metaphors and Realities*, John Wiley, Chichester, UK, 1993.

Milner, M. "Jobs Gloom Could Breed Protectionism," *Guardian* (Manchester, UK) (2/1/93), 1993, p. 31.

NCC *Complex Contracting Out for IT: Critical Success Factors*, NCC Guidelines for IT Management no.179, National Computer Centre, Manchester, UK, 1993.

Parvatiyar, A. and Gupta, Y.P. "Synergistic Pay-offs in Indo-US Strategic Alliances," *Technovation* (14:6), 1994, pp. 395-406.

Patane, J.R. and Jurison, J. "Is Global Outsourcing Diminishing the Prospects for American Programmers?," *Journal of Systems Management* (45:6), 1994, pp. 6-10.

Polilli, S. "Is Outsourcing a Bargain?," *Software Magazine* (13:4), 1993, pp. 36,40.

Sauvant, K.P. and Lavipour, F.G. *Controlling Multinational Enterprises*, Westview Press, Boulder, CO, 1976.

Schware, R. "Software Industry Entry Strategies for Developing Countries," *World Development* (20:2), 1992, pp. 143-64.

Takac, P.F. "Outsourcing: a Key to Controlling Escalating IT Costs?," *International Journal of Technology Management* (9:2), 1994, pp. 139-55.

Tilley, L. "A Passage to India," *Financial Times* (17/5/90), 1990, p. 36.

UNCTC *Transnational Corporations in World Development*, United Nations, New York, 1988.
Widge, N. "Uncle Sam Wants You," *Dataquest* (India), March 1990, pp. 74-93.

SECTION-5

Global Support Systems and Technologies

It is important to keep in mind that on tope of the complex networks of data centers and information warehouses sits a layer of applications which helps multinational enterprises to function more efficiently and effectively. The activities of office workers as they coordinate their work around the world is being re-engineered by information technology, particularly groupware, as described in the chapter by Sharma et al. Developments in management support systems are continuing to progress so that they are beginning to encompass the grand scale and scope of the international enterprise, as shown by Sean Eom. At the same time, developments in inter-organizational networking are being further facilitated by EDI and the rise of the Internet and electronic commerce as means to facilitate trade, a s described in the chapters by Saxena and Wagenaar as well as Roche.

18 Global Transfer Of EDI Technology: A Multi-Level Approach

K.B.C. Saxena
Indian Institute of Management, India

R.W. Wagenaar
Erasmus University, The Netherlands

Electronic Data Interchange (EDI) is a technology which has shown significant impact not only at the individual organization level, but at industry-sector and even at the country-level. As the issues to be addressed at these levels are different, a systemic study of EDI technology transfer incorporating multiple levels is necessary for developing a holistic understanding of the transfer process. This chapter provides such a framework of global EDI technology transfer which can be used for analyzing and planning EDI implementation within a country, an industry-sector, or an organization. The chapter explores EDI implementation across two dimensions: breadth and depth. The breadth dimension focuses on the scope of EDI technology transfer -- a country, an industry-sector, or an organization. The depth dimension focuses on the maturity of EDI usage, which is differentiated into three levels roughly corresponding to "learner", "practitioner" and "expert" levels. The chapter then identifies critical success factors across these two dimensions. These factors are grouped into "critical success areas" which are used to define a conceptual framework of EDI technology transfer, and to apply this framework to some countries and industry-sectors as example. Finally, the chapter uses the framework for proposing an approach for planning the EDI technology transfer process.

INTRODUCTION

Technology could be defined as knowledge that can be studied, codified, and taught to others (Weick, 1990). *Technology transfer* basically refers to the application of such knowledge and can cover the entire spectrum of events from conceptualization of a new technology to its industry-wide use. An important component of the transfer process, *technology implementation* refers to the process of large scale institutionalization of the new technology in organizations. Often the technologies of interest deal with physical products or processes whose scope is limited to only a few organizations or at the most an entire industry-sector. However, some technologies have much wider impact as they deal with inter-organizational information flows affecting business performance and relationships of organizations across multiple industry-sectors in several countries. The transfer of such technologies, therefore, needs to be studied *globally* in order to improve our understanding of the issues related to their successful implementation. *Electronic data interchange* (EDI) is such a technology, which can be defined as the *inter-organizational, computer-to-computer exchange of business documents in a standard, machine-processable format* (Emmelhainz, 1993). Some key features of EDI are: (a) the use of an electronic transmission medium; (b) the use of structured, formatted messages based upon agreed standards; (c) relatively fast delivery from sender to receiver; and (d) direct processing by computer application software, generally resulting in a response to the sending organization (Wrigley et al, 1994).

EDI technology gives organizations an opportunity to exchange electronic messages instead of paper business documents, and leads to a new way of doing business -- *electronic commerce*. Because of the need for a structured form and agreed standards, the introduction of EDI requires considerably more planning and coordination than while introducing other forms of electronic communication. Direct benefits of EDI include labor-savings in the areas of data transcription, controls, and error investigation and correction, and fewer delays in data-handling. As a consequence, EDI (Emmelhainz, 1993): (a) improves internal operations of a firm from a reduction in process-cycle time, (b) improves responsiveness to customers, (c) helps improve trading partner relationships, and (d) increases ability to compete, both domestically and internationally. These *indirect* benefits of EDI may prove to be even more significant strategically than the direct ones, but can only be obtained from closer integration among related functions within different organizations.

Many industrialized and newly industrialized countries, such as the USA, Canada, Japan, Australia, and Singapore have been successful in exploiting the strategic potential of EDI, especially in international trading (Farhoomand, 1992; Clarke, 1994; Masson, 1992; McCubbrey et al, 1994; Neo, 1994). EDI is also very attractive to many developing countries, who intend to strategically compete in the international market by reducing the length of *procurement/ delivery cycle* through EDI. As a consequence, many developing countries are actively considering EDI technology even though the technology infrastructure required for EDI in these countries is not very adequate (Doukidis 1993). However, there are also many countries such as Hong Kong (Damsgaard et al, 1994), who have' not been very successful in adopting EDI technology to their own environments. The major barriers to the successful transfer of EDI technology as often found are:

(a) limited EDI awareness,
(b) lack of government support,
(c) weak technological infrastructure such as value-added networks and other services,

(d) high percentage of small and medium-size enterprises, having small volume of transactions insufficient to justify EDI investment,

(e) bureaucratic "paper-oriented" business culture and public administration,

(f) primitive "batch-oriented" business information technology environments, and

(g) cheap human labor in case of developing countries.

Thus an interesting question relates to factors which contribute towards successful transfer of EDI technology into a country. Furthermore, as EDI adoption varies between different industry-sectors (even within a country), another question posed is that for a given industry-sector, what factors contribute towards the successful implementation of EDI technology within the organizations in that sector. There have been many studies of EDI implementation (as for example Banerjee et al, 1994; Bouchard, 1993; Cox et al, 1995; Holland et al, 1992; Krcmar et al, 1994; Mackay, 1993; Pfeiffer, 1992; Reekers, 1994; Reekers et al, 1993; Reekers et al, 1994; Saunders et al, 1992; Scala et al, 1993; Thissen et al, 1992). Unfortunately most of them have focused mainly at the organizational-level characteristics and not on either country-level or industry level characteristics.

Whereas successful transfer of any technology depends on some key factors, EDI technology is different from many other technologies in the sense that these factors are not merely technological or organizational in nature. They are also *environmental*, needing intervention of governments and international organizations. For instance, successful EDI technology transfer needs large scale availability of low-cost value added telecommunication services. But it also needs willingness of trading partners to enter into formalized business relationships, and even more important, legal acceptance of electronic documents and regulatory structure for global electronic commerce.

Because issues in EDI technology transfer are complex and dynamic, a structure is needed to analyze the issues. A *framework* provides that structure as it identifies and organizes context variables for research and practice (DeSanctis, 1993). Frameworks do not lend good insight into cause/effect relationships, rather the power of frameworks is that they provide a short-hand language for describing the relation. They highlight important dimensions as well as suggest which dimensions may be unimportant (Neumann, 1994). Frameworks are *not* theories; they are only a classification language. Therefore a framework could be applied for analyzing the issues in the EDI technology transfer. Furthermore, in order to make the analysis more meaningful, a framework could relate the issues to the stakeholders in the transfer process.

This chapter provides a conceptual framework of global EDI technology transfer which can be applied *universally*, i.e. in industrialized, *newly* industrialized as well as developing countries. It explores EDI implementation across two dimensions of its *breadth* and *depth*. The breadth dimension includes three levels in descending order of *scope*: country, industry-sector, and individual organization (Figure). This *multi-level* approach is deemed necessary because each level has its unique characteristics, nature of EDI impact, success factors, and resource requirements.

The depth dimension of EDI technology transfer captures three *maturity-levels* of organizational use of EDI. These levels refer to *discovery*, *operational use*, and *strategic use* of EDI. They roughly correspond to using EDI as a "learner", "practitioner", and "expert". Again, the need for multiple levels arises from our finding that each one differs in its impact, success factors, and resource requirements.

EDI implementation at the organization-level has been studied extensively. Therefore, this chapter will discuss *critical success factors* of EDI implementation at the country and industry-sector levels, spanning across the entire depth dimension within each level. The chapter is organized as follows. The next two sections describe the levels of EDI technology transfer *scope* and the EDI *usage maturity* respectively. The subsequent three sections define the CSFs of EDI technology transfer and describe those CSFs at the country- and industry-sector levels. The two subsequent sections describe a framework for global EDI technology transfer and identify stakeholders in the country-level EDI technology transfer. The section following it applies the framework to some selected countries. Finally, an approach for planning EDI technology transfer is given, followed by the conclusion and recommendation for further research.

EDI TECHNOLOGY TRANSFER SCOPE (BREADTH) LEVELS

This dimension defines various "units of analysis" for understanding the EDI technology transfer process, which are: (a) the *country*, (b) the *industry-sector/community*, and (c) the individual *organization*. These three units are chosen for analysis because: (a) they provide a continuum of a broad to a narrow analytical focus (Figure), (b) each unit can be identified as a distinct behavioral entity having its unique set of characteristics, and most important (c) the three units together facilitate a systemic study of global EDI technology transfer.

EDI Technology Transfer at Country-Level

Countries have characteristics such as geographical location, economic structure, government policies, national values and culture, technological infrastructure, etc., and may compete globally for economic growth and development (Porter, 1990). Many of these factors may affect EDI technology transfer and in turn be affected by it (Clarke et al, 1992). Many countries perceive EDI as a critical technology for facilitating their economic growth and improved quality-of-life, but either lack resources for its country-wide implementation or are unable to promote its adoption in crucial sectors. Thus, a country-level analysis of EDI implementation success factors is very important.

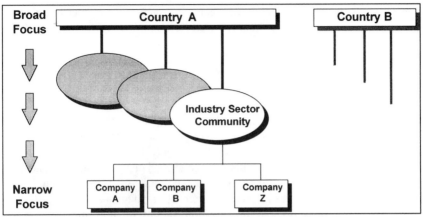

Figure 1: Levels of Scope of EDI Technology Transfer

EDI Technology Transfer at Industry Sector/ Community Level

An *industry-sector* represents a collection of distinct but inter-related industries which share resources or concerns or both. Examples are the transportation, retail, health-care and financial industry sectors. A *community* is a collection of distinct industries from one or many sectors and public administration bodies, which are inter-related through a *business network*, i.e. the structure of inter-dependent relationships between the activities of those organizations which influence each other's strategies (Kambil et al, 1994). Communities are seldom identifiable, concrete entities, but can be conceptualized as *virtual* sectors in order to improve understanding of *coordination* between inter- and intra-sectorial as well as public administration organizations resulting in economic activities of mutual interest. For example, a "port community" can be conceptualized as a virtual sector composed of a number of organizations such as the port authority, customs, shippers, forwarders, importers, exporters, plus a number of other roles (Wrigley et al, 1994).

An industry-sector or a community has many characteristics, such as concentration level (i.e. the extent to which market share is *concentrated* among few dominant firms), coordination needs, industry-level critical success factors (Rockart, 1979), importance in the government policy context, etc. These affect EDI technology transfer and an understanding of their inter-relationship is highly desirable. Furthermore, often the EDI implementation studies assume competition playing a major role in EDI adoption, but in some industries, such as health-care and telecommunications, competition is often heavily constrained. Thus, such studies need to consider an overall view of industry-sectors, not so much in the context of a centrally planned economy but rather as a linked set of organizations whose freedom of action is constrained (Clarke, 1992). Therefore, the conventional and limited view of EDI implementation from an individual organization's perspective needs to be complemented by a broader and deeper appreciation of the relevant industry-sector/community view (Clarke, 1992; Lobet-Maris, 1994).

EDI Technology Transfer at Organization Level

Organization is the most common unit of analysis for studying EDI implementation as it provides a highly tangible boundary for understanding business entities. Moreover, EDI is now seen as essential to successful business operation, and in many countries soon there may not be much choice over whether or not to use EDI. Even this level of analysis provides ample challenge in understanding the EDI implementation process due to complex interaction of various organizational characteristics such as strategy, structure, culture, technology, etc. Therefore, an organization should be the smallest unit of analysis for understanding EDI implementation success factors.

"EDI MATURITY LEVELS" IN EDI TECHNOLOGY TRANSFER

The *EDI usage maturity* refers to the extent to which EDI-based solutions have been adopted and integrated to achieve business objectives. It is an important dimension for understanding EDI technology transfer as the higher the usage maturity, the more wide or outward-looking, dynamic and complex are the issues involved (Figure 2).

The EDI usage maturity could be described using the concept of an *EDI life cycle* which has three main stages of the EDI implementation process (Holland et al, 1992):

Discovery Stage

This stage signifies awareness of EDI technology, developing an understanding of the concept of *electronic commerce*, generating interest in the need for, and opportunities to achieve sustainable business benefits through EDI. A country (or city-state) should be considered in the discovery stage if the majority of its major industry-sectors/communities is in the discovery stage and none of them in either the operational or the strategic use stages. Similar criteria could be stated for categorizing an industry-sector/community in the discovery stage, using organizations belonging to the sector/community as a basis.

Operational Use Stage

This stage signifies a working EDI system by gaining the inter-organizational ability of electronic document exchange. A country (or city-state) is in the operational stage if the majority of its major industry-sectors/communities is in the operational use stage and none of them in the strategic use stage. Similar criteria could be specified for operational use stage of an industry-sector/community.

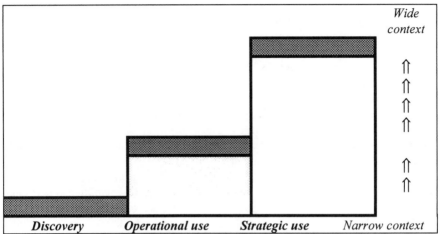

Figure 2. The EDI Maturity Level Staircase

Strategic Use Stage

This stage builds on the expertise gained in the earlier stages to exploit EDI for improving the *competitive position* of the business, an industry-sector, or a country (Leyland, 1993). As a by-product, such use may also lead to new products/markets, new business relationships, new organizational forms, and/or new sector/community structures. A country is in the strategic use stage if either (a) it has an explicit formulation of its "strategic vision" and the majority of its major industry-sectors is at least in operational use stage; or (b) if at least half of its major industry-sectors is in the "strategic use" stage. An industry-sector is in the strategic use stage if the sector as a whole has, and is working for realization of, a "strategic vision" and a majority of organizations in the sector are in operational use stage.

These stages appear to represent an *evolutionary* path from discovery to operational use and finally to strategic use; but in many cases it could also be *iterative* as well. Organizations make mistakes and have to rectify some of their initial errors, for example mistake due to lack of education and training, or lack of understanding of changes in the industry-structure or the global business environment, etc. This may push their move back from strategic use to operational use, and so on.

CRITICAL SUCCESS FACTORS OF EDI TECHNOLOGY TRANSFER

Critical success factors (CSFs) are those characteristics, conditions, or variables that when properly sustained, maintained, or managed can have a significant impact on the competitive success of an organization, an industry-sector, or a country (Rockart, 1979). In the context of EDI technology transfer, CSFs refer to the *critical enablers* in the successful development, use and diffusion of EDI applications (Krcmar et al, 1994). This section will describe the CSFs for successful EDI technology transfer using the dimensions of technology transfer scope and EDI usage maturity. The *scope* dimension would cover CSFs at the country- and industry-sector levels, and within each of these, it will include CSFs for the three usage-maturity levels.

Identification of CSFs is a long-term "watch-dog" exercise which, given the relatively short history of EDI and the complexity of *combining* long-term observations of countries, industries and organizations together would be very difficult to do purely by empirical methods. Therefore the CSFs were identified using a combination of analytical and empirical methods:

(a) *Systemic analysis* (Checkland et al, 1990) of EDI technology transfer based on the hierarchy of country, industry-sector and organization and their emergent properties.
(b) *Content analysis* (Weber, 1990) of published empirical research on EDI implementation and secondary sources such as industry analyses, EDI directories and reports.
(c) Comparative analysis of similarities and differences among various socio-economic characteristics, and EDI implementation success or failures in some selected countries and industry-sectors.

Effective management of CSFs requires that these should be only a few in number (Rockart, 1979). Therefore, if the number of CSFs turns out to be large, they should be aggregated, if possible, into broader groups for parsimony, conceptual clarity and manageability. This happens to be the case here because the number of CSFs for all the maturity-levels is rather large at the country as well as industry-sector levels (as we shall see in Tables 1 and 2). We would therefore categorize them into a few broader but homogeneous groups in order to make them conceptually more meaningful. Our research on CSFs made it clear that the CSFs can be broadly grouped into six categories, which are the *same* at the country (Table 1) as well as at the industry-sector (Table 2) levels. These categories, called the *critical success areas*, are: (a) strategy development, (b) EDI technology infrastructure, (c) IT maturity of businesses, (d) EDI coordination, (e) EDI education and expertise, and (f) business culture. The latter refers to characteristics of the business practices, the business environment and the business people (Randlesome et al, 1993).

CSFs AT THE COUNTRY-LEVEL

Discovery Stage

During this stage the issues of critical importance are the country's economic strategy, its technological infrastructure, awareness about EDI and its perceived need, and people's skills in IT.

Perceived Need: EDI implementation efforts depend on its *need* as perceived by the government and/or industry firms in a country. For example, countries having export-oriented economies with distant markets for their products may perceive need for EDI more than those having less export emphasis or having nearby markets. Similarly EDI need may be perceived by countries who intend to improve the cost-effectiveness of public services such as health-care, etc.

Strategic Vision Development (Envisioning): Strategic vision of a country describes the *image* of the country's possible and desirable future state, and is required by any country planning for radical economic change. Vision provides a broad-directive target to help countries plan when they cannot easily predict. Some countries view EDI as a core technology to realize their strategic vision, and are more successful in EDI adoption compared to some other countries who do not. For example, trade has been Singapore's main source of survival and prosperity, therefore Singapore's strategy has been to enhance its global competitiveness as a trading nation (Neo, 1994). This strategy was translated into a vision of being one of the pioneering nations to have *electronic trading* by implementing an EDI-based community trading system. On the contrary, export-dependent Hong Kong lacked such vision and perceived EDI merely as a replacement for trade paperwork; which delayed the adoption of EDI even until now (Damsgaard et al, 1994).

Technological Infrastructure Planning: A major requirement for EDI to be tenable is the availability of sufficiently sophisticated and reliable data communication networks and value-added network services, extending at least to the major industrial and commercial centers (Juric, 1994). As the infrastructure may not be developed overnight, planning for overcoming infrastructure weaknesses is essential for moving from discovery to operational use stage. For example, telecommunications should be liberalized in order to facilitate availability of low-cost value-added network (VAN) services.

IT Diffusion in Business: Developing countries are often dominated by small and medium-size enterprises, which are often slow in adopting IT. Senior management of these organizations tend to lack awareness of IT and feel that either they do not need it or could not afford it (Gable et al, 1992). EDI is a sophisticated technology and poor diffusion of IT in business environment will mean general lack of appropriate technology required for EDI implementation. Specific IT education and development programs, such as the Small Enterprise Computerization Program (SECP) initiated by Singapore in 1986, may be necessary to overcome IT diffusion problems.

Critical Success Areas	Stage		
	Discovery	**Operational use**	**Strategic use**
Strategy development	Perceived need Strategic vision development	Vision implementation	Vision review/ modification
EDI technology infrastructure	Technological infrastructure planning	Infrastructure development	Infrastructure upgrading
IT maturity of businesses	IT diffusion in business		
EDI coordination	EDI coordination mechanism	Government use of EDI EDI standardization Regulatory/ legal structure	International liaison Strategic EDI planning
EDI education & expertise	EDI education and promotion	EDI knowledge diffusion	EDI expertise management
Business culture	Formalized business relationship development	Willingness to compete internationally	Structural change in industries

Table 1. Critical Factors for Successful EDI Implementation at the Country-level

EDI Coordination Mechanism: *Coordination* refers to managing dependencies between activities (Malone et al, 1994). Coordination of various activities such as government regulations, EDI standardization, liaison with potential users and EDI service providers within and between various industry-sectors, etc. is extremely important at the country-level EDI implementation. Most countries have some type of coordination body, such as EDIforum in the Netherlands, which facilitates these activities.

EDI Education and Promotion: The business community's adoption of telecommunication-based applications in general, and EDI in particular, is often delayed generally due to lack of understanding of potential strategic benefits which can accrue from their effective utilization. There is, therefore, a strong need for business people to gain a wider education on EDI. For example, in the Netherlands, the VEDI program was initiated to provide EDI experience to organizations in various sectors (Van Der Net et al, 1992). In many countries such as Greece and UK, *EDI awareness centers* have been opened who play a major role in EDI promotion and training.

Formalized Business Relationship Development: EDI enforces a *formal* cooperative business relationship which may be contrary to the business culture of a country. Thus, an important issue is the need for 'maintenance' or 'enforcement' of the cooperative business relationship over a longer period of time in order to forge this relationship into an alliance as well as to overcome the threat of opportunism, i.e. behavior involving self-interest seeking with guile (Williamson, 1975). One extreme for reducing opportunism is that of explicit contracts and legal enforcement which forms the foundation of Anglo-Saxon business practices (Willcocks et al, 1995). These have tended to over-emphasize litigation, law and regulation at the cost of institutionalizing trust throughout society. On the other extreme are societies where trust and reputation take on greater importance, such as in the Asian business environment. A third type of situation faces organizations doing business in areas such as Eastern Europe and developing regions such as Africa, where there is neither strong legal enforcement nor high levels of trust in society. Since EDI enforces formalization in cooperation, it favors the first extreme. Therefore, in countries where formal contract is not the common business practice, this cultural barrier may also need to be overcome to promote international cooperation through EDI.

Operational Use Stage

The CSFs for this stage are the factors which would ensure EDI start-up and its continual growth along with the associated benefits.

Vision Implementation: The realization of vision requires planning and committing resources for projects and programs for leading the country towards the envisioned state. A prerequisite for this would be a national IT plan describing these projects and programs (Doukidis, 1993). Singapore had its National Information Technology Plan in 1986 which identified EDI implementation as part of the plan (Raman, 1993).

Technological Infrastructure Development: Infrastructure development which was planned during the discovery stage, such as availability of low-cost VAN services, must be in place during the operational use stage. A national IT plan would greatly facilitate this development, as in the case of Singapore (Raman, 1993) and Greece (Doukidis, 1993).

Government Use of EDI: Government may set an example for the non-adopters by using EDI in areas such as tendering, taxation returns, etc., and can provide a stimulus for the development of infrastructure and culture necessary for EDI's widespread use (Clarke et al, 1992). As an example, EDI use in trading would not be very successful if the government agencies (such as customs) themselves do not start using it [Gotschlich, 1992].

EDI Standardization: Standards make a vital contribution to the EDI infrastructure. The acceptance of a common message standard is a fundamental requirement of EDI. Ideally, standards should be common across various industry-sectors in a country. This would provide a wider market for EDI messages, and thus has the potential for reduced EDI costs. In addition, a commonly accepted standard would also reduce the occurrence of a "hub" enterprise forcing its small trading partners to use a *proprietary* EDI standard. It is for this reason that an internationally accepted UN/EDIFACT standard has been developed, but other standards such as ANSI X12 also exist.

Regulatory/ Legal Structure: The regulatory structure imposed by government may be a constraint to EDI implementation and require change, in some cases through changes to the law (Clarke et al, 1992). For example, contract definition may need to be changed legally to accept electronic in lieu of paper documents. Similarly liberalization in telecommunication may be necessary for encouraging third-party VAN services for EDI.

EDI Knowledge Diffusion: Early adopters of EDI develop valuable knowledge out of their EDI experiences. In order to avoid recurrence of costly mistakes by late adopters, there should be mechanisms for diffusion of this knowledge, such as EDI user associations, industry-specific associations, and EDI publications.

Willingness to Compete Internationally: EDI facilitates comparative advantage which is gained through cooperation with other countries. Thus, willingness to compete globally through international trade, investment, travel, and commercial innovations is a factor critical to successful EDI implementation (Clarke et al, 1992). Without it, there could be hardly EDI-based international trading, which may hamper EDI diffusion in other sectors.

Strategic Use Stage

The CSFs for this stage mostly relate to the national and international environment for finding and exploiting innovative/ strategic opportunities involving EDI use.

Vision Review/ Modification (Re-visioning): Experience with EDI use during the operational use stage creates valuable knowledge. This knowledge coupled with the changes in the global environment may open new opportunities, which may require a critical appraisal of existing vision, perhaps even formulation of a new vision. For example, Singapore now has a new vision of an intelligent city as defined in its new IT2000 plan (Soh et al, 1993).

Technological Infrastructure Upgrading: New developments in the technology (such as multi-media messaging) may help identify new opportunities for EDI use (such as electronic graphic communication in construction and health-care industries). Thus monitoring of new developments in technology and planning for improving the infrastructure is critical to successful strategic use of EDI.

International EDI Liaison: may help in joint discovery of new opportunities through global alliances and other inter-organizational mechanisms. Such liaison could be between the level of national and international EDI coordinating bodies.

Strategic EDI Planning: EDI diffusion should be monitored by government bodies, user associations or other coordinating bodies through routine surveys of EDI use (Clarke, 1994; Masson, 1992). With the increasing level of EDI maturity, it would be necessary to carry out strategic planning for identifying innovative use of EDI as dictated by the new vision and consequent need for a change in the infrastructure.

EDI Expertise Management: With the increasing levels of EDI maturity and expertise, there would be a need to manage this expertise effectively for growth and diffusion among other users. Diffusion of expertise could take place through publication of case studies (Swatman, 1994) and consultancies.

Structural Change in Industries: EDI use may change structure of industry-sectors. These changes may be *functional reallocation*, in which functions are transferred among corporations; *architectural re-structuring*, in which some organizations are destroyed and new ones may be created; and *industry redefinition*, in which the entire industry undergoes major changes (Clarke, 1992). For example, construction industry, which is inherently very fragmented, has been found to change structurally with the increasing diffusion of EDI (O Brien et al, 1993). Monitoring such changes and feeding them back into the strategic EDI planning process may give rise to new EDI opportunities or may warn for corrective actions.

CSFs AT THE INDUSTRY SECTOR/ COMMUNITY LEVEL

There are hardly any global sector-level empirical studies of EDI implementation available. Therefore CSFs at the industry-sector level are proposed here more on the basis of analytical reasoning rather than empirical evidence.

Discovery Stage

During this stage, the choice of sector(s) for EDI implementation is the most important CSF, as different sectors may have different structures, coordination needs, technological maturity, and importance for the country.

Choice of Industry-sector/Community: The choice of industry-sector/ community is critical in two ways: the importance of the sector/community to the country, and its characteristics in promoting successful EDI adoption. For example, in the case of the Netherlands, the VEDI project was initiated during 1989-92 for identifying industry-sectors of strategic importance for Netherlands (van Der Net et al, 1992). Similarly trade and transportation were economically important to Singapore and, therefore, they were selected for initial EDI implementation in Singapore (Neo, 1994).

As for structural characteristics, industry-sectors having high *concentration rates* and *coordination needs* are likely to accept EDI more readily (Lobet-Maris, 1994). A highly concentrated industry-sector is dominated by a small number of dominant players, and the degree of concentration is generally expressed in terms of market share. High concentration within a sector reduces the complexity of agreeing the form of electronic trading. Coordination needs vary widely from sector to sector and depend on production processes. General mass production based industries have higher coordination needs compared to those based on flow or project based production (Lobet-Maris, 1994). EDI enhances the efficiency of coordination process through standardization and long-term business relationships. For example, retailing has a higher level of concentration compared to construction in most countries, and retailing is also based on mass production whereas construction is project-based. Consequently EDI adoption level is much higher in retailing in these countries compared to that in construction.

Critical Success Areas	Stage		
	Discovery	Operational use	Strategic use
Sector-level strategy development	Choice of sector/ community	Strategic thinking in the sector/ community	Strategic vision of the sector/ community
			Strategic sector/ community level planning
			Industry environment monitoring
EDI technology infrastructure		Technology infrastructure support	Technology infrastructure upgrading
IT maturity of businesses	IT diffusion in the sector/ community		
EDI coordination	EDI coordination planning in the sector	EDI coordination support in the sector	International EDI coordination
		Government support EDI Standardization	
EDI education & expertise	EDI education and promotion	EDI knowledge diffusion	EDI expertise consulting
Business culture in the sector	Cultural change	Collaborative needs	Sector/ community structure monitoring

Table 2. CSFs for EDI Implementation at the Sector/Community Level

IT Diffusion in the Industry-sector: Even in countries where IT diffusion in business is high, it is *not* uniform across all sectors. A sector/community having high diffusion of IT is more likely to have appropriate technology necessary for EDI implementation, and thus more ready for EDI adoption.

EDI Coordination Planning: Fragmented industries need a mechanism or institution to mediate between organizations, negotiating the form of EDI and coordinating its implementation. Industry may support EDI by setting-up such mediator organizations, commonly called EDI user associations, and giving them legitimacy through the organizations which support them (Metcalf, 1993). Examples of such associations in Netherlands are ODETTE in the automotive sector and UAC-Transcom in retailing.

EDI Education and Promotion: Lack of common understanding and limited education about EDI, its "business" value and justification have also been identified as one of the major barriers to EDI adoption (Scala et al, 1993). Also, existing EDI education and promotion programs may be too general for organizations within a specific sector/community. Thus education and promotion programs specifically customized for a sector/community should be available.

Sector-specific EDI user associations could play a major role in accomplishing it.

Cultural Change: Cooperation among business partners can prove very difficult to achieve if different organizations have widely differing cultures. For example, if most organizations perceive transactions in the "paper-form" only, they might go as far as fax, but may not agree for EDI easily. Such differences can inhibit communication and make working relationships hard to negotiate and maintain for the EDI environment to exist. Thus, there may be a need for changing the business culture, which should be one of the major goals of EDI education.

Operational Use Stage

During this stage some leading organizations, called the EDI *champions*, would have already introduced EDI and the aim would be that the successes of these early adopters should motivate other organizations to adopt EDI.

Strategic Thinking in the Industry: Strategic thinking promotes competitive orientation. An industry dominated by strategy-conscious organizations is more likely to adopt EDI as an enabler of organizational strategies; especially if their strategy is based on reduction in the procurement/delivery cycle, or some other comparative advantage.

Technology Infrastructure Support: There is an increasing tendency, specially in Europe, Australia and Asia, for even the largest organizations to use third-party value-added network services rather than to perform the function themselves (Clarke et al, 1992). Lack of such services customized for a specific sector(s) may inhibit EDI adoption in the sector.

EDI Coordination Support: The EDI user associations specific to chosen industry-sectors should be in operation in this stage. They have a very important role in several critical areas such as EDI promotion and education in the sector, liaison with government for its EDI related support, promoting EDI standardization, and overseeing development of technology infrastructure for EDI use in the sector.

Government Support: Departments which directly interface with a specific sector/community should be encouraged to use EDI in order to rationalize their operations. Government should also modify various laws and court-rules, particularly in the areas of evidence and contract, in order to facilitate EDI-based trade.

EDI Standardization: EDI standards could be proprietary, industry specific, or international (d'Udekem-Gevers, 1994). As EDI becomes increasingly inter-sectorial and international, de facto industry-specific standards, such as ODETTE in European automotive industry, become increasingly restrictive and impede the attainment of international trading. There is, therefore, an increasing trend within sectors to upgrade their standards in conformity with international standards such as UN-EDIFACT.

EDI Knowledge Diffusion: Early adopters of EDI within a sector/community develop experiential knowledge related to managerial aspects of EDI, which could be a valuable learning source for late adopters. This knowledge could be shared through EDI user group conferences and case study publications.

Collaborative Needs: With the increase in EDI adoption, a sector-wide EDI implementation scheme is more likely to emerge (Clarke et al, 1992). This may be partly due to competitors' tendency to move for neutralizing the advantage of "first mover" organizations, and partly to industry and regulatory bodies' tendency to perceive a successful EDI scheme as one which is widely adopted and not limited to few organizations (who could retain the competitive advantage!). Although this sector-based *collaboration* might seem to reduce the competitiveness of the sector concerned, EDI tends to open up new possibilities for competition among the organizations. Thus, development of cooperative needs benefits the industry's customers, and hence the economy and society as a whole.

Strategic Use Stage

During this stage, the sector/community has matured in terms of EDI use. There must, therefore, be an increasing strategic-orientation within the sector/community and it must open up for international EDI coordination.

Strategic Vision of the Industry-sector: With successful collaboration in operational stage, companies may start thinking of "global competitiveness" rather than a national or regional one; and may facilitate development of a vision for the entire sector. As for example, the shipping and maritime industry may start identifying itself as an "ocean port community" and analyze various alternative strategies to attain EDI integration (Wrigley et al, 1994).

Strategic Industry-sector Level Planning: Developing a vision alone is not enough unless it is supported by strategic sector-level planning for implementing it. For example, Singapore has not only identified critical sectors for its vision of an "intelligent city" in its IT2000 plan, but has also initiated sector-level planning (Soh et al, 1993).

Industry Environment Monitoring: In most industries, business environments are highly turbulent. This makes early detection and rapid interpretation of weak environment signals about impending structural change and discontinuities most critical. For example, the shipping industry within the transportation sector is experiencing a change in terms of customers demand (one point service, "door-to-door" delivery), emphasis on safety and environmental protection, and shift towards multimodal transportation (European Commission, 1994). Such environmental change, if monitored continuously, may highlight emerging opportunities for EDI use, such as multimodal transport based EDI networks, etc.

Technology Infrastructure Upgrading: Strategic applications of EDI may demand additional developments in the technological infrastructure, such as multi-media messaging required for electronic graphic communications (EGI) in construction and health-care industries.

International EDI Coordination: As most strategic applications of EDI are global in nature and scope, there may be a need to coordinate EDI activities internationally. Thus, during this stage, the EDI coordination should be extended to EDI coordination bodies for the same sector in other countries/ regions and international EDI bodies.

EDI Expertise Consulting: Strategic EDI applications are often innovative and it would be desirable for other organizations to know about such innovative use in order to enhance the global competitiveness of the entire sector/community. Such knowledge should therefore be disseminated to other organizations through consultancies or case studies for possible replication or even improved innovation.

Industry Structure Monitoring: EDI implementation may impact the industry structure, which should be monitored closely for identifying new innovative EDI opportunities. For example, EDI's impact on construction industry in UK in terms of enhancing the concentration means that rate of EDI diffusion could be enhanced by changing the strategy to one which is more appropriate for a high-concentration sector. For instance, EDI may be used to implement a vertical integration strategy in the construction industry, as in Japan.

EDI IMPLEMENTATION IN SOME SELECTED INDUSTRY SECTORS

In the near absence of empirical studies of industry sector-level EDI implementation, it may be worthwhile to discuss *analytically* EDI technology transfer in some specific sectors on the basis of their structural and economic characteristics. It illustrates how the CSFs may play their role in the implementation process. We will consider three industry-sectors as examples: transport services, retailing, and construction. Transport services is perhaps the most common sector for implementing EDI; retailing is a sector having a high level of IT diffusion and more adopting to EDI generally; and construction is a highly fragmented sector normally considered non-adopting for EDI.

Transport Services

Transport is a crucial sector for the economy of any country. The transport services sector is engaged directly or indirectly in the conveyance of goods and passengers. Direct involvement relates to the actual conveyance of goods and passengers by various modes of transport. Indirect involvement includes services as handling when changing modes, traffic guidance, freight brokerage, storage, customs clearance, etc. The demand for transport depends on the level of national and global economic and social development at any specific time. It also depends on other factors such as the trend towards flexible production methods, e.g. Just In Time (JIT), leading to lower stock levels but more frequent deliveries of lower volumes.

For countries such as the Netherlands and Singapore, transport services is a very important sector in achieving their strategy of acting as a "logistic hub" for Europe and South Asia respectively. Consequently, there has been a continued high level of government support in improving the efficiency of this sector, specially sea transport, through EDI. For example, the port community of Rotterdam has INTIS and many other inter-linked EDI networks, and that of Singapore has TradeNet and PortNet EDI networks to provide highly efficient sea transport services in these countries. Such high levels of support and promotion were necessary because of the fragmented nature of sea transport sub-sector. For the purpose of comparison, transport is not a strategic sector for the UK, and consequently the level of government support for, and implementation of EDI in the transport sector in UK has been relatively lower compared to other sectors such as retailing.

Retailing Industry

For the majority of consumer goods, retailing is the final link in the distribution channel starting from the product manufacturer to the customer. It is a dynamic and complex sector involving a range of organization types of varying scale. Its structure reflects the cultural characteristics of the society it serves, and therefore sociological, economic and technological developments would have an impact on retail trade. In many industrialized countries, retailing has a high level of concentration and close vertical links between manufacturers, wholesalers and retailers. Since low inventory levels is a critical factor for competitive success, there has been a relatively higher level of EDI adoption in this sector compared to many others such as construction, clothing, etc. A CSF exemplified by this sector is the relatively high level of IT diffusion. This is because retailing is heavily dependent on many IT products such as electronic article numbering (EAN), bar-coding, point-of-sale (POS) terminals, etc.

Construction Industry

Construction is traditionally divided into *building* and *civil engineering*. Civil engineering mainly involves public infrastructure in other sectors such as transport, energy, etc. Construction sector is a highly fragmented sector (i.e. many similar firms compete for market share) in most countries. For example, the total number of construction firms in Netherlands is 41,000; out of which only 5 to 10 are large, a small number medium-sized, and all the others are small (European Commission, 1994). This fragmentation is due to many factors which result from the diversity of construction technology, customers and market sectors. The need to repair and maintain the existing built environment means the retention of competence in most of the technologies that were ever used in construction. Furthermore, many construction firms specialize in one or a group of related technologies and are involved with other firms only during a particular project as part of the project team. The fragmented nature of the sector is somewhat reduced by long-term business contracts among firms, as in Japan and to some extent in USA

Construction sector is generally considered to be a laggard sector for EDI technology. This is generally due to the fragmentation but also, at least in Europe, characterized by small-scale firms, due to the tendency to avoid risks and look for short-term profit, and finally due to a preference for traditional work methods (European Commission, 1994). Therefore, in spite of its strategic importance for countries such as the Netherlands and UK, the construction sector is not so successful in implementing EDI as it is weak with respect to several CSFs. IT diffusion is generally low in this sector as most firms are small in size; EDI education has been lacking due to the conservative thinking of most firms; and worst of all the products and parts standardization is very low (till recently there were hardly any standards available at the construction project level).

However, recently there seems to be a growing tendency towards EDI implementation in countries such as the Netherlands and the UK. In fact, the Dutch government has put in lot of effort in promoting EDI within this sector (Thissen et al, 1992) in spite of the sector's non-EDI adopting nature. This could perhaps be explained by the fact that the Dutch construction market is reasonably large but there are no such large construction firms compared to those in UK, Germany, France and Japan (i.e. Japanese firms operating in Europe) (European Commission, 1994). Thus, the Dutch construction sector is open for large competitors from other European countries, and this vulnerability makes it an important sector for the Netherlands. On the other hand, the construction sector is important for UK because of the large European market which the big firms in UK would like to capitalize on.

A FRAMEWORK FOR GLOBAL EDI TECHNOLOGY TRANSFER

Having described the CSFs for EDI technology transfer at the country- and industry-sector levels and the status of EDI implementation in three industries, we will attempt to conceptualize linkages between these CSFs and the level of adoption of EDI technology. We will primarily focus on the six parsimonious "critical success areas" identified earlier (Tables 1 and 2) rather than the large number of CSFs themselves. Since the second and third critical areas - EDI technology infrastructure and IT maturity of business - both deal with technological issues, they will be combined into one broader category "Technology Infrastructure Development". We propose a framework of EDI technology transfer which inter-relates the ensuing five *critical success areas*: strategy development, technology infrastructure development, EDI education and expertise, EDI coordination and business culture change (Figure 3).

Strategy development is a critical area in EDI technology transfer because it provides a clear purpose and sets the direction for the entire country or for a specific industry-sector. Traditionally strategy depends on perceived needs/opportunities and after articulating a *vision* and objectives, a strategic plan is chalked out to achieve these objectives. These objectives and the strategic plan may promote the *demand* for EDI technology. Cases of recent EDI successes (e.g. countries such as Singapore, Australia, Netherlands) are almost always associated with the explicit formulation of a strategy. Once a strategy has been developed, it needs to be implemented.

This requires two things -- the *knowledge/skills* for the execution of various implementation tasks; and the necessary *technological infrastructure* to enable implementation. The three critical areas, which need to be successfully managed simultaneously are: *strategy* development, *infrastructure* development, and *education* (including expertise). This needs effective co-ordination (Malone et al, 1994) of these areas. Therefore the EDI implementation process needs to be coordinated between various stakeholders from governments to international business communities, to industry firms, depending on the level at which coordination is considered. Finally, the outcome of successful EDI implementation should be a desirable change in the *business culture*, i.e. characteristics of the business practices, the business environment and the business people (Randlesome et al, 1993). Thus, at the country-level, the business culture will include characteristics of business environment and practices favoring the willingness to compete internationally whereas at the industry sector-level, it would include characteristics such as basic business philosophy, *trust* in buyer-seller relationships, etc.

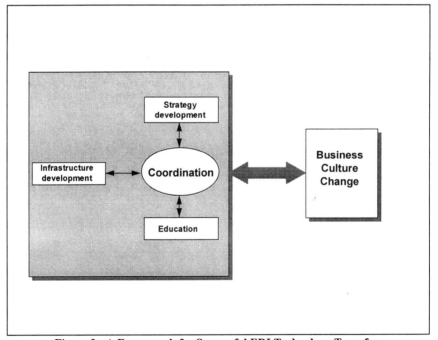

Figure 3: A Framework for Successful EDI Technology Transfer

Thus, a framework for successful transfer of EDI technology could be proposed for both the country and the industry-sector levels (Figure 3). According to this framework, simultaneous development of *strategy*, *technological infrastructure*, and *education* are the initial critical areas for EDI implementation, which need to be coordinated properly to ensure *success*. Thus the fourth critical area for success is a *mechanism for coordinating* strategy development, infrastructure development and education. Without proper co-ordination of the three areas, the transfer of EDI technology may not be successful. The success of EDI technology transfer may be ascertained through the *business culture change* at the level the EDI implementation was planned. The changed business culture would, in turn, facilitate for a deeper transfer of EDI technology by affecting demand for change in the other critical success areas, which is indicated by bi-directional arrows in Figure 3.

To understand the implications of this framework at the country-level (as an example), let us assume that initially the business culture lacks "formalized business relationship". Then, the country would have to develop appropriate strategy, infrastructure and education programs, and coordinate them in an appropriate manner such that the business community develops "formalized business relationships". This would be the "discovery" stage for the country. The changed business culture would now require changes in the strategy, infrastructure and educational programs in order to move the country into the "operational use" stage. These three areas need to be appropriately coordinated in order to change the business culture further, this time to develop "willingness to compete internationally". This would be the "operational use" stage for the country. Similar action would be required to move the country into the "strategic use" stage, and may perhaps require much more effort compared to that required for the "operational use" stage. Different countries may require different amounts of effort in different critical areas. For example, in east European countries, business culture change may need more effort compared to countries in the Asia pacific region.

APPLICATION OF EDI TECHNOLOGY TRANSFER FRAMEWORK TO SELECTED COUNTRIES

In this section, we will apply the above framework of Figure 3 to some of those countries which have either already adopted EDI technology or are trying to adopt it, such as Singapore, Hong Kong, Australia, Netherlands, Greece, Slovenia, etc. In addition to the five critical success areas identified in the framework, another factor, presence of *dominant* (such as large multinational) organizations, has also been included here because, as explained above, their presence could overcome weakness (if any) in the strategy development area. This has been done in order to show what could happen when the technology is available but a national strategy is missing (as in the case of Hong Kong)! In such a case the dominant industry firms could also pressurize their trading partners to have private EDI links with them for continuation of the partnership. The relationship between the critical success areas and EDI implementation success in example countries has been shown in Table 3.

From Table 3, it appears that strategy development plays the most crucial role in successful EDI technology transfer, as in the case of Singapore, Australia and Netherlands. This may be because in the absence of proper strategy, there may not be a proper evaluation of the technology infrastructure and educational requirements and, therefore, any weaknesses in these areas may not be even noticed. However, if an explicit strategy and IT policy are being articulated, plans for developing or upgrading the infrastructure as well as educating the business community could be initiated as in the case of Greece and Slovenia.

	Singa-pore	Hong Kong	Austra-lia	Nether-lands	Greece	Slove-nia	Colum-bia
National EDI Strategy development	Yes	No	Yes	Partial	Evolving	Evolving	Yes
EDI technology infrastructure	Yes	Yes	Yes	Yes	Limited	Limited	Fast deve-loping
IT maturity of businesses	Yes	Yes	Yes	Yes	Limited	Limited	Limited
EDI education & expertise	Yes	Yes	Yes	Yes	Limited	Yes	Yes
EDI coordination	Yes	No	Yes	Limited	No	Limited	Yes
Pressure from dominant industry firms	Limited	Yes	Yes	Yes	Limited	No	Limited
EDI technology transfer	Success-ful transfer	Limited; private EDI	Success-ful transfer	Success-ful transfer	Limited; slow transfer	Limited; slow transfer	Limited, fast transfer

Table 3: Application of EDI Technology Transfer Framework: A Multi-country Perspective

In countries having developed strategies, EDI implementation would be successful if other critical success areas are properly managed, as in the case of Singapore and Australia. A particular interesting case is that of Columbia: encouraged by a well articulated national EDI strategy and telecommunications deregulation policy, EDI technology is currently transferred at a high pace (over 4000 users have been reported). This case confirms the importance of developing a national strategy in the successful transfer of EDI. However, in countries where development of strategy is weak, evolving or non-existent, presence of dominant industry firms become more important in order to pressurize government for necessary infrastructure (as in the Netherlands) or to pressurize their trading partners to have private EDI links for continuation of business with them (as in Hong Kong).

STAKEHOLDERS IN COUNTRY-LEVEL EDI TECHNOLOGY TRANSFER

Having previously discussed the CSFs at the country-level, an important question is who should have the responsibility for managing them. There are many stakeholders in the EDI technology transfer process at the country-level: the government of the country, IT vendors, EDI user associations,

Stakeholder	Responsibility area	Relevant CSFs
Government	Strategy development	Perception of EDI need *Envisioning* Vision implementation *Re-visioning*
	Technology infrastructure	Infrastructure planning Infrastructure development Infrastructure upgrading
	Technology maturity	IT diffusion in business
	EDI coordination	EDI coordination mechanism Regulatory/ legal structure Government use of EDI Strategic EDI planning
	Business culture	Willingness to compete internationally
IT vendors	Technology infrastructure	Infrastructure development Infrastructure upgrading
	Technology maturity	IT diffusion in business
	EDI education	EDI education and promotion EDI knowledge diffusion
EDI user association	EDI coordination	EDI standardization International liaison Strategic EDI planning
	EDI education	EDI education and promotion EDI knowledge diffusion EDI expertise management
EDI awareness center	EDI education	EDI education and promotion EDI knowledge diffusion EDI expertise management
Industry firms	Strategy development	Perception of EDI need
	Technology maturity	IT diffusion in business
	EDI coordination	Strategic EDI planning
	EDI education	EDI knowledge diffusion EDI expertise management
	Business culture	Formalized business relationship Willingness to compete internationally Structural change monitoring *EDI use in business*

Table 4: Stakeholders' Roles in Managing CSFs at Country Level

EDI awareness centers, and the industry firms themselves. Each one of these should play an active role in the EDI implementation process by sharing responsibilities for some critical areas which would facilitate effective management of CSFs. These managerial roles of the various stakeholders are shown in Table 4.

From this table it is obvious that the government has some responsibility in *most* of the critical success areas and a major responsibility for strategy development. Countries where governments play such a *pro-active* role are generally more successful in EDI technology transfer compared to countries where governments play merely a *reactive* or an *inactive* role.

EDI technology transfer success also depends heavily on the industry firms who will ultimately be the adopters of EDI technology. They constitute the other most important stakeholder as they also have some responsibility in *all* critical success areas. The more *pro-active* the industry firms in a country, the less effort the government has to make for successful EDI implementation. Moreover, if the industry firms have some dominant big players (as in high concentration industries) who perceive a pressing *need* for EDI, they can pressurize a reactive (or even an inactive) government to at least facilitate transfer of EDI technology by managing CSFs which no other stakeholder can manage, such as "regulatory/ legal structure".

PLANNING FOR EDI TECHNOLOGY TRANSFER

The nature of required coordination varies during different levels of EDI maturity. Therefore, the EDI technology transfer should be conceptualized as a "staged" process for implementing EDI. Such an approach seeks to strike a balance between strategy development, education and expertise development, as well as technology infrastructure development. Therefore, planning for EDI

Responsible Stakeholder(s)	Tasks
Government	• Define strategic scope, scale and direction. Clarify the strategic direction and target technological infrastructure. Develop a vision and determine the strategic objectives. • Decide on the scale of infrastructure change required and the core industry-sectors for EDI implementation. • Set up an EDI coordination body (or bodies) such as EDI user association, EDI awareness center, etc.
EDI user association EDI awareness center	• Raise awareness of, understanding of, and interest in EDI.
Government, IT vendors, Industry firms	• Promote IT diffusion in core sector businesses (if necessary) through education, training, subsidies, and consultancies.

Table 5. Planning EDI Technology Transfer: Initiation Stage

technology transfer should be carried out in the following stages: (a) initiation (*discovery* level), (b) institutionalization (*operational use* level), and (c) exploitation (*strategic use* level). The tasks and the stakeholders responsible during the three stages are shown in Tables 5, 6 and 7.

It is obvious that the government initiative plays a very important role during the "initiation" stage in terms of defining the strategic direction, changing the infrastructure, and establishing a coordination mechanism. Thus, without strong government support and leadership, EDI technology may not take-off on a large scale in a country! During the institutionalization stage, the role of EDI user association and awareness center becomes more important because of the need for effectively coordinating the EDI education programs as well as development of technology infrastructure such as EDI standardization, etc.

Responsible Stakeholder(s)	Tasks
Government	Undertake necessary changes in the regulatory and legal structure (e.g. deregulation of telecommunications, modification in the contract law, etc.).
Government, EDI user association, Industry firms	Initiate EDI standardization at least for the selected core sectors.
Government/ IT vendors, EDI user association	Develop EDI infrastructure (e.g. reliable telecommunication networks and VAN services).
EDI user association, IT vendors, Industry firms	Promote EDI use in core sectors through training programs.
IT vendors, User association	Provide EDI support technology and services.
Government, EDI user association	Introduce EDI in government, at least in those departments which interface with core sectors.
EDI user association, EDI awareness center, Industry firms	Diffuse EDI experiential knowledge through EDI user group meetings and conferences as well as publication of case studies.

Table 6: Planning EDI Technology Transfer: Institutionalization Stage

Finally, during the exploitation stage, the industry firms need to play an active role in perceiving themselves as a "community" rather than merely as an industry, searching for innovative opportunities involving EDI use, and more important, acquiring the necessary skills and the technology for the desired innovative EDI use.

CONCLUSION AND FUTURE RESEARCH DIRECTION

EDI is a sophisticated technology which has shown significant impact at multiple levels -- country, industry-sector, and individual organization. Therefore, a holistic understanding of EDI technology transfer process requires an understanding of the issues to be addressed and the success factors at the three levels. This chapter has proposed a general framework of EDI technology

Responsible Stakeholder(s)	Tasks
Government, EDI user association	Plan for liaison with international EDI bodies.
Government, EDI user association/ IT vendors, Industry firms	Develop international EDI links.
User association, Awareness center, Industry firms	Monitor EDI expertise through sector-specific user group meetings and seminars.
Government, EDI user association, Industry firms	Ensure a continuous review of EDI achievements and opportunities world-wide through national and international user conferences and industry delegations.
EDI user association, EDI awareness center, Industry firms	Monitor core industry-sector structures through industry surveys to assess EDI impact and potential for new sector-specific EDI opportunities.
IT vendors, EDI user association, Government	Maintain EDI technological infrastructure through *continuous incremental improvements* as well as occasional fundamental changes to it.

Table 7: Planning EDI Technology Transfer: Exploitation Stage

transfer, which fulfills this need because it takes into account these multiple levels and identifies the CSFs at the first two levels. The framework gives an insight into the key areas to be managed for the successful transfer of EDI technology into a country or an industry-sector. Furthermore, the chapter also describes a planning approach for EDI technology transfer, which is based on the framework, and could be used for formulating or evaluating the EDI implementation strategies of a country and/or industry-sector by the policy planners. It can also be used by the senior IS management of multinational corporations for planning EDI implementation in their subsidiaries in different countries. Empirical research involving detailed case studies at the country level, is being planned to validate the framework and the role of stakeholders in these countries (using data from a much larger population of countries) and thus will enhance its value even more.

References

Banerjee, S. and Golhar, D.Y. "Electronic Data Interchange: Characteristics of Users and Nonusers", *Information & Management*, (26), February 1994, pp. 65-74.

Bouchard, L. "Decision Criteria in the Adoption of EDI", *Proc. Fourteenth International Conference on Information Systems*, Orlando, Florida, December 5-8, 1993, pp.365-376.

Checkland, P. and Scholes, J. *Soft Systems Methodology in Action*, John Wiley, Chichester, 1990.

Clarke, R. "A Contingency Model of EDI's Impact on Industry Sectors", *Journal of Strategic Information Systems*, (1:3), June 1992, pp.143-151.

Clarke, R. "EDI in Australian International Trade and Transportation", *Proc. Seventh International EDI-IOS Conference*, Bled, Slovenia, June 6-8, 1994, pp.114-137.

Clarke, R.; DeLuca, P.; Gricar, J.; Imai, T.; McCubbrey, D. and Swatman, P. "The International Significance of Electronic Data Interchange", in *The Global Issues of Information Technology Management*, Palvia, S.; Palvia, P. and Zigil, R. (eds.), Idea Group Publishing, Harrisburg, Penn., U.S.A., 1992, pp.277-307.

Cox, B. and Ghoneim, S. "Implementing a National EDI Service: Issues in Developing Countries & Lessons from the UK", *Proc. IFIP WG9.4 International Conference on Information Technology and Socio-Economic Development: Challenges and Opportunities*, Cairo, Egypt, January 8-11, 1995, pp.125-147.

Damsgaard, J., Lyytinen, K. "Can the Dragon Jump the EDI Bandwagon?", *Proc. Second SISnet Conference*, Barcelona, Spain, September 1994.

DeSanctis, G. "Theory and Research: Goals, Priorities, and Approaches", *MIS Quarterly*, (17:1), March 1993, pp.vi-viii.

Doukidis, G.I. "E.D.I. in Less Developed Environments: An Information Systems Perspective", *Proc. Seventh International EDI-IOS Conference*, Bled, Slovenia, June 6-8, 1993, pp.100-115.

d'Udekem-Gevers, M. "Classification of EDI Standards and Their Implications", *Proc. Seventh International EDI-IOS Conference*, Bled, Slovenia , June 1994, pp.280-290.

Emmelhainz, M.A. *EDI: A Total Management Guide*, 2nd edn., Van Nostrand Reinhold., New York, N.Y., U.S.A., 1993.

European Commission *Panorama of EU Industry 94*, European Commission, Brussels, Belgium, 1994.

Farhoomand, A. "A Snapshot of Electronic Data Interchange in the 1990s", *EDI Forum*, (5:4), 1992, pp.27-31.

Gable, G.G. and Raman, K.S. "Government Initiative for IT Adoption in Small Business", *International Information Systems*, (1:1), January 1992, pp.68-93.

Gotschlich, G.D. "Customs Changing to Market Economies: Modern Customs Procedures with a Single Administrative Document (SAD) First Step to Use EDI", *Proc. Fifth International EDI Conference*, Bled, Slovenia, September 1992, pp.36-40.

Holland, C.; Lockett, G. and Blackman, I. "Electronic Data Interchange Implementation: A Comparison of U.S. and European Cases", *International Information Systems*, (1:4), October 1992, pp.14-37.

Juric, J. "Electronic Commerce and VAN", *Proc. Seventh International EDI-IOS Conference*, Bled, Slovenia., June 1994, pp.162-169.

Kambil, A. and Short, J.E. "Electronic Integration and Business Network Redesign: A Roles-Linkage Perspective", *Journal of Management Information Systems*, (10:4), Spring 1994, pp.59-83.

Krcmar, H.; Bjorn-Andersen, N.; Eistert, T.; Griese, J.; Jelassi, T.; O'Callaghan, R.; Pasini, P. and Ribbers, P. "EDI in Europe -- Empirical Analysis of a Multi-Industry Study", *Proc. Seventh International EDI-IOS Conference*, Bled, Slovenia, June 6-8, 1994, pp.200-220.

Leyland, V. *Electronic Data Interchange: A Management View*, Prentice-Hall, Englewood Cliffs, N.J., U.S.A., 1993.

Lobet-Maris, C. "EDI Diffusion: Controversies and Realities", *Proc. Seventh International EDI-IOS Conference*, Bled, Slovenia, June 6-8, 1994, pp.170-179.

McCubbrey, D.J. and Imai, T. "EDI/IOS in the U.S. and Japan: Contrasts and Conjectures", *Proc. Seventh International EDI-IOS Conference*, Bled, Slovenia, June 6-8, 1994, pp.32-39.

Mackay, D.R. "The Impact of EDI on the Components Sector of the Australian Automotive Industry", *Journal of Strategic Information Systems*, (2:3), September 1993, pp.243-263.

Malone, T.W. and Crowston, K. "The Interdisciplinary Study of Coordination", *ACM Computing Surveys*, (26:1), March 1994, pp.87-119.

Masson, D.J. "The State of U.S. EDI", *EDI Forum*, (5:4), 1992, pp.8-12.

Metcalf, T. "Organization and Management Structures for EDI - User Groups", *Proc. Sixth International EDI-IOS Conference*, Bled, Slovenia, June 7-9, 1993, pp.377-382.

Neo, B.S. "Managing New Information Technologies: Lessons from Singapore's Experience with EDI", *Information & Management*, (26:6), June 1994, pp.317-326.

Neumann, S. *Strategic Information Systems: Competition Through Information Technologies*, Maxwell Macmillan, 1994.

O Brien, M.J. and Al-Soufi, A. "Electronic Data Interchange and the Structure of U.K. Construction Industry", *Construction Management & Economics*, (11:6), November 1993, pp.443-453.

Pfeiffer, H.K. *The Diffusion of Electronic Data Interchange*, Springer-Verlag, 1992.

Porter, M.E. "The Competitive Advantage of Nations", *Harvard Business Review*, March-April 1990, pp.73-93.

Raman, K.S. "Electronic Data Interchange in Singapore", *Proc. Sixth International Conference on Electronic Data Interchange and Interorganization Systems*, Bled, Slovenia, June7-9, 1993, pp.47-59.

Randlesome, C.; Brierley, B.; Bruton, K. and Gordon, C. *Business Cultures in Europe*, 2nd edn., Butterworth-Heinemann, 1993.

Reekers, N. "Electronic Data Interchange Use in German and US Organizations", *International Journal of Information Management*, (14:5), October 1994, pp.344-356).

Reekers, N. and Smithson, S. "EDI in Europe: A Comparative Study of Implementation and Use", *Proc. Sixth International EDI-IOS Conference*, Bled, Slovenia, June 7-9, 1993, pp.61-75.

Reekers, N. and Smithson, S. "EDI in Germany and the UK: Strategic and Operational Use", *European Journal of Information Systems*, (3:3), July 1994, pp.169-178.

Saunders, C.S. and Clark, S. "EDI Adoption and Implementation: A Focus on Interorganizational Linkages", *Information Resources Management Journal*, (5:1), Winter 1992, pp.9-19.

Scala, S. and McGrath, R. "Advantages and Disadvantages of Electronic Data Interchange: An Industry Perspective", *Information & Management*, (25:2), August 1993, pp.85-91.

Soh, C.; Neo, B.S. and Markus, L. "IT2000: A Critical Appraisal of Singapore's State-wide Strategic Planning Process for Information Technology", *Journal of Strategic Information Systems*, (2:4), December 1993, pp.351-372.

Swatman, P.M.C. "Business Process Redesign Using EDI: the BHP Steel Experience", *Australian Journal of Information Systems*, (2:1), 1994, pp.55-73.

Thissen, W.A.H. and Stam, W.J. "Electronic Data Interchange in an Industrial Sector: The Case of the Netherlands' Building Industry", *Information & Management*, (23), 1992, pp.15-30.

van der Net, D.J. and de Bruijn, D.J. "EDI in the Netherlands: The VEDI Project", *EDI Forum*, (5:4), 1992, pp.86-90.

Weber, R.P. *Basic Content Analysis*, 2nd ed., Sage, 1990.

Weick, K.E. "Technology as Equivoque: Sensemaking in New Tachnologies", in *Technology and Organisation*, Goodman, P.S. et al (eds.), Jossey-Bass, 1990.

Willcocks, L. and Choi, C.J. "Co-operative Partnership and 'Total' IT Outsourcing: From Contractual Obligation to Strategic Alliance?", *European Management Journal*, (13:1), March 1995, pp.67-78.

Williamson, O.E. *Markets and Hierarchies*, Free Press, New York, 1975.

Wrigley, C.D., Wagenaar, R.W., Clarke, R.A.: Electronic Data Interchange in International Trade: Frameworks for the Strategic Analysis of Ocean Port Communities. *Journal of Strategic Information Systems* (3:3), September 1994, pp.211-234.

19 The Multinational Enterprise In An Age Of Internet and Electronic Commerce

Edward Mozley Roche
Seton Hall University, USA

The rise of electronic commerce will produce many challenges and opportunities for multinational enterprises. Unfortunately, because of many historical developments as well as entrenched habits, many entrprises are not well suited to cope with these new developments in the exploding cyberspace. Multinational companies must learn to adjust to new competition in these electronic markets by acquiring new skills in systems development, by reshaping their advertising strategies for presentation of information in cyberspace, by being prepared to reengineer their distribution channels, by building new managerial systems which implement computer supported co-operative work across internatinal borders, by accelerating the ability to scan the external environment for acquiring critical intelligence information, by personalizing international customer support through expanded use of IT, and by working harder to use electronic commerce to expand more rapidly into the high growth emerging markets of the world.

INTRODUCTION

Business managers today face two major trends: continued transformation in the structure and operations of global business enterprises, and a rapidly growing use of network-intensive business applications.

In terms of trend I, companies need to examine what will happen as the rush towards "globalization" subsides and is replaced by new strategies for the multinational corporation. If the 1960's was the age of centralization, the 1970's of decentralization, the 1980's a period of globalization, then perhaps the 1990's will be about the emergence of global virtual enterprises based on an entirely new set of operational principles.

We see the development of a "post-global" enterprise. Multinational firms will cease to centralize administrative functions yet further. They will "de-integrate" into a looser confederation of task-related enterprises. We will see the emergence of global "virtual" corporations formed of loose confederations of quasi-independent enterprises tied together through contractual relations. (See Goldman, et al 1995). Global corporations will cease to act as hierarchical organizations and will transform into a confederation of cooperating business nodes.

In terms of trend II, there is currently a siege-like mentality in the information systems function today as it watches the blistering growth of the Internet, open systems, inter-organizational systems, and the potentialities for electronic commerce with electronic trading, inter-organizational information systems, on-line catalogues and marketing. Yet, although the use of electronic commerce technologies appears to promise great potential for cost-savings, re-engineering, and other benefits, managing the organizational and technological transition to take advantage of this potential presents a stiff challenge.

The larger question is how these changes will shape the future of international business enterprises. How will new strategies develop? What types of organizational changes will be possible and preferable? Which companies are best suited to make the transition to the "age of electronic commerce" and what are some of the steps being taken by the more successful firms?

The purpose of this chapter is to explain how the rise of electronic commerce and network-intensive applications will challenge the operations and structure of international business enterprises, and to suggest the best areas to focus management attention.

EARLIER TRANSITIONS IN INTERNATIONAL BUSINESS ENTERPRISES

The international business structure which we see today is the product of an age-old series of transformations in the international political, economic, industrial and technological environment. How information technology and control systems are used is a reflection in a structural mirror of how these systems have been established over the past 800 years.

The foundations of the current international trading regime and the businesses which rise and fall within its context reach back to old Europe - a Europe before the renaissance (Landes, 1965). It was during this time the first developments in chemistry and mining of ores for process metallurgy started to raise Europe above the rest of the world in its technological prowess and practical accomplishments. At the same time, we can see the initial development of trading systems reaching first into Middle Europe through the trade fair and river system then into the Middle East where Europeans traded their chemical and metallurgical goods for drugs and spices. These initial trading arrangements gave rise to a regular system of commerce, supplemented by a functioning bureaucracy, emergence of legal customs, and systems of accounting capable of handling the complexities of transnational trading, which was forced into existence by the absence of a standardized currency or system of exchange.

We can see this in Northern Europe where along the coasts of Scandinavia and Germany, reaching from the Atlantic eastwards to what is now St. Petersburg, the Hanseatic League set up a complex trading system in which lumber and other raw materials from Russia were exchanged for agricultural and ocean products, such as preserved herring, coming from the

Atlantic West. The opening up of the New World with its influx of gold and silver into the financial system of Europe disturbed the equilibrium of exchange as much as had the hundreds of pounds of gold delivered to Egypt from the Nigerian King Abuja making his way on pilgrimage to Mecca had done several hundred years earlier.

The technological advances in transportation by ship as well as the supremacy of Europe brought about by its world explorations and search for tradable and profitable materials gave rise to a critical need to build administrative infrastructures capable of supporting the command and control needed to maintain efficiency over such far flung geographical distances. Communication was measured in units of weeks and months, not the seconds and days we use today. It was during this earlier period, and not hundreds of years later, that the underlying concepts and practices of headquarters to subsidiary control and coordination were worked out and applied in a systematic manner, as we can easily see by studying the records of Genoa and Venice (Braudel, 1972).

In the age of mercantilism, the control and development of enterprise was seen as the natural prerogative of the state, and in many nations, an umbilical cord between state enterprise and international business was formed. The logical and inevitable result of this was easy to predict: state military power eventually was used to support the business operations of private and semi-private enterprise, and to enforce their contracts.

During the Second Forty Years War in Europe - the First World War followed by the Second World War (1915-1955) with a brief inter-war period - the nation state increased even more its economic power and control. It became commonplace to think of government as having the natural right to control all economic activity and enterprise so as to harness it to the national interest. The "national security state" as it has been called, has taken several forms, some with oriental or despotic variations, each of which was derived from 19th century thinking in Europe. It was easy to come to the view that international enterprises were a thinly-disguised extension of state power.

In the early post-war period (the 1950s and 1960s), the national security state rose to its height in power based on the need for coordination of military production, steering of capital investment, and the subsequent control of enterprise and human resources this necessitated.

In the 1960s, however, we saw the rapid rise of a new economic form, the multinational corporation, which although at first was a vehicle for national interest, having become entrenched eventually sought to transcend the boundaries and associated administrative controls of the nation state. These MNCs became a great investment vehicle and powerful figures in the organization of international trade. Their giant scale quickly dwarfed the power of all but the largest nation states. As alarm bells in the pinnacles of state power started to ring, efforts, through international treaties, international organizations, and varying regimes of national legislation, were taken to attempt to place a new bridle of state control over this new form of investment and economic activity, and this struggle continues even today.

Restrictions on computers and telecommunications systems can be seen as only one of many forms of nation state control over multinationals.

The origin of this interference by the nation state in international commercial transactions and the computer and telecommunications infrastructure which supports them has its roots in the need to preserve national security, and encourage development of the national economy. These restrictions include transborder data flow restrictions, government purchasing requirements, controls on how computer applications might be used, taxes and surcharges on personnel and supplies, including tariffs on computer equipment, as well as many other leverage points at which the multinational is vulnerable to state intervention (Roche et al, 1992). Much of the nation state response might have been due to cultural shock at the new technology (Abdul-Gader, 1993). In any case, it is clear that the administrative control systems - many of which have come to rely ever more strongly on electronic data processing - put into place by MNCs have by necessity conformed to the pre-existing arrangements, based as they are on a long historical development. As the new technologies such as electronic commerce are put into place, we will see even further state inteference.

Early Forms of Control

Control of the extended enterprise started early, and involved solving most of the "classical" problems which we see persisting even today including the recognition of the centrality of management strategy in directing the enterprise. This developed as the complexity and risk of overseas operations strained even the most careful of enterprises of Spain, Italy and later Holland. Another eternal problem faced was management of the relationship with host countries. In the early days, in past centuries, this was a far more uncertain and risky problem than it would ever be considered today. Unknown governments with unpredictable ways of working and paths of influence as well as language problems and differences in habit and custom all made for a higher level of uncertainty. In the 15th-19th centuries it was not possible to call a service or even one's own diplomatic corps to obtain reliable and efficient translation. Perhaps the greatest difficulty lay in the lack of a legal regime governing state and state-corporate relationships. Indeed, in many nations of the world, the concept of "corporation" did not even exist and could not be separated from the exercise of national power by the country of the originating enterprise. Neither was it the case that this connection was entirely unfounded.

The development of highly variegated ownership structures also evolved much earlier, and we must recall that the joint stock company is more than 100 years old. The use of foreign direct investment in cooperation with businesses partially owned by local governments was also worked out. Virtually all forms of ownership had been solved long before the advent of information technology.

Floating above these many early developments was the system of reporting relationships which formed the nervous system of the enterprise. Over the centuries, the greatest change in these reporting relationships has not been their essentially hierarchical nature, but rather the speed at which they have been executed. Faster ships made as great an impact if not greater than faster chips.

Over time firms have modified their structures, changing from joint stock ventures in which each foray into foreign markets was legally organized as a separate enterprise, to more vertically integrated firms engaged in closely-related lines of business and then to the divisional form capable of accommodating the diversified and semi-autonomous product lines found in giant conglomerates.

Legacy Systems

The historical pre-requisites for the multinational corporation insure us that its legal and administrative structures were put into place well before information and telecommunications came into use. The early forms of information technology and telecommunications networks, in the 1960s and 1970s, did not allow the types of distributed databases and remote access to information possible today and made it inconceivable that there could have been notions of decentralized management or of the "networked" firm, as defined by Hagström (1991).

Computer architectures forced centralized models on corporations, but international telecommunications did not allow transnational centralization. In the formative stages, there was only telegraph and telex, apart from sea mail. As a result, firms had been organized around the existence of strong national managers and the replication of all key functional areas within each nation state. This was not the product of a grand strategy. It was the result of practicality, for there was little if any other way to manage such geographically distributed enterprises.

When computers were introduced in the 1960s, they immediately accelerated the tendencies towards centralization within principal individual host countries. These technologies were too weak to do this on a global scale. As this accelerator towards centralization gained force, a reverse effect took place at the international level: the strengthening of centralization within individual corporate units in nation states necessitated a weakening of the tendency towards global centralization. It is only correct to say that the impact of the mainframe computer was to both hinder and accelerate centralization of administrative procedures - but at different levels of analysis as one peers at the corporate form.

If it is true that the early mainframes which we are claiming had such a strong centralizing force were in actuality weaker in processing power than an Intel 486, Pentium or P6 machine of today, then how could they have had such a major effect? Certainly the installation of a 486-class machine in an overseas subsidiary today would have virtually no effect whatsoever on the management structure of the firm. How can this be explained?

The explanation lies in the human web supporting computing. In the case of the mainframe, a large number of persons and a considerably greater share of financial and other resources were required to operate the machinery, in contrast to the personal computer of today which is most often a one-person affair using packaged software. Early machines had little pre-made software, and a large amount of resources were required to get them up, running, and embedded into the social and business fabric of the firm. The allocation of such resources to an activity which re-shaped how information was handled and processed at the firm-wide level was strong enough to move the bureaucratic structure towards stronger centralization. This phenomena continued as long as the mainframe played an important role, that is, up until the early 1980s.

The inability to centralize transnationally has caused a growth of much excess computational capacity. A great uncoordinated mass of under-powered systems have emerged virtually impossible to intelligently manage. Harnessing the information systems we see today into the service of playing a lead role in supporting multinational firm strategy is proving to be an enduring challenge for management. The rapid spread of re-engineering methods in firms indicates the disappointment with many current information systems. Part of the answer to this lies in the crisis of flexibility which has become so great as to cause a serious managerial problem in contemporary business.

Managerial Flexibility and the Virtual Firm

The powerful and integrated firms which we see today dominating the world's economy are threatened. Their lifetime is limited. One has only to look at a roster of the Fortune 50 of a decade ago, and the decade before that, and so on, to appreciate how short-lived can be the life of a large enterprise. Long-standing industrial giants are being surrounded by newer more flexible, but considerably smaller, companies which are able to move faster with innovation. The larger firms which dominate many markets of the world are able to take advantage of their scale of operations, but they are many times not able to sustain the rate of innovation found in smaller firms. In the high-technology sector, for example, smaller firms have long held sway on innovation.[1]

The large companies of the world have found themselves straddled with aging technology holding up a nation-state centered rather than global oriented structure. The transition to integrated international data processing systems has been slow because of the general technical complexity of the task, the limitations of available technologies, and the existence of entrenched systems set up previously under a regionalized structure. As demands have arisen for more flexible management, information systems have stood in the way. Expensive to install, and even more expensive to change, information systems can be one of the major barriers to innovation in a global enterprise.

Under globalization, specific functional areas of the enterprise are rationalized, primarily through elimination of redundancies, which generally implies strong centralization. The elimination of duplicated facilities, human resources and practices in selected functional areas can save a great deal, and also make on-going operations smoother as the resulting infrastructure is less complex, thus less expensive to manage. Re-engineering and head-count reduction for globalization has spread to the information systems function through two mechanisms: change driven by simplification of administrative functions; also, change driven by the introduction of new technology itself, independent of the functional areas it supports.

Re-engineering for globalization has allowed the giant integrated international business enterprise to lower its operating costs to compete with other large integrated enterprises. It has enabled management to squeeze more value out of the business to raise shareholder value, and is still an ongoing process in almost every major firm of the world.

Unfortunately, continued re-engineering for globalization may be a historical anachronism, for just as firms are working hard to globalize, a new superior industrial model has emerged: the "networked" or "virtual" enterprise.

The "new" form which has started to replace the older hierarchical firm is based on an entirely different model. Instead of all essential functional areas of the firm being contained within a single organization, as in the global model, they are "attached" to the firm through a network relationship to outside organizations. Instead of being linked together through an ownership relation, whether co-located or not, these firms are linked together through a contractual relationship. It is the contractual relationship which determines how one firm interacts with another, and it is the information networks between the firms which allow the relationship to operate.

It has been argued that the networked firm emerged first in Silicon Valley, and is represented best by companies such as Hewlett Packard and Sun Microsystems. This type of industrial organization has proven to be completely superior to the older hierarchical form, as is evidenced by the rapid decline of Route 128 (near Boston) companies such as Wang and DEC at the same time that HP and Sun were rising (Saxenian, 1994). All of these firms had the same sets of opportunities to explore, it was how they were organized that made the key difference in their success and failure. These new companies were able to successfully compete against the largest multinational corporations of all times. Some firms have recognized the inherent superiority of this model and have started to re-position industrial structures to match the new competitive form. Re-engineering, outsourcing, and the search for "core competencies" are examples of firms attempting to simplify their hierarchically-organized internal structures to adopt a networked form. This transformation towards the "virtual" model of the firm is working in some places, but it is always far more difficult to re-engineer a pre-existing form of industrial organization than to create a new company which starts from the very beginning with a corporate culture operating on entirely different assumptions.

Will There Be a "Virtual" Multinational Enterprise?

Information technology has eased the need for centralized control, as new models of headquarters-subsidiary coordination have developed. The networked multinational will emerge as a form of industrial organization which operates through an international alliance system to coordinate shifting coalitions of technology, production, and marketing skills (Yoshino and Rangan, 1995; Gerlach, 1992; Gilroy, 1993).

This change is being made possible by the sustained and rapid drop in the cost of interconnection between firms being brought about by the accelerating use of open systems, such as the Internet. Although interorganizational systems have been written about much in the past, they have been generally difficult to implement because of technical problems. In addition, a large amount of negotiation between parties was necessary in order to finalize legal arrangements, and this tended to push up the price even further.

With open systems, however, the cost reduction may be as much as 70% or more, thus making interorganizational activities far more cost-effective than in the past. The comparatively easy implementation of interorganizational systems will accelerate the use of electronic commerce, the buying and selling of goods and services through networks. But as this technology spreads to a global scale, what will be the challenges it poses for the multinational corporation?

THE AGE OF ELECTRONIC COMMERCE AND THE TRANSFORMATION OF THE MULTINATIONAL

The rise of computer networking availability throughout the entire population, particularly through the Internet, has made possible the rise of electronic markets in sectors which have never experienced them before. Although equities, bonds, and pork bellies (commodities) have long been traded through electronic markets, most other sectors of the economy (home appliances, cars, used goods, clothes, consumer goods, etc.) have been sold by traditional methods of advertising and distribution. Comparison shopping for either final or intermediate consumers has been a paper-based affair. The "purchasing officer" as a specialized administrative function focused solely on finding the lowest prices has grown in importance.

The age of electronic commerce means that more sections of the economy will be subject to rigorous market competition. Changes such as the disappearance of geographical boundaries, the rapid flow of pricing information, and the ability of electronic markets to force instant price comparisons, as well as their associated structural elements will alter profoundly the organization of industry, killing off some firms, and growing some to undreamed of size.

Several key technologies are driving this electronic phenomena. First, information technology will make it possible to increase the matching of offers with prices, much like what is done in traditional stock markets. This will be accomplished by one of two ways: bulletin-board type listing services and intelligent search engines. The bulletin board model is well understood because it works primarily like the stock exchanges we see today. The model is based on the existence of a centralized listing service for prices. Every trader sees the same prices and is able to react with their bids. The rise of "electronic storefronts", "electronic shopping malls" and "cyber-malls" are examples of how networking technology can be used to provide critical information to consumers of goods and services. In cyberspace, there are no "regional" or "neighborhood" shops.

The intelligent search engine model works by the shopper using artificial intelligence software to search through cyberspace for the best deal.[2] It is not necessary to have a single market in which to compare information on prices. The intelligent search engine covers multiple markets simultaneously.

A second key technology of electronic commerce is Electronic Data Interchange (EDI) - the passing of commercial information through networks between firms. In the Internet world, this technology has been stalled temporarily through concerns regarding privacy and security of data transmission. These problems have been solved with encryption technologies such as Secure HTTP from Enterprise Integration Technologies and Single Sockets Layer from NetScape. There are several double key systems being put into place by companies such as Premenos, and momentum is growing to have the United States Post Office serve as the central repository of public keys.[3]

EDI and the Pre-Visual World

The foundations of electronic commerce are found in early timesharing and electronic data interchange (EDI) systems (See Sokol, 1995). There were at one time many timesharing and messaging systems pioneers in providing value-added services such as EDI, but few survived the onslaught of the mini and personal computer. Like dinosaurs, these large systems declined, were bought out and absorbed by other entities, or had to re-engineer their offerings. An example would be Tymnet which still survives under management of British Telecom and now MCI in the United States. Many of the surviving Value Added Network (VAN) providers we see today - GEISCO, Advantis, Tymnet, etc. - have well-established EDI systems based on a web of customers organized into Closed User Groups (CUGs) which have adopted their networks to exchange much vital commercial information.

EDI has moved through three distinct stages in its evolution. Like the Internet, it started with activities in the U.S. Government, particularly in the massive purchasing operations supporting the U.S. Department of Defense. During the 1980s, EDI spread into private enterprise, as the UN Edifact and X.12 standards were better refined, including their subsets which have been applied in specific industries such as groceries, hardware, retail and pharmaceuticals. Generally, EDI has failed to take off substantially in the past because its implementation has been highly technical although these few sectors have progressed rapidly.

The third phase in EDI's evolution is towards OpenEDI based on transmission through the Internet using completely open standards. This phase is starting now, and it is rapidly becoming one of the foundations of electronic commerce. Most word processors and World Wide Web browsers are now shipping with EDI capabilities. This will mean that any user of Internet-oriented software will be able to send standardized EDI messages back and forth with commercial enterprises through the Internet, and will be able to do so with a minimum of cost.

Although there are many concerns about security, legal liability, traceability and other problems being expressed in the popular press regarding electronic commerce, in reality, most of the problems have already been worked out with EDI.

The effect of using the Internet as an EDI delivery mechanism will be strong. First, it will no longer be necessary to engage high-cost VANS in order to take advantage of EDI as transmission over the Internet is only 20% to 30% of the cost of VANs; Second, it will not be necessary for purchasers to pay expensive licensing and software fees to EDI service vendors. Instead, this software will become part of generally available programs such as Lotus Notes, or operating systems, such as Microsoft Windows-95.

Electronic commerce will cause many changes in the way we conduct business. As shown by Ellsworth & Ellsworth (1994), employees in companies will be able to get far more information more quickly than in the past. The rapid deployment of inter-linked trading and communications between firms will help solidify the competitive advantage of different "technopoles" of the world, as seen by Castells and Hall (1994) and Scott (1993), and will be a key factor in international high technology competition, particularly intra-industry trade (see Scherer, 1992). According to Russell (1995) it will be a reflection of a type of "global brain" phenomena in which businesses will be even more inter-linked than ever before. According to Slouka (1995), even basic perceptions of reality are changing, and being commercialized. Corporations are adopting internal structures based on "virtual work spaces" (Pruitt & Barrett, 1992). We can expect that these are being applied to the international enterprise, perhaps as part of a new "techno-vision" (see Wang, 1994).

CHALLENGES FOR THE POST-GLOBAL MULTINATIONAL

Even though the bulk of management literature has been pointing towards "globalization", the age of electronic commerce will make the concept obsolete. In fact, the opposite trend is a better indicator of success in the future. Instead of firms becoming more global, they are breaking down more into giant alliance structures, supported by new forms of multimedia technology, virtual space technologies (teleconferencing), and the global information superhighway

(Baran, 1995). Work in global enterprises is done through distributed teams dependent upon computer communication systems (Manheim, 1993). The possibilities for international computer networking with advanced telecommunications systems based on ATM (Asynchronous Transfer Mode) indicate dozens of "services" or applications that can be operated through the same network simultaneously (Heldman, 1992). In large organizations, the impact of these new telecommunications systems will be to create network-type rather than traditional hierarchical-type organizations (Lipnack and Stamps, 1994). The "networked corporation" or "virtual corporation" is becoming the most successful corporate form. Firms which survive this transition period will likely be the giant multinationals and not the small enterprises. They will be able better to sustain and institutionalize what is learned and advantageous from innovation. In so doing, however, they will face many challenges in adopting their business operations to the age of electronic commerce, as listed below.

Adjust to Competition in Electronic Markets: Moving into the world of electronic commerce means that stable pricing is gone forever. There is every indication competition will increase tremendously as shoppable markets grow in number. Firms must be able to face competition from cut-price suppliers and must learn how to scan markets for changing prices so as to be able to react quickly to aggressive moves by competitors. Above all, even if the number of networks and distribution channels served increases, the competitive firm must be able to operate well within any individual market, and not favor one market over another.

For the multinational, it will become increasingly difficult to maintain the practice of posting different prices for the same good or service in different national markets or regions.

Acquire Skills for Systems Development of Electronic Commerce: The key systems development challenges involve matching the web server with back-office production systems. With the number of "hits" on some web servers reaching more than 2,000,000 per day, it is necessary to anticipate the processing requirements needed to accommodate a large number of incoming orders, as it is impractical for this to be a manual process. In most cases, this problem is being solved by sending SQL commands from the WWW interface. This allows the Web site to access the database. The world wide web server emulates an additional terminal for the order processing system, which in any case is busy with the mainstream orders handled at telemarketing centers.

One implication of this type of arrangement is that as the percentage of orders processed through the web interface increases, then the need for telemarketing employees will decrease. When these technologies are in place, the firm is then set up for electronic commerce operations.[4]

Define New Advertising Strategy: When a firm places a page on the World Wide Web - how can they ensure their customers will be able to find them? Cronin (1995) calls this the "home page advantage". Should traditional advertising be done with pointers towards the WWW page? Will certain services, "electronic malls", collect fees for providing a central or regional point for collection and display of HTTP pointers? GNN is already charging $7,500 per week to place a pointer to a company page on its "hot list" which is seen by millions of persons per day. Silicon Graphics pays Hot Wired magazine $15,000 per month to have a direct link to its home page. Netscape Communication is charging $40,000 for a three-month placement on its Web site, pointing out that it received more than 400,000 "hits" per day. Is it worth it?

The World Wide Web provides a potentially superior form of advertising, in comparison with other media. In the case of regular print advertising, it is not possible to determine how many persons see an advertisement. It is possible to determine circulation figures, but this is only an indirect measure of exposure. In contrast, web technology allows the host to measure exactly how many hits are taken against a particular advertising target. It is also possible to determine the type of viewer - e.g. whether they are from the government, from a commercial enterprise, from the military, or from an educational establishment, etc. and potentially even more details. This is a type of accuracy which has never been possible with print advertising, or with television advertising. From the point of view of its empirical reliability, web-based advertising is superior in virtually every way to print or other media forms of advertising.

As the Internet starts to be recognized as an important advertising channel, traditional advertising will be able to demand less fee, and Web-based advertising will be able to demand more.

Madison Avenue will no doubt quickly adjust to this new reality by purchasing the talent needed, but the deeper question is how will marketing change in electronic commerce? What new niches or opportunities are available? How will the cost structure change? How will consumer testing and technical production change? What will happen to models, photographers, sound effects persons - the entire industry, as the world moves towards advertising on the Internet with resolutions of only 72-110 lines per inch instead of the 2400 or higher customary in the print world? Surely, if the present growth rates continue, large parts of the traditional advertising sector are threatened.

For the multinational corporation and the companies it has hired to handle its advertising, even more questions emerge. Accustomed to advertising in national markets, with different messages, different cultural patterns, and different brand images, the World Wide Web provides a stiff challenge. Web sites are available from anywhere in the world, regardless of national or cultural borders.[5] Handling different languages is an on-going technical problem. For IBM's page on the web, the problem has been solved by having buttons on the page leading to different languages. If Rupert Murdoch is correct, and the information superhighway will have its greatest impact in 15-20 years in the developed countries and in approximately 50 years in developing countries, then much talk of the changes which will take place in advertising may be premature. Nevertheless, it is clear that a major transformation in management of global advertising for the multinational corporation is coming, and it is sure to challenge much of the way business has been conducted and managed in the past.

Re-Engineer Distribution Channels: The rise of electronic commerce will bring chaos to traditional distribution channels. The role of the middle-man (intermediate enterprise) will wither away as large firms can provide direct access to sales without the logistical jerkiness of old-style supply chains. It may be that interactive networks (Internet, Prodigy, CompuServe, etc.) will become "super networks" and start to grab so much of the transaction value they will be able to drive traditional distributors out of business. The age of electronic commerce might bring to an end the intermediate enterprise. Perhaps old-style distributors will be building their own ordering networks. Perhaps all the players will settle down into a type of synergy. But whatever the case, distribution channels as we know them are going to be changed, and therefore, one can surmise electronic commerce is a severe threat to some industries, and a great opportunity for others.

International enterprises also face difficulties with channel management. Accustomed to providing different technical standards, different guarantees, and above all, different prices in different markets of the world, traditional companies will find that the rise of electronic commerce will blur distribution channels. It is technically the same for someone to place an order in one national jurisdiction as in another. How will the Value Added Tax (VAT) in Europe be applied to Internet-based orders in Cyberspace where shipment is via an international courier service? What will be the case within the European Community itself? If a good is purchased from Mexico but the transaction takes places in the United States, then what is the price, and how is the legal guarantee handled? This is a major problem in the consumer goods industry, where companies must carefully define consumer rights. On the other hand, if prices are considerably less expensive in Mexico, then why should United States citizens not take advantage of this? Surely such orders could be handled by *maquiladora* warehouses along the border.

The inevitable conclusion is that electronic commerce is going to cause severe headaches for companies in their channel management for distribution and pricing of goods and services - not only domestically within national markets, but at the international level as well.

Implement Computer Supported Cooperative Work (CSCW) for International Teams: Technology is making it possible for the way work is accomplished within the multinational corporation to be completely changed. Technologies such as desktop videoconferencing, computer conferencing, group decision support systems and email are making the sharing of information easier. Lotus Notes is emerging as one of the greatest forces in promoting large-scale cooperative work projects, and is used widely by companies like Andersen Consulting, which is able to coordinate very large systems integration projects spanning time zones and geographical distances. These types of CSCW technologies promise to further integrate the management of international businesses. (See Henderson, 1989)

Accelerate Corporate Intelligence and Environmental Scanning: The continued rapid pace at which the world is becoming "wired" into a global cyber-society will make employees able to communicate with large numbers of persons, counterparts, and databases and other connections outside of their own company. It is amazing to notice today how many companies are skeptical about letting their employees have access to the outside world. They maintain special approvals and proceures in order to screen applicants for email and computer accounts accessible to the cyberspace outside. Why is there so much reluctance? One reason is the fear employees will engage in unproductive activity by spending too much time "surfing" the Internet; another fear is that more connection to the outside world will increase the vulnerability of the firm; but perhaps the most fundamental fear is that exposure to the outside world will permit employees to better organize themselves to resist abusive corporate practices; or to form networks with interested sympathetic parties outside the company. One example might be the use of email and international video-conferencing for unions to help organize against cut-backs and rationalization of plants. Ultimately, it is a question of trust. The corporations which do not trust their employees, attempt to keep them in the dark. In this sense, the Internet and the World Wide Web represent more of a challenge than an opportunity for the multinational corporation. Certainly if we accept the model of the enterprise as a "learning machine", employee access to cyberspace should not be limited.

Personalize International Customer Support: Companies can build database gateways which can link customers from anywhere to detailed corporate information, such as parts information, product guides, and other highly technical data which it is normally difficult or time consuming to get. This will allow customers to get direct access to the information, at any time of day, without having to go through a toll free number, which the company must pay for, to reach a phone bank of trained technical experts, which the company also must pay for. The ability to provide highly technical information, including color diagrams, manuals, parts numbers, ordering interfaces, and order tracking information can greatly reduce the difficulty customers have in conducting business. This information can be made available to many locations of the world which normally are not serviced by near-by company offices (e.g. technical spare parts information for off-shore oil wells). At the same time, the cost of providing such high quality service is greatly reduced.

Expand to Emerging Markets: Although the growth rate of telecommunications networks in developing countries has been slow, the rise of large outsourcing operations, such as those in the Phillipeans and India, have done much to accelerate their growth. Internet and World Wide Web access has been spreading faster than any other technology. As a result, multinational corporations should be able to take advantage of this new access into these markets.

Apply Strategic Management to Corporate Alliance Systems: The successful competitors will emerge as a system of alliance networks, and the methods of analysis used in diplomatic history might be a better tool to understand business in the age of electronic commerce. Perhaps a type of "new medievalism" will become prevalent in the giant electronic business networks in the future. The task of "management" will become much more similar to diplomacy between sovereigns, but instead of nation states, the players will be parts of virtual enterprises.

So too might the work of Niccolò Machiavelli even after 500 years yet remain useful reading for the entrepreneur. After all, many of the foundations of modern business were built hundreds of years ago.

References

Abdul-Gader, Abdulla Hasan. 1993. "Globalization of Information Systems Education: Host Countries' Perspective" in Mehdi Khosrowpour and Karen D. Loch, Eds. Global Information Technology Education: Issues and Trends. Harrisburg: Idea Group Publishing.

Baran, Nicholas. 1995. Inside the Information Superhighway. Scottsdale: The Coriolis Group, Inc.

Braudel, Fernand. 1972. The Mediterranean and the Mediterranean World in the Age of Philip II. New York: Harper Colophon.

Castells, Manuel and Peter Hall. 1994. Technopoles of the World: The Making of 21st Century Industrial Complexes. London; New York: Routledge.

Cohen, Frederick B. 1995. Protection and Security on the Information Superhighway. New York:John Wiley & Sons, Inc.

Cronin, Mary J. 1995. Doing More Business on the Internet. [2nd ed.] New York: Van Nostrand Reinhold.

Ellsworth, Jill and Matthew Ellsworth. 1994. The Internet Business Book. New York: John Wiley & Sons, Inc.

Gerlach, Michael L. 1992. Alliance Capitalism: The Social Organization of Japanese Business. Berkeley: University of California Press.

Gilroy, Bernard Michael. 1993. Networking in Multinational Enterprises: The Importance of Strategic Alliances. Columbia: University of South Carolina Press.

Goldman, Steven L., Roger N. Nagel, Kenneth Preiss. 1995. Agile Competitors and Virtual Organizations: Strategies for Enriching the Customer. New York: Van Nostrand Reinhold.

Hagström, Peter. 1991. The 'Wired' MNC: The Role of Information Systems for Structural Change in Complex Organizations. Stockholm: Institute of International Business, Stockholm School of Economics.

Heldman, Robert K. 1992. Global Telecommunications: Layered Networks' Layered Services. New York: McGraw-Hill, Inc.

Henderson, Jeffrey. 1989. The Globalisation of High Technology Production: Society, Space and Semiconductors in the Restructuring of the Modern World. London: Routledge.

Landes, David S. 1965. "Technological Change and Development in Western Europe 1750-1914" in H.J. Habakkuk and M. Postan, Eds. The Industrial Revolutions and After: Incomes, Population and Technological Change, part I, of The Cambridge Economic History of Europe, Volume VI, pp. 274-457.

Lipnack, Jessica and Jeffrey Stamps. 1994. The Age of the Network: Organizing Principles for the 21st Century. Essex Junction, Vermont: Oliver Wight Publications, Inc.

Manheim, Marvin. 1993. "Integrating Global Organizations through Task/Team Support Systems" in Linda M. Harasim, Ed. Global Networks: Computers and International Communication. Cambridge, Massachusetts; London, England: The MIT Press.

Pruitt, Steve and Tom Barrett. 1992. "Corporate Virtual Workspace" in Michael Benedikt, Ed. Cyberspace: First Steps. Cambridge, Massachusetts; London: The MIT Press.

Roche, EM, Goodman, SE, Chen, H. 1992. The Landscape of International Computing. Advances in Computers (35)

Russell, Peter. 1995. The Global Brain Awakens: Our Next Evolutionary Leap. [2nd ed.] Palo Alto: Global Brain Inc.

Saxenian, Annalee. 1994. Regional Advantage: Culture and Competition in Silicon Valley and Route 128. Cambridge, Mass.; London: Harvard University Press.

Scherer, Frederic M. 1992. International High-Technology Competition. Cambridge, Massachusetts; London: Harvard University Press.

Schwartau, Winn. 1994. Information Warfare: Chaos on the Electronic Superhighway. New York: Thunder's Mouth Press.

Scott, Allen J. 1993. Technopolis: High-Technology Industry and Regional Development in Southern California. Berkeley: University of California Press.

Slouka, Mark. 1995. War of the Worlds: Cyberspace and the High-Tech Assault on Reality. New York: BasicBooks.

Sokol, Phyllis K. 1995. From EDI to Electronic Commerce: A Business Initiative. New York: McGraw-Hill, Inc.

Wang, Charles B. 1994. Techno Vision: The Executive's Survival Guide to Understanding and Managing Information Technology. New York: McGraw-Hill, Inc.

Yoshino, Michael Y. and U. Srinivasa Rangan. 1995. Strategic Alliances: An Entrepreneurial Approach to Globalization. Boston: Harvard Business School Press.

Endnotes

[1]   Large integrated firms can sustain innovation by setting up semi-autonomous "creative" units able to act as if they are small start-up companies.

[2]   A similar technology has developed to aid librarians in their search for reference information through the Internet.

[3]   The USPO has several advantages in this regard - besides having locations throughout the United States, it operates an investigative arm and a private police force which can fight vigorously against fraud and prosecute offenders - something which no private enterprise can hope to offer. Because of the stakes involved, there will be a need for a strong government presence in cyberspace to combat organized crime (see Schwartzu, 1994). Protection of security on the emerging information superhighway has been an increasing concern and is requiring companies to take aggressive measures to combat crime (Cohen, 1995).

[4]   A note on security. Although it has been pointed out that using the Internet for financial transactions is not secure, even today no home banking application uses encryption. Using a web browser with built-in encryption may be _more_ secure than the systems in place today.

[5]   Some countries have placed limitations on Internet access for their citizens, in violation of the United Nations Declaration of Human Rights. These types of limitations imposed by nation states, are sure to have an impact on advertising through the World Wide Web.

20 Global Management Support Systems: The New Frontiers in MIS

Sean B. Eom
Southeast Missouri State University, USA

Over the past decade, we have experienced several significant changes in business and technological environments that have contributed to the globalization of business and to the increasing interdependence of the global economy. With this changing global environment, a new type of information systems, the global management support system (GMSS), is emerging. This chapter reviews prior research on the development and application of global management support systems and suggests a definition, functional requirements, and an architecture of the GMSS that consists of a network of management support systems (MSS) which link parent companies with foreign subsidiaries. Survey results of operational GMSSs in the real world are presented. Finally, future directions in GMSS research and several issues in the design and implementation of GMSSs are discussed. Key Words and Phrases: Management Support Systems, Multinational Corporations, Global Strategic Planning and Control,Conflict Management,Global Management SupportSystems.

INTRODUCTION

One of the most significant business and economic trends of the late 20th century is the stateless corporation. A new type of company is emerging. Global companies do research wherever necessary, develop products in several countries, promote key executives regardless of nationality, and even have shareholders on all continents. With the continuing trend of globalization, many globe-spanning companies are making decisions with little regard to national boundaries. Many heads of the world's largest companies believe that the trend toward statelessness is unmistakable and irreversible (Holstein, et. al., 1990). With this changing global environment, a new type of support system, global management support system (GMSS), is emerging.

The purpose of this chapter is to inform academicians and practicing managers of the emergence of global management support systems by:

i) reviewing prior research on the development and application of global management support systems;

ii)   suggesting a definition, the functional requirements, and an architecture of GMSSs that   consists of a network of decision support systems (DSS) which link parent companies with foreign subsidiaries;

iii) reporting survey results of operational GMSSs in the   real world; and

iv)   discussing future directions for GMSS research.

REVIEW OF LITERATURE AND EVOLUTION OF DECISION SUPPORT SYSTEMS

Global issues in information systems are being increasingly studied among information systems researchers (e.g., Palvia, et al., 1992; Roche, 1992). Iyer and Schkade (1987) briefly described the characteristics, potential applications, and fundamental requirements of multinational decision support systems and multinational executive support systems. King and Sethi (1992) reviewed five areas of global information systems literature up to 1990, including general issues, planning, decision support, transborder data flows, and contingency applications.

As the global marketplace expands, many MNCs have been influenced by mounting pressures to develop worldwide communication, distribution, and information networks that facilitate the free flow of information and goods across national boundaries. Telecommunication technologies are significantly changing the traditional ways of manufacturing, marketing, financing, decision making, etc. For example, International Aero Engines was established in 1984 as a joint-venture of five world leaders in jet engine manufacturing to produce the turbofan engine of the Airbus (Ryerson and Pitts, 1989). The companies are Pratt & Whitney (U.S.), Rolls-Royce (U.K.), MTU (Germany), Fiat Aviazione (Italy), and Aero Engines Corp. (Japan). Each of the five companies shares responsibilities for producing particular engine modules or sections to be assembled as one final product. In the process of manufacturing the engine modules, each manufacturing location generates large volumes of data such as master parts lists, bills of materials, parts catalogs, etc. Further, each plant has access to the data generated from the other locations. Without the five-nation data network, it might not have been possible for five companies in five countries to function as one (Ryerson and Pitts, 1989).

Global management support systems are playing vital roles in the complex decision making process at MNCs. For example, when Dow Chemical noticed the recent decline in European demand for a certain solvent product, the decision support system at the company responded quickly to suggest reducing production of the chemical product at a German plant and shifting the idle production capacity to another chemical product that was imported from the U.S.A. Several decision support systems have been developed to support global decisions such as global financing and capital structure decisions (Eom, et al., 1988), international marketing channel selection decisions (Shrivastava, et al., 1984), global manufacturing plant location decisions (Breitman and Lucas, 1987), and global production capacity optimization (Holstein, et al., 1990).

In the area of finance, the major world financial communities have invested heavily to develop international networks, real-time securities tracking systems, and global electronic trading systems for on-line stock quotations, settlements, and electronic mail. Morgan Stanley's "Trade Analysis and Processing Systems"(TAPS) is an example of such a system. The TAPS system tracks, in real time, the company's inventory of financial instruments such as bonds, equity, and currency exposure in multiple currencies (Maranoff, et al., 1987). Ballester and Marcarelli (1992) also reviewed the use of expert systems in the management of international investment in the major world capital markets including New York City, London, and Tokyo.

In the area of logistics, Min and Eom (1994) provided practical guidelines for the design of an integrated knowledge-based decision support system for global logistics (IDSSGL) linked by worldwide communication networks. The IDSSGL they proposed is a worldwide network of multi-user knowledge-based DSSs that integrates the MNCs' various logistics operations and standardizes databases across national, legal, and cultural boundaries. The IDSSGL consists of a set of DSSs linked electronically in the MNC's headquarters to a set of local DSSs at foreign business partners, branch offices, suppliers, and third party logisticians. The major goals of the IDSSGL are to coordinate international distribution plans, share a central communication backbone network, and evaluate tradeoffs throughout the global logistics system.

By conducting surveys of DSSs over the past two decades, we have been able to identify the development pattern of DSS and predict the future pattern of development as shown below (Eom and Lee, 1990).

1970s
1. Discrete Functional DSS
2. Cross-functional DSS

1980s
3. Strategic DSS for Functional and Business Level Strategy
4. Group DSS
5. Distributed Decision Making Systems

1990s
6. Organizational DSS
7. Global DSS
8. Integration of DSS Technology in a Total System

The eight different stages of DSS development can be interpreted as evolutionary steps toward a total computer-based information system. While an evolution pattern is apparent, different organizations may follow some variations of the general trend.

In a uninational (i.e., single nation) environment, information systems have evolved from transaction processing systems (TPS) and management information systems (MIS) to decision support systems. The same developmental pattern can be found in the global dimension of information systems.

Since the early 1980s, there have been increasing developments of global transaction processing and management information systems, which can be attributed to the development of telecommunication infrastructures. Such developments of telecommunication infrastructures allow many MNCs to implement global communication networks as a strategic weapon to help survive fierce global competition, to provide a real-time communication link with foreign and domestic subsidiaries, and to enable worldwide production, marketing, and other critical information on a daily basis. Such a network enables the company to streamline its far-flung, worldwide operations (Pantages, 1989). An increasing number of companies have been building global communication networks to link all of their major business units worldwide through an all-digital system integrating voice, data, and video.

THE EMERGENCE OF GMSS

In the early 1970s, DSS focused on helping an individual user in an organization at a single location. In the 1980s, many companies shifted their attention to the application of DSS technology to large-scale, organizational decision making and global decision making. For example, Citgo Petroleum Corporation designed and implemented an integrated, knowledge-based DSS (KBDSS) to optimize its marketing and distribution network of 48 contiguous states in the U.S. The model in the KBDSS consists of approximately 3000 equations to support top management in making refinery production capacity decisions, inventory decisions at each location in the 48 states, pricing decisions, etc. A significant direct benefit of the KBDSS was the $91.3 million reduction in inventory. This is just one of the numerous success stories of a large scale DSS (Phillips, et al., 1986). General Motors (GM), in association with EDS company, has developed PLANETS: A modeling system for business planning. The automotive section of GM manages thousands of products manufactured and distributed by several hundred facilities worldwide (Breitman and Lucas, 1987). The DSS of GM supports analysts and managers in making, either independently or simultaneously, decisions relative to capacity expansion at existing plants, buying or building for new facilities, and optimal allocation of production volume among existing plants as well as other decisions. GM has developed the 80 major applications of this DSS software, resulting in over $1 billion cost savings and approximately 2 or 3 percent capital expenditure savings.

Nature of Global Decisions

What makes a management support system global? Is a GMSS just a DSS containing global data? The essential role of the GMSS is to support global decision making which must deal with multidimensional complexity. This multidimensional complexity stems from the multiplicity of global environments in which MNCs operate. The global environment consists of legal (patent and trademark laws, laws affecting multinational operations, etc.), cultural (languages, customs, value systems, religious beliefs, etc.), economic (currency, tax, inflation, interest rates, monetary and fiscal policy, etc.), and political (form and stability of government, governmental policy toward MNCs, etc.) forces.

In international business planning, it is essential to understand several important global risks that are unique to MNCs' operations. They include political risks, foreign exchange risks, tax risks, and market risks. A further complication arises due to the combined effects and conflicting nature of the various risks. A global decision will accompany some/or all risks. Each decision alternative may have different degrees of composite risk levels. In addition, management of global operations necessitates the consideration of conflicts of interest among home government, host government, parent company, and foreign subsidiaries.

Can our existing DSS theory, framework, tools, and techniques lend support in making global decisions with such multidimensional complexities/risks? The answer is a resounding "No."

Definition of GMSSs

The term "management support systems" is defined as a computer-based information system to support management in improving the effectiveness of managerial decision making. Four types of decision making technologies are collectively termed as management support systems -- decision support systems, expert systems, executive information systems, and artificial neural networks (ANN).

A global management support system is defined as a management support system to:

- Support managers of multinational corporations in their decision making processes; and
- Deal with one or more variables that constitute the multidimensional complexities of global decision making.

This simple point of view clearly differentiates a GMSS from an MSS in a pure domestic corporation. GMSSs can be further classified by the three different levels of management -- operational, tactical, and strategic. Moreover, GMSS is an evolving concept to support the decision making process of MNCs.

FUNCTIONAL REQUIREMENTS OF GMSS

Operational Management Support Requirements

There are several functional requirements of GMSS, distinguishable from those of a uninational MSS. Global MSSs build on management support systems in a uninational environment. The complexities of global decision making necessitate several distinctive, requirements in addition to the generic functional requirements of DSSs, ESs, and EISs in a uninational environment. Generic functions of DSS classified by Steven Alter (1980), for example, include on-line retrieval, display, and manipulation of data (current, historical, internal, and external), inventing decision alternatives, and choosing an alternative based on computation of the consequences of each decision alternative. Several distinctive, additional, functional requirements are classified into two different levels: operational (requirements #1 through #4) and tactical/strategic (requirements #5 through #8).

Requirement #1: Global Data Access: The unimpeded access to information from a company location anywhere in the organization is an important functional requirement of GMSSs. To many global companies, on-line access to corporate data has already become vital for their success in managing numerous overseas subsidiaries.

An essential function of GMSSs should be to allow corporate managers desktop, on-line access to corporate information in order to monitor global operations from the company headquarters. Ideally, global networks of MNCs will provide a real-time communication link with foreign and domestic subsidiaries around the globe through an all-digital system integrating voice, data, and video. Many MNCs such as General Electric, Texas Instruments, and Hewlett Packard, to name a few, have completed or are progressing toward the complete worldwide linkage of corporate data bases.

The functions of EISs may be even more important in the management of MNCs due to increased global and domestic competition and governmental regulations. To respond to changes in the business environment, many corporations have initiated broad structural changes. The acceptance of EISs in many U.S. corporations signifies these changes. Tracking performances of the consolidated corporation, as well as each subsidiary, against plans is indeed the critical activity of the top management of MNCs.

The case in point is the executive support system at Hertz Corporation. The system, using touch-screen icons to execute commands, has become an integral part of decision making for executives at Hertz's New Jersey headquarters in assessing market shares in a contested area, gauging price levels in relation to costs, projecting the rental volume needed to offset a price decrease, measuring cost changes against historical data, and performing 'what-if' scenarios to determine the long-term effect of pricing trends. Eventually, the ESS at Hertz will be a global system to link all its managerial people in the U.S.A. and abroad, enabling them to work from a common knowledge base (McCartney, 1989).

Requirement #2: Global Consolidated Reporting: Many global companies realize that consolidated global reporting is a vital tool for their success in managing numerous overseas subsidiaries. Numerous accounting and financial reports need to be integrated into a global consolidated report.

Consolidating financial statements is a crucial activity for sensitivity analysis of any global decision making.

GMSSs should be able to provide accurate, timely information for planning, controlling, and budgeting. Other reports for internal control include inventory, receivables, sales, cash flow by currency, cash and capital expenditure budgets, and product line income statements of each foreign subsidiary, the parent company, and the consolidated entity. In addition to consolidated reporting, GMSSs should allow MNCs to compare financial accounting data between various foreign subsidiaries. Due to differences in accounting procedures and regulatory policies, special care must be given to such comparisons.

To meet the increasing demand of many MNCs, dozens of vendors of financial software in the U.S.A. and Europe have recently begun to aggressively market their products which have the following capabilities: i) electronic funds transfer, ii) conversion of multiple currency, iii) multilingual translations, iv) value-added tax reporting, v) conversion of weights and measures between metric and English units, and vi) conversion of financial data between different fiscal calendar and time zones (Goodwin, 1991).

Requirement #3: Providing Effective Means of Communication between MNC Headquarters and Its Subsidiaries: To facilitate the organization-wide planning process, GMSSs should provide an effective means of communication between the MNC headquarters and its subsidiaries. The last two decades' advancement in management support systems technology certainly facilitates multinational planning, communication, and joint decision making. The technology includes distributed decision making (DDM) systems (Rathwell and Burns, 1985) and four group decision support systems (GDSS) alternatives (local area decision networks, wide area decision networks, decision rooms, and teleconferencing systems). For example, the decreasing costs of computer hardware and software and emerging worldwide standards have made teleconferencing and video conferencing systems powerful tools for executive meetings, research and development.

Requirement #4: Short-term Global Foreign Exchange Risk Management Support: A mix of freely floating (without any government intervention), managed floating, and fixed exchange rates characterizes today's international monetary system. Relative value of a currency vis-a-vis other currencies is changing every day. Consequently, an essential task of management of global corporations is to minimize the negative impact of fluctuations between the currencies of the parent company and the currency of other operating countries.

There are numerous examples of real world companies which were forced out of business due to mismanagement of foreign exchange risks, such as in the case of the British company-Laker-Airways (Srinirasulu, 1983). To effectively manage foreign exchange risks, many companies developed and deployed expert decision support systems. Morgan Stanley's "Trade Analysis and Processing Systems" (TAPS) and Manufacturers Hanover Trust's

"Technical Analysis and Reasoning Assistant" (TARA) are tracking in real time the company's inventory of financial instruments such as bonds, equity, interest rates, and currency exposure in multiple currencies. These systems, consisting of optimization programs and knowledge bases of trading strategies, examine large quantities of data and their historical trends, and predict changes in price in real time to assist foreign currency traders to make the decision to buy or sell.

"Inspector" is another example of an expert system for monitoring worldwide foreign exchange trading activities developed and deployed at Manufacturers Hanover Trust (MHT). Inspector is designed to examine every one of the thousands of trades executed by more than twenty locations around the world every day, in order to spot unauthorized or fraudulent foreign exchange trades. In doing so, extensive knowledge of foreign exchange trading procedures, operational control procedures, multinational accounting practices, and auditing procedures must be applied to every recorded deal (Byrnes, et al., 1990). Inspector is a multi-technology application of expert systems, a global communication network (GEONET), and a relational database management system (ORACLE). Data on foreign exchange deals from around the world are recorded in a relational database management system, transmitted to New York City, MHT's foreign exchange headquarters, and passed to Inspector for evaluation.

At the *tactical/strategic* levels, a host of complex management tools must be utilized to deal with various multinational management issues such as multinational risk management and conflict management among host and home governments, parent companies, and foreign subsidiaries. Requirements #5 through #8 are meant for *tactical/strategic* management support.

Requirement #5: Strategic Planning Process Support: Support of strategic management processes is the core role of GMSSs. The strategic planning and control systems of MNCs aim at rationalizing resources more effectively on a global basis to respond to rapid environmental changes, such as increased political and foreign exchange risks and global competition (Dymsza, 1984).

According to Dymsza (1984), the strategic planning process begins with the reevaluation of the company's philosophy, mission, and definition of business (Step A of Figure 1). Figure 1 is adapted from Dymsza (1984). The next step is a realistic and subjective evaluation of the firm's present strengths and weaknesses and an assessment of major competitors (Step B). An analysis of major opportunities and risks and the specification of key strategic issues for entire corporate units (Step C) are needed to formulate objectives and goals for each unit of the MNC (Step D). The specific objectives and goals are to increase the firm's return on investment by expanding investment in profitable product lines and countries and divesting countries and product lines that do not meet the firm's mission and definition of business.

The next step is the choice of a strategy among four generic, international competitive strategies-- global high share strategies, global niche strategies, national high share strategies, and national niche strategies (for a

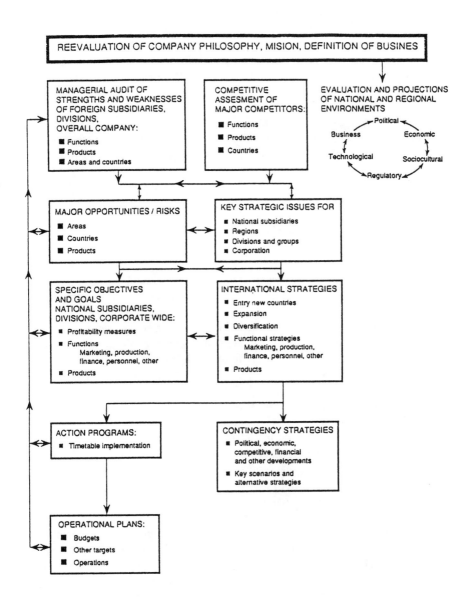

Figure 1: Model for Comprehensive Strategic Planning for MNCs

detail of each strategy, see Leontiases, 1985). A subsequent step is the formulation of various global competitive strategies, including new entry, expansion, diversification, and functional strategies, translated from specific objectives and goals of corporate headquarters and foreign subsidiaries. Another subsequent step is the formulation of contingency strategies, action programs, and operational plans.

In step A, scanning the international environment (political, economical, etc.) is a crucial activity. A survey revealed that international environmental scanning activities had been integrated in many cmpanies as a part of information systems to regularly monitor a broad range of environmental and foreign risk factors (Preble, et al., 1988). GMSSs should be capable of effectively collecting, analyzing, and interpreting environmental scanning data to extract meaningful information. Therefore, in step A, EIS subsystems of GMSS should be a major element.

In steps B, C, and D, GDSSs such as decision room and teleconferencing systems can increase the effectiveness of idea generation and evaluation processes. In step E, corporate goals are converted into global strategies, which can be most effectively supported by a GMSS. In this conversion, the multiplicity of economic, political, legal, and cultural forces in global environments must be taken into consideration. Management decisions of global operations are complicated by a significantly uncertain decision environment that stems from the multiplicity of global environments. For example, Onan Corporation, a leading U.S. manufacturer of electrical generator sets and industrial engines, designed and implemented a comprehensive DSS for international investment planning to support global decision making. The system lends support in country and strategy selection, evaluating operational risks for selected strategic choices, and evaluating strategic choices for integration into existing or planned structures (Iyer, 1988).

GMSSs should be capable of analyzing multinational, multifunctional, or multibusiness consequences of decisions and evaluating the tradeoffs between long-term and short-term impacts. Often, long-run profit and other corporate goals are attained at the expense of current profits by undertaking development projects that may enhance future profitability or stability. Long-range planning should not be considered as an activity separate from and independent of short-range planning. The GMSS should be able to balance the conflicting goals of long-range and short-range planning.

Requirement #6: Conflict and Political Risk Management Support
A major difference in the decision making of an MNC and a domestic company is that global decisions of an MNC must always take into consideration the conflicting objectives of MNCs, national governments, and multilateral organizations. Conflict management in MNCs is critical for survival. The focus of conflict management in MNCs is not conflicts between individual managers, or interpersonal conflicts among executives, or intra-organizational conflicts within a firm. Rather, it is on inter-organizational conflict among MNCs, host governments, home governments, and multilateral organizations.

The multiple-criteria decision making (MCDM) approach and MCDM-model based decision support systems (MCDSS) can be instrumental in managing global conflicts among MNCs and governments of home and host countries (Eom, in press-b). In addition, applications of group decision making technology, such as electronic meeting systems, or negotiation support systems may be of help to the management of global conflicts.

Requirement #7: Long-Term Foreign Exchange Risk Management Support: Many MNCs have developed more integrative strategic planning systems to rationalize resources more effectively on a global basis to respond to rapid environmental changes, such as increased political and foreign exchange risk and global competition (Dymsa, 1984). When formulating a worldwide financing strategy, financial managers of MNCs must resolve several issues including long-term foreign exchange risk management. Essentially, there are three fundamental issues in global financing decisions. They are (1) the conflicting nature of financing objectives, (2) financial market imperfections and effective management of foreign exchange risks, and (3) the firm's financial structure. To resolve these issues, Eom and others (1987/1988) designed a model-based decision support system for global financial planning to simultaneously consider all risks and tradeoffs in order to design the best long-term financing strategies.

Requirement #8: Global Tax Risk Management Support: Global tax planning has been an extremely important topic in international financial management. Effectively designing tax risk management systems requires a complex knowledge of international finance, international monetary systems, international tax law concerning the legal structure of parent and subsidiaries, etc. Due to the extremely complex nature of global tax planning, several expert systems have been developed and are being used in planning multinational corporations' income tax and selecting locations for new subsidiaries (Phillips, et al., 1993), in managing property transferred offshore under section 367 of the US tax code (Phillips, et al., 1993), and in deciding transfer pricing for inventory and equipment moved across international boundaries (Freundlich, 1990). In the 1990's, more and more expert systems will be developed and deployed in the area of worldwide tax planning.

Requirement #9: Global Joint Decision Support Between Headquarters and Overseas Subsidiaries: A central issue the managers of MNCs face in the management of global operations is headquarters control over subsidiary activities (Doz and Prahalad, 1984). Therefore, a most critical task of MNCs' top management is to structure a decision making process between headquarters and its subsidiaries, through which an appropriate balance between national responsiveness and multinational integration can be reached.

Strategic planning involves participation of all units of the corporation, which include headquarters, foreign subsidiaries, regional offices, divisions, and groups. Global strategic management requires stimulative inputs from planners at functional, business, and corporate levels of each operating country. This interactive/iterative flow of information is extremely important for strategic planning of MNCs.

Electronic meeting systems (EMS) are playing an important role in supporting the joint decisions between headquarters and overseas subsidiaries. EMSs can be effective in improving decision-making performance and augmenting traditional audio-conferencing by strengthening the medium and allowing additional communication cues to be exchanged among participants. As businesses expand globally, such systems will provide instant communication capabilities and help coordinate dispersed decision-making activities (Chidambaram and Jones, 1993).

Most of the GDSS research has focused on simultaneous and concurrent communication-based studies. But these technologies are not yet readily available (Gray and Olfman, 1989). Smith and Vaneck (1990) conducted a quasi-experiment to compare the decision effectiveness of a non-simultaneous computer conferencing system and face-to-face groups. Although their experiments suggest that non-simultaneous computer conferencing may be less effective than a face-to-face meeting, the research in the non-simultaneous computer conferencing area will be very important in that, in some cases, the non-simultaneous computer conferencing can be an effective means of communication between foreign subsidiaries and headquarters operating in different time zones.

ARCHITECTURE OF GMSS

Prior to designing an architecture for GMSSs, three general decision making behaviors of MNCs need to be considered. Generally speaking, all levels of strategic decisions are made at the headquarters. Tactical decisions are made jointly by the home office and the overseas subsidiary. Operational decisions are made primarily at the subsidiary levels. Some functional areas of decision making, such as finance, rely heavily on centralization of decision making.

To support centralized decision making at the headquarters, MNCs may not need complex architectures as described here. Rather, the necessary local data from foreign subsidiaries, other branch offices, and suppliers would have to be transmitted to the MNC headquarters. Today's data communication and database management system technologies have made it possible for MNCs to build database files from the data originating in many international locations. Many tactical decisions can be effectively supported by DSS technologies such as teleconferencing systems and remote decision making systems.

The generic architecture of GMSSs described here is primarily to support joint decision making of the home office and overseas subsidiaries with high levels of interaction. GMSSs may be designed as a network of management support systems that links a set of DSS (single-user DSS, group DSS, and distributed decision making systems), ES, and EIS in the headquarters with a set of DSS, ES, and EIS in each foreign subsidiary. The purpose is to integrate organizational decision making across functional fields, planning horizons (long-range, medium-range, and short-range) and national boundaries to create *a coordinated global strategy*.

Design of GMSSs requires a different specification of each subsystem of data, model, and dialogue. Many MNCs are progressing toward the complete worldwide linkage of corporate distributed data bases in many foreign subsidiaries. Distributed DBMSs are evolving to satisfy all transparency requirements such as location transparency-- e.g., a user in an operating unit in an MNC can submit a query that accesses distributed objects, without having to know where the objects are. Models in GMSSs can be broadly classified into global models and local models. Global models are the models that are shared by each entity of an MNC. Local models are used to support the local decisions of foreign subsidiaries. The crucial function of GMSSs should be to create *a coordinated global strategy*. The essence of global decision making is to deal with high degree of task (decision) interdependency between the parent company and its foreign subsidiaries. Global sales forecasting, for example, is a sequential task. The output of sales forecasting for each foreign operating country must be used as input to a global forecasting model in the GMSS of the parent company. Therefore, the model of each operating unit must be linked as shown in Figure 2.

The functions of GMSSs are augmented by other information and communication technologies such as electronic data interchange (EDI), value added networks (VAN), integrated services digital network (ISDN), and the Internet. These elements are essential for GMSSs to deal with geographical separation among operating units in heterogeneous and diverse environments. EDI, for instance, can reduce time delay through paperless intra- and inter-organizational communication. The VAN allows MNCs to interconnect an assortment of terminals, microcomputers, and workstations to establish quickly an EDI network among suppliers, and customers. ISDN streamlines the operations of the MNC through high-speed transfer of voice, image, text, video, and audio. Other benefits of ISDN include improved database access for multiple users, greater network reliabilities and securities, and fewer transmission errors (Kessler, 1993).

SURVEY RESULTS OF OPERATIONAL GMSS's IN REAL WORLD

Although there are no existing systems that meet all the functional requirements of GMSSs that we have described, there are numerous systems that can partially fulfill our specifications.

ES Utilization in Global Management

Table 1 lists 13 expert systems in use in the international business area, based on a survey of publications between 1980 and 1993. As discussed earlier, an increasing number of financial institutions have deployed expert

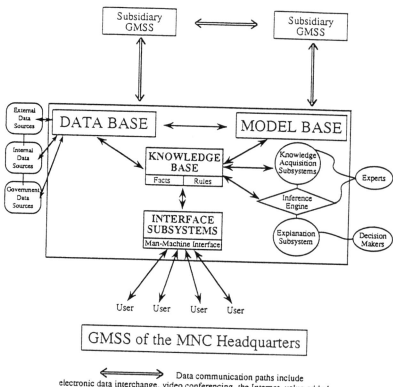

Figure-2: A Generic Architecture of GMSSs

---

1. Foreign Exchange Risk Management
* Monitoring and developing strategies for trading foreign currency options (Arend, 1989; Byrnes, et al., 1990; Harmon, 1988)
* Monitoring worldwide trading activities in foreign exchange (Byrnes, et al., 1989)

2. International Financing
* Designing new financial products that combine swaps and options in different currencies to procure capital with minimum risk, and interest (Expert Systems, 1992b)

3. International Taxation
* Planning multinational corporations' income tax and selecting locations for new subsidiaries (Phillips, et al.,1993)
* Property transferred offshore under section 367 of the US tax code (Phillips, et al., 1993)
* Transfer pricing for inventory and equipment moved across international boundaries (Freundlich, 1990)

4. International Telecommunication Network Control
* The network controller assistant for the Society for Worldwide Interbank Financial Telecommunication (SWIFT) (Phelps, et. al., 1990)

5. International Trade Support
* Advice on the legal aspects of trade transactions between the US and Canada (Harmon, 1988)
* Complying with US regulations on the export and re-export of US technical items (Expert Systems, 1990)
* Detection of discrepancies between the letter of credit and accompanying documents (Harmon, 1988)

6. International Marketing, Logistics, and Transportation
* Scheduling crude oil delivery vessels (Lee, et al., 1991)
* the evaluation and selection of an international freight forwarder (Ozsomer, et al., 1993)

7. Others
* Analyzing the business implications of the single European market (Expert Systems, 1992a)

Table 1: Operational Expert Systems in International Business

systems to monitor worldwide trading activities in foreign exchange and develop strategies for trading foreign currency options. In the area of international financing, the Dai-Ichi Kangyo Bank has implemented an expert system, Mr. Genius, for designing new financial products that combine swaps and options in different currencies to procure capital with a minimum of risk, at the lowest interest for corporate investors. In international marketing, logistics, and transportation management, an expert system assists decision makers in selecting the freight forwarder which best fits their needs, utilizing quantitative and qualitative decision-analytic techniques to provide a systematic methodology for forwarder evaluation and selection. Yu-Kong Company in Korea has developed and implemented an expert system for worldwide scheduling of crude oil delivery vessels. ESs are used to manage international tax risks, to support international trade, and to monitor international telecommunication networks.

Business expert systems are emerging as a predominant area of applications. Many ESs shrink the time required for tasks from days to hours, minutes, or seconds. Supporting global business activities, however, is becoming an important task, and we can expect to see more global management applications in the 1990's, in domains such as political risk management, global tax management, and international accounting and financial reporting.

DSS Utilization in Global Management

Since the early 1970s, a wide variety of DSS applications has been developed in many different fields for profit and not-for-profit organizations. A survey of DSS applications between 1971 and April 1988 indicated that in corporate management, international business and accounting/auditing were relatively minor fields for DSS application.

During the 1970s, the impact of computer-based information and decision support systems on strategic planning at business and corporate levels was insignificant. It was not until the 1980s that DSS development efforts began to shift to the formulation of business and corporate strategies. During the period of 1981 through 1985, the number of DSS applications increased significantly as did the number of DSS, for functional strategy. In the first half of the 1980s, all levels of decision support systems emerged to support all levels of strategic decisions except global corporate strategy. Since 1985, a few DSS's for global corporate strategy formulations have been developed. This trend, however, must be carefully interpreted. Although we have witnessed a whole range of DSS's to support all levels of organizational decision making in the late 1980s, the majority of DSS applications continue to support operational, tactical, and functional strategic decisions (Eom and Lee 1990). Since then, a few more operational DSS's have been developed or are under development. Here are two examples. Federal Express Corporation is developing an integrated decision support and information system, the Global Operations Control Center (GOCC) system. The system is expected to support critical decision making concerning future operations of the 2,500 trucks, 252 jet transports, and approximately 200 feeder aircrafts, as well as to keep track of what is happening in the far-flung courier and freight operation. The core of the GOCC system includes Total Airspace and Airport Modeler (TAAM) to optimize all cargo loading (weight and balance) operation, and a decision support module for fast and real-time simulations of aircraft and airport operations. The GOCC system will be a strategic decision making tool to quickly and accurately evaluate the impact of operational, tactical, and strategic management decisions (Ott, 1992).

Another example is the case of The Global Decision Support System implemented at The Military Airlift Command's (MAC) new command and control center in the U.S. Department of Defense. The system is built on a wide area network that tracks aircraft and air crews worldwide in near real time for vastly improved command and control. The wide area network consists of seven local area networks (LAN's). Each LAN is comprised of digital computers that can simultaneously update databases at all other sites (Hughes, 1988).

CONCLUSIONS

Global Management Support Systems the newest frontiers of computer-based decision technologies that must be conquered as we enter the age of the global village, where geographic and temporal boundaries are shrinking rapidly. Multinational decision making indeed presents today's managers with unprecedented challenges which can only be managed properly by the emerging tools of global management support systems. Nevertheless, global management support systems are no longer a subject of conceptual discussion. They have indeed become a real world technology to deal with the real world managerial complexities of global corporations. This chapter attempted to lay important groundwork for further development of GMSSs. We also presented a generic architecture of GMSSs, which consists of a network of DSSs, ESs, and EISs to link parent companies with foreign subsidiaries.

We are in an early stage in the development life cycle of global management support systems. In this stage, foundations of the new field must be laid by providing definitions, concepts, architectures, taxonomies, developments, and evaluation criteria. Information systems are an applied discipline that should be evaluated by its impact on practice and applications. In the next stage of the GMSS development life cycle our attention must shift to the development of theories, concepts, frameworks, methods, techniques, and tools that can be applied in practice.

Numerous new challenges and opportunities await researchers in the GMSS area. The simple Data-Dialogue-Model architecture of decision support systems in a single location must be expanded to deal with multiple data, multiple models, and multiple dialogue systems that can handle multiple language interfaces. For instance, due to transborder data flow restrictions and certain advantages of distributed database management systems, MNCs in general have located their database files at multiple sites in many foreign subsidiary locations. The current information technology cannot provide full support to manage heterogeneous distributed databases that consist of database files of different data models (relational, hierarchical, or network) running under different computer systems (mainframes, minis, microcomputers) of different manufacturers. New information technologies and decision paradigms will be needed to scale the global frontiers.

References

Alter, S.L. Decision Support Systems: Current Practice and Continuing Challenges, Addison-Wesley, Reading, MA, 1980.

Arend, M. "AI: Expert Keeps Up with Bank's Currency Events," Wall Street Computer Review (6:9), 1989, pp. 22-24, 91-92.

Ballester, G. and Marcarelli, E. "The Impact of Global Information Technology on International Investment Managers and Custodians," in: Global Issues of Information Technology Management, S. Palvia, P. Palvia, and R.M. Zigli (eds.), Idea Group Publishing, Harrisburg, PA, 1992, pp. 356-382.

Breitman, R.L. and Lucas, J.M. "PLANETS: A Modeling System for Business Planning," Interfaces (17:1), January-February 1987, pp. 94-106.

Byrnes, E., Campfield, T., and Connor, B. "TARA: An Intelligent Assistant for Foreign Traders," in Innovative Applications of Artificial Intelligence, H. Schorr and A. Rappaport (eds.) Vol. 1, AAAI Press/The MIT press, Menlo Park, CA, 1989, pp. 71-77.

Byrnes, E., Campfield, T., Henry, N., and Waldman, S. "Inspector: An Expert System for Monitoring World-Wide Trading Activities in Foreign Exchange," in Innovative Applications of Artificial Intelligence, A. Rappaport and R. Smith (eds.) Vol. 2, AAAI Press/The MIT Press, Menlo Park, CA, 1990, pp. 15-24.

Chidambaram, L. and Jones, B. "Impact of Communication Medium and Computer Support on Group Perceptions and Performance: A Comparison of Face-To-Face and Dispersed Meetings," MIS Quarterly (17:4), December 1993, pp. 465-491.

Dymsza, W.A. "Global Strategic Planning: A Model and Recent   Developments," Journal of International Business Studies, (15:2), Fall 1984, pp. 169-184.

Doz, Y.L. and Prahalad, C.K. "Patterns of Strategic Control Within Multinational Corporations," Journal of International Business Studies, (15:2), Fall 1984, pp. 55-72.

Eom, H.B., Lee, S.M., Snyder, C.A. and Ford, N.F. "A Multiple Criteria Decision Support System for Global Financial Planning," Journal of Management Information Systems, (4:3), Winter 1987, pp. 94-113.
Eom, H.B. and Lee, S.M. "A Survey of Decision Support System   Applications (1971-April 1988)," Interfaces (20:3), May-June 1990, pp. 65-79.

Eom, S.B. "A Survey of Operational Expert Systems (1980-1993)," Interfaces (in press-a).

Eom, S.B. "Mapping the Intellectual Structure of Research in Decision Support Systems Through Author Cocitation Analysis (1971-1993)," Decision Support Systems (in press-b).

Expert Systems "News: Applications," (7:2), 1990, p. 125.

Expert Systems "News: Applications-top twenty from IAAI," (9:1), 1992a, p. 51.

Expert Systems "News: Applications," (9:2), 1992b, p. 99.

Goodwin, C. "Financial Software: Some Hard Choices," Accountancy (107:1171), March 1991, pp. 114-118.

Freundlich, Y. "Transfer pricing: Integrating expert systems in MIS environments," IEEE Expert (5:1), 1990, pp. 54-62.

Gray, P. and Olfman, L. "The User Interfaces in Group Decision Support Systems," Decision Support Systems (5:2), 1989, pp. 119-137.

Harmon, P. "Appendix: Expert Systems in Use," In The Rise of the Expert Company, E. Feigenbaum, P. McCorduck, and P. Nii (eds.), 1988," Times Books, New York, 1988, pp. 273-315.

Holstein, W.J., Reed, S., Kapstein, J., Vogel, T., and Weber, J.J., "The Stateless Corporation," Business Week, May 14, 1990, pp. 98-105.

Hughes, D. "MAC Command and Control Center to Serve as Defense Dept. Model, Aviation Week & Space Technology (129:3), July 18, 1988, pp. 55, 57.

Iyer, R.K. and Schkade, L.L. "Management Support Systems for Multinational Business," Information & Management (12:2) February 1987, pp. 59-64.

Iyer, R.K. "Information and Modeling Resources for Decision Support in Global Environments," Information & Management (14:2), February 1988, pp. 67-73.

Kessler, G.C. ISDN: Concepts, Facilities, and Services, 2nd Ed., McGraw-Hill, New York, NY, 1993.
King, W.R. and Sethi, V. "A Framework for Transnational Systems," in: Global Issues of Information Technology Management, S. Palvia, P. Palvia, and R.M. Zigli (eds.), Idea Group Publishing, Harrisburg, PA, 1992, pp. 214-248.

Lee, J.K., Song, Y.U., Suh, M.S., and Yun, H.S. "UNIK-PCS: A Crude Oil Delivery Scheduling System," in Operational Expert System Applications in the Far East, J.K. Lee, R. Mizoguchi, D. Narasimhalu, and D.S. Yeung (eds.), Pergamon Press, New York, 1991, pp. 109-121.

Leontiases, J.C. Multinational Corporate Strategy, Lexington Books, D.C. Heath and Company, Lexington, MA, 1985.

Maranoff, J., Tate P. and Whitehouse, B. "Around the World in 24 hours" Datamation, January 1987, pp. 15, 75-77

McCartney, L. "How ESS Keeps Hertz Managers Out in Front," Business Month (134:1), July 1989, pp. 46-47.

Min, H-K. and Eom, S.B., "An Integrated Decision Support System for Global Logistics," International Journal of Physical Distribution & Logistics Management (24:1), 1994, pp. 29-39.

Ott, J. "Federal Express Develops C3I-Based Information System," Aviation Week & Space Technology (137:21), November 23, 1992, pp. 57-60.

Ozsomer, Aysegul; Mitri, Michel; and Cavusgil, S. Tamer, "Selecting International Freight Forwarders: An Expert Systems Application," International Journal of Physical Distribution & Logistics Management (23:3), 1993, pp. 11-21.

Palvia, S., Palvia, P., and Zigli, R.M. The Global Issues of Information Technology Management, Idea Group Publishing, Harrisburg, PA 1992.

Pantages, A. "TI's Global Window," Datamation, September 1, 1989, pp. 49-52.

Phelps, R.; Ristori, F.; Mukherjee, D.; Thomae, L.; and Steinier, J. 1990, "INCA-An innovative approach to constructing large-scale real-time expert systems," in Innovative Applications of Artificial Intelligence, A. Rappaport and R. Smith (eds.) Vol. 2, AAAI Press/The MIT Press, Menlo Park, CA, 1990, pp. 3-14.

Phillips, D., Steiger, W.R. and Young, W. "The Challenges and Success Factors in Implementing an Integrated Products Planning System for CITGO," Interfaces, (16:3), May/June 1986, pp. 1-19.

Phillips, M.E. and Brown, C.E. "A Survey of Expert Systems Used in the Practice of Public Accounting," In Expert Systems in Business and Finance: Issues and Applications, P.R. Watkins and L.B. Eliot (eds.), John Wiley and Sons, Chichester, UK, 1993, pp. 341-356.

Preble, J.F., Rau, P.A., Reichel, A. "The Environmental Scanning Practices of U.S. Multinationals in the Late 1980's," Management International Review, (28:4), Fourth Quarter 1988, pp. 4-14.

Rathwell, M.A. and Burns, A. "Information Systems Support for Group Planning and Decision Making Activities," MIS Quarterly, (9:3), September 1985, pp. 254-270.

Roche, E.M., Managing Information Technology in Multinational Corporations, Macmillan Publishing Company, New York, 1992.

Ryerson, W.M., and Pitts, J.C. "A Five-Nation Data Network for Aircraft Manufacturing," Telecommunications, October 1989, pp. 45-48.

Shrivastava, P., Etgar, M., and Licht, S. "A Decision Support System for Strategic Marketing Decisions," Systems, Objectives, Solutions(4), 1984, pp. 131-139.

Smith, J.Y. and Vanecek, M.T. "Dispersed Group Decision Making Using Nonsimultaneous Computer Conferencing," Journal of Management Information Systems (7:2), Fall 1990, pp. 71-92.

Srinirasulu, S.L. "Currency Denomination of Debt: Lessons From Rolls-Royce and Laker Airways," Business Horizons (26), September/October 1983, pp. 19-21.

Tobias, A.J. "Multinationals Spearheading Worldwide Financial Trust," Software Magazine, May1988, pp. 64-70.

21 Design and Implementation Issues for Groupware in the Global Organization

Ravi Sharma
Deutsche Telekom Asia, Singapore

Shailendra Palvia
Long Island University, USA

Lai Lai Tung, Wooi Boon Goh, and Schubert Foo
Nanyang Technological University, Singapore

Groupware facilitates and supports collaboration within groups that may be physically and/or temporally separated. While much work has been done in establishing the concept of groupware and the impact of a variety of factors on the efficiency and effectiveness of its use; there is no seminal work that thoroughly investigates experimentally the design and implementation problems associated with such systems. In the area of design and implementation, some work has been done in regard to groupware for same time and place situations (e.g. meeting rooms) but there is a general vacuum in regard to groupware for groups that are geographically dispersed and cross time zones. In this chapter, we present a framework and an experimental methodology that addresses the problem of matching groupware design with its proposed use. Stated briefly, groupware is only effective when the system is considered in the context of group objectives, stakeholder roles and environmental constraints. Our research methodology is simple: prototyping and field testing beta versions of four main classes of groupware. We have gleaned a comprehensive list of parameters for the design and implementation of such systems. As a result, we have a provisional list of guidelines for the design and implementation of groupware which is particularly relevant to the global organization.

INTRODUCTION

There is considerable agreement that the work group or task team has become the cornerstone of the post-industrial organization. Cummings (cited in Cannon-Bowers et al., 1992, p355) describes work groups as the "basic components comprising organizations and contexts within which workers work". It is easy to see that the primary advantage of a work group would be the handling and analysis of input data from multiple sources to help in solving the increasingly complex problems of corporations today. In the era of the "global village" and "information age", the post-industrial organization is increasingly multinational in outlook - both in terms of its strategies employed as well as in organizational infrastructure (Mintzberg, 1979). Consequently, the work groups within these organizations are dispersed geographically and across several time zones so as to bring together the best resources for the various tasks undertaken. The technological support that seeks to augment and complement group work must necessarily bridge this time and/or space separation.

Groupware or Computer Supported Cooperative Work (CSCW) systems facilitate interaction among the group whose members may be physically or temporally distributed. It is arguably the most needed component of a global organization's portfolio of information technology applications. Effectively managing such systems therefore becomes a critical element of any chief information officer's strategy. Although the terms "groupware" and "CSCW systems" are often used interchangeably, Ellis et al. (1991) clarify that the former define exclusively the technical system per se whereas the latter also relate to the social dynamics of group work. In any case, the objective of such systems is to support generic group relationships such as communication, coordination, cooperation, collaboration and control. Researchers (Ellis, 1991; Rodden, 1991) have generally classified groupware or CSCW systems into the following classes: messaging, conferencing, meeting-room support, and co-authoring tools. Rodden (1991) also provides a comprehensive survey of a number of developed systems over the four classes in such diverse domains as office work, design and manufacturing, distance education and personal communications. Greenberg (1993) has an even more extensive annotated list of readings on the entire subject of groupware.

Interest in groupware resurged in the mid 1980s after a twenty-year hiatus. The Association for Computing Machinery (ACM), for instance, has held annual inter-disciplinary conferences in CSCW research since 1984. Many vendors now make claims of being able to support collaborative work over enterprise networks. Given the current world-wide penchant for organizational rightsizing and re-engineering its work flow, industry leaders are actively developing technical systems and environments that would facilitate group work. Since the underlying technologies of communications networks, multimedia processing and group interfaces have proven feasible, research efforts in groupware focus increasingly on relating architectures to applications. But as Grudin [1994] insightfully points out, there are reasons other than technical feasibility that account for the successful utilization of groupware that must be factored into the design equation. The development of superior groupware therefore is a complex and time-consuming problem which warrants the efforts of researchers and practitioners alike in seeking a solution.

But why is groupware more difficult to design and evaluate than single-user applications? Grudin in fact goes on to list eight challenges for the developers of groupware, with three of them being probable reasons for the above question. (1). Participants have differing backgrounds, past experiences and work styles which may not easily be reconciled with a common toolbar and/or palette. In addition, there may be differences in culture, regulatory regimes, languages, norms and time zones arising from the global dimension of groupware. e.g., in global groupware, it can be confusing to say "today at 2 pm" - we must specify the local time and date to avoid confusion. (2). In any collaborative activity different users adopt different roles and role-switching may occur. (3). Group dynamics and processes are not well understood or monitored and may vary between groups. There have been cases where miscommunication between parties in Internet discussions (for example) resulted in dissatisfaction, protests and even abuse from participants. Researchers and practitioners, therefore, cannot ignore the wider scope of technology in developing groupware.

This chapter documents the findings of an on-going program investigating the design and implementation issues for groupware. The central thrust of this research is to determine the best fit between technical features and characteristics of groupware on one hand and the contextual factors such as the task at hand, stakeholder roles, group traits as well as organizational structure on the other hand. In short, the objective is to determine how groupware ought to be configured in a given situation so that it may be effectively utilized. In the next section, we review some frameworks and models that have been suggested in the organization theory / behavior literature. Following that, we present a brief description of our own distillation of the issues governing the design and implementation of groupware especially in the global context. Next, is a methodology to test the validity of such a framework. We conclude with some preliminary findings and comments of what is to come.

BACKGROUND REVIEW

Research in groupware may be roughly divided into two thrusts: (1) developing and testing prototypes in order to investigate the features and characteristics that would be useful for various tasks; and (2) modeling the nature of group processes so as to specify the type of support required. While Ellis et al. (1991), Rodden (1991) and others have categorized groupware along time-space dimensions and application areas, little work has been done in developing implementation theories that fit features and characteristics to the context of group work. On the other hand, the social theory perspective such as McGrath's pioneering model and latter modifications (McGrath and Hollingshead, 1994) for understanding groups, do not provide the level of detail required for technical specifications. In this section, we critique the latter- the social theory perspective - so as to enable a fusion with the former - the conceptual frameworks that had been developed.

Classically, there are two fundamental dimensions that taxonomize groupware. First, the nature of interaction may either be synchronous or asynchronous. That is, the group work is being performed in real time or it is not. Second, the group that is being supported can be physically in one location or distributed over several locations. Thus, groupware must be designed to provide support for one of the four possible combinations shown in Figure 1(a). The 2x2 matrix is hardly new, having been used for expository purposes by many researchers and practitioners alike.

	SAME TIME	DIFFERENT TIMES
SAME PLACE	Face-to-Face Interaction *e.g. electronic meeting room, Group DSS room*	Asynchronus Interaction *e.g. information kiosk, project management team room*
DIFFERENT PLACES	Synchronus Distributed Interaction *e.g. conference calls, videoconference, screen*	Asynchronus distributed interaction *e.g. electronic mail, voice mail*

Figure 1(a):   Time and Space Classification of Groupware

To illustrate, a conventional meeting requires participants to be in the same room at the same time. Groupware for such an application might provide support for decision-making activities such as the provision of electronic white-boards for brainstorming or input devices for conducting voting procedures. In contrast, when real-time interaction is not necessary, like in the case of office directories and information kiosks, then groupware would include storage and retrieval facilities that allow consistent and up-to-date information interchange. The third scenario is when a group may be spread out geographically but may be working on parts of a task at the same time. Examples would be co-editing a text or graphics document or running a sequence of jobs in a distributed environment. Finally, electronic mail allows asynchronous communication between members of a distributed group. Effective time and space management by groupware therefore becomes a critical success factor and the technology must provide for these contexts. The same holds for combinations of all the contextual factors to be identified in our framework.

This broad time and space 2 x 2 matrix needs to be probed further in the global context. When originally developed, it appears that its scope was same country/same culture and/or same time zone. But barriers of operating within single or limited time zones and within the borders of a country or culture are fast falling apart. Increasingly, one has to be aware that the groupware may be used by a workgroup representing several time zones within a single country/culture/operating environment (e.g., Russia or U.S.A. or Canada) or different countries in the same time zone (e.g., countries in Europe or Pan-Pacific region) or the ultimate group representing several countries/cultures and several time zones. Thus, Figure 1(b) captures this new global dimension of groupware.

	SAME TIME ZONE	DIFFERENT TIME ZONES
SAME COUNTRY/ CULTURE	Unicultural Interaction *India*	Unicultural Interaction *United States*
DIFFERENT COUNTRY/ CULTURE	Multicultural Interaction *western Europe, East Asia*	Multicultural Interaction *the entire globe*

Figure 1(b): Global Dimension of Groupware.

Essentially, the same country/culture represents a homogeneous operating and regulatory environment; certainly more so than the different country/culture case! This is important because, as we shall observe in the next section, group work is very much influenced by the operating context. The same time zone and different time zone taxonomy influences whether or not synchronous, concurrent work processes may be feasibly initiated and engaged in.

The most common model for group support is the one adopted from McGrath's framework for group research (McGrath, 1984). Particularly in the domain of Group Support Systems (GSS), many researchers have adapted this research framework to formulate more specific models for empirical studies. The essence of McGrath's framework is that group outcomes are governed by group, task and contextual characteristics. The group characteristics that can affect processes and outcomes include group size, proximity, history, expertise, etc. Task characteristics include the task complexity and the activities involved in completing a task such as idea generation or choosing among alternatives. Contextual characteristics that have been looked at in the literature include cultural differences, time, conflict, and so on. (McGrath and Hollingshead, 1994 contains a thorough survey of the relevant variables). From an input-process-output viewpoint, this framework shows that the process outcome (efficiency and effectiveness) is dependent on the group process which is in turn affected by its group, task and contextual characteristics.

One way of looking at this "process" box is to examine how groupware actually affects the group process itself. Nunamaker et al. (1993) suggested that a GSS affects the balance of process gains and losses through four mechanisms: (1) process support, (2) process structure, (3) task structure, and (4) task support. Process support refers to the communication infrastructure (media, channels, and devices) that facilitates communication among members, such as an electronic communication channel or blackboard (parallel communication, group memory, and anonymity). Process structure is the set of rules or process techniques that direct the pattern, timing, or content of this communication such as an agenda, or process methodology such as the nominal group technique and following a strategy/agenda to perform the task. The task structure refers to the techniques, rules, or models for analyzing task-related information to gain new insights, such as those within computer models or decision support systems while task support refers to the information and computation infrastructure for task-related activities, such as external databases and pop-up calculators.

McGrath and Hollingshead (1994) have also proposed a revised conceptual framework for studying the impact of technology on groups. Here they have attempted to encompass "a full panoply of potentially relevant variables" and place them in a functional relation to one another. Briefly stated, the model comprises the following: (1) *the input factors*: member attributes, group attributes, task purposes, technology, and context factors; (2) *the process variables*: participation, information processing, consensus generating, and normative regulation; (3) *the outcome factors*: task performance effectiveness, user reactions, and member relations.

However, the McGrath framework and its refinements are essentially models that consider group behavior and processes in the meeting room support context. Specifically, its appeal lies in its applicability to general small group decision making, but lacks the specification needed for research of the kind that seeks a unified theory for supporting group work in general. Its other major limitations are: (1) it does not distinguish between the different types and functions of groupware; (2) it does not consider the different roles played by stakeholders; (3) the outcome factors are measured post-hoc, in terms of performance and perception; (4) it does not establish theoretical inter-relationships between the system and its context; (5) it does not define the other types of tasks that employ groupware and focuses exclusively on decision-making processes. Thus, the McGrath framework by itself is not sufficient to guide our research on the design and implementation issues for groupware.

Lately, there has been a trend to define platforms or toolboxes for the developers of groupware. Alarmingly, these attempts have not been based on any underlying foundation or theory. Our long term objective is to develop a field-tested framework for the design and implementation of global groupware whereby the developer is guided on what features and characteristics "best fit" a given context. This would seem to be the inspiration behind the "ecological" approaches suggested by Cannon-Bowers et al. (1992) and Sundstrom et al. (1990). Likewise, we may define a context by the type of task at hand, required solution, stakeholder roles, and organizational structure. Such a framework necessarily assumes a socio-technical understanding of both systems and work variables.

DESIGN AND IMPLEMENTATION FRAMEWORK

The concept of a socio-technical system arose from the field projects undertaken during the postwar reconstruction of the British coal mining industry. These early field studies showed that the performance of a new technology - in the particular case of these field studies, innovative mining methods - relied on the mutual support of its technical and social components. The observations from the British coal mines were later confirmed in projects involving other industries and jurisdictions.

Trist and Bamforth, in the very first public usage of the term "socio-technical system", distinguished between the "technological system" and "social structure". The essence of their philosophy is best captured by the following quote from Trist (1981):

... a work system depends on the social and technical components becoming directly correlated to produce a given goal state. They are co-producers of the outcome. The distinctive characteristics of each must be respected else their contradictions will intrude and their complementarities will remain unrealized. (p24)

Thus in the same parlance, when designing a system to be "socio-technical", there is a "joint optimization" or trade-off between optimizing the technical subsystem and the social subsystem. The term socio-technical may therefore be taken to mean considering the technology in the context of its application environment. In formulating our framework, we have drawn inspiration from this school of thought (Trist,1979; Trist, 1981). Figure 2 shows a condensed version of our proposed framework.

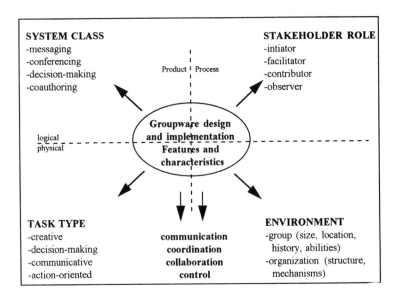

Figure-2: The Relationship between Technology and Context

We posit that the design and implementation characteristics and features of groupware are affected by the context of: *class of system, type of task, role of the stakeholders* and *environment*. Roughly speaking, these allude to the support solution, group objective, user participation and constraints respectively. Our model attempts to map a close fit between the design and implementation variables on the one hand and the context defined above. We contend that a good fit leads to enhanced communication, coordination, cooperation, collaboration and control. Discounting process losses from the process gains, we should ideally have a situation of cost savings, improved quality, greater product variety, better customer service and faster response.

Four distinct classes of groupware have been identified by researchers (Ellis et al., 1991; Rodden, 1991): messaging, conferencing, decision-making and co-authoring systems. McGrath (1984) lists 4 types of group tasks: communicative, decision-making, creative and action-oriented. There seems to be a noticeable isomorphism between the above 2 sets that strongly suggests the need for further study. The literature (Nunamaker et al., 1993) has identified the various and sometimes interchanging roles of stakeholders: initiators, facilitators, contributors and observers. Finally, organizational theorists (Mintzberg, 1979) believe that some of the more pertinent parameters of the environment are: unit size, physical location, background history, skills and expertise, grouping, control and liaison mechanisms.

In consultation with ideas from researchers and practitioners, the framework is used to spawn design and implementation issues for groupware. For example, Ellis et al. (1991) state that the key concepts to groupware design are: shared context, group window, telepointer, synchronous/asynchronous interaction, and session/role. Reinhard et al. (1994) describe a universal architecture for CSCW tools which comprises cooperation management, application sharing, telepointing, and audio-visual conferencing modules. In a similar vein, Dourish and Bellotti (1992) identify the issues for successful collaboration to be: effective information sharing, awareness of group and individual activities, and fluid and seamless coordination. Likewise, McGrath and Hollingshead (1994) have adapted the list of tools and modules for task performance support systems first proposed by Nunamaker et al. to include system management, electronic brainstorming, evaluation and voting, policy formulation, organizational infrastructure, and communications channels.

All the above sources provide details of the mechanisms that achieve these concepts. We have culled from the literature [e.g. Greif, 1982; Kraemer and King, 1988; Olson et al., 1993; Reinhard et al., 1994; Wilson, 1991; Malone et al., 1992; Bly et al., 1993; Loeb, 1992; Hellman, 1992) and our own exposure to developing prototypes, the provisional list of features and characteristics for the socio-technical implementation of groupware as listed in Table 1.

The features and characteristics outlined in Table 1 serve as instances of the links between design / implementation on the one-hand and application on the other. They span both the logical requirements and the physical specifications of groupware. By "logical", we mean conceptual or abstract whereas "physical" refers to the more tangible. Also referred to in Table 1 is the subtle distinction between "product" factors which spell out the desired end-result and "process" factors which articulate the possible means by which the desired end-result can be achieved. In total, Table 1 lists some of the nuances in establishing communications, coordination, cooperation, collaboration and control that have been spawned from the framework outlined in Figure 2. These design and implementation factors are now subject to empirical validation.

	PRODUCT APPLICATION SPECIFICATIONS	PROCESS IMPLEMENTATION FACTORS
logical issues	notification information sharing:- granularity, monotonicity, sequencing awareness interface:- (display space, #windows, time, population, congruence) presentation vs. viewing centralized vs. distributed groups synchronous vs. asynchronous work	access control:- floor control concurrency control:- locking mechanisms coordination strategy:- scheduling quality of service requirement:- delay, reliability security:- privacy and authentication integrity and consistency
physical issues	WYSIWIS vs. overlay vs. personal media:- standards audio - audio bandwidth, lip synch, echo cancellation images - bitmap vs. vector drawn video - frame rate, size, resolution, color sampling	utilities :- archive for logs/diaries backup for recoverability connectivity:- medium, topology, protocols

Table 1: Groupware Specifications and Design Factors.

RESEARCH METHODOLOGY

The method that we adopted in determining the design and implementation issues for groupware is experimental in nature. Drawing from the guidelines proposed by Adams and Schvaneveldt [1985], Babbie [1986] and the field research experience of Saraph et al. [1989], we have taken the first steps that allow us to validate the general tenets of our framework. The fundamental research question is: Are the design and implementation issues and the contextual factors that we have uncovered both comprehensive and parsimonious?

We began with a literature review of the issues governing the development of groupware. An extensive list of sources was drawn from the areas of group support systems, communications and networking, multimedia, computer human interaction, organizational behavior, and research methods. The end of the chapter includes selected references. We were then ready for some prototyping activity to get insights into the design issues. Where the applications were substantial (for example, decision support and multimedia

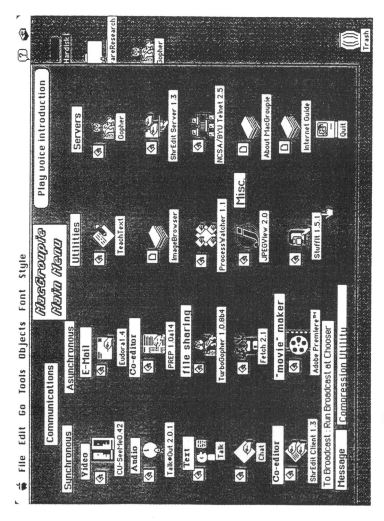

Figure 3:   MacGroupie - a desktop conferencing system
             configured from intefnet shareware

conferencing systems), we obtained off-the-shelf software and peripherals for further customization and experimentation. Finally, we conducted field tests to determine and document usage experiences.

The systems that we developed and configured were:

- a desktop conferencing system that we call MacGroupie (configured from internet shareware) [Figure 3]
- a GUI-based Group Decision Support System or GDSS - Group System V (acquired off-the-shelf) [Figure 4]
- CommIT - a shared white-board / group editor developed in-house [Figure 5]
- an MIME (Multipurpose Internet Mail Extension) -based multimedia e-mail system for a heterogeneous environment [Figure 6]

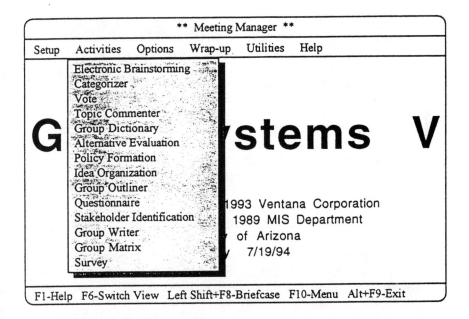

Figure 4:   GroupSystem V - a GUI-based Group Decision
Support System from University of Arizona

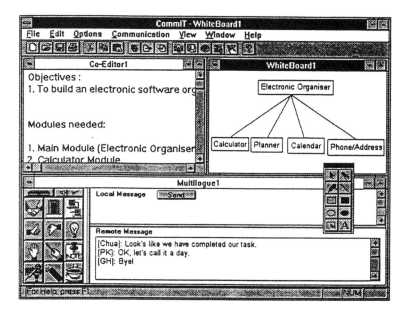

**Figure-5: CommIT - a Shared Whiteboard/Group Editor
Developed at Nanyang Technolgical University**

The nature of our experiments was varied. First, we were mostly interested in the critical success factors when various classes of systems are used (messaging, conferencing, decision-making and co-authoring) for different types of tasks (creative, decision-making, communicative, and action-oriented) with a range of stake holder roles (initiator, facilitator, contributor and observer). To a limited extent, we could also change the environment - especially group size, location and history. Structure and mechanisms are harder to monitor and control.

The objective of this research methodology was to determine the necessary features and characteristics for each possible combination of contextual variables. Field-testing prototypes under varying circumstances and following up with "thought experiments" was supposed to provide insights into what the key parameters of success may be. We document these insights into design and implementation rules for developers of groupware (that we call assertions). In order to establish face and construct validity, we also undertook a delphi procedure to improve the level of agreement for our assertions. The results of our empirical work are documented in the next section.

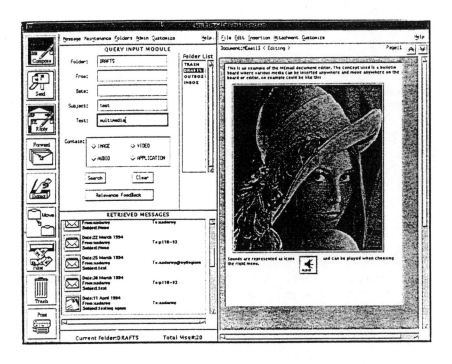

Figure-6: Memail's Control Panel
Incorporating the Query Tool

Despite what may appear to be a factorial design, there is some order in the relationship between the variables that we hope to glean from the exercise. The end-result is some sound and practical guidelines on developing groupware to fit the context.

RESULTS AND DISCUSSION

Preamble

The design and implementation issues for groupware lead to factors that must be considered by developers/configurers of such systems in the context of their applications. The following assertions have been derived using the methodology suggested above. Drawing from Ellis et al. [1991], we categorize them as relating to Group Interfaces, Group Processes, Concurrency Control, (Other) System Issues and Global Considerations.

Group Interfaces

1. The group interface must concentrate on high priority activities and downplay background processes. More specifically, screen space management must optimize the main window while minimizing any interference from secondary or inactive windows. For instance, when co-editing a text/graphics document, having full 320*240 pixel video windows of all participants would be more of a distraction that an aid. Cosmetically, the interface may even be multilingual so as to fit the local context or may adopt icons which are internationally understood.

2. A relaxation of the What-You-See-Is-What-I-See (WYSIWIS) paradigm is conducive to collaboration. Strict WYSIWIS enforces full sharing of group information which may be intrusive. Thus, a relaxation of WYSIWIS is a tradeoff between the individual's privacy and the group's access to shared information. In a global context, it must be borne in mind that the notion of privacy is different, even between Europeans and Americans. Thus, full WYSIWIS, may not be uniformly enforceable.

Group Processes

3. The issue of group awareness generally addresses the "who's doing what" question. Awareness encompasses design of the interface, notification scheme, locking mechanism, granularity and communications channel. Awareness must be set at the right level - too much becomes distracting, too little impedes cooperation. For example, video is useful for establishing authentication but is sometimes an overhead. Likewise, telepointers (cursors which may be manipulated to point to an object of interest on the window that is viewed by the work group) generally increase group

awareness, but for a large group size this can be a nuisance without adequate color coding. In a global context, a video channel may establish authentication and cooperation. Since there is a good chance that participants may have differing linguistic abilities and preferences, facial expressions and gesticulations are important components of communication.

4. The media (i.e. text, graphics, images, audio or video) and the nature of input/output operations must complement each other. In other words, the choice of media used must take into account the nature of the other processes - a text-based communications channel clashes with text-editing whereas "hands free" audio is complementary, or alternatively voice annotations or communications clashing with the editing of sound files. By the same token, if there is a need for real-time language translators or dictionaries, their presentation must complement (not distract) the collaboration.

5. The greater the extent of integration of groupware features - e.g. file formats, interactive help screens, applications switching, dictionaries - the greater will be the propensity for usage. Help screens should be accessible while the group process is going on.

6. Design must take into consideration design process issues such as making it easy to create applications with common features (perhaps through the use of templates as in Lotus Notes). In addition, popular processes should be easy to activate, retrieve and modify (e.g., through the use of desktop icons), while lesser used processes should be hidden in order not to clutter the desktop. This should, ideally, be locally customizable.

7. Designers may want to take into consideration what are the popular "sequences" of tools that a user may engage in, and design applications that run these application of tools. Users who want to use a prearranged sequence of tools can select that option and the system will guide the user through the sequence of tools without further prompting from the user - a user profile of sorts. This option will help novice users get accustomed to groupware.

Concurrency Control

8. Concurrency control is influenced mainly by the parallelizability or serializability of a task. The choice between synchronous and asynchronous groupware is determined by whether or not the task is parallel or serial. For example, work that is divisible into independent modules (e.g. software coding) or is to be performed concurrently by all members of a group (e.g. brainstorming) may be amenable to synchronous collaboration whereas non-interactive communication like e-mail is by nature asynchronous and have

chronological dependencies. The effectiveness of concurrency control is limited if significant contention and coordination effort is required.

9. Floor control policies (like turn-taking) are critical issues in synchronous collaboration. Ineffective or unsuitable floor control introduces contention and requires time-consuming coordination in synchronous group work. On the other hand, the establishment of stakeholder roles (e.g. author-reviewer relations) facilitates asynchronous collaboration. A minor corollary is that members of a group who are separated by over eight time zones effectively do not have the benefit of synchronous collaboration in that they would be working at awkward times for one or all. Under these circumstances, asynchronous tools are better suited.

10. The history of the group is a factor in choosing between technical and social protocols such as presentation and viewing, floor control and turn-taking. Members of a group who are already familiar with each other do not need constraining technical protocols imposed by the system as the existing social norms will prevail. In a global context, it must not appear that the moderators or initiators of the session dominate by virtue of the technology.

Other System Issues

11. The idea of security in groupware is volatile. Privacy and anonymity, for example, are not always desirable as they may be for voting procedures. Anonymity may run counter to "considering the source" during a brainstorming session in that an idea is accepted especially when it comes from an expert. As well, privacy may shield inactive members, therefore complicating credit assignment and reward. Monitoring the performance of individual members of the group is therefore not straightforward and is fraught with cultural and regional practices, and taboos.

12. Notification reduces potential for conflict during groupwork, especially when conveyed prior to finalizing a change or decision. Locking - or preventing others in the group from interrupting a sequence of actions being taken - is a critical issue in action oriented tasks, analogous to floor control in communicative tasks.

Global Considerations

13. In the category of global considerations, the issue that eclipses all other is the necessity of conforming to standards, open systems and interoperability. Bluntly put, groupware in a global dimension will certainly fail if there was not a strict adherence to global standards (such as those directed by the International Standards Organization, International Telecommunications Union or even the Internet Engineering Task Force) and a deep commitment

to open architectures which encourage multi-vendor interoperability. At the simplest of instances, imagine the chaos if there was no Greenwich Mean Time to specify a standard, world-wide reference to time and date!

14. Another unique aspect about global groupware is that - for perhaps the first time in the field of designing information systems - there is a need for instantaneous understanding of differing cultural contexts. Examples include: spoken and written language translators, generally accepted accounting and engineering norms and practices, and even the more subtle expressions of human expression - hand-shaking, waving, kissing and so on. While the use of multimedia channels may be an improvement on text alone in getting around much of these differences, it is possible that despair :-(or happiness :-) or jest ;-) may well be misunderstood via voice and images. An integral challenge to global groupware is therefore to grapple with the differences within the group.

15. While the issue of mobility was not studied in itself, it emerged when a global perspective for groupware was sought. Mobile (or wireless) connections allow access and portability - two issues that are more critical in a global context than a national one.

CONCLUDING REMARKS

We are presently in the process of finalizing our list of design and implementation issues and shall subject them to a Delphi panel for refinements. In a parallel track, we have completed the development / installation of systems in each of the four classes - ME-mail, MacGroupie, Arizona's GroupSystemV, and CommIT - which gave us invaluable insights. Usage experiences and thought experiments enabled us to synthesize our findings. However, more remains to be done.

For example, do windows, icons, menus, pointers and color improve decision-making? And a higher hardware configuration (in terms of CPU, memory, andVDU)? What is the effect of adding multi-media to an e-mail system within an organization? For example, in two independent trials that were completed, observations were made with respect to carrying out a technical conversation and co-editing a file with MacGroupie and CommIT. Involving MBA and undergraduate students, we are currently performing and studying trials of how groups utilize these types of systems and to what effect. Some of the research questions (and answers!) we seek are deliberately basic in nature so as to enable an understanding of what the important questions really are.

Such on-going inter-disciplinary research is necessary to obtain a better understanding of the complex issues surrounding the design and implementation of groupware. The team of researchers involved in this project is now spread over four locations. In MacGroupie, we have a platform that allows the permanent establishment of links between the researchers via the internet. What must follow therefore is sustained use and reporting of experiences.

The findings reported in this chapter are provisional, but they illustrate the nature of the problem. This project is a first and small step in attempting to unravel some of the design and implementation questions that will enable developers of global groupware to better understand the context of group work. In the long term, our results would serve as a starting point to developing tools and environments (perhaps in the form of macros or APIs) that would assist in the prototyping of groupware so as to enable further field trials. Therefore, while the philosopher's stone remains elusive, it must nevertheless be sought. This is an important lesson for systems administrators of global information technology solutions.

The circumstances emerging for global groupware are clear: the post-industrial organization has evolved into an information-based and transnational entity that critically requires interaction within project teams that span time zones and continents. The rapidly increasing maturity and decreasing costs of technology has, by and large, supported this evolution by making computing and communications links feasible solutions for collaborative work. In a global marketplace of deregulation and competition, groupware is emerging as the strategic advantage with which to enjoy economies of scale and stay in tune with worldwide customers. In time to come, the global dimension of groupware might be the single-most fundamental issue that determine its implementation success.

Acknowledgments

This project was funded by an Applied Research grant from the Nanyang Technological University. The principal investigator was Ravi Sharma who was then with the Division of Computer Engineering at NTU. We would like to acknowledge the advice of David Conrath, then a Visiting Professor at the School of Accountancy and Business. We would like to put on record the role played by our undergraduate and postgraduate students - Ng Aik Pin and Ong Yee May for configuring MacGroupie; Foo Ji Bin and Goh Kheng Wee for implementing and testing CommIT; and Daroy Consolador for developing ME-mail - without whom we could not have undertaken the experiments in the first place. We are also grateful to the numerous developers of shareware that were available on the internet which served as invaluable learning and experimental tools.

References
Genral Concepts

CA Ellis, SJ Gibbs and GL Rein, "Groupware: some issues and experiences", *Communications of the ACM*, **34** (1), pp 38-58, January 1991.

S Greenberg, An annotated bibliography of computer supported cooperative work, Research Report, Department of Computer Science, University of Calgary, Alberta, 1993.

I Greif, "Computer Support for Cooperative Office Activities", *Proceedings of the Office Automation Conference*, San Francisco, April 5-7 1982, pp 105-113.

J Grudin, "Groupware and Social Dynamics: eight challenges for developers", *Communications of the ACM*, **37** (1), pp 92-105, January 1994.

K.L. Kraemer and J.L. King, "Computer-Based Systems for Cooperative Work and Group Decision Making," *ACM Computing Surveys*, **20** (2), pp 115-146, June 1988.

JE McGrath, Groups: Interaction and performance, Prentice Hall, Englewood Cliffs, 1984.

JE McGrath and AB Hollingshead, Groups Interacting With Technology, Sage Publications, Thousand Oaks, 1994.

H Mintzberg, The Structuring of Organizations: a synthesis of the Research, Prentice-Hall, Englewood Cliffs, New Jersey, 1979.

JS Olson, SK Card, TK Landauer , GM Olson, T Malone, and J Leggett, "Computer-supported co-operative work: research issues for the 90s", *Behavior and Information Technology*, **12** (2), pp115-129, 1993.

T Rodden, "A survey of CSCW systems", *Interacting with Computers*, **3** (3), pp 319-353, 1991.

W Reinhard, J Schweitzer, Gerd Volksen and Michael Weber, "CSCW Tools: Concepts and Architectures", *IEEE Computer*, **27** (5), pp 28-36, May 1994.

P Wilson, Computer Supported Cooperative Work: an introduction, Kluwer Publishers, Norwell, MA 1991.

Models, Frameworks and Methodology

G.R. Adams and J.D. Schvaneveldt, Understanding Research Methods, Longman, London, 1985.

E. Babbie, The Practice of Social Research [4th edition], Wadsworth Publishing, Belmont, California, 1986.

SR Buckley and DC Yen, "Group Decision Support Systems: Concerns for Success", *The Information Society*, **7**, pp 109-123, 1990.

JA Cannon-Bowers, R Oser and DL Flanagan, "Work Teams in Industry: A Selected Review and Proposed Framework", in Teams: Their Training and Performance, edited by Swezey and Salas, Ablex Publishing, Norwood, New Jersey, 1992.

R Kling and C Dunlop, "Controversies about Computerization and the Character of White Collar Worklife", *The Information Society*, **9** (1), pp 1-29, January-March 1993.

KJ Lyytinen and OK Ngwenyama, "What does Computer Support for Cooperative Work Cooperative Work Mean? A Structurational Analysis of Computer Supported Cooperative Work", *Accounting Management & Information Technology*, **2** (1), pp. 19-37, 1992.

JF Nunamaker, AR Dennis, JS Valacich, DR Vogel, and JF George, "Group Support Systems Research: Experience from the Lab and Field", in Group Support Systems: New Perspectives , edited by LM Jessup and JS Valacich, Macmillan Publishing Company, New York, 1993.

J.V. Saraph, P.G. Benson and R.G. Schroeder, "An Instrument for Measuring the Critical Factors of Quality Management," *Decision Sciences*, **20** (4), p 810-829, Fall 1989.

E Sundstrom, KP De Meuse and D Futrell, "Work Teams: applications and effectiveness", *American Psychologist*, **45** (2) pp 120-133, February 1990.

E Trist, "Collaboration in Work Settings: A Personal Perspective", *Journal of Applied Behavioral Science*, **13** (3), pp 268-278, 1977.

E. Trist, "The evolution of socio-technical systems: a conceptual framework and an action research program," Issues in the Quality of Working Life Ocasional Paper # 2, Ontario Ministry of Labour, Toronto, June 1981.

Applications / Case Studies

L Chidambaram and WG Chismar, "Telecommunications Technologies: Use and Investment Patterns in US Multinational Corporations", Journalof Global Information Management, 2 (4), pp 5-17, Fall 1994.

H Lewe and H Kremar, "The Design Process for a Computer-Supported Cooperative Work Research Laboratory: The Hohenheim CATeam Room", *Journal of Management Information Systems*, **8** (3), pp 69-85, Winter 1991.

TW Malone, C Fry and KY Lai, "Experiment with Oval: A Radically Tailorable Tool for Cooperative Work", *CSCW '92 - Proceedings of the Conference on Computer Supported Cooperative Work*, pp 289-297, Toronto, 31 October - 4 November 1992.

Enabling Technologies - Networks and Distributed Computing

H Ricke and J Kanzow (editors), BERKOM - Broadband Communication within the Optical Fibre Network, R. v. Decker's Verlag, Heidelberg, 1992.

JA Short, E Williams and B Christie, The social psychology of telecommunications, Wiley, London, 1976.

A Sinha, "Client-Server Computing: Current Technology Review, *Communications of the ACM*, **35** (7), pp 77-98, July 1992.

Enabling Technologies - Multimedia Systems

SA Bly, SR Harrison and S Irwin, "Media Spaces: Bringing People Together in a Video, Audio and Computing Environment", *Communications of the ACM*, **36** (1), pp 28-47, January 1993.

D Le Gall, "MPEG: a video compression standard for multimedia applications", *Communications of the ACM*, **34** (4), pp 46-58, April 1991.

S Loeb, "Architecting Personalized Delivery of Multimedia Information", *Communications of the ACM*, **35** (12), pp 39-50, December 1992.

Enabling Technologies - Group Interfaces and Computer Human Interaction

R.W. Bailey, Human Performance Engineering: a guide for system designers, Prentice-Hall, Engelwood Cliffs, 1982.

P Dourish and V Bellotti, "Awareness and Coordination in Shared Workspaces", *CSCW '92 - Proceedings of the Conference on Computer Supported Cooperative Work*, pp 107-114, Toronto, 31 October - 4 November 1992.

R Hellman, "Combining CSCW and user support techniques to design collaborative user interfaces", *Interacting with Computers*, **4** (1), pp 41-67, 1992.

SECTION-6

Global Information Technology
Strategy and Management

Choosing an appropriate IT strategy and structure to match the business mission of a multinational company is not an easy task. One way to understand this relationship clearly is to examine how information technology can support a specific functional area of the corporation, or how it can support a critical activity. This is the approach taken by Sirkka Jarvenpaa, Blake Ives, and Keri Pearlson who present a chapter on how IT can aid companies in the computer and communications industry in providing the high level of customer service and support required for any successful company. A more theoretical discussion of this question is presented by Peter Hagström who takes the view that the purpose of the IT infrastructure in the multinational enterprise is to serve as a "service delivery" platform, thereby aiding grand strategy. In order to see the varying texture of this problem, one might apply the "GLITS" model which has been developed by Prashant Palvia and is presented herein. This model allows key information strategists in a multinational enterprise to work through a series of analyses which will create a clear picture of the most effective ways to use IT in global strategy. The model is capable of being extended to include even more variables and factors as they are identified and developed.

22 Global Customer Service for the Computer and Communications Industry

Sirkka L. Jarvenpaa[1]
University of Texas

Blake Ives
Southern Methodist University

Keri Pearlson[2]
University of Texas

Global customer support is emerging as an important part of the competitive strategy of multinational firms and will become important for many others in the near future. Information technology is a critical enabler of information and knowledge flows allowing a supplier organization to quickly and flexibly respond to the demands of its global customers. Information technology can be also a catalyst for new organizational designs that can be focused towards customer support. Here we present a set of requirements elicited from global customers of computer and communications firms. We conclude with alternative ways that supplier firms address such requirements through the use of organizational design and information technology.

INTRODUCTION

"There are no vendors that can effectively service firms of our size on an international scale. They can handle corporate giants, but not the mid-sized firms. Every vendor is a collection of national subsidiaries. I am virtually at war with them. In the U.S., our primary computer vendor sees me to be a significant customer, but to their office in Singapore I am just a flea on a gnat's bottom. Nevertheless, that midsize computer in Singapore is an integral part of our worldwide network" (Chief Information Officer of a Fortune 500 Company).

"At stake is a fast-growing $10 billion market in private networks for large corporations that want telephone and computer links between their offices on different continents. These customers increasingly want to buy their services in a single package from a single vendor, rather than dealing with an international patchwork of private and government-run telecommunications carriers" (*New York Times*, June 3, 1993, page A1).

As firms with operations in several countries transform themselves into an integrated whole, their buying decisions will increasingly be based on how they are served globally by their suppliers. They will seek suppliers who can treat them as a single global entity and provide them with consistent and cost effective service that spans national borders (Daniels and Daniels, 1993). A supplier must be able to quickly respond to an inquiry on the customer's worldwide business with the supplier, discuss the customer's local position anywhere in the world, handle global supplier-related problems, and make a last minute reallocation from one customer factory to another. Firms who can not provide worldwide support will lose customers to suppliers who can. The supplier who can carefully interweave their international customer service strategy with appropriate organizational design, control and incentive mechanisms, as well as globally integrated databases and communication systems will have a decisive advantage over firms that continue to preside over a loose federation of national customer service units.

In the past, not meeting international support requirements usually meant a relatively small lost exporting opportunity. Now the threat is the potential loss of a sizable share if not the entire worldwide account. A corporate customer recently compared the reactions of two value-added telecommunications suppliers who had been asked to put together a global electronic mail network. According to a manager, "Our regular supplier spent a few minutes pulling together a list of office phone numbers for their foreign subsidiaries and wished us good luck. The second firm offered to handle the complete job, from specification to training and installation in all of our remote locations. Guess who got the job, and a big share of our domestic business?"

In Europe, Citibank refused to sign separate computer service contracts with the same supplier in different countries. Instead they signed up with a new vendor, Phillips, that offered a unified sales and support strategy for the 650 offices of Citibank's European consumer banking network (Financial Times, 1992). Similarly, as Unilever adopted a global strategy for its deployment of systems, they demanded from Hewlett Packard a single worldwide contact point (Financial Times, 1992). According to Unilever management, the vendor's single global contact point reduces the customer's administrative costs, allows economies of scale in purchasing, promotes compatibility in purchased services and products between countries, and makes global integration of a customer's operations more likely.

The Challenge for the Suppliers

Integrated global customer service presents major challenges even for suppliers that have operated internationally for years. Various country units value particular elements of customer service differently. Kanter (1991) found that while U.S. managers rated customer service as the most important element, West German and Japanese managers, respectively, thought that work force skills and product development were more important than customer service. Country units with their own profit and loss accountability and parochial marketing organizations see little incentive to coordinate across borders. Each country unit's customer, order, and sales support information systems have likely evolved independently and differ markedly in functionality, data structures, hardware platforms, and even in the ways the customer is identified. Even in the domestic context, marketing and customer service systems are notorious for being local standalone entities that do not integrate with the organization's other systems such as manufacturing, finance, or engineering (Li et al, 1993).

Integration is also hampered by language diversity, geographical distance, the regulations of various host governments including different accounting and tax rules, and so on. Some country units may have also benefited from disparities in pricing structures from one country to another. Disparities motivate the sister units with lower prices to steal business from the firm's other units, resulting in highly competitive and hostile relationships. For example, Polaroid Corporation was integrating its order management systems in Europe partly in response to remarketers who have purchased Polaroid Film in one market and resold it to others, gaining a profit from disparities in Polaroid's pricing policy or its slowness to respond to currency fluctuations (Linder, 1990).

Servicing a global customer requires broad worldwide access to knowledge about, and accountability for, the customer that is scattered throughout the firm. There must be individuals responsible for dealing with key customers on a global basis. Billing systems will have to be able to handle payments stretched out through time, originating from many sources, and potentially paid in various currencies. Databases must record detailed buying habits of the customer's different units. Electronic highways must ferry structured and unstructured messages between customer account personnel and the firm's other staff worldwide. The firms must be able to help a customer learn about solutions already employed by the same customer or by other customers elsewhere in the world. Similarly, specialized expertise, even if located at some relatively remote location of the firm, should be readily available to customers. Providing such far reaching integrative, yet intimate services may be a competitive advantage today, but it will be a competitive necessity in tomorrow's global marketplace (Treacy and Wiersema, 1994). For example, the computer maker, Dell, plans to become the "Nielsen" of the computer business. By using new systems to track customers' detailed buying habits anywhere in the world, Dell hopes to anticipate the customers' needs and thus market products they are most likely to purchase (Sager, 1994).

Supporting integrated global customer service requires major transformations in organizations. It requires new organizational forms and structures; it requires information and communication technologies to enable daily effective functioning of those new forms; and it requires revamping the compensation schemes to motivate and reward new behaviors. According to the CIO of 3M, a lot of people within the firm would like worldwide information on key customers, but no one is providing it because there are no individuals with direct business accountability for the worldwide customer set (Flax, 1992).

A Definition of Global Customer Service

We begin with a definition of global customers and customer service. First, "global customers" are multinational organizations, or consuming entities, that have interdependent needs in multiple countries. This is different than a customer with operations in multiple nations around the globe that do not interact with each other. Hence, a global customer has intertwined business processes that cross country boundaries. Second, "customer service" refers to all customer-specific marketing, sales, and service activities including order management, service delivery and after sale service.

Global Customer Service

Among the first to focus executives' attention to customer service on a broad scale were Peters and Waterman in their book In Search of Excellence (1982). They found most of the excellent companies they studied were "obsessed with service." Writing five years later, Tom Peters, in *Thriving on Chaos*, extolled executive leaders to "launch a customer revolution." In 1992, in his book on *Liberation Management*, Peters challenged firms to build symbiotic relationships and intimately intertwine with customers.

The customer is increasingly seen as the most valuable asset an organization has. A recent Computer Sciences survey of information system managers at U.S. and European corporations found that customer service is the No. 1 focus of their companies' investments in technology (Computer Sciences Corporation, 1994). Although these and other works about managing customers report on service strategies in multiple countries, they do not specifically address the unique environment of global customers.

Much of the global marketing research published in the 1970s and 1980s considered how an organization might market to customers in foreign countries (e.g., Wiklund, 1987; Kaynak, 1985). Classic studies analyzed topics such as global convergence and commonality of products, global business and marketing strategies, and global trends in specific markets (e.g., Levitt, 1986; Yip, 1992). Heskett (1986) considers the multinational development of service industries as a global trend whereby domestic service companies expand their market through multi-national expansion. Unfortunately, little of the work to date considers the unique aspects of the role of advanced technologies in managing the necessary information flows of a company servicing global customers.

In the domestic context, a few studies postulate the future impact of information technologies on marketing such as those included in Robert Buzzell's anthology of landmark works, *Marketing in an Electronic Age* (1985).

Buzzell presents a marketing scenario for 10 years in the future that is ladden with hypothetical information systems to aid marketing activities. This work describes two types of marketing information systems: sales and distribution systems and marketing decision support systems. However, these information systems are discussed in the context of supporting domestic marketing activities rather than international customer service activities. Similarly, a more recent book, *The Marketing Information Revolution* by Blattberg, Glazer, and Little (1994), presents a wealth of information technology solutions in marketing and customer activities in U.S. operations, but no chapter explicitly addresses the information technology solutions in service of global customers.

A few writings in the information technology literature echo the importance of IT in enabling global customer integration. According to Roche (1992) "Information technology enables a company to present one consistent face to (global) customers, view the total relationship with key customers and mobilize worldwide resources quickly to meet customer needs. Digital Equipment Company, for example, uses electronic mail and electronic conferencing to assemble service teams worldwide. Digital can locate service personnel for any problem and put them to work on it immediately" (p. 371). In the 1993 writing, Roche similarly provides examples of the use of technology in service of global customers. In one case, United Technologies Automotive devised an information technology strategy to link together 130 manufacturing locations around the world in order to service Ford Motor Company, an important customer that had interdependent needs across its own global operation.

There are a number of case studies that deal with the requirements of global customers and their suppliers' plans to meet the new emerging requirements (see Keen et al, 1982; Ives and Jarvenpaa, 1992; Ives and Jarvenpaa, 1994; Reponen and Copeland, 1985; Jarvenpaa and Tuomi, 1995). A number of authors also discuss how the suppliers' inability to provide global customer support was a barrier for customer organizations' global plans (Ives and Jarvenpaa, 1991; Steinbart and Nath, 1992).

The Global Customer

Globally competing firms in the transportation, financial services, management consulting, and semiconductor firms must pay close attention to the service needs of their worldwide customers. They can do so in either *reactive* or *proactive* mode.

There are five interrelated conditions under which a supplier is likely to find itself *reactively* responding to the requirements of global customer service. The first condition involves customers seeking to transform themselves into transnational firms. This means that the customer is trying to reengineer its own business processes for global operations. For example, Electronic Data Systems (EDS) was driven to move from a regionalized business strategies to global and transnational as its clients became increasingly transnational in their operations (Financial World, 1993).

The second condition for reactive response is when customers optimize the use of a resource on a global scale. This is less often seen in business processes than in administrative processes such as the customer seeking one common billing statement or global volume discounts and price agreements. It does not take long to realize how the supplier's lack of integration will constrain the customer's own integration attempts. Dougherty et al (1992) found that firms that had integrated their own logistics operations were found to be able to handle integrated requests better from their customers than those that had not integrated their own operations.

The third condition is when a customer has worldwide total quality programs in place. These programs force customers to examine and manage their relationships across the company. Customers want, and may require, their vendor to assist their global efforts. For example, JcPenney uses color fax technology with its Far East suppliers to increase the quality of its international merchandise.

A fourth condition is when worldwide demand begins to emerge for a product that was initially intended to be offered only in limited markets. For instance, the Internet's worldwide web provides an inexpensive distribution channel, but one that, because of its worldwide reach, may exceed a firm's ability to actually deliver products or services.

The fifth condition is when the customer's own customers meets any of the above four conditions. It is only a matter of time until the pressure reaches the supplier organization. Exhibit 1 contains a list of questions to begin to identify if a company' or its customers will begin exerting pressure to provide global customer service.

Firms can also take a *proactive* stance and differentiate themselves via global customer service, particularly in new niche markets. For instance, QAD, a software company with headquarters in the United States, designed their manufacturing, financial, and distribution management software to focus on integrated global companies whose requirements were not satisfied by regionally focused software vendors. The manufacturing and distribution

---

• Are they becoming transnational firms?
• Does scale/scope matter to them?
• Do they have total quality management programs?
• What are their customers doing?
• What are their and our competitors doing?

Exhibit 1: Will Customers Force Integrated Customer Service?

---

management software system runs on a wide range of platforms from personal computers to networks, in mini- and mainframe environments, and under a variety of operating systems. The product provides multiple currency transactions, support for local tax structures, and concurrent multiple language capability. QAD specifically designs its products for the global market place, that is for transnational firms who have dispersed their value chain internationally. This approach to designing software is different from the more usual approach of releasing the software first in one market and then after additional changes (" internationalizing the product") release it in other countries.

Exhibit 2 illustrates business visions of companies that emphasize global customer service in their strategies. A logistics firm, for example, imagines itself eventually acting as the logistics arm for global customers. This vision is described as a "partnership between us and the customer to manage the customer's total costs and quality of the logistic pipeline."

There is also a major indirect benefit from focusing on global customer service. Global customer service is an external business driver and hence can be communicated as a more compelling force for organizational change than internal drivers such as economies of scale or risk reduction (Ives et al, 1993). Given that the legacy of the multinational firm is often the highest barrier to global coordination, the most fertile field for initial global coordination activities often lies at the global customer's feet. Meeting the needs of these increasingly important customers can begin to build much needed collaboration within the supplier organization. Specific country unit resistance to common customer support applications may be relatively low if their own large corporate customers are expecting to be treated as a single worldwide entity. Country unit managers see that they will reap the benefits of a coordinated approach. The requirements (or demands) of just one major customer can be enough to overcome organizational inertia. Customer requirements for consistent products can later be used to fuel the drive for information systems in support of worldwide procurement, human resources management, logistics, and globally integrated engineering.

In summary, to some suppliers, the need for globally integrated customer service will come as a mandate from their globally competing customers. To others, this force presents an opportunity. Customers facing information intensive activities, complex products, untrained workers, and limited information processing resources quickly and recurringly respond to a helpful supplier's well conceived notions of assistance. Domestic customers that seek global expansion might be a better starting point for some suppliers than established international customers. As we have noted above, resistance to integration is more likely among firms used to operating internationally but autonomously. Consequently, the supplier's integration efforts might be seen by a customer firm's subsidiary managers as leading down a path towards internal centralization and loss of local control. Newly globalizing firms might be better able to see the added value and therefore be willing to pay for 'soft' support services from suppliers.

Publishing	**Logistics**
We want our customer to be able to call their local Singaporean book store and get the latest status information on availability and orders on books and magazines being printed in the U.S. and England. Our firm's global reach must be available to the customer with a single phone call. Today a librarian placing orders with our firm has to go directly to each business unit.	We want to be our customer's logistics expert, managing from an intial order, the demands for raw material, manufacturing work-in-process and finished goods inventories and delivery to a customer. Our customer has within its figure tips a fully integrated worldwide network that ties, customers, warehousing, and logistics in 78 countries. All the information on the customer is in one place.

Engineering	**Chemicals**
Our objective is to design and manufacture on a worldwide basis to be able to offer the least cost structure to our customers. Transparent to the customer, an engineer located in the U.S. or Europe could be working on any Asian project at anytime. This will help us to leverage the talent and expertise residing in our larger organization for the benefit of a customer.	We want to be able to give a remote mining operator in our Peruan site, within 24 hours, whatever pertinent information we have within the company worldwide so that he can readily satisfy the customer's request.

Exhibit 2: Four Global Customer-Based Visions of Multinational Firms

Global Customer Requirements in the Computer and Communications Industry

The four industries most often associated with the global customer support are computer and communication companies, transportation suppliers, integrated logistics providers, financial services, and advertising firms. In the short run, the suppliers that are likely to find the greatest opportunity, as well as pressure, to provide global customer service include suppliers of components or raw materials for which there are opportunities to achieve global economies of scale (i.e, computer chips, aviation fuel). It will also include providers of the means to global integration and coordination. Among this latter group are professional firms and providers of information technology and communications.

One might expect the computer and communications industry to be at the forefront of this transformation to customer service for global corporations. After all, the communication and information technology have been the drivers of globalization in many industries such as transportation and financial services. Others have presented information technology as the glue of global coordination and control that will link the transnational organizations across national borders (Keen, 1991; Feeny et al, 1990; Reck, 1989). Surely if information technology is to make global integration a reality, then the suppliers of that technology must be prepared to support their own emerging global customers.

U.S. Multinational's Satisfaction With Their IT Vendors

A field study of 20 U.S. multinationals (Ives and Jarvenpaa, 1991) surfaced the lack of vendor support as a significant problem for the executives charged with managing information technology on a global scale. IBM was the most common primary computer vendor of the 20 companies' international IT activities. But customers' frustrations mirrored IBM's difficulties in coordinating its operations globally with an organization structure designed from a confederation of national business units that have historically enjoyed considerable autonomy. Historically IBM innovations tended to be developed in the U.S. and then were exported to the relatively autonomous IBM country units. Each country unit modified the innovation to meet anticipated local requirements and after some delay, introduced it in the local marketplace. The delays, inconsistencies, and unavailable products and services had been agonizing to IBM customers seeking to establish worldwide integrated systems.

These problems were by no means unique to IBM. They were shared widely by hardware, software, and communications vendors mentioned in our interviews. The senior information technology executives who oversaw the acquisition and purchase of hardware and software for global use expressed the following types of complaints:

"IBM, DEC, and HP have put together an international group to serve their large global customers. But little customers are not going to get access to these groups."

"IBM has separate P&L sheets in each country so there is little incentive for them to respond to the needs of the greater organization."

IBM developed OS in six languages - one of them was Spanish which I can speak. Our operations staff included a Colombian, Chilean, and a Bolivian, all fluent in Spanish. None of us could figure it out. I went up to World Trade IBM and asked them what language the OS-Spanish version was. My operations around the world are now using the English language version."

"The biggest problem is the cost and availability of parts. The problems are accentuated by government limitations on importation and exportation, dollar quotas, long delays, and lead times."

"Some of the dealers selling the vendor offerings double or triple the price of the software on overseas markets."

"When the vendor has their own branches in overseas locations, you can push for worldwide support. In Malaysia we don't do much business with a particular vendor but we have lots of worldwide clout so we get pretty good local support when we need it. But, that strategy doesn't work if you are dealing through local agents rather than the vendor's own branch offices."

Similar results were accumulated from a study of 108 U.S. headquartered companies (Jarvenpaa and Ives, 1993). The responding firms represented diversity in industries, in size, and in international coverage. Two firms operated in over 160 countries, but the typical respondent operated in 20 to 40 countries.

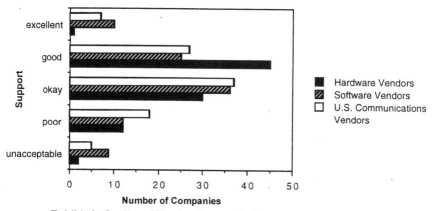

Exhibit 3: Quality of Vendor Support in International IT Activities

The survey found moderate satisfaction among the customer firms. Major U.S. hardware vendors were seen to provide better global support than major U.S. software companies. Generally, hardware vendor support was related as "good," whereas software vendor support was more likely to be described as "okay" (Exhibit 3). Lack of adequate copyright protection, incompatibility, multiple languages, currency conversions, multiple versions of software releases, and unreliable local dealers produced a minefield of dissatisfying experiences. Similar problems among the often highly regulated telecommunications providers had led to considerable disenchantment among multinationals who are critically dependent on international information technology to manage their operations in a globally coordinated manner. The customers complained about the ability of the U.S. telecommunication vendors to develop partnerships with foreign-based state owned telecommunication authorities (so called PTTs).

The survey ratings may have over-estimated levels of satisfaction. Although customers request global customer assistance, in many instances expectations were so low that virtually any type of support resulted in moderate satisfaction. The firms most dissatisfied were either mid-sized multinational firms changing their business approach from a multidomestic to a transnational strategy, or small firms moving into foreign markets. New innovative, information-based, support structures and organizational arrangements are needed to meet the requirements of this new cadre of global customers.

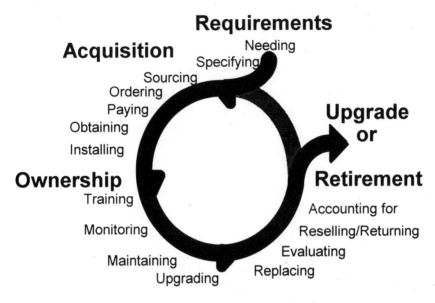

Exhibit 4: The Customer Service Life Cycle

Using the Customer Service Life Cycle Framework[3]

The Customer Service Life Cycle, or CSLC, Framework formulated by Ives and Learmonth (1984) looks at the product or service being provided from the perspective of a customer's interfacing processes with a supplier. This perspective includes the following steps: assist the customer in specifying, acquiring, owning, or disposing of the product or other resources used in conjunction with the product or service. The CSLC, in Exhibit 4, depicts the subprocesses that a customer traverses from initial realization of the need for a product/service, through to its acquisition, ownership, and eventual retirement. The CSLC framework can be used to envision new ways to use information to augment a service or product.

The Requirements Stage: In the requirements phase, the customer realizes the need for a product/service and specifies the requirements on a worldwide basis. Here is an example of such a need expressed by an international bank on its electronic funds transfer system:

"The electronic payment system will pull the multinational bank's existing clearings   into one integrated position...The system will improve the bank's capabilities for risk management and funds management, and gives Treasurers immediate visibility of the bank's overall position... In the future, the system will need to support real-time gross settlement.The system will use internationally compatible message formats and protocols for EDI... The system provides both English and Arabic user-interface support."

The emphasis in the first stage is on recognizing and specifying both the global and local needs. Global customers are looking for a partner that can inform, educate, and advise on the requirements, "We want the supplier to work with us in helping us understand our requirements and alternative solutions." Customers want the vendor to provide differing levels of support from one country to another in identifying requirements, "Our own operations vary in expertise. We need different levels of hand holding from one country to another." Customers also stress timely response to international requirements, "Our vendor has global electronic mail and videoconferencing, but for account representatives to get their peers to response in other countries, they have to get on the phone and on the plane."

Customers setting up worldwide systems tend to look for products and services that share the same functionality and quality no matter in which country they are acquired. But they also seek the ability to customize products to the local environment (e.g., different keyboard requirements, software interfaces in different languages, training courses). Customers complain about the vendor's local representatives wanting to modify the software further resulting in incompatibilities of products across countries, "There is a pride of ownership at the local sites; they want to put their own handprints on the offerings." Barring legal regulations, customers expect the vendor to be able to sell a product it has developed elsewhere in the world. Customers also expect cosmopolitan and bilingual vendor personnel,

"After two years we had still not gotten the vendor to find us a single bilingual consultant. They agreed to give us a software version in Japanese - but have only just delivered that. The costs have been far higher than we anticipated. We faced one situation where one of their consultants went into a country and left us with a $5,000 telephone bill."

Exhibit 5 presents some of the support requirements of global customers at the Requirements Stage.

The Acquisition Stage: Having made the decision to acquire the product or service, the customer becomes involved in acquisition: sourcing, ordering, paying, obtaining, and installing. For the acquisition steps, customers expect the supplier to provide global planning, negotiation, and ordering, but local implementation and country-based billing. This requires the establishment of a worldwide customer identity to ensure a single vendor image for sourcing, pricing, ordering, order tracking, and contract negotiations. Customers relate stories where local vendor representatives are unwilling to push the sale politically upwards to headquarters for a more competitive bid reflecting the customers' worldwide buying power. Customers also expect multilingual and multicurrency support throughout the acquisition step. A customer recalled, "When we said 'bid' the local vendor representative could not comprehend beyond price. But, what we were talking about included the terms of the agreement, service level guarantees, problem escalation processes, etc."

CSLC Activity	Support Requested by Global Customers
Needing	Global view of the customer's use of vendor solutions (i.e., helping the customer see the global applicability of vendor solutions)
	Worldwide directory of vendor's products
	Differentiated help, as needed, in each country (i.e., the level and degree of vendor support match the customer need for support)
	Vendor's knowledge of customer's relative competitive position in using vendor's products (i.e., use of the vendor intelligence to understand whether the customer is trailing or leading in the use of certain technologies)
	Vendor support at customer's headquarters city despite it not being an international city such as New York or Los Angeles (i.e., the existence of global support in the customer's headquarters despite where it might be)
	Flexibility in vendor relationships (i.e., formal contracts provide a flexible working framework)
	Cosmopolitan and multilingual account team (i.e., vendor representatives are globally trained and experienced)
Specifying	Vendor participation in key management meetings of a customer (for example, for joint requirements development)
	Knowledge of local environment and regulations (e.g., power and safety requirements, laws)
	Worldwide directory of products and services by country and their availability to customers in other countries

Exhibit 5: Customer Support Needs at the Requirements Stage of the CSLC

Vendors are also expected to take an order in one location for delivery in another, including a delayed commitment for a delivery point. One executive remarked, "We want to plan in Belgium, install locally, and pay on a country-by-country or region-by-region basis. The vendor must be able to handle the account balances internally." Customers are also looking for suppliers that will partner if necessary with other suppliers to provide a customer with a one stop shopping environment. One customer, for example, described his vision for the installation of a worldwide private network: "I would like to place an order with one service provider and that provider places orders with all the necessary parties, coordinates schedules, install, bills, and maintains the service."

Customers also expect the application of international volume discounts and global license agreements covering all major countries where it does business. Customers complain bitterly about the idiosyncratic country-based pricing schemes and the difficulty of getting suppliers to base volume discounts on total yearly purchases rather than by purchases made by product category within a single country unit. According to one executive, "We would like to have consistent pricing around the world. Pricing of identical equipment varies beyond monetary reasons such as cost of doing business, shipping costs, exchange rates, etc. The pricing has to do with the vendor's market position and strategy in a particular country. There has been little thought given to the requirements of a multinational customer."

The Ownership Stage: In the ownership step, the customer seeks support for changes in status, the need for upgrades, monitoring operations, continuous maintenance, training, documentation etc. Customers look for consistent maintenance regardless of location (see Exhibit 7). Maintaining high quality standards often means "big favors in out-of-the-way places." It sometimes means being willing to support technology produced by other vendors. Some vendors use "flying consulting teams" to ensure smooth and timely software upgrades at a customer's sites. Customers desire a global 24-hour help desk to provide access to the best expertise the firm has to offer. Worldwide service level agreements should be translated to local language and local work practices to ensure consistent look and feel. For example, one customer illustrated how the same vendor instructions resulted in a four-hour installation in U.K and Germany and two-day installation in Italy. Several executives have commented that while the vendors are eager to agree to common service principles, there are always major discrepancies in practice. The account management team in the parent company seems to have little ability to enforce common practices on their foreign counterparts. Consequently, according to one manager, "We have to make different kinds of demands in different countries to get the same level of service."

In fact, we were told that while the management instructions from the firm's headquarters tend to travel well outward to the local level, they travel less effectively the other way around. This causes problems as customers try to escalate a problem from the local office to the corporate level. Two customers, however, stressed that although a cross-border escalation procedure needs to be

CSLC Activity	Support Requested by Global Customers
Sourcing	Physical presence in the customer's major foreign locations
	Global discount schemes that are enforced from country to country
	Logical and consistent pricing between vendor divisions (reduce the incentive to shop among the supplier's divisions for price breaks)
	Global customer identification (i.e., treating the customer as one global entity)
	Global offering of ancillary and third-party services (e.g., a large hardware vendor agreeing to partner with a small software vendor and take liability in the case of failure of the smaller partner
	Globally integrated inventory information on products and services
	Worldwide directory of sales agents and account managers
	Consistent and compatible products and services that are scalable to fit to the size of a particular country
Ordering	A single global order point (a customer can submit one order that covers many diffe countries)
	Global order tracking system (one single vendor contact point can inform the status an order or a set of orders that covers a customer's different country units)
	Ordering in one country and delivery in another (i.e., being able to order from one country goods to be installed in another)
	Delayed commitment for delivery (at the time of the order, the delivery date is not specified)
Negotiating and paying	Global proposals (i.e., ability to generate proposals quickly that include input as we as consensus/agreements from key vendor personnel from all impacted countries)
	Single (corporate) representative for negotiation, yet local execution of the contract
	International volume pricing discounts applied consistently across all countries
	Worldwide site licenses which do not penalize a customer that has a decentralized organization structure (i.e., many independent but related businesses around the wor
	Ability to deal with multiple currencies (i.e., billing at different local currencies eve in cases where the order is submitted centrally at one vendor's location)
	Local sales people understand and are motivated to achieve global account objective
Obtaining	Close to simultaneous global release of products and services
Installation	Intimate and seamless partnerships with local firms
	Uniform quality and time standards for installments across countries

Exhibit 6: Customer Support Needs at the Aquisition Stage of the CSLC

formalized in the contracts, it should not replace relationship building on the local level. "For responsive customer service, it is important to encourage the people at the local level to first deal with the problems."

The use of distributors by vendors in countries with limited market opportunities presents problems. Customers want their vendors to have a better knowledge of, as well as a partnership with, their distributors. In one instance, a manager remarked, "One of our software vendors doesn't have a big enough work force to have a presence everywhere where we have significant operations. Rather, they work through independent distributors. The problem is that the vendor can't bring enough pressure to bear on the distributor. We get sloppy software and sloppy service."

Many acknowledge that vendors, particularly hardware vendors are sufficiently better than 10 years ago. Positive changes include online documentation, online databases on most frequently asked questions, electronic mail, fax, global account managers, online catalogs of products, online ordering capability, etc. One customer noted, "the vendor's use of technology is starting to help, but the quality of customer service is still really dependent on the quality of the account manager. In our case, we have an account manager serving us who has done a terrific job finding out about our business and communicating to our key stakeholders around the world. Since he came on board, the service has been 300% better I have seen him mobilize resources that I would not have thought were possible."

The Retirement Stage: For the last step, retirement, customers looked for discounts on upgrades and consulting help on replacement timing and next generation technologies. Multinationals sometimes sought to resell the technology solution to another site within a firm that was less technologically advanced. However, the vendors representatives in the recipient countries tended to see this as lost revenue rather than building the goodwill of the customer.

Exhibit 8 summarizes the salient dimensions that emerged from eliciting requirements for global customer service. Customers expect globally consistent or compatible products and services that can be ordered any place with the appropriate multilingual and multicurrency support. Customers also expect "hand-holding" in defining and managing the order. More and more customers are also expecting to have their vendors confirm to world-wide service and support standards.

Most vendor companies are far from meeting the above requirements. Many large customers appear to have created their own ways of coordinating hardware and software purchases globally. Some have global internal support groups that buy hardware and software centrally and then distribute it throughout the firm's global operations. These same groups are also flying around the world to perform major implementation and upgrade activities. Others compensate for the lack of support in building slack in schedules and resources. A few have to make alternative technology architecture decisions because of unsatisfactory vendor support.

CSLC Activity	Support Requested by Global Customers
Training and use	Consistent look and feel of product or service regardless of location Ability to adapt to local requirements
Maintaining	Worldwide service level standards Local support by local people Cross border mechanism for political and technical escalation (pushing the problems up the management chain to the regional and global level) Willingness to support products and services of third parties that are used in conjunction with vendor's products Ability to quickly mobilize vendor resources in country where a customer has a small presence and hence a small count with a vendor Seamless communication flow across vendor divisions
Upgrading	The same as in 'training and use' and in 'maintaining'

Exhibit 7: Customer Support Needs at the Ownership Stage of the CSLC

> • Consistent product and service offerings
> • Multilingual, multicurrency support
> • Worldwide discount structure
> • Expertise, central planning, but local delivery
> • Worldwide ordering, order tracking, billing
> • Quality tracking data
> • Big favors in out of the way places
> • Worldwide service standards
> • Local support and tailoring

Exhibit 8: Global Customer Expectations: Summary

Customers face another dilemma. Many firms are centralizing globally their main computing facilities with data communications and workstations dispersed to each country. This, however, often means that the customer presents even a smaller business base in many local countries. The customer's image diminishes in the eye's of the local vendor organization because of the decreased local revenue stream. One executive explained, "Although we have inexpensive workstations in a particular country, those are as critical as the mainframe would be. The vendor has to fix the workstation or network problems with equal priority as if it were a central mainframe."

Organizational Response to Global Customer Service Requirements

Vendors were found to experiment with three structures to provide globally coordinated service for their largest customers: *international transfers, global account executive, and the global account team.* The first two structures were often present together, the first focuses on socialization as a means of coordination and the second on formalization and centralization. A fourth structure discussed here, the *virtual team*, was not used by any of the suppliers, except in highly exceptional cases. Finally, *information technology* solutions supported these structures by primarily facilitating communications and information flow (informating up or down), not automating or transforming business processes.

International Transfers and Exchanges

International transfers, a common approach to global customer service, was simply to transfer managers between country locations. This simple organizational solution helped to facilitate the formation of an interpersonal network across personnel serving global customers. Senior level account management positions were filled with individuals who had, via extensive transfers and travel, built up a portfolio of management connections in the supplier's foreign locations. They were expected to understand the local culture, be multilingual, and be able to deal with people from various backgrounds and origins.

The problem with international transfers is the instability of the established network and the increasing psychological and administrative costs of such transfers. Each assignment results in a manager uprooting his or her family and risking a move from a pleasant situation to an unpleasant one. Compensation schemes usually dictate that the manager receive not only his full compensation, but also that the company pay for the employee and family's home leaves as well as services in helping to find schools for children, etc. Moreover, the international service network is then tied to a particular individual. When that individual manager leaves the company so does the established network. Some of the vendors mentioned that because of the belt tightening in their own organizations, transfers and foreign travel had been cut. One manager complained, "Now that we are having expense pressures, some managers who are not used to international deals believe that you can do 100% of your job with email and fax. I spent two years without getting out there and I was 100% more effective once I got out there regularly."

Increasingly, rather than transfers, the vendors used quarterly, twice a year, or yearly global managers' meetings to bring the executives together and share their experiences. These more informal exchanges seem to be good investments for building global networks. Many vendors had regional rather than global international sales meetings if their global customers were regionally rather than globally structured.

Global Account Executive

All the large supplier firms had appointed a senior level manager as the global account executive for the firm's top accounts. This individual had global responsibility for all of a client's sales and service activities around the world. The global account executive provided the client with a single point of contact for their multinational activities. Further, the global account manager was usually located near client headquarters to provide a consistent presence of vendor for senior customer managers. However, a single individual is not a global entity, therefore the global account executive relied on the loyalty of the individual country organizations and the hierarchical power afforded to him or her by virtue of the global position. One manager stated, "the account managers are really general managers who have the corporate power over the local country. They can directly appeal to our executive VPs if the country managers do not cooperate." The obvious advantage to this approach was the customer's perception of a unified, global customer service operation. The customer could deal with the supplier as one entity rather than as many different country-based companies. One company specifically sought for non-home country nationals to serve as global account executives in the headquarters' location.

One manager explained how the structure works in his organization, "The global account executive has to establish yearly international account plans for a multinational client. This provides the basis for each country unit signing up to provide a certain resource to a client and receive a share of the revenue from the client. The account plan is signed off by local country management and the customer management. The plans also prioritize the customer needs and set up 'International Customers Bill of Rights'."

The problem with the global account executive concept appears to be its highly centralized approach. Major decisions are made by one manager who is then also responsible for the surveillance of their execution around the world. This type of personal and direct control reduces responsiveness and flexibility of local units. Moreover, the approach is likely to become ineffective in the highly volatile and complex environments characterized by global markets. Rapidly changing situations require local authority and global coordination of local information and experiences. After all, the global account executive can only be in one place at a time and it is doubtful that one person alone can understand all the facets of the major customer's diverse operations. Moreover, managers, even the best global managers, are known for their nearsightedness; they tend to manage what they know the best, and that typically was the customers closest to home (Ohmae, 1989). This structure also appeared to be fraught with account imbalances between countries that had to be dealt on an exception basis. Some vendors also found customer resistance, "We have heard from customers that they don't always like to go through a single representative. They prefer to work with their local vendor contact. We have to have good relationships between the customer and vendor by country. The account managers should only get involved in problem escalation."

Global Account Team

Whereas the global account executive presents a centralized approach to global service, the global account team represents a cooperative arrangement. We found only one firm having established global account teams that involved a well-defined network of equals assigned to a common task of servicing the customer. The team approach assumes that each major country has an individual who is part of a task force or a team to support the customer. The members of the team are individually responsible for local activities as well as collectively responsible for global coordination. The team appears to the global customer as a single well-defined organization rather than a loosely coupled set of employees who work for the same multinational firm. This team operates as a single unit when global needs emerge and as a collection of individual local units, when local needs are addressed providing both a centralized and a decentralized support structure. This approach promotes hiring nationals in each country unit to provide a local look and using the team and information technology to provide a global look.

The problems with the team approach are the general problems with teams. Additionally, in the global context, the initial investment in socializing and training is more complex than in a domestic context. To be really effective the firm must be equipped with groupware technology to facilitate coordination and communication among team members dispersed around the world. Information technologies must be used to support and replace some of the individual, face-to-face communication for this approach to be workable. In addition, problems arise from individual recognition and compensating the team members for their team activities. One executive explained, "When we were first rolling out global sales teams there was great resistance from the sales people in the UK to work for sales teams elsewhere in the world - they were afraid they would lose compensation. We recognized that we had to balance the targets and bonuses for sales people, that had been traditionally tailored to particular markets. We often have to make a one off payment to ensure equitable rewards for working on a global deal."

Global Virtual Team

A more flexible approach than a permanent global account team is to exploit the concept of a virtual team. A virtual team is comprised of globally dispersed members that are brought together to solve one time customer problems - say to help design a worldwide communications network. The team might meet face-to-face on an occasional basis, but is largely enabled by the use of information and communication technology. Computerized databases serve as the institutional memory of the past customer-supplier exchanges; no longer is the history of the customer relationship tied to any particular employee. The team is constantly evolving; as the needed expertise to solve a customer's problem changes so does the team membership.

Nohria and Eccles (1992) refute the notion that a team can be successful without regular face-to-face contact. They argue that as the use of electronic media increases within the team, so must face-to-face meetings. In their view, electronic media can not substitute, only complement, for social processing that occurs in face-to-face meeting. This was echoed in the vendor interviews, "Videoconferencing will help us tremendously once everyone has it on their desktop and feels comfortable with it. But till then, we need to speak face to face." Nohria and Eccles maintain that electronically-enabled virtual teams can only handle relationships that are "impersonal, unambiguous, standardized, and atomistic." The global customer-supplier exchanges are likely to be just the opposite: ambiguous, uncertain, highly knowledge intensive, and so on. On the other hand, as communications bandwidth increases and becomes less expensive, we will see increasingly more life-like electronic meetings take place.

All the above approaches are certainly costly for a supplier firm. Several suppliers did complain that customers request for integration services, but are not willing to pay for them. Wiersema and Thompson (1991) argue that "adopting a partnering strategy is one way to strike a balance between customers' requirements and willingness to pay for service. Partnering suppliers share data, plans, and forecasts with customers to smooth the relationship and spread out the burden of maintaining information" (p. 10). Anderson and Narus (1991) discuss the pitfalls of partnering from a supplier's point of view.

Information Technology Solutions

In terms of information technology, we heard of little beyond telephone, fax machines, desk top publishing, electronic mail, videoconferencing, and online catalogs or support information on the Internet. One highly centralized global vendor has a global customer database as well as global order management system that is used by all major sites. Another discussed the development of such systems. One vendor discussed their global online proprietary sales directory. Customers could access vendor announcements, product, pricing, and technical help information. Another vendor claimed to have over 60 databases in service of its international sales, " I can access online information such as what is installed for each customer by location, and who the customer's purchasing reps are worldwide. I can find out with a few strokes who the account executive is for a customer in a particular country. There is also a wealth of general information on each country. We also have databases on the available products and services by country and whether ordering requires special permissions. We also have a database of trends by industries by countries." In many companies, the Internet, and particularly the Worldwide Web had became the place to get the most up to date information on the firm. Some were allowing the customer to order hardware, software, and services, configure systems, generate price quotations, and test run products. This had brought in another set of challenges for vendors. Now, their customers were often more up to date with the details of new products than their sales personnel. And, in many instances, product information that was now readily accessible from throughout the world described products that were unique to a particular market.

But, largely global service, if it existed, was provided via manual coordination being stitched together with fax transmissions and plane tickets. This was in dark contrast to domestic service where sophisticated marketing, order fulfillment, and customer service systems existed to provide consistent service within the U.S.

Although interpersonal relations remain as the most important coordination and integration device in a global context, technology should be able to facilitate those relationships. Laptop computers with built-in modems, could let an account representative determine, from the customer's premises, who the customer's account representative is in what country, as well as what products and services are available in a given country, and what services are available through special bidding. Access to local databases of prior purchases by customer location can be another critical source of information that helps a supplier better understand the customer requirements and alternative solutions. For example, a supplier might help the customer see the applicability of solutions already being employed by the customer elsewhere. These electronic highways and global databases will also help to convince the customer of the supplier's global reach and international expertise. For example, videoconference hookups could be used to demonstrate to the potential customers outside the headquarters' market that the specialized expertise located in headquarters' facility is readily accessible to them.

Supporting a global customer can be an expensive proposition for a supplier. Information technology should reduce the cost of coordination and integration. Lower costs should enable firms to provide global services not only to their largest accounts, but to small and midsize customers as well. Dell is investing heavily in a global information system that will, among other things, enable a repairperson or a customer in any country to pull up data on any Dell PC -- in his or her native tongue, including trouble shooting information. Customers can also access online catalogs, order a PC, and receive shipment without ever talking to a salesperson (Sager, 1994).

Building Global Support Structures

Whether to organize around a single global manager, a global account team, or to use the international transfer option is best decided from an analysis of the customer. Customer organizations who have centralized decision making in a single country or location prefer to have a representative of their suppliers at that location. Customers with a more decentralized decision making culture would work best with a vendor team where well-informed vendors are available in each location around the world. Customer organization form is also a factor. Customers with global organizations prefer well-coordinated global customer support, which implies a team or global account manager scenario versus an international transfer scenario. Customers with international, transnational, or multinational organization forms want local vendor support hence a less tightly coupled global account management structure can suffice. The type of customer service requirements is a third factor. Customers may require full scale, occasional help, or product-only service. This factor would help decide what level of organizational structure must be offered to service the customer. Finally, customer size, billings, and frequency of service would be a factor in what customer service support structure to offer. The larger the customer, the larger the billings, or the more frequent the service, the more well coordinated customer service structure is necessary.

There are vendor characteristics which are also factors in deciding which global support structure to offer. Size is an important factor. If the vendor is a relatively small to midsize organization with limited resources, it may not be possible to offer to global customers an account team, rather, the preferred solution might be the global account manager with established reliable contacts in the local area for customers requiring global support. Complexity of the product/service offered is another factor. Complex products tend to require more service than simple products, hence an organization with complex products would need to set up a more elaborate global customer service structure. Exhibit 9 lists both the customer and vendor characteristics that should be considered in deciding the global support structure.

Customer Factors	Company Factors
• Decision Making Authority • Organization Structure and Services • Service Requirements • Size • Billings • Frequency of Service	• Size • Complexity of Products

Exhibit 9: Contingency Factors for Global Customer Service Organizations

Implications for Practice

Below we list implications for managers who understand the urgency of moving toward global customer service.

1. To capture the global customer, a company must begin to look capable of supporting global customers. It is important to have some type of plan, rather than no plan at all, when addressing customers. Creating a vision of how global customers will be supported will help both customers and employees move in that direction.

2. Don't wait for the first mover to move in the industry. Once the first mover has begun to implement global customer service, other competitors will have to offer something bigger, better and probably more expensive. It is important to begin now, and be the first mover. You should also plan to continue to invest to maintain the first mover advantage.

3. A survey of customers of all levels in the company can produce a laundry list of important issues for global customer support. This laundry list is a "where to begin" list. We found that customer "wish lists" were very similar to their "must have list." From such lists, a vision can be developed to address these desires.

4. The emerging worldwide web provides companies in high tecnology industries with a relatively low cost way to provide support information on a worldwide basis. Such opportunities should be exploited, but with the recognition that such information will further raise customer expectations of a consistent worldwide product line and support services.

5. It is not important to provide global customer service today if none of the customers are global customers. It is important to be 1 or 2 steps ahead of those customers, however. By understanding exactly where the customers are headed, it is possible to plan a customer support organization to assist that customer. A basketball player described his success, "I anticipate and go where the ball will be, not where the ball is now." This same philosophy applies to providing world class customer service. Go where the customers are going, not where they are today.

CONCLUSIONS

The need for global customer service is still emerging in many industries. We are rapidly entering a global economy where firms will distribute value chain activities throughout the world. Those globalizing firms, and the global customers they serve, will require and demand global customer service from their suppliers. Firms that are unable to meet those needs will run the risk of losing business from some of their biggest customers. On the other hand, firms that learn to provide integrated global service have an opportunity to pick up market share throughout the world and be pulled by their global customers into new geographical markets. Historically, customer service has been viewed as culturally dependent and therefore to be left to local business units. It should continue to be so for truly local requirements. But customer needs for worldwide consistency and coordination will grow and must be accommodated.

Endnotes

[1] The author was funded by the Center for International Business Education and Research at the University of Texas at Austin and the Faculty Research Grants, Graduate School of Business, University of Texas.

[2] The author was funded by the Faculty Research Grants, Graduate School of Business, University of Texas at Austin.

[3] To understand the needs of global customers in the computer and communications industry, we interviewed senior most IT managers in 22 organizations from many industries including transportation, financial services, high technology manufacturing, consumer product manufacturing (see the interview template in Appendix). These organizations were selected because they were moving toward a transnational form structure and that were in the midst of building global information systems to support their firm's global integration. These customers were in the midst of large global projects that demanded global support from their computer and communications suppliers.

References

Anderson, J. C. and Narus, J.A. "Partnering as a Focused Market Strategy," *California Management Review*, Spring 1991, 95-113.

Blatterberg, R.C., Glazer, R., and Little, J.D.C. *The Marketing Information Revolution*, Harvard Business School Press, Boston, MA, 1994.

Buzzell, R.D. (ed.), *Marketing in an Electronic Age*, HBS Press, Boston, MA, 1985.

Computer Sciences Corp., Cambridge,Mass., Based on 782 survey responses from senior information systems executives, 1994.

Daniels, J.L. and Daniels, N.C. *Global Vision*, McGraw-Hill, Inc, New York, New York, 1993.

Daugherty, P.J., Sabath, R.E., and Rogers, D.S. "Competitive Advantage Through Customer Responsiveness," *Logistics and Transportation Review*, 28, 3 (September 1992), 257-271.

DeMyer, A. "Tech-Talk: How Managers Are Stimulating Global R&D Communication," *Sloan Management Review*, Spring 1991, 49-58.

Financial World, "Blowing through the barrier," 162, 14 (July 6, 1992), 24-26.

Feeny, D., Earl, M., and Stevenson, H. "Information Technology and Global Strategy: From Tradeoffs to Simultaneities," Working Paper, Oxford Institute of Information Management, Templeton College, Oxford OX1 5NY, England, 1990.

Financial Times, "Taking A Global Approach to IT," FinTech Electronic Office, October 7, 1992.

Flax, S. "Gobal IT Without Tears," *Beyond Computing*, an IBM Magazine, August/September 1992, 18-26.

Heskett, J.L. *Managing in the Service Economy*, HBS Press, Boston, MA 1986.

Ives, B. and Jarvenpaa, S.L. "Applications of Global Information Technology: Key Issues for Management," *MIS Quarterly*, March 1991, 33-49.

Ives, B., Jarvenpaa, S.L., and Mason, R.O. "Global Business Drivers: Aligning Information Technology to Global Business Strategy," *IBM Systems Journal*, 32, 1 (1993), 143-161.

Ives, B. and Jarvenpaa, S.L. "Air Products and Chemicals, Inc.: Planning for Global Information Technology," *International Information Systems*, 1,2 (1992), 77-99.

Ives, B. and Jarvenpaa, S.L. "MSAS Cargo: Global Freight Management," in Jelassi, T. and Ciborra, C. (eds.), *Strategic Information Systems: A European Perspective*, 1994.

Ives, B. and Learmonth , G.P. "The Information System as a Competitive Weapon," *Communications of the ACM*, 27, 12 (December 1984), 1193-1201.

Jarvenpaa, S.L. and Ives, B. "Organizing for Global Competition: The Fit of Information Technology," *Decision Sciences*, Spring 1993.

Jarvenpaa, S.L. and Tuomi, I. "Nokia Telecommunications: Redesign of International Logistics," a teaching case study, University of Texas at Austin, MSIS Department, Austin, TX 78712.

Kanter, R. M. "Transcending Business Boundaries: 12,000 World Managers View Change," Harvard Business Review, May-June 1991, 151-164.

Kaynak, E. *Global Perspectives in Marketing*, Praeger Publishers, New York, New York, 1985.

Keen, P.G.W. *Shaping the Future: Business Design Through Information Technology*, Harvard Business School Press, Boston, MA, 1991.

Keen, P.G.W., Bronsema, G.S., and Zuboff, S. "Implementing Common Systems: One Organization's Experience," *Systems, Objectives, and Solutions*, 2 (1982), 125-142.

Leavitt, T. *The Marketing Imagination*, Free Press, New York, New York, 1986.

Li, E.Y., McLeod, R. Jr., and Rogers, J.C. "Marketing Information Systems in the Fortune 500 Companies: Past, Present, and Future," *Journal of Management Information Systems*, Summer 1993, 10, 1, 165-192.

Linder, J. "Polaroid Corporation: Leading from the Back Office," Harvard Business School Case Study, No. 9-191-003.

New York Times, "British-Telecom will Buy 20% Stake in MCI in Big U.S. Foray," June 3, 1993, A1.

Nohria, N. and Eccles, R. "Face-to-Face: Making Network Organizations to Work," Chapter 11 in Nohria and Eccles (eds.), *From Networks and Organizations*, Harvard Business School Press, 1992.

Ohmae, K, "Managing in a Borderless World," *Harvard Business Review*, March-April 1989, 152-161.

Peters, T. and Waterman, R. H. *In Search of Excellence*, Harper and Row, 1982.

Peters, T. *Liberation Management*, Alfred A. Knopf, New York, New York, 1992.

Peters, T. *Thriving on Chaos*, Alfred A. Knopf, New York, New York, 1987.

Reck, R.H. "The Shock of Going Global," *Datamation*, August 1, 1989, 76-79.

Reponen, T and Copeland, D. "Finnpap/Finnboard," Harvard Business School, 9-186-30, 1985.

Roche, E.M. *Managing Information Technology in Multinational Corporations*, Macmillan Publishing, New York, New York, 1992.

Roche, E. M. "Managing Systems Development in Multinational Corporations: Practical Lessons from 7 Case Studies," in Palvia, s., Palvia, P, and Zigli, R.M., *The Global Issues of Information Technology Management*, Idea Group Publishing, 1993.

Sager, I. "The Great Equalizer," *Business Week,* June 6, 1994, 100-107.

Steinbart, P.J. and Nath, R. "Problems and Issues in the Management of International Data Communcations Networks: The Experiences of American Companies," *MIS Quarterly*, March 1992, 55-73.

Treacy, M. and Wiersema, F. *The Discipline of Market Leaders,* Addison-Wesley Publishing Company, Reading, MA, 1994.

Wiersema, F. and Thompson, J. "Consistent Customer Contacts for Repeat Business," *Information Strategy: The Executive's Journal*, Winter 1991, 6-12.

Wiklund, E. *International Marketing Strategies*, McGraw Hill, New York, New York, 1987.

Yip, G.S. *Total Global Strategy: Managing for Worldwide Competitive Advantage*, Prentice-Hall, Englewood Cliffs, New Jersey, 1992.

Appendix: *Interview Template*

1. Name of Interviewee, Position, Company

2. Help us to understand Firm Y's requirement for worldwide IT vendors?

3. Can we look at a particular application for which such integration was important.

4. Focus on a particular hardware vendor. How well do they meet these requirements?

5. What are their barriers to successfully meeting these needs? Are there variations from one part of the world to another?

6. Can you recall any compromises or "work arounds" that you were required to make so as to compensate for the vendors inability to support your global requirements?.

7. Have you seen improvements by this vendor? In what ways?

8. What about major software vendors for mainframe or workstation -based products?

9. Software for PC products - e.g., LOTUS or Microsoft

10. Are there other people in your organization who face similar problems dealing with vendors for the provision of integrated supplies or services?

11. Turning now to your own customers? What requirements, if any, do you face in serving global customers?

12. What role does IT play?

23 Strategic Applications of Information Technology in Global Business: Using the "GLITS" Model and Instrument

Prashant C. Palvia
The University of Memphis, USA

Information technology (IT) has become absolutely essential in the conduct of global business in multi-national corporations. Global information systems (GISs) provide a new order of world-wide connectivity in the day-to-day, and even minute-to-minute, operational activities of global firms. While the use of technology for operational support may itself be construed strategic in nature, there are numerous specific opportunities for a firm to utilize information technology in a strategic manner. Surely anecdotal cases of strategic use of IT for global competitive advantage have been reported in the literature, but how can strategic opportunities for a firm be identified more systematically? This chapter provides a model, called the GLITS model, and an accompanying instrument for the identification of strategic opportunities in a firm, and for the measurement of strategic use of IT. The instrument, while based on a small sample, has undergone extensive statistical testing and exhibits high levels of reliability and validity. Besides obvious practical benefits to global organizations, a validated model and instrument provide the foundation for productive and rigorous research in international information systems.

INTRODUCTION

Numerous examples exist and many reports have been published on the use of information technology (IT) for enhancing a firm's competitive position. Explicitly or implicitly, these reports focus on the use of IT to enhance domestic/national competitiveness, i.e., within the firm's own national borders. Nonetheless, as the Landmark MIT study (Arthur Young 1989) predicted, information technology can and would be a vital resource for competing in the global marketplace of the 1990s and beyond. Today, many progressive organizations (e.g., American Express, Dow Chemicals, Federal Express, DEC, GM, Texaco) consider information technology an essential component of worldwide corporate strategy. However, while there are several anecdotal cases of IT application for global competitive advantage, the larger American and the world business communities have no validated models for analyzing the strategic impact of information technology on global firms.

In this chapter, we provide an initial model which identifies the various areas for strategic use of information technology in global business, and supplement it with a validated instrument for firms to assess their own use (or potential for future use) of information technology for the said purpose. The model and the instrument are extensions of the ones proposed by Mahmood and Soon (1991) in the domestic context. Throughout the chapter, we will refer to the model as the global IT strategic model or the GLITS model.

With continuous and relentless business globalization, the model and instrument have a direct bearing on corporate chief executives and information officers. The model provides a much-needed and validated reference for explicating and measuring the strategic and competitive impact of information technology at a global scale. By taking an inventory of the corporate position with respect to each item in the instrument, a firm will be able to identify its own stance in the use of IT for strategic global advantage. A careful examination of the model and instrument components can also point to the strengths and weaknesses in IT application, and to promising areas for future development. Further research, based on the current model, can lead to the development of a contingency evaluation of the model components based on organizational, industry, and national characteristics. Thus organizations may be able to customize the model to their own unique needs. We will explore the various applications of the model in greater detail towards the end of the chapter

THE UNDERLYING LITERATURE

While there is little direct literature on the role of IT for global competitiveness, there are two streams of literature which have bearing on the development of the GLITS model. The first of these is the general literature on the use of information systems as competitive weapons. Such systems, known as strategic information systems (SIS) for competitive advantage, have been developed and studied largely from a national perspective (e.g., Beath and Ives 1986; Rackoff et al. 1985; Wiseman 1985; Wiseman and MacMillan 1984). In the mid 1980s, such systems were billed as one of the ten IT megatrends in the U.S. (Kanter 1985). A few well-known examples of such systems are: American Airlines' SABRE reservation system, Merril Lynch's Cash Management Account, and American Hospital Supply's order-processing system (Rackoff et al. 1985; Wiseman and MacMillan 1984).

Several researchers, led by Michael Porter, have developed frameworks (Bakos and Treacy 1986; Benjamin et al. 1984, McFarlan 1984; Palvia et al. 1990, Porter 1980; Porter and Millar 1985) for the application of SIS. Porter's framework consists of three dimensions for strategic applications of IS: strategic target (supplier, customer, competitor), strategic thrust (differentiation, cost, focus, innovation, growth, alliance), and strategic mode (offensive, defensive). Ives and Learmonth (1984) suggested a 13-stage customer resource cycle for identifying SIS opportunities. Based on the above works, Mahmood and Soon (1991) developed a model for the potential IT impact on domestic strategic variables, and provided a validated instrument.

The above reports examine competitiveness of firms in the domestic arena (primarily in the U.S.A.). They have generally not been extended to the international context. The second stream of research relevant for the GLITS model relates to international/ global information systems in general. This stream is still young and exploratory. For example, the early works of Deans et al. (1991), and Ives and Jarvenpaa (1991) explored key issues in managing global information technology in multinational corporations. Specifically, Ives and Jarvenpaa identified business drivers for global IT, which included both operational and strategic variables. Manheim (1992) discussed the various global IT issues as well as strategic opportunities due to technology. Porter (1986) probed competitive forces and changes in the international arena; his focus was on general business strategies. Simon and Grover (1993) examined the strategic use of IT in international business within an integration-responsiveness framework. Wetherbe et al. (1994) discussed fast cycle development enabled by IT as a source of competitive advantage. Several other articles discuss the strategic benefits (e.g., effectiveness, efficiency, responsiveness) attainable by global firms by the use of IT (Cheung and Burn 1994; Nelson and Clark 1994). Several recent books on global IT (Bradley et al 1993; Butler Cox 1991; Deans and Kane 1992; Palvia et al. 1992; Roche 1992) discuss the strategic implications of information technology for the global firm.

The above works in domestic SIS and international MIS literature contain numerous examples and recommendations for utilizing IT in a strategic manner in a global firm. These were systematically analyzed and used in developing the GLITS model.

DEVELOPMENT OF THE GLITS MODEL

An overview of the model development process is provided herein; details can be found in (Palvia 1995). Global organizational variables, that information technology may be able to influence, were generated by reviewing the literature (those cited above plus additional works). Mahmood and Soon's study (1991) provided the initial impetus for the identification of variables. Initially, there were a total of twenty seven specific variables plus one overall variable. Seventeen of these were derived from the domestic SIS literature, and were chosen on the basis of their applicability at the global level (e.g., variables like: customers, market, pricing, and flexible operations). Six new variables from the international IS literature were generated (e.g., country requirements, worldwide physical resources, and time zones). Finally, there were four variables that related directly to technology impacts (e.g., coordination, and responsiveness). An additional variable "overall" was created to assess the overall impact of IT. Specific items were developed for each variable (e.g., one item in the "customers" variable is: IT helps serve customers in different countries with different needs). There was a total of 255 items under the 27 variables, and 6 items under the "overall" variable. These constituted the preliminary instrument.

The preliminary instrument underwent extensive refinement. Steps of refinement included: self-examination by the researchers, two-staged pilot test, and the full study. In the full study, an intermediate version of the instrument was completed by thirty six senior executives of U.S. international firms. While the

Variable (Variable Code)	# of Items	Cronbach's α
1. Customers (CS)	3	.7702
2. Competitive Rivalry (CR)	4	.8976
3. Suppliers (SU)	2	.9457
4. Market (MK)	4	.8971
5. Products and Services (PS)	4	.8280
6. Economies of Scope (SP)	2	.9586
7. Internal Organizationall Efficiency (EF)	2	.8986
8. Interorganizational Efficiency (IO)	4	.8632
9. Business RiskReduction (BR)	2	.9501
10. Downsizing/ Outsourcing (DO)	3	.9162
11. Learning Curve/ Knowledge Transfer (LK)	2	.9488
12. Flexible Operations (FO)	7	.9563
13. Resources (RS)	2	.9660
14. Government & Country Requirements (GC)	5	.9362
15. Human Resources (HR)	2	.9031
16. Alliance and Growth (AG)	2	.8953
17. Time Zones (TZ)	2	.9020
18. Coordination (CD)	2	.9468
19. Integration (IG)	2	.8363
20. Information Systems (IS)	2	.9730
ENTIRE INSTRUMENT	58	.9866

Table 1: Cronbach's Reliability Coefficients for the Final 58 Item, 20 Variable Final Instrument

sample size is somewhat small, it was deemed adequate given the exploration of new ground, use of homogeneous sampling method, and level of rigor applied in subsequent tests.

Numerous statistical tests were conducted at different stages. As a result, many items were eliminated, many were modified, many variables were eliminated, and many were regrouped. Validation tests included: reliability evaluation using Cronbach's α (Cronbach 1951), construct validity (Cohen and Cohen 1975), criterion-related validity (Kerlinger 1978), item-variable correlations, and convergent and discriminant validity (Campbell and Fiske 1959). The final GLITS model has 20 variables plus one overall variable. The instrument that captures these variables has 58 items for the 20 variables, and 2 for the overall variable.

The model and the accompanying instrument scored well on all validity tests. Table 1 shows the reliability of the 58 item final instrument as well as the reliability coefficient for each of the updated variables. The reliability of the entire instrument is 0.9866. Nunnaly (1978) has suggested a minimum reliability of .80 for basic research and .90 for application. Except for the "customers" variable, all variables have adequate reliabilities. The "customers" reliability is .77, which is only slightly lower than the .80 mark. The 20-variable model and the 58-item instrument, having undergone extensive evaluation and validation, represents significant progress towards the development of a standard instrument for measuring the strategic impact of information technology at a global level. Moreover, the instrument is simultaneously comprehensive and precise.

THE GLITS MODEL DESCRIPTION

The GLITS model is shown in Figure 1, and the instrument in Exhibit 1. The model can be viewed as a 3-level hierarchy. The first and the highest level describes the total strategic impact of information technology on a global business. The second level subdivides the total impact into impact on each of the twenty variables. An organization can therefore identify how IT is being used or may be used in specific areas. Finally, the third level breaks each variable down into its constituent items. At this level, an organization can surmise the specific ways IT can be put to use for global strategic advantage.

Some general comments are offered on the efficacy of the model, followed by a brief description of each variable. First, the model and theinstrument are more comprehensive than the domestic model developed by Mahmood and Soon (1991). They had ten variables in their model, and we have twenty. This was expected as we were extending their basic model, developed in the domestic setting, to a global context. Many of the model variables are therefore unique to the global environment and carry a special significance, e.g., physical resources, country requirements, human resources, flexible operations, time zones, and knowledge transfer.

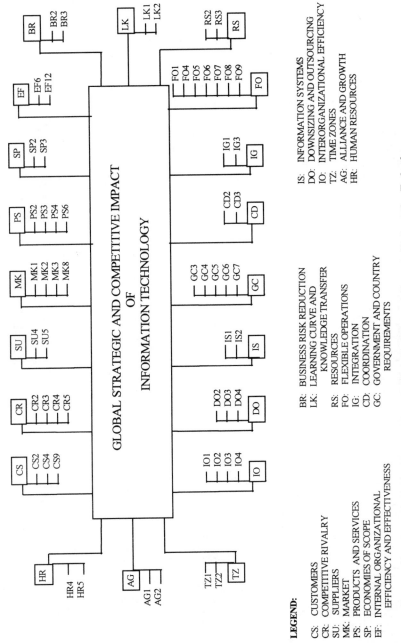

Figure 1: A Model For the Global and Strategic Impact of Information Technology

LEGEND:

CS: CUSTOMERS
CR: COMPETITIVE RIVALRY
SU: SUPPLIERS
MK: MARKET
PS: PRODUCTS AND SERVICES
SP: ECONOMIES OF SCOPE
EF: INTERNAL ORGANIZATIONAL EFFICIENCY AND EFFECTIVENESS

BR: BUSINESS RISK REDUCTION
LK: LEARNING CURVE AND KNOWLEDGE TRANSFER
RS: RESOURCES
FO: FLEXIBLE OPERATIONS
IG: INTEGRATION
CD: COORDINATION
GC: GOVERNMENT AND COUNTRY REQUIREMENTS

IS: INFORMATION SYSTEMS
DO: DOWNSIZING AND OUTSOURCING
IO: INTERORGANIZATIONAL EFFICIENCY
TZ: TIME ZONES
AG: ALLIANCE AND GROWTH
HR: HUMAN RESOURCES

Further, as Emery (1993) commented, in today's global economy, a global organization will be the norm and a domestic firm will be the special case. The model, while developed in the global context, also has relevance for purely domestic firms or those contemplating venturing into the global arena at a later date. The model and the variables for a domestic firm are a subset of the complete model, and can be extracted by simple examination. In fact, firms may choose only the variables that have particular significance for their own unique environment. For example, a firm that is just beginning to globalize its operations, may wish to focus on a different set of specific international variables for IT application, compared to the firm with an extended history of global operations. It is, therefore, possible for one model and instrument to serve the needs of both a domestic and an international organization.

The instrument was completed by executives in thirty six firms. Their responses were used to prioritize the relative impact of IT on each. organizational variable. The variable ranks are listed in Table 2. The variables are discussed

Rank	Variable
1	Customers
2	Time Zones
3	Products and Services
4	Economies of Scope
5	Integration
6	Interorganizational Efficiency
7	Coordination
8	Market
9	Competitive Rivalry
10	Suppliers
11	Information Systems
12	Internal Organizational Efficiency and Effectiveness
13	Flexible Operations
14	Government and Country Requirements
15	Downsizing and Outsourcing
16	Human Resources
17	Learning Curve and Knowledge Transfer
18	Business Risk Reduction
19	Resources
20	Alliance and Growth

Table 2

below in the same order. As a caveat, these ranks require further interpretation and qualification before being generalized to the larger base of U.S. companies or even a single organization for that matter. We are using them merely to facilitate the following discussion.

Customers

Per our sample, IT has the potential of making a substantial impact on the relationship between the company and its customers. As an inhibiting factor, McFarlan (1984) has stated that information systems can build switching costs so that customers will have to spend too much time and money to change suppliers. IT can increase customer's cost of switching to other suppliers and reduce buyer power (Bakos and Treacy 1986). In a more positive and facilitative role, IT can be used to help worldwide customers learn about the company's products and services by making company databases available to them. It can ultimately allow a company to be more responsive to the unique needs of people and customers in different countries by providing relevant information concerning their needs, wants, and preferences (in the form of worldwide customer databases). Another manner to serve customers is by improving customer service. Customer oriented information systems can differentiate products or services through customer service, while simultaneously strengthening customer ties (Learmonth and Ives 1987, Porter and Millar 1985).

Time zones

Different countries operate in different time zones creating barriers to the simultaneous conduct of business. Information technology is conquering both time and space barriers in international business. Telecommunications based technologies, such as email, EDI, fax, wide area networks, telnet, FTP, teleconferencing, etc., are permitting communication between two parties at any place and at any time. Not only have such barriers to normal patterns of business been removed, but also new opportunities to conduct business operations during all twenty four hours of the day have been created (McFarlan 1992). For example, while one 8-hour day shift is concluded in U.S.A., work can be taken over by a day shift in a subsidiary in Singapore (while all necessary work-related information is routinely transmitted over telecommunication lines). Another example is in international investments (Ballester and Marcarelli 1992), where there is always someone somewhere around the world trading securities and foreign exchange. While New York City sleeps, Tokyo trades, and London is the bridge between the two.

Products and Services

IT provides opportunities for products and services innovation as well as enhancement of product/service performance and quality. Good examples of products and services enabled by IT include Merryl Lynch's Cash Management Account (Wiseman and MacMillan 1984) and American Express' "Authorizer's Assistant" expert system for credit authorization (Davenport and Short 1990). IT can further facilitate the globalization of a firm's product (e.g., rapid dissemination of information about the product, worldwide sales and service support, etc.). Additionally, it can help coordinate worldwide operations and technologies, such as CIM (computer integrated manufacturing), CAE (computer aided engineering), and CAD (computer aided design) can help build customized products rapidly (Martinson 1993; Rackoff et al. 1985). Finally, IT can enhance post-product-sale services.

Economies of Scope

Scope economies may be viewed in terms of the synergistic benefits gained through multilateral exchange of resources, competencies and know-how among organizational units or divisions (Teece 1980). Information technology provides numerous opportunities for economies of scope. First, by removing space and time barriers, IT can significantly increase the number of markets a firm can serve in the world with existing financial and human resources. Second, resources can be utilized more effectively. For example, an expertise that exists in one country, can be easily tapped by other locations in the world. Third, operations can be rationalized (Ives and Jarvenpaa 1991), and more products and services can be generated. For example, different subsidiaries may build different parts of the same product or different products based on their comparative advantages.

Integration

Integration is of paramount importance in a global firm; the myriad of activities performed in various countries need to be integrated to produce a unified whole. Integration provides MNCs the opportunity to maximize their total system-wide margins and exploit imperfections in labor and financial markets (Neo 1991). IT allows worldwide integration of activities within the firm as well as with external value-chain business units, e.g., suppliers, distributors, wholesalers, or retailers (Ives et al. 1993). Further, it is a critical resource for building integrated worldwide operations, manufacturing, logistic, and distribution networks. IT also permits the formation of integrated teams that encompass design, engineering, and manufacturing.

Interorganizational Efficiency

Strategic use of IT includes interorganizational applications. Cooperative systems serving the firm and its worldwide customers, distributors, wholesalers, and retailers will have a strategic impact on the firm's performance, efficiency, and competitiveness. Furthermore, they will improve communication and coordination with these external entities (Bakos and Treacy 1986; Porter and Millar 1985). Likewise, IT permits communication and formal agreements with other organizations worldwide. McFarlan (1992) provided an interesting example in this respect: an IBM marketing representative, in 48 hours, assembled electronic documentation from around the world from 8 people he had never met to prepare a 200-page, multi-million dollar project proposal for a customer.

Coordination

The essence of coordination is the communication and processing of information (Malone et al. 1987). The number and complexity of the linkages between various units of a global firm increase rapidly (Neo 1991). Information technology provides information systems, information, and the conduits to transport information in order to support, monitor, and control subsidiary operations. Additionally, IT provides control of logistic and distribution activities.
The effective, timely, and accurate communication of information between headquarters and subsidiary operations facilitates coordination.

Market

Information technology can be used to alter the market structure in order to gain competitive advantage (Bakos and Treacy 1986; Li et al. 1994), and to discover and develop new and profitable worldwide markets (Simon and Grover 1993). Further, IT makes new businesses technologically feasible, and allows a firm to identify worldwide market trends and to focus on product/market niches (Deans and Kane 1992). It helps reduce marketing costs by providing pertinent local market knowledge and sales information, facilitating distribution of the product worldwide and enhancing sales forecast accuracy. As a recent example of IT's role in this domain, Internet and World Wide Web are becoming new tools for a firm to reach and penetrate new markets.

Competitive Rivalry

Information technology provides global competitive advantage in several ways (McFarlan 1984; Rackoff et al. 1985; Wiseman and MacMillan 1984). First, it helps differentiate the firm's products and services from its competitors. Second, it enables the firm to make a preemptive strike against competitors (i.e., by introducing new products and services). Third, it helps build customized products rapidly. Fourth, it can mount barriers against less technologically advanced companies wishing to compete in existing markets, or entering into new markets. Fifth, it lets a firm access global markets that were previously inaccessible. Sixth, it can reduce the home-court advantage of local firms by allowing a global firm to make information about its own products and services available readily to local clients. Finally, it can allow the firm to lock in suppliers and customers. In fact, by definition of the GLITS model, practically all variables directly or indirectly lead to competitive advantage. However, this specific variable focuses on items that are directly targeted at competitors.

Suppliers

IT affects the relationship between the company and its suppliers in multiple ways. A global firm may have suppliers from different parts of the world. For example, in almost any automobile manufactured in U.S.A. and Japan, many of the parts are produced in and supplied by different countries. IT not only reduces the company's transaction costs by simplifying the order process but also minimizes supplier's transaction costs by facilitating the purchasing process. EDI is a technology being increasingly used internationally to process customer-vendor transactions (Clarke et al. 1992). IT further increases the bargaining power of the company by increasing the potential number of available suppliers (Bakos and Treacy 1986) and locating substitute products/services on a worldwide basis. Moreover, the monitoring of the quality of products and services can be performed with the use of IT. IT is also used to implement just-in-time manufacturing, which requires close coordination with the suppliers.

Information Systems

Competitive advantages, that were previously even inconceivable, are provided in the global market by special purpose information systems. Besides many of the operational systems discussed earlier, IT can be used to build decision support systems (DSS), executive information systems (EIS), and expert systems (ES) in other countries (Sauter 1992) as well as build such systems with increasingly global scope. Through the provision of such systems, IT provides rapid and worldwide access to internal and external databases (Deans and Kane 1992; Ives and Jarvenpaa 1991). For example, global EIS (GEIS) can be used to provide quick access to demographic, market, customer, and financial data from other countries (Palvia et al. 1995). On the other hand, special purpose expert systems may provide an opportunity for the inexpensive transfer of technology and expertise to subsidiaries in other countries (Eom 1995).

Internal Organizational Efficiency and Effectiveness

While the past use of information technology was for improving the efficiency of the organization, recent efforts have targeted the use of IT to enhance organizational effectiveness. In fact, Keen (1989) observes that an emerging strategic use of IT will be for *organizational advantage* through the design of adaptive, responsive, and flexible organizations. Globalization involves increased coordination, operation across time zones and locations, increased breadth of activities, time stresses due to geographic dispersion and shortening of planning and delivery cycles, and increasing deregulation. Properly conceived and designed systems can enable a global company to meet such requirements effectively, e.g., the PRISM system at Federal Express Corporation (Palvia et al. 1992). In addition, IT improves the process and quality of decision making in both the centralized and decentralized modes. It can effectively extend these forms of decision-making into the global arena. Furthermore, IT improves strategic planning by providing appropriate data, decision models, and communication facilities to the decision makers.

Flexible Operations

Flexibility in operations provides a hedge against vagaries of the marketplace, e.g., labor shortages or strikes, raw material shortages, strains in supplier relationships, etc. (Ives and Jarvenpaa 1991). Information technology provides requisite flexibility in locating and relocating worldwide operations and in scheduling operations/manufacturing (Boggs 1988). IT can also be used to support just-in-time inventory and manufacturing systems and allows manufacturing of different parts in different countries. For example, Seagate Technology (Palvia and Lee 1995) manufactures different parts of its disk read-write heads in U.S.A., Northern Ireland, Malaysia, Thailand, and Singapore. Information systems act as the glue holding together the various operations. Finally, IT allows the firm to share facilities across the world and eliminates duplication of effort in various country subsidiaries.

Government and Country Requirements

Information technology is a powerful tool in dealing with government, regulatory, and legal requirements of countries. Sipior and Townsend (1993) provide an example of the use of multimedia technology for training General Electric employees in laws, regulations, and contractual specifications of the U.S. government. Similar systems could me made available for other countries, or perhaps could be part of a global EIS. Software can also be made readily available to automatically decipher differences in accounting and financial practices, currency variations, and language differences between countries. For example, Aiken et al. (1994) have developed a prototype multi-lingual group decision support system which translates the sender's comments into the receiver's language.

Downsizing and Outsourcing

Organizations have used downsizing and outsourcing for cost containment, particularly through the achievement of economies of scale and operational efficiencies. The IT function itself provides opportunities for downsizing and outsourcing, as seen in the classic cases of Eastman Kodak (Computer World 1991) and Continental Bank (Huber 1993). Besides cost control, benefits of outsourcing include: improved financial outlook, control of key operations, return to core competencies, and retention of strategic focus (Lacity and Hirschheim 1993). Globalization dramatically broadens a company's outsourcing options. IT, through its coordination and integration mechanisms, allows a firm to profitably outsource activities to outside firms in its own country as well as other countries. Once again, the IT function itself provides an outstanding example of international outsourcing, where software outsourcing to countries like India, Ireland, and Phillipines have provided savings in the order of 35 to 40% (McFarlan 1994). Private and public international data highways have permitted such collaborations.

Human Resources

As international outsourcing illustrates, the use of skilled labor (both technical and management) from other countries is being made possible through the application of information technology (Swierczek 1991). Work within the company can be allocated and transferred to specialized or under-utilized employees across the globe. Not only IT allows the transfer of work to other parts of the world, but it also permits distant employees to work together on common tasks (Jarvenpaa and Ives 1994). For example, groupware or collaboration software (such as Lotus Notes) offers the possibilities for geographically dispersed work groups to come together and work on joint projects (Ellis et al. 1991). This type of software provides the needed elements of communication, coordination, cooperation, collaboration, and control.

Learning curve and Knowledge Transfer

Learning curve effects reflect enhancements in processing, performance and retention capacities by way of increasing knowledge and experience. Information technology accelerates the firm's movement up the learning curve ladder. It permits the rapid acquisition of knowledge about subsidiaries by headquarters personnel (Deans and Kane 1992, Korson and Vaishnavi 1992). By the same token, new business units, especially new subsidiaries, can learn about the core business much more rapidly (Neo 1991). Through systems such as CAD/CAM, multimedia & hypermedia systems, and expert systems, IT helps firms learn about new processes and technologies faster, thus accelerating knowledge transfer (Federowicz et al. 1992, Eom 1995).

Business Risk Reduction

Information technology can also be used to reduce business, market and technical risks. Ives and Jarvenpaa (1991) state that risks associated with currency

conversions, multiple global markets, and multiple traders are managed effectively with global IT applications (e.g., applications that provide real time monitoring and financial exposure reporting). They provide examples of a petroleum company which developed a global system for bidding on crude oil contracts, and of a multinational bank which
implemented a global risk management system for currency trading. In the international investment arena, IT based information systems are indispensable for the customized design and redesign of global financial products, such as mutual funds, pension funds, and endowments (Ballester and Marcarelli 1992).

Resources

While human resource is important in and of itself and was listed earlier as a separate variable, we pool the remaining global resources that can be leveraged by IT under this category. These resources include raw materials, semi-finished goods, finished goods, and financial resources, and can be procured from any part of the world. Global information systems can coordinate the utilization of joint and scarce resources (Ives and Jarvenpaa 1991). As the earlier example illustrated (Ballester and Marcarelli 1992), financing arrangements for new ventures may actually require raising capital from various financial markets of the world, where the use of IT would be pivotal. In the same vein, quick financial support to host country subsidiaries can be provided through the use of IT.

Alliance and Growth

Firms can expand by forging partnerships by way of joint ventures, mergers, and acquisitions (Porter 1980). An international firm typically forms strategic alliances with host country partners in order to expedite market entry. An excellent example of this is the automobile parts industry in Japan and U.S.A. Manufacturers in each country have made alliances with part manufacturers in the other country. Interorganizational information systems provide the necessary linkages to reduce costs and to make the alliances workable. Another growth area is the formation of spin-off companies. The example of the spinoff Kids "R" Us is well-known, where Toys "R" Us, the number one toy company in U.S.A., could leverage its information system's expertise and resources to venture into a new business (Wiseman and MacMillan 1984). International markets may present more of such openings, and the "IT ready" companies will be the ones who can move in quickly and capitalize on such opportunities.

PRACTICAL AND THEORETICAL APPLICATIONS

The provision of a comprehensive and statistically validated construct for the strategic application of global IT should be useful to both practitioners and academicians. It forms the necessary base for practical applications as well as for conducting research that is grounded in theory.

Practical Applications

A validated model and instrument for assessing the role of IT in global competitiveness have significant practical value for business organizations. Information technology is vital for an international business' very existence, and it can no longer be ignored from close scrutiny and proper management. The model and the instrument identify the strategic areas for the global application of information technology. Just as the strategic "options generator" developed by Wiseman and MacMillan (1984) provided firms a way to scan opportunities for SIS application in the domestic context, a careful application of this instrument should reveal numerous opportunities to explore information technology on a global scale.

The instrument may be applied in the following ways. First of all, a senior IS executive (e.g., the CIO) or several executives may complete the instrument to assess the *current* impact or use of IT for each of the 58 items. The impact is assessed on a 5-point likert scale, where 1 refers to no impact, and 5 refers to greatest impact. The sum of the scores on all items will provide a measure of the current use of IT in the organization for global strategic advantage. Note that the sum for 58 items can range between 58 and 290. Some guidelines on the range of values for this measure may be developed to indicate what is effective and what is ineffective technology use. Additionally, the executives may complete the instrument a second time, this time assessing the *potential* impact of IT on the 58 items given the organization's internal and external environment. This exercise will yield areas for future application of IT. A careful comparison of the current and potential scores on each item will also allow the organization to identify its IT strengths and weaknesses.

Thus, by taking an inventory of the items contained in the instrument, a firm can determine whether IT can be used at an international level for financial gain or competitive advantage, or for preventing the firm from sliding into competitive disadvantage. Furthermore, the individual variables of the model can be used to separately measure IT's impact on a firm's products or services, economies of scale, optimization of resources, global product, global customer, etc. Based on analysis of the current and potential impacts, a firm can conduct a contingency analysis based on its own unique requirements, and determine the variables of particular relevance to the firm. It can, then, maximize its return on IT investment by focusing on the selected areas.

Another practical application for an organization is to evaluate and monitor itself against industry practices. If industry practices are widely reported or if the instrument is administered to a representative sample of companies in a specific industry, then a particular firm will be able to assess its relative position, and take necessary actions.

Theoretical Applications

While the model provides an initial set of validated and useful variables, there is scope for improvement, as with any model development. Researchers may further refine the model and the underlying construct by using a larger sample, a more focused or a more homogeneous sample, samples from other countries, and using other statistical techniques, such as factor analysis. The current model provides an excellent base from which to seek further refinements.

Another worthwhile research pursuit is to conduct a detailed examination of the specific variables. It may be that some variables are more meaningful for certain firms or industries, and further insights into these variables may be of interest. For example, if "downsizing & outsourcing" is identified as an important variable for a class of firms, specific hypotheses related to it may be formulated and tested in future studies. An illustration of such a hypothesis may be that "IT related global outsourcing is facilitated by heavy investments in telecommunications technology".

Another area of interest is to investigate the relationship between actual organizational strategic performance and global IT competitive impact. A positive relationship between the two should encourage higher IT investment. A detailed analysis could look into which specific elements of global IT variables are correlated with organizational performance, with the implication that these would be the ones that need to be emphasized in terms of investment.

Finally, we recommend that a contingency analysis of the impact variables be undertaken. It seems reasonable to postulate that different variables and items have varying degree of importance to different firms. What are the contingency factors which drive the impact of each variable, and what is the amount of the impact? Some possible factors from the literature are: global organizational structure (Bartlett and Ghoshal 1989), business strategy (Miles and Snow 1978), industry (Deans et al. 1991), firm size, and host country culture (Hofstede 1980). Relationships between these factors and the model variables at present are unknown or speculative; research needs to firmly establish these relationships.

CONCLUSIONS

This chapter has provided a comprehensive and concise model and instrument for assessing the strategic impact of information technology in global firms. The model was formulated along the lines of a single-country domestic model (Mahmood and Soon 1991), but was augmented with variables extracted from the international IT literature. While details of model and instrument development are not reported, both were carefully crafted using extensive evaluation and validation procedures. This work represents significant progress towards the creation of a standard global IT impact measurement model and instrument; nevertheless, efforts should be carried out to further refine and extend the model.

The model has practical as well as theoretical and research applications. In terms of practical applications, a validated model provides a much-needed tool for assessing the role of IT in the global competitiveness of a firm. Senior executives may complete the instrument to evaluate the current use of IT for global effectiveness, as well as assess its future potential. They may further hone in on specific areas of interest. In terms of implications for researchers, the model provides a theoretically grounded initial instrument which can be used to base further research on and to test contingency based hypotheses.

EXHIBIT 1: THE INSTRUMENT

Instrument to Measure Global Strategic and Competitive Impact of Information Technology (The GLITS Instrument)

Definition: Information Technology (IT) includes all aspects of computers (hardware and software), information systems, telecommunications, and office automation.

Q1. From your own firm's point of view, to what extent do you think **Information Technology (IT)** can **do** or can **assist** with the following in providing **strategic and competitive advantage** over other firms on an **international level**. Do not be concerned about IT's current role, but its potential role in your firm. Please circle **one** choice using the following scale.

Scale: 1 = No Extent, 2 = Little Extent, 3 = Some Extent,
4 = Great Extent, 5 = Very Great Extent

Customers (CS)

CS2   Makes the products/services database available to worldwide customers.
CS4   Helps provide administrative support (such as billing, collection, inventory management) to worldwide customers.
CS9   Helps serve customers in different countries with different needs.

Competitive Rivalry (CR)

CR2   Helps to make first/preemptive strike against competitors (i.e., a new product/service).
CR3   Helps the firm provide substitutes before competitors do.
CR4   Helps the firm match an existing competitor's offering.
CR5   Assists in overcoming the home-court advantage of local firms in host country.

Suppliers (SU)

SU4   Helps the firm identify alternative supply sources on a worldwide basis.
SU5   Helps the firm locate substitute products/services on a worldwide basis.

Market (MK)

MK1   Makes new business technologically feasible worldwide.
MK2   Identifies worldwide market trends.
MK3   Discovers and develops new and profitable worldwide market.
MK8   Aids in selling the product in different parts of the world.

Products and Services (PS)

PS2   Enhances product/service performance and quality.
PS3   Allows the firm to bundle more information with products/services.
PS4   Allows the development of new products/services.
PS6   Enhances the after-product-sale services and activities.

Economies of Scope (SP)

SP2   Increases number of markets that can be tapped with existing resources.
SP3   Increases number of countries business can be conducted in with existing resources.

Internal Organizational Efficiency and Effectiveness (EF)

EF6   Improves strategic planning.
EF12   Facilitates organizational change in the firm.

Interorganizational Efficiency (IO)

IO1   Improves communication/coordination with worldwide businesses (e.g., suppliers, wholesalers, retailers).
IO2   Improves communication/coordination with worldwide customers.
IO3   Permits communication/formal agreements with other organizations worldwide.
IO4   Facilitates the making of worldwide financial investments.

Business Risk Reduction (BR)

BR2   Reduces risk by allowing to work with multiple global traders and suppliers.
BR3   Reduces risk by allowing to conduct business in multiple global markets.

Downsizing/Outsourcing (DO)

DO2   Allows to profitably contract/outsource activities to firms in its own country.

DO3   Allows to profitably contract/outsource activities to firms in other countries.

DO4   Allows to consolidate operations all over the world.

Learning Curve/Knowledge Transfer (LK)

LK1   Allows foreign subsidiaries to learn technical and business knowledge much faster.

LK2   Helps the firm to learn about subsidiaries much faster.

Flexible Operations (FO)

FO1   Allows flexibility in locating and relocating worldwide operations.

FO4   Allows the manufacture of different parts in different countries.

FO5   Eliminates duplication of effort in other country subsidiaries.

FO6   Provides for rapid adjustments to the firm's logistics/distribution network.

FO7   Allows the firm to share facilities across the world.

FO8   Allows the sharing of computer software across multiple world facilities.

FO9   Allows the firm to utilize excess capacity in any part of the world.

Resources (RS)

RS2   Assists in procuring semi-finished/finished goods from the most beneficial worldwide sources.

RS3   Allows financing arrangements from the most desirable world sources.

Government and Country Requirements (GC)

GC3   Assists in the advancement and social policy objectives of host countries.

GC4   Helps address accounting/financial/internal control requirements of countries.

GC5   Helps deal with different currencies/physical units of other countries.

GC6   Helps address taxation requirements of other countries.

GC7   Helps address language barriers in other countries.

Human Resources (HR)

HR4   Facilitates the coordination of global research and development efforts.

HR5   Allows to assign work to underutilized employees across the globe.

Alliance and Growth (AG)

AG1   Facilitates the formation of spinoff companies in other countries.
AG2   Permits alliances/acquisitions/joint ventures in other countries.

Time Zones (TZ)

TZ1   Overcomes barriers due to time differences in various countries.
TZ2   Expands the time during the 24-hour day to conduct international business.

Coordination (CD)

CD2   Provides information support to subsidiaries.
CD3   Permits better monitoring and control of subsidiary operations.

Integration (IG)

IG1   Allows worldwide integration of business with suppliers, distributors, wholesalers, or retailers.
IG3   Helps build an integrated worldwide logistics/distribution network.

Information Systems (IS)

IS1   Expedites transfer/development of operational information systems in other countries.
IS2   Expedites transfer/development of decision support/expert/strategic systems in other countries.

Overall (OA)

OA1   Provides an international competitive advantage to the firm.
OA2   Supports the firm in becoming a global business.

References

Aiken, M.W., Martin, J.S., Paolillo, J.G.P., and Shirani, A.I. A Group Decision Support System for Multilingual Groups. Information & Management. Vol 26, 1994, pp. 155-161.

Arthur Young, The Landmark MIT Study: Management in the 1990s, 1989.

Bakos, J.Y. & Treacy, M.E. Information Technology and Corporate Strategy: A Research Perspective. MIS Quarterly, 1986, 10(2), pp. 107-119.

Ballester, G.B. and Marcarelli, E.A. The Impact of Global Information Technology on International Investment Managers and Custodians. in The Global Issues of Information Technology Management, eds. Palvia, S., Palvia, P., and Zigli, R. Idea Group Publishing 1992, pp. 356-382.

Bartlett, C.A. and Ghoshal, S. Managing Across Borders: The Transnational Solution. Boston, MA, 1989, Harvard Business School Press.

Beath, C.M. and Ives, B. Competitive Information Systems in Support of Pricing. MIS Quarterly, 10, 1986.

Benjamin, R.I., Rockart, J.F., Scott Morton, M.S., & Wyman, J. Information Technology: A Strategic Opportunity. Sloan Management Review, 1984, 26, pp. 3-10.

Boggs, R. A. Implications of formal production information systems for production management. International Journal of Operations & Production Management, Vol 8, No 4, 1988, pp. 22-33.

Bradley, S.P., Hausman, J.A., and Nolan, R.L. Globalization, Technology, and Competition, Harvard Business School Press, Boston, MA, 1993.

Butler Cox Foundation. Globalization: The IT Challenge, Amdahl Executive Institute, Sunnyvale, 1991.

Campbell, D.T., & Fiske, D.W. Convergent and Discriminant Validation by the Multitrait-Multimethod Matrix. Psychological Bulletin, 1959, 50, pp. 81-105.

Cheung, H.K. and Burn, J.M. Distributing Global Information Systems Resources in Multinational Companies - A Contingency Model. Journal of Global Information Management, vol 2, no 3, pp. 14-27.

Clarke, R., DeLuca, P., Gricar, J., Imai, T., McCubbrey, D., and Swatman, P. The International Significance of Electronic Data Interchange. in The Global Issues of Information Technology Management, eds. Palvia, S., Palvia, P., and Zigli, R. Idea Group Publishing 1992, pp. 276-307.

Cohen, J. and Cohen, P. Applied Multiple Regression/Correlation Analysis for the Behavioral Sciences, Lawrence Erlbaum Assoc., Hillsdale, NJ, 1975.

Computerworld, September 30, 1991, p. 1.

Cronbach, L.J. Coefficient alpha and the internal structures of tests. Psychometrika, 1951, 16, pp. 297-334.

Davenport, T.H., and Short, J.E. The New Industrial Engineering: Information Technology and Business Process Redesign. Sloan Management Review, Vol 31, No 4, Summer 1990, pp. 11-27.

Deans, P.C., and Kane, M.J. International Dimensions of Information Systems and Technology, PWS-Kent, Boston, MA, 1992.

Deans, P.C., Karwan, K.R., Goslar, M.D., Ricks, D.A., and Toyne, B. Identification of Key International Information Systems Issues in U.S. Based Multinational Corporations. Journal of Management Information Systems, Vol. 7, No. 4, Spring 1991, pp. 27-50.

Ellis, C.A., Gibbs, S.J., and Rein, G.L. Groupware: Some Issues and Experiences. Communications of the ACM, Vol 34, No 1, January 1991, pp. 38-58.

Emery, J.C. The Global Organization as the Norm. Journal of Global Information Management, Vol 1, No 3, Summer 1993, pp. 3,4,31,44.

Eom, S. R. Global Management Support Systems: The New Frontiers. in Global Information Technology and Systems Management: Key Issues and Trends, eds. Palvia, P., Palvia, S., Roche, E. Ivy League Publishing, 1995.

Federowicz, J., Oz, E., Berger, P.D. A Learning Curve Analysis of Expert System Use. Decision Sciences. Vol 23, No 4, 1992, pp. 797-818.

Hofstede, G. Cultural Consequences: International Differences in Work Related Values, Sage, Beverly Hills, 1980.

Huber, R.L., "How Continental Bank Outsourced its Crown Jewels", Harvard Business Review, January-February 1993, pp. 121-129.

Ives, B., and Jarvenpaa, S.L. Applications of Global Information Technology: Key Issues for Management. MIS Quarterly, Vol. 15, No. 1, March 1991.

Ives, B., Jarvenpaa, S. L., Mason, R. O. Global Business Drivers: Aligning Information Technology to Global Business Strategy. IBM Systems Journal, Vol 32, No 1, 1993, pp. 143-161.

Ives, B. and Learmonth, G.P. The Information System as a Competitive Weapon. Communications of the ACM, 1984.

Jarvenpaa, S. L. & Ives, B. The Global Organization of the Future: Information Management Opportunities and Challenges. Journal of Management Information Systems, Vol 10, No 4, 1994, pp. 25-57.

Kanter, J. Ten Information Systems Megatrends. The Executive's Journal, Fall 1985.

Keen, P.G.W., "Information Technology and Organizational Advantage" in MoIS, Management of Information Systems, P. Gray, W. King, E. McLean, and H. Watson (eds.), The Dryden Press, Hinsdale, IL, 1989.

Kerlinger, F.N. Foundations of Behavioral Research, McGraw-Hill, NY 1978.

Korson, T. D., Vaishnavi, V. K. Managing Emerging Software Technologies: A Technology Transfer Framework. Communications of the ACM, Vol 35, No 9, 1992, pp. 101-111.

Lacity, M.C., and Hirschheim, R., "The Information Systems Outsourcing Bandwagon", Sloan Management Review, Fall 1993, pp. 73-86.

Learmonth, G.P., and B. Ives, "Information System Technology Can Improve Customer Service," Data Base, Winter 1987, pp. 6-10

Li, E. Y., McLeod, R. Jr., Rogers, J. C. (1994). Marketing information systems in the Fortune 500 companies: Past, present, future. Journal of Management Information Systems, vol 10, no. 1, 165-192.

Mahmood, M.A., and Soon, S.K. A Comprehensive Model for Measuring the Potential Impact of Information Technology on Organizational Strategic Variables. Decision Sciences, Vol. 22, No. 4, Sept./Oct. 1991.

Malone, T.W., Yates, J., and Benjamin, R.I. Electronic Markets and Electronic Hierarchies. Communications of the ACM, June 1987.

Manheim, M. Global Information Technology: Issues and Strategic Opportunities. International Information Systems, Vol. 1, No. 1, 1992.

Martinson, M. G. A strategic vision for our information age. Executive Development, 6, 5, 1993, pp. 21-25

McFarlan, W.F. Some Implications of the International Data Highway. Journal of Global Information Management, Vol 2, No 4, Fall 1994, pp. 3-4.

McFarlan, W.F. Multinational CIO Challenge for the 1990s. In The Global Issues of Information Technology Management, edited by Palvia, Palvia, & Zigli, Idea Group Publishing, 1992, pp. 484-493.

McFarlan, W.F. Information Technology Changes the Way You Compete. Harvard Business Review, 1984, 62(3), pp. 98-103.

Miles, R.E., and Snow, C.C. Organizational Strategy, Structure, and Process, McGraw-Hill, 1978.

Nelson, K.G., and Clark, T.D. Cross-Cultural Issues in Information Systems Research: A Research Paradigm. Journal of Global Information Management, vol 2, no 4, Fall 1994, pp. 19-29.

Neo, B. S. Information Technology and Global Competition. Information & Management, Vol. 20, 1991, pp. 151-160.

Nunnally, J.C. Psychometric Theory, McGraw-Hill, New York, 1978, p. 245.

Palvia, P. GLOSCIT: A Model for Global and Strategic Impact of Information Technology. Working Paper, The University of Memphis, 1995.

Palvia, P., Kumar, A., Kumar, N., and Hendon, R. Information Requirements of a Global EIS: An Exploratory Macro Assessment. Forthcoming in Decision Support Systems, 1995.

Palvia, P., Perkins, J.A., and Zeltmann, S.M., "The PRISM System: A Key to Organizational Effectiveness at Federal Express Corporation", MIS Quarterly, September, 1992, pp. 277-292.

Palvia, P., Palvia, S., and Zigli, R.M. Models and Requirements for Using Strategic Information Systems in Developing Nations, International Journal of Information Management, June 1990.

Palvia, S., and Lee, K.F. Seagate Technology: Developing Global Information Systems. in Global Information Technology and Systems Management: Key Issues and Trends, eds. Palvia, P., Palvia, S., Roche, E. Ivy League Publishing, 1995.

Palvia, S., Palvia, P, and Zigli, R.M. The Global Issues of Information Technology Management, Idea Group Publishing, 1992.

Porter, M.E. Changing Patterns of International Competition. California Management Review, Winter 1986.

Porter, M.E. Competitive Strategy: Techniques for Analyzing Industries and Competitors, Free Press, 1980.

Porter, M.E. & Millar, V.E. How Information Gives You Competitive Advantage. Harvard Business Review, 1985, 63 (4), pp. 149-159.

Rackoff, N., Wiseman, C., and Ulrich, W.A. Information Systems for Competitive Advantage, MIS Quarterly, 9, 1985.

Roche, E.M. Managing Information Technology in Multinational Corporations, Macmillan, New York, U.S.A., 1992.

Sauter, V.L. Cross-Cultural Aspects of Model Management Needs in a Transnational Decision Support System. In The Global Issues of Information Technology Management, edited by Palvia, Palvia, & Zigli, Idea Group Publishing, 1992.

Simon, S.J., and Grover, V. Strategic Use of Information Technology in International Business: A Framework for Information Technology Application. Journal of Global Information Management, vol 1, no 2, spring 1993, pp. 29-42.

Sipior, J. C. & Townsend, J. A case study of General Electric's multimedia training systems. Information Resources Management Journal, vol 6, no 4, 1993, pp. 23-31.

Swierczek, F. W. The Management of Technology: Human Resource and Organizational Issues. International Journal of Technology Management. Vol 6, No 1-2, 1991, pp. 1-14.

Teece, D.J. Economies of Scope and the Scope of the Enterprise. Journal of Economic Behavior and Organization, 1, 1980, pp. 223-247.

Wetherbe, J.C., Vitalari, N.P., and Milner, A. Key Trends in Systems Development in Europe and North America. Journal of Global Information Management. Vol 2, no 2, Spring 1994. pp. 5-20.

Wiseman, C. Strategy and Computers: Information Systems as Competitive Weapons, Homewood, Ill, Dow Jones-Irwin, 1985.

Wiseman, C., and MacMillan, I.C. Creating Competitive Weapons from Information Systems, Journal of Business Strategy, Fall 1984.

24 Information Systems in MNCs as an Infrastructure for Service Delivery

Peter Hagström
Harvard Business School, USA

In this chapter we propose to look at international information systems from the general manager's point of view and in the process suggest a practical, non-technical scheme with which to do so. The basic, simple proposition is that new information and communication technologies not only are an improvement over previously employed technologies and means of communication, but rather that the modern electronic information infrastructure in advanced multinational corporations (MNCs) represents a more dramatic change in the way MNCs can operate. Traditional managerial approaches and mind-sets are likely not to be sufficient in order to perceive, evaluate, and act on these unfolding opportunities. Similarly, less familiar primitive concepts would be needed to describe and explain new firm behavior. One possible way to begin is to view new information and communication technologies as allowing for a novel and different transport system for information-based services to evolve. This has implications for how a complex firm can operate, and for which managerial procedures and tools that are available.

After an impressionistic description of present-day activities in MNCs, this chapter gives an interpretative overview of the roots of the rapidly evolving academic research field that simultaneously addresses issues of international business and of information systems. A context for the simple, intuitive conceptualization of a firm transport infrastructure for information-based services is then provided and some of its implications explored. Some existing aggregate data on firm activities and communication patterns are presented to illustrate the discussion. The chapter attempts to demonstrate how even a simple conceptualization can inform our understanding of how to deal with issues like centralization vs. decentralization, which activities are performed within the firm and which are externalized, and why have geographically dispersed operations.

INTRODUCTION

If an MNC is a dynamic network, then geographical location must be continuously adjusted if the firm is to reap the inherent advantages of being multinational. Many activities can become extremely foot-loose, to the point where they are 'unplugged', shifted, and 'replugged' into the network. Many financial activities fall into this category. For instance, during the 1980s, many Swedish

MNCs moved parts of their treasury function to Brussels in order to take advantage of a more favorable tax regime. Several firms moved more than once, something that would have been impossible without information systems in place. Typically, subsidiaries lose many of their financial responsibilities, which instead are concentrated and recombined to get economies of scale, not least in the form of improved expertise. ASEA, now comprising half of the better known ABB (Asea Brown Boveri), put its corporate trading and counter-trading unit in London, its international financing activities in Switzerland, and most of its portfolio management in New York. Verifone, the US credit card equipment verification manufacturer, claims to let its professionals live wherever they want as long as they can maintain a link to the corporate information system. The company likes to think of this as being located at 'the intelligence points'. Unbundling and relocating activities can also be illustrated with an example from Ericsson, manufacturer of telecommunications equipment. Stand-by servicing of the software (which is a major part of value-added) in an AXE telephone exchange is in principle carried out from Stockholm, irrespective of where in the world a malfunction occurs. The software block is 'lifted ' from the exchange, transmitted over the telephone network, and then replaced when corrected. In IBM, professionals can sell their 'unused' time by the hour on internal labor exchanges, everything going through the data communications network.

From a different angle, are these descriptions best characterized as centralization or decentralization? Traditionally, centralization conjure up a picture of corporate-wide responsibility, residing at the very top of the organization and likely to be physically located at the head-office. ASEA's important international financing certainly was 'centralized' to experts, but not to the head-office, nor would it have been possible to say that it was organizationally located anywhere near something of a hierarchical apex. Improved possibilities for specialization can lead to geographical concentration, but calling it centralization would be a misnomer. The now common shifting out of global product mandates to far-flung organizational units in manufacturing MNCs is more a process of dismembering the divisional or head-office than any dilution of the global responsibility. Strategic coordination and adjustment would be impossible without a well-functioning international information systems. A Swedish battery-maker found that working with common CAD/CAM systems internationally both made it possible to leverage expertise from all over the company and induced common work practices. This allowed it to develop solutions for some of its most critical designs and implement them corporate-wide for the first time ever. In the process, the metric system was introduced to its US subsidiaries virtually overnight; something they had tried to do unsuccessfully for more than fifty years.

The formal organization seems to be losing much of its relevance. These days, few MNCs have any detailed charts for the whole organization. Where charts exist in parts of the organization, they tend to be partial and inconsistent. Organizational units have different and varying roles. Keeping track of unwieldy organizations is possible only with international information systems. In ABB, the corporate reporting system ABACUS is now the only corporate-wide application and the main tool for holding together the more than 5000 profit centers world-wide. Nor is formal organizational location and status necessarily anything to go by. The strategically critical unit that coordinates production and distribution in SKF, the world-leading bearing-maker, is hidden deep 'down' in one of its four divisional structures, yet in constant and direct contact with the corporate office. The Forecasting and Supply Office retains its name, although there has been a clear shift from traditional planning to clearing. This corporate communications hub is furthermore located in Belgium, and the headquarters in Sweden.

With an effective information systems infrastructure in place, spontaneous coordination can arise. Information is increasingly sought, rather than sent and, hopefully, received, be it technical or commercial information. As a rather dramatic example, consider the desperate SKF subsidiary manager from a few years ago who needed a particular type of bearing for a customer, a type that would not become available for several weeks. Remembering that the Middle East/Africa regional warehouse often complained about unreliable transport and customers leaving them with capital tied up in inventory, he inquired there. The order was placed over the standard electronic mail system and paid through the corporate netting system. Today, that single transaction has spontaneously grown into an international electronic clearing house or internal market where excess quantities of bearings are bought and sold. The example illustrates how international information systems can facilitate coordination, how dispersed decision-making can be effective, and how an organizational unit can be without physical existence (it is now labelled Global Bearing Trade).

These descriptions of MNC activities serve to demonstrate the relevance of international information systems for MNCs; a complex reality that both managers and researchers have to contend with.

EVOLUTION OF RESEARCH ON INFORMATION SYSTEMS USAGE IN MNCS

Although MNCs and new information systems have prompted much attention and research separately over at least the last quarter of a century, the intersecting set of the two has only over the last few years started to produce a rich stream of research. The main source of this surge is a merger of two fields of research; viz. information systems has come to incorporate telecommunications, and traditional telecommunications research has come to focus more on users, i.e. firms.

The seminal article by Nanus (1969), *"The Multinational Computer"* set the stage for much of the ensuing managerially-oriented research efforts. In Nanus's bold conception, the use of computer power as multinational in scope as the MNC itself would decisively strengthen the MNC as a pervasive institution in economic life, ultimately accelerating the international convergence of tastes, attitudes, product preferences and behavioral patterns. Corporate-wide use of information systems could then counteract the - at that time common - excessive decentralization of MNC operations. Instead of having a "disjointed composite of small businesses", the MNC should build on its main competitive advantage; "...its ability to consider opportunities throughout the world." (Nanus, 1969:9). Large-scale computer-based information systems would, in Nanus's vision, offer the advantages of economies of scale and better decision-making by improving the amount and quality of information available to the organization and its subsequent corporate-wide exploitation. His fundamental notion was one of more efficient and flexible utilization of a given MNC structure and set of resources primarily through improvement in the coordination of decision-making at all levels in the MNC.

Two main strands of research later picked up on issues raised by Nanus. They can be characterized as being primarily concerned with either management of information systems in the context of firm strategy, or with policy issues relating to telecommunications.

The former tended to follow strategy as - and if - it 'spilled over borders', but typically without acknowledging any distinct concerns being prompted by moving onto the international arena. The dominant strategic issues have instead largely been ones of the possibilities to create new or modified products or services with a greater information content and of the competitive opportunities brought by inter-organizational information systems. The research has mostly been set in the context of the registered enhanced efficiency of firm operations and management of the information systems function. Some influential contributions from the formative period of this managerially-oriented tradition are McFarlan and McKenney (1983), McFarlan et al. (1983), Parsons (1983), Benjamin et al. (1984), Rockart and Scott Morton (1984), Cash and Konsynski (1985), Porter and Millar (1985), and Earl (1987 and 1988).

One can also find a very small number of writings which depart somewhat from this mainstream agenda in two aspects that are particularly relevant here. First, Buss (1982) very early addressed the international dimension, but from the narrower vantage point of functional management of information systems. Second, Clemons and McFarlan (1986), Keen (1986), and Davenport and Cronin (1988) expanded the standard area of inquiry by highlighting the importance of bringing telecommunications into the analysis.

The second main strand of research focused on instead regulatory and other policy issues. Traditional telecommunications research dealing with international issues has been almost exclusively concerned with traffic flows (cf. the review by Snow, 1988), in practice meaning voice telephony between countries (for an illustrative example, see Kellerman, 1990).

Again, two subsidiary lines of inquiry have, however, addressed international data communications and in many cases done this from the perspective of the firm. One line has directly followed the regulatory trail. The observed growth of 'transborder data flows' within MNCs early on was seen either to have likely strong adverse effects on the international division of labor and consequently possibly prompting reconsideration of existing regulatory regimes (e.g. Sauvant, 1983; Jussawallah and Cheah, 1983; and UNCTAD, 1984), or to be an expression of legitimate business practices that was being threatened or thwarted by national telecommunications regulation (e.g. Buss, 1984, and Samiee, 1984). Subsequent empirical investigations (e.g. Kane and Ricks, 1989; and Sambharya and Phatak, 1990) have, however, not found such regulation to have had significant impact on MNC activities so far. - The other, related line of research to focus on international data communications has been more concerned with the larger issue of competitiveness - national competitiveness and the competitiveness of firms in different countries. Most of the early comprehensive work took place under the auspices of the Organization for Economic Co-operation and Development (e.g. OECD, 1980; Antonelli, 1981; OECD, 1983; and Parry, 1983; see also UNCTC, 1982). An important contribution to come out of this research was to make the individual firm and its *de facto* usage of international data communications the primary unit of analysis. In the process, it was clearly demonstrated how both analytical tools and reliable empirical data were sorely lacking.

The last few years have seen an impressive surge in the research on firms' usage of international data communications. Issues relating to firm strategy and management have emerged as the key concerns. Most contributions employ an information systems perspective; a research approach that lately also has become much more receptive to telecommunications issues. Notwithstanding this evolution, international information systems research is arguably still very much in its infancy. Considerable effort goes into systematically identifying the key issues (see Deans and Ricks, 1993; Ives and Järvenpää, 1991; Karimi and Konsynski, 1991; and Palvia and Saraswat, 1992). The persisting dearth of empirical data means that most research is exploratory in nature. Relevant secondary data are basically not available, either because they are not collected or because they are kept outside the public domain (often by telecommunications service providers). Attempts at alleviating this lack of data have come in a variety of ways, in particular through extensive surveys using questionnaires and/or interviews (e.g. Deans et al., 1991; and Stück and Schroeder, 1994), mainly descriptive cross-sectional case studies (e.g. OECD-BRIE, 1989; and Roche, 1992), and longitudinal in-depth case studies (e.g. Hagström, 1990 and 1991; and for a varied menu, see also the contributions in Palvia et al., 1992).

Much research remains to be done. Indeed, when surveying research on MNCs, Hedlund (1991) identified the consequences of modern information technology as one of the single most important avenues for future research.

DISPERSAL OF ACTIVITIES IN MNCs

There is a clear link between international information systems and MNCs on a fundamental level. Historically, it was technical developments in transportation and communications (notably the railroad and the telegraph) that made large and geographically dispersed corporations a viable proposition (Chandler, 1977; Caves, 1980; and Williamson, 1981). The argument is extended *à fortiori* to the advent of the first industrial MNCs at the turn of the century (Chandler, 1986). The related, early conceptions of (corporate) structure focussed on organization design for administrative purposes, encompassing both the lines of communication and the information that flow through them (Chandler, 1962:14). Structural change was found to be a response to loss of managerial control over firm operations as the firm grows. Being able to maintain complex administrative structures that reach across international borders is a necessary condition for MNCs to exist at all. Innovations in communication technologies then explain why MNCs could emerge (cf. Chandler, 1986).

Control and Coordination

The traditional emphasis on *control* of geographically dispersed operations as a key facet of MNC structure can be taken a step further. Computer and telecommunications technologies can be seen to be particularly well suited for control purposes. Indeed, forceful arguments have been put forth that maintenance of control of economic activity within organizations is *the* prime function of information technology (see Ackoff,1967; Boddy and Buchanan, 1986; and Beniger, 1986).

Much modern, managerial research puts more emphasis on integration of MNC operations. Rather than searching for explanations why MNCs arose, the MNC is taken as a given, and research worries more about how it is maintained and about what possible advantages possibly accrue to an existing, internationally dispersed firm. Dynamic *coordination* of a complex network of resources becomes relatively much more important. As a corollary, the formal organization then becomes much less important than the more elusive informal methods of coordination such as management systems, staffing, normative values, and modes and patterns of internal communication[1]. The main reason for focusing on corporate integration and coordination across markets is the identified qualitative change in the way MNC business practices have evolved in conjunction with global market segments appearing, more rapid diffusion of technology and radically improved access to multiple geographical markets (cf. Bartlett, Doz and Hedlund, 1990).

In an economic sense, the main advantages of being an internationalized firm have been identified as economies of scale and scope, operating flexibility, and successive learning about varying local conditions (cf. Kogut, 1983 and 1990). Fundamentally, economies of scale and scope hinge on classical ideas of division of labor and specialization. The firm is a bundle of different activities, divided up to the point when the benefits of specialization no longer outweigh the costs of the additional coordination that any fragmentation brings with it.

Operating flexibility translates into to the superior ability MNCs have over domestic firms in responding to changing external conditions. Similarly, learning from several local environments benefits the firm both on the input and the output side; knowledge picked up in one locality can be applied elsewhere, and an MNC is well-poised to detect commercial opportunities wherever they appear (a "global scanner" in Vernon's (1979) words).

The bottom line is that the gains from these advantages in MNCs are greater than the additional costs incurred when operating in many different countries while under one and the same management. Effective exploitation of a geographically dispersed network of organizational units requires careful monitoring of firm activities and managing interdependencies among them. In other words, maintaining control and achieving coordination are more pressing managerial challenges in MNCs than in other firms.

Location of Activities

A remaining problem is *where* these activities are carried out and the fact that they can shift their location. A case in point is MNC operating flexibility. It can be seen as a form of arbitrage, not only financial such, but also involving other resources. For instance, production can be shifted in response to persistent exchange rate movements, and research and development (R&D) can be located where a particular skill is available in the labor force.

The MNC does epitomize the geographical aspect of location, but location can also be seen to have an organizational dimension. First, there is an issue of where in the organization particular activities are performed. Consider how some activities may be geographically concentrated, but remain in the periphery of the formal organization. A logistics center in a manufacturing MNC is a common example. Conversely, activities may be geographically dispersed while being concentrated core activities in the organization. An illustration would be the top management team in a multidivisional MNC, like ABB where several Executive Committee members have their respective offices at main ABB subsidiaries. Again, the problem with the terms of centralization and decentralization are highlighted. Which of the two would best describe a situation of an organizationally concentrated activity that is geographically dispersed?

Second, there is the issue of the boundary of the firm, or whether an activity at a particular time should be carried out by the firm itself or be contracted out. 'Outsourcing' has become increasingly popular lately, but the opposite is also common. For instance, many MNCs have internalized financial activities previously carried out by banks.

Organizing and labelling these dimensions of location would then give the following, intuitive taxonomy[2]:

1. geographical location   (spatial distribution of activities)

2. 'organizational location'   (internal location of activities and
                                   their location in relation to the
                                   organizational boundary)

       a) 'hierarchical location'   (where inside the organization
                                          activities are performed)
       b) 'institutional location'   (whether related activities are
                                          external or internal to the
                                          organization)

This simple classification has the advantage of providing a terminology for the changing configuration of activities in a complex MNC. However defined, activities can be moved around and some of them are eminently suited for using the firm international information systems.

INTERNATIONAL INFORMATION SYSTEMS AS AN INFRASTRUCTURE

The standard argument explaining why a data communications network is established is twofold, putting it down to utilization of distant computer processing power, and to the need to access data located elsewhere (cf. Martin, 1981). The first reason springs from a need to overcome local insufficient processing power and the second from data being collected and stored in different locations, notably, different from the locations where they may be needed. The advent of relatively cheap and more powerful small computers means that the second reason has come to dominate, especially since commercial transactions make up the bulk of traffic and typically do not require much in the way of computer power.

However, not only data, but also applications are normally found at different locations. Consequently, access to applications - as opposed to data - is conceivably also an important rationale for establishing a data communications network.

A second point is that the important function of being a system for communication needs to be given its due weight. This function can be perceived as divorced from what is commonly called "obtaining data for computer processing" (as in Martin, 1981), unless the latter is given such a wide domain as to render it virtually meaningless. Consider, for instance, electronic mail. True, processing is involved, but it is minute and largely confined to enabling transmission. True, data are transmitted, but not really for local machine processing at the receiving end. Rather, we can typically conceive of electronic mail primarily as a delivery system; a message is sent to be received unchanged for subsequent human 'processing'[3]. In short, the idea of enhanced communications - without reference to the twins 'processing' and 'data' - is an additional motivation for having a data communications network.

The network essentially constitutes the infrastructure for making information systems (and therewith associated data) available at geographically dispersed locations. The information systems also determine the type of data that can be handled within the data communications network, subject to the restrictions set by the communications hard- and software (and, in exceptional cases, by government regulations). The implied communications network, plus the set of systems and pattern of availability or access make up the information systems infrastructure of the organization.

To clarify, the network can be seen as akin to economies of scope, whereas the computer applications (commonly called "systems") belong to the realm of economies of scale. Economies of scope cannot be attributed to any particular product or function, while economies of scale relate to achieving an efficient scale for a specific product or function. The network can be used across activities, whereas the computer applications are intended for a more specific purpose. Types of, access to, and the actual use of computer-based systems by different organizational units then say more about the intended functionality of use. But just as economies of scale and scope are not neatly separable, the network and systems categories exhibit some overlap.

The network allows the firm to exploit the economies of scale inherent in specific computer applications. Different organizational units having access to the services offered by these applications is tantamount to services being transported across space and organizational boundaries. Hence, we have *a transport system for information-based services*, where the network provides the transport and the specific applications determine which services are transported. In turn, that has implications for where geographically, and where in the organization, activities are carried out.

This function of networks and systems implies an element of *standardization* that goes beyond mere technical compatibility issues. Including the 'basic communications services'[4], the network insures standardization so that transmitted data are intelligible at the receiving end. Access, and remote usage of computer applications, thus presuppose such standardization.

Recall the example of SKF's internal electronic trading of excess quantities of bearings. The market could arise because of this wider standardization having been instituted. The example also sheds some light on the contentious issue of whether dedicated interorganizational information systems will 'degenerate' into electronic markets or not. Much of that debate deals with the importance of induced standardization. The question is how likely that is to make competition bring about open electronic markets where there are dedicated bilateral information links (see Malone et al. 1989; and Bakos, 1991). The SKF illustration gives a different, and so far neglected, angle by pointing to the evolution of firm *internal* markets; electronic markets where an 'open' and standardized communications infrastructure is likely to exist already. Hence, the tendency of common standardization to undermine interorganizational information links with restricted access receives some support.

Potential for Transporting Information-Based Services

How significant is the possibility to deliver services over the network for the MNC? Some evidence of the potential can be found in an investigation from

1986 of *all* Swedish manufacturing firms with more than 200 employees. Backed by the Federation of Swedish Industries, Eliasson et al. (1990) could allocate internal labor costs and the costs of externally purchased services for the firms' Swedish as well as international operations (see Table 1). Costs were expressed as a proportion of total internal labor costs and distributed by function with the aim to get robust measures for the extent of service activities in manufacturing firms.

It is remarkable that only some 20-25 percent of internal labor costs could be attributed to direct production; the rest being different kinds of services, primarily found to be information-based services. The share of direct production drops even further if services purchased externally are taken into account. Although measurement by labor costs gives a somewhat exaggerated view of the relative importance of services (with their high labor content), and although not even all information-based services are transportable by electronic means, the results constitute a strong - albeit indirect - indication of the possible significance of data communications networks. On the other hand, by implication a stronger case can be made regarding the same potential in service firms, particularly information service firms.

Functions	Percent
Information production and use	
Creation of new knowledge	
R&D	5.2
Design etc.	4.6
Total	9.8
Coordination	
Marketing and distribution	21.3
Administration	7.9
Other	1.2
Total	30.4
Internal knowledge transfer (training)	3.0
External purchase of services	22.0
Goods manufacturing	
Work preparation	16.5-21.5
Direct work scheduling	3.5
Technical work preparation, service, control etc.	8
Direct production	20-25
Internal transports, inventories	3-8
Total	56.7
Total - all above	122.0

Source: Manufacturing firms or divisions with more than 200 employees; global operations; 1986; percent of total internal labor costs. Adapted from Eliasson et al. (1990).

Table 1: Wage and Salary Costs of Swedish Firms Distributed on Different Functions

By offering transportation and automation of some information-based services, data communications-cum-computer applications can conceivably change the nature of activities performed in firms. Activities can be subdivided, or fragmented, differently by partial automation and recombined in new ways. For instance, the keeping of sales records can be largely automated and then combined with other data for new kinds of analyses and forecasting. With transport, the activities can be performed in new locations, also outside the firm. The keeping of sales records can more readily be externalized, local records can be kept at a different location, dispersed sales records analyzed and used within the R&D function for planning purposes etc. The advent of new information systems can allow un- and rebundling of activities to be done economically.

Innovations in goods transport have made dispersed component manufacture and subsequent assembly commonplace. In addition to improved means of transport, these innovations include the systemic switch to container transport. Similar possibilities now exist for information-based services. Particularly the 'containerization' associated with electronic transmission of data (cf. from analog to digital over telecommunication links) has greatly added to the transportation capacity. Moreover, many services are 'pre-packaged' for transport, a case in point being software. However, one significant difference between physical components and 'service components' is that the latter also includes traditional managerial activities, thus implying that service transport is likely to have more profound impact on the management of firms than the familiar transport revolution after the World War II. Clearly, these developments are especially pertinent for MNCs.

Usage of International Information Systems

One fairly recent survey of all leased lines with one terminal point in Sweden provides some measure of the extent of data communications usage[5]. The limited geographical and technical coverage inspires caution in the interpretation of the findings. However, a few observations are in order. First, Sweden is the home country of a relatively very large number of MNCs, which also tend to be highly internationalized by any standard measure (e.g. Hörnell and Vahlne, 1986). Second, telecommunications services are similarly well developed, largely as a result of the MNCs being very demanding customers (Thorngren, 1990). A related point is that Swedish MNCs exhibit relatively early and very intensive use of data communications (Thorngren, 1990; OECD 1983; UNCTC, 1982). Third, leased lines for data communications are arguably a fairly good approximation of advanced usage since they have for long been the most reliable (and in many cases the only) way to establish international data connections. Leased lines have dominated international data transmission, especially for large amounts of data. Nevertheless, this 'leased line approximation' deteriorates with better quality and availability of alternative services and with increased reliance on third-party carriage[6]. Leasing lines is very often still the preferred option (cf. Andresen, 1993).

The survey does include third-party carriage, although in that case the final customer (part-leasee) cannot be identified. The underlying data are the technical records of the configuration of all international lines leased for data communications. The existing stock of lines was registered on two occasions, at year-end 1987 and 1989. Institutional changes motivate this timing, since 1987 represents the very last year before large scale third-party carriage, and in 1990 the records went from being implicitly to explicitly classified as confidential. Although no legal monopoly has ever been awarded to Swedish Telecom, all international lines had to be leased from it due to simple physical availability. Thus, the turn of the year 1987/88 represents the last chance to obtain a complete picture of user categories, and 1989/90 similarly was the last opportunity to measure the total stock of international leased lines. Some salient features of the data are:

- a total of 600 leased lines for data communications were recorded 1987/88;
- the net increase in the number of lines and number of customers was slightly more than ten percent over the two years;
- the average number of leased lines per user remained largely stable at 2.5;
- the total transmission capacity (Mbps) increased more than three- fold during the same time;
- well over half of the leased lines were 9.6 kbps connections; and
- capacities of 14.4 kbps - 2 Mbps made up more than half of total capacity 1987/88, whereas 2 Mbps only accounted for close to two-thirds 1989/90.

The picture that emerges is one of a fairly stable population with rather few links. However, the large increase in capacity is an effect of a migration of leasees to third-party carriage and less of a dramatic upgrading of connections. The true increase in the number of connections at the two times of measurement, i.e. allowing for this switch, was somewhere in the range 40 - 50 percent. Taken together with the known capacity distribution, it appears that very modest links dominate. That is consistent with the observation that data communications is primarily used for internal and external control purposes, or at least for financial and similar data which do not require much in the way of capacity (in particular if compared to technical uses).

One significant advantage of the data is that they allow looking at the distribution of users by main activity, thus obtaining a fairly detailed view of which types of organizations generate international data communications. Table 2 below provides such a classification, one which closely follows the International Standard Industrial Classification (ISIC). Some subdivisions were, however, made to single out particular activities, and one heading ("Mass media.....") was adjusted to better reflect the underlying data.

Leased Lines by Main Activity of Customer in Sweden
(Shares of total leased lines; unweighted and weighted by actual line capacity)

Industry/Activity (No. of organizations for 1987/1988; and 1989/90)	1987/88 (%)	1987/88 Weighted (%)	1989/90 (%)	1989/90 Weighted (%)
Foods (3; 3)	0.5	0.3	0.5	0.1
Textile and apparel (3; 4)	0.8	0.5	0.9	0.2
Wood and wood products (3; 3)	1.0	0.6	1.5	0.6
Paper and paper products (8; 9)	2.0	1.0	1.8	0.4
Chemicals, pharmaceuticals, petroleum etc. (20; 24)	5.3	3.3	7.2	1.8
Metal products, machinery and equipment (52; 53) *	30.2	23.9	26.2	10.1
of which computer equipment (26; 26)	[16.5]	[14.9]	[14.8]	[6.9]
Miscellaneous manufacturing (8; 8)	2.3	1.5	2.5	0.5
Trade (15; 14) *	7.5	5.8	7.3	2.9
Transport and travel (39;48)*	16.7	34.6	16.2	23.8
Communications (8; 7) *	2.2	1.8	4.5	47.5
Financial services (21; 24) *	13.7	15.1	14.1	7.8
of which banks, cards and insurance (13; 16)	[3.0]	[1.9]	[3.3]	[0.9]
Business services (24; 30)	8.8	6.3	7.9	2.2
of which computer services (20; 25) *	[8.2]	[5.9]	[7.2]	[2.0]
Public administration (3; 3)	1.0	0.5	1.1	0.2
Research and scientific institutions (3; 5)	0.8	0.5	1.4	0.6
Mass media, incl. publishing, printing and news agencies (20; 18)	5.2	3.2	4.0	0.8
of which (non-financial) news agencies (3; 3)	[1.3]	[0.7]	[1.1]	[0.2]
Total - all above (230; 253)	98.0	98.9	96.9	99.5
Total - six main(*) above (155; 171)	78.4	87.2	75.4	94.1

Note: Main activities with only one or two organizations recorded at any one occasion are not listed. These are mining (2; 1); glass and pottery products (2; 3); basic metal production (1; 1); electrical and gas industry (1; 3); construction (2; 4); hotels (1; 2); and cleaning etc. services (0; 1). The remaining (2; 2) organizations could not be classified.

Table 2: Leased Lines by Main Activity of Customer in Sweden (Shares of total leased lines; unweighted and weighted by actual line capacity

The overall pattern emerging from Table 2 appears to confirm previous research (e.g. OECD-BRIE, 1989; OECD, 1983; and UNCTC, 1982) in that service industries and the computer industry (which here also includes telecommunications equipment) account for a lion's share of international leased lines. Some discrepancies do occur, however. The relatively high share for manufacturing industry, and low one for the banking, credit cards and insurance category stand out. The former, 'overrepresentation' is a reflection of the category covering most of Sweden's well-known and highly internationalized MNCs. Scrutinizing financial services demonstrates that it is the financial information providers, not the traditional financial firms as typically assumed, that dominate strongly.

Taking also capacity into account, the dramatic growth in third-party carriage becomes clear. The communications category captures most of that development[7]. Computer services, and to some extent computer equipment, could be expected to conceal demand for international data transmission by other firms. However, the raw data suggest that most traffic is more directly related to the firms' own activities. In addition and contrary to common, earlier perceptions, there is little evidence of any computer service bureaus activity. In computer services, one finds mostly small, local firms in the software business with one or a few subsidiaries in neighboring countries.

One could argue that there are still rather few connections and most often of modest capacity. That may invite the suspicion that there is more hyperbole than substance in the discussion about the importance of international data communications. On the other hand, individual firms come out as very avid users. Both the aggregate data and the underlying records indicate that instead of sector (as is often assumed), *firm characteristics* are a more important determinant of international data communications activity. For instance, in Table 2 above this translates into a high share of communications falling in the engineering sector, a sector where most experienced Swedish MNCs are active. In financial services, a very high scoring intersection is "connections to the UK; financial information provision sector; non-Swedish-owned firms, firm internal communications", which would be a good description of a firm like Reuters. The survey also found a preponderance of firm internal over external links[8], which lends additional support to the firm being more relevant as a unit of analysis than industry. Finally, the remarkable rise of plain third-party carriage, as opposed to elaborate value-added transmission services, suggests that the technical capabilities rest with the user[9].

Modern communication technologies offer opportunities, but the key to their exploitation is dependent on *individual firm capabilities*. The link between effective use of these technologies on the one hand, and knowledge about the firm itself and its business on the other, is much stronger than commonly held. With information systems representing an enabling condition, and with new uses and services evolving rapidly, much is left to managerial creativity.

Scope of the MNC

Perhaps the greatest managerial challenge posed by the advent of new information and communication technologies is the need to 'rethink' which activities the firm performs. If new possibilities to transport information-based services can prompt significant changes internally, so they can with external parties. For instance, the unbundling property means that information systems can make it possible to externalize an activity that previously could not be separated out from other activities. By opening for possibly increased specialization (as in the analogous case of internal specialization) unbundling can, of course, also lead to internalization of activities previously performed by other parties (e.g. internalization of specific financial services). However, the scope for specialization is normally greater on the market. Information systems enabling new choices therefore tend to favor selective externalization of some 'old' internal activities, rather than internalization of totally new activities. Using SKF as an illustration, its extreme specialization of production translates into a potential logistics nightmare with a dramatically increased number of product shipments. Previously, shipping was a complex activity, but being able to separate out pure transport from planning, inventory management, picking, sequencing, follow-up etc., SKF could contract out the transport, letting the trucks run on prespecified routes according to a set timetable. This critical activity could only be externalized once SKF was able to separate it out and keep total control over it; something its information systems infrastructure enabled it to do.

So, there is an additional quality to many information systems-mediated external relationships, a quality that has to do with control (and, indirectly, with inter-firm coordination). 'Marginal' cases of externalization (i.e. where the benefit thereof is very small) can change with the advent of information systems. A common argument has it that assuring quality control of critical upstream activities is an important motive for backward integration (e.g. Casson, 1987); a more general motive being reducing uncertainty (Arrow, 1975). The contention here is that those needs can be satisfied through information systems thus reducing the need for vertical integration. The more general argument is that if control of a relationship improves with information systems, legal incorporation of that particular activity becomes less of a necessity. We are also reminded by Ashby (1965) that it is always cheaper to control, or monitor, a system than to manage it outright. In addition, the combination of unbundling and control means that many unbundled activities are externalized, not to an arm's-length market, but to a 'controlled' external relationship. In other words, loss of control from loss of ownership can, in part, be compensated for by maintained control through information systems.

Down-stream internalization of activities has attracted more attention as evidenced by the popularity of add-on services. Here, information systems offer new opportunities for differentiation among customer relationships, not least by their offering a distinct mode of delivery in addition to un- and rebundling of services. Common examples are different direct ordering services, as in the case of a large manufacturer *vis-à-vis* small distributors. Shorter lead-times translate into inventory reductions. If better and more timely information is made available to the distributor (delivery schedules, current prices, product data etc.), the accuracy and timeliness of the distributor's ordering will tend to improve, thereby allowing further stock reductions for both parties. Perhaps less obvious is the further step of using accumulated customer order histories. Being much more easily accessible when stored in electronic format, the manufacturer can use the data to better anticipate a small distributors ordering. More accurate knowledge of ordering patterns means that smaller buffers are required. Finally, by combining the accumulated information on the particular distributor with aggregate customer order histories and aggregate forecast demand the manufacturer can advise the distributor on his ordering procedures, stock levels and stock mix. Better inventory management by the small distributor improves his customer service and can thus increase the manufacturer's sales at a given level of inventory. At the end of the day, a significantly changed supplier-customer relationship has been enabled through information systems usage.

The example serves to illustrate the range of options that have become available, the likely blurring of organizational boundaries, and the potential value of the information of information systems. With many applications becoming easily to copy, competitive advantage has come to rest more with the accumulated information, and in the experience of how to accumulate information and how to use it, than with a particular application or information link.

CONCLUDING REMARKS

The discussion has attempted to show how activities can be reconfigured and how the rules of the game have changed. Competitive dynamics drive the process and firms ignore these opportunities at their peril. Looking at the problem through the simple lens of the multidimensional (re-)location of activities may help in making sense of what is happening and which are the opportunities that present themselves.

The view of international information systems as essentially a transport system for information-based services has several implications, not least of which is the need to rethink what the organization does, and where and when it is done. Given that MNCs already are dispersed geographically, tend to be complex organizationally, and are more likely than others to have a coherent information systems infrastructure in place, they are in the best position to take advantage of new opportunities and to the greatest effect.

Information systems improves the ability to maintain control over what appears to be in the process of becoming ever more complex and unorthodox organizations. In addition, spontaneous coordination between far-flung organizational units unleashed by the existence of a solid information systems infrastructure in such an organization can be strikingly effective. Maintaining and developing this infrastructure then becomes a key managerial imperative.

Endnotes

[1] Recent, comprehensive conceptions of this kind, which explicitly distance themselves from MNC structure as a question of organizational form, are Bartlett (1986), Hedlund (1986), Bartlett and Ghoshal (1988 and 1989), and White and Poynter (1990). Hagström (1992) applies this type of approach to the area information systems in MNCs.

[2] For a fuller argument, see Hagström (1991).

[3] The gist of our argument remains, although electronic mail messages frequently have attached files, or contain other information, which eventually is processed by a computer.

[4] The main such services, which are intimately associated with a network, are interactive traffic, remote job entry, file transfer, different (technically determined) gateways, and connections to external systems and networks. The concept of 'basic' services corresponds well to the International Standards Organization's (ISO) Open Systems Interconnection (OSI) model for data communication, although that model was developed for technical and regulatory purposes (cf. ISO, 1986; and Tanenbaum, 1989). The services included here relate to the three top layers of the model (i.e. session, presentation, and application). For instance, file transfer is specified in the top layer.

[5] Reported in extenso in Hagström (forthcoming).

[6] The most relevant services here are particularly X.25/X.28 (to a limited extent also X.21), and carriage refers to carriage basically void of value-added services, a case in point being straight resale of excess capacity.

[7] An early, large, but temporary, third-party carrier (SAS, the airline) inflate the 1987/88 figures.

[8]The figure for 1987/88 was 66 percent and for 1989/90 67 percent of the number of leased lines. About 10 percent and 15 percent, respectively could be identified as going between two different firms. The remaining lines could not be classified with certainty.

[9] It also casts some doubt over the assertion that national telecommunications service availability and their degree of sophistication are a key determinant of usage and, in turn, of business competitiveness (for instance, as in OECD-BRIE, 1989).

References

Ackoff, R. L. (1967), "Management Misinformation Systems", **Management Science**, Vol. 14, No. 4, pp. (B)147-(B)156.

Andresen, J. (1993), "Leased Line Choices for High-Speed Data", **Telecommunications (International Edition)**, Vol. 27, No. 12, pp. 21-24+.

Antonelli, C. (1981), "Transborder Data Flows and International Business - A Pilot Study", **Directorate for Science, Technology and Industry**, Working Party on Information, Computer and Communications Policy, Expert Group on Transborder Data Flows, DSTI/ICCP/81.16. Paris: OECD.

Arrow, K. J. (1975), "Vertical Integration and Communication", **Bell Journal of Economics**, Vol. 6, No. 1, pp. 173-183.

Ashby, W. R. (1965), **An Introduction to Cybernetics**. London: Methuen & Co.

Bakos, J. Y. (1991), "Information Links and Electronic Marketplaces: The Role of Interorganizational Information Systems in Vertical Markets", **Journal of Management Information Systems**, Vol. 8, No. 2, pp. 31-52.

Bartlett, C. A. (1986), "Building and Managing the Transnational: The New Organizational Challenge" in Porter, M. E., ed., **Competition in Global Industries**. Boston, Mass.: Harvard Business School Press, pp. 367-401.

Bartlett, C. A., Doz, Y. and Hedlund, G. (1990), "Introduction: The Changing Agenda for Researchers and Practitioners" in Bartlett, C. A., Doz, Y. and Hedlund, G., eds., **Managing the Global Firm**. London: Routledge, pp. 1-12.

Bartlett, C. A. and Ghoshal, S. (1988), "Organizing for Worldwide Effectiveness: The Transnational Solution", **California Management Review**, Vol. 31, No. 1, pp. 54-74.

Bartlett, C. A. and Ghoshal, S. (1989), **Managing Across Borders: The Transnational Solution**. Boston, Mass.: Harvard Business School Press.

Beniger, J. R. (1986), **The Control Revolution: Technological and Economic Origins of the Information Society**. Cambridge, Mass.: Harvard University Press.

Benjamin, R. I., Rockart, J. F., Scott Morton, M. S. and Wyman, J. (1984), "Information Technology: A Strategic Opportunity", **Sloan Management Review**, Vol. 25, No. 3, pp. 3-10.

Boddy, D. and Buchanan, D. A. (1986), **Managing New Technology**. Oxford: Basil Blackwell.

Buss, M. D. J. (1982), "Managing International Information Systems", **Harvard Business Review**, Vol. 60, No. 5, pp. 153-162.

Buss, M. D. J. (1984), "Legislative Threat to Transborder Data Flow", **Harvard Business Review**, Vol. 62, No. 3, pp. 111-118.

Cash, J. I. Jr. and Konsynski, B. R. (1985), "IS Redraws Competitive Boundaries", **Harvard Business Review**, Vol. 63, No. 2, pp. 134-142.

Casson, M. (1987), **The Firm and the Market: Studies on Multinational Enterprise and the Scope of the Firm**. Oxford: Basil Blackwell.

Caves, R. E. (1980), "Industrial Organization, Corporate Strategy and Structure", **Journal of Economic Literature**, Vol. XVIII, No.1, pp. 64-92.

Chandler, A. D. Jr. (1962), **Strategy and Structure: Chapters in the History of the American Industrial Enterprise**. Cambridge, Mass.: The M.I.T. Press.

Chandler, A. D. Jr. (1977), **The Visible Hand**. Cambridge, Mass.: The Belknap Press of Harvard University Press.

Chandler, A. D. Jr. (1986), "The Evolution of Modern Global Competition" in Porter, M. E., ed., **Competition in Global Industries**. Boston, Mass.: Harvard Business School Press, pp. 405-448.

Clemons, E. K. and McFarlan, F. W. (1986), "Telecom: Hook Up or Lose Out", **Harvard Business Review**, Vol. 64, No. 4, pp. 91-97.

Davenport, L. and Cronin, B. (1988), "Strategic Information Management: Forging the Value Chain", **International Journal of Information Management**, Vol. 8, No. 1, pp. 25-34.

Deans, P. C., Karwan, K. R., Goslar, M. D., Ricks, D. A. and Toyne, B. (1991), "Identification of Key International Information Systems Issues in U.S.-Based Multinational Corporations", **Journal of Management Information Systems**, Vol. 7, No. 4, pp. 27-50.

Deans, P. C. and Ricks, D. A., (1993), "An Agenda for Research Linking Information Systems and International Business: Theory, Methodology and Application", **Journal of Global Information Management**, Vol. 1, No. 1, pp. 6-19.

Earl, M. J. (1987), "Information Systems Strategy Formulation" in Boland, R. J. Jr. and Hirschheim, R. A., eds., **Critical Issues in Information Systems Research**. Chichester: John Wiley & Sons, pp. 157-178.

Earl, M. J. (1988), "IT and Strategic Advantage: A Framework of Frameworks" in Earl, M. J., ed., **Information Management: The Strategic Dimension**. Oxford: Clarendon Press, pp. 33-53.

Eliasson, G., Fölster, S., Lindberg, T., Pousette, T. and Taymaz, E. (1990), **The Knowledge Based Information Economy**. Stockholm: Almqvist & Wicksell International.

Hagström, P. (1990), "New Information Systems and the Changing Structure of MNCs" in Bartlett, C. A., Doz, Y. L. and Hedlund, G., eds., **Managing the Global Firm**. London: Routledge, pp. 164-185.

Hagström, P. (1991), **The 'Wired' MNC: The Role of Information Systems for Structural Change in Complex Organizations**. Stockholm: IIB/Gotab.

Hagström, P. (1992), "Inside the 'Wired' MNC" in Antonelli, C., ed., **The Economics of Information Networks**. Amsterdam: North Holland/Elsevier Science Publishers, pp. 325-345.

Hagström, P. (forthcoming), "International Data Communications - A Survey of All Leased Lines by User Category in Sweden 1987-1990", forthcoming in **Information Economics and Policy**.

Hedlund, G. (1986), "The Hypermodern MNC - A Heterarchy?", **Human Resource Management**, Vol. 25, No. 1, pp. 9-35.

Hedlund, G., ed. (1991), **Organization and Management of the TNC**. New York, N.Y.: United Nations Centre on Transnational Corporations.

Hörnell, E. and Vahlne, J.-E. (1986), **Multinationals: The Swedish Case**. London: Croom Helm.

International Standards Organization (1986), "Open Systems Interconnection", **Advance Technology Alert System (ATAS) Bulletin**, Centre for Science and Technology for Development, United Nations Secretariat, New York, Issue 3, June, pp. 33-34.

Ives, B. and Järvenpää, S. L. (1991), "Applications of Global InformationTechnology: Key Issues for Management", **MIS Quarterly**, Vol. 15, No. 1, pp. 31-49.

Jussawalla, M. and Cheah, C.-W. (1983), "Emerging Economic Constraints on Transborder Data Flows", **Telecommunications Policy**, Vol. 7, No. 4, pp. 285-296.

Karimi, J. and Konsynski, B. R. (1991), "Globalization and Information Management Strategies" **Journal of Management Information Systems**, Vol. 7, No. 4, pp. 7-26.

Kane, M. J. and Ricks, D. A. (1989), "The Impact of Transborder Data Flow Regulation on Large United States-Based Corporations", **Columbia Journal of World Business**, Vol. 24, No. 2, pp. 23-29.

Keen, P. G. W. (1986), **Competing in Time: Using Telecommunications for Competitive Advantage**. Cambridge, Mass.: Ballinger Publishing Company.

Kellerman, A. (1990), "International Telecommunications Around the World", **Telecommunications Policy**, Vol. 14, No. 6, pp. 461-475.

Kogut, B. (1983), "Foreign Direct Investment as a Sequential Process" in Kindleberger, C. P. and Audretsch, D., eds., **The Multinational Corporation in the 1980s**. Cambridge, Mass.: The M.I.T. Press, pp. 38-56.

Kogut, B. (1990), "International Sequential Advantages and Network Flexibility" in Bartlett, C. A., Doz, Y. and Hedlund, G., eds., **Managing the Global Firm**. London: Routledge, pp. 47-68.

McFarlan, F. W. and McKenney, J. L. (1983), **Corporate Information Systems Management: The Issues Facing Senior Executives**. Homewood, Ill.: Richard D. Irwin.

McFarlan, F. W., McKenney, J. L. and Pyburn, P. (1983), "The Information Archipelago - Plotting a Course", **Harvard Business Review**, Vol. 61, No. 1, pp. 145-156.

Malone, T. W., Yates, J. and Benjamin, R. I. (1989), "The Logic of Electronic Markets", **Harvard Business Review**, Vol. 67, No. 3, pp. 166-170.

Martin, J. (1981), **Computer Networks and Distributed Processing**. Englewood Cliffs, N.J.: Prentice-Hall.

Nanus, B. (1969), "The Multinational Computer", **Columbia Journal of World Business**, Vol. IV, No. 6, pp. 7-14.

OECD (1980), **Policy Implications of Data Network Developments in the OECD Area** (No. 3 in the "Information, Computer and Communications Policy" Series). Paris: OECD.

OECD (1983), "Transborder Data Flows in International Enterprises: Based on Results of a Joint BIAC/OECD Survey and Interviews with Firms" (Note by the Secretariat), **Directorate for Science, Technology and Industry**, Committee for Information, Computer and Communications Policy, DSTI/ICCP/83.23, Paris.

OECD-BRIE (1989), "Information Networks and Business Strategies: An OECD-BRIE Project on Competitiveness and Telecommunications Policy", BRIE Working Paper 38, **Berkeley Roundtable on the International Economy**, University of California, Berkeley.

Palvia, S., Palvia, P. and Zigli, R. M., eds. (1992), **The Global Issues of Information Technology Management**. Harrisburg, Penn.: Idea Group Publishing.

Palvia, S. and Saraswat, S. P. (1992), "Information Technology and the Transnational Corporation: The Emerging Multinational Issues" in Palvia, S., Palvia, P. and Zigli, R. M., eds., **The Global Issues of Information Technology Management**. Harrisburg, Penn.: Idea Group Publishing, pp. 554-574.Parry, T. G. (1983), "Multinational Enterprises' Structure and Transborder Data Flows: Main Trends in the Evolution of Multinational Enterprise Structure", **Directorate for Science, Technology and Industry**, Committee for Information, Computer and Communications Policy, DSTI/ICCP/83.24, Paris.

Parsons, G. L. (1983), "Information Technology: A New Competitive Weapon", **Sloan Management Review**, Vol. 25, No. 1, pp. 3-14.

Porter, M. E. and Millar, V. E. (1985), "How Information Gives You Competitive Advantage", **Harvard Business Review**, Vol. 63, No. 4, pp. 149-160.

Roche, E. M. (1992), **Managing Information Technology in Multinational Corporations**. New York, N. Y.: Macmillan Publishing Company.

Rockart, J. F. and Scott Morton, M. F. (1984), "Implications of Changes in Information Technology for Corporate Strategy", **Interfaces**, Vol. 14, No. 1, pp. 84-95.

Sambharya, R. B. and Phatak, A. (1990), "The Effects of transborder Data Flow Restrictions on American Multinational Corporations", **Management International Review**, Vol. 30, No. 3, pp. 267-289.

Samiee, S. (1984), "Transnational Data Flow Constraints: A New Challenge for Multinational Corporations", **Journal of International Business Studies**, Vol. 15, No. 1, pp. 141-150.

Sauvant, K. P. (1983), "Transborder Data Flows and the Developing Countries", **International Organization**, Vol. 37, No. 2, pp. 359-371.

Snow, M. S. (1988), "Telecommunications Literature: A Critical Review of the Economic, Technological and Public Policy Issues", **Telecommunications Policy**, Vol. 12, No. 2, pp. 153-183.

Stück, J. M. and Schroeder, D. L. (1994), "Transborder Data Flows Usage by U.S. Subsidiaries in Mexico and Hispanic South America: A Preliminary Regional Study", **Journal of International Business Studies**, Vol. 25, No. 2, pp. 389-401.

Tanenbaum, A. S. (1989), **Computer Networks**. Englewood Cliffs, N.J.: Prentice-Hall International.

Thorngren, B. (1990), "The Swedish Road to Liberalization", **Telecommunications Policy**, Vol. 14, No. 2, pp. 94-98.

UNCTAD (1984), "Services and the Development Process", **United Nations Conference on Trade and Development**, The Secretariat, TD/B/1008, United Nations, Geneva.

UNCTC (1982), "Transnational Corporations and Transborder Data Flows: A Technical Paper", **United Nations Centre on Transnational Corporations**, ST/CTC/23, United Nations, New York.

Vernon, R. (1979), "The Product Cycle Hypothesis in a New International Environment", **Oxford Bulletin of Economics and Statistics**, Vol. 80, No. 2, pp. 190-207.

White, R. E. and Poynter, T. A. (1990), "Organizing for World-Wide Advantage" in Bartlett, C. A., Doz, Y. and Hedlund, G., eds., **Managing the Global Firm**. London: Routledge, pp. 95-113.

Williamson, O. E. (1981), "The Modern Corporation: Origins, Evolution, Attributes", **Journal of Economic Literature**, Vol. XIX, No. 4, pp. 1537-1568.

SECTION-7

| GLOBAL IT APPLICATIONS |
| *AND CASES* |

True to the top-down philosophy used for organization of chapters in this book, this final section takes a microscopic view of key global IT management issues within the domain of specific MNCs.

First chapter in this section by Palvia and Lee describes the key factors contributing to the successful development and implementation of the GIS application **Seaserv** in Seagate Technology International. Besides other factors, the presence of a virtual project team, worldwide definition of users' requirements, and a global groupware to monitor and control the project were cited as critical to the success of the Seaserv GIS application.

The second chapter by DiNardo describes the installation of a GIS being currently implemented in Citibank's Global Consumer bank in the Asia Pacific region. This system uses the classical three tiered architecture (client, local server, and centralized superserver). This chapter documents insights into factors like "centers of excellence", network cost, regulatory constraints, cross border cooperation, and country to country differences.

Finally, the chapter by Sankar and Terase describes the strategic alliances that General Motors forged with many different car manufacturers, supplier, and dealers worldwide to be a successful global player. Realizing the ability of information technology to reduce costs of production and increase the quality of products, GM has been aggressively implementing global MIS applications and telecommunication networks. This chapter also discusses the key commonalties and differences between interorganizational systems (IOS) and internal MIS applications developed by GM.

25 Developing and Implementing Global Information Systems: Lessons from Seagate Technology

Shailendra Palvia
Long Island University, U.S.A.

Kenny Lee
Nanyang Technology University, Singapore

Seagate Technology, headqaurtered in California, is a world leader in disk drive manufacturing. Distinct from its competitors, it is a highly vertically integrated company with manufacturing operations located primarily in Singapore, Thailand and Malaysia; and for design centers located in U.S.A. Information Technology functions are centrally controlled out of California while providing substantial autonomy to worldwide manufacturing locations for IT operations. To utilize economies of scale, to provide similar and consistent services, and to facilitate responsiveness to its customers worldwide, Seagate develops and implements Global Information Systems (GISs). One such GISs is the Seaserv application, which provides a centralized global after-sales service capability for repairing faulty disk drives. This application, through one of the largest VAX-based Warranties database, and system availability close to 100% throughout 24 hours of the day and 365 days of the year, has become a source of major competitive advantage for Seagate. This chapter captures successfully with a case approach, the key factors responsible for successfully developing and implementing a GIS like the Seaserv application.

INTRODUCTION

Seagate Technology, located in Scotts Valley, California, is one of the world's largest disk drive manufacturers. Its operations are higly vertically integrated. In 1984 its management took a decision to relocate its key plants into three countries in Southeast Asia, beginning with Singapore, to take advantage of the cheaper skilled labour. It was a bold move in a volatile and technology-intensive industry, one that stretched the company's resultant value chain across large geographic distances and made the organization ever more dependent upon Information Technology (IT). Today, Seagate uses global IT (GIT) and its global Information Systems (GIS) applications to not only link American-based senior management, Asian

manufacturing plants, and R&D centres in four   locations in the U.S., but also
to practise Just-In-Time (JIT) and Total Quality Management (TQM).

Singapore   continues to be Seagate's regional   headquarters for its
Asian operations. With two major data centres   located in Singapore and
significant IT operations in Penang (Malaysia) and Bangkok (Thailand), it is also
the regional headquarters for Seagate's Far East Asian IT operations. Two of
Seagate Far East's Global Information Systems (GIS) applications are featured
in this case - SEASERV, which is key to Seagate's strategic hard disk service
and repair operations in Singapore and worldwide, and the Thailand Local
Currency Accounting system which when operational will significantly
simplify the Thai Seagate unit's tax accounting in its native location.

On July 1, 1994 Seagate Technology closed its books on another
record year. Revenue for the Scotts Valley,   California, based   company
exceeded US$ 3.5 billion, up 15% from the previous year's, while net income
grew to US$ 225 million and primary net income per share increased to US$
3.08, compared to US$ 2.80 the previous year. Also as of the end of 1993, the
disk drive giant employed over 58,000 employees worldwide of whom some
48,000 are based in South East Asia.

SEAGATE AND THE DISK DRIVE INDUSTRY

More About the Company

For Seagate and its competitors, the disk drive manufacturing industry
has proven to be a   fast-growing,   price-sensitive, high-technology, and often
times volatile (owing to the cyclical nature of the demand for the industry's
output) business that is witness to both high growth rates and equally rapid
reversals.   Major players in this business include   Conner Peripherals,
Quantum (now a part of Digital), Western Digital, Maxtor, and Micropolis.
Competition is fierce, with   price erosions of 5-8% per quarter being common.
Being in the computer industry in which the technology and its engineering
tolerances improve an order of magnitude every couple of years, technology
factors such as higher MTBFs (Mean Time Between Failure), higher storage
densities, and higher access speeds; better quality; lower costs; and resilience
of manufacturing operations to volume swings are critical to success.

In addition to setting high standards in many of the above areas,
Seagate prides itself on being a nimble and   lean organisation, and has
maintained prudent fiscal policies that have resulted in very low debt levels
and substantial cash reserves. The policy has stood the company in good stead
during periods of industry downturns when its competitors had been forced
towards other palliative measures. Finally Seagate's employees play an
important role in the realisation of its mission and its quality philosophy.
The company continues to invest heavily in its people in Singapore and
elsewhere, by way of training, and use of industry-leading personnel policies.

Seagate Technology has four design centres located in the US - two in California, one in Minneapolis, one in Oklahoma City; and three major manufacturing facilities along with some basic engineering development capability in the Far East in Singapore, Thailand, and Malaysia. Geographically, therefore, the company's operations are far-flung with the workflow beginning in the US at product design, and going on for manufacturing and engineering to the Far East.

The company manufactures all the components and subassemblies that go into their disk drives - the printed circuit boards (PCBs), the motors including most of the components, the actual disk media, and the most important semi-conductor heads (the key technology in this business). Thus, Seagate effectively controls all the critical technologies. There is very little sub-contracting - presently the company subcontracts some of the motor manufacturing, but it has the capability of fully manufacturing the motors on its own. By contrast the other disk drive manufacturers (all of whom are represented in Singapore), can be referred to essentially as "glue factories". They hardly do any manufacturing, instead they simply design at the top level, outsource for the requisite components, bring these all together at the final assembly level, test the drives, and finally ship them out. They are therefore extremely dependent upon outside suppliers for their components.

Seagate's strategy of vertical integration has so far worked. However Todd Bakar, an analyst who tracks the company for Hambrecht & Quist in San Francisco, cautions, "in a market upturn, when demand is growing and capacity is constrained, vertical integration is positive. But in a downturn, all the extra overhead works against you."

Traditionally a single-product (disk drive) company, Seagate's current technology acquisition and development strategy is directed towards taking advantage of the market opportunities created by the shift to client/server architecture and the development of the global information infrastructure. Seagate founder, Chairman and CEO, Alan F. Shugart in the Company's latest annual report to shareholders says, "As a leading provider of data storage technology, Seagate is a vital contributor to the latest technology trends such as distributed and client/server computing. With a strong balance sheet built from our success in storage devices, the company has begun acquiring and developing additional enabling technologies that can facilitate its expansion into emerging and established data industry markets, including data access and data management ....Seagate will maintain its focus as a Technology Company and continue to participate in the high growth markets emerging from rapidly transitioning technology".

One such instance is the recent acquisition of Palindrome Corporation, a developer of the state-of-the-art data management and protection software. Palindrome met a very important goal of Seagate - venturing into advanced technology. Through this acquisition, Seagate plans to leverage its technical expertise and market position to tap into the broader storage management market, especially in enterprise network computing.

Seagate's Shugart is regarded in some ways as the father of the disk drive, having begun his career in the early 60s as an engineer in IBM, then moving on to Memorex where he developed the first plug-compatible disk drive, following which he went on to found several ventures in this new technology. Seagate Technology itself was founded by Shugart only as recently as in 1981, and has since grown rapidly to become the Fortune 500 company that it is today, completely dominating the technology and its industry. It continues to sell its disk drive products into two basic markets - major computer manufacturers and also directly to customers under its own label through approved distributors worldwide. As an OEM supplier it supplies its drives to computer manufacturers such as Sun Microsystems, AT&T/NCR, and the IBM-compatible PC makers. At its core, Seagate remains very much an engineering-driven company with a significant R & D investment. In a business in which the recording head constitutes the key technology, Seagate today controls many of the significant head patents and innovations.

Competition in the Disk Drive Industry

In the computer industry slump during early 1990s, while its competitors had been slashing costs, closing factories, firing employees, and becoming assemblers of other companies' components, Seagate managed to stay vertically integrated and consistently profitable. While the combined losses of its biggest competitors - Conner Peripheral, Quantum, Western Digital, Maxtor, and Micropolis - amounted to around $400 million in 1993, Seagate earned $195 million, or $2.85 per share.

Seagate's strategy is to maintain the same margin of profit even when there is tremendous price cutting pressure to stay competitive. They do this by cost cutting through control of technology and manufacturing. "By maintaining control of our technology and our manufacturing, we do not give away our margins," says Al Shugart, the CEO of Seagate Technologies. Seagate's gross margins, have been holding up in the 18%-22% range, even though disk drive prices have been witnessing price erosions at an average of 5-8% a year.

Fiscal 1994 was a record year for Seagate Technology. Revenue soared to $3.5 billion, while net income grew to $225 million. Primary net income per share increased to $3.08, compared to $2.80 in the previous fiscal year. See Appendix-1 for Selected Financial Data for 1990 through 1994. Net sales in 1994 were 15% higher than those reported for 1993. The increase was primarily due to higher level of unit shipments inspite of price erosion due to intense competition. Although price erosion for the company's lower capacity products slowed considerably during the last half of 1994, it became more severe for the company's higher capacity products - particularly due to aggressive marketing from large OEM computer manufacturers. The decrease in gross margin as a percentage of nett sales can be also attributed to this price erosion. Compared to 1993, product development expenses increased by 12%; and marketing and administrative expenses increased by 6%.

Investment in Technologies

Since 1988, Seagate has spent an average of 20% more per year per dollar of sales on new plant and equipment compared to its five competitors. In October 1989, Seagate acquired $450 million of Control Data Corporation's high-capacity disk drive business. According to Shugart, "the deal added $1 billion to Seagate's sales, but the technology alone was worth the deal."

Over the years, Seagate has improved its technological strength in two areas. First, the area of "thin-film" recording heads in which the heads read changes in the magnetic flux on the disk surface which are then amplified, filtered and converted to digital representation by the electronics of the disk drive's circuit boards. Second, magneto-resistive (M-R) heads which actively "read" the disk by passing a slight but steady current through the head and measuring resistance of the head to the flow of electricity. The M-R technology allows a 30% increase in the number of tracks that can be put on a disk, and about 15% increase in the number of bits per track. Seagate has also developed expertise in tiny precision motors and spindles and other components. According to Shugart, "The control of the above technologies gives you cost advantage because if you manage it properly, your time-to-market should always be better than competitors who are just designing and assembling drives from other other people's components."

Seagate's competitors are hot on developing and perfecting 1.3" disk drives. Shugart expects that the storage density of disks (number of bits per square inch) will continue to double every two to three years for the next decade. Such miniature drives have their potential use in mobile computing. "But you can solve the memory problems for laptops and smaller devices, like personal digital assistants (PDAs) with semi-conductor flash memories," says Shugart. Seagate bought a 25% stake in Sundisk, a flash memory maker, in January 1993. Shugart believes that there is room for lot more increase in disk capacity. For example, right now, there are no magnetic disk drives that can handle motion pictures digitally (1.5 terabytes for a single motion picture).

EDI IN THE GLOBAL VALUE CHAIN

Seagate Technology, like many manufacturing companies, works to a master production schedule which in itself is driven by a sales forecast. Given Seagate's highly vertically integrated approach, this means that the master production schedule drives supply chain needs and capacity planning all the way down to the lowest levels of the organisation. Many of Seagate's plants therefore, are dependent for their components upon direct shipments from plants the next level below. An example is the manufacture of the semi-conductor heads, which begins with the production of the wafers at one of the two worldwide locations - Minneapolis in the US, or Springstown in Northern Ireland. The wafers are then air-shipped into Penang where they are shaped electronically into the flying heads that read the disk surfaces. The flying heads are subsequently processed at the assembly plants in Malaysia and Thailand into head-arm assemblies and then into disk-arm assemblies. Finally, these subassemblies are put together into a head-disk assembly in Singapore.

The company is therefore its own customer and supplier at each stage of the supply chain. This allows Seagate far tighter control over its operations than if it was dealing with outside suppliers; however at the highest levels it is extremely vulnerable to supply line breaks. For instance the plants in Singapore are dependent upon three flights daily from Thailand for shipments of components and subassemblies; upon arrival these are put directly onto the assembly lines. Should there be a disruption of this part of the supply chain then the Singapore assembly line would be seriously affected, as it is the practice that many of the Seagate plants do not carry buffer stocks. This kind of vertical integration provides Seagate with flexibility in reducing work-in-progress inventories. Given that the customer-supplier relationship is an interplant (intragroup) relationship in most cases, Seagate exemplifies a bold demonstration of the use of JIT concepts for managing production schedules.

To get the JIT concept to work, there needs to be a free flow of physical materials, dependable transportation, good working relationship with the various national customs authorities, and most important, exchange of electronic information between plants. Says Rod Mackinlay, Seagate's IT Director for the Far East, "We are very dependent upon our IT and on interplant EDI to make all this happen". For example within minutes of a shipment leaving its plant in Thailand for Singapore, an in-transit record with all the details of the shipment is received electronically in Singapore, and a few hours later the same physical shipment is received in Singapore against the previous electronic document. Along with shipment documentation intercompany billing is also done electronically through EDI.

ABOUT SEAGATE FAR EAST

Automation of the disk drive manufacturing technology has progressively driven down the labour cost component to the extent that the labour cost accounts for less than 5% of the total value of a drive. Still the total labour cost component is considered to be significant given the sheer volumes of drives that are produced each day. To avail of the cheaper skilled labour available, Seagate's management took a bold decision in 1982 to relocate its key manufacturing plants into three countries in Southeast Asia beginning with Singapore in 1982, Bangkok (Thailand) in 1984, and Penang (Malaysia) in 1988.

Of the 48,000 Seagate employees in this part of the world, Singapore accounts for about 13,000, and Thailand employs majority of the remaining 35,000 employees. This makes Seagate Technology one of the largest private sector employers in both Singapore and Thailand. In Singapore the three Seagate plants are located at Kallang, at Sembawang, and at Jurong. As an indication of the improved productivity achieved through the steady automation of Seagate's manufacturing processes over the years -- it should be noted that the 13,000 employees of Seagate who produced 8,000 drives a day six years back have since ramped up their daily output to over 40,000 drives today without any additional employees.

Singapore continues to be Seagate's regional headquarters for its Asian operations. With two major data centres located in Singpaore as well as significant IT operations in Penang and Bangkok, it is also home to Seagate's Far East Asia IT operations.

Seagate Far East IT Operations

Rod Mackinlay joined Seagate in 1988. As Director of MIS for the Far East business and based in Singapore's Kallang plant, he is responsible for IT operations in Singapore, Penang, and Thailand. Like Schugart he has worked many years in the disk drive industry, including at IBM and a number of years at Memorex before coming to Seagate. He reports directly to the VP, MIS located at Scotts Valley along with four other MIS directors worldwide and in the U.S., but is responsible on a dotted line basis to Javed Chaudhary, the VP and General Manager, Seagate Technology International, Singapore/Chokchai Operations.

MIS, especially systems development, at Seagate Technology is centralised and controlled out of Scotts Valley, California. Operations however, are decentralised into the manufacturing facilities and each major factory has its own data centre that runs applications for that plant. Wherever feasible, standard IS applications run at each of these data centres. In the Far East, consistent with this philosophy, IT has been decentralised into the Seagate operations in Singapore, Thailand, and Malaysia, with the result that each of the three countries now possesses significant MIS capabilities. The idea is to organise MIS in such a way as to assure a high level of IT availability at local level, so that local management feels that IS applications meet their needs and that they have control over the IT resources. The MIS management challenge, says Mackinlay, is "to provide Manufacturing (the plants) with solid local operational support from MIS, but at the same time to stay in control (of MIS)", and it appears that they have achieved this balance.

Commenting on the achieved level of integration of the technology with user processes, Rod Mackinlay lauds the high service levels provided by his MIS Managers in the respective countries they support, adding "Plant managers get the impression that they are the ones (and not IS) who have the control of IS", as indicative of the rapport and close working relationships achieved   by IS with their users. Acknowledging the user role   in the partnership's success, he enthuses, "For example we have extremely IT-literate engineering users in our organisation,   and they do some really classy presentation graphics with our downloaded data (on their workstations and PCs)".

Seagate Singapore MIS Organisation

Seagate   is a Digital shop, and Singapore's multiple VAXes are networked locally and worldwide into a large international wide-area network that includes Sun Microsystems workstations and PCs.   The organisation is globally dependent upon this network and the near-seamless integration of data, telecommunications, applications,   and technology infrastructure that has painstakingly been built over the years.

The   Singapore   MIS operations are currently   geared   around decentralised data centres at Kallang and at Senoko, whereas Tuas operations shares the Kallang facilities over a high speed   data link.   The   MIS management is currently in the process of consolidating the operartions into a single large data center operation in order to realise benefits of scale. Application systems just like hardware and software platforms are common from plant to plant, to facilitate compatibility and consistency.

The overall IS manpower count in Singapore was 46 as of the end of June 1994, with most of these personnel being located in   the Kallang facility under a Singapore MIS   Director. Applications support and development teams are organised by functional/application area - Manufacturing System development and   Finance/HR System development. Some of the   IS applications were developed in Singapore, most were sourced from Scotts Valley or from other locations in the US. Most early applications had been developed in either 3GLs or using packaged vendor software, e.g.   the   MANMAN manufacturing package. The   more   recent applications are written in 4GLs and are based on the use of a relational database management system -- INGRES. Seagate prides itself in providing extensive continuing training to its IS professionals and also in deploying newest technologies.

The transaction levels that are managed in Singapore are extremely high to support the business processes in the core manufacturing operations of order management, shipping, and packaging for the 40,000-plus disk drives that are produced each day. The response and performance requirements for these systems are very high since these must conform to very high levels of availability in order to ensure that shipment schedules are met. All of these applications are tightly integrated and are ultimately networked via global telecommunications links, 24 hours a day, into databases in the countries that Seagate has operations in.

DEVELOPING GLOBAL INFORMATION SYSTEMS

The development of international informations systems can give multinational firms a basis for increased coordination and control or direct competitive advantage in global markets. From a successful multinational company's perspective global IS (GIS) applications enable the company to avail of the economies of scale and scope in its manufacturing and marketing operations.

The reasons for building GIS at Seagate are several. First, GISs encourage Seagate's operations around the world to build similar business processes (e.g. for procurement, for tracking, for inventory, etc) "that gives us a common face to the customer; it also gives us a common way of looking at data," says Rod MacKinlay. Second is economies of scale. According to Rod, "instead of building five different fixed assets systems and three different human resource information systems around the world, we can obviously benefit if we can build one of each, and accomodate the local customisation requirements of the country at the same time. Also common applications running on standard hardware/software platforms increase economies of scale." The third motivation is more effective utilisation of IS or user skills - "if we have a specialist already who's developed and implemented a certain application, and that individual is stationed in one of our plants, we can, by finding a way to put together a worldwide development team that includes that person, pass on the benefits in implementation and time to other sites" explains Mackinlay.

What factors must be considered in GIS development? One factor is deciding on project team mix or composition. It may be necessary to strike a balance between getting representation from the various countries (as well as from the major plants) onto the team, versus making use of the skills that already exist. "More emphasis on skills could sometimes result in a less-than-homogeneous team that is biased towards the country where the skills were," says Rod MacKinlay. Another factor is that cultural and communications skills differences in the various countries where Seagate operates need to be recognised, especially when eliciting requirements.

Key global IS applications at Seagate include systems for multi-plant materials and capacity planning, materials requirements planning, and a repair service tracking system called SEASERV. "High on my list of priorities is the question -- how do we develop and implement high-value IS in a cost-effective way that attempts to avoid pitfalls such as duplicate development, as well as being meaningful in terms of meeting the real business requirements (of the local countries)?" says Mackinlay. The following sections depict some of the classic problems, issues, and challenges that Seagate faced in building its two GIS applications -- its strategic SEASERV application and its Thai Local Currency Accounting system.

The SEASERV Application

An IT-based after sales-service can provide strategic competitive advnatage to a firm in any industry. For a global company like Seagate, a global after-sales service capability without sacrificing special local needs, is critical for sustaining competitive advantage in the volatile disk drive manufacturing industry. Such a global IS application does exist for Seagate's global customers for repiring faulty disk drives and is called SEASERV. Implemented in 1994 at Kallang in Singapore, SEASERV is a GUI-based system whose development in-house was led by the MIS group at Minneapolis using the ABF/VISION (4 GL) code generator on top of an INGRES (Relational DBMS) platform.

SEASERV links Seagate's three major repair centres -Amsterdam, Oklahoma City, and Singapore to a central warranties database through Seagate's worldwide network. SEASERV has extensive interfaces to other plant functions worldwide through the company's MANMAN manufacturing package and other application databases. System availability is close to 100% and the system runs 24 hours a day in order to support customer service activities around the globe. "SEASERV is a strategic system for competitive advantage and survival. SEASERV is an asset (to our business), and Seagate's Customer Service and Repair (CSR) division has extremely close relationships with Marketing, Design, and with Manufacturing," says Mackinlay. Exhibit - 1 captures the worldwide nature of this application spanning several locations around the globe.

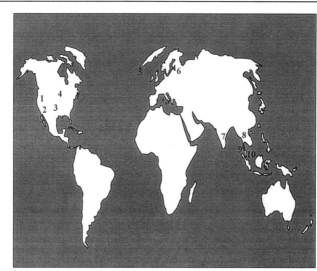

1- Scotts Valley, CA
2- Location-2, CA
3. Oklahoma City, OK
4. Minneapolis, MN
5. Springstown, Ireland
6. Amsterdam, Holland
7. Bangalore, India
8. Bangkok, Thailand
9. Penang, Malaysia
10. Singapore

Exhibit 1: Worldwide Locations of Seagate Operations

SEASERV provides Seagate with the kind of global after-sales service that this far-flung company needs to support its products. Although the company's disk drives are entirely produced in the Far East, only 11% of the drives manufactured here end up in the Asian and Pacific Rim area - the rest end up mostly in the US (60-70%) and Europe (12-15%). However when a customer calls Seagate for service in Singapore, which is Seagate's largest CSR operation, from anywhere in the world, SEASERV can get the customer's details and the serial numbers up onto the screen immediately, verify if the warranty was valid, then schedule the faulty shipment of drives for repair. SEASERV can even tell if a disk was a stolen drive! (in which case the drives concerned could be trapped if they subsequently showed up for repairs)!

Prior to the SEASERV system, repair and service procedures were essentially manual. Seagate's sales agents had to take the customer complaints and requests for repair manually or over the phone and then fax the information to the main plant in order to verify the warranty on the drives concerned. In the new system, there exists a single worldwide Warranty database containing information on every disk drive that has ever been shipped, along with its entire history. Access is online and data can be shared by any number of locations. Every drive is serial numbered, even though up to 50,000 are produced a day, and information captured includes the date and place of manufacture of the drive, where and to which customer the disk was shipped to, whether it had failed at some point in its history, and if so when, along with details of the failure, the date of repair, and of return to the customer. The database is reportedly one of the largest VMS-based databases in the world.

A customer's faulty drives are usually replaced immediately by Seagate with new drives. Occassionally however, the customer prefers to have the faulty drives fixed and returned to him, in which case the drives are accepted and scheduled for service or repair. SEASERV then tracks the process of rectification of the faulty hard disks all the way from acceptance through billing (if the warranty is expired, or invalidated, as is the case sometimes), and the generation of statistics (on turnaround time, repair time, etc). The trapping of such failure statistics is a valuable by-product of the CSR (Customer Service & Repair) disk servicing and repair activity for these provide Seagate engineers with a rolling picture of failures, e.g. as a disk model matures in the field, failures of a particular type by customer are encountered. The data is also deployed to project warranty exposure, and to track and analyse field failures. Such information is critical and SEASERV plays a central role in getting it fed back to various functions including Quality, Engineering, Design, Manufacturing, and Marketing.

The Thai Local Currency Accounting System

North American MNCs like Seagate Technology that have operations in a number of countries do their management accounting and performance reporting in the currencies of the respective host countries. Such

MNCs also have to discharge their local corporate accounting responsibility in the local native currency - as tax rates, tax algorithms, statutory requirements, depreciation procedures etc., are different in different countries. A common practice by most MNCs, including Seagate, is to customise an existing general ledger application to the local operating unit's requirements.

In the case of Seagate, the US operations were using a general ledger and a management reporting system from a major package vendor; however the package had neither multi-currency nor local currency reporting capability. So when Penang (Malaysia) required a local currency accounting system a couple of years back, Rod Mackinlay assigned an analyst from the Minneapolis office to Penang to do the customisation. More recently, the Bangkok operations required a computerised local currency accounting system. MacKinlay intended to use the the expertise of the Minneapolis analyst to customize the global accounting system.

ISSUES AND CHALLENGES IN GIS DEVELOPMENT

Drawing on the development and implementation experience of these two GISs studied, some issues and factors are proposed in the following pages, which may be critical to the development of successful Global ISs.

Obtaining Management Buy-in

The project request for the SEASERVsystem was originally made by CSR back in the US. At Seagate, the ideas for GISs may be conceived at and originate from any level, but often times they come from Head Office, e.g. from the Vice President of Materials Management. At other times, these may originate from the operations side, whether from Head office or overseas. Frequently Rod MacKinlay's boss, the worldwide VP of MIS (formerly, a senior user-manager in the Materials Management area himself), scans the business environment for new IS application opportunities and personally champions many such ideas.

Rod MacKinlay figures that his MIS boss' role in the birth of a project is crucial, because "he knows the Seagate business as well as, or better than, anyone around". The VP of MIS is constantly looking for opportunities for improvement in the processes and procedures in various functional areas. Typically when an opportunity is spotted, he follows up by going down into the specific functional area to do the requisite hard selling. Then an outline system is sketched out, following which the division involved reviews the proposed system's objectives - whether the system agrees with the overall objectives and vision and figure out how to get the project off the ground.

In the context of the development of SEASERV (and other GISs), Mackinlay recalls some early stage key factors in developing excellent GISs, "identifying the right project scope, agreeing with the objectives, getting the management buy-in and commitment levels, which in many cases may involve the services of a management consultant or of an outside specialist....if we do this (early stage) correctly then chances are that we'll get an application that is usable, accepted, and one that contributes to the competitiveness of Seagate International". Elaborating on what he meant by the right project scope, Mackinlay continues, "developing an application that has the right basics (like) locating the centre of the project in the right country; spreading the risk; assuring the availability of professional people (resources); and developing systems with multi-plant capability, on compatible platforms".

Avoid Duplicate Application Development

Applications requests, regardless of where they originate from, are first checked out on a networked global database of recently developed applications worldwide to avoid duplication of development effort and waste of resources. If a similar application already exists elsewhere in the worldwide organisation, then its developer may be contacted and a networked demonstration arranged remotely before deciding whether to develop the new system. In 50% of the cases, Seagate gets the "insurance factor" of an outside consultant (industry or application specific specialists) to confirm the business relevance of the proposed system. The use of consultant resources is always directed, i.e. the purpose is for the consultants to assess, then to confirm/endorse (or even to reject) the project direction, not to "come and tell us what to do" according to MacKinaly. Getting the consultant's confirmation of the project in this fashion lends legitimacy to its subsequent phases. Project steering committees are not used much within Seagate. Presently there is one in the Finance function but its focus is more towards systems implementation, rather than towards idea generation or idea validation.

Where Does the Expertise Lie?

"Assuming that everything is fine, and that we've got management buy-in, a budget, and some high-level objectives - and even an acronym (like SEASERV) - now we've got a project. The next question is -- where will it be done?" continues Rod MacKinlay. "Here the critical factor is "where are the resources that are needed to do this", i.e. where does the expertise lie that is needed - and this could be anywhere - in Singapore, the US, or in Thailand".

For the Thai local currency accounting case, the requirements were local (in Bangkok), and the programming resources were also in Bangkok; however the systems expertise was in Minneapolis. They wanted the services of a Minneapolis based analyst who had previously designed the Malaysian Local Currency Accounting system for the Thai project. A related consideration is that of cost. For the Thai local currency accounting system case, if cost had been the sole consideration, then the entire project would likely have been done in Thailand. On the other hand if the key determinant was the right type of people to customize the GIS, then it was more likely that the project would have been done in the US (which would have been expensive). The option chosen was an optimal way combining low costs of Thailand with the expertise of Mineapolis.

The Virtual Project Team

What finally transpired was that the project was carved up and partitioned in such a way that Seagate Thailand initially provided the MIS personnel to do the local requirements determination, following which the Minneapolis-based analyst was stationed out in Bangkok for a few weeks, supervising three local MIS professionals, and specifying the design.

But before the Minneapolis analyst arrived in Bangkok, he would engage in some information exchange and discussion via e-mail and video-conferencing with the Thai IS personnel. While in Bangkok, he would work with the Thai personnel to come up with design specifications and then return to his home base in Minnesota. At the beginning of the next critical phase, he would return to Thailand again, and so forth until implementation time, when he would return finally to oversee the execution of this critical stage. Throughout these phases, the team was assisted by a firm of contractors from Bangalore (India), from where one member was flown out to Thailand periodically. The Bangalore-based member of the team had worked on other Thailand projects for Seagate and so was familiar with the people and business environment. This geographically extended project structure was organized regardless of the location of the best resources from around the world with the project leader (the Minneapolis-based analyst) reporting to Mackinlay. On those occasions that such people resources were not available internally, then the organisation would turn to outside sources.

In the case of SEASERV the IS development team comprised key IS personnel from Minneapolis, Scotts Valley, and Singapore. Extensive video conferencing and telephone conferencing facilities were deployed to link the team together, to reduce travelling time and expense - for instance with video conferencing and a document camera, project schedules, graphic specifications and so forth could be reviewed and discussed by the team to very great levels of detail.

Insourcing and Outsourcing- Using the Best Resources Worldwide

In the case of the Thai Local Currency Accounting project the Bangalore outsourcer had recently installed a leased line linking its office via satellite to the Seagate Vaxes in the Singapore IT offices. In this way, and until such time as the outsourcer installed his own VAX, his programmers would have access to Seagate Singapore's machine resources to build and test the

Bangkok programs. This arrangement is typical of numerous other GIS projects at Seagate worldwide, past and present.

Worldwide Requirements Definition

When asked what was different about developing GIS as opposed to local IS, Mackinlay responded, "When the functionality of an IS is built from the point of view of the headquarter country, performance may be suboptimal when subjected to the high transaction volumes and specific or exceptional demands of the decentralised (local) location." Many of the successful GIS that are eventually implemented in Seagate's overseas locations have their development roots in the host MNC country but the requirements focus is always the local user. SEASERV is no exception in this regard.

In the SEASERV case, the system was built entirely in Minneapolis. This was simply because the MIS people who knew about customer service were based there. However pains were taken during requirements analysis to accomodate the local requirement worldwide. The makeup of the project team reflected this effort of the fourteen personnel that formed the development team, two were from Seagate Singapore.

From the outset user surveys were administered throughout Seagate's worldwide operations to determine the need for replacing the old system, and to identify broad requirements for the new system. This was followed by a White Paper on the system's feasibility. A Design Action paper was then circulated comprising problem identification, project definition, user requirements, and functional specifications. The requirements were then developed interactively with the Minneapolis CSR (Customer Service Repair) users using an INGRES-based prototype. Subsequently the prototype was used to extract the detailed design specifications that formed the blueprint for SEASERV.

The system was then written in the INGRES 4GL/VISION at a level of requirements that was common to Seagate's three worldwide CSR sites. The idea was to develop a standard parameter-driven system that could be customised to each site using country-specific parameters, system flags, and commands.

Such worldwide elicitation of requirements is a sound long term investment for the life of the system. For one thing, it promotes global ownership of the system and helps in smoother implementation after design and development. Also, ongoing support can be spread globally.

Testing and Implementation - the Right Pilot

Testing was carried out at the three CSR sites in the Netherlands, in Singapore, and at Oklahoma City. All test results had to be first approved by the customer service organization centrally organized in Minneapolis. The prototype proved to be extremely difficult to volume-test as there was lot of logic embedded in the   system.   Low-volume site Amsterdam was logically chosen as the first test site, followed by Singapore, and lastly, Oklahoma City. However when   it came   to   high-volume testing it   was   found   that significant modification to the prototype's design was   necessary for   the database to manage the high transaction volumes encountered.

Following this SEASERV was pilot-implemented at Oklahoma City. In Singapore SEASERV was implemented in 1994 and already further changes to the system have been necessary to   accomodate the steadily increasing transaction volumes.

Maintenance Strategy

System support for SEASERV continues to   be centralised in Minneapolis. Consistent with the SEASERV theme   of centralised   GIS development and centralised database management is the practice of centralised change control, in which all major system revisions and changes are centrally controlled out of Minneapolis. This strategy is not unique to SEASERV, but is also true for other major GIS at Seagate. Local reporting requirements and urgent change requests however, may be handled locally but changes to the database are allowed only by the Minneapolis IS office, in the interest of assuring data consistency and integrity.

The Continual Sell

A fast-moving   organisation   like   Seagate Technology   needs to continually adjust with the volatile market forces of its industry and to continuously align its organisation structures - a characteristic of the industry. This frequently causes a change of senior-level management, and potentially impacts the GIS project sponsorship of new applications and of projects-in-progress. Says Mackinlay of this industry-specific factor, "If you don't spend the continual extra effort to make sure that people understand the goals and objectives of the new application, you may start off fine but as the project progresses, core functionality will be compromised thereby endangering the workability of the application."

The danger in this business is that, over the new project's finite life-span (which may be a year or more), the company has changed significantly in the way it has been doing business, possibly even in the type of products sold, and in the manufacturing processes employed, and the senior managers are now a new set of people. Then, says Mackinley, "if you haven't been selling the new IS' objectives all along, you've got a real problem. Because you've used up your budget, and you've got a system that's ready to go in, and a bunch of middle management people who've been with the system all along - so you've got a user group who believe in it and who want to do it - but the senior guys don't even know what it's all about, and the natural tendency is for them to question what was done by the previous set of management. So then you'll have to go out and sell the project all over again..."

BUSINESS STRATEGY FOR THE FUTURE

To achieve Seagate CEO Shugart's vision of providing relatively inexpensive massive disk storage capacity and to capture a major share of this potential market, Shugart hired Stephen Luczo from Bear Sterns in 1993 to be the Senior Vice President of corporate development. Luczo's assigned goal is to double Seagate's sales in the next five years, no easy feat for a company whose sales have been growing only at about 7% a year. "What we'll be looking for," says Luczo (Kindel, 1994), "are products that we can sell, maybe with services, maybe without, and we'll sell them either bundled or unbundled. But we're not looking to get out of the product business, because once you do, you can never get back in. You lose all of the day-to-day incremental knowledge that makes you competitive."

Furthermore, Seagate is targetting at broadening the scope of its product from data storage to data management. Towards this goal, Seagate plans four or five acquisitions in the year ahead. Shugart wants Seagate to be a global company and to meet this goal, he is seeking companies strong in speech recognition or other forms of natural language interface between man and machine. He said, "There have been changes in the business and home environment. The challenge is to manage interfaces in the home environment...the keyboard is the wrong thing for the home."

A few months ago, Seagate bought software publisher Crystal Services. In the summer of 1994, it acquired 25% of Dragon Systems of Massachusetts, a company that develops advanced speech recognition technology for PCs and workstations. Seagate is also eyeing CD-ROMs for multimedia software. "With multimedia...the convergence of audio and video is absolutely huge," states Shugart (Leow, 1994). Meanwhile Seagate cannot make enough of its new, highest capacity 9-gigabyte Elite-9 disk drive.

Another possible avenue of exploration for Seagate is the new memory card technology, the popularity of which could lead to their replacing the floppy drive in laptop-notebook computers. While the replacement of hard drives with memory cards is technologically feasible, it is not yet economically feasible. However success in the latter area would be more likely if memory cards initially replaced the floppy. Technically, the card outperforms the floppy in several areas, chief among them being robustness - cards can withstand 1000Gs of impact, as compared to 70Gs for floppy drives and 10Gs for a small form factor hard drive. Replacement of the floppy drive by the memory card slot may be most attractive to users of operating systems with graphical user interfaces (GUI) and for mobile personal computer users who also have home or office desktops. The combination of the ROM and flash technologies in cards will give the users the ability to run software and temporarily store work on cards.

The product cycles in this business keep getting shorter and shorter. In trying to position itself as the visionary data technology company, Shugart (Leow, 1994) recognizes that, "with an increasing dependency on global interaction comes the requirement for global solutions... that means the access and exchange of data on a global basis...through an extensive global communications infrastructure... Seagate is committed to the essential core technologies for the efficient storage, management, access and delivery of data, Seagate continues to invest in the development and marketing of data technology products that increase the capabilites and effectiveness of global business information systems."

References

Kindel Stephen, "Maverick," *Financial World* (TWO), vol. 163, Issue 2, January 18, 1994.

Leow, Claire, "Seagate wants to be Leader in Data Technology," *Business Times*, September 12, 1994.

26 Regional Banking and Credit Card Processing at Citibank Consumer Banking and it's Global Implications

George P. DiNardo
Citibank & Nanyang Technological University,
Singapore

This chapter documents the planning, implementation, and control issues faced by Citibank while implementing a regional Information System. The system uses the classic three tiered architecture (client server and centralized super server) with an end to an end hub and spoke configuration. The vision of this system development and implementation is driven by the "citibanking" concept which simply means that the system development will be such that the customers will have the same set of services in any of citibanks' branches throughout the world to provide a "universally uniform" experience. The chapter emphasizes a novel approach of "centers of excellence": which utilizes geographically dispersed expertise and experience for development and implementation of the Credit Card application in the South East Asia region. The chapter also recommends paying attention to network cost, regulatory constraints, cross border cooperation, network sizing, and country to country differences.

INTRODUCTION

This chapter is devoted to a case study and presents a real world installation of a Global Information System which is currently being implemented in Citibank's Global Consumer Bank in the Asia Pacific region. This system uses the classical three tiered architecture (client, local server and centralized super server) with an end to end hub and spoke configuration. This configuration provides, at the output end, customer services (through client devices) such as cash withdrawals, deposits or payments etc. at a teller or an ATM, which can be transacted at any of the customer service locations in any of the 15 Asia Pacific Consumer Banking (APCB) countries. The other end of this continuim is the hub, located in Singapore that does the transaction handling, account updating and application processing (i.e. customer account balance) on large IBM mainframes. The transformation is from the current local independant systems in each country to a regionalized super server (a large IBM mainframe) located in Singapore (the hub), connected to a communications controller (concentrator) in each country. The communications controller in turn talks to at least one server in each Citibank branch. The server is then connected to client stations at Teller, ATM and Customer Service Workstations.

Connectivity is achieved via a traditional SNA backbone network. The wide area networks (WANs) are primarily terrestrial fibre links or fast path statelite links. The WANs are then connected to the 17 local countries via telecommunication controllers (IBM 37XX). Transmission throughout the country is via Telecommunication Control Protocol (TCP). These backbone networks are engineered primarily as digital data networks. They can of course also carry voice and "voice over data" transmission where voice sending over unused data bandwidth will be tested shortly.

THE ORIGINATION OF GLOBALIZATION

Citibank is and has been a global bank for its large corporate customers for more than 100 years. With physical locations across the entire world and offshore services that include
global cash management, foreign exchange, letters of credit, wire transfer, custody management etc, Citibank's position as a leader in global wholesale banking remains a true strength.

The Global Consumer Bank however, is far younger than its corporate counterpart. Although exhibiting a long and luxurious history in New York city in the USA, the consumer bank is less than 25 years old in terms of truly global physical presence and service. Accordingly, although the consumer bank has provided global service via interconnected ATMs, wire transfer and securities transactions, it has for the last five years or so adopted a novel concept called "Citibanking". This is simply defined as a system where the customers will have the same set of services in any of Citibank's branches throughout the world. The customer "experience" will be universally uniform.

Regionalization

Toward this end, the Asia Pacific Consumer Bank of Citibank has been working on an open client server teller and platform system (SABRE) for all of its branches. Sabre uses a Windows Graphical User Interface (GUI) and NT operating system, which is the Citibank corporate standard. For screen text, Visual Basic is the standard, as is C++ for the server language.

The presentation will begin with an analysis of the underlying strategy surrounding regionalization. Accordingly, regionalization for the APCB consists of two basic elements that occur simulataneously:

a) The consolidation of computer hardware from 15 countries, i.e. Singapore, Malaysia, Thailand, Indonesia, Hong Kong, Korea, Philippines, Guam, India, Taiwan, Saudi Arabia, United Arab Emirates, Australia, Pakistan and Turkey into large IBM computers housed in two separate Data Centers in one country (Singapore). The primary mainframes are located in a fully engineered facility in a very colloquial area. This facility performs the majority of the production operation and houses the master consoles that control this and the backup site. The backup site, is an unmanned facility (lights out) located several miles away that handles all of the program testing and development as well as some production. This site is designed to take over the primary load within 15 minutes. When this backup complex (with the primary and backup site located in Singapore) is fully tested and debugged, the backup site will then be relocated to another country so as to eliminate any country risk. It will however always remain a lights out facility!

b) The conversion of the current back end processor functions from a panoply of legacy systems running on decentralized hardware located in each country with the attendant (in country) operating and programming support, to a set of integrated backend systems running on regionalized large IBM hardware located in Singapore, is currently under progress.

These current back end processor application systems include basic banking systems such as CORE and COSMOS[1], DEVINE[2] and OASIS/BASIS[3] which will all be converted to the SYSTEMATICS ASSET & LIABILITY SYSTEMS. In addition, an entire suite of additional back end systems such as CIITPLUS (multi-currency time deposits), SHARE HOLDER RECORD KEEPING (mutual fund sales at branches), SHARE FINANCING (stock purchase on the margin) etc, will be constructed as contemporary Object Oriented Mainframe systems. The objects and the code will be structured, although code generation via Texas Instruments Interactive Engineering Facility (IEF) is also under current evaluation as a mainframe tool.

Management of The Regionalization Process: The idea for regionalization of the computer center, as well as the conversion to common back end system was incubated as a APCB Group process. The planning and decision making was done as a top down process. Buy in at the country level came later.

Country technology heads were then brought in to have the plan presented to them in early Spring 1994. Their suggestions were incorporated and a preliminary schedule drawn up for three groups (AS400, IBM Mainframe and UNIX) of countries. Positional swaps at the contry to country level were encouraged. The projects was then presented to country managers at a meeting in late Spring 1994. All other geographic areas of Citibank were kept fully appraised of the process with the most interest coming from Europe via presentation and citimail.

The countries were expected to establish a strong management team and to manage the project especially the USER ACCEPTANCE TESTING (UAT). Integrated Consumer Banking Systems (ICBS) managed by Dan Hartman and Sergio Araneda in the case of the AS400 countries would provide a team of professionals experienced in SYSTEMATICS to handle the conversion. The Singapore conversion team, managed by Ajit Kanagasundram handled the Singapore conversion, provided experienced staff to ICBS, assisting with Turkey and will soon start the Malaysia conversion. Hong Kong, originally scheduled to execute its own conversion, will probably be helped by the Singapore team. India is scheduled to do its own conversion and will assist Dubai. Much of the Dubai work is now scheduled to be handled by a third party vendor. I suspect this might change over time and they will seek more assistance from ICBS.

Multiple conversion teams were established in order to parallel the effort and therefore reduce the overall duration of the conversion periods.

Management Information Systems Approach: This regionalization project also include a very serious overhaul of the Asia Pacific Consumer Bank's MIS effort! Effective April 1995, a regional MIS team under the direction of S. Ramakrishnan has been formed, with the express charter of establishing a more effective (in terms of information quality and cost) MIS approach. Initial plans call for the creation of a consolidated MIS database made up of controlled (in proof) data extractions from the various regionalized back end and Global Relationship Banking (GRB) systems. This consolidated MIS database is frequently referred to as an Information Warehouse. A standard set of MIS reports is currently being assembled, and is projected to serve 75% of our MIS needs. The savings for this project were not part of the original Major Expenditure Proposal (MEP), but could achieve (save) an additional US$4-5 million per year. We will with this part of our effort, move from being "Awash to the gunnels with data" to "being filled with management information".

Staffing: Our staffing plans are based on two principles:

1. Conversion of each country's computer center to a regionalized computer center. Country (local) requirements would then be reduced to producing transmitted reports, microfiches etc. Labor reductions occur in the area of computer operators and sytem programmers.

2. The establishment of several applications development "Center of Excellence" for the production and maintenance of backend systems for all countries simultaneously. Centers of Excellence, plus the implementation of Systematics, result in a reduced number of applications programmers.

Therefore net personnel reduction from regionalization approaches 150 staff members. Attrition will be the rationalization vehicle for this reduction down!"

Commodity Versus Strategic Systems

The basic theme is then to switch the back end processing systems to vendor produced packages where the systems are of a COMMODITY nature and to build internally with the latest tools a series of modern user friendly parameter driven systems for STRATEGIC products.

It is important to note that this regionalization is part of a much larger APCB technology strategy that is being implemented country by country at the same time. Specifically, we are rolling out to those countries who convert to the Systematics back end our feature rich open Client Server Branch Teller and Platform System (Sabre Teller and Sabre Platform). We are also rolling out to those same countries our proprietary Automated Teller Machine (ATM) system built by a Citibank owned company. This ATM is in the Citibank parlance called "CAT"[4] (Customer Activated Terminal) and has the ability to be accessed universally (i.e. anywhere in the world where Citibank has installed a CAT). We call our version "ASIA CAT". 'PC CAT" and Home Banking are varients on the CAT theme and are also being rolled out.

Today's world of sophisticated consumer bank servicing is coupled to the customers overall bank relationship. The customer's value is determined by both the absolute value of the customers balances as well as the number of the customer accounts! At Citibank, this customer relationship system is certainly more powerful and sophisticated than most, and is accomplished by a computer applications system called GRB[5] (Global Relationship Banking). Current global relationshps are structured around a recently updated GRB system that has been modernized to suit each countries'needs as well as the needs of CITIBANKING. We are also PROCESS RE-ENGINEERING during and after regionalization, Systematics and Sabre. Consolidation of appropriate clerical operations to regional sites is the final part of our program and will commence in 1996.

TESTING THE CONCEPT

Our concept was tested and verified using the credit card application. A modestly equipped computer center was constructed in Singapore and labelled the Regional Card Center (RCC). A large air cooled IBM mainframe was installed. Telecommunications were engineered and initial installation undertaken. Although bandwidth was much less than that required for the full banking system, it was felt that it would be a good pro-forma test of the future system. A modern credit card software system was designed, coded and made operational in late 1993. This system was specifically designed for IBM large mainframes The performance of the early phases of this regionalized credit card system was very satisfying. Uptime was greater than 99.9%, costs were substantially reduced and cycle time for new products and features was infact reduced by more than 60%.

Regionalization of all countries (except India), and processing on a new and vibrant system will be completed by November 1995. Both Card and Banking will run on the same hardware, thus facilitating a single GRB thereby dramatically aiding CITIBANKING as well as providing large, computer economies of scale.

What this means quite simply, is that in Citibank Asia, the Global Consumer Bank will process both credit card and banking applications on the same regionalized computer, using GRB. This of course enhances our ability to fold in the credit card services and balances into the overall Citibank customer relationship.

Elements of Control

It is important to note that the elements of control, security and high volume capacity were the determining factors in selecting client-local server-super server (mainframe) architecture. Stated another way, Citibank's APCB group technology office selected the three-tiered architecture because no other available architecture had the flexibility and user friendliness of the client server front end while at the same time provided the control features of IBM mainframe super server. These control features include:

a) very robust data and operating system security features
b) substantial (industrial strength) data processing capacity needed to service the requirements of the APCB
c) good backup, backout and recovery capability
d) powerful multi-tasking operating system
e) a strong set of vendor provided utilities and application programs.

These criteria apply in many situations, but are critical for interconnected consumer banking networks that have more than 500 branches.

Citibank, like General Motors, produces many products for many markets. It is true therefore, that Citibank has substantial experience in developing and in fact vending various banking systems. Specifically, Citibank technology in India in concert with the Nucleus Systems Group have produced a very novel and feature-rich banking system running on RISC hardware. This system called OASIS/BASIS provides full service consumer banking using the UNIX operating system. It is novel in that it emulates IBM multi-tasking by hooking many UNIX CPUs together to one single console, control station. One UNIX CPU is in reality driving and controlling all other clustered CPUs. Specific applications (i.e. current accounts) are confined to a CPU thus rudimentary multi processing is accomplished.

Thus, individual applications can be run in a single RISC computer which is tied to common input/output (I/O) equipment, and a single operator console. To a degree, this UNIX banking system is comparable to a mid-range IBM mainframe. A careful analysis, however, indicated that we could not use this system as our back end as it did not have enough capacity nor security nor recoverability for our needs.

Citibank also produces and vends through a subsidiary (CITTL) in Bangalore, India, a very tight and feature rich banking system that is called MICROBANKER. This system is wrapped around a STRATUS "non-stop" computer and is absolutely ideal for small (i.e. those with deposits below US$500 million) banks. Again, this system was rejected as being inadequate for the large environment.

Thus, the Asian Consumer Bank considered the alternatives and selected large IBM Mainframe processors as its super server. Our decision finds a great degree of common support in the financial services industry. Support can also be found in a chapter by Roche (1992), within the book entitled Global Issues of Information Technology Management, wherein the author states that "Global Strategy Means Centralized Computing".

Conversion Planning

Planning for the bank regionalization commenced in earnest in late 1993. Australia converted to Systematics in November 1994 and Singapore completed its conversion on April 1995. Australia will move its data processing to Singapore in the 4th quarter of 1995. Hong Kong will move its data processing to Singapore in June of 1995 and convert to Systematics in 1996. The full conversion schedule is included as Figure 1.

ACTIVITY	IMPL	3Q95	4Q95	1Q96	2Q96	3Q96	4Q96	1997
GRB/SI	AUS SIN	TUR GRB/DB2		GUAM	PHIL MAL AUS (GRB)	THAI TWN* HKG	INDO	KOR - 1Q UAE - 1Q IND - 4Q PAK - 2Q
SABRE-TELLER	SIN		MAL THAI TUR	GUAM	TUR (P2) AUS	TWN* IND	INDO PHIL	UAE - 1Q KOR - 1Q HKG - 1Q PAK - 2Q
SABRE-PLATFORM (Liabilities)				HKG SIN	TUR AUS			
SABRE-PLATFORM (Asset & Liabilities)					HKG MAL PHIL SIN AUS	TUR GUAM THAI TWN* IND	INDO	KOR - 1Q UAE - 1Q PAK - 2Q

* indicated dependent on double byte support

Figure 1: Asia Pacific Consumer Bank - Project Schedule

Our regionalization systematics conversion strategy is centered around conversion teams populated by Citibank staff. We initially tested Systematics corporation as a conversion resource (an outsourcer), and while they performed satisfactorily (they converted Australia), they are simply too expensive, considering the magnitude of our conversion. The Australia conversion approached US$12 million in cost while our internal team converted Singapore for less than US$4 million. It was therefore decided that, with over 13 conversions left to go in Asia alone, a Citibank team would be more effective. Hiring commenced and these teams were established in 1994.

Currently, we have segmented our countries into four groups for conversion:

1. Those using large IBM Mainframe (ESA) hardware and COSMOS software:
   - Singapore, Malaysia and Hong Kong. (3 countries)

2. Those using IBM AS400s and CORE software:
   - Philippines/Guam, Indonesia, Thailand, Korea and Taiwan
   (5 countries)
3. Those using RISC UNIX hardware and DEVINE or OASIS BASIS software:
   - India, Dubai, Saudi Arabia, Pakistan (4 countries)
4. Additional Countries:
   -Turkey will be initiated with the SYSTEMATICS/SABRE/ASIA CAT system
   - Japan (although not a part of APCB) is already using the regional
   card center (RCC) and considering SABRE and SYSTEMATICS processed out of Singapore
   - It is important to note, that as our plans began to become reality, a number of other Citibank department solicted the APCB to process (outsource) their Asian computing requirements. We agreed to almost all requests and have just signed a contract with the "Private Bank" and will begin their processing in January of 1996.

We are already seeing the benefits from new back end systems. They replace systems formerly built individually by each country (normally on a PC) and suffering therefore, from problems of efficiency, security, uniformity and reliability. A good example is the recently implemented mutual fund record keeping system where the India developed Oasis/Basis system was modified and moved to Singapore as a hub system available to all countries. This project, managed by S. S. Raghavan, was completed in six months and made operational on May 16, 1995. This topic will be discussed further under "Control Issues".

Internal conversion staff have been hired and trained for the COSMOS and CORE countries. Singapore is completed and work is underway on Philippines/Guam, Malaysia and Turkey. Training for India and Dubai is underway and Pakistan is formulating its plans. The plan covers all the countries in APCB although a final decision is still pending on SYSTEMATICS for SAMBA (Saudi American Bank, Saudi Arabia).

Systems Development and Implementation

The primary benefit from this project is to enable APCB to dramatically reduce the cycle time (by 50%) for development and delivery of product to market and then to process this product in a much more controlled and uniform manner.

So as to facilitate this reduced cycle time, state of the art development capabilities were added to the Singapore Computer Center. Upper case tools were added to aid development, trace and display tools to aid debugging and a panoply of other productivity oriented development tools necessary to handle client, server and mainframe needs. These include stand alone tools like MICRO FOCUS and the dedication of an entire IBM mainframe to testing. Of course standard tools like: Project Management, Abnormal Termination quick print and the like were made part of the programmers workbench. Now taking on the responsiblity and commitment to reduce cycle time by 50% requires more than the addition of a set of tools and the dedication of MIPs on a mainframe. The following is in our view, a reasonably inclusive list of the additional requirements.

Centers of Excellence: Our solution was to create Centers of Excellence as described below, but first, two salient points:

a) There must be an overt commitment to this new and agressive development cycle. Management must make its position clear through Mission Statements and various other forms of communication. There is involved here, a strange new paradigm for veteran technology staff. Minimally, we are using a set of new tools and a 50% improvement objective. We are then contemplating another dramatic paradigm shift, which is the move to an Upper Case development tool. Upper Case tools, are in general, those that have the complete tool kit supplied by one vendor. These tools also tend to provide service from the beginning of the development cycle through to the ultimate object construction and/or the code generation. The impact of Upper Case tools can therefore be quite traumatic on the long time analyst programmer who is anxious to get down and code.

Suffice to say that serious retraining must be undertaken and the attrition rate may exceed 40 percent. Not everybody approves of this new world and we must accept some level of rejection.

b) Adequate and qualified staff must be added to the development group and to the overall technology group as well. This is a difficult proposition given the tremendous variance across Asia in terms of cultural differences, salary and cost of living expenses and of course market place needs as we combine the developed countries with these emerging countries.

Now, as mentioned previously, commodity asset and liability systems were converted to the Systematics package. Strategic Asian systems such as mortgage power, share finance securities (purchase on the margin) etc were chosen to be written in house. Centers of Excellence were selected for at least the design of the new back end systems. A Center of Excellence is defined (for APCB) as a country willing to take on the design and development of back and/or front end systems. The design must be functional for more than one half of the countries in the Asia Pacific region. Subsequent releases will support all users who decide to avail themselves of the subject system. Accordingly, Citibank Hong Kong was selected as the Center of Excellence for the development of the Multi Currency (20 currencies) certificate of deposit system. Hong Kong was also selected as the Center of Excellence for SABRE Phone which is the underlying automation for Citibank's citiphone, a 24-hour x 7 days a week service. Both of these will probably be programmed in Beijing. Taiwan will be the Center of Excellence for image capture of credit card Korea for loan origination image and Australia for insurance and mortgage origination.

A Center of Excellence is then, a country who has a sufficient level of expertise in a given product, a good amount of technical talent and is willing to step forward and support other countries.

PAYOFFS OF THE SYSTEM

Tangible Benefits

There will of course be substantial cost reductions. Considering the regionalization alone, the Major Expenditure Proposal (MEP) calls for an US$80 million investment with an annual cost avoidance of more than US$50 million. Current efforts are underway to see how more tangible dollar savings can be added to the above, although again, cost reduction is only secondary consideration.

We are in addition committed to reducing the processing cost per account to each country by 10% to 20% per year, for at least the next 5 years. We have already demonstrated reductions of this magnitude are achieveable in our credit card regionalization efforts. User service contract commitments have been signed, and we are commencing our efforts. This has been accomplished with the Regional Card Center. This will be of course be accomplished by dedicated efforts to improve computer use efficiency, implementation of improved application development tools and the fact that we will develop a backend system once as opposed to 15 times and that backend system will be very efficient.

Customer demand for cross border services and more sophisticated productsare also influential factors in our regionalization move. All of these more sophisticated product requirements call for access to cross border data. This is much more efficiently accomplished in a regional environment.

If, we view the benefits of SABRE (i.e. faster teller close out in a multi-currency world, point of source data entry) and the benefits of countryprocess process re-engineering (image check processing, intelligent data capture etc), then the benefits approach US$200MM per year.

Intangible Benefits

Although we are very early in the cycle, the significant outcomes so far are:

1. Our project is definitely doable and will meet or exceed our financial and operational goals.

2. We will see the expense saves as predicted, with concommitant improvements in customer service via reduced disconnect potential, error tracking systems and substantially improved "Levers of Control".

3. The entire APCB is participating in regionalization and is scheduled over the next three years. To date, we are proceeding in an "on time, under budget conversion schedule". This will continue, but our over-riding "credo is to do it right the first time and if necessary we will slow down!"

GLOBAL ISSUES & LESSONS LEARNED

Although this project is still in its early stages, there have been a substantial number of lessons learned and are communicated as follows:

International (Cross Border) Telecommunications Management is at Best Difficult, at Worst it is Impossible

Although the project is still in progress, the title of this subsection pretty much captures the complexity of global telecommunications management.

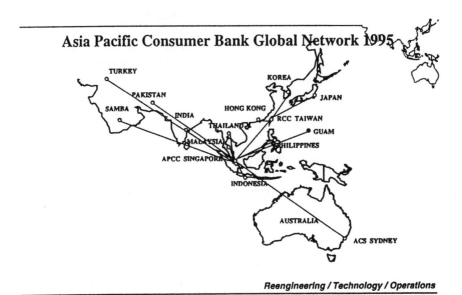

Asia Pacific Consumer Bank Global Network 1995

Reengineering / Technology / Operations

Network Cost

The network pictured in Figure 2 is now installed and operating across the entire Citiibank Asia Pacific domain. Based on an initial set of bandwidth requirements (determining bandwidth is a problem in itself and discussed later in this chapter) the network was designed, engineered and installed. Although cost reduction, as mentioned earlier was not a major driver and network optimization was not fully employed, the initial network costs were shocking in their overall magnitude. Summing up the result, it can be reasonably stated that, on a per unit basis, wide band telecommunications in Asia are at least one order of magnitude greater than those in the United States and at least four times greater than those in Europe.

It appears also true that while on a absolute basis, all rates (worldwide) are decreasing, the relative difference (the delta) between Asean telecommunication costs and the United States telecommunication costs are increasing. This is simply due to the fact that with the large base of installed technology in the US, it is relatively easy to upgrade that technology. It appears that we have a case of the "big getting bigger".

Regulatory Constraints and Lack of Cross Border Cooperation

Telecommunications in the Asean Pacific basin are still not deregulated and are for the most part run by country/government Postal Telephone and Telegraph units (PTTs). Although privatization is beginning, these PTTs are still very heavily regulated. They are also quite monopolistic. Competition from external providers (i.e. AT & T and British Telecommunications) etc. is just beginning. One country PTT will frequently not talk to another country PTT unless long, formal and notorized forms are filled out by the client and approved by local ministers. The point is that the installation, management and operation of an Asean backbone network requires a high level of technology and management skill. It also requires a high level of diplomatic/political and negotiating skills as well. Finding an individual capable of doing all the above is critical to the successful implementation of a global network.

There were other incidents where country PTTs acted in a manner that totally ignored the impact of their actions on another countries PTT and of course the customer. There was one instance where a certain PTT increased the gain (power) on its transmission to a satellite such that it interfered (blocked) out the reception of the transponders in a neighbouring country, thus shutting down use of this system for several days. Was this event intentional? One cannot be sure, but it took substantial diplomacy to smooth things out and get back to normal. There are also times when PTTs favour one local vendor over another. As an in country backup, we decided to experiment with Very Small Aperature Transmission (VSAT). Our application (and our backup) was held up for 9 months because the local PTT favored one supplier over the one we preferred. Again, substantial diplomacy was required to get action even though we were willing to accept either vendor. The point is simply to re-enforce how much skill is demanded of the Telecommunications Manager.

Network Sizing

Typical network configurations, in this case Singapore to Philippines and Guam, are illustrated in Figures 3 & 4. The effort in trying to estimate the bandwidth requirements was very theoretical at best. The SABRE LAN traffic

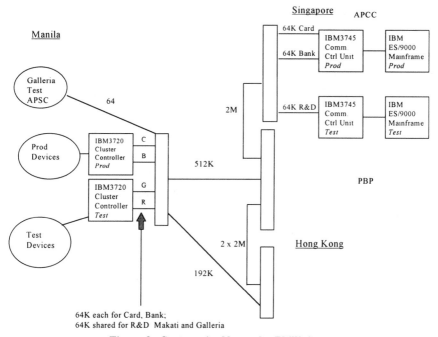

Figure 3: Systematics Network - Phillipines

was still under design and we had to mathematically model the country specific teller/platform network component load. This was then combined with the CAT loading on a TCP IP network connected to the IBM 3745 at country headquarters. This then combined with file transfer requirements (including remote printing) become the bandwidth demand on the SNA backbone. Simulation and mathematical models were employed and a 20% safety factor added. The results were used as the basis for circuit engineering and designing. There was however not a great amount of confidence over the results. Accordingly consultants were brought in to conduct their own study. They produced what turned out to be much more quantifiable results and the network bandwidth was revised. We had to wait however until the first node (country) was installed in the regionalized network so that line traces could be taken and a true model created. After the traces a resonably predictive model was built that serves well.

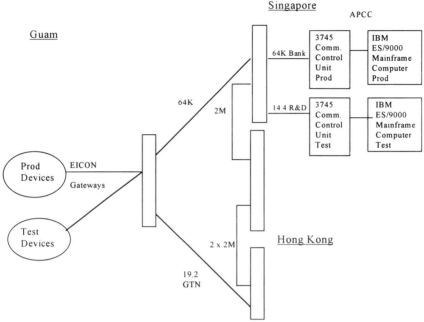

Figure 4: Systematics Network - Guam

Country To Country Differences

Finally, it is important to point out that this very large project was undertaken as a consolidation process. Its increased control, security and cost improvements were key, but it was designed to provide similar products that could, if so desired, be used by all countries. Use was not mandated, but was optional. Systematics was a parameter driven system so that setting a parameter would allow for system changes that would accommodate country differences.

Unfortunately, Asia turned out to be more diverse than we expected. Each country averaged 4-5 changes per application system above and beyond the parameter capabilities. Suffice it to say that all of the country change requests were accommodated. Future changes are handled in semi-annual releases with regulatory changes made when required.

Our original goal was to have only one version of the Systematics software. The amount of change for each country has made this goal a little more difficult to achieve. Suffice it to say that it is still our goal, but it will be achieved later than we planned.

CONCLUSIONS

The best way to capture the essence of this chapter is the following quote from Machavelli (circa 1500) which emphasizes the immense difficulties that an organization can face when initiating, designing, and implementing change:

> *There is nothing more difficult to plan, more doubtful of success, nor more dangerous to manage than the creation of a new system. For the initiator has the enmity of all who would profit by the preservation of the old system and merely lukewarm defenders in those who would gain from the new one.*
>
> **-Machiavelli, circa 1500**

Endnotes

[1] CORE is an asset and liability system written by a vendor in 1982 and runs on AS400s. COSMOS is an asset & liability system written by Citibank in 1975 and runs on IBM Mainframes.

[2] DEVINE is a purchased Asset & Liability system that runs on prime computers.

[3] OASIS/BASIS is a recently completed UNIX asset/liability system.

[4] CAT is Customer Activated Terminal, Citibank's version of an ATM.

[5] GRB is global relationship banking and is CIF plus other banking relationships, service pricing models and combined statement etc. GRB is a tailored and uniquely Citibank system that uses the IBM data base management system DB2.

References

Roche, Edward M., "Managing Systems Development in Multinational Corporations: Practical Lessons from Seven Case Studies," in The Global Issues of Information Technology Management, edited by Shailendra Palvia, Prashant Palvia and Ronald M Zigli, Idea Group Publishing, 1992

27 Information Systems that Support Global Alliances at General Motors

Chetan S. Sankar and Naohiro Terase
Auburn University, USA

Since General Motors had consistently made a profit in markets outside USA, an increase in their international market share was of advantage to the company. Understanding this need, GM had embarked on strategic alliances with many different car manufactures, suppliers, and dealers worldwide. Effective information transfer formed the backbone that supported the worldwide alliance operations. Realizing the ability of information technology (IT) to reduce costs of production and increase the quality of products, GM has been aggressively implementing global MIS and telecommunications networks. This chapter discusses the inter-organizational systems (IOS) and internal MIS applications developed by GM. A comparison of these systems indicated that IOS were designed and used differently compared to the internal MIS applications. Future research and documentation of the efforts of GM and other multinational corporations to create IOS to nurture strategic alliances is critical to the study of global information systems.

INTRODUCTION

In the automobile industry, many multinational companies are using strategic alliances to expand their market and to enhance their competitive advantages. Information systems are expected to play an important role in supporting these alliances. General Motors (GM), being the largest company in the world, has also formed many different global alliances with other automobile manufacturers and parts suppliers in European and Asian countries. The information reported in this chapter is based on a literature review of GM's operations from articles in academic and practitioner journals and books. This chapter will:

1. Identify and describe the successful as well as unsuccessful global alliances formed by GM during the past decade.
2. Describe the role of MIS in supporting GM's global alliances (inter-organizational systems) and internal operations (internal systems).
3. Compare and contrast the inter-organizational systems and internal systems.

This case study could help a student learn how a large multinational company has used different kinds of MIS in order to support its alliances as well as internal operations. Based on such case studies, researchers could refine past models (Johnston and Vitale, 1988) that identify the role of inter-organizational systems in supporting global alliances.

CRITICAL ROLE OF GLOBAL ALLIANCES FOR GM

General Motors (GM) is the largest manufacturing company in the world and global alliances have been responsible for a large share of its profits. Its total sales in 1994 was $155 billion and its number of employees was more than 710,000. GM had been losing heavily during 1990-1992 as indicated in Table 1. During 1993 and 1994, GM made a little recovery in net income, but still had a far less profit compared to average profits during the 1980's. In order to understand the reasons for the loss, Table 2 breaks down GM's 1994 financial data into its operations areas. The table shows that GM's automotive products operations are its core strength accounting for $123 billion sale, constituting 81% of its revenue, and about $6 billion in profit.

	1990	1991	1992	1993	1994
Sales	124,705	123,108	132,242	138,219	154,951
Net Income	1,985	4,452	23,498	2,465	4,900
Income as % of sales	-4.1%	-8.0%	-38.3%	2.1%	5.2%

Table 1: GM's sales and Net Income for last five years (in $ millions)

1994	Automotive Products	Financing and Insurance Operations	Other Products	Total
Net Sales	$ 123,253	$ 9,418	$ 17, 919	$150,590
Other Income	N/A	N/A	N/A	$4,360
Total Income	N/A	N/A	N/A	$154,951
Operating Profit (loss)	$ 6,116	N/A	$ 2,105	$8,221

Note: * After elimination of intersegment transactions
Table 2: Sales Analyzed by Operations in 1994 (in $ millions)

We further analyzed the 1994 sales of GM's automotive product line across different market areas: United States, other North America, Europe, Latin America, and all other countries. The data in Table 3 shows that GM's automotive division had the lowest income as percent of sales in the USA. This division returned a higher profit share in every other part of the world. The table also shows that 28% of sales revenue for GM originated outside the United States. This proportion had increased significantly since 1985 when it was only 11%. Table 4 shows the percent share of GM in the European and Asian-Pacific automobile market. Historically GM had consistently made increasing profits in markets outside USA. Clearly, a strategy focusing on an increase in their international market share would be of advantage to GM. Understanding this need, GM had embarked on strategic alliances with many different car manufactures, suppliers, and dealers worldwide. These alliances are described in the next section.

Region:	United States	Other North America	Europe	Latin America	All Other	Total
Sales (outside)	101,186	8,377	24,850	5,305	1,456	141,172.8
% of sales	71.1%	5.9%	17.6%	3.8%	1.0%	100%
GMAC, other income	N/A	N/A	N/A	N/A	N/A	13,778
Net sales	N/A	N/A	N/A	N/A	N/A	N/A
Net Income (loss)	1,362	1,133	1,337	829	257	4,901
Income as % of sales	1.3%	13.5%	5.4%	15.6%	17.6%	3.5%

Table 3: Regional Automotive sales for 1994 (in millions)

Region/Country	GM	Industry	GM'spercent share
Western Europe	1.6 million	12.6 million	12.70%
Asia Pacific	273,300	10.61 million	2.57%
Japan	13,300	7.5 million	0.18%
South Korea	151,000	1.15 million	13.13%
China	0	630,000	------
Australia	86,100	511,000	16.85%
Taiwan	14,300	489,000	2.92%
Indonesia	0	263,000	------
New Zealand	6,000	69,000	8.70%

Table 4: Automobile Sales in European and Asian Countries in 1991 (number of cars)

GM'S GLOBAL ALLIANCES

GM had formed global alliances with other car manufacturers, parts suppliers, and car dealers to attain increased global share of the automobile market. With alliances, GM was able to expand its market and quickly introduce products in many different markets. In the USA and European Community (EC), GM sold all types of automobiles. In EC, GM used allianceswith Isuzu, Saab, and Lotus for manufacturing and selling small and luxury cars. In Japan, GM used Yanase for distribution of its automobiles. The other alliance partners are identified in Table 5.

| Countries | <u>Type</u> <u>of</u> <u>Car</u> | | |
	Small Car	Compact Car	Luxury Car
USA	NUMMI(Toyota)		
Asia - Pacific	Yanase	Yanase	
	Daewoo		
European Community	Opel	Opel	Saab
	Isuzu cars		IBC/Lotus

Table 5: GM's Worldwide Partners

EUROPEAN ALLIANCES

GM's automotive operations are especially profitable in the European market. GM had the second largest share in European passenger car sales in 1992 and sold 1.7 million cars making $1.2 billion in profits. This success was from record sales of its Opel/Vauxhall cars. For instance, the small Opel Kadett was the second most popular car in Germany (Sasseen, 1991). Also, unlike GM's North American operations, GM's Opel had highly productive assembly plants in Germany (Feast, 1993).

An example of high productivity could be seen in the plant located at Eisenach, East Germany. Eisenach was an old plant located in previous East Germany and was used to produce the Watburg sedan. Opel completely modernized this plant and eliminated inefficient operations. Its production started in October 1990 and the products included the compact Astra and subcompact Corsa. The plant employed about 2,000 workers and produced 150,000 cars, averaging production of 100 cars per worker-year. It took 18.3 hours to produce a car compared to 30 hours at GM's other Opel plants in Europe at Bochum, Germany, and Zargoza(Feast, 1993).

GM introduced many new ideas in this factory, especially the concept of lean production system (Motor Report International, 1992). The lean production system was introduced by Japanese auto makers and consisted of several new concepts. First, it grouped assembly line workers into teams. Second, it used continuous quality improvement process called Kaizen. In the plant, large red clocks continuously showed how many minutes were lost since the start of each shift, telling the employees, not to pass on a defect. Third, it used the just-in-time schedule for delivery by suppliers. Eight suppliers were within a 30-minute drive and another 15 were within an hour of the factory. The factory had gained by reducing inventory, speeding up production, reducing production costs, and increasing quality (Feast, 1993).

While GM's Opel operation had been successful, GM's alliances with other European car makers had shown some troubles. For instance, Saab Automobile AB, the joint venture between GM and Saab-Scania AB, lost $376 million in the first eight months of 1992. This joint venture was started in December 1989 when GM paid $600 million for a 50% stake and management control of Saab (Sasseen, 1992). The initial plan of this joint venture was to sell 180,000 cars annually. However, in 1993 it sold only 51,000 cars. The primary objective of this joint venture was to expand GM's share of luxury car market in Europe. Also, GM's European plants were operating under full capacity and this joint venture provided additional production capacity to GM (Ward's Auto World, 1991). However, the alliance suffered loss and a major reason was the outdated production system. GM had shut down four Saab plants, but in the long term it hoped to induce economics of scale by sharing technology between itself and Saab; for example, two Saab models shared a chassis with Opel. Despite these problems, GM benefited in at least two ways from this joint venture. First, it gave GM additional production capacity to produce Opel cars. Second, Saab used GM's worldwide distribution system to sell its cars. For instance, Saab started to sell 9000 series of cars in Brazil through GM dealers (Ward's Auto World, 1991).

Another alliance of GM in Europe was the acquisition of Group Lotus Cars. GM paid 22.7 million pounds in 1986 to buy 66% share of Lotus Car (Motor Report International, 1993). The primary reason of this acquisition of Lotus Car was to gain an entry into the luxury sport sedan market. However, GM did not make any profit with this acquisition. In 1992, Lotus showed a pre-tax loss of 36.6 million pounds. Lotus produced 2,241 Elans and the company made a loss on each car sold. In 1992, Lotus decided to stop the production of Elans. After terminating the production of Elan, Lotus produced only the Esprit model. It produced only 350 Esprit cars in 1992. In 1993, GM finally decided to sell out Group Lotus to Bugatti International SAH (Ward's Auto World, 1993).

GM entered into several other alliances in Europe. These alliances were aimed at overcoming the shortage of production capacity and expanding market share. In 1991, GM made agreement with Isuzu to sell all Isuzu cars in Europe under GM's brand name. Especially beneficial to GM was the production of Isuzu's light-trucks, since GM did not have additional capacity to produce light-trucks in Europe. This agreement made it possible for GM to hold a market share in the light-truck market (PR Newswire, 1991).

In the future, intensified competition in the European market could expose weaknesses of GM. Capitalization remained low and falling profits might dent the funds available for build-up (Sasseen, 1991). GM's North American operations may become too involved in their own survival to help European operations. If survival in the US was at stake, the costly plants for Saab in eastern Europe could quickly be downgraded. Jones, European research director for a five-year study of the global auto industry said:

> *"So far, GM hasn't fundamentally altered its manufacturing process,
> it's simply squeezed more cars out of the same bricks and mortar. GM's
> European operations face a huge risk of being milked to bail out the US.
> I doubt they'll be able to sustain the investment necessary to keep
> momentum going."*

However, the President of the European division of GM disagreed:

> *" It's going to get awfully bloody out there. There's not a chance in 10
> [not even a 1 in 10 chance] that all of Europe's major players today will
> still exist in a decade's time. All our capital needs are being met and we
> expect that to continue. If you get the product right, the other problems
> in this industry become far easier to solve. We lead in that area. Our
> success with Opel Kadett is due to its distinctive style and now is the
> second-most popular car in Germany. We boast second-best
> productivity, measured in cars per worker-year. Plants have been
> modernized and union relations have been improved. A global sourcing
> program has weaned Opel purchasing managers off their
> overdependence on high-cost German suppliers. It has led to savings
> that account for two fifths of the improvement in GM's bottom line."*

GM had coped well with the recession in Europe during 1993 since it
was reasonably lean and fit. The company had risen to second place by selling
around 760,000 cars in the first half of 1993 (Automotive Industries, 1993).

ASIAN ALLIANCES

Fueled by some of the highest economic growth rates in the world and
decades of pent-up demand, analysts expect the Asia-Pacific region to account
for sale of 15 million new cars and trucks by the end of the decade - double the
volume of 1993 and about equal to the expected size of the North American and
European markets (Johnson, 1994). This high sales volume is attributed to an
expected increase in automobile demand in Japan, South Korea, China, India,
and ASEAN countries - Thailand, Malaysia, Indonesia, Philippines, Singapore,
and Brunei.

GM had formed many alliances for its operations in Asia, but its sales
of automobiles had been very low in this region (Table 4). The biggest obstacle
to penetrating the Asian market was competition from the Japanese automobile
makers who dominate the market. Also, some Asian countries had heavily
protected their local companies.

GM made several alliances to gain a significant market share in the
Asian market. One example was the alliance with Daewoo Motor in South
Korea. GM and Daewoo invested about $100 million for a Pontiac LeMans
coupe production (Aftermarket Business, 1992). However, the result of this

investment was not successful. The joint venture began to crumble when GM refused to invest more capital into upgrading of the plant. Another factor was Daewoo Motor's interest in expanding its market to Eastern European countries. GM tried to block Daewoo Motor's efforts to expand into that market. As a result of these problems, GM agreed to let Daewoo Motor buy out their operations in South Korea (Aftermarket Business, 1992).

GM made an agreement with China to manufacture a 1-ton pickup. The strategy of GM in China was to limit the number of models and to reduce its cost of manufacturing. In China, GM's plant made only one model with a capacity of 20,000 vehicles annually. One of the biggest problems for Chinese operation was to get foreign exchange to pay for imports. GM could obtain only 25% of the vehicles' sales price in dollars (Aftermarket Business, 1992).

GM's market share in Japan was only 0.18%, although Japan was the second largest automobile market in the world. Even though GM did not gain a large share of the Japanese market, it made alliances with several companies to get high quality suppliers, to develop new cars, and to learn Japanese production systems.

For selling cars, GM made a contract with Yanase corporation in Japan, an automobile dealer company that specialized in selling many foreign cars, including the Mercedes Benz, Volvo, Audi, Lotus, and VW. It had many dealerships in Japan and excellent reputation for its customer services. However, this company had a reputation of selling luxury cars; therefore, this alliance of GM and Yanase was not that successful. Also, GM was criticized for not selling cars to meet the local customers' demand. GM did not produce right-hand drive vehicles that were critical for sales in Japan. Although GM announced a plan to produce a right-hand drive Saturn, it may not be shipped for several years (Nauss, 1993).

GM made an alliance with Isuzu Motors in Japan and held 37.5% share of this company. This alliance did not make any particular joint-development in Japan nor did GM use Isuzu to sell its cars in Japan. The primary reason of this alliance was to gain the knowledge of small car production. GM learned that Isuzu's cost of producing a car was about $2,857 whereas GM's cost was about $5,781 (Lowry , 1992). The knowledge gained by this alliance was successfully used in the production of Opel Cars in Europe.

While GM had made efforts to develop more cost effective and attractive small cars, it realized a need to have a partner who had such a knowledge. GM selected Toyota as another partner in 1984. Both companies agreed to establish a joint venture called New United Motor Manufacturing Inc., (NUMMI) in Fremont, California, USA. This venture employed 4,250 people and produced about 300,000 cars a year, and its products included Chevrolet Geo, Prizm, the Toyota Corolla, and the Toyota compact pickup truck. This plant was highly successful economically. NUMMI produced an average of 63 cars per worker per year, 40 percent more than an average GM plant. Also, the defect ratio at this plant was 45 defects per 100 cars compared to 135 defects per

100 cars from a comparable GM plant. Absenteeism at NUMMI was 2 percent compared to 20 percent in some of the other GM plants (Kauffman, 1992; Chappell, 1993).

This alliance with Toyota was not only economically beneficial, GM also learned many important lessons. First, GM learned Toyota's production system and techniques to improve quality of the product. Second, it taught GM the importance of long-term supplier relationship. Third, it demonstrated need for gradual improvement, not sudden change. Fourth, it taught GM about Toyota's avoidance of over-engineering to retain flexibility (Furukawa, 1993). As a result of these benefits and economic successes, both companies agreed to expand their joint venture indefinitely in 1994.

NUMMI was not the only joint effort made between GM and Toyota. For instance, GM signed a contract with Toyota in 1993 to build 20,000 right hand drive cars to be sold as Toyota cars in Japan. This agreement will triple GM's sales in Japan in 1996. Also, this would give an opportunity for GM to penetrate Japanese car market (Nauss, 1993).

SUMMARY OF GM'S GLOBAL ALLIANCES

GM 's participation in these global alliances led to increased market share worldwide. GM seemed to have understood the need to produce low cost and high quality cars. It had gained considerable market share in other countries by collaborating with local automobile manufacturers and upgrading the facilities. Also, knowledge gained by collaborating with Japanese small car makers had been effectively transferred to production of small cars in Europe. Some of the key benefits obtained by the alliances seemed to be gaining ready distribution networks, bypassing nationalistic policies, and overcoming tariff barriers. Information transfer formed the backbone that supported the worldwide alliance operations. Realizing the ability for information technology (IT) to reduce costs of production and increase the quality of products, GM had aggressively implemented global MIS and telecommunications networks as described in the next section.

GM'S GLOBAL MIS APPLICATIONS AND GLOBAL TELECOMMUNICATIONS NETWORKS

Before 1984, each GM division operated its own wide-area networks typically using analog facilities. In October 1984, GM purchased the outsourcing firm, Electronic Data Services (EDS), for $2.5 billion. EDS consolidated GM's networks into a network called EDS-Net. It is one of the world's largest voice and data networks and is the information systems platform on which EDS provides its outsourcing services (Crockett, 1990). In 1990, GM paid EDS Corp. $3.2 billion to run all of GM's telecommunications and computers operations. This amount spent on IT comprised about 2.5% of GM's sales, compared to 1.6% for Ford and 0.9% for Chrysler (Caldwell, 1991). This clearly indicates that GM made a strong commitment to the use of information technologies worldwide.

EDS-Net migrated the disparate facilities onto a common digital backbone that served as a shared information highway connecting GM's data centers and business units. GM utilized EDS's technologies and expertise to integrate its diverse and complex information systems (Perkowski, 1990). In all, about 30 to 40 GM data centers, managed separately by different divisions were consolidated into about six EDS-operated information processing centers connected by EDS-Net in 1990. This network integrated 100 separate networks into a single backbone network. It consisted of 540 domestic and 100 international digital switches, 900 multiplexers, 264,000 telephones, 280,000 terminals and data devices, 700 T1 circuits, 130 T3 circuits, 20 microwave terminals, 100 X.25 packet assemblers/disassemblers, 2 leased satellites, 60 two-way earth stations, and 11 C-band earth stations operating in five continents (Livingston, 1990).

Although the development of EDS-Net required significant development costs, 2,000 development personnel, and three years of development time, EDS-Net provided a variety of benefits for the company. For instance, EDS-Net reduced GM's voice network cost. Before EDS-Net was implemented, GM used AT&T's software defined network (SDI) service and it cost 18 cents per minute for voice communication. GM reduced this cost to under 13 cents with EDS-Net (Wallance, 1989), and the cost has been reduced further due to the competition among the telecommunications carriers. EDS-Net was used to centralize purchase and obtain efficiencies of scale when negotiating with suppliers of parts(Boudette, 1990). It also provided a capability to communicate with many automobile dealers worldwide. Overall, this centralized IT architecture had many advantages for GM such as cost reduction, high utilization of information resources, and improved manageability.

Some of the MIS applications based on the centralized IT architecture were used to support the global alliances and others were used to improve the internal operations at GM. Occasionally, the same application was used to support both the interorganizational and internal systems. We discuss these next.

Inter-organizational MIS Applications to support Worldwide Alliances

GM developed electronic data interchange (EDI), internet, C4-systems, video conferencing, and groupware applications in order to support its worldwide alliances.

Electronic Data Interchange (EDI): GM had been an active user of electronic data interchange standards during the past. It paid many of its bills electronically and refused to deal with banks that did not support EDI applications (Korzeniowski, 1989). The company used EDI to link 2,000 suppliers in West Germany, Spain, Italy, Belgium and the Netherlands to the company's central European computer system in Antwerp, Belgium.

A major difficulty for GM in using EDI worldwide was a lack of global standards. The most common standards for EDI were the American National Standards Institute's X.12 that outlined how data could be exchanged. Many industries had tailored the standards resulting in about 35 different subsets of ANSI X.12. Also, Europe had its own standard called General Trade Document Interchange (GTDI). None of these standards defined the records and fields of documents. Consequently, it required tremendous effort for GM to connect equipment using different EDI standards (Korzeniowski, 1989). Antiquated laws also presented problems since EDI required transfer of real-time information. Such transfer of information violated existing laws in countries such as Hong Kong. Consultant Guilbert said, "I don't expect global EDI to move like gangbusters. The new has to blend with the old and companies are not going to throw out their current applications."

EDI was used to connect the suppliers of NUMMI to the plant in order to provide Just-in-Time schedules. Suppliers for NUMMI were selected not because they submitted the lowest bid on an order but because they showed a willingness to adopt to the rigors of a Japanese Just-in-Time schedule. For local California suppliers, NUMMI kept as little as two to three hours of inventory on hand; for suppliers in the Midwest, three to four days; and for engines and transmissions that came from Japan, one week. Frequent deliveries meant that mistakes were discovered hours, not days or weeks after parts were manufactured. Workers, engineers, and executives traveled between plants to learn from each other and correct mistakes before they became catastrophes (Kauffman, 1992). GM enhanced EDI technologies by creating C-4 systems.

C-4 Systems: The acronym C-4 stands for computer-aided design (CAD), computer-aided engineering (CAE), computer-aided manufacturing (CAM), and computer-integrated manufacturing (CIM). This integrated application would use a standardized system of electronic data exchange for GM's design and manufacturing operations worldwide. A global telecommunications network would link all GM product development teams and their suppliers via a common electronic data format.

C-4 was a response to GM's recognition that it was trailing its competitors in product development time and cost, and that it must execute new-vehicle programs more efficiently and bring products to market faster and cheaper on a program-by-program basis. One of the keys to the C-4 program was the replacement of two-dimensional engineering drawings of products and tools with the 3-dimensional forms of geometrically complete representations (Automotive News, 1989).

The company has been a major user of computer-aided design (CAD) and computer-aided manufacturing (CAM) software tools. The Chassis System Center (CSC) was a test center to use CAD/CAM software tools. CSC integrated CAD and CAM tools which designers in the center used for designing, analyzing, and manufacturing tasks (Trego, 1992). The system eliminated any recreation of data and manual data transfer. Since the part geometry could be changed quickly, this system was able to generate, check, and optimize first-order designs 85% faster. Several layouts were produced per day compared with typical production of one layout in several weeks. Also, CAD software tools were connected with the Object Manufacturing System which could automatically produce a full-size prototype for a design object. The rapid prototyping system could make prototype parts in days rather than months in a traditional factory (Demmler,1994).

Video-Teleconferencing System to Connect to Dealers: The company had implemented a video-teleconferencing system as well as two-way data transmission system called Pulsat that connected GM's headquarters and its 10,000 dealer showrooms using satellite communication systems (Harler, 1991). It would allow GM to conduct face-to-face meetings, discuss and decide promotional literature, conduct sales and service training, and make marketing presentations anywhere a car dealer had a satellite dish. It would also include electronic shop manuals, electronic vehicle invoicing, and next-generation vehicle diagnostics. Schreitmueller, leader of the GM team that designed the Pulsat network system, said:

> *"Communicating pictorially is more economical and more effective. It becomes both the medium and the message. The leadership in telecommunication technology may provide the edge needed for GM to move into the 21st century. The success of this system did not depend on how good an idea was but on how well that idea was implemented."*

In addition to divisional communications and training uses, Pulsat was expected to help GM with inventory control. In addition, GMAC, the financial arm of the corporation, would be able to get faster financial information turnaround.

Groupware Systems

GM had been using many different E-Mail software packages since different divisions of GM and alliance partners preferred different software. However, using different software created many problems for the company. Files could not be easily transferred using the incompatible e-mail systems. Special communication devices and software had to be installed in order to connect the different e-mail systems. Also, employee training costs on all the different software became very expensive. In order to circumvent this issue, in 1991, GM distributed 15,000 copies of Lotus Notes to suppliers and dealerships in 13 European countries. Using Lotus Notes, suppliers and dealers were able to communicate with each other even if they individually used different e-mail systems. This decision significantly reduced training costs for GM and was heralded as one of the most popular IT decisions. In 1994, GM distributed 100,000 copies of Notes throughout organization (Bride et al., 1991).

Internet and Worldwide Web to Connect to Partners

GM had traditionally used private telecommunications networks in order to connect to its alliance partners. An advantage of this strategy was the assurance of security in its connections to the partners. During August 1994, the Automotive Industry Action Group (AIAG) announced that GM will adopt the TCP/IP standard and will use Internet for data communications (Messmer, 1994). An advantage of using TCP/IP was that it was a widely used international standard and was inexpensive to use. Using internet could provide GM cost advantages and increased connectivity to its partners. However, using the most popular public world wide network, the Internet, could create substantial security concerns for GM and its alliance partners.

Parts Catalog on CD-ROMs to Dealers

GM Canada had stopped sending paper parts catalogs (Buckler, 1992) replacing them with information on compact-disk systems. This version was expected to save the dealers quite a bit of shelf space, since 8 to 10 volume manuals would be replaced by a thin disk. Also, with the CD-ROM version, the dealers would be able to search for parts by car model, year, and the part of the car. They could also see a picture of the part on the computer screen.

GM not only had developed MIS applications to support global alliances, it also had developed applications to support internal operations of the company. These will be discussed next.

MIS APPLICATIONS TO SUPPORT GM'S INTERNAL OPERATIONS

'Factory' Training Software

Recruiting and training were very important consideration for a company such as GM that wanted to project a high-quality image throughout the world. As GM used more powerful software to improve its operations, training cost in turn became more expensive and unavoidable. GM tried to reduce these costs using a software called 'Factory.' Many modern factories had computer controlled equipment that relayed performance data to a centralized monitoring system. It required extensive training for managers in order to learn the new systems and plan new schedules. GM's CIM & Networking group decided to take a simple solution to this training problem. They developed an add-in module called 'factory' for Lotus 1-2-3, and this add-in module had all capabilities to collect data from factory equipment. Since most managers were familiar with Lotus 1-2-3, they did not receive any special training to analyze data collected by this add-in module. With the use of 'factory,' GM saved significant amount of training cost. The managers performed "what-if" analysis based on the familiar screens of Lotus 1-2-3 (Teresko, 1990).

Integrated Scheduling Project

Another application called Integrated Scheduling Project (ISP) was expected to replace 30 different materials and scheduling systems to handle inventory, manufacturing, and financial data. This just-in-time manufacturing system let the plant managers receive orders from the various car divisions for the number and type of vehicles to be built, and to create an estimated 20-week manufacturing scheduling for itself and its suppliers.

Computer-Aided Manufacturing

GM transformed its Pontiac East pickup-truck plant into a computer integrated factory (Boudette, 1990) from customer order to delivery. A GM's dealer sent customer orders through EDS-Net and the factory's computer reviewed these orders. It, then, sent these orders to the plan's production support system that coordinates all production processes. The system also integrated with the computer controlled testing system, the material control system, and GM's corporate accounting system. The system managed 25 miles of conveyor and 146 robots. The result of this integrated system was a fast production processes in this plant. The plant produced 960 trucks each day and it took about 22 hours to produce one truck.

Consistent Office Environment

In the office, GM made another plan to standardize its information technologies. The project called Consistent Office Environment (COM) was a three year plan to standardize desktops and equipment. It involved replacing a mix of network operating system, application development tools, and desktop models. Under this plan, GM reduced the list of technology platforms and vendors. Compaq and Lotus Development Corporation were chosen as the main vendors for this application. With this project, the company made it easy for complex information systems to interact easily (Booker, 1994).

Comparison of Global Inter-Organizational Systems and Internal Systems

General Motors, had entered into strategic alliances with many different automobile manufacturers and suppliers globally in order to lower costs and increase profits. The examples in this chapter show that the company had a mix of successes and failures in these strategic alliances. GM in the 1980s had realized that IT was a major essential infrastructure that needed to be pervasive throughout the entire GM value chain from procurement to service support. This realization led to the acquisition of EDS and eventual consolidation of GM's networks and MIS applications. The chapter shows a few examples of the interorganizational systems that were used to nurture the global alliances and internal systems that were used to manage the internal operations. We compare and contrast these two categories of systems next.

Interorganizational systems (IOS) - defined as automated information systems shared by two or more companies - were expected to significantly contribute to enhanced productivity, flexibility, and competitiveness for many companies (Cash, et al., 1992; Johnston and Vitale, 1988). The major differences between the two categories of systems for GM are shown in Table 6. The first four factors were drawn from the research of Cash et al. (1992). The last three factors were added based on analyzing GM's experience in setting up these systems.

The first factor was control of the MIS applications and telecommunications networks. In an IOS, this activity crossed organizational boundaries and companies had to agree to common protocols such as EDI standards. For the internal systems, GM's corporate MIS group could dictate standards, but, for IOS, it would be impossible. Thereby, prevalence of IOS systems made the MIS organizations partner with other organizations.

Factors	Interorganizational Systems	Internal Systems
Control	Crossed organizational boundaries	Within the company
Government regulations	Critical	Not that critical
Presence of facilitators	Important	Not that important
Broader competitive impact	Took manufacturing ideas from Japan and used them in Europe	Improved productivity within plants
Value Chain impact	Cut across all levels from inbound logistics to service	Focused on core competency
Training costs	Had major impact on multiple firms	Impact within a firm
Standards	Critical	Not that critical

Table 6: Factors that Differentiate Inter-Organizational Systems from Internal Systems

The second factor was the presence of governmental control in IOS. Companies in foreign countries was subject to tariff and legal regulations that are very different than those faced by GM and its partners in U.S.A. When GM became multinational, its MIS applications had to accommodate legal regulations from other countries. This became much more critical as IOS systems were introduced. For example, it was impossible to open a factory in many developing countries without equity participation from a local company.

The third factor was the importance of facilitators for IOS compared to internal systems. For examples, CCITT is a facilitating body that made many internal standards. IOS systems had to abide by these standards. In contrast, GM's internal systems could be run based on proprietary protocols. Another facilitator for GM had been EDS, which worked as a separate division within the company. The increasing complexity of computer systems often made it more cost-effective for businesses to outsource their information management and data processing systems to companies like EDS. EDS, in 1995, had $36 billion in contracts, and was originating $8-$10 billion in new contracts per years. GM had gained by utilizing EDS to create its MIS applications since the cost of creating these systems was shared with other companies. An example was the creation of EDS-Net. This network not only served the needs of GM, but also the needs of many other companies. Thereby, the cost of developing the applications for GM was shared with other companies. Since EDS was a unit of GM, proprietary systems that could provide competitive advantage might not be offered to competitors of GM. Also, the knowledge gained by EDS in developing systems for companies in other industries might be used by GM in order to enhance its MIS applications.

IOS systems could produce a much broader competitive impact for the company compared to the internal systems. This is the fourth factor. For example, GM learnt lean production techniques by its association with Japanese companies and transferred this knowledge to European automobile production. This led to substantial advantages to the company as seen by the emergence of the small car - Opel - as a market leader in Europe. GM had been using alliances with suppliers and other manufactures in order to have high growth globally.

The fifth factor is that IOS systems cut across the complete cycle of the value chain of the company starting from suppliers to those who serviced the company's cars. It formed the backbone that supported the entire GM value chain worldwide. In contrast, the internal MIS applications normally concentrated on supporting the activities that provided core competency to the company - for example, control of the manufacturing plant.

The sixth factor is that IOS systems due to standardization could cut down the training costs of the cooperative organizations significantly. For example, the use of Lotus Notes by GM's dealers, suppliers, and internal personnel made it possible for all of them to use similar syntax and user interface. That could in turn lead to standardization of groupware within GM's operations itself. When external pressure from suppliers and dealers was applied to a company such as GM to standardize its Groupware product, most divisions responded to customer needs and changed the systems. If the mandate came from the central MIS division, many divisions might have ignored the command and stuck to their proprietary systems.

The seventh differentiating factor was that national and global standards essential for making IOS applications possible. These could not be closed proprietary systems owned and leased by a few companies. It was possible for GM to work with proprietary systems for its internal systems, but, they had to be made open when IOS systems started to be implemented. The gradual changeover to TCP/IP protocol was a good example of adhering to global standards.

SUMMARY

This chapter reviewed the global alliances formed by GM and described the benefits and drawbacks of the collaboration. It also provided examples of the interorganizational and internal MIS applications developed by GM to support its alliances and internal operations. As GM's domestic operations did not seem to be highly profitable, its global alliances and IT strategies were becoming much more critical in creating profits. This might be an important lesson for other companies in that profits might be frequently outside the head-quarters of a multinational company. Sasaki, General Manager at Toyota (Sasaki, 1993) recommended that GM stop changing its partners so often. He believed that GM's future will depend on its effort to restore competitive pricing and to create new dramatic products with high customer satisfaction, from small cars to luxury cars and featuring high technology. A comparison of IOS and internal systems indicated that IOS systems were designed and used differently compared to the internal MIS systems. But, literature on the study of these differences is limited. Global information systems require strategic alliances and IOS might play a large role in their success or failure. Therefore, future research and documentation of the efforts of GM and other multinational corporations to create IOS systems to nurture strategic alliances is critical to the study of global information systems.

References

Boudette, E. Neal, (1990, June 18), "GM Computers in Symphony," Industry Week, v. 239, n. 12, p. 59.

Booker, Ellis, (1994, March 14), "GM Seeks Consistency," Computerworld, v. 28, n. 11, p. 1.

Bride, Ed, Bucken, Mike, Frye, Colleen, Gronert, Elke, Melewski, Deborah, (1991, November), "GM spreads Lotus Notes throughout Europe," Software Magazine, v.11, n.13, p. 14.

Buckler, Grant, (1992, April 13), "GM Canada to Put Parts Catalog on CD-ROM," Newsbyte.

Caldwell, Bruce, (1991, June 10), "GM: Putting IS in the Driver's Seat," Information Week, n. 324, p. 38.

Cash, James, I., Jr., McFarlan, Warren, F., and McKenney, James, L., Corporate Information Systems Management: The Issues Facing Senior Executives, IRWIN, Homewood: IL, 1992.

Chappell, Lindsay, (1993, July 5), "It's NUMMI Forever, or NUMMI No More," Automotive News.

Crockett, Barton, (1990, August 27), GM, "EDS Looks to Future with Strategic Net Project," Network World, v. 7, n. 35.

Demmler, Al, (1994, August), "Rapid Prototyping with Paper," Automotive Engineering, v. 102, n. 8, p. 35.

Feast, Richard, (1993, November), "Europe's Lean Warriors," Automotive Industries, v. 173, n. 11, p. 43.

Furukawa, Tsukawa, (1993, July 5), "Toyota, GM to Extend Venture; New Agreement Would Continue NUMMI Indefinitely," American Metal Market, v. 101, n. 128, p. 7.

"GM to be Exclusive Isuzu Light-Truck Distributor in Europe," (1991, October 7), PR Newswire.

"GM Sets Up Joint Venture in China, Cuts Link with Daewoo," (1992, April 1), Aftermarket Business, v. 102, n. 4, p. 11.

"GM Sells Lotus to Bugatti," (1993, September), Ward's Auto World, v. 29, n. 9, p. 10.

"GM Foresees C4," (1989, September 25), Automotive News, E12.

Harler, Curt, (1991, March), "General Motors to Launch World's Largest VSAT Network," Communication News, v. 28, n. 3, p. 6.

Johnson, Richard, (1994, March 7), " For Carmakers, All Roads Lead to Pacific," Crains Detroit Business, v. 10, n. 10, s. 2.

Johnston, Russell, H. and Vitale, Michael, R. (1988, June), "Creating Competitive Advantage With Interorganizational Information Systems," MIS Quarterly, v. 12, n. 12, pp. 153-166.

Kauffman, Richard, (1992, April), "Working Partners," Diablo Business, v. 28, s. 1, p. 22.

Korzeniowski, Paul, (1989, March 15), "Overseas Signals Making More Sense: Worldwide EDI Is Taking Years To Jell, But Tests This Year Will Run EDIFACT Through Paces," Software Magazine, v. 9, n. 4, p. 22.

"Lean Production Is The Aim At Eisenach, "(1992, October 12), Motor Report International, p. 8.

Livingston, Dennis, (1990, Febuary), "How EDS Built World's Biggest Private Network," System Integration, v. 23, n.2, p. 34.

Lowry, Karen, (1992, Febuary 10), "GM and Isuzu: A Waste of Synergy," Business Week.

Messmer, Ellen, (1994, August 8), "Auto Industry Takes To The Open Highway," Network World, v. 11, n. 32, p. 1.

Nauss, W. Donald, (1993, November 20), "GM Getting On Right Side Of Hard-To-Pierce Japan Market," Business Dataline(R).

Perkowski, Mike, (1990, January 18), "Systems Integrations: The Strategy For The Future," Computing Canada, v. 16, n. 2, p. 9.

"Saab's Story: Future Brighter," (1991, Febuary), Ward's Auto World, v. 27, n. 2, p. 17

Sasaki, Toru, (1993, December), "What the Japanese have Learned from Strategic Alliances," Long Range Planning, v. 26.

Saseen, Jane, (1991, Febuary), "GM Moves Up A Gear," International Management, v. 46, n. 1, p. 46.

Teresko, John, (1990, May 7), "Lotus 'Discovers' The Factory Floor," Industry Week, v. 239, n. 9, p. 43.

"The Big Three Do Europe," (1993, October), Automotive Industries, v. 173, n. 10, p. 33.

Trego, E. Linda, (1992, April), "General Motors Links CAD And CAE Software For Concurrent Engineering," <u>Automotive Engineering</u>, v. 100, n. 4, p. 27.

Wallance, Bob, (1989, April 3), "GM Migrates To SDN In Net Optimization Plan," <u>Network World</u>, v. 6, n. 13, p. 47.

"Write-Off Worsens Group Lotus Losses," (1993, August 16), <u>Motor Report International</u>, n. 670, p. 2.

About the Authors

Dr. Lore Alkier

Lore Alkier is Assistant Professor of MIS at the Vienna University of Economics and Business Administration (WU) and is currently a Visiting Scholar at the Leonard N. Stern School of Business at New York University. Her recent research interests include information management in multinational corporations, strategic and long term information systems planning, corporate strategy and information technology, and information management at universities. Besides her research interest she served as Director of the WU Computing Center for several years and works as a management consultant. She has been teaching post-graduate, graduate and undergraduate MIS courses at WU, and in the joint International MBA program of WU and the University of South Carolina.

Dr. Paul Alpar

Paul Alpar is Professor of Business Administration and Management Information Systems in the School of Business Administration and Economics at the Philipps-University at Marburg, Germany. He has also taught or done research at the University of Illinois, Chicago, Goethe-University, Frankfurt, Germany, Tel-Aviv University, Tel-Aviv, Israel, University of New Mexico, Albuquerque, and University of California, Berkeley. Paul received his doctorate degree from Goethe-University, Frankfurt, Germany. He has published in various national and international journals such as Journal of MIS, Information & Management, IEEE Transactions on Engineering Management, Decision Support Systems, Journal of Organizational Computing, International Journal of Research in Marketing, and Annals of Operations Research. His current research interests are economics of information systems, AI-based decision support, and online business.

Dr. Chrisanthi Avgerou

Dr. Avgerou is a lecturer in Information Systems at the London School of Economics and Political Science (UK). She teaches postgraduate courses on government IT policy issues and information systems in developing countries. She has acted as advisor on IS management to government institutions and corporations in different countries, and enjoys links with academics, IS practitioners, and research organizations on several continents.

Dr. Janice Burn

Janice Burn obtained her Masters Degree in the UK and her Doctorate in Hong Kong. She is currently employed as an Associate Professor at the Hong Kong Polytechnic University and previously held posts in the UK and Canada. Her research interests are in the areas of information systems strategies, globalization of information technology, information systems research framework and information resources management. Her particular focus over the last five years has been directed towards Asia and cross cultural studies. She has published over forty papers, co-authored three books and is currently editing a book on "Global Information Systems Technology - the role of Hong Kong" as part of an international series.

Dr. Elia Chepaitis

Elia Chepaitis is an associate professor of computer information systems at Fairfield University, She worked in Russia in 1991, 1992, and the spring of 1994, and in Morocco in the fall of 1994 as a consultant and Fulbright fellow. With the assistance of a grant from the Lattanze Center for Executive Information Systems and five Sterling fellowships from Yale University, Dr. Chepaitis has developed information strategies for a group of U.S.-based corporations. She also holds twelve international patents for an alternative to Braille.

Mr. Hin-Keung Cheung

Hin-Keung Cheung received his B.A. (Hons) Degree in Computing Studies from Hong Kong Polytechnic in 1991 and his Masters Degree in Information Management from Lancaster University U.K. in 1992. He is currently studying for his doctorate at the Hong Kong Polytechnic University (formerly named as Hong Kong Polytechnic). His main research interests relate to globalization of information technology and cross cultural influences on effective utilization of information systems resources.

Mr. George DiNardo

George DiNardo is a veteran MIS practitioner and adjunct Professor of MIS. He was honored as the CIO of the Year in the 1980s. Currently, he is the Chief Information Technology Officer at the Asia Pacific Consumer Banking of Citibank headquaretered in Singapore. He also teached M.B.A. classes at the Nanyang Technological University.

Dr. Amitava Dutta

Amitava Dutta is Professor of Decision Sciences and MIS in George Mason Univeristy's School of Business Administration. Previously, he was on the faculty of The University of Iowa and The Simon Business School at the Univeristy of Rochester. His research interests include telecommuniations management/policy and decision support systems. He has a speical interest in the reform processes underway in the telecommunications sector in developing countries. Dutta's research has appeared in several journals including IEEE Transactions on Communications, The European Journal of Operations Research, IIE Transactions, Operations Research and Management Science. Dutta is on the editorial boards of several IS journals, and is a member of the IEEE, ACM and INFORMS.

Dr. Sean B. Eom

Sean B. Eom is the Copper Dome Faculty Fellow in Research and Professor of Management Information Systems (MIS) in the Department of Management at Southeast Missouri State University. Professor Eom received a Ph.D. in Management Science with supporting fields in MIS and Computer Science from the University of Nebraska - Lincoln in 1985. His other degrees are from Korea University (B.A.), Seoul National University (M.B.A. in International Management), and the University of South Carolina at Columbia (M.S. in International Business). He is on the editorial board of theJournal of Global Information Management. His primary research areas include Decision Support Systems, Expert Systems, and Global Information Systems Management. He has published over 35 refereed journal articles.

Mr. Jorge Fagundes

Jorge Fagundes is an Assistant Professor at the Núcleo De Estratégias Empresariais Comparadas of the Faculdades Cândido Mendes-Ipanema, Rio de Janeiro. His main lines of research are Industrial Economics and Information Technologies, and he has been working with Profs. La Rovere and Tigre on a research about the telecommunications sector in Brazil.

Dr. Schubert Foo

Schubert Foo is a Senior Lecturer and Sub-Dean in the Scool of Applied Science at Nanyang Technological University. He received his PhD in Mechchanical Engineering from the University of Strathclyde.

Dr. Rick Gibson

Rick Gibson received his Ph.D. in Information Systems from the University of Maryland in 1992. Several years of teaching computer science and business management in Italy, Germany, Belgium, Korea, Japan, and the Philippines provided the impetus for adopting a global perspective regarding information systems. International consulting assignments in the area of software engineering have provided further opportunities to examine the role and impact of international information systems. Related research interests include the evolutionary internationalization of the information systems curriculum and the revolutionary application of chaos theory to information systems development.

Dr. Lee Gilbert

As a practitioner, Lee Gilbert designed software for energy and aerospace firms, directed advanced data centres, then assisted varied private and public sector clients in Asia, Europe, North America and the Middle East to acquire and implement computing and telecommunications solutions to business problems. He served the United Nations Secretariat as Regional Adviser for

Technology Transfer and Development, Harvard Business School as Future Information Systems Faculty Fellow, the Institue of Systems Science as leader of its executive education programme, and SRI International as senior managemnet consultant.

Dr. Wooi Boon Goh

Goh Wooi Boon is a Senior Lecturer in the Division of Computer Engineering of Nanyang Technological University. He received the MSc in Electrical Engineering and Computer Science from the University of Warwick (UK).

Dr. Peter Hagström

Assistant Professor Peter HagstrÖm is affiliated to the Management Information Systems and General Management areas at the Harvard Business School. He teaches Global Strategy and Management, a second year elective course in the MBA program. His research primarily concerns the use of data communications by international firms as a way to understand how these firms function and are structured. Peter received his M.B.A. and Ph.D. from the Stockholm School of Economics in Sweden and holds an M.A. in Political Science and Languages from the University of Stockholm.

Dr. Ulrich Hasenkamp

Ulrich Hasenkamp is Professor of Business Administration and Management Information Systems in the School of Business Administration and Economics at the Philipps-University at Marburg, Germany. He has previously taught at the University of Cologne, Germany, where he received his doctorate degree. He was a visiting scientist with IBM (San Jose Research Lab) and the University of Hawaii at Manoa. In addition to numerous publications in German journals he is editor-in-chief of "Wirtschaftsinformatik", the leading German journal on Management Information Systems. His current research focuses on computer supported cooperative work and electronic data interchange.

Dr. Richard Heeks

Dr. Richard Heeks is a Lecturer in Information Systems and Development at the Institute for Development Policy and Management, University of Manchester, U.K. He has an Mphil in information systems and a PhD on the development of the Indian software industry. He is currently researching the development of Asian IT industries, and the implications of new information systems for accountability in development organizations. He can be contacted about this research at the University of Manchester (email: richard. Heeks @man.ac.uk).

Dr. Blake Ives

Dr. Blake Ives is a visiting faculty member at the University College Dublin and is Constantin Distinguished Professor of the Management Information Sciences Department at the Cox School of Business at Southern Methodist University. Professor Ives has been a distinguished Fellow at the Oxford Institute for Information Management at Templeton College, Oxford and a Marvin Bower Faculty Fellow at the Harvard Business School. He has also served on the faculty of Dartmouth College. He is currently an Honorary Research Associate at Victoria University of Wellington, N.Z. an Associate Fellow of Templeton College, and a visiting faculty member at London Business School. Professor Ives serves on the editorial boards of several U.S. and international information systems and journals and has published over 50 articles and book chapters. He is the Senior Editor of the Management Information Systems Quarterly and Editor-in-Chief of MISQ Discovery, a new electronic publication. He chairs the governance committee and is chief champion for ISWorld Net. He was until recently on the board of directors of the Society for Information Management International. He has taught in executive education programs in Australia, France, Germany, England as well as in a variety of institutions in the U.S.

Dr. Sirkka L. Jarvenpaa

Dr. Sirkka L. Jarvenpaa is an associate professor of information systems at the University of Texas at Austin. She served as a Marvin Bower Fellow at Harvard Business School the calendar year of 1994. She received her Ph.D. in management information systems and her MBA from the University of Minnesota. Dr. Jarvepaa serves as the associate editor for the following journals: Management Science, Information Systems Research, MIS Quarterly, Database, and Journal of Computer-Mediated Communication. Dr. Jarvenpaa has published over 30 articles and numerous case studies. Her current research projects focus on global information technology, electronic commerce, and the use of IT in radical organizational transformations.

Dr. Renata Lebre La Rovere

Renata Lèbre La Rovere is an Associate Professor of the Economics Department and a researcher at the Instituto de Economia Industrial of the Federal University of Rio de Janeiro (IEI/UFRJ) since 1992. Prof. La Rovere obtained her Ph.D degree at the Université Paris 7, France, and was a visiting scholar at the MIS Department of the University of Arizona during 1991 and 1992. Her research interests include Information Technologies and the Telecommunications Industry.

Mr. Kenny Lee

Kenny Lee is Senior Lecturer at the Nanyang Business School, Nanyang Technological University, Singapore where he teaches Information Systems courses at both undergraduate and graduale levels. Prior to that he worked in industry for ten years, holding IS management responsibilities at country and international levels in a number of multinational businesses. His research interests are in the areas of international IS management, IT architecture, and the impact of IT on organisations. He possesses a Masters in Systems Engineering from the University of London.

Dr. F. Warren McFarlan

F. Warren McFarlan is the Ross Graham Walker Professor of Business Administration at the Harvad Business School where he is currently Senior Associate Dean of Research. McFarlan, with three degrees from Harvard,has been on the Harvard Business School faculty since 1964 where his work has continuously been in the field of information systems. He has published a number of books and articles in the field and was Senior Editor of the MIS Quarterly during 1986-88. He is a member of several profit and non-profit boards.

Dr. Effy Oz

Effy Oz is the coordinator of the Management Information Systems Program at Wayne State University School of Business Administration. He holds a MBA degree from the Hebrew University and a doctorate from Boston University. For eleven years, Dr. Oz served as an executive for a large aerospace corporation. He published articles in academic and professional journals among which are: MIS Quarterly, Communications of the ACM, Decision Sciences, Information & Management, Omega, Journal of Systems Management, and Journal of Global Information Management. He is the author of three books: Ethics for the Information Age, Ethics for the Information Age: Cases Wm.C. Brown), and the forthcoming Principles of Management Information Systems (Irwin).

Dr. Prashant C. Palvia

Prashant Palvia is Professor of Management Information Systems at the University of Memphis. He received his Ph.D, M.B.A. and M.S. from the University of Minnesota, and B.S. from the University of Delhi, India. In addition to twelve years in academics, he has nine years of industry experience. Dr. Palvia is the Editor-in-Chief of the *Journal of Global Information Management*, and is on editorial board of several journals. He was the conference chair of the 1991 International Conference of the Information Resources Management Association. His research interests include international information systems, strategic information systems, database design, and software engineering. He has published over forty five articles in journals such as *MIS Quarterly, Decision Sciences,*

Communications of the ACM, Information & Management, Decision Support Systems, and *ACM Transactions on Database Systems.*

Dr. Shailendra Palvia

Shailendra Palvia is an Associate Professor at the Long Island University. In industry he has worked with IBM, Conrol Data, Federal Reserve Bank and Hennepin County for 10 years. In academia he has taught at the University of Minnesota, Babson College and Singapore for over 11 years. His research interests include management of the systems development process, modes of use in problem solving, MIS/DSS implementation issues, and information management issues of MNCs. He has published in Communications of the ACM, MIS Quarterly, Journal of Global Information Management, Internatinal Information Systems, Information & Management etc. He was the Program Chair of the CISR (MIT) - IMARC (NTU) conference held in Singapore in July, 1993. Dr. Palvia has given invited talks before professional groups in Singapore, Boston, and Stuttgart (Germany).

Dr. Keri E. Pearlson

Dr. Keri E. Pearlson is a member of the faculty at the Graduate School of Business at the University of Texas in Austin. She teaches management information systems, business reengineering, and creativity management course to MBAs and executives. Her research activities involve topiocs in reengineering, personal portable technologies, and customer service support systems. Prior to joining UT, Dr. Pearlson held various positions in academia and industry at Harvard Business School, AT&T, CSC/Index, and Hughes Aircraft Company. Dr. Pearlson holds a Doctorate in Business Administration (DBA) in Management Information Systems from the Harvard Business School and both a Masters Degree in Industrial Engineering and Engineering Management and a Bachelors Degree in Applied Mathematics from Stanford University.

Dr. Edward M. Roche

Dr. Roche worked in management consulting for 9 years with The Diebold Group and with Booz-Allen & Hamilton, Inc. He was an associate editor for the journal International Information Systems. He is a contributing editor to Transnational Data Report, and a book review editor for Journal of Global Information Management. He received an M.Phil and Ph.D. from Columbia University in the City of New York with a thesis on the international telecommunications systems of multinational corporations. He also holds a M.A. in International Relations from the Johns Hopkins School of Advanced International Studies in Washington, D.C. He serves on the IFIPS 9.4 working sub-committee on information technology in developing countries. He is the author of two books: "Managing Information Technology in Multinational

Corporations" and "Telecommunications and Business Strategy". He founded the IFIP Working Group 8.7 Informatics in International Business Enterprises.

Dr. Chetan S. Sankar

Chetan S. Sankar is an Associate Professor of MIS at the Auburn University's College of Business. He has eight years of work experience in management information systems. He worked at AT&T Bell Laboratories with multinational companies in desighning telecommunications networks. He received his Ph.D. from the Wharton School, University of Pennsylvania and has worked as an Assistant Professor at Temple University. His current research interests include global telecommunications management, career progression of technologists to managers, case study research, and user interfaces. He has published more than 85 papers in journals, book chapters, and conference proceedings. He can be reached at sankar@business.auburn.edu.

Dr. K.B.C. Saxena

Dr. K.B.C. Saxena is a Visiting Professor at the Indian Institute of Management, Bangalore, India. Prior to this position, he was an Assistant Professor of Information Systems at the Faculty of Business Administration, Erasmus University, Rotterdam, the Netherlands and a Reader in Computing Studies at the Hong Kong Polytechnic University, Hong Kong. His current research interests are broadly focused on decision and information support in organisations and its strategic implications. Specifically his research interests include decision support in public administration, business process re-engineering in the public sector, information strategy for small/medium size organisations, global transfer of EDI technology, and IT in developing countries. He has authored or co-authored more than 60 papers on management support systems and information systems management, and business process re-engineering in the public sector.

Dr. Ravi S. Sharma

Ravi S Sharma is presently Director (R&D-Berkom) at Deutsche Telekom Asia. Prior to this he was a Member of Academic Staff in Computer Engineering and Acting Director of the MSc (Information Studies) programme at Nanyang Technological University, Singapore. He received the BSc in Computer Science from Brandon University, Manitoba, the MSc in Computer Science from the University of Regina, Saskatchewan, and the PhD in Information Systems from the University of Waterloo, Ontario. He began his career as assistant professor of Mathematics and Computing Sciences at St. Francis Xavier University, Nova Scotia ten years ago. Dr Sharma's current research interests are in collaborative computing and multimedia teleservices. He has published about fifty technical papers in international journals and conferences and has served as consultant to several organizations. He is a Senior Member of the IEEE and a registered Chartered Engineer (UK).

Dr. Barry Shore

Barry Shore is a Professor of Decision Sciences at the Whittemore School of Business and Economics, The University of New Hampshire. He received his Ph.D from the University of Wisconsin. Professor Shore is the author of four books published by McGraw-Hill and Hewlett-Holt Rinehart and Winston. He has worked for Boeing Company, General Electric, Hewlett-Packard and Arthur D. Little. His research interests are primarily in the area of global information systems and has recently published in such journals as the jJournal of Global Information Management, Information and Management, Journal of Strategic Information Systems, and Journal of Computer Information Systems.

Dr. Steven John Simon

Steven John Simon is an assistant professor of Information Technology and International Business at the Meinders School of Business at Oklahoma City University. He received his Ph.D. from the University of South Carolina, specializing in Mis and International and his Bachelor and Masters degrees from the University of Georgia system. Before entering the doctoral program he spent eighteen years in the private sector in management and computer operations. His current researcg interests include information determinants of international business structures, IS training and learning issues, and military applications of Business Process Redesign. He is also an officer in the United States Naval Reserve whose past assignments included serving as Information Resource Management Officer to the Commander of the Second Naval Construcyion Brigade. He has previously published in *Database* and *The Journal of Global Information Management.*

Dr. Ewan Sutherland

Ewan teaches and researches in informatics at the University of Wales, Lampeter. He has previously worked at the Universities of Stirling, Westminster and Wolverhampton and as a visiting member of staff at Georgetown University. He is a graduate of the Universities of Glasgow and Strathclyde. He is an active member of the International Telecommunication Users Group (INTUG). His URL for the World Wide Web is http://www.lamp.ac.uk/~ewan

Mr. Naohiro Terase

Naohiro Terase is a master's student at Auburn University. He received the Master of Business Administration degree in the Auburn University and currently enrolled in the management information systems program. He is from Japan and obtained his undergraduate business degree from Geogia Colleg. His interests include IT strategy, global business strategy, and IT resource management. He has conducted few case studies in companies such as AFLAC, NEC, GM, and 7-11 Japan. He has written a few related articles in Japanese. He had previously worked in the Japanese Research Institute where he participated in several IT research projects.

Dr. Paulo Bastos Tigre

Paulo Bastos Tigre obtained his D.Phil at the SPRU, Sussex, in 1982. He was a director of Cobra Computers between 1986 and 1988, and since then he is an Associate Professor of the IEI/UFRJ. Prof. Tigre has written two books about the informatics industry and its impacts on economic development in Brazil. His main lines of research are Industrial Economics and Information Technologies.

Dr. Lai Lai Tung

Tung Lai Lai is a Lecturer at the Nanyang Business School and Associate Director of Information Management Research Centre. She received the PhD in Business Administration from the University of Indianna.

Dr. Nicholas P. Vitalari

Nicholas is a senior vice president of CSC Index Research and Advisory Services and executive director of CSC Index's global information technology research programs. Dr. Vitalari researches and consults widely on distributed models of the firm, information technology strategy, best practices in technology implementation, and executive alignment. He is host and commentator for Index Summit's video series on best practices in technology implementation and is a member of the CSC corporate technology steering committee. Dr. Vitalari recently co-authored Systems Analysis and Design: Best Practices with Dr. James C. Wetherbe. He has served on the editorial boards of *MIS Quarterly* and *Data Base*. Dr. Vitalari holds a Ph.D. in management with a minor in sociology from the University of Minnesota, where he also earned his M.B.A., and a B.S. in business administration from Marguette University.

Dr. R.W. Wagenaar

Dr. Wagenaar is an Associate Professor in Business Telecommunications at the Faculty of Business Administration, Erasmus University at Rotterdam, The Netherlands. His main areas of research are within telematics and electronic commerce. His research focuses on the impact of telematic systems and services on trading relationships between firms and how this influences existing industry structures. He did extensive research on the role of EDI for the strategic positioning of ocean port communities. He contributed numerous papers on these topics to European journals and conferences. He holds a PhD in computer science and physics.

Dr. James C. Wetherbe

Dr. Wetherbe is a Federal Express Professor of Excellence and Director of the Center for Cycle Time Research, Fogelman College of Business, University of Memphis; and professor of MIS and director of the Management Information Systems Research Center, Carlson School of Management, University of Minnesota. Internationally known as a dynamic and entertaining speaker, author, and leading authority on the use of computers and information systems to improve organizational performance and competitiveness, Dr. Wetherbe has over twenty-five years experience in higher education and technical positions in industry. He has served as a consultant for a broad spectrum of private and public organizations, and is rated as one of the top dozen consultants and lecturers on information technology by *Information Week*. He is the author of 15 highly regarded books, over 200 articles, regular columns and serves as the consulting editor for publishing companies. Dr. Wetherbe holds a Ph.D. in Management Information Systems and Computer Science Management, and an M.B.A. in Management Information Systems from Texas Tech University. His undergraduate degrees were obtained from New Mexico State University.

List of Abbreviations

IDRC   International Development Research Programme
GATT   General Agreement on Tariffs and Trade
NAFTA North American Free Trade Agreement
OECD   Organization for Economic Cooperation and Development
UNDP   United Nations Development Programme
IT   information technology
IS   information systems
JAD   joint application development
TDQM Total Data Quality Management
IRM   Information Resource Management
MNCs Multinational corporations.
TDF   Transborder Data Flow
EDI   Electronic Data Inter
change
CCE   Communication Cost Economics
CCITT Comiti Consultatif International Tiligraphique et Tiliphonique
CEPT Confirence Europienne des Administrations des Postes et des
Tilicommunications
Datex Data Exchange (Public Digital Network)
Datex-L Line-switching Datex
Datex-P Packet-switching Datex
DFN   Deutsches ForschungsNetz (German research network)
DM   Deutsche Mark (German currency unit)
EDI   Electronic Data Interchange
EDIFACT Electronic Data Interchange for Administration, Commerce and
Transport
EU   European Union
FRG   Federal Republic of Germany
GEIS General Electric Information Services
GNP   Gross National Product
HV   High Monthly Volume
IBM   International Business Machines Network
ISDN Integrated Services Digital Network
ISO   International Organization for Standardization
ISP   Internet Service Provider
KIT   Kernel for Intelligent communication Terminals
KB   KiloByte
LAN   Local Area Network
LV   Low Monthly Volume
MAN   Metropolitan Area Network
OSI   Open System Interconnection
SMTP Simple Mai

l Transfer Protocol
SNA   Systems Network Architecture
SWIFT   Society of Worldwide Interbank Financial Telecommunication
TCE   Transaction Cost Economics
TCP/IP   Transmission Control Protocol / Internetwork Protocol
UN   United Nations
VAN   Value Added Network
WWW   World Wide Web

Glossary of Terms

ADSL: see Asymmetric Digital Subscriber Loop

ATM: See Asynchronous Transfer Method.

ASEAN - Association of Southeast Asian Nations

Asymmetric Digital Subscriber Loop: Using standard copper cables to provide television quality video

Asynchronous Transfer Method: A 53-byte fixed-length packet (or 'cell') of data used in telecommunications.

Body Shopping: Software outsourcing involving onsite provision of programming services.

Business Culture: Characteristics of the business practices, the business environment and the business people.

Business Network: Structure of inter-dependent relationships between the activities of those organizations which influence each others strategies.

Centralized Federation: This IT organization is characterized by one-way knowledge flows from the headquarters to the subsidiary unit. Information flows from the subsidiary to the headquarters do exist but are restricted to procedural data flows such as sales reporting data.

Client: The organization for which services are provided.

Client-Server Architecture: An arrangement of different computer and communications equipment that caters primarily to the needs of an individual client...typically, this architecture consists of LANs and WANs, Server and Client computers.

Closed User Group: A group of companies using a network in such a way that they are not accessible to others.

Community: A collection of distinct industries from one or more sectors and public administration bodies, which are interrelated through a business network.

Computer Aided Design (CAD): The use of computers in the design, modeling and drafting process for creating specifications for manufacture of goods.

Computer Integrated Manufacturing (CIM): A combination of systems linked by computer technology to achieve greater efficiency and effectiveness in the transformation processes of materials and/or services into products that serve customer needs.

Connectivity: The degrees to which hardware, software, and databases can be easily linked together in a telecommunications network

Coordination: Managing dependencies between technology transfer activities such as government regulations, standardization, etc.

Coordinated Federation: Subsidiaries in this organization operate in areas that require extensive modification of products for use in their markets. These subsidiaries are forced to rely on their parent company for new processes and ideas. This dependency requires an extensive knowledge flow from the headquarters to the subsidiary. Since the subsidiaries operate in an independent manner, in widely differing markets, we expect to find little in the way of knowledge flows between the subsidiaries.

Core Competency: The skills in a firm which can not be reproduced by other firms.

Critical Success Factors (CSFs): Those characteristics, conditions, or variables that when properly sustained, maintained or managed can have a significant impact on the competitive success of an organization, an industry-sector or a country. In the context of technology transfer, CSFs refer to the critical enablers in the successful development, use and diffusion of technology applications.

Critical Success Areas: Broader but homogeneous groups of CSFs conceptualized to improve their interpretation when the number of CSFs is large.

CHUG: See Closed User Group.

Cyber Mail: A host site connected to the Internet where 'visitors' can purchase goods and services.

Data Centre: A computer centre (center) that processes ongoing jobs using various computer systems.

Data Communications - Transfer of data between two electronic devices using telecommunications technologies

Decentralized Federation: Both information and knowledge flows in this structure are quite informal. The organization supported by this structure is composed of highly autonomous national companies that have little interaction with either headquarters or other subsidiaries. Information flows can be characterized by procedural information similar to that found in the centralized federation with knowledge flows almost nonexistent.

Decision Support Systems (DSS): Computer-based systems that help decision makers confront ill structured problems through direct interaction with data and analysis models.

Delphi Survey: An iterative survey of a focused group with aim of obtaining convergence.

EDI Implementation: Process of large scale institutionalization of EDI in organizations.

Electronic Brainstorming: Rapid generation of ideas by a focus group using a networked collection of computers.

Electronic Commerce: The buying and selling of goods or services through telecommunications networks either with EDI or the Internet.

Electronic Data Interchange (EDI): Technology of inter-organizational, computer-to-computer exchange of business documents in a standard, machine-processable format.

Electronic Storefront: See Cyber Mail.

Ethnocentrism: Regarding of one's own culture as superior to others'.

Expert Systems (ES): A computer application that guides the performance of ill-structured tasks which usually require experience and specialized knowledge (i.e. expertise).

Ergonomic characteristics: The elements related to the human side of a system or work.

FTP: Protocol for file transfers between computers using the TCP/IP network protocol.

Foreign subsidiary: A company owned by a parent company that is located in a country other than the home country of the parent company.

Geocentricism: Tending to take a world view; tending to be oriented toward the global marketplace.

Globalization: Integrated production of goods and services in more than one country.

Global DSS: see Global MSS

Global Information Systems (GIS): An IS application meant for use in different operations of a multinational corporation.

Global Management Support Systems (GMSS): systems such as DSS, EIS, ESS, ES that support managers in a global organization.

Global Outsourcing: outsourcing the development or maintenance of information processing to sub-contractors. This delegation of work may be internal or external to the company.

Global Software Outsourcing: Outsourcing of software development to sub-contractors outside the home country of the client organization.

Global Sourcing: The consideration of the purchasing function across organizational links so as to prevent duplication and to take advantage of quantity discounts through order aggregation.

Global Technology Transfer: The entire spectrum of events from conceptualization of a new technology to its countrywide use.

Global Value Chain: When the different operations of a company that add value to their products and services (from the perspective of current or potential customers) are spread around different parts of the world.

Going Global - Operating as a single, unified company worldwide, balancing resources across the entire company to implement a structure to compete with other firms and maximize total customer value.

Gopher: TCP/IP based protocol for menu-oriented structured presentation of distributed information frequently offered on the Internet.

Government purchasing requirements: Laws which reserve the market for national firms; serves to discriminate against foreign corporations.

Hanseatic League: A trading system operating in the medieval period along the Northern coasts of Europe.

Head-count reduction: Laying off people.

Hit:(noun slang) The accessing of information from a World Wide Web site by a user.

Information Architecture: A high level map of the information requirements of an organization.

Information Culture: Set of values and practices shared by those members of an organization involved in information activities including MIS professionals, managers and end-users.

Information Poverty: A long-standing and deep-rooted paucity of robust information and a lack of the means to develop information resources.

Information Society: European equivalent of the Information Superhighway, emphasizing the impact of technology on the society and the individual.

Information Superhighway: A web of networks, computers, databases, and consumer electronics that presents information to users where and whenever needed. Frequently used synonyms are "Information Society" or "National Information Infrastructure".

Information System (IS): The wide variety of computer resources to perform transaction processing, to provide processing for a formal information and reporting system, and to accomplish managerial-decision support.

Information Technology (IT): the combination of computer and telecommunication technology to create (business) applications.

Integrated Network: This structure is the most complex of the four types in the topology and resembles that of a matrix organization. It is characterized by conditions where subsidiaries and headquarters are considered as equal partners, information is dispersed throughout the organization, and widely used two-way communication channels are common. Subsidiaries operating under this structure have been referred to as holographic, suggesting that as with a hologram, each piece contains a complete image of the whole. Knowledge and information flows are extensive and occur throughout the organization at all levels.

Intellectual Property Rights: Rights to property that is produced by mental effort.

Internet: A global network, consisting of thousands of participating networks all over the world that are interconnected by the communications protocol TCP/IP.

International Information Technology Architecture: A high level map of the information and telecommunications technological capabilities of the firm as a global entity, composed of physical elements of computing, data, communications and applications, and inclusive of logical elements of planning, organizing and control.

IS Downsizing: reducing the size of IS resources such as personnel, operations and hardware. Some IS downsizing can be achieved through outsourcing.

ISDN: Integrated Services Digital Network, offering different communications services like data and voice communications on one network.

Just-In-Time Inventory: Management practices leading to saving costs of storing good and parts by receiving them in in-house warehouse just prior to their planned use.

Leapfrog Computing:Rejecting the conservative, proven, evolutionary approach and employing client/server technology, multimedia i.e. whatever is state -of-the art.

Maquiladora:This industry consists of plants just south of US-Mexico border. It is exempt from paying tariffs on imported raw materials provided the fina l product is exported. The plants are engaged in assembling operations for US companies.

MTBF: A measure of the quality of a computer equipment...it indicates the mean time (measured in hours or days or weeks or years) that elapses before a specific computer equipment will fail.

M-R Technology: Magneto-Resisitive heads for disk drives actively "read" the disk by passing a slight but steady current through the head and measuring resistance of the head to the flow of electricity....this technology allows about 30% increase in the number of tracks and about 15% increase in the number of bits per track.

Multinational Corporation: A company operating in more than one country

National Culture: The common mental programming of a group of people who live or lived in the same social environment.

National Information Infrastructure (NII): see Information Superhighway

OEM: Original Equipment Manufacturer: Signifies companies who manufacture the primary computer equipment which may be modified later on by non-OEM companies....examples of such companies being IBM, AT&T, Apple Computers, Sun Microsystems etc.

Open Systems: Information technology or telecommunications systems which use standards not covered by patents.

Open EDI: The transmission of EDI through the Internet in such as way as to remain secure.

Organizational Culture: The collective programming of the mind that distinguishes the members of one organization from another.

Outsourcing: Hiring outside professional services to meet in-house needs.

PAN: Public Access Network, the interactive videotex system of the Austrian PTT.

Polycentrism: Tending to regard each culture as a separate entity; tending to be oriented towards individual foreign markets.

Postal, Telephone, and Telegraph (PTT): The state-owned telecommunications monopoly present in most countries and responsible for provision of all telecommunications services. In some countries (U.S., U.K., Japan) the PTT's are becoming privatized.

Regiocentrism: Tending to be oriented towards regions larger than individual countries as markets.

SEASERV: A GIS developed by Seagate Technology International to serve to the needs of its customers who request the repair of faulty disk drives.

Second Forty Years War: A terms which includes the entire historical period of World War I and World War II including the inter-war period.

Secure HTTP: A standard for encryption of messages transmitted with the hypertext transfer protocol.

Single Sockets Layer: See Secure HTTP.

S-HTTP: See Secure HTTP.

Software: The instructions used to direct the operations of a computer or other hardware.

Strategy: A plan of action that requires commitment of significant resources to achieve a major objective.

Sub-contractor: The organization which provides the services when hired by the main service provider.

Structure: The division of the firm into subunits and the associated distribution of authority and resources, including information.

Surf. (verb. slang): To view information on the World Wide Web.

Technology-Intensive Industry: An industry that depends heavily on the use of state-of-the-art technology for competitive advantage and survival.

Technology Transfer: Process containing all the events related to application of a new technology starting from its conceptualization to its industrywide use in a country.

Technopole: A geographical concentration of high technology industry, such as Silicon Valley.

Total Quality Management: Giving utmost attention to quality in all aspects of an organization's operations with a customer focus, zero-defects, and continuous improvement.

Transborder Data Flow Restrictions: National controls against international computer networks used to inhibit international trade.

UN EDIFACT: An international standard for transmission of electronic data interchange messages.

VAN: see Value Added Network

Value Added Network: A third party computer network provider. In the case of EDI the VAN acts as a clearinghouse for the EDI transactions.

Value-Chain: Sequence of distinct operations within an organization which add value to the products or services sold from the perspective of current or potential customers.

Vertically Integrated: Most operations from raw materials acquisitions to various manufacturing operations to marketing to selling to after-sales support services performed in-house by the company such a company typically abhors subcontracting its operations.

Virtual Enterprise: A company which operates as a federation of enterprises through contractual rather than ownership relationships.

Virtual Work Space: The psychological space in a set of one or more offices connected together with advanced communications technologies, such as groupware and teleconferencing.

Volatile Industry: An industry in which the sales fluctuate significantly by seasons or economic conditions.

World Wide Web (WWW, Web): Logical network of docu
ments linked by hypertextcommands. The hypertext links open connections to physical hosts that carry the documents when requested by the user.

Web Browser: Typically graphical user interfaces (well known browsers are Netscape Navigator or NCSA Mosaic) that are broadly used to navigate the information provided on the World Wide Web.

X.12 : A standard for EDI developed in the United States.

INDEX OF TERMS

PURCHASE ORDER FORM

Postal orders: **Ivy League Publishing, Limited,**
32 Brackenwood Drive
P.O. Box 7225, Nashua, NH - 03060-7225

Fax orders: (603) 891-4125

Telephone orders: (603) 891-0669

Customer Information:

Name: _____

Phone: _____

Organization Name if applicable (corporation /library / bookstore):

_____

Address:_____

_____

Signature : _____ Date: _____

Name of Book:

Global Information Technology and Systems Management: Key Issues and Trends
(US$ 79.00) *Palvia/ Palvia/ Roche;* ISBN 0-9648382-0-6   (Ivy League Publishing)

	Per Book	Quantity		Total
Price	$79.00 x	_____	=	_____
Shipping & handling			=	_____

($ 3.95 for first book and $1.95 for each additional book)
(For rush orders, $7.95 per book by express mail)

Total   ==========

[NOTE: All individual orders must be accompanied with a check; organizations may send a check or request to be billed.]

LIBRARY RECOMMENDATION FORM

Dear _____,   Date: ____/____/_____

(librarian's name)

I would like to recommend the purchase of the book *Global Information Technology and Systems Management: Key Issues and Trends(Palvia/Palvia/Roche)* ISBN: 0-9648382-0-6 ($79.00). This is a publication of Ivy League Publishing and can be ordered directly or through your jobber. Questions or orders may be forwarded to:

Ivy League Publishing, Limited   **Phone:** (603) 891-0669
32 Brackenwood Drive   **Fax:**   (603) 891-4125
P.O. Box 7225
Nashua, NH 03060-7225

Recommended by:_____

Department:_____

The degree of benefit to the different library patrons is indicated below:
(A----> highest benefit, B----> moderate benefit, C --- lowest benefit)

A   B   C   Graduate Students: I plan to utilize this book as a prescribed
                                    or reference book for MIS courses.

A   B   C   Undergraduates: I plan to recommend chapters from this
                                    book as reference material.

A   B   C   Researchers: Our MIS professors will use this book to
                                    refer to the latest developments and
                                    paradigms in the global information
                                    technology arena.